Fundamentals of
Human Resources
in Healthcare

**Third
Edition**

Fundamentals of
Human Resources
in Healthcare

Carla Jackie Sampson | Bruce J. Fried

GATEWAY

TO HEALTHCARE MANAGEMENT

HAP

AUPHA

Health Administration Press, Chicago, Illinois
Association of University Programs in Health Administration, Washington, DC

Library of Congress Cataloging-in-Publication Data

Library of Congress Cataloging-in-Publication Data is on file at the Library of Congress, Washington, DC.

ISBN: 978-1-64055-379-8

The paper used in this publication meets the minimum requirements of American National Standard for Information Sciences—Permanence of Paper for Printed Library Materials, ANSI Z39.48-1984. ∞ ™

Manuscript editor: Lori Meek Schuldt; Cover designer: James Slate; Layout: PerfecType

Found an error or a typo? We want to know! Please e-mail it to hapbooks@ache.org, mentioning the book's title and putting "Book Error" in the subject line.

For photocopying and copyright information, please contact Copyright Clearance Center at www.copyright.com or at (978) 750-8400.

Health Administration Press
A division of the Foundation of the American
   College of Healthcare Executives
300 S. Riverside Plaza, Suite 1900
Chicago, IL 60606-6698
(312) 424-2800

Association of University Programs
   in Health Administration
1730 Rhode Island Ave NW
Suite 810
Washington, DC 20036
(202) 763-7283

We express our great appreciation to Myron Fottler, who has been an active participant in all editions of this book and played a central role in developing the framework guiding this text.

BRIEF CONTENTS

DETAILED CONTENTS

PREFACE

Healthcare is undergoing major changes as a result of a multitude of factors, including rapidly changing technology, cost pressures and value-based payment models, unprecedented consumer access to information, globalization and global changes, changing demographics, and new levels and forms of competition among healthcare organizations. Whereas some changes have been somewhat predictable, others have occurred abruptly, with little warning. The COVID-19 pandemic is the most notable of these changes, affecting every aspect of healthcare delivery. Change is a staple in healthcare: a Google search for "health care change" generates close to eight million results.

Human resources—that is, people—represent the bedrock of US healthcare organizations. As of this writing, the healthcare industry employs more than 22 million workers, or 14 percent of all US workers (Laughlin et al. 2021). Even with these astronomical numbers, we face severe staffing shortages with the confluence of the aging of the population and of the healthcare workforce. For many years, healthcare workforce data have shown that many communities experience chronic shortages among a wide range of healthcare workers, and there are widespread disparities in the geographic distribution of the healthcare workforce. For those unconvinced by the data, workforce shortages resulting from the pandemic unequivocally sent the message that healthcare workers are a scarce resource that we should nurture, develop, and treat with the utmost care. Yet if we speak with a random group of workers in the healthcare workforce, it is doubtful that we would find the sentiment reflected that they are treated with the respect and care required of a scarce resource. It's not that we don't know how to manage healthcare workers; rather, it is a question of how well healthcare managers understand the fundamental principles of effective human resources management.

Anybody who has worked in any type of organization—whether a hospital, a sports team, the military, or an educational institution—knows that planning is the easy part. A soccer team prepares to meet its opposition by understanding its own strengths and weaknesses and those of the opposition. However, putting this plan into practice—implementation—is fraught with all kinds of obstacles. These obstacles are particularly intense in healthcare organizations, and the possibility of failed implementation can be catastrophic. When implementation fails in a sports team, a team loses and fans feel disappointed for a day or two. In a healthcare organization, patients may die, employees may be injured, and the organization's very survival can be put at risk.

This book is about putting plans into practice. Specifically, we address what is indisputably the most important part of implementation: the workforce. All too often, managers become so enraptured and self-satisfied with their plans that they ignore the people who are responsible for putting plans into practice. If we value employees who are patient oriented and empathetic, are we considering these qualities when we hire people? If we want to retain our employees (and not have them leave if they are offered an additional dollar per hour by another organization), do we know the factors that are related to employee turnover and retention? If we want our managers to help employees improve, do we train our managers in how to conduct performance reviews and coach employees toward success? As this book illustrates, solutions to workforce challenges are complex, and managers need to be cognizant of a multitude of factors that affect the quality and sustainability of the workforce. These factors include the manner in which we select and supervise employees, perceptions of fairness and equity in compensation, and the way we work with diverse populations of workers and patients.

The challenges encountered in motivating and managing the workforce are not lost on entrepreneurs, consultants, and "pop business" writers (if you are in doubt, visit an airport's bookstore or google "books on managing people"). What we frequently find are books that are billed as the *latest* solution to workforce challenges; all too often, they are put forward as commonsense cure-alls. Books that present the topic as complex don't sell; simplicity sells.

The fact is, managing the workforce *is* complex—and uncertain. There is no magic single solution. If there were, we would not have a flourishing market for management cure-alls. This book is in many ways a back-to-basics approach. Managers frequently rely on common sense in managing people, but common sense is not always correct, and situations do not present themselves neatly tailored to our theories and expectations.

This book sets forth fundamental concepts that will help healthcare managers do the most important and most difficult part of their job: managing the people. Having a strong knowledge base in what works is fundamental to good management, and that is what we offer in this book. We acknowledge the complexity of managing people. Needless to say, you will not find simple answers in this book; that would be a recipe for failure. What we do offer in this book is information, best practices, ways to analyze workforce problems, evidence about what works and under what circumstances, and tangible evidence-based strategies for successfully working with employees so that our carefully laid-out plans are effectively implemented.

This book is intended for current and aspiring managers, and not solely for people employed in human resources departments in organizations. Our philosophy is that everyone manages relationships with others, whether one is a supervisor or an employee who must manage relationships with coworkers and with one or more bosses. In sum, *we are all human resource managers.*

CHAPTER OVERVIEWS

Workforce management requires an understanding of multiple disciplines and functions, such as employee motivation, compensation, and training strategies. A successful manager will understand the multitude of disciplines required for managing the workforce. However, they must also be able to synthesize these areas of knowledge and recognize that organizations are systems, and as in systems, changes in one part of an organization affect other parts of the organization. For example, if we change the way we pay employees, how will it affect employee motivation, productivity, and turnover? Although this book is divided in a disciplinary manner for ease of presentation, it should be understood that effective managers will master these areas and also develop the ability to view management and organizations systemically.

Chapter 1, by Carla Jackie Sampson, introduces the concept of strategic human resources management. For many years, human resources management has had an often well-deserved reputation for playing a passive role in organizations. In contrast to such functions as marketing and research and development, which were seen as contributing to organizational growth and performance, the personnel department did not appear to support the organization but instead appeared to keep it from flourishing. Rather than finding ways to promote progress in the organization, the personnel department was often perceived as standing in the way of innovation and change.

In this first chapter, Sampson sets the stage for this entire volume. The approach stresses the need to ensure that the way in which we manage people supports the organization's mission, strategies, and goals. The chapter emphasizes the importance of positive employee outcomes, particularly inclusion, belonging, and well-being for positive organizational outcomes. It presents a vision for human resources in which the responsibility for managing people is not restricted to a particular department but is the responsibility of everyone in the organization. The remainder of this book expands on this simple framework: aligning our human resources management practices with the interests of the organization.

Chapter 2, by Patrick D. Shay and Dolores G. Clement, provides the reader with an understanding of the variety of professionals working in healthcare organizations. Highlighting the major health professionals, the authors describe the unique characteristics of these professions, paying particular attention to their functions in healthcare, educational requirements, licensure, changing roles, and future prospects for professional groups. They also address issues such as academic progression for nurses and advanced practice nurses, the supply challenges facing nursing, and some emerging and evolving roles.

Like much of healthcare management, effective human resources management requires an understanding of an enormous body of laws and regulations. Written by Drake Maynard, chapter 3 provides an overview of laws related to such topics as employee rights, discipline and privacy, sexual harassment, discrimination, equal employment opportunity, and the protections for LGBTQ+ persons. A later chapter addresses the specific laws related to unionization and union–management relations.

In chapter 4, Sean A. Newman and Paige N. Ocker discuss job analysis and job design, which form an essential foundation for virtually every other human resources management function. Effective job analysis provides managers with an understanding of the purpose and content of jobs, which in turn allows us to create job descriptions and identify the qualifications for particular jobs. Such goals as effective recruitment and fair compensation depend on having a clear understanding of the requirements of a job. The authors discuss the increasing application of analytics and algorithms and other tools to job analysis, and they explore workgroup redesign, telecommuting, and other workplace developments. Newman and Ocker contend that the deliberate structuring of work can lead to improved individual, group, and organizational performance.

Staffing and keeping competent employees pose an increasing challenge for healthcare organizations. In chapter 5, Gabriela "Gabbi" J. Maris and Bruce J. Fried address the interrelated topics of recruitment, selection, and retention. Reasons that employees choose to accept jobs, strategies for successful selection of employees, and evidence about why healthcare employees stay with or leave organizations are the focus of this chapter. The authors also look at staffing from a global perspective and address such controversial topics as the global migration of healthcare workers and the ethics of foreign recruitment of physicians and nurses. This chapter also examines the role of technology in recruitment and selection, including social media screening, and discusses the impact of the COVID-19 pandemic on retention.

With the rapid changes in healthcare, employees and organizations require continual renewal. Organizational and employee development is a characteristic of all successful organizations, yet many healthcare organizations pay scant attention to the link between these initiatives and the organizational culture. In chapter 6, Carla Jackie Sampson and Julene Campion provide insights on the link between employee engagement and organizational effectiveness. They discuss employee engagement interventions, onboarding, succession planning, coaching, and mentoring. They explore trends for the future of organizational and employee development, such as microlearning and on-demand training.

Performance measurement and improvement have become central features of healthcare organizations. In many instances, healthcare organizations are financially rewarded for excellent performance. However, excellent organizations depend on high-performing employees. Performance management seeks to improve employee performance by accurately evaluating employee performance, providing feedback to employees, coaching, designing strategies for improvement, and evaluating the effectiveness of improvement efforts. In chapter 7, Bruce J. Fried offers a variety of approaches to performance management. He argues that effective performance management often requires a change in the organizational mind-set because performance evaluation is often viewed as a punitive and judgmental process, rather than a positive and collaborative experience.

In chapter 8, Bruce J. Fried, Brigid K. Grabert, and John Cashion discuss the complex topic of compensation in healthcare organizations. Compensation is anything but a routine function. This chapter addresses the organizational challenge of balancing internal equity and external competitiveness in compensation policy, and the role of labor market conditions in determining compensation. The chapter also discusses physician pay-for-performance compensation and the changing relationship between physicians and organizations, which affects how physicians are compensated.

Organizational reward systems are not limited to compensation. A significant portion of staff costs in organizations is related to employee benefits. In chapter 9, Melissa G. McCraw and Dolores G. Clement bring their collective knowledge and experience to the topic and provide a highly readable and comprehensive review of employee benefits, including history, current practices and issues, budgetary implications, and benefits administration. They also discuss new directions in benefits, such as including mental health, wellness, and fitness programs.

The role of labor unions in healthcare organizations continues to evolve, along with the legal landscape of unionization and union–management relations. Healthcare and the public sector remain the two major targets for unionization in the United States. Carla Jackie Sampson, Bruce J. Fried, and Donna Malvey bring their expertise to this topic in chapter 10, where they examine legislative and judicial rulings that affect management of organized labor in healthcare settings. They also address the role played by social media in union organizing, collective bargaining, and contract administration, as well as the implications of the COVID-19 pandemic on labor relations and organizing activity.

With an increasingly diverse US population, American healthcare organizations must understand diversity, inclusion, and belonging to retain diverse employees and reflect the populations they serve. In chapter 11, Carla Jackie Sampson, Bruce J. Fried, and Jeffrey Simms stress the importance of inclusive leadership to shape the culture of the organization. They champion concrete actions to move the organization toward greater inclusivity for the many dimensions of diversity. The chapter emphasizes that diversity is the result of belonging and has expanded content on the culture change necessary to support these sustained activities.

Quality improvement is now a mainstay of healthcare organizations. While much attention has been focused on quality improvement methods, relatively little has been given to the workforce aspects of developing and implementing quality improvement initiatives in healthcare organizations. In chapter 12, Hilary K. Hecht and Bruce J. Fried address quality improvement and implementation science from the perspective of the healthcare workforce. They illustrate the role of implementation science for successful quality and patient safety improvements and compare the differences and complementarity of implementation science and quality improvement methodologies. They examine the role of teams in this crucial work and explain how to engage and motivate team members.

Finally, in our response to the COVID-19 pandemic, we were forced to reckon with the scarcity of healthcare workers. Stress and burnout became part of the layperson's vocabulary, and healthcare managers prioritized strategies to help ensure positive outcomes for their employees. Thus, employee well-being is the focus of a new chapter 13 in this third edition. Written by Amanda Raffenaud and Tina Yeung, the chapter outlines burnout concepts in the health professions and describes specific concerns for physicians, nurses, medical students and residents, and healthcare executives. This timely addition provides strategies to address stress and burnout in healthcare organizations and foster employee well-being.

A NOTE ABOUT LANGUAGE

So that all people of Latin descent may see themselves represented in this book, the editors have specifically selected *Latine* over *Latino/a/x*. We understand that words ending in the letter *X* are difficult for native Spanish speakers to pronounce. Thus, using the gender-inclusive term *Latinx* may unintentionally erase a spectrum of Latine diversity not represented in the feminine and masculine *Latina* or *Latino*, respectively. For more information, see Chery (2022). Health Administration Press also recognizes the use of *they*, *them*, *their*, and *theirs* as gender-neutral singular pronouns.

REFERENCES

Chery, S. 2022. "A Guide to How Words Like Latinx and Hispanic Came About." *Washington Post*. Published October 1. www.washingtonpost.com/lifestyle/2022/10/01/hispanic-latino-latinx-latine-words-history/.

Laughlin, L., A. Anderson, A. Martinez, and A. Gayfield. 2021. "Who Are Our Health Care Workers?" US Census Bureau. Published April 5. www.census.gov/library/stories/2021/04/who-are-our-health-care-workers.html.

INSTRUCTOR RESOURCES

This book's Instructor Resources include an Instructor's Manual and test bank.

For the most up-to-date information about this book and its Instructor Resources, go to ache.org/HAP and search for the book's order code (2484I).

This book's instructor resources are available to instructors who adopt this book for use in their course. For access information, please email hapbooks@ache.org.

ACKNOWLEDGMENTS

I wish to express heartfelt thanks to my wife, Nancy, for her unrelenting patience and support. As a clinical social worker, Nancy knows a great deal about working with people and dealing effectively with the most difficult situations. She has taught me more than I could ever imagine about perseverance and dealing courageously with personal adversity. Through our children—Noah, Shoshana, and Aaron—I have learned about coping with the large and small challenges of life while continuing to grow and develop. They have been outstanding teachers.

Bruce Fried, PhD
University of North Carolina at Chapel Hill

I thank Dr. Myron Fottler, editor of the previous editions of this text, for the opportunity to try on his shoes. Although my parents did not get see who I grew up to be, I am still grateful for the enthusiastic encouragement they gave their bespectacled bookworm. Books are still my respite from the world and my opportunity to learn something new every day.

I thank my family and my chosen family for putting up with my lengthy disappearances behind my laptop, and the calls I have yet to return. I am grateful for your grace and understanding that the lime (the 868 diaspora will get this) can still go on without me.

I could only do this book project with the stellar support of the Online MHA team at NYU Wagner. Tiffany, Erica, and Henrie, thank you all for your time and talents in supporting the health programs and preparing the next generation of Wagner leaders. Everyone deserves a team as talented as they are. Every day they prove my maxim: people matter.

Carla Jackie Sampson, PhD, MBA, FACHE
New York University

This book would not have been possible without our collaborative authors, who worked hard and creatively to put their expertise into a readable, textbook format. They were extremely patient with us as we asked for revisions and clarifications. Our authors came through, and we are grateful for their generosity. Michael Cunningham, Molly Lowe, La'Toya Carter, and Kevin McLenithan at Health Administration Press have been supportive and exercised remarkable patience throughout this process. The authors also acknowledge the excellent, timely, and high-quality editorial services provided by Lori Meek Schuldt, who did an exceptional job in bringing this book to completion.

Bruce Fried and Carla Jackie Sampson

CHAPTER 1

STRATEGIC HUMAN RESOURCES MANAGEMENT

Carla Jackie Sampson

LEARNING OBJECTIVES

After completing this chapter, you should be able to

➤ define strategic human resources management;

➤ outline key human resources functions;

➤ discuss the significance of strategic human resources management to present and future healthcare executives;

➤ describe the organizational and human resources systems that affect organizational outcomes; and

➤ outline the need for a balance between positive employee and organizational outcomes.

VIGNETTE

Kamla Seers is the administrator of the Sunset Assisted Living Center in Orlando, Florida. Three years ago, they brought board members, medical staff, and a top management team together to develop a new strategic plan for the organization. The new plan identified a series of goals and objectives in the areas of marketing, finance, and information systems. In addition, the organization set a goal of annual growth in resident census of 10 percent. The strategic planning group assumed that human resources would be available to implement the plan as needed. Then they lurched into the pandemic.

Now Kamla has discovered that Sunset has not been able to recruit and retain adequate numbers of nurses and other allied health personnel needed to implement the strategic plan. Worse, current operations are hampered by a chronic staffing shortage because of burnout. Further, several senior clinical and administrative staff have indicated their plans to retire within the next year. Overall employee turnover averaged 22 percent per year in the last three years, and for the current year turnover has reached 49 percent to date. They will now have to report to the board that the resident census goals cannot be reached because of the organization's inability to adequately staff the facility.

INTRODUCTION

The previous vignette illustrates a critical error that many healthcare organizations make when they develop and attempt to implement their strategic business plan without consideration of human resources. Sunset failed to consider the crucial role of an adequate quantity and quality of human resources in the successful implementation of its business strategy.

Like most other service industries, the healthcare industry is labor intensive. One reason for healthcare's reliance on an extensive workforce is the real-time interaction between healthcare consumers and healthcare providers—an integral part of the delivery of health services. Another reason is that employees from several professions are required to provide a defined service as specified by their licenses to practice. Given the dependence on healthcare professionals to deliver service, the possibility of wide variations in service quality must be recognized within an employee as skills and competencies change over time and greatly depend on the well-being and vitality of the workforce.

The intensive use of labor and the variability in professional practice require that leaders in the healthcare field manage the performance of the people involved in the delivery of services. Effective management requires that healthcare executives understand the factors that influence the performance of their employees. These factors include the traditional **human resources management (HRM)** activities (i.e., recruitment and selection, training and development, performance management, compensation, and employee relations) and the environmental and other organizational aspects that inform human resources (HR) activities.

human resources management (HRM) The processes (recruitment, selection, training and development, performance management, compensation, and employee relations) performed within the organization or external to it and more informal management of employees performed by all administrators.

DEFINITION AND SIGNIFICANCE OF STRATEGIC HUMAN RESOURCES MANAGEMENT

Strategic human resources management (SHRM) is the comprehensive set of managerial activities and tasks related to developing and maintaining a qualified and engaged workforce. This workforce contributes to organizational effectiveness, as defined by the organization's strategic goals. SHRM occurs in a complex and dynamic environment within the organizational context. HR managers must adopt a strategic perspective of their job and recognize the critical links between organizational and HR strategies. To produce the required staff competencies and behaviors, the healthcare organization needs to implement the right mix of recruitment, selection, compensation, performance management, employee development, and other HR strategies, policies, and practices.

This book explains methods for increasing the probability of hiring competent people and of those people ably performing needed tasks after hire. To implement these methods and practices, organizations must

strategic human resources management (SHRM) The process of formulating and executing human resources (HR) policies and practices that produce employee competencies and behaviors required for the organization to achieve its strategic objectives.

◆   determine requirements for positions,

◆   recruit and select qualified people,

◆ train and develop employees to meet future organizational needs,

◆ evaluate job performance, and

◆ provide adequate rewards to attract and retain top performers.

All these functions must be managed within society's ethical as well as legal constraints—legislation, regulation, and court decisions.

This chapter emphasizes that HR functions are performed within the context of the overall activities of the organization. These functions are influenced or constrained by the environment, the organizational mission and strategies that are being pursued, and the organization's internal systems.

Why study SHRM? How does this topic relate to the career interests or aspirations of present and future healthcare executives? Staffing the organization, designing jobs, building teams, developing employee skills, identifying approaches to improve performance and customer service, protecting employee well-being, and rewarding employee success are as relevant to *line managers* (those with formal authority to direct or supervise others) as they are to HR managers. A successful healthcare executive needs to understand human behavior, work with employees effectively, and be knowledgeable about numerous systems and practices available to put together a skilled and engaged workforce. The executive also has to be aware of political, economic, technological, social, and legal issues that affect human resources and, in turn, facilitate or constrain efforts to attain strategic objectives.

Healthcare executives do not want to hire the wrong person, experience high turnover, manage unmotivated employees, be taken to court for discrimination actions, be cited for unsafe practices, have their patients' satisfaction undermined by poorly trained staff, or commit unfair labor practices. Despite their best efforts, executives often fail at HRM because they hire the wrong people or do not motivate or develop their staff. You are likely to manage people at some point in your career in healthcare management. Carefully studying this book and implementing effective HR management techniques will help you avoid these mistakes.

Healthcare organizations can gain a competitive advantage by effectively managing their human resources. This competitive advantage may be in the form of cost leadership (e.g., being a low-cost provider), product differentiation (e.g., having high levels of service quality), or innovation (new ideas). Today's healthcare leaders are competing on the *value of care*—the highest quality of patient outcomes at the lowest cost to payers—under new healthcare reimbursement methods. Thus, attention to service delivery quality is a key component in the management of healthcare organizations for which human capital is a critical component (Khatri, Gupta, and Varma 2017).

Achieving competitive advantage through human resources must be based on the combination of an organization's human capital strategies and core capabilities that are unique to the organization. Healthcare executives cannot simply rely on the benchmarks and strategies of others, even though they may be suggestive of better approaches to managing people. Instead, leaders who successfully develop and implement their own HR strategies can achieve sustained competitive advantage in their markets. However, improving organizational outcomes is heavily dependent on employee motivation and engagement (Melián-González et al. 2015). Thus, ensuring positive employee outcomes is a mandate for all leaders at every level of the organization. The future belongs to healthcare executives who can improve and sustain organizational performance while managing change through engaged and committed employees.

Organizations can position themselves for sustainable competitive advantage through SHRM by doing the following:

◆ Linking organizational capabilities and culture to desirable traits and behaviors for the recruitment and performance management processes

◆ Investing in employee learning and development such that employee knowledge and competencies are unmatched by competitors

◆ Deploying strategies to retain top talent

◆ Leveraging human capital to improve organizational efficiency and effectiveness

◆ Harnessing the power of analytics to inform SHRM

Organizations achieve competitive advantage through SHRM for the following reasons:

◆ SHRM requires proactive rather than reactive behavior.

◆ SHRM requires evidence-based decision making.

◆ Company goals are communicated explicitly.

◆ Focus is the gap between the current and desired situation.

◆ Line managers are involved in the HR planning process.

◆ Opportunities and constraints are identified in implementing strategic plans.

A STRATEGIC PERSPECTIVE ON HUMAN RESOURCES

Managers at all levels are becoming increasingly aware that critical sources of competitive advantage include appropriate systems for attracting, developing, motivating, and managing the organization's human resources. Adopting a strategic view of human resources involves considering employees as human assets and developing appropriate policies and programs to increase the value of these assets to the organization and the marketplace. Effective organizations realize that their employees have value, much as the organization's physical and capital assets have value, and investing in these assets prepares the organization for the future.

The American College of Healthcare Executives (ACHE) conducts an annual survey of hospital CEOs. For almost two decades CEOs consistently ranked financial challenges as their number one concern—until 2021. In that year, shortages for all employee positions, including physicians, eclipsed finance as the most pressing challenge (ACHE 2022). Forward-thinking healthcare leaders recognize the critical role of HR in future performance and address these concerns with short- and long-term solutions. In the short term, strategic investments in staffing, employee development, and well-being will be required. In the long term, leaders will invest in HR as an asset and create pathways to build capacity for success (Kupletsky 2022).

Viewing human resources from an investment perspective, rather than as variable costs of production, allows the organization to determine how to best invest in its people, which leads to a dilemma. An organization that does not invest in its employees may be less attractive to current and prospective employees, which causes inefficiency and weakens the organization's competitive position. However, an organization that does invest in its people needs to ensure that these investments are not lost by developing strategies to retain employees long enough to realize an acceptable return on its investment in employee skills and knowledge.

Not all organizations realize that human assets can be strategically managed from an investment perspective. Management might not appreciate the value of its human assets relative to its other assets such as brand identity, distribution channels, real estate, and facilities and equipment. Organizations may be characterized as HR-oriented or not, based on their answers to the following questions:

◆ Does the organization see its people as central to its purpose and strategy?

◆ Do the organization's mission statement and strategy objectives mention or espouse the value of human assets?

◆ Does the organization's management philosophy prevent the depreciation of its human assets?

◆ Does the organization prioritize a positive work environment for all employees?

◆ Does the organization consider what skills will position its operations most favorably in the future?

An HR-oriented organization would answer yes to all these questions.

Organizations often hesitate to adopt an HR investment perspective because it involves making a longer-term commitment to employees. Because employees can leave and most organizations use only short-term performance measures, investments in human assets are often ignored. Well-performing organizations may feel no need to change their HR strategies. Those that are not doing as well usually need a "quick fix" and therefore ignore longer-term investments in people. However, although investment in human resources may not yield immediate results, it yields positive outcomes that are likely to last longer and are more difficult for competitors to duplicate.

THE SHRM APPROACH

A strategic approach to human resources management begins with the organization's mission and includes the following:

◆ Assessment of the organization's environment

◆ Business strategy formulation

◆ HR specifications based on the business strategy

◆ Comparison of the current HR inventory—numbers, characteristics, and practices—with future strategic requirements

◆ Development of HR strategy based on the differences between the current inventory and future requirements

◆ Implementation of the appropriate HR practices to reinforce the business strategy and to attain competitive advantage

Changes in the external and internal environments have a direct impact on how organizations are run and people are managed. Some external changes represent opportunities for the organization, and others represent threats. *Environmental scanning* is the systematic monitoring of major environmental forces affecting the organization. Internally, changes may also occur in terms of the organization's strengths and weaknesses as leadership, culture, and organizational capabilities change. In addition, the likelihood of unexpected events requires the organization to be flexible and agile while moored to the mission and values.

The organization's mission, vision, and values must also be assessed to determine an appropriate business strategy. Examples include being a low-cost provider or differentiating the organization based on a unique service or outstanding customer service or social responsibility. After the business strategy has been determined, the organization must develop an HR strategy that will execute the business strategy by making sure that talent is available in the right numbers, with the right skills, and at the right time.

The *HR strategy* generally refers to a company's development, deployment, and retention of its employees to create value. More specifically, the HR strategy commonly includes approaches that direct staffing, training, and compensation activities. To optimize performance in the face of constant change, organizations today must devote more attention to business strategy implementation and execution. The HR strategy facilitates business strategy implementation and execution.

Exhibit 1.1 illustrates some strategic HR trends that affect job analysis and planning, staffing, training and development, performance management, compensation, employee rights and discipline, and employee and labor relations. These trends are discussed in greater detail in later chapters. The key point of exhibit 1.1 is that organizations have moved to higher levels of flexibility, collaboration, decentralization, and team orientation and are using technology and analytics to transform work.

The SHRM Model

As illustrated in exhibit 1.2, a healthcare organization is made up of systems that require constant interaction within the environment. To remain viable, an organization must extend

Exhibit 1.1
Strategic Human
Resources Trends

Old HR Practices	Current HR Practices
Job Analysis/Planning	
Explicit job descriptions	Broad job classes
Detailed HR planning	Leverage technology and analytics to transform work
Detailed controls	Flexibility
Efficiency	Innovation and technology integration
Staffing	
Supervisors make hiring decisions	Team makes hiring decisions
Emphasis on candidate's technical qualifications	Emphasis on fit of applicant within the culture
Layoffs	Incentives to retire voluntarily
Letting laid-off workers fend for themselves	Providing continued support to laid-off workers
Workforce diversity is the result of recruitment activities in compliance with equal opportunity	Workforce diversity is defined in the context of the mission and is the result of an inclusive culture

Old HR Practices	Current HR Practices
Training and Development	
Individual training	Team-based training
Job-specific training	Generic training emphasizing flexibility and optimizing talent
"Buying" skills by hiring experienced workers	"Upskilling" or "reskilling" workers to meet new or expected demands
Organization responsible for career development	Employee responsible for skills development according to personal interests matched to organizational or project priorities
Performance Management	
Uniform appraisal procedures	Customized appraisals
Control-oriented appraisals	Developmental appraisals linked to organizational goals
Supervisor input only	Appraisals with multiple inputs
Compensation	
Seniority	Performance-based pay
Centralized pay decisions	Decentralized pay decisions
Fixed fringe benefits	Flexible fringe benefits (cafeteria approach)
Employee Rights and Discipline	
Emphasis on employer protection	Emphasis on employee protection
Informal ethical standards	Explicit ethical codes and enforcement procedures
Emphasis on discipline to reduce mistakes	Emphasis on prevention to reduce mistakes
Employee and Labor Relations	
Top-down communication	Bottom-up communication and feedback
Adversarial approach	Collaborative approach
Preventive labor relations	Employee freedom of choice

EXHIBIT 1.1
Strategic Human Resources Trends
(continued)

its strategic planning and thinking to external changes because the internal components of the organization are affected by these changes.

The characteristics, performance levels, and alignment in operating practices among these systems improve organizational and employee performance. HR goals, objectives, process systems, culture, technology, and workforce closely align with one another (internal alignment) and with various levels of organizational strategies (external alignment) (Ford et al. 2006).

INTERNAL AND EXTERNAL ENVIRONMENTAL ASSESSMENT

Environmental assessment is a crucial element of SHRM. Changes in the legal and regulatory climate, economic conditions, and labor market realities mean that healthcare organizations face constantly changing opportunities and threats. These opportunities and threats make particular services or markets more or less attractive.

Among the trends currently affecting the healthcare labor environment are greater workforce diversity, aging of the workforce, union organizing, protracted skilled labor shortages, changing worker values and attitudes, and advances in technology. Healthcare executives have responded to these external environmental pressures through various internal structural changes, including developing network structures, joining healthcare systems, participating in mergers and acquisitions, forming work teams, leveraging continuous quality improvement, allowing telecommuting, leasing employees, outsourcing work, using additional temporary or contingent workers or internal floating pools, and positioning for medical tourism. In addition to assessing their organizational strengths and weaknesses, healthcare executives need to assess their internal systems; their human resources' skills, knowledge, and abilities; and their portfolio of service markets. Managers should develop HR policies and practices that are closely related to, influenced by, and supportive of the strategic goals and plans of their organization.

Organizations, either explicitly or implicitly, pursue a strategy in their operations. Deciding on a strategy involves determining the products or services that will be created and the markets to which the chosen services will be offered. After the selections are made, the methods to compete in the chosen market must be identified from among the available or potential internal resources.

As shown in exhibit 1.2, strategies should consider environmental conditions and organizational capabilities. To take advantage of opportunities and circumvent threats, managers must have detailed knowledge of the current and future operating environment and link SHRM to organization risk management processes. Knowing internal strengths and weaknesses allows managers to develop plans based on an accurate assessment of the organization's ability to perform as desired in the marketplace.

Exhibit 1.2 indicates that the SHRM process starts with the identification of the organization's purpose, mission, and business unit, as defined by the board of directors and the senior management team. The process ends with HR serving as an adviser to

environmental assessment
A crucial element of strategic human resources management in which an organization reviews the changes in the legal and regulatory climate, economic conditions, and labor market realities to understand current opportunities and threats.

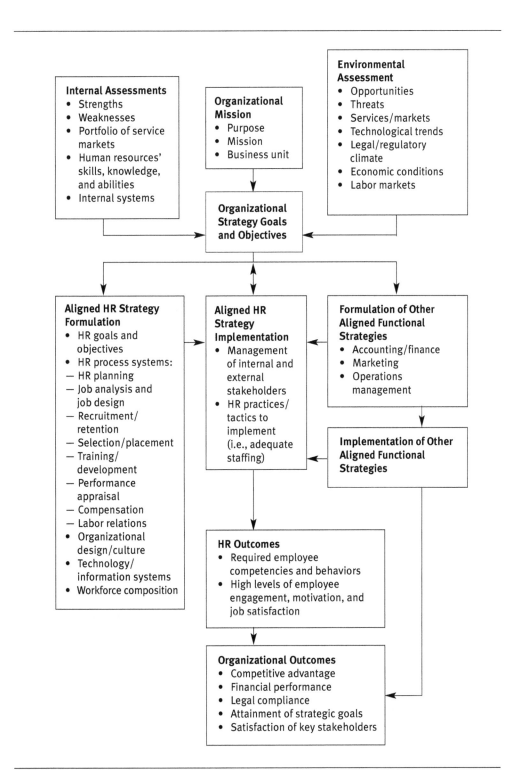

EXHIBIT 1.2
Strategic Human
Resources
Management
Model

Internal Assessments
- Strengths
- Weaknesses
- Portfolio of service markets
- Human resources' skills, knowledge, and abilities
- Internal systems

Organizational Mission
- Purpose
- Mission
- Business unit

Environmental Assessment
- Opportunities
- Threats
- Services/markets
- Technological trends
- Legal/regulatory climate
- Economic conditions
- Labor markets

Organizational Strategy Goals and Objectives

Aligned HR Strategy Formulation
- HR goals and objectives
- HR process systems:
  - HR planning
  - Job analysis and job design
  - Recruitment/retention
  - Selection/placement
  - Training/development
  - Performance appraisal
  - Compensation
  - Labor relations
- Organizational design/culture
- Technology/information systems
- Workforce composition

Aligned HR Strategy Implementation
- Management of internal and external stakeholders
- HR practices/tactics to implement (i.e., adequate staffing)

Formulation of Other Aligned Functional Strategies
- Accounting/finance
- Marketing
- Operations management

Implementation of Other Aligned Functional Strategies

HR Outcomes
- Required employee competencies and behaviors
- High levels of employee engagement, motivation, and job satisfaction

Organizational Outcomes
- Competitive advantage
- Financial performance
- Legal compliance
- Attainment of strategic goals
- Satisfaction of key stakeholders

the operations. Under this view of human resources management, the HR manager's job is to help operating managers achieve their strategic goals by serving as a partner in all employment-related activities and issues.

ORGANIZATIONAL MISSION AND CORPORATE STRATEGY

An organization's **purpose** is its basic reason for existence. The purpose of a hospital may be to deliver high-quality clinical care to the population in a given service area. An organization's **mission**, created by its board and senior managers, specifies how the organization intends to manage itself to most effectively fulfill its purpose. The mission statement often provides subtle clues about the importance the organization places on its human resources.

The first step in formulating a corporate and business strategy is doing an analysis of the organization's strengths, weaknesses, opportunities, and threats—a **SWOT analysis**. Managers may then use the organization's strengths to capitalize on environmental opportunities and cope with environmental threats. Managers can also overcome identified weaknesses to deal with environmental threats or minimize weaknesses to avoid environmental threats. Human resources play a fundamental role in SWOT analysis because the employees' skills (or lack thereof) and the organization's ability (or inability) to attract new talent represent significant strengths (or weaknesses). Human resources has a bigger role when the organization takes an even closer look at units of the enterprise to find opportunities to direct resources and improve value when conducting a **value chain analysis**. The analysis divides the whole organization into smaller units of activity, like links in a chain, and examines them to identify new sources of advantage. An organizations that proactively and strategically links its talent with value is better positioned to achieve its goals than one that does not (Barriere, Owens, and Pobereskin 2018).

Most organizations formulate strategy at three basic levels: corporate, business, and functional. **Corporate strategy** is a set of strategic alternatives from which an organization chooses as it manages its operations simultaneously across several industries and markets. **Business strategy** is a set of strategic alternatives from which an organization chooses to compete in a particular industry or market most effectively. **Functional strategies** consider how the organization will manage each of its major functions, such as marketing, finance, and human resources.

A key challenge for HR managers in organizations using a corporate growth strategy is recruiting and training the many qualified employees needed to provide services in added operations. Training programs may also be needed to onboard and update the skills of incoming and existing employees. When HR is a true strategic partner, all organizational parties consult with and support one another.

HR STRATEGY FORMULATION AND IMPLEMENTATION

After the organization's corporate and business strategies have been determined, managers can develop an HR strategy. This strategy commonly includes a staffing strategy (planning, recruitment, selection, and placement), a developmental strategy (performance management, training, development, and career or succession planning), and a compensation strategy (salary structure, benefits, and employee incentives). Formulating an aligned strategy necessitates asking the following questions:

◆ What types of individuals do we need to attract and retain?

◆ How will we develop individual skill sets that we will need in the future?

◆ How will we reward these individuals to better enhance employee productivity and protect their well-being?

A **staffing strategy** is a set of activities used by the organization to determine its future HR needs, recruit qualified applicants with an interest in the organization, and select the best of those applicants as new employees. This strategy should be put into place only after a careful and systematic development of the corporate and business strategies so that staffing activities mesh with other strategic elements. For example, if a reduction of the workforce is part of the business strategy, the staffing strategy will focus on determining which employees to retain and how to redeploy or lay off the others.

A **developmental strategy** helps the organization enhance the quality of its human resources. The developmental strategy must be consistent with corporate and business strategies. For example, if the organization wishes to differentiate itself from competitors through customer focus and service quality, it will need to invest heavily in training its employees to provide the highest-quality service and to ensure that performance management focuses on measuring, recognizing, and rewarding performance—all of which lead to high service quality. Alternatively, if the business strategy is to be a leader in innovation, the developmental strategy may focus on training to enhance teamwork, design thinking, and creative problem solving.

A **compensation strategy** must also complement the organization's other strategies. For example, if the organization is pursuing a strategy of related diversification, its compensation strategy must be geared toward rewarding employees whose skills allow them to move from the original business into related businesses—for example, inpatient care to telehealth or hospital-at-home. The organization may choose to pay a premium to highly talented individuals who have competencies that are relevant to one of its new businesses or that may be deployed across the organization.

---

business strategy
A set of strategic alternatives from which an organization chooses to compete in a particular industry or market most effectively.

functional strategies
Strategies that consider how the organization will manage each of its major functions, such as marketing, finance, and human resources.

staffing strategy
A set of activities used by an organization to determine its future human resources needs, recruit qualified applicants with an interest in the organization, and select the best of those applicants as new employees.

developmental strategy
A set of methods that facilitate the enhancement of an organization's human resources' quality.

compensation strategy
The set of rewards that organizations provide to staff in exchange for their performance of various organizational tasks and jobs.

workforce composition
The demographics of the workforce, including factors such as gender, age, ethnicity, marital status, and disability status.

Finally, **workforce composition** and trends also affect HR strategy formulation and implementation. The American workforce has diversified in numerous ways. It has more women, older employees, Latin, Asians, African Americans, workers born outside the United States, people who are differently abled, single parents, lesbian, gay, bisexual, transgender, or queer/questioning (LGBTQ) individuals; and people with special dietary needs or preferences than it did during the twentieth century. Then, most employers observed a fairly predictable employee pattern: People entered the workforce while young, maintained stable employment (with the same employer) for many years, and retired at the usual age—at or around age 65. This pattern has changed and continues to evolve as a result of demographic factors, improved health, changing attitudes to work, employee geographic mobility, and the abolition of mandatory retirement.

By 2045, the American workforce is expected to be "majority minority," that is, the US Census Bureau expects that by 2045, more than half the population will be from a minoritized group or have two or more races, with the latter group the fastest growing of all races/ethnicities. With immigration as the largest driver of population growth in the United States, by 2028, the percentage of foreign-born US citizens and residents will be at the highest level in more than two centuries. By 2040, there will be more adults older age 65 than there are minors aged 17 or younger (Vespa, Armstrong, and Medina 2020). The challenge for healthcare leaders will be how to identify, utilize, develop, retain, and replace the necessary human resources to deliver high-quality health services given the anticipated demographic changes (US Bureau of Labor Statistics 2022). The best strategic HR plans may fail when specific HR programs and tactics are poorly chosen and implemented. They are more likely to be successful when they are compatible with the business strategy, environment, organization structure, culture, and HR capabilities. HR strategies are also more effective when they reinforce one another rather than work as cross forces. For example, work teams are more likely to be successful if performance appraisals use workgroup performance rather than individual performance as a criterion.

The HR strategy implementation requires motivational and communication processes, goal setting, and leadership. Specific practices or tactics, such as training, are also necessary to implement the HR strategy. Methods for implementation also need to be chosen. For example, should the training be provided in-house or outsourced? How will each employee's success in applying the principles learned be measured and rewarded? The answers to such questions provide the specific tactics needed to implement the HR strategy.

EMPLOYEE OUTCOMES AND PERFORMANCE

An organization should provide its workforce with job security, meaningful work, safe conditions of employment, equitable financial compensation, and a satisfactory quality of work life. Organizations cannot attract and retain the number, type, and quality of professionals required to deliver quality health services if the internal work environment is unattractive or the HR practices are ineffective. Employees are a valuable stakeholder group whose concerns are important to the healthcare organization because of the complexity of the services they provide. High employee performance requires employee motivation and commitment to achieve positive organizational outcomes (Kaufman 2015). As was shown in exhibit 1.2, the organization must seek a balance between employee and business outcomes. These outcomes feed back into both internal and environmental characteristics, and the whole process is continuous, evolving, and changing. A sense of belonging, job satisfaction, commitment to the organization, employee engagement, motivation, level of job stress, well-being, and other constructs are the usual measures of employee attitude and positive employee outcomes and are discussed in more detail in later chapters of this book.

MEASURING THE HR FUNCTION

HR metrics are measures of HR outcomes and performance. Part of HR's role as a strategic business partner is to measure the effectiveness of both the HR function as a whole and the various HR tasks. Specifically, the questions often focus on the return on investment (ROI) of HR activities.

HR metrics
Measures of human resources outcomes and performance.

Human capital metrics determine how HR activities contribute to the organization's bottom line (Feffer 2017). Some employers gather data on the ROI of various recruitment sources, such as internet and social media advertising, college recruitment, internal transfers, and career fairs. Other employers track productivity using cost metrics such as the time to fill positions, the percentage of diverse candidates hired and turnover in this population, interview-to-offer ratios, offer-to-acceptance ratios, hiring manager satisfaction, new hire satisfaction, cost per hire, head count ratios, turnover costs, financial benefits of employee retention, and the ROI of training.

Such metrics relate to specific HR activities and also measure the overall contribution of the HR function to organizational performance and outcomes. The HR scorecard is one method to measure this contribution. This tool is basically a modified version of the balanced scorecard, which is a measurement and control system that examines a mix of quantitative and qualitative factors to evaluate organizational performance (Kaplan and Norton 1996). The *balance* in the balanced scorecard reflects the need for short-term and long-term objectives, financial and nonfinancial metrics, lagging and leading indicators, and internal and external performance perspectives. The organization should select a set of metrics that serve as good indicators for the HR activities that support the strategic initiatives critical to organizational outcomes (Mondore 2018). Based on the assumption that what gets measured gets managed, an HR balanced scorecard can measure and monitor many input and output HR indicators that are aligned with the organization's mission and strategic goals.

The Society for Human Resource Management (SHRM 2022) provides a benchmarking service that enables employers to compare their own HR metrics with those of similar employers in the same geographic region and size. While such benchmarks show

how an organization's HR metrics compare to those of competitors, they do not show the extent to which they support its strategic goals. By contrast, *strategy-based* HR metrics do show the extent to which these metrics will achieve the organization's strategic goals. For example, customer service training should contribute to patient satisfaction, customer compliments, and intent to return to the organization.

Examples of HR metrics from SHRM (2022) include the following:

◆ HR to employee ratio

◆ HR expenses to operating expense ratio

◆ HR expense to FTE [full-time equivalency] ratio

◆ Number of positions filled

◆ Time to fill positions

◆ Cost per hire

◆ Annual overall turnover rate

◆ Annual voluntary turnover rate

◆ Annual involuntary turnover rate

◆ Physicians within the organizational succession plan

◆ Percentage of employees participating in tuition reimbursement

◆ Revenue per FTE

evidence-based HRM
Human resource management decisions based on critical thinking applied to available data, internal business metrics, or results of research studies.

The process of using metrics (i.e., data, facts, and scientific rigor) and critically evaluated research to support HR proposals, decisions, strategies, and tactics is often referred to as **evidence-based HRM.** Strategic HR metrics provide material to allow healthcare managers to apply scientific thinking to "evidence"—data, information, research—to support their decisions. Thinking like scientists requires the manager to be both objective and experimental in evaluating and gathering information about what works and does not work in terms of HR strategies, which may facilitate strategic goals. For example, if you wish to evaluate the particular training program of a patient satisfaction plan, don't wait to implement the plan on all staff members. Instead, implement it for an "experimental" group, which receives the training, and do not implement it for a similar control group. Then compare changes over time between the experimental group and the control group in terms of patient satisfaction scores.

Strategic HR metrics can give healthcare leaders insights on human resources strategies as well as operational and strategic goals. However, managers must approach these metrics with a good understanding of the link between the human resources and strategic outcomes to leverage these insights effectively (Huselid 2018). The strategic HR metrics selected for monitoring will support the mission and outcomes prioritized by management and will be reflected in the selected strategies, tactics, and HR practices.

Examples of strategic HR metrics (SHRM 2022) include the following:

◆ Average percentage of employees hired based on a validated test

◆ Average number of hours of training for new employees

◆ Average percentage of employees receiving a regular performance appraisal

◆ Average percentage of employees eligible for incentive pay

◆ Average percentage of employees routinely working on teams

◆ Employees receiving relative financial and operational reporting information

◆ Number of qualified applicants per position

Ready availability of data that drive all HR metrics can extend organizational capabilities from a *retrospective* (backward-looking) HR view to one that is *prospective* (forward-looking). Organizations also can leverage **predictive HR analytics** to inform decisions about organizational and people outcomes. Predictive HR analytics uses modeling techniques to mine existing data to identify potential causes for HR outcomes. These results can then be used to indicate future organizational or people outcomes, where appropriate (Edwards and Edwards 2019). However, these models built with historical data are only as robust as the quality of the data available. Leaders must be aware that these techniques can replicate biases in the underlying historical data (Hamilton and Sodeman 2020). Since these data were originally classified and collected by a person, the technique then replicates what or even who is included or excluded in the models, and how the data are categorized.

predictive HR analytics
Data mining and modeling techniques to identify potential causes for human resource outcomes, which then indicate future outcomes.

Growth, profitability, ROI, market share, legal compliance, strategic objectives attainment, and key stakeholder satisfaction are outcome measures that can be used to determine how well the organization is performing in the marketplace and whether it is producing a service that is valued by consumers. Key stakeholder satisfaction may include such indexes as patient satisfaction, cost per patient day, and community perception.

The mission and objectives of the organization are reflected in the outcomes that management stresses and in the strategies, general tactics, and HR practices the organization chooses. For example, almost all healthcare organizations need to earn some profit for continued viability. However, an organization might refrain from initiating possibly profitable new ventures that do not fit its overall mission of providing high-quality services needed by a defined population group. Conversely, an organization may start services that are break-even propositions at best because those services are viewed as critical to their mission and the needs of their community.

An organization's concerns are reflected in the services it offers, the HR approaches it uses, and the outcome measures it views as important. A quality-centric organization likely emphasizes assessment criteria that stress the provision of high-quality care more than criteria concerned with efficient use of supplies and the maintenance of staffing ratios. This prioritization does not mean that the organization is ignoring efficiency of operations; it just signals that the organization places greater weight on the quality-care criteria. The outcome measures used to judge the institution should reflect its priorities.

Another institution may place greater emphasis on economic return, profitability, and efficiency of operations. Quality of care is also important to that organization, but the driving force to become a low-cost provider causes the organization to make decisions that reflect its business strategy; therefore, it stresses maintenance or reduction of staffing levels and strictly prohibits overtime. Its recruitment criteria stress identification and selection of employees who will meet minimum job requirements and expectations and, possibly, will accept lower pay levels. In an organization that strives to be efficient, less energy may be spent on social maintenance activities designed to meet employee needs and keep them from leaving or unionizing. The outcomes in this situation will reflect higher economic return and lower measures of work–life quality.

Regardless of their specific outcome objectives, most healthcare organizations seek competitive advantage over similar institutions. The ultimate goal of the HR function should be to develop a distinctive brand so that employees, potential employees, and the general public view that particular organization as the choice rather than as the last resort.

The HR Brand

branding
The organization's corporate image or culture.

In HR, **branding** refers to the organization's corporate image or culture. Because organizations are constantly competing for the best talent, developing an attractive HR brand is important. A brand embodies the values and standards that guide employee behavior. It indicates the purpose and perception of the organization, the profiles of people it hires, and the results it recognizes and rewards. If an organization can convey that it is a great place to work, it can attract the right people (Adams 2022). Being acknowledged by an external source is a good way to create a recognized HR brand. Inclusion on national "best" lists, such as the following, helps an organization build a base of followers and enhances its recruitment and retention programs:

- *Fortune's* 100 Best Companies to Work For
- *Working Mother's* 100 Best Companies
- *Becker's Healthcare* 150 Top Places to Work in Healthcare

- *Computerworld*'s Best Places to Work in IT

- *Modern Healthcare*'s Best Places to Work

- The Great Place to Work Institute's best lists, which include the *Fortune* list

Being selected for *Fortune*'s 100 Best Companies list is so desirable that some organizations try to change their culture, philosophy, and brand to gain these designations. Organization leaders and their employees credit some combination of the following approaches as the secret to their success:

- Healthy organizational cultures that emphasize diversity, equity, and inclusion

- Comprehensive benefits packages

- Zero-tolerance approaches to workplace violence or incivility

- Employee well-being and work–life integration as top priorities

- An employee-centric focus on patient safety

HR Best Practices

Exhibit 1.3 summarizes HRM practices that appear to enhance the effectiveness and outcomes of organizations. These practices tend to be present in organizations that are effective in managing their human resources, and they recur repeatedly in studies of high-performing organizations. In addition, these themes are interrelated and mutually reinforcing; it is difficult to achieve positive results by implementing just one practice on its own (Saridakis, Lai, and Cooper 2017).

While these HR practices generally have a positive impact on organizational performance, their relative effectiveness may also vary depending on their alignment (or lack thereof) among themselves and with the organization's mission, values, culture, strategies, goals, and objectives, and this link is not very clear (Paauwe and Farndale 2017). HRM practices may vary in their impact on various types of healthcare organizations, depending on how well each one is aligned with and reinforces the others as well as how well it is aligned with various aspects of the overall business strategy. Earlier in this chapter, we described a model in exhibit 1.2—the strategic human resources management model—that attempts to explain this phenomenon.

The bad news about achieving competitive advantage through the workforce is that it takes time to accomplish (Pfeffer 1998). The good news is that, once achieved, such competitive advantage is likely to be more enduring and harder for competitors to duplicate, provided that that talent is retained.

Exhibit 1.3
Effective HRM
Practices for
Healthcare
Organizations

Category	Practices	
HR planning, job analysis	Encourage employee involvement so there is strong "buy-in" of HR practices and managerial initiatives. Encourage teamwork so employees are more willing to collaborate. Provide employment security.	Include self-managed teams and decentralization as basic elements of organization design to minimize management layers. Use analytics to support and develop the HR plan.
Recruiting, staffing	Be proactive in identifying and attracting talent. In selecting new employees, use additional criteria beyond basic skills (e.g., attitudes, diversity, customer focus, cultural fit). Actively review application and hiring process from the prospective employee perspective.	Be transparent about culture, staff development, and advancement opportunities to support the employee value proposition. Track and analyze retention and turnover rates.
Training, organizational development, and employee engagement	Invest in training and organizational programs to enhance employee skills related to organizational goals. Provide upskilling and reskilling opportunities to current employees to prepare them for future roles. Provide employees with future career opportunities by giving promotional priority to internal candidates.	Include customer service in new employee onboarding and skill development. Provide opportunities for employee growth so employees are "stretched" to enhance all their skills. Give employees a voice in decision making.

Category	Practices	
Performance management and compensation	Recognize employees by providing monetary and non-monetary rewards.	Reduce status distinction and barriers such as dress, language, office arrangement, parking, and wage differentials.
	Offer high compensation contingent on organizational performance to reduce employee turnover and increase attraction to high-quality employees.	Base individual and team compensation on goal-oriented results.
Employee rights	Communicate effectively with employees to keep them informed concerning major issues and initiatives.	Provide employment security for employees who perform well so they are not downsized because of economic downturns or strategic errors by senior management.
	Share financial, salary, and performance information to develop a high-trust organization.	
	Give higher priority to internal candidates for promotion to enhance employee motivation.	
Culture	Prioritize healthy organizational culture and positive work culture.	Promote employee resilience, and self-care.
	Develop strategies to enhance employee work–life balance.	Actively monitor burnout.

EXHIBIT **1.3**
Effective HRM Practices for Healthcare Organizations *(continued)*

Sources: Chuang and Liao (2010), Gomez-Mejia and Balkin (2011); Pfeffer (1995, 1998); Wright et al. (2005).

WHO PERFORMS HR TASKS?

All healthcare managers must deal effectively with HR issues regardless of their functional area and the size of their organization. There has been a clear trend toward reducing the size of the HR department and shifting traditional HR functions (i.e., recruitment, selection, performance management, and training) to line managers. This trend empowers managers to take ownership of decisions about people in their own units and teams with support from the HR team (Blumenfeld et al. 2022).

In recent years, there has been no typical HR department, and organizations vary in how and where HR tasks are carried out. In some instances, HR tasks may be centralized in the HR department; in other cases, HR facilitates and monitors HR tasks that may be decentralized to functional departments. Internal restructuring often results in a shift of who carries out HR tasks, but it has not eliminated those functions identified in exhibit 1.3. In fact, in some healthcare organizations, the HR department continues to perform the majority of HR functions.

The evolution of HR raises the following questions:

◆ Which HR tasks can be performed more effectively and efficiently by line managers?

◆ Which HR tasks should be outsourced to an integrated HR service provider?

◆ Can some HR tasks be centralized or eliminated altogether?

◆ Can technology perform HR tasks that were once previously done by HR staff?

The number of HR staff members continues to decline as others have begun to assume responsibility for certain HR functions. Outsourcing, shared service centers, and line managers now assist in many HR functions and activities. While most organizations are expected to outsource even more administrative HR tasks in the future, the strategic components of HR and key functions such as compensation and employee engagement will likely remain within the organization as partners to top management (Blumenfeld et al. 2022).

The shift toward strategic HR permits the HR function to shed its administrative image and to focus on more mission-oriented activities. This shift also means that all healthcare executives need to become skilled managers of their human resources. More HR professionals are assuming a strategic perspective when it comes to managing HR-related issues. As they do so, they continually upgrade and enhance their professional capabilities. More HR professionals now have a seat at the board of directors' table to help the chief

The chief human resources officer (CHRO) is a role that continues to grow in strategic importance to the organization. The role is vital to shaping the organization's climate and preparing the organization for the future.

For example, the CHRO's portfolio might include any of the following:

- Operational and strategic HR analytics
- Diversity, equity, and inclusion
- Employee engagement and company culture
- Organization and employee development
- Compensation strategy and structure
- Employee HR experience
- Health and safety, including employee well-being
- HR ethics, compliance, and privacy
- Business strategy development and governance

A diverse set of leadership competencies is critical because a CHRO is equal parts strategist and tactician. The CHRO must identify and execute initiatives that leverage business opportunities and hedge against risks (Boudreau, Navin, and Creelman 2017).

officers, senior management, and board members make appropriate decisions concerning HR matters in the role of chief human resources officer (CHRO), also known as chief people officer (CPO). The three critical HR issues to which this HR professional can lend expertise and therefore help organizational governance are (1) selecting the incoming CEO, (2) tying the CEO's compensation to performance, and (3) identifying and developing optimum business and HR strategies.

The CHRO must think strategically and tactically to advise human capital investment decisions to support organizational outcomes. This means that the CHRO has a vital role in developing and selecting HR metrics and must appreciate the underlying drivers for each metric selected. The CHRO can contribute to leveraging HR's role in major change strategies (such as mergers and acquisitions), sustain employee engagement, and help line managers achieve their unit goals.

HR Trends Affecting the Healthcare Industry

A survey was sent to 1,327 community hospital CEOs who were ACHE members in 2021. Of the 310 CEOs who responded, their top five pressing concerns were (1) personnel shortages, (2) financial challenges, (3) patient safety and quality, (4) behavioral health or addiction issues, and (5) government mandates. From this list, only the governmental mandates issue is not directly related to human resources management (ACHE 2022).

HR practices and policies are crucial in creating and maintaining a positive work culture. Such an environment is characterized by well-trained, engaged employees who have the tools they need to do their jobs, the opportunity to participate in decisions affecting their jobs, and the services and support they need from other organizational members. The benefits for healthcare organizations able to deliver high service quality that yields customer satisfaction include reduced cost because of higher employee retention and reduction in errors, resulting in enhanced quality of service. Thus, HR can be a strategic leader in ensuring that policies, procedures, and practices produce employee behaviors that are supported, rewarded, and contributing toward a superior-quality service climate.

Much of the growth of the HR function since the 1930s is attributable to the crucial role of keeping all employers out of trouble with the law. Most large healthcare organizations are deeply concerned about whether their personnel decisions may violate laws, regulations, and court decisions at the federal, state, or local government levels. The result has been an administrative nightmare that grows by the day so that no individual can comprehend its scope and depth. This challenge is exacerbated by the fact that the regulatory burden on employers continues to increase in the United States, and that employers must protect their HR brand by doing what is right.

Patient satisfaction has been studied since the 1970s, and various metrics to measure it are highly correlated with a positive work environment (Carthon et al. 2021). This research shows that hospitals where nurses have the lowest burnout rates and most supportive work environments also have the highest patient satisfaction. A similar relationship exists for physician burnout and patient satisfaction and safety (Panagioti et al. 2018). HR has a key role to perform in enhancing patient satisfaction by creating and sustaining a workplace culture of HR management practices and initiatives that encourage, reward, and support behavior focused on high-quality service.

Personnel shortages in healthcare affect most clinical occupations, although the severity of such shortages tends to vary over time. Shortages of nonclinical staff have been problematic for lower-skilled occupations as a result of the deficiencies of public education systems. As a result, healthcare leaders have begun to support local high schools and university programs to supply resources for potential hires and create pathways to careers in healthcare organizations. These initiatives also demonstrate a social responsibility to communities they serve and address the upstream health determinants (Koh et al. 2020). They have also enhanced their own organizational and hiring efforts, which will be discussed in chapters 5 and 6 of this book.

The nursing profession has exhibited periodic shortages of registered nurses over many decades. Among nurses surveyed in 2021, 52 percent responded that they intend to leave or are considering leaving the profession (American Nurses Foundation 2022). One contributor to the nursing shortage is the availability of qualified nursing faculty, which limits the number of nursing students who can be accepted into education programs. Another source of such shortages is the role conflict between work requirements and family necessities, which affects nursing as well as other female-dominated professions. Work–family conflict lowers job satisfaction, increases the intent to leave the job and profession, and is positively affected by age, health, and family responsibilities (Unruh, Raffenaud, and Fottler 2016). Various attempts to mitigate such conflict will enhance nurse retention on the job and in the profession, thus reducing the negative impact of an aging workforce and mitigating nursing shortages. Once again, the work stressors of nurses are not unique. The experience of the pandemic has changed general attitudes toward work. Unless all organizations support mechanisms to keep stress manageable and promote employee well-being, both individuals and organizations will pay a heavy price.

SUMMARY

In healthcare, the intense need for an array of professionals to consistently deliver high-quality services requires organizations to focus attention on strategic HR management. Healthcare leaders must be aware of the factors that influence employees' performance. To assist healthcare executives in understanding this dynamic, this chapter presents a model that explains the interrelationship among corporate strategy, selected organizational design features, HRM activities, employee outcomes, and organizational outcomes.

The outcomes achieved by the organization are influenced by numerous HR and non-HR factors. The mission determines the organization's direction and goals. The amount of integration or alignment of mission, strategy, HR functions, behavioral components, and non-HR strategies defines the level of achievement that is possible.

A sophisticated, valuable healthcare human resources management system is responsive to the highly competitive marketplace, aligned with and informative to the business strategy, jointly conceived and implemented by both line and HR managers, and focused on the highest-priority organization and employee performance indicators. Such indicators might include clinical quality, customer service, productivity, and employee engagement and retention. These outcomes, in turn, will enhance market share in various measures of financial performance.

Healthcare organizations are increasingly striving to impress a distinctive HR brand image on employees, potential employees, and the general public by modifying their cultures and working hard to be included on various national lists of best companies. Successful HR branding yields competitive advantage in labor and service markets. Organizations are also increasing the volume and quality of HR metrics to align their HR strategies with their business strategies. Finally, the locus of HRM is shifting as strategic functions are retained by HR professionals within the organization while administrative tasks are outsourced or delegated to line managers.

Key points to remember include the following:

- Managing HR strategically is critical to the viability and success of any healthcare organization.
- HR must be integrated and aligned with the business strategy.
- Healthcare organizations identified as "best to work for" have a competitive advantage.
- Healthcare organizations need to determine which HR functions should be performed in-house and which should be outsourced.
- Employee well-being is vital to positive organizational outcomes, including patient satisfaction and safety.

FOR DISCUSSION

1. How may an organization's human resources be viewed as a strength or a weakness when doing a SWOT analysis? What could be done to strengthen human resources if it is seen as a weakness?

2. What factors under the control of healthcare managers contribute to the decrease in the number of people applying to health professions schools? Describe the steps that healthcare organizations can take to improve this situation.

3. What are the organizational advantages of integrating strategic management and human resources management? What are the steps involved in such an integration?

4. One healthcare organization is pursuing a business strategy of differentiating its service product through providing excellent customer service. What HR metrics do you recommend to reinforce this business strategy? Why?

5. In what sense are all healthcare executives human resources managers? How can executives best prepare to perform well in this HR function?

6. Why are knowledge and proficiency in HRM concepts and techniques important to all healthcare managers?

7. Consider the vignette at the beginning of this chapter. Outline three to five initiatives that Kamla should undertake to achieve the strategic goals.

EXPERIENTIAL EXERCISES

EXERCISE 1

Before class, review the effective HRM practices shown in exhibit 1.3. Consider how your current or most recent employer follows any three of these practices. Write a one- to two-page summary that lists the three practices you selected and their compatibilities or incompatibilities with your employer's HRM practices.

In class, form a group of four or five students and share your perceptions. Discuss the following:

- What similarities and differences arise among the chosen employers' practices?
- Which of the practices seem to be least often followed, and why?

EXERCISE 2

Each year, *Fortune* magazine publishes a list of the best companies to work for in the United States. Editors of the magazine base their selections on an extensive review of the HR practices of many organizations as well as on surveys of those organizations' current and former employees.

Identify three healthcare organizations on the latest *Fortune* best companies list. Next, visit the websites of these organizations, and review the posted information from the perspective of a prospective job applicant. Then, as a potential employee, answer the following:

- What information on the websites most interested you, and why?
- Which organization's website is best, and why?

Based on the information posted on these websites, what are the implications for you as a future healthcare executive who will be planning and implementing HRM practices? What information will you include on your organization's website that will attract and retain employees?

REFERENCES

Adams, B. 2022. "Make Your Employer Brand Stand Out in the Talent Marketplace." *Harvard Business Review*. Published February 8. https://hbr.org/2022/02/make-your -employer-brand-stand-out-in-the-talent-marketplace.

American College of Healthcare Executives (ACHE). 2022. "Top Issues Confronting Hospitals in 2021." Published February 4. www.ache.org/learning-center/research/about-the-field/top-issues-confronting-hospitals/top-issues-confronting-hospitals-in-2021.

American Nurses Foundation. 2022. *COVID-19 Two-Year Impact Assessment Survey: Younger Nurses Disproportionally Impacted by Pandemic Compared to Older Nurses; Intent to Leave and Staff Shortages Reach Critical Levels.* Pulse on the Nation's Nurses Survey Series. Published March 1. www.nursingworld.org/~492857/contentassets/872ebb13c63f44f6b11a1bd0c74907c9/covid-19-two-year-impact-assessment-written-report-final.pdf.

Barriere, M., M. Owens, and S. Pobereskin. 2018. "Linking Talent to Value." *McKinsey Quarterly* 4 (2): 1–9.

Blumenfeld, L., N. Gandhi, A. Komm, and F. Pollner. 2022. "Reimagining HR: Insights from People Leaders." McKinsey & Company. Published March 1. www.mckinsey.com/business-functions/people-and-organizational-performance/our-insights/reimagining-hr-insights-from-people-leaders.

Boudreau, J., P. Navin, and D. Creelman. 2017. "Why More Executives Should Consider Becoming a CHRO." *Harvard Business Review.* Published May 3. https://hbr.org/2017/05/why-more-executives-should-consider-becoming-a-chro.

Carthon, J., M. Brooks, L. Hatfield, H. Brom, M. Houton, E. Kelly-Hellyer, A. Schlak, and L. Aiken. 2021. "System-Level Improvements in Work Environments Lead to Lower Nurse Burnout and Higher Patient Satisfaction." *Journal of Nursing Care Quality* 36 (1): 7.

Chuang, C. H., and H. Liao. 2010. "Strategic Human Resource Management in Service Context." *Personnel Psychology* 63 (2): 153–96.

Edwards, M. R., and K. Edwards. 2019. *Predictive HR Analytics: Mastering the HR Metric*, 2nd ed. London: Kogan Page.

Feffer, K. 2017. "9 Tips for Using HR Metrics Strategically." Society for Human Resource Management. Published September 21. www.shrm.org/hr-today/news/hr-magazine/1017/pages/9-tips-for-using-hr-metrics-strategically.aspx.

Ford, R. C., S. A. Sivo, M. D. Fottler, D. Dickson, K. Bradley, and L. Johnson. 2006. "Aligning Internal Organizational Factors with a Service Excellence Mission: An Exploratory Investigation in Healthcare." *Health Care Management Review* 31 (4): 259–69.

Gomez-Mejia, L. R., and D. B. Balkin. 2011. *Management: People, Performance and Change*. Upper Saddle River, NJ: Prentice-Hall.

Hamilton, R. H., and W. A. Sodeman. 2020. "The Questions We Ask: Opportunities and Challenges for Using Big Data Analytics to Strategically Manage Human Capital Resources." *Business Horizons* 63 (1): 85–95.

Huselid, M. A. 2018. "The Science and Practice of Workforce Analytics: Introduction to the HRM Special Issue." *Human Resource Management* 57 (3): 679–84.

Kaplan, R. S., and D. P. Norton. 1996. The Balanced Scorecard. Boston: Harvard Business School Press.

Kaufman, B. E. 2015. "Evolution of Strategic HRM as Seen Through Two Founding Books: A 30th Anniversary Perspective on Development of the Field." *Human Resource Management* 54 (3): 389–407.

Khatri, N., V. Gupta, and A. Varma. 2017. "The Relationship Between HR Capabilities and Quality of Patient Care: The Mediating Role of Proactive Work Behaviors." *Human Resource Management* 56 (4): 673–91.

Koh, H. K., A. Bantham, A. C. Geller, M. A. Rukavina, K. M. Emmons, P. Yatsko, and R. Restuccia. 2020. "Anchor Institutions: Best Practices to Address Social Needs and Social Determinants of Health." *American Journal of Public Health* 110 (3): 309–16.

Kupletsky, J. 2022. "How Healthcare Organizations Can Shift the Paradigm and Make HR a Strategic Asset." *Forbes*. Published May 20. www.forbes.com/sites /forbesbusinesscouncil/2022/05/20/how-healthcare-organizations-can-shift-the -paradigm-and-make-hr-a-strategic-asset/?sh=578c8d1b40da.

Melián-González, S., J. Bulchand-Gidumal, and B. González López-Valcárcel. 2015. "New Evidence of the Relationship Between Employee Satisfaction and Firm Economic Performance." *Personnel Review* 44 (6): 906–29.

Mondore, S. P. 2018. "3 Steps for Building the Business-Focused HR Scorecard." Society for Human Resource Management. Published May 3. www.shrm.org/resourcesandtools /hr-topics/organizational-and-employee-development/pages/3-steps-for-building -the-business-focused-hr-scorecard.aspx.

Paauwe, J., and Farndale, E. 2017. *Strategy, HRM, and Performance: A Contextual Approach*. Oxford: Oxford University Press.

Panagioti, M., K. Geraghty, J. Johnson, A. Zhou, E. Panagopoulou, C. Chew-Graham, D. Peters, A. Hodkinson, R. Riley, and A. Esmail. 2018. "Association Between Physician Burnout and Patient Safety, Professionalism, and Patient Satisfaction: A Systematic Review and Meta-Analysis." *JAMA Internal Medicine* 178 (10): 1317–31.

Pfeffer, J. 1998. *The Human Equation: Building Profits by Putting People First*. Boston: Harvard Business School Press.

———. 1995. "Producing Sustainable Competitive Advantage Through Effective Management of People." *Academy of Management Executive* 9 (1): 55–69.

Saridakis, G., Y. Lai, and C. L. Cooper. 2017. "Exploring the Relationship Between HRM and Firm Performance: A Meta-Analysis of Longitudinal Studies." *Human Resource Management Review* 27 (1): 87–96.

Society for Human Resource Management (SHRM). 2022. "Benchmarking Human Capital Metrics." Accessed August 12. www.shrm.org/resourcesandtools/business-solutions /pages/benchmarking.aspx.

Unruh, L. Y., A. Raffenaud, and M. D. Fottler. 2016. "Work–Family Conflict Among Newly Licensed Registered Nurses: A Structural Equation Model of Antecedents and Outcomes." *Journal of Healthcare Management* 61 (2): 129–45.

US Bureau of Labor Statistics (BLS). 2022. "Occupational Outlook Handbook: Healthcare Occupations." Updated September 8. www.bls.gov/ooh/healthcare/home.htm.

Vespa, J., D. M. Armstrong, and L. Medina. 2020. *Demographic Turning Points for the United States: Population Projections for 2020 to 2060*. Report no. P25-1144. Washington, DC: US Department of Commerce, Economics and Statistics Administration, US Census Bureau. Revised February. www.census.gov/content/dam/Census/library /publications/2020/demo/p25-1144.pdf.

Wright, P. M., T. M. Gardner, L. M. Moynihan, and M. R. Allen. 2005. "The Relationship Between HR Practices and Firm Performance: Examining Causal Order." *Personnel Psychology* 58 (2): 409–46.

CHAPTER 2

THE HEALTHCARE PROFESSIONAL

Patrick D. Shay and Dolores G. Clement

LEARNING OBJECTIVES

After completing this chapter, you should be able to

➤ identify the roles of healthcare professionals in healthcare organizations;

➤ define the elements of a profession, with an understanding of the theoretical underpinnings of the healthcare professions in particular;

➤ describe the major healthcare professions and the required educational levels, scopes of practice, and licensure issues for each;

➤ relate knowledge of the healthcare professions to selected human resources management issues and systems development; and

➤ comprehend the changing nature of existing and emerging healthcare professions in the healthcare workforce.

Kara, a sophomore student at New State University, is weighing potential majors and is meeting with Dr. Fontelera, a faculty member in the Department of Health Professions, to learn more about its undergraduate major and potential career options.

"Tell me," Dr. Fontelera begins, "what makes you interested in healthcare management?"

Kara thinks for a moment and replies, "Well, I've always admired the work that doctors and nurses do in caring for patients. At the same time, I've never really wanted to be a doctor or a nurse, because being around blood creeps me out, and so I guess I kind of ruled out a career in healthcare for a long time. But when I came to college and saw that you offer a major in healthcare management, I got very curious. I really like the idea of being involved in a field that directly cares for people in need, and I'm good at problem solving and feel like I have natural administrative skills. So, I suppose I'm interested in healthcare management because even if I can't be a doctor or nurse who treats patients, maybe I could help those doctors and nurses by being an administrator for them."

"I like your passion," Dr. Fontelera replies, "and I'm excited about your interest in our field. I also think that as you learn more about healthcare management, you'll realize that it's perhaps a much broader field that you may currently imagine. Doctors and nurses each play critical roles in health services, and they have historically been the face of healthcare. But the work of healthcare managers extends well beyond serving doctors and nurses; we serve a vast array of healthcare professionals. I think you're going to be amazed about the opportunity to make a meaningful difference across a broad industry of professionals dedicated to improving the health and well-being of others."

Kara feels intrigued and inspired. Drawn further to explore this potential major, Kara is eager to understand the varied healthcare professions and the issues and challenges they face across healthcare organizations.

INTRODUCTION

Healthcare professionals are central to the delivery of high-quality healthcare services. Extensive training, education, and skills are essential to meet society's needs for safe, competent healthcare. The specialized techniques and skills that healthcare professionals acquire through systematic programs of study are the basis for socialization into their profession. The healthcare industry is labor intensive and distinguished from other service industries by the number of licensed and registered personnel in various healthcare fields. These healthcare fields have emerged as a result of numerous trends, including the specialization of medicine, the increased scope of advanced practice nursing, the development of public health, an increased emphasis on health promotion and prevention, and technological advances.

Because of the division of labor within medical and health services delivery, many tasks that were once the responsibility of physicians are now shared with or delegated to other healthcare professionals. Today, healthcare is commonly delivered by interprofessional teams with the physician at the helm, with a greater emphasis on patient- and family-centered care. Such collaboration raises important questions for the industry: What healthcare professions are involved in delivering healthcare? What is the extent of their scope of practice?

In this chapter, we respond to these questions by defining key terms, describing the healthcare professions and labor force, explaining the role of human resources (HR) in healthcare, and discussing key HR issues that affect healthcare delivery.

PROFESSIONALIZATION

Although the terms *occupation* and *profession* often are used interchangeably, they can be differentiated from each other.

An **occupation** is the principal activity that supports one's livelihood. It is different from a profession in several ways. An occupation typically does not require a high level of skill specialization. An individual in an occupation is usually closely supervised, adheres to a defined work schedule, and earns an hourly wage.

A **profession** requires specialized knowledge and training. Compared with nonprofessionals, a professional has more authority and responsibility and must adhere to a code of ethics. A professional usually has considerable autonomy in determining the content of the service provided and in monitoring the workload. A professional generally earns a salary, obtains higher education, and works with more independence and mobility than nonprofessionals do.

The distinction between an occupation and a profession is important because as healthcare evolves, it requires more and more professionals who are empowered to make decisions in the absence of direct supervision. The proliferation of knowledge and skills needed in the prevention, diagnosis, and treatment of disease has required increasing levels of education. Undergraduate or graduate-level degrees are now required to enter virtually

occupation
One's principal activity and means of support.

profession
A calling that requires specialized knowledge and training. Professionals have more authority and responsibility than people in an occupation and adhere to a code of ethics.

every professional healthcare field. Some professions, such as pharmacy, physical therapy, and nursing, are moving toward professional doctorates (i.e., doctor of pharmacy [PharmD], doctor of physical therapy [DPT], and doctor of nursing practice [DNP], respectively) for practice.

Countering this increase in professionalization, healthcare organizations are finding fewer financial resources available because of consolidation, demands for efficiency, and ongoing changes in the mechanisms for delivery and payment of services. As a result, healthcare organizations face pressure to replace highly trained—and therefore more expensive—healthcare professionals with unlicensed support personnel. Those with advanced degrees are required to supervise more assistants who are functionally trained for specific roles.

functional training
Training that produces personnel who can perform tasks but who may not know the theory behind the practice.

Functional training produces personnel who can perform tasks but may not know the theory behind the practice. However, understanding theory is essential to becoming fully skilled and making complex management and patient care decisions. Conversely, knowing the theory without having the experience also makes competent practice difficult. When educating future healthcare professionals, on-the-job training or a period of apprenticeship is needed in addition to basic coursework. (See also the accompanying Critical Concept sidebar "Five Stages of Ability.")

HEALTHCARE PROFESSIONALS

Healthcare is the largest and most powerful industry in the United States. It constitutes more than 10 percent of the country's total labor force (US Bureau of Labor Statistics [BLS] 2022b) and 19.7 percent of gross domestic product (Centers for Medicare & Medicaid Services [CMS] 2022). Healthcare professionals include physicians, nurses, dentists, pharmacists, optometrists, psychologists, nonphysician practitioners (e.g., physician assistants and nurse practitioners), healthcare managers, and allied health professionals. *Allied health* encompasses a vast array of professionals, including therapists, medical and radiologic technologists, social workers, health educators, and other ancillary personnel. Exhibit 2.1 provides a sample of professional associations representing healthcare professionals, and other key organizations in the health sector, including accrediting associations and trade associations.

Healthcare professionals work in a variety of settings, including hospitals, ambulatory care centers, managed care organizations, and long-term care organizations; behavioral health organizations; pharmaceutical companies; community health centers; physician offices; laboratories; research institutions; and schools of medicine, nursing, and allied health professions. According to the BLS (2022a), healthcare professionals are employed by the following types of organizations:

◆ Hospitals (32 percent)

◆ Nursing and personal and residential care facilities (18 percent)

◆ Physician offices and clinics (17 percent)

◆ Home health care services (10 percent)

◆ Dentist offices and clinics (6 percent)

◆ Other health service sites (17 percent)

> ⓘ **CRITICAL CONCEPT**
> Five Stages of Ability
>
> Dreyfus and Dreyfus (2009) contend that both theoretical knowledge and practiced response are required to acquire skill in a profession. These authors describe five stages in becoming a professional:
>
> 1. *Novice.* The novice learns tasks and skills that enable them to determine actions based on recognized situations. Rules and guidelines direct the novice's energy and action at this stage.
> 2. *Advanced beginner.* The advanced beginner has gained enough experience and knowledge that certain behaviors become automatic, and they can begin to learn when tasks should be addressed.
> 3. *Competent.* The competent individual has mastered definable tasks and processes and has acquired the ability to deal with unexpected events that may not conform to plans.
> 4. *Proficient.* The proficient individual has the ability to discern a situation, intuitively assess it, plan what needs to be done, decide on an action, and perform the action more effectively than in the earlier stages.
> 5. *Expert.* At this final stage, the expert can accomplish the goals without realizing that rules are being followed because the skills and knowledge required to reach the goal have become second nature.
>
> *Theoretical understanding* is melded with practice in each progressive stage. Functional training can help an individual progress through the first three stages and provide the individual with the ability to apply and improve theories and rules. At the proficient and expert levels, one has the ability to challenge and improve theories and rules learned. Healthcare professionals need to become experts in fields where self-direction, autonomy, and decision making for patient care are required (Dreyfus and Dreyfus 2009).

EXHIBIT 2.1
Resource Guide
for Healthcare
Professionals

Organization	Target Audience	Website
Accrediting Organizations		
Accreditation Association for Ambulatory Health Care (AAAHC)	Ambulatory healthcare facilities	www.aaahc.org
Accreditation Commission for Education in Nursing (ACEN)	Nursing education and transition-to-practice programs	www.acenursing.org
Accreditation Council for Graduate Medical Education (ACGME)	Graduate medical education programs	www.acgme.org
American Association of Blood Banks	Blood banks	www.aabb.org
American College of Radiology (ACR)	Diagnostic imaging	www.acr.org
American College of Surgeons (ACS)	Surgeons	www.facs.org
American College of Surgeons: Cancer Programs	Cancer programs	www.facs.org/cancer
American Osteopathic Association	Osteopathic hospitals and health systems	www.osteopathic.org
CARF International	Rehabilitation facilities	www.carf.org
College of American Pathologists (CAP)	Clinical laboratories	www.cap.org
Commission on Accreditation of Healthcare Management Education (CAHME)	Graduate healthcare management programs	www.cahme.org
The Joint Commission	Hospitals and health systems	www.jointcommission.org
National Committee for Quality Assurance (NCQA)	Health plans	www.ncqa.org
Professional Associations		
American Association for Homecare	Home health care administrators	www.aahomecare.org
American Association for Physician Leadership	Physician executives	www.physicianleaders.org

Organization	Target Audience	Website
American Association for Respiratory Care (AARC)	Respiratory therapists	www.aarc.org
American Association of Nurse Anesthetists (AANA)	Nurse anesthetists	www.aana.com
American College of Health Care Administrators (ACHCA)	Long-term care administrators	www.achca.org
American College of Health-care Executives (ACHE)	Healthcare executives	www.ache.org
American Health Informa-tion Management Associa-tion (AHIMA)	Medical records and information manage-ment professionals	www.ahima.org
American Medical Tech-nologists (AMT)	Medical technologists	www.americanmedtech.org
American Nurses Associa-tion (ANA)	Registered nurses	www.ana.org
American Occupational Therapy Association (AOTA)	Occupational therapists	www.aota.org
American Organization for Nursing Leadership (AONL)	Nurse executives	www.aonl.org
American Physical Therapy Association (APTA)	Physical therapists	www.apta.org
American Society for Clini-cal Pathology (ASCP)	Pathologists and labora-tory professionals	www.ascp.org
American Society for Healthcare Human Resources Administration (ASHHRA)	Healthcare HR professionals	www.ashhra.org
American Society of Health-System Pharmacists (ASHP)	Health system pharmacists	www.ashp.org
American Society of Radio-logic Technologists (ASRT)	Radiologic technologists	www.asrt.org
American Speech-Language–Hearing Asso-ciation (ASHA)	Speech-language pathol-ogists; audiologists; and speech, language, and hearing scientists	www.asha.org

EXHIBIT 2.1
Resource Guide for Healthcare Professionals *(continued)*

(continued)

EXHIBIT **2.1**
Resource Guide
for Healthcare
Professionals
(continued)

Organization	Target Audience	Website
Association for Healthcare Documentation Integrity (AHDI)	Medical transcriptionists	www.ahdionline.org
Healthcare Financial Management Association (HFMA)	Controllers, chief financial officers, and accountants	www.hfma.org
Healthcare Information and Management Systems Society (HIMSS)	Health information and technology	www.himss.org
Medical Group Management Association (MGMA)	Physician practice managers and executives	www.mgma.com
National Association of Health Services Executives (NAHSE)	African American healthcare executives	www.nahse.org
National Association of Latino Healthcare Executives (NALHE)	Latine healthcare executives	www.nalhe.org
National Cancer Registrars Association (NCRA)	Cancer registry professionals	www.ncra-usa.org
National League for Nursing (NLN)	Nurse faculty and educators	www.nln.org
Trade Associations		
American Hospital Association (AHA)	Hospitals, health systems, and personal membership groups	www.aha.org
America's Health Insurance Plans (AHIP)	Health insurers	www.ahip.org
Association of American Medical Colleges (AAMC)	Teaching hospitals and health systems	www.aamc.org
Catholic Health Association (CHA) of the United States	Roman Catholic hospitals and health systems	www.chausa.org
Federation of American Hospitals (FAH)	Investor-owned hospitals and health systems	www.fah.org

The US Department of Labor recognizes about 400 specific job titles in the healthcare sector; however, many of these job titles are not included in the definition of *healthcare professionals* used in this chapter. For example, the BLS (2022b) categorizes many positions in the healthcare sector as "healthcare support occupations." Curiously, however, it does not consider these healthcare support occupations part of the patient care team or directly delivering healthcare services. These occupations include nursing aides, home health aides, personal attendants, and other aides, assistants, and support workers who are indeed critical to the delivery of healthcare services.

In its consideration of healthcare professions, this chapter further explores the roles and issues relating to nurses, pharmacists, selected allied health professionals, and healthcare administrators, with each category discussed in the following sections.

Nurses

The art of caring, combined with the science of healthcare delivery, is the essence of nursing. Although diverse types of nurses work across a variety of healthcare settings, the nursing process serves as a common thread that embodies nurses' delivery of holistic, patient-focused care. As outlined by the American Nurses Association (ANA 2022), the nursing process has five components:

1. *Assessment*: Collecting and analyzing physical, psychological, sociocultural, spiritual, economic, and lifestyle factors about a patient

2. *Diagnosis*: The nurse's clinical judgment about the client's response to actual or potential health conditions or needs

3. *Outcomes/planning*: Based on the assessment and diagnosis, involves writing an individualized care plan in the patient's record so that nurses as well as other members of the interprofessional team have access to it

4. *Implementation*: Includes supervising or carrying out the treatment plan and documenting it in the patient's record

5. *Evaluation*: Continuous assessment of the plan and modifications as needed

Nurses also serve as patient advocates, interprofessional team members, managers, executives, consultants, researchers, and entrepreneurs.

Nurses comprise the largest group of licensed healthcare professionals in the United States. According to the 2020 National Nursing Workforce Survey conducted by the National Council of State Boards of Nursing (NCSBN), the United States has 4.2 million licensed registered nurses (RNs), of whom roughly 3.5 million (84 percent) are actively employed in healthcare organizations (Smiley et al. 2021). Approximately 60 percent of employed

RNs, or 1.9 million, work in hospitals, while 18 percent work in ambulatory settings (BLS 2022f). Complementing this workforce are nearly 950,000 licensed practical nurses (LPNs), or licensed vocational nurses (LVNs), as they are known in some states (Smiley et al. 2021). Employment for LPNs and LVNs has been projected to increase 6 percent between 2021 and 2031, comparable to the average growth rate for all occupations (BLS 2022c). For other demographic findings from the national survey, see the accompanying "Did You Know?" sidebar.

All US states require nurses to be licensed to practice. Licensure requirements include graduation from an approved nursing program and successful completion of a national examination. Educational preparation distinguishes the two levels of nurses: RNs must complete an associate's degree in nursing, a diploma program, or a bachelor of science degree in nursing (BSN) to qualify for the licensure examination, while LPN/LVNs must complete a state-approved program in practical nursing—often offered at community colleges, post-secondary learning institutions, or hospital systems' own vocational nursing programs—and achieve a passing score on a national examination. Each state maintains regulations and practice acts that delineate the **scope of practice**—that is, the services that their role permits them to perform given their professional license—for RNs and LPN/LVNs. For RNs, the

scope of practice
The services a healthcare professional's role permits them to perform given their professional license.

 DID YOU KNOW?
Demographics of Nurses in the United States

Demographic profiles from the 2020 National Nursing Workforce Survey (Smiley et al. 2021) revealed the following:

- Whereas most nurses are women, men are a growing demographic, accounting for 9.4 percent of the RN workforce and 8.1 percent of the LPN/LVN workforce, an increase of 0.3 and 0.4 percentage points, respectively, from 2017.
- In 2020, the median age of RNs was 52, while the median age for LPN/LVNs was 53, with both groups exhibiting an increasing median age over time.
- Although the proportion of minority groups among nurses continues to grow, white/Caucasian nurses represent the majority of the nursing workforce, with nurses from racial and ethnic minority backgrounds representing about 19 percent of RNs and more than 30 percent of LPN/LVNs.

Despite some gains in recruiting underrepresented minorities into nursing, more work must be done to increase the numbers of men and persons from racial and ethnic minority backgrounds.

time required to complete educational preparation to qualify for licensure examination can vary. Associate's degree programs generally take two years to complete and are offered by community colleges. Hospital-based diploma programs can be completed in about three years. The fastest-growing avenue for nursing education is the BSN, which typically can be completed in four years and is offered by colleges and universities.

For decades, prominent voices and academic studies have supported higher levels of education in the nursing profession to prepare nurses for the more complex care needs of sicker patients and the sophisticated technologies for providing care (e.g., Djukic, Stimpfel, and Kovner 2019; Gerardi, Farmer, and Hoffman 2018). A 2011 National Academy of Medicine report titled *The Future of Nursing: Leading Change, Advancing Health* recommended increasing the proportion of nurses holding a BSN to 80 percent by 2020. However, despite increased education at initial licensure across the nursing workforce since 2013, the 2020 National Nursing Workforce Survey reported that efforts to meet that goal have fallen short, with roughly 67 percent of RNs and 3 percent of LPN/LVNs holding a bachelor's degree or higher (Smiley et al. 2021).

In light of widespread calls for a more highly educated nursing workforce, academic progression has become a key focus of efforts to improve the deployment of the nursing workforce. **Academic progression** refers to efforts to promote the advanced education of the nursing workforce (e.g., LPN to RN, RN to BSN, BSN to MSN [master of science in nursing] or other graduate nursing degree). It is valued largely because of evidence that higher proportions of nurses with BSNs and MSNs are associated with improved patient outcomes (Harrison et al. 2019; O'Brien, Knowlton, and Whichello 2018; Sloane et al. 2018). Academic progression efforts are supported by the American Association of Colleges of Nursing, the National League for Nursing, the American Nurses Association, the American Organization of Nurse Leadership, and the Robert Wood Johnson Foundation's Academic Progression in Nursing Program (Farmer et al. 2018).

academic progression Efforts to promote the advanced education of the nursing workforce, including LPN to RN, RN to BSN, and BSN to MSN or other graduate nursing degree.

During the twenty-first century, educational transformation and academic progression have been observed in the US nursing workforce. Still, challenges and barriers to academic progression persist, most notably including social and economic disruptions, increased stress and burnout, and organizational changes resulting from the COVID-19 pandemic (Fernandez et al. 2022). As a result, further commitment and investment across diverse healthcare stakeholders will be required to advance BSN degree attainment in the US nursing workforce (T. Jones, Yoder, and Baernholdt 2019; Ma, Garrard, and He 2018).

In addition to licensure and educational achievements, some nurses obtain certification in nursing specialty areas such as acute and critical care, infection control, trauma/emergency, acute care surgery, or obstetrics. Certification in these areas requires additional specialty education, practical experience, and successful completion of a national examination. Some nurses obtain certification in these specialty areas because doing so helps them maintain their competence and membership in professional associations. Continued employment, continuing education units, or reexamination may be required to remain certified.

Beyond specialty certification, some nurses also receive education and preparation to work as advanced practice registered nurses. An *advanced practice registered nurse* (APRN) is a registered nurse who has completed an accredited graduate-level education program and obtained certification and licensure to practice in one of the four roles recognized by the NCSBN (2022): certified nurse practitioner (CNP), clinical nurse specialist (CNS), certified registered nurse anesthetist (CRNA), or certified nurse-midwife (CNM). Broadly, APRNs assume responsibility and accountability for health promotion or maintenance as well as the assessment, diagnosis, and management of patient problems, which includes the use and prescription of pharmacological and nonpharmacological interventions (NCSBN 2022). Each of the specific APRN roles builds on the competencies of RNs by demonstrating a greater depth and breadth of knowledge, a greater synthesis of data, increased complexity of skills and interventions, and greater role autonomy.

CNPs are the largest subset of APRNs, who may further specialize in primary or acute care, adult care or gerontology, neonatology or pediatrics, women's health, or psychiatric and mental health. CNPs have developed an autonomous role in which their collaboration is encouraged, and they generally have the legal authority to implement management actions. In contrast, the CNS scope of practice is not as broad: CNSs are often employed by hospitals as nursing experts in particular specialties, working with a specialty population under a circumscribed set of conditions, and the patient management authority still rests with physicians. CRNAs complete additional education to specialize in administering anesthesia and analgesia to patients, often working collaboratively with surgeons and anesthesiologists as part of the perioperative care team. CNMs specialize in low-risk obstetric care, including all aspects of the prenatal, labor and delivery, and postnatal processes. The workforce of CRNAs, CNMs, and CNPs comprised 300,000 jobs in 2021, with an expected growth of 40 percent—an increase of more than 118,000 APRNs—by 2031 (BLS 2022d).

PHARMACISTS

Up to the late twentieth century, pharmacists performed the traditional role of preparing drug products and filling prescriptions. Today, pharmacists are key members of healthcare teams and experts for clients and patients on the effects of drugs, drug interactions, generic drug substitutions for brand-name drugs, and other issues. Pharmacists also oversee the work of pharmacy technicians, who assist pharmacists in filling and dispensing prescription medications.

To be eligible for licensure, pharmacists must graduate from an accredited bachelor's degree program in pharmacy, successfully complete a state board examination, and obtain practical experience or complete a supervised internship. After passing a national examination, a registered pharmacist (RPh) is permitted to carry out the scope of practice outlined by state regulations. Since 2000, most schools of pharmacy have begun offering only the six-year PharmD degree. The extensive training of doctorally prepared pharmacists allows them to pursue careers in research, education, healthcare management and leadership, or clinical pharmacy as a member of interprofessional patient care teams. This educational preparation also requires successful completion of a state board examination and other practical clinical experience, as outlined by state laws.

In 2021, pharmacists comprised more than 323,000 jobs within the healthcare workforce, and total employment of pharmacists in the United States was projected to increase 2 percent by 2031, with about 7,700 openings for pharmacists anticipated each year as a result of workers retiring or transferring to other occupations (BLS 2022e).

OTHER HEALTH PROFESSIONALS

A wide range of health professionals work collaboratively with physicians, nurses, and pharmacists, and these professionals are commonly categorized as *allied health professionals*. The United States Code defines an allied health professional as follows (Title 42, Chapter 6A, Subchapter V, Part G § 295p):

A health professional (other than a registered nurse or a physician assistant)—

(A) who has received a certificate, an associate's degree, a bachelor's degree, a master's degree, a doctoral degree, or postbaccalaureate training, in a science related to health care;

(B) who shares in the responsibility for the delivery of health care services or related services, including—

(i) services relating to the identification, evaluation, and prevention of disease and disorders;

(ii) dietary and nutrition services;

(iii) health promotion services;

(iv) rehabilitation services; or

(v) health systems management services;

and

(C) who has not received a degree of doctor of medicine, a degree of doctor of osteopathy, a degree of doctor of dentistry or an equivalent degree, a degree of doctor of veterinary medicine or an equivalent degree, a degree of doctor of optometry or an equivalent degree, a degree of doctor of podiatric medicine or an equivalent degree, a degree of bachelor of science in pharmacy or an equivalent degree, a degree of doctor of pharmacy or an equivalent degree, a graduate degree in public health or an equivalent degree, a degree of doctor of chiropractic or an equivalent degree, a graduate degree in health administration or an equivalent degree, a doctoral degree in clinical psychology or an equivalent degree, or a degree in social work or an equivalent degree or a degree in counseling or an equivalent degree.

The exclusiveness and inclusiveness of this definition continue to be debated. Some healthcare observers consider nursing, public health, and social work to fall under the umbrella of allied health, but these professions are often categorized as separate groups. Exhibit 2.2 lists the major categories that make up allied health professions, along with job titles and a sample of positions that generally fall under each category.

According to the Association of Schools Advancing Health Professions (ASAHP 2022b), licensed and unlicensed personnel traditionally included in the allied health professions constitute up to 60 percent of the healthcare workforce in the United States. Although this number excludes physicians, nurses, dentists, pharmacists, veterinarians, chiropractors, optometrists, and podiatrists, its members are integral to interprofessional teams. With a wide variety of nonnurse, nonphysician professions, this collection of health professions is the most heterogeneous of the personnel groupings in healthcare.

Although no single, commonly defined list of allied health professions exists, they are generally divided into two categories: (1) therapists/technologists and (2) technicians/assistants (Shi and Singh 2022). In general, the therapist/technologist category represents those with higher-level professional training and often responsible for supervising those in the technician/assistant category. Therapists/technologists usually hold a bachelor's or higher-level degree, and are trained to evaluate patients, understand diagnoses, and develop treatment plans in their area of expertise. Technicians/assistants are most likely to have two years of postsecondary education or less, and they are functionally trained with procedural skills for specified tasks.

Some job titles shown in exhibit 2.2 may not easily fit into the categories of therapists/technologists or technicians/assistants, such as community health workers or dietitians. However, these roles collectively work to optimize health outcomes across patients and communities through the evaluation, treatment, and management of disease, as well as the promotion of wellness, and the provision of dietary and rehabilitation services (ASAHP 2022b).

Educational and training programs for these health professions are sponsored by a variety of organizations in an array of academic and clinical settings. They range from degree offerings at colleges and universities to clinical programs in hospitals and other health facilities. The ASAHP (2022a) membership includes 124 academic institutions as well as numerous accreditation bodies and professional organizations. Not only four-year undergraduate institutions but also community colleges, vocational or technical schools, and academic health centers can sponsor allied health programs. These programs can stand alone when they are aligned with an academic health center, or they may operate under the auspices of the school of medicine or nursing if a specific school of allied health professions does not exist. Dental and pharmacy technicians/assistants may be trained in their respective schools or a school of allied health professions.

The Commission on Accreditation of Allied Health Education Programs (CAAHEP) accredits a vast number of health professions programs. CAAHEP is intended to simplify

The following lists include examples of professional titles within the allied health professions; the lists are not all-inclusive.

Behavioral Health Services
- Community health worker
- Home health aide
- Mental health aide
- Mental health assistant
- Substance abuse counselor

Clinical Laboratory Sciences
- Associate laboratory microbiologist
- Biochemist
- Laboratory associate
- Laboratory microbiologist
- Laboratory technician
- Microbiologist

Dental Services
- Dental assistant
- Dental hygienist
- Dental laboratory technologist

Dietetic Services
- Assistant director of food service
- Associate supervising dietitian
- Dietary assistant
- Dietitian

Emergency Medical Services
- Ambulance technician
- Emergency medical technician

Health Information Management Services
- Assistant director of medical records
- Coder
- Data analyst
- Director of medical records
- Health information manager
- Medical record specialist
- Senior analyst of medical records

Medical and Surgical Services
- Ambulatory care technician
- Biomedical engineer
- Biomedical equipment technician
- Cardiovascular technologist
- Dialysis technologist
- Electrocardiograph technician
- Electroencephalograph technician
- Electroencephalograph technologist
- Medical equipment specialist
- Operating room technician
- Surgical assistant

Occupational Therapy
- Occupational therapist
- Occupational therapy aide
- Occupational therapy assistant

Ophthalmology
- Ophthalmic technician
- Optician
- Optometric aide

Orthotics/Prosthetics
- Orthopedic assistant

Physical Therapy
- Physical therapist
- Physical therapy assistant

Radiological Services
- Diagnostic medical sonographer
- Medical radiation dosimetrist
- Nuclear medicine technician
- Nuclear medicine technologist
- Radiation technician
- Radiologic (medical) technologist
- Ultrasound technician

Rehabilitation Services
- Addiction counselor
- Addiction specialist
- Art therapist
- Dance therapist
- Exercise physiologist
- Music therapist
- Psychiatric social health technician
- Recreational therapist
- Recreation therapy assistant
- Rehabilitation counselor
- Rehabilitation technician
- Sign language interpreter

Respiratory Therapy Services
- Respiratory therapist
- Respiratory therapy assistant
- Respiratory therapy technician

Speech-Language Pathology/Audiology Services
- Audiology clinician
- Speech clinician
- Staff audiologist
- Staff speech pathologist

Other Allied Health Services
- Central supply technician
- Chiropractic assistant
- Health unit coordinator
- Home health aide
- Medical illustrator
- Podiatric assistant

the accrediting process, be more inclusive of health professions programs that provide entry-level education, and serve as an initiator of change. Some health professions graduate programs, such as physical therapy and occupational therapy, are accredited through professional and specialized professional accreditation agencies.

HEALTHCARE MANAGERS

Healthcare managers organize, coordinate, and oversee the delivery of health services; provide leadership; and guide the strategic direction of healthcare organizations. The variety and numbers of healthcare professionals they employ, the complexity of healthcare delivery, and environmental pressures to provide access, high quality, and efficient services make healthcare institutions some of the most complex organizations to manage.

Healthcare management is taught at the undergraduate and graduate levels in various settings, including schools of medicine, public health, business, and allied health professions. A bachelor's degree in health administration allows individuals to pursue positions such as nursing home administrator, supervisor, or middle manager in healthcare organizations. Most students who aspire to a career in healthcare management go on to earn a master's degree.

Graduate education programs in healthcare management are accredited by the Commission on Accreditation of Healthcare Management Education. The most common degrees include the master of health administration (MHA), master of business administration (MBA) with a healthcare emphasis, master of public health (MPH), and master of public administration (MPA). However, the MHA degree, or its equivalent, has been the accepted training model for entry-level managers in the healthcare industry. The MHA program, in contrast to the MPH program, offers core courses that focus on building business management competency, quantitative and analytical skills, and experiential learning. In addition, some MHA programs require students to complete three-month internships or 12-month residencies as part of their two- or three-year curricula. Some graduates complete postgraduate fellowships that are available in selected hospitals, health systems, managed care organizations, consulting firms, and other health-related organizations.

A growing number of healthcare managers are physicians and other clinicians. Membership in the American Association for Physician Leadership (AAPL 2022) increased to more than 11,000 in 2022, more than double the number in 1990. Physicians, nurses, and other clinicians may refocus their careers on the business side of the enterprise, getting involved in the strategy, decision making, resource allocation, and operations of healthcare organizations. A traditional management role for physician executives is the chief medical officer (CMO, or a similar position) in a hospital, overseeing the medical staff and serving as a liaison between clinical care and administration. Likewise, a typical management career path for nurses is to become the chief nursing officer (CNO), with responsibility for the clinical care provided by employed professional staff.

Typically, CMOs begin their careers practicing medicine and then transition into management roles. Physician executives work at every level and in every setting in healthcare. Many physician executives earn a graduate degree, such as an MHA or an MBA. As reported by the Association of American Medical Colleges (AAMC 2022), as of 2022, 85 medical schools offer a combined MD/MBA program. MD/MHA degrees have also proliferated.

Nursing home administrator programs require students to pass a national examination administered by the National Association of Long Term Care Administrator Boards (NAB). Passing this examination is a standard requirement in all states, but the educational preparation needed to qualify for this exam varies among states. One-third of states still allow less than a bachelor's degree as the minimum academic preparation (NAB 2022). However, the demand and educational requirements for long-term care administrators are predicted to increase as the population continues to live longer, along with the growth of educational programs targeted to this sector.

CONSIDERATIONS FOR HUMAN RESOURCES MANAGEMENT

The role of HR management in healthcare organizations is to develop and implement systems according to regulatory guidelines and licensure laws for the selection, evaluation, and retention of healthcare professionals. In light of this role, HR personnel should be aware that each healthcare profession, and often the subspecialties within the profession, will have specific requirements that allow an individual to qualify for a job in their chosen profession. The requirements of national accrediting organizations (e.g., The Joint Commission), regulatory bodies (e.g., CMS), and licensure authorities (e.g., state licensure boards) should be considered in all aspects of HR management. This section briefly discusses some of the issues that a healthcare organization's HR department must consider when dealing with healthcare professionals.

QUALIFICATIONS

In developing a comprehensive employee compensation program, HR personnel must include the specific skill and knowledge required for each job in the organization. Those qualifications must be determined and stated in writing for each job. The job description usually contains the level of education, experience, judgment ability, accountability, physical skills, responsibilities, communication skills, and any special certification or licensure requirements. HR personnel need to be aware of all specifications for all job titles within the organization. This knowledge of healthcare professionals is necessary to ensure that essential qualifications of individuals coincide with job specifications, and it is also necessary for determining wage and salary ranges.

LICENSURE AND CERTIFICATION

An HR department must have policies and procedures that describe how licensure is verified upon initial employment. Also, HR must have a system in place for tracking the expiration dates of licenses and for ensuring licensure renewal. Therefore, HR team members must be conscious of whether the information received is a **primary verification** (i.e., the information comes directly from the licensing authority) or a **secondary verification** (i.e., the candidate submits a copy of a document indicating that licensure has been granted, including the expiration date). Certifications must be verified during the selection process, although certifications and licenses generally are not statutory requirements. Many healthcare organizations accept a copy of a certification document as verification. If the certification is a job requirement, systems must be in place to track expiration dates and access new certification documents.

primary verification
Information directly received from the licensing authority that verifies a new hire's license.

secondary verification
A copy of a document that indicates licensure has been granted and shows the license's expiration date.

EDUCATIONAL SERVICES

Healthcare professionals require continuous, lifelong learning. Healthcare organizations must have training and development plans to ensure that professionals achieve competency in new technologies, programs, and equipment and are aware of policy and procedure changes.

In addition to providing training programs, healthcare organizations should provide onboarding for all new employees, including interprofessional team training. Such training enables leadership to share the values, mission, goals, and policies of the institution and indicate how to be successful in that organization. Some professions and licensing jurisdictions may require profession-specific continuing education. (See also the "Did You Know?" sidebar on career pathways.)

> **(?) DID YOU KNOW?**
> Career Pathways
>
> Many healthcare organizations have *career pathways*, which are mechanisms by which healthcare professionals advance within the organization or assume additional responsibilities. Career pathways are based on the Dreyfus and Dreyfus (2009) model of novice to expert (explained earlier in this chapter), and experience may be used as a criterion for assigning an individual to a particular job category. In addition, healthcare organizations may conduct annual reviews of employees who have leadership and management potential. Such reviews entail HR working with senior management to assess the competency, ability, and career progression of employees on an ongoing basis.

PRACTITIONER IMPAIRMENT

Healthcare professionals are accountable to the public for maintaining high professional standards. By statute, the governing body of a healthcare organization is responsible for the quality of care rendered in the organization, but instances of practitioner impairment can easily jeopardize an organization's quality of health services. An **impaired practitioner** is a healthcare professional who is unable to carry out their professional duties with reasonable skill and safety because of a physical or mental illness, including deterioration through aging, loss of motor skill, or excessive use of drugs and alcohol.

Mechanisms to identify and deal with the impaired practitioner—such as policies and procedures that describe how the organization will handle investigations, subsequent recommendations for treatment, monitoring, and employment restrictions or separation— must be in place. Hospitals, for instance, usually have a process in place for the governing board (which has the ultimate responsibility for the quality of care delivered in the organization) to review provider credentials and performance and to oversee any employment actions. Each national or state licensing authority maintains legal requirements for reporting impaired practitioners.

impaired practitioner
A healthcare professional who is unable to carry out their professional duties with reasonable skill and safety because of a physical or mental illness, including deterioration through aging, loss of motor skill, or excessive use of drugs and alcohol.

THE CHANGING NATURE OF THE HEALTHCARE PROFESSIONS

Changes in the organization and financing of healthcare services have shifted delivery from hospitals to outpatient facilities, the home, long-term care facilities, and the community. This trend is largely the result of three major forces: (1) a shift in reimbursement to outpatient settings and a focus on cost containment; (2) technological advances, such as telehealth and electronic health records; and (3) medical innovation—specifically, the fact that the science of medicine has progressed to the point that complicated procedures that once required several nights of stay in a hospital can now be treated with a simple procedure or even solely with medication.

As the settings for care delivery have changed, so have arrangements between physicians and healthcare organizations. For instance, physicians can function as individual providers (in either solo or group practice) and refer patients to the hospital. Typically, these private practice doctors have admitting privileges to the hospital but are not governed by the hospital, do not serve as attending physicians, and infrequently participate on hospital committees. Physicians considered "on staff" at any hospital refer and treat patients at that hospital. They are credentialed by the hospital credentialing committee and are governed by the medical staff bylaws. This scenario is a common type of hospital–physician arrangement.

However, a trend toward employment of physicians by hospitals has been steadily growing, with more than half of US physicians now employed by hospitals or hospital-based systems (Physicians Advocacy Institute 2022). In this arrangement, physicians are on staff, referring to and treating at only the hospital that employs them. Because they are considered employees, physicians are not only held to the organization's HR policies but also governed by the medical staff bylaws. Physicians who are employed by a hospital can also maintain a private practice.

Finally, the field of hospital medicine, often called *hospitalists*, has also seen rapid growth, with hospitalists practicing at the vast majority of US hospitals (Ryskina et al. 2021; Wachter and Goldman 2016). Typically, these physicians do not run their own practice aside from their hospital employment. Hospitalists work full-time for the hospital and are trained in delivering specialized inpatient care. Regardless of the type of arrangement, most hospitals have a CMO, or a similar position, who oversees the roles and responsibilities of the hospitalist as a member of the medical staff. The HR department typically manages the hospitalist's employee issues and responsibilities. These hospital–physician arrangements get more complex in academic medical centers, which must integrate the roles and responsibilities of the physicians, the hospital, and the medical school.

As a result of the changing healthcare environment and declining reimbursements, the majority of physicians now work outside *private practice* (i.e., a practice wholly owned by physicians), and only 5.8 percent of physicians work as independent contractors (Kane 2021). Among physician practices, recent trends show that more than 25 percent of US physician practices are owned by hospitals or hospital-based systems, and another 27.2 percent are owned by corporate entities such as insurance companies and private equity firms (Physicians Advocacy Institute 2022). Many of the remaining practices are large

 DEBATE POINT

Employment of physicians and acquisition of physician practices are key elements in the consolidation of the US healthcare industry. However, debates have grown regarding the potential benefits and consequences of such activity. Some opponents raise concerns that physician consolidation and employment by hospital systems may limit patient choice, inhibit transparency, stifle collaboration, and minimize physician autonomy, while proponents suggest that this activity can ensure financial viability, clinical network stability, physician work–life balance, and improved coordination of care (O'Hanlon 2020; O'Hanlon, Whaley, and Freund 2019; Richards, Seward, and Whaley 2022). What might be the impact of hospitals' increased employment of physicians and acquisition of physician practices on access to care, the cost of care, and the quality of care provided to communities? Who benefits from such consolidation, and what are some intended and unintended consequences? For health services administrators, what challenges and considerations might they have to navigate as a result of increased consolidation and employment of physicians?

physician-owned medical groups (Kane 2021), which offer several advantages to physicians, including competitive advantage with vendors and manufacturers, improved negotiating power with managed care organizations, shared risk and decision making, and enhanced flexibility and choice for patients. Physicians who own or share ownership in the group practice are also responsible for its business operations. Typically, group practices employ an office manager who works closely with physicians to manage day-to-day operations. A full-time administrator may also formulate strategies and oversee personnel, billing and collection, purchasing, patient flow, and other functions. Many group practices opt to outsource their business functions, including HR, to specialized firms.

These shifts in healthcare settings and arrangements have changed the roles, functions, and expectations of the healthcare workforce and have led to the emergence of the issues of supply and demand; complementary, alternative, and integrative therapies; nonphysician licensed independent practitioners; emerging and evolving roles; and innovation and entrepreneurship. These issues are discussed in the sections that follow.

SUPPLY AND DEMAND

Labor markets for various health professions have cycled through periods of shortages and surpluses. Indicators of demand include numbers of vacancies, turnover rates, and increases in salaries. To fill positions, hospitals—the largest employers of nurses and health professionals—have raised salaries, provided scholarships, and given other incentives such as sign-on bonuses and tuition reimbursement.

In addition to the challenges facing the nursing workforce (as described in the accompanying Current Issue sidebar "Supply Challenges Facing Nurses"), shortages of other health professionals persist, including behavioral health professionals, information technology professionals and analysts, laboratory technicians, and certified nursing assistants, among others (American Hospital Association [AHA] 2020). As a result, the recruitment of nursing and other health profession students has become a major focus of practitioners, professional associations, and academic institutions. Furthermore, healthcare organizations (in addition to increasing salaries) are developing innovative ways to recruit and retain health professionals. Such developments include opening or sponsoring new schools, offering shorter and more flexible shifts, issuing tuition reimbursement or loan repayment, providing child care, and aligning recruitment and retention processes to emphasize the organization's mission of serving others (AHA 2020).

COMPLEMENTARY, ALTERNATIVE, AND INTEGRATIVE MEDICINE THERAPIES

Complementary and alternative medicine (CAM) therapies continue to gain acceptance and popularity. A turning point was a seminal study of the prevalence of the use of alternative

CURRENT ISSUE
Supply Challenges Facing Nurses

The supply of nurses and other health professionals is reflected in the number of students in educational programs and those available for the healthcare workforce. The future supply of nurses is a challenge, as reflected by the following factors:

- *The aging of the nursing workforce.* More than 50 percent of all RNs and LVN/LPNs in the healthcare workforce are aged 50 or older, with nurses aged 65 or older representing nearly 20 percent of their peers (NCSBN 2022). As the current nursing workforce continues to age, a new generation of nurses will need to be educated and introduced to the field.

- *The aging of nursing faculty.* The American Association of Colleges of Nursing (AACN 2021) reports that nursing schools have restricted enrollment, in large part because of an insufficient number of nursing faculty. Related to this issue, the average ages of doctoral-prepared professors, associate professors, and assistant professors who serve as nurse faculty are 62.6, 56.9, and 50.9, respectively, while the average ages for master's-prepared nurse faculty are 57.1, 56.0, and 49.6, respectively (AACN 2020). The lack of younger nurses in faculty positions may contribute further to both the shortage of nursing school faculty and barriers to educating the next generations of nurses.

- *The barriers to available educational resources.* According to the National League for Nursing's biennial survey of schools of nursing, nursing programs turn away significant percentages of qualified applicants—including 29 percent of BSN program applicants as well as 35 percent of associate's degree program applicants and 17 percent of diploma degree program applicants (Mazinga 2021). The survey found that a lack of clinical placement settings and a shortage of faculty are obstacles to program capacity expansion and increased nursing education opportunities (Mazinga 2021). In an American Association of Colleges of Nursing faculty vacancy survey, the 884 schools of nursing that responded had an average of 1.69 full-time faculty vacancies per school and a range of 1 to 31 vacancies (AACN 2022). A key challenge to recruiting potential nurse educators—and retaining current nurse educators—to address such faculty vacancies is the higher compensation that nurses can earn in clinical and private-sector settings in comparison to teaching positions (AACN 2020).

or unconventional therapies (Eisenberg et al. 1993). In that study, Eisenberg and colleagues concluded that one in three adults relied on treatments and interventions that are not widely taught at medical schools in the United States, such as acupuncture, chiropractic, and massage therapies. Consumers are increasingly using and paying for CAM approaches (Scott et al. 2022; Stussman et al. 2020), and more than half of office-based physicians recommend CAM approaches to their patients (Stussman et al. 2020).

In recognizing the growing demand for CAM therapies, health systems are increasingly pursuing the integration of conventional medical care with CAM therapies, often referred to as "integrative health" (Ng et al. 2022). Some common challenges that systems may face in the further embrace of complementary, alternative, and integrative medicine therapies include initial costs associated with developing CAM or integrative medicine programs, teams' disagreement on conflicting treatment approaches, and a lack of knowledge or education about integrative medicine among clinicians to support its expansion (Gannotta et al. 2018).

NONPHYSICIAN LICENSED INDEPENDENT PRACTITIONERS

As a result of the Affordable Care Act, healthcare organizations are relying more on nonphysician licensed independent practitioners (LIPs). Collaborative practice models that include nurse practitioners, physician assistants, pharmacists, and other therapists are appropriate in both acute and long-term healthcare delivery. Advances have been made in the direct reimbursement for some LIP services, which is an impetus for further collaboration in practice. Evidence points to a growing LIP presence in primary care practices, as primary care providers are increasingly embracing interdisciplinary configurations in efforts to improve access and advance healthcare delivery (Barnes et al. 2018; Cornell et al. 2020; A. Jones et al. 2022; Poghosyan et al. 2020; Stephenson et al. 2019).

At the same time, debates persist regarding the appropriate roles of LIPs within healthcare delivery (Perloff et al. 2019; Smith 2022; see also the accompanying Debate Point sidebar). These debates include each role's scope of practice and diverging views surrounding the progressive expansion of practice for LIP roles to gradually include responsibilities that were traditionally viewed as the role of physicians, also referred to as **scope creep**. Given the varied scope of practice regulations and restrictions across states (Frogner et al. 2020), as well as the restrictiveness of LIP privileging practices among individual hospitals (Pittman et al. 2020), such debates are likely to persist. However, recent healthcare reform efforts, as well as increasing demand for health services, have led to a growing recognition of the value of LIPs, highlighting opportunities to more effectively plan for their utilization and integrate them into healthcare delivery (Knodel 2019; Perloff et al. 2019; Pittman et al. 2020; Smith 2022).

scope creep
The progressive expansion of the scope of practice for specific healthcare professional roles, encompassing responsibilities previously viewed as outside a specific role's scope of practice or pertaining to another healthcare professional role.

DEBATE POINT

In the midst of widely reported shortages of primary care providers, many leaders have called for expansion of the scope of practice for nurse practitioners (NPs) to meet patients' needs and demand for primary care services. However, this argument has proven to be controversial and contentious, with sharp differences in an understanding of appropriate roles in the primary care workforce. Advocates for the expansion of NPs' scope of practice suggest that they can be effectively utilized to meet primary care needs, particularly in underserved communities and provider shortage areas, as well as to better support current primary care physicians who struggle under demanding work schedules to meet existing and future demand. In contrast, opponents question whether the quality of care provided by NPs is comparable to that of physicians, despite studies indicating similar or improved patient outcomes (Kleinpell et al. 2019), and they raise concerns that NPs may actually lead to increased costs of care as well, again in contrast to study findings, including among "complex patients"—that is, patients with multiple chronic conditions (Morgan et al. 2019). What might be arguments both for and against expansion of NPs' scope of practice, particularly with respect to the potential impact on access to care, cost of care, and quality of care? For health services managers, what challenges and considerations might they navigate in addressing the debate surrounding scope of practice?

EMERGING AND EVOLVING ROLES

Critical roles within the healthcare workforce continue to emerge and evolve because of multiple factors, including the continued shift toward outpatient care, the increasing emphasis on population health management, the growth of healthcare consumerism, the increased prevalence of chronic disease, the proliferation of technology, and the expansion of value-based care models (e.g., accountable care organizations [ACOs]). Such roles include the increased involvement of LIPs, with a notable increase in LIPs as participating clinicians in ACOs (Nyweide, Lee, and Colla 2020). Additionally, we see the emergence of positions focused on such areas as patient experience, clinical informatics, diversity, and innovation (Rohan and Brandt 2016). These developments have led to positions that are more focused and may even be interdisciplinary. Specifically, care coordination has been recognized as a dominant role domain in recent years, drawing on those with nursing, social work, and physical therapy backgrounds and education (Frogner, Stubbs, and Skillman 2018). Community health workers (CHWs) have also taken on a more prominent role in care delivery, as described in the accompanying Critical Concept sidebar "Changing Roles of Community Health Workers."

> **CRITICAL CONCEPT**
> Changing Roles of Community Health Workers
>
> As the US healthcare delivery system has faced calls for increased efforts and change surrounding population health management, preventive care, health equity, and investments in public health and primary care, the roles of community health workers (CHWs) have seen increased emphasis and value in recent years. CHWs generally serve as community members who are intimately familiar with their communities and trusted to serve as valuable voices for health promotion, health literacy and education, and disease prevention. Although they have historic roots as lay members of the community or trained public health workers, they have recently seen a shift toward employment in hospitals and hospital-based systems (Malcarney et al. 2017), and their value in connecting the needs and experiences of community members to specific medical and social services has been made apparent, particularly in the midst of the COVID-19 pandemic (Ballard et al. 2020; Peretz, Islam, and Matiz 2020). As a result, CHWs play a critical role in the healthcare industry. Experts suggest that healthcare leaders must work diligently to recognize CHWs' value as frontline team members of healthcare and public health; better integrate them into the work of hospital systems and healthcare organizations; increasingly utilize their ability to enhance primary care services; support their positive interactions with multiple healthcare professional roles; and selectively recruit and retain CHWs for competencies in empathy, cultural humility, and community engagement (Hartzler et al. 2018; LeBan, Kok, and Perry 2021; Malcarney et al. 2017; Peretz, Islam, and Matiz 2020).

INNOVATION AND ENTREPRENEURSHIP

In the face of complex challenges and increasing demands on healthcare professionals, researchers have highlighted the need for health professions educators to incorporate innovation as a core skill set for healthcare professionals (Boms et al. 2022; McLaughlin et al. 2019). Many healthcare professionals are already seasoned inventors, applying creative problem solving to address the challenges they face in caring for patients.

Design thinking is an approach to innovation that suggests that meaningful, lasting solutions must be not only technically feasible and financially viable but also genuinely desirable to the user or recipient of the innovation. Thus, design thinking emphasizes an understanding of the perspective and desires of end users, embracing an empathy-driven approach to creative problem solving that is also referred to as *human-centered design*.

Numerous observers have suggested design thinking as a valuable tool for health systems, and leading healthcare organizations have embraced design thinking (Altman,

Huang, and Breland 2018; Wheelock, Bechtel, and Leff 2020). However, despite its growth in recognition and esteem, the principles of design thinking are still not fully adopted by today's healthcare organizations. A 2018 survey of US healthcare executives and clinical leaders found that an overwhelming majority—more than 90 percent—believed design thinking is useful for healthcare organizations as well as healthcare delivery in general, yet less than 25 percent employed design thinking principles on more than an occasional or seldom basis (Compton-Phillips and Mohta 2018). More than 50 percent of the survey respondents pointed to care coordination as the current issue that would benefit the most from such creative problem-solving approaches. However, the same number highlighted limited buy-in from decision makers as a barrier to design thinking, with nearly as many suggesting they lacked an understanding of design thinking techniques (Compton-Phillips and Mohta 2018). Gaps in education and the lack of support from leadership are current barriers to exercising innovation.

Entrepreneurship is another aspect of the changing nature of the healthcare professions. Given the bureaucratic nature of organizations, the regulation of the healthcare industry, and additional constraints imposed by payers and managed care, many healthcare professionals are choosing to pursue opportunities on their own. The service economy, coupled with knowledge-based professions, may encourage the pursuit of new and different ventures for individuals who have the personality, skills, and tenacity to go into business for themselves. An entrepreneur must have a mix of management skills and the means to depart from a traditional career path to practice on their own.

SUMMARY

Healthcare professionals make up a large segment of the US labor force. Historically, the development of healthcare professionals has been related to the following trends:

- Supply and demand
- Increased use of technology
- Changes in disease and illness
- The impact of healthcare financing and delivery

The healthcare workforce is diverse in many respects. The levels of education, scopes of practice, and practice settings of healthcare professionals contribute to the complexity of managing this workforce. Some reforms within the healthcare professions are likely in the coming decades in response to increasing pressures to finance and deliver healthcare with higher-quality, lower-cost, and measurable outcomes.

FOR DISCUSSION

1. Describe the process of professionalization. What is the difference between an occupation and a profession?

2. Describe the major types of healthcare professionals (excluding physicians and dentists) and their roles, training, licensure requirements, and practice settings.

3. Describe and apply the issues of HR management and systems development to healthcare professionals.

4. How have financing and reimbursement policies affected the healthcare professions?

5. Which nonphysician practitioners provide primary care? What is their role in the delivery of health services?

EXPERIENTIAL EXERCISE

The purpose of this exercise is to allow you to explore one healthcare profession in detail. From all of the healthcare professions, select one for analysis. Exhibit 2.1 from earlier in the chapter provides a starting point for selection. Describe the following characteristics of the profession you selected:

*   Knowledge base
*   Collective goals
*   Training
*   Licensure (this varies by state)
*   Number of professionals in practice, categorized according to
    –   Vertical differentiation (position, experience, education level)
    –   Horizontal differentiation (geography, practice setting, specialty)
*   History and evolution of the profession
*   Professional associations and their roles
*   Competitor professions
*   Strategic issues that face the profession and the profession's position on these issues

    To get started on this exercise, you may wish to go to the websites of professional organizations and state licensing boards. You may also interview members of the profession as well as leaders in the field.

REFERENCES

Altman, M., T. T. K. Huang, and J. Y. Breland. 2018. "Design Thinking in Health Care." *Preventing Chronic Disease* 15. Published September 27. https://doi.org/10.5888/pcd15.180128.

American Association for Physician Leadership (AAPL). 2022. "Membership with the American Association for Physician Leadership." Accessed June 30. www.physicianleaders.org/.

American Association of Colleges of Nursing (AACN). 2022. *Special Survey on Vacant Faculty Positions for Academic Year 2020–2021.* Accessed June 30. www.aacnnursing.org/Portals/42/News/Surveys-Data/2020-Faculty-Vacancy-Report.pdf.

———. 2021. "Data Spotlight: Insights on the Nursing Faculty Shortage." Published August 17. www.aacnnursing.org/News-Information/News/View/ArticleId/25043/data-spotlight-august-2021-Nursing-Faculty-Shortage.

———. 2020. *Fact Sheet: Nursing Faculty Shortage.* Updated September. www.aacnnursing.org/Portals/42/News/Factsheets/Faculty-Shortage-Factsheet.pdf.

American Hospital Association (AHA). 2020. *Trendwatch: Hospital and Health System Workforce Strategic Planning.* Published January. www.aha.org/system/files/media/file/2020/01/aha-trendwatch-hospital-and-health-system-workforce-strategic-planning2_0.pdf.

American Nurses Association (ANA). 2022. "The Nursing Process." Accessed June 30. www.nursingworld.org/practice-policy/workforce/what-is-nursing/the-nursing-process/.

Association of American Medical Colleges (AAMC). 2022. "Medical School Admissions Requirements (MSAR)." Accessed June 30. https://mec.aamc.org/msar-ui/#/landing.

Association of Schools Advancing Health Professions (ASAHP). 2022a. *2021 Annual Report.* Accessed June 30. www.asahp.org/s/2021-Annual-Report-compressed.pdf.

———. 2022b. "What Is Allied Health?" Accessed June 30. www.asahp.org/what-is.

Ballard, M., E. Bancroft, J. Nesbit, A. Johnson, I. Holeman, J. Foth, D. Rogers, J. Yang, J. Nardella, H. Olsen, M. Raghavan, R. Panjabi, R. Alban, S. Malaba, M. Christiansen, S.

Rapp, J. Schechter, P. Aylward, A. Rogers, J. Sebisaho, C. Ako, N. Choudhury, C. Westgate, J. Mbeya, R. Schwarz, M. H. Bonds, R. Adamjee, J. Bishop, A. Yembrick, D. Flood, M. McLaughlin, and D. Palazuelos. 2020. "Prioritising the Role of Community Health Workers in the COVID-19 Response." *BMJ Global Health* 5 (6): e002550. https://gh.bmj .com/content/5/6/e002550.

Barnes, H., M. R. Richards, M. D. McHugh, and G. Martsolf. 2018. "Rural and Nonrural Primary Care Physician Practices Increasingly Rely on Nurse Practitioners." *Health Affairs* 37 (6): 908–14.

Boms, O., Z. Shi, N. Mallipeddi, J. J. Chung, W. H. Marks, D. C. Whitehead, and M. D. Succi. 2022. "Integrating Innovation as a Core Objective in Medical Training." *Nature Biotechnology* 40 (3): 434–37.

Centers for Medicare & Medicaid Services (CMS). 2022. *National Health Expenditures 2020 Highlights*. Accessed June 30. www.cms.gov/files/document/highlights.pdf.

Compton-Phillips, A., and N. S. Mohta. 2018. "Care Redesign Survey: How Design Thinking Can Transform Health Care." *NEJM Catalyst*. Published June 7. https://catalyst.nejm .org/doi/full/10.1056/CAT.18.0159.

Cornell, P. Y., C. W. Halladay, J. Ader, J. Halaszynski, M. Hogue, C. E. McClain, J. W. Silva, L. D. Taylor, and J. L. Rudolph. 2020. "Embedding Social Workers in Veterans Health Administration Primary Care Teams Reduces Emergency Department Visits." *Health Affairs* 39 (4): 603–12.

Djukic, M., A. W. Stimpfel, and C. Kovner. 2019. "Bachelor's Degree Nurse Graduates Report Better Quality and Safety Educational Preparedness than Associate Degree Graduates." *Joint Commission Journal on Quality and Patient Safety* 45 (3): 180–86.

Dreyfus, H. L., and S. E. Dreyfus. 2009. "The Relationship of Theory and Practice in the Acquisition of Skill." In *Expertise in Nursing Practice: Caring, Clinical Judgment, and Ethics*, 2nd ed., edited by P. Benner, C. A. Tanner, and C. A. Chesla, 1–24. New York: Springer.

Eisenberg, D. M., R. D. Kessler, C. Foster, R. E. Norlock, D. R. Calkins, and T. L. Delbanco. 1993. "Unconventional Medicine in the United States." *New England Journal of Medicine* 328 (24): 246–52.

Farmer, P., T. Gerardi, P. Thompson, and B. Hoffman. 2018. *Academic Progression in Nursing (APIN): Final Program Summary and Outcomes*. Published March. https://nepincollaborative.org/wp-content/uploads/2018/03/FINAL-APIN-REPORT.pdf.

Fernandez, R., H. Green, R. Middleton, E. Halcomb, and L. Moxham. 2022. "Development and Evaluation of the Altered Student Study Environment Tool: A Tool to Measure Nursing Student Concerns Relating to Academic Progression During the COVID-19 Pandemic." *Nursing Education Perspectives* 43 (3): 147–51.

Frogner, B. K., E. P. Fraher, J. Spetz, P. Pittman, J. Moore, A. J. Beck, D. Armstrong, and P. I. Buerhaus. 2020. "Modernizing Scope-of-Practice Regulations—Time to Prioritize Patients." *New England Journal of Medicine* 382 (7): 591–93.

Frogner, B. K., B. A. Stubbs, and S. M. Skillman. 2018. *Emerging Roles and Occupations in the Health Care Workforce*. Seattle, WA: Center for Health Workforce Studies, University of Washington.

Gannotta, R., S. Malik, A. Y. Chan, K. Urgun, F. Hsu, and S. Vadera. 2018. "Integrative Medicine as a Vital Component of Patient Care." *Cureus* 10 (8): e3098. Published August 4. https://doi.org/10.7759/cureus.3098.

Gerardi, T., P. Farmer, and B. Hoffman. 2018. "Moving Closer to the 2020 BSN-Prepared Workforce Goal." *American Journal of Nursing* 118 (2): 43–45.

Harrison, J. M., L. H. Aiken, D. M. Sloane, J. M. Brooks Carthon, R. M. Merchant, R. A. Berg, and M. D. McHugh. 2019. "In Hospitals with More Nurses Who Have Baccalaureate Degrees, Better Outcomes for Patients After Cardiac Arrest." *Health Affairs* 38 (7): 1087–94.

Hartzler, A. L., L. Tuzzio, C. Hsu, and E. H. Wagner. 2018. "Roles and Functions of Community Health Workers in Primary Care." *Annals of Family Medicine* 16 (3): 240–45.

Jones, A. L., A. T. Kelley, Y. Suo, J. D. Baylis, N. K. Codell, N. A. West, and A. J. Gordon. 2022. "Trends in Health Service Utilization After Enrollment in an Interdisciplinary Primary Care Clinic for Veterans With Addiction, Social Determinants of Health, or Other Vulnerabilities." *Journal of General Internal Medicine*. Published February 22. https://doi.org/10.1007/s11606-022-07456-x.

Jones, T. L., L. H. Yoder, and M. Baernholdt. 2019. "Variation in Academic Preparation and Progression of Nurses Across the Continuum of Care." *Nursing Outlook* 67 (4): 381–92.

Kane, C. K. 2021. "Recent Changes in Physician Practice Arrangements: Private Practice Dropped to Less Than 50 Percent of Physicians in 2020." *American Medical Association Policy Research Perspective*. Published May. www.ama-assn.org/system/files/2021-05/2020-prp-physician-practice-arrangements.pdf.

Kleinpell, R. M., W. R. Grabenkort, A. N. Kapu, R. Constantine, and C. Sicoutris. 2019. "Nurse Practitioners and Physician Assistants in Acute and Critical Care: A Concise Review of the Literature and Data 2008–2018." *Critical Care Medicine* 47 (10): 1442–49.

Knodel, L. J. 2019. "As Healthcare Changes, So Must the People Who Deliver It." *Frontiers of Health Services Management* 35 (4): 21–24.

LeBan, K., M. Kok, and H. B. Perry. 2021. "Community Health Workers at the Dawn of a New Era: CHWs' Relationships with the Health System and Communities." *Health Research Policy and Systems* 19: article no. 116. Published October 12. https://doi.org/10.1186/s12961-021-00756-4.

Ma, C., L. Garrard, and J. He. 2018. "Recent Trends in Baccalaureate-Prepared Registered Nurses in U.S. Acute Care Hospital Units, 2004–2013: A Longitudinal Study." *Journal of Nursing Scholarship* 50 (1): 83–91.

Malcarney, M. B., P. Pittman, L. Quigley, K. Horton, and N. Seiler. 2017. "The Changing Roles of Community Health Workers." *Health Services Research* 52 (Suppl 1): 360–82.

Mazinga, G. 2021. "NLN Biennial Survey of Schools of Nursing Academic Year 2019–2020: Executive Summary." *Nursing Education Perspectives* 42 (5): 333–34.

McLaughlin, J. E., M. D. Wolcott, D. Hubbard, K. Umstead, and T. R. Rider. 2019. "A Qualitative Review of the Design Thinking Framework in Health Professions Education." *BMC Medical Education* 19: article no. 98. Published April 4. https://doi.org/10.1186/s12909-019-1528-8.

Morgan, P. A., V. A. Smith, T. S. Z. Berkowitz, D. Edelman, C. H. Van Houtven, S. L. Woolson, C. C. Hendrix, C. M. Everett, B. S. White, and G. L. Jackson. 2019. "Impact of Physicians, Nurse Practitioners, and Physician Assistants on Utilization and Costs for Complex Patients." *Health Affairs* 38 (6): 1028–36.

National Association of Long Term Care Administrator Boards (NAB). 2022. "State Licensure Requirements." Accessed June 30. www.nabweb.org/state-licensure-requirements.

National Council of State Boards of Nursing (NCSBN). 2022. "APRNs in the U.S." Accessed June 30. www.ncsbn.org/aprn.htm.

Ng, J. Y., T. Dhawan, E. Dogadova, Z. Taghi-Zada, A. Vacca, L. S. Wieland, and D. Moher. 2022. "Operational Definition of Complementary, Alternative, and Integrative Medicine Derived from a Systematic Search." *BMC Complementary Medicine and Therapies* 22: article no. 104. Published April 12. https://doi.org/10.1186/s12906-022-03556-7.

Nyweide, D. J., W. Lee, and C. H. Colla. 2020. "Accountable Care Organizations' Increase in Nonphysician Practitioners May Signal Shift for Health Care Workforce." *Health Affairs* 39 (6): 1080–86.

O'Brien, D., M. Knowlton, and R. Whichello. 2018. "Attention Health Care Leaders: Literature Review Deems Baccalaureate Nurses Improve Patient Outcomes." *Nursing Education Perspectives* 39 (4): E2–E6.

O'Hanlon, C. E. 2020. "Impacts of Health Care Industry Consolidation in Pittsburgh, Pennsylvania: A Qualitative Study." *INQUIRY: The Journal of Health Care Organization, Provision, and Financing* 57. Published November 24. https://doi.org/10.1177/0046958020976246.

O'Hanlon, C. E., C. M. Whaley, and D. Freund. 2019. "Medical Practice Consolidation and Physician Shared Patient Network Size, Strength, and Stability." *Medical Care* 57 (9): 680–87.

Peretz, P. J., N. Islam, and L. A. Matiz. 2020. "Community Health Workers and Covid-19—Addressing Social Determinants of Health in Times of Crisis and Beyond." *New England Journal of Medicine* 383 (19): e108. https://doi.org/10.1056/NEJMp2022641.

Perloff, J., S. Clarke, C. M. DesRoches, M. O'Reilly-Jacob, and P. Buerhaus. 2019. "Association of State-Level Restrictions in Nurse Practitioner Scope of Practice with the Quality of Primary Care Provided to Medicare Beneficiaries." *Medical Care Research and Review* 76 (5): 597–626.

Physicians Advocacy Institute. 2022. *COVID-19's Impact on Acquisitions of Physician Practices and Physician Employment 2019–2021*. Updated April. www.physiciansadvocacyinstitute.org/PAI-Research/Physician-Employment-and-Practice-Acquisitions-Trends-2019-21.

Pittman, P., B. Leach, C. Everett, X. Han, and D. McElroy. 2020. "NP and PA Privileging in Acute Care Settings: Do Scope of Practice Laws Matter?" *Medical Care Research and Review* 77 (2): 112–20.

Poghosyan, L., A. Ghaffari, J. Liu, and M. W. Friedberg. 2020. "Physician-Nurse Practitioner Teamwork in Primary Care Practices in New York: A Cross-Sectional Survey." *Journal of General Internal Medicine* 35 (4): 1021–28.

Richards, M. R., J. A. Seward, and C. M. Whaley. 2022. "Treatment Consolidation After Vertical Integration: Evidence from Outpatient Procedure Markets." *Journal of Health Economics* 81: article no. 102569. https://doi.org/10.1016/j.jhealeco.2021.102569.

Rohan, J. E., and C. Brandt. 2016. "Emerging Roles in Value-Based Care." *Healthcare Executive* 31 (5): 64–65.

Ryskina, K. L., K. Shultz, M. A. Unruh, and H. Y. Jung. 2021. "Practice Trends and Characteristics of US Hospitalists from 2012 to 2018." *JAMA Health Forum* 2 (11): e213524.

Scott, R., R. L. Nahin, B. J. Sussman, and T. Feinberg. 2022. "Physician Office Visits Which Included Complementary Health Approaches in U.S. Adults: 2005–2015." *Journal of Integrative and Complementary Medicine* 28 (8). Published May 13. https://doi.org/10.1089/jicm.2021.0331.

Shi, L., and D. A. Singh. 2022. *Delivering Health Care in America: A Systems Approach*, 8th ed. Burlington, MA: Jones & Bartlett Learning.

Sloane, D. M., H. L. Smith, M. D. McHugh, and L. H. Aiken. 2018. "Effect of Changes in Hospital Nursing Resources on Improvements in Patient Safety and Quality of Care: A Panel Study." *Medical Care* 56 (12): 1001–8.

Smiley, R. A., C. Ruttinger, C. M. Oliveira, L. R. Hudson, R. Allgeyer, K. A. Reneau, J. H. Silvestre, and M. Alexander. 2021. "The 2020 National Nursing Workforce Survey." *Journal of Nursing Regulation* 12 (1 Suppl): S1–S96.

Smith, L. B. 2022. "The Effect of Nurse Practitioner Scope of Practice Laws on Primary Care Delivery." *Health Economics* 31 (1): 21–41.

Stephenson, M. D., K. Lisy, C. J. Stern, A. M. Feyer, L. Fisher, and E. Aromataris. 2019. "The Impact of Integrated Care for People with Chronic Conditions on Hospital and Emergency Department Utilization." *International Journal of Evidence-Based Healthcare* 17 (1): 14–26.

Stussman, B. J., R. R. Nahin, P. M. Barnes, and B. W. Ward. 2020. "U.S. Physician Recommendations to Their Patients About the Use of Complementary Health Approaches." *Journal of Alternative and Complementary Medicine* 26 (1): 25–33.

US Bureau of Labor Statistics (BLS). 2022a. "Economic News Release: Table B-1; Employees on Nonfarm Payrolls by Industry Sector and Selected Industry Detail." Updated October 7. www.bls.gov/news.release/empsit.t17.htm.

———. 2022b. "Occupational Outlook Handbook: Healthcare Occupations." Updated September 8. www.bls.gov/ooh/healthcare/home.htm.

———. 2022c. "Occupational Outlook Handbook: Licensed Practical and Licensed Vocational Nurses." Updated September 8. www.bls.gov/ooh/healthcare/licensed-practical-and-licensed-vocational-nurses.htm.

———. 2022d. "Occupational Outlook Handbook: Nurse Anesthetists, Nurse Midwives, and Nurse Practitioners." Updated September 8. www.bls.gov/ooh/healthcare/nurse-anesthetists-nurse-midwives-and-nurse-practitioners.htm.

———. 2022e. "Occupational Outlook Handbook: Pharmacists." Updated September 8. www.bls.gov/ooh/healthcare/pharmacists.htm.

———. 2022f. "Occupational Outlook Handbook: Registered Nurses; Work Environment." Updated September 8. www.bls.gov/ooh/healthcare/registered-nurses.htm#tab-3.

Wachter, R. M., and L. Goldman. 2016. "Zero to 50,000—The 20th Anniversary of the Hospitalist." *New England Journal of Medicine* 375 (11): 1009–11.

Wheelock, A., C. Bechtel, and B. Leff. 2020. "Human-Centered Design and Trust in Medicine." *JAMA* 324 (23): 2369–70.

CHAPTER 3

THE LEGAL AND ETHICAL ENVIRONMENT

Drake Maynard

After completing this chapter, you should be able to

➤ define *employment-at-will*, *dismissal for cause*, and *due process*;

➤ describe the strategies that organizations use to prevent and identify discrimination in the workplace;

➤ discuss the key features of the Americans with Disabilities Act, including the concepts of undue hardship and reasonable accommodation;

➤ describe the legal definitions of *sexual harassment*; and

➤ explain the concept of progressive discipline and the steps required for employee termination.

After three weeks as assistant administrator of a medical group practice, Jessica Mont-
gomery spends the weekend pondering how to deal with some events that happened at
work. The job was all she hoped it would be—she worked in a highly regarded practice
and felt professionally challenged and up to the job. She was disturbed, however, by
some of the interactions with one of the physicians in the practice, Dr. Curtis Sanford.
Dr. Sanford is a well-respected physician who has been with the practice for almost 20
years. During Jessica's first week, he made a number of sexually suggestive remarks to
Jessica that she felt were unprofessional and demeaning. Because she did not want to
stir up trouble or seem overly sensitive, she chose to remain silent. On Friday of her third
week, Jessica had lunch with two female coworkers, Maria and Denise, who verified that
Dr. Sanford tends to pick on new female employees. "When the next female employee is
hired, Dr. Sanford will stop this behavior and transfer it to the new girl. Just give it some
time," said Maria. However, Maria and Denise also noted that several highly competent
female employees had left after only two weeks on the job. Although Jessica understands
that this may be a form of sexual harassment, she believes that she can live with the situation until it ends. However, she also feels a legal and ethical obligation to put an end to
this physician's behavior. As of Sunday night, going into her fourth week, Jessica is still
not sure how to deal with this situation.

INTRODUCTION

Jessica's story illustrates one of the many ways legal issues affect the workplace. This instance includes a potential ethical issue and possible illegal activity on the part of Dr. Sanford. This chapter discusses the complex set of laws that affect human resources management (HRM). Understanding the impact of the many laws affecting the workplace is critical for healthcare managers. What's important is not just the wording of laws but also the manner in which courts and regulatory agencies have interpreted them.

The laws that govern the relationship between employer and employee reflect society's attempt to achieve a balance between allowing managers to pursue their legitimate business goals and keeping employees free from injury, prejudice, and duress. While the US legal system seeks to protect employee rights, laws also protect management rights. In light of the greater relative power of employers in the employer–employee relationship, US laws tend to emphasize protection of the employee.

When any individual in an organization violates the law, senior managers and board members may be liable. Perhaps an even more compelling reason for managers to understand and comply with legal requirements is this: Compliance implies good management practice. A central idea in laws providing equal opportunity is that the job description and an employee's competencies—instead of factors such as race and age—should guide human resource decisions. This idea is consistent with good management practice.

An important consideration is the ambiguity of laws and regulations. Virtually every employment-related US law has been subject to extensive and far-reaching interpretation by the courts—including the US Supreme Court—and quasi-judicial administrative agencies, such as the **National Labor Relations Board (NLRB)** and the **US Equal Employment Opportunity Commission (EEOC)**. For this reason, employment law cannot be understood by simply reading the text of existing laws. We must also look at how laws have been interpreted by courts, which affects how they are enforced.

KEY FEDERAL AND STATE EMPLOYMENT LAWS

The respective rights and responsibilities that govern the workplace are documented in federal and state statutes, administrative agency regulations, case law interpretations of various state and federal legislation and regulations, written and verbal employment agreements, and employee handbooks. Among the most important federal statutes that directly or indirectly affect the employment setting are the Fair Labor Standards Act (FLSA), the Civil Rights Act of 1964, the Family and Medical Leave Act (FMLA), the Americans with Disabilities Act (ADA), and the Health Insurance Portability and Accountability Act of 1996 (HIPAA), each of which will be discussed in greater detail later in the chapter. Exhibit 3.1 presents federal sources of equal employment opportunity law.

National Labor Relations Board (NLRB)
An independent federal agency that protects the rights of private-sector employees to join together, with or without a union, to improve their wages and working conditions. It was established by the National Labor Relations Act (NLRA) to investigate alleged NLRA violations.

US Equal Employment Opportunity Commission (EEOC)
A federal agency responsible for ending employment discrimination. The EEOC files lawsuits on behalf of alleged victims of discrimination in the workplace.

Exhibit 3.1
Sources of Equal
Employment
Opportunity Law

Source	Purpose	Coverage	Administration
First Amendment, US Constitution*	Protection of free speech, protection of assembly (for example, joining a union)	All individuals	Federal courts
Fourth Amendment, US Constitution*	Protects against unreasonable searches	All individuals (from government activity)	Federal courts
Fifth Amendment, US Constitution*	Protects against federal violation of due process	All individuals (from government activity)	Federal courts
Fourteenth Amendment, US Constitution*	Provides equal protection for all citizens and requires due process in state action	All individuals (from government activity)	Federal courts
Civil Rights Acts of 1866 and 1871	Establishes the rights of all citizens to make and enforce contracts	All individuals	Federal courts
Equal Pay Act of 1963	Requires that men and women performing equal jobs receive equal pay	Employers engaged in interstate commerce	Equal Employment Opportunity Commission (EEOC) and federal courts
Civil Rights Act of 1964, Title VII, as amended in 1991	Prohibits discrimination on the basis of race, color, religion, sex, or national origin	Employers with 15 or more employees working 20 or more weeks per year; labor unions; employment agencies	EEOC
Executive Orders 11246 (1965) and 11375 (1967)	Prohibit discrimination by contractors and subcontractors of federal agencies, and require affirmative action in hiring women and minorities	Federal contractors and subcontractors with contracts of or greater than $10,000	Federal, Office of Federal Contract Compliance Program (OFCCP)

Source	Purpose	Coverage	Administration
Age Discrimination in Employment Act (ADEA) of 1967	Prohibits discrimination in employment against individuals aged 40 or older	Employers with 15 or more employees working 20 or more weeks in the current or preceding calendar year; labor unions; employment agencies	EEOC
Rehabilitation Act of 1973	Protects persons with disabilities against discrimination in the public sector and requires affirmative action in the employment of individuals with disabilities	Government agencies; federal contractors and subcontractors with contracts of or greater than $2,500	OFCCP
Americans with Disabilities Act (ADA) of 1990	Prohibits discrimination against individuals with disabilities	Employers with more than 15 employees	EEOC
Family and Medical Leave Act (FMLA) of 1993	Requires employers to provide 12 weeks of unpaid leave for family and medical emergencies, childbirth, and other serious personal events	Employers with more than 50 employees	US Department of Labor
Americans with Disabilities Act Amendments Act (ADAAA) of 2008	Provides a more flexible and inclusive definition of a qualifying disability	Employers with more than 15 employees	EEOC

EXHIBIT 3.1
Sources of Equal Employment Opportunity Law *(continued)*

* *Note*: Only government employees—federal, state, county, and municipality—are covered by the Bill of Rights. Government as employer implies that government agencies are bound by employment regulations put forward by the US Constitution. Private-sector employers are not obligated in the same way by the Constitution. For example, while employee free speech may be constitutionally protected in the public sector, private-sector employees do not enjoy this and other constitutional provisions.

KEY POINT

Federal law establishes many legal requirements for managing the workforce. These laws include the Civil Rights Act (Title VII), the Fair Labor Standards Act, and the Americans with Disabilities Act. State and local laws also play an important role in the workplace. Sometimes state and local laws extend the provisions of federal law, while in other cases, new regulations are put into place. For example, until recently, several jurisdictions provided protection against discrimination because of sexual orientation. Recent court interpretations of federal law now extend federal protection against discrimination because of sexual orientation. Federal law currently does not provide protection against discrimination because of weight. However, some jurisdictions do provide such protection. Numerous other state and local laws govern a wide range of other issues in the workplace.

In addition to federal law, state laws address additional rights and responsibilities for employees. For example, in North Carolina, an employer many not withhold money from an employee's paycheck to recoup money the employee owes, unless the employee was given prior notice and has authorized the transaction (NC Gen. Stat. Sections 95–25.8 to 95–25.10). Other states, such as California, have enacted statutes that supplement federal statutes—for example, in the area of pregnancy leave (CA Govt. Section 12945).

In this chapter, attention is focused primarily on laws at the federal level, but it is critical to understand that there are myriad laws and administrative arrangements at the state and local level, and in some instances, there are dramatic differences in scope and purpose.

EMPLOYMENT LAWS AND THE LAWS OF EQUAL EMPLOYMENT OPPORTUNITY

Federal agencies administer and enforce laws regarding employment generally (FLSA, FMLA) and nondiscrimination in employment (Title VII, the Age Discrimination in Employment Act [ADEA], and the Americans with Disabilities Act Amendments Act of 2008 [ADAAA]). *Equal employment opportunity (EEO)* efforts are governmental attempts to ensure that all individuals have equal access to employment, regardless of age, race, religion, disability, and other non-job-related characteristics. EEO applies to every aspect of employment; to quote Title VII, it applies to every "term, condition or privilege of employment." To accomplish EEO aims, the federal government has used constitutional amendments, legislation, executive orders, and courts and quasi-judicial bodies.

> ### ⓘ CRITICAL CONCEPT
> Exempt and Nonexempt Employees
>
> The Fair Labor Standards Act establishes minimum national labor standards, including payment for time worked beyond 40 hours in a workweek. Most employees, because of their job duties, are eligible for overtime compensation. However, based on job duties, some types of employees are exempt from this overtime compensation. Classifying employees as *exempt* from overtime compensation or *subject to* (nonexempt) overtime compensation is a critical aspect of HRM. Failure to make the correct classification can have expensive consequences for an employer.

The oldest national employment law in the United States is the **Fair Labor Standards Act** (**FLSA**), which was passed in 1938 and has been amended many times since. The FLSA sets the minimum wage; establishes a standard workweek of 40 hours; requires that employers pay time-and-a-half compensation for work beyond the standard workweek (but see the Critical Concept sidebar "Exempt and Nonexempt Employees"); forbids the employment of children in hazardous occupations such as mining, logging, woodworking, meatpacking, and certain types of manufacturing; and sets specific guidelines related to working hours for children. Prior to the FLSA, there were absolutely no legal restrictions placed on child labor.

THE 1960S AND FEDERAL ANTIDISCRIMINATION LAW

The 1960s was a period of significant social activism in the United States. New federal legislation extended civil rights and equal opportunity in a variety of areas—housing, voting, education, and employment. The basic premise of all of these laws is that employment decisions—including hiring, promotion, compensation, benefits, and training opportunities—should be based on the requirements of the job and an individual's qualifications, and not on an individual's age, gender, race, or disability.

Title VII of the Civil Rights Act of 1964 prohibits discrimination in voting, public accommodations, use of public facilities, public education, and employment. It is the most far-reaching and significant of all antidiscrimination statutes. Title VII is that portion of the Civil Rights Act that prohibits discrimination in employment. The act bars discrimination in hiring, promotion, compensation, training, benefits, and other human resources (HR) aspects. Discrimination on the basis of race, color, religion, sex, and national origin is specifically prohibited. Exhibit 3.2 describes the key provisions of Title VII. Although

Fair Labor Standards Act (FLSA)
The 1938 law that establishes a federal minimum wage, establishes a standard 40-hour workweek, and contains provisions for work performed beyond the standard workweek. It also sets limits on child labor.

Title VII of the Civil Rights Act of 1964
That portion of the law prohibiting discrimination in employment on the basis of race, sex, religion, national origin, or color. This was the first nationwide antidiscrimination law.

this legislation was established in the 1960s, its provisions still face challenges today (see the Current Issue sidebar "Prayer Breaks for Muslim Employees" discussing the issue of discrimination based on religion).

A key Supreme Court decision in 2020 made it illegal under federal law to discriminate based on sexual orientation. Previously, 17 states and the District of Columbia had passed laws prohibiting sexual orientation discrimination in private employment. Six states had laws that prohibit sexual orientation discrimination in public workplaces only. At least 225 cities and counties prohibit employment discrimination based on gender identity. These ordinances cover public and private employers (Human Rights Campaign 2022).

In the US Supreme Court case *Bostock v. Clayton County*, two conservative Supreme Court justices joined the liberal minority in finding that discriminating against someone

---

EXHIBIT 3.2
Key Provisions of
the Civil Rights Act

Section 703a Title VII of the Civil Rights Act is specific in its definition of discrimination:

(a) Employer practices
  It shall be an unlawful employment practice for an employer—
  (1) to fail or refuse to hire or to discharge any individual, or otherwise to discriminate against any individual with respect to his compensation, terms, conditions, or privileges of employment, because of such individual's race, color, religion, sex, or national origin; or
  (2) to limit, segregate, or classify his employees or applicants for employment in any way which would deprive or tend to deprive any individual of employment opportunities or otherwise adversely affect his status as an employee, because of such individual's race, color, religion, sex, or national origin.

The Civil Rights Act outlaws discrimination in a wide variety of organizations:

- All private employers involved in interstate commerce that employ 15 or more employees for 20 or more weeks per year
- State and local governments
- Private and public employment agencies
- Joint labor–management committees that govern apprenticeship or training programs
- Labor unions that have 15 or more members or employees
- Public and private educational institutions
- Foreign subsidiaries of US organizations that employ US citizens
- Federal government employees covered by section 717 of the Civil Rights Act and Civil Service Reform Act

---

Source: Civil Rights Act of 1964, Title VII, 42 U.S.C. § 703 (2000).

because of their sexual orientation was a form of sex discrimination and therefore a violation of Title VII. As the conservative Justice Neil Gorsuch wrote in the court's 2020 decision, "it is impossible to discriminate against a person for being homosexual or transgender without discriminating against that individual based on sex" (590 US). This Supreme Court decision was among the most significant and far-reaching decisions in US history.

Prior to the 1960s, it was legal to give different rates of pay to men and women for the same work. To rectify this situation, Congress passed an amendment to the FLSA, the Equal Pay Act of 1963. This act requires that men and women in the same organization who perform equal jobs receive equal pay. The Equal Pay Act outlaws the once-prevalent practice of paying women less simply because of their gender. This practice was commonly defended using the argument that a married man needed a higher salary to support his family. Sometimes determining what constitutes equal work may be difficult. The Equal Pay Act specifies that jobs are the same if they are equal in terms of skill, effort, responsibility,

CURRENT ISSUE
Prayer Breaks for Muslim Employees

Ariens Company, a Wisconsin manufacturer, had previously allowed its Muslim employees five unscheduled prayer breaks during the workday, as is required for devout Muslims. Following complaints from non-Muslim employees, and after an earnings report allegedly showed losses that the company attributed to lack of productivity during prayer breaks, Ariens told its Muslim employees that they were limited to two ten-minute breaks per workday. Subsequently Ariens fired seven Muslim employees for violating its work break policy; a number of other Muslim employees quit in protest over the new break policy. Prior to the change in break policy, Ariens had 53 Muslim employees (Barrett 2016). The EEOC was asked to investigate possible religious discrimination, and it ended up filing a lawsuit on the workers' behalf.

Title VII requires employers to accommodate employees' religious beliefs if it can be done without "undue hardship." Court decisions have defined *undue hardship* as efforts that are too costly or difficult for the employer to provide.

Does Ariens have the right to make its employees abide by its break policy even if it violates a religious belief? Would allowing employees to continue taking five unscheduled work breaks a day place "undue hardship" on the company? How do you think the case was decided?

After you have considered these questions, read the final disposition of this case (see Wiessner 2021 for link). Did it turn out the way you thought it would? Why or why not?

and working conditions. As discussed in chapter 8, pay equity legislation in some jurisdictions extends the scope of equality to include not just equal pay for equal work but equal pay for equivalent value to the organization.

Although the Equal Pay Act has been law for more than 40 years, substantial gaps in earnings between men and women persist. According to the US Department of Labor, in 2020, women overall made 83 cents for every dollar earned by men, with an even greater disparity among women of color. Black women were paid 64 cents and Hispanic women (of any race) were paid 57 cents for every dollar of what white non-Hispanic men were paid (Glynn and Boesch 2022).

*Age Discrimination
in Employment Act
(ADEA)*
Federal law passed in
1967 that prohibits
employment
discrimination against
employees and
applicants aged 40 or
older.

The **Age Discrimination in Employment Act (ADEA)** of 1967 forbids discrimination against men and women aged 40 or older by employers, unions, employment agencies, state and local governments, and the federal government. As with Title VII and the Equal Pay Act, enforcement of the ADEA is the responsibility of the EEOC, which is among the most influential federal government agencies. The EEOC can file suit on behalf of employees who allege discrimination.

The Older Workers Benefit Protection Act (OWBPA), passed in 1990, is an amendment to the ADEA. Overall, the act requires that benefit plans be nondiscriminatory. Although it has a variety of applications, an important goal is to protect older workers who are offered early retirement or severance plans. In return for an early retirement plan, employers often ask older employees who take early retirement to sign a statement, or waiver, indicating that they will not pursue a discrimination lawsuit (that is, sue the employer). At times, however, these waivers are unclear and misleading. The OWBPA requires that waivers be written in plain English and give employees a 21-day consideration period. The waiver language must also encourage employees to consult legal counsel and provide a 7-day period during which they can back out of the agreement.

EXPANSION OF ANTIDISCRIMINATION LAW UNDER THE ADA

Discrimination against individuals with disabilities was first prohibited in federally funded activities by the Vocational Rehabilitation Act of 1973. The **Americans with Disabilities Act (ADA)** grew out of the Vocational Rehabilitation Act and prohibits discrimination against individuals with disabilities in all aspects of employment, including job application procedures, hiring, termination, promotions, compensation, and training.

*Americans with
Disabilities Act (ADA)*
The federal civil
rights law passed in
1990 that prohibits
discrimination based
on disabilities.

The ADA Amendments Act of 2008 broadens the definition of *disability* (see the accompanying Critical Concept sidebar "How the ADAAA Defines *Disability*"). The amendments expand the list of major life activities and broaden the interpretation of substantial limitation of one or more of the major life activities. The act also eliminates consideration of mitigating measures in determining whether an individual has a disability. For example, under the original legislation, it was not clear whether someone with epilepsy would be covered if the condition is controlled by medication. The amendments indicate with certainty that an individual with a disability is covered under the act even if the symptoms are controlled by medication, assistive devices, prosthetics, or other aids. However, persons whose vision can be corrected with eyeglasses or contact lenses are not considered to have a disability.

The ADA also provides protection for people who are regarded as having an impairment, such as burn victims and individuals with disfiguring conditions. For example, the ADA protects individuals who may be denied employment because an employer believes that coworkers will have negative reactions to that individual's physical appearance. Although these categories are rather broad, the ADA specifically excludes the following from the definition of a disability:

- Homosexuality and bisexuality (as noted earlier, Title VII of the Civil Rights Act now provides protection against discrimination based on sexual orientation)

- Crossdressing, transsexualism, gender identity disorders that do not result from physical impairment, or other sexual behavior disorders

- Compulsive gambling, kleptomania, or pyromania

- Psychoactive substance abuse disorders resulting from current illegal use of drugs

The ADA does not require an organization to hire someone who has a disability but does not meet the requirements to do the job. In the language of the ADA (42 USC § 12111[8]), "the term 'qualified individual' means an individual who, with or without reasonable accommodation, can perform the essential functions of the employment position that such individual holds or desires." (See also "Did You Know?" sidebar.)

The ADA specifically states that it is the employer's responsibility to make **reasonable accommodation** to the physical or mental limitations of an employee with a disability, unless doing so will impose an undue hardship on the organization. Reasonable accommodation includes taking such measures as adjusting an employee's working conditions or schedules, restructuring jobs, reassigning individuals to other tasks, adjusting training materials, and providing readers or interpreters. Reasonableness is determined on a case-by-case basis. The EEOC and many courts now take the position that it is the employer's responsibility to engage in what is known as the "interactive process," which is a discussion between the employer and the employee about the disability and what, if any, reasonable accommodations can be made. The employer's responsibility to begin this process has been found even where the employee did not raise a disability issue or request an accommodation.

reasonable accommodation The concept that it is the employer's responsibility to make adjustments—within reasonable limits—for employees with physical or mental disabilities. Reasonableness is determined on a case-by-case basis.

> ⚠ **CRITICAL CONCEPT**
> How the ADAAA Defines *Disability*
>
> The language of the original Americans with Disabilities Act (ADA), like other legislation, was somewhat vague and thus was open to judicial interpretation. The revised ADA Amendments Act of 2008 (ADAAA) still uses the original three-pronged definition of disability (ADAAA 2008):
>
>   The term "disability" means, with respect to an individual
>
>   (A) a physical or mental impairment that substantially limits one or more major life activities of such individual;
>   (B) a record of such an impairment; or
>   (C) being regarded as having such an impairment.
>
> However, since the 2009 revisions were a reaction to court decisions restricting the definition of *disability* and thus access to reasonable accommodation, the new law specifically interprets certain phrases to avoid a repetition of those court decisions. For example, the law now defines "substantially limits" to mean "significantly restricted," a much lower standard. "Major life activities" is now defined to include major bodily functions. Under these new definitions, many conditions not previously determined to be a disability, such as diabetes, are now considered to be a disability (diabetes being a dysfunction of the body's endocrine system). Under court decisions interpreting the ADA, it became almost impossible to show a disability; the changes in the ADAAA now make that showing much easier.

compensatory damages
Payment to compensate a claimant in a court decision for loss, injury, or harm suffered by another's breach of duty.

punitive damages
Payment to compensate a claimant in a court decision beyond actual damages suffered.

PENALTIES FOR BREAKING EEO LAW

Organizations found guilty of breaking equal employment opportunity law are subject to a variety of penalties. Prior to 1991, the Civil Rights Act limited damage claims to *equitable relief*, such as back pay, lost benefits, front pay, and in some cases, attorney's fees. In 1991, enforcement provisions were strengthened to allow compensatory and punitive damages when intentional or reckless discrimination is proven. **Compensatory damages** may include payment to offset future monetary loss, emotional pain, suffering, and loss of enjoyment of life. **Punitive damages** are intended to discourage discrimination by providing for payments to the plaintiff beyond actual damages suffered.

Over the years, the types of discrimination cases brought before the EEOC have been relatively consistent. Between 1997 and 2021, the total number of claims fluctuated, ranging from a low of 61,331 in 2021 to a high of 99,947 in 2011. About 35 percent

DID YOU KNOW?
Facts About People with Disabilities in the United States

Drawing information from the 2021 American Community Survey, the US Bureau of Labor Statistics (BLS 2022), the US Census Bureau (2022a, 2022b), and the National Disability Institute (Goodman, Morris, and Boston 2019), the following statistics relate to Americans with disabilities:

- In 2021, the total civilian noninstitutionalized population aged 16 or older with a disability numbered more than 31 million people, 21.3 percent of whom were active in the labor force.
- In 2019, 19.8 percent of the civilian noninstitutionalized population in West Virginia had a disability—the highest rate of any state in the nation. Utah, at 9.3 percent, had the lowest rate.
- The total civilian noninstitutionalized population with a disability who were aged 18–64 and employed in 2019 numbered 7.9 million people.
- Across all age groups in 2021, persons with disabilities were much less likely to be employed than persons with no disabilities.
- In 2021, 19.1 percent of persons with a disability were employed, up from 17.9 percent in 2020.
- In 2021, 29 percent of workers with a disability were employed part-time, compared with 16 percent of workers with no disability.
- In 2021, 18.2 percent of persons with a disability worked in service occupations, compared with 15.9 percent of persons with no disability.
- In 2021, the unemployment rate for men with a disability was 10.1 percent, the same as the rate for women.
- A larger share of workers with a disability were self-employed in 2021 than were those with no disability (9.6 percent versus 6.4 percent).
- In 2021, persons with a disability were less likely to have completed a bachelor's degree or higher than persons with no disability.
- Among persons with a disability, the jobless rates for Blacks (15.1 percent) and Hispanics (13.3 percent) were higher than the rates for Whites (9.3 percent) and Asians (8.5 percent) in 2021. The rates for Whites, Asians, and Hispanics decreased from 2020 to 2021, while the rate for Blacks showed little change.
- In 2015, the poverty rate for adults with disabilities (27 percent) was more than twice the rate for adults with no disability (12 percent).
- In 2015, almost 40 percent of African Americans with disabilities lived in poverty, compared with 24 percent of non-Hispanic Whites, 29 percent of Latinos, and 19 percent of Asians.
- In 2015, working-age adults with disabilities were four times more likely to live with significantly low or very low food security than adults without disabilities.

of charges were brought on the basis of race, and this proportion has been stable since 1997. Similarly, charges based on sex discrimination have accounted for about 30 percent of all complaints over the same period. Of all the bases for charges, complaints based on allegations of retaliation have seen the greatest increase: 18,198 charges (20.3 percent of all charges) were filed in 1997, compared with 34,332 (36.2 percent of all charges) in 2021 (EEOC 2022b). Exhibit 3.3 shows charges filed with the EEOC in 2021 by basis of charge (EEOC 2022b). Exhibit 3.4 shows trends in the types of charges filed from 2007 to 2021 (EEOC 2022b).

affirmative action
A set of procedures designed to eliminate and prevent unlawful discrimination among applicants, including taking race, gender, ethnicity, disability, and veteran status into consideration in an attempt to promote equal opportunity; often used in hiring practices.

IMPLEMENTING EQUAL EMPLOYMENT OPPORTUNITY

Under Executive Order 11246, all federal contractors are required to complete an *affirmative action plan*. **Affirmative action** can be defined as "a set of procedures designed to eliminate unlawful discrimination among applicants, remedy the results of such prior discrimination, and prevent such discrimination in the future" (Legal Information Institute 2022). Thus, the goal of an affirmative action plan is to demonstrate the positive steps that an organization will take to recruit and advance qualified members of racial and ethnic minorities, women, persons with disabilities, and covered veterans. The plan may include such activities and

EXHIBIT 3.3
Equal Employment Opportunity Commission Charge Statistics, 2021

Basis of Charge	Number of Charges	Percent of All Charges Filed
Total charges	61,331	*
Retaliation	34,332	56.0%
Disability	22,843	37.2%
Race	20,908	34.1%
Sex	18,762	30.6%
Age	12,965	21.1%
National origin	6,213	10.1%
Color	3,516	5.7%
Religion	2,111	3.4%
Equal Pay Act	885	1.4%
Genetic information	440	0.7%

*Note: Percentages add up to more than 100 percent because some charges allege multiple bases.
Source: EEOC (2022b).

Exhibit 3.4
EEOC Charge Statistics, 2007–2021

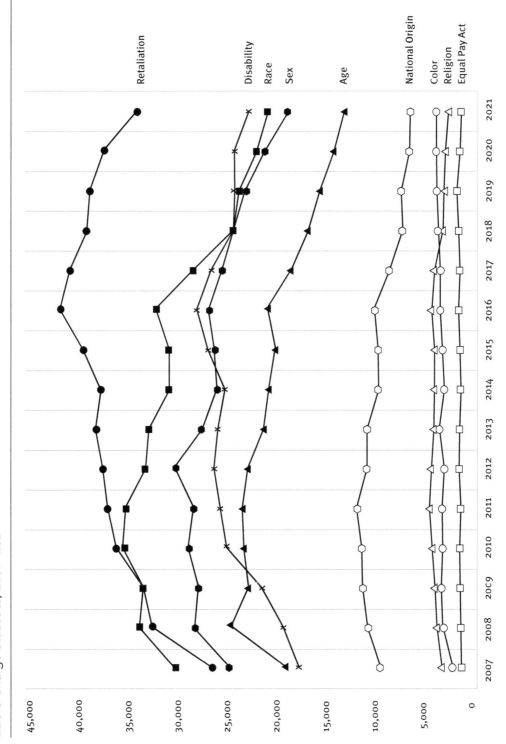

Source: EEOC (2022b).

DEBATE POINT

Is affirmative action still necessary? *Affirmative action* refers to a set of procedures that ensure that traditionally underrepresented groups are given an equal chance in the workplace. Affirmative action is not a quota system, but it does require that organizations document their strategies for ensuring equal employment opportunity. Affirmative action principles have been applied to hiring, compensation, training, and other areas of employment. Traditionally used to address racial disparities in the workplace, affirmative action has been extended to include women and other marginalized groups. Some people claim that affirmative action has outlived its purpose and that discrimination is not as pervasive as it once was, and that the documentation required for affirmative action is cumbersome, time-consuming, and unnecessary. Others claim that while racial and gender discrimination are decreasing, the group that is currently most neglected includes those who are economically disadvantaged. Thus, some people call for class-based affirmative action. Has discrimination been reduced enough to abandon affirmative action? What evidence would you need to help make a decision about this issue?

initiatives as training programs and outreach efforts. In addition, the law requires these plans to be reviewed and updated on an annual basis.

Affirmative action is frequently misunderstood as a quota-driven system that requires companies to hire and promote individuals based on demographic characteristics rather than on job qualifications. However, affirmative action simply asks employers to analyze their workforce and relevant labor markets and then determine the steps needed to improve the representation of their workforce.

Employees may sue an employer or a potential employer for violations of employment law. Various types of discrimination are recognized by law. **Disparate impact** discrimination refers to an employment practice that appears to be unbiased but has a discriminatory effect on a group protected by legislation. The landmark case in this area is *Griggs v. Duke Power Company* in 1971 (401 US 424), in which an employee's request for a promotion to a supervisory position was denied because he was not a high school graduate. Willie Griggs, an African American man, claimed that this job standard was discriminatory because it did not relate to job success and because the standard had an adverse impact on a **protected class**. Duke Power could not demonstrate that an employee needed a high school diploma to perform effectively as a supervisor. In this case, the employment practice had the effect

disparate impact
The result of a practice that may appear to be neutral but has a discriminatory effect.

protected class
A group of individuals protected under a particular law.

of excluding a protected class and was thus found illegal. The US Supreme Court's decision in favor of Griggs established two important principles:

1. Employer discrimination need not be overt or intentional to be present and illegal.

2. Employment selection practices must be job related, and employers have the burden of demonstrating that employment requirements are job related or constitute a business necessity.

More common than disparate impact is **disparate treatment**, when individuals in similar employment situations are treated differently because of race, color, religion, gender, national origin, age, or disability. The most obvious case of disparate treatment is when an employer decides whom to hire on the basis of race, religion, gender, or other illegal criteria. Disparate treatment may also be more subtle, such as asking female job applicants to demonstrate a particular skill when male applicants are not asked to do the same. The defining case in this area is *McDonnell Douglas Corp. v. Green* in 1973 (411 US 792), in which a qualified African American man applied and was rejected for a job and the company continued to advertise for the position. This case established the following four-part guideline for determining disparate treatment:

disparate treatment When employees are treated differently because of race, color, religion, gender, national origin, age, disability, or other protected class category.

1. The person is a member of a protected class.

2. The person applied for a job and is qualified.

3. The person was rejected for the job.

4. The position remained open to applicants with equal or fewer qualifications.

A number of defenses can be made against charges of disparate treatment. One defense is that whereas a candidate may have had the qualifications for a particular job, the employer hired someone else with superior qualifications. Another defense is that a characteristic such as gender may be a **bona fide occupational qualification (BFOQ)**. There are situations where being of a certain age, gender, race, or other characteristic is key to job success (see the accompanying Critical Concept sidebar "Bona Fide Occupational Qualifications").

Employers may also claim that a particular characteristic is a business necessity. For example, in some circumstances, a religious organization may legally hire or refuse to hire someone on the basis of the job applicant's religious affiliation. However, a great debate brews over what constitutes a BFOQ or business necessity, and court rulings are inconsistent in this area.

bona fide occupational qualification (BFOQ) A specific employment qualification that requires some kind of discrimination because the job requires someone of a particular age, gender, race, or other characteristic.

> ### ⚠ CRITICAL CONCEPT
> Bona Fide Occupational Qualifications
>
> Civil rights laws prohibit discrimination on the basis of age, gender, religion, and other factors. However, if one of these characteristics is a *bona fide occupational qualification* (BFOQ), it is legal to discriminate in favor of someone who meets these characteristics, or against someone who does not possess these characteristics. According to the ADEA, a BFOQ based on age must meet the following criteria:
>
> - The age limit is reasonably necessary to the essence of the business.
> - All or substantially all individuals excluded from the job because of age are not able to perform it safely or efficiently.
> - Some of the individuals excluded possess a disqualifying trait or susceptibility that cannot be explained except by the use of an age-based qualification.
> - There is a legal age requirement to perform a particular aspect of that type of work. (For example, it is illegal for someone underage to serve alcohol in a restaurant.)
>
> *Source*: Age Discrimination in Employment Act of 1967 (ADEA), 29 USC §§ 621–634 (2000).

As a result of the complexity of EEO laws, organizations may find it difficult to know how to comply with the law. The federal government responded by issuing Uniform Guidelines on Employee Selection Procedures, guidelines that summarize and synthesize the employment-related implications of these laws (EEOC 1978). The document provides basic guidance on compliance in virtually every human resources function and is a valuable tool for managers.

negligent hiring
A situation in which an employer could have discovered a new employee's problematic conduct through due diligence but failed to do so, making the employer liable for damages caused by the employee.

EMPLOYEE SCREENING AND SELECTION PROCEDURES

Effective screening of potential employees is a necessary step in minimizing employer liability and in preventing the need for employee discipline in the future. The amount of screening to be performed must be balanced against the level of risk associated with the open position. Employers are expected to more thoroughly screen candidates for positions that carry greater risk, such as those that give the employee access to master keys, narcotics, finances, children, the elderly, or individuals with disabilities.

To avoid claims of **negligent hiring**, employers have an obligation to prescreen employees for, at a minimum, references, education, and professional license status. However,

CURRENT ISSUE
Using Social Media in the Hiring Process

Once the province of the tech savvy, social media are now in the mainstream of American culture. Many employers now use social media as one of the tools in their recruitment and selection processes. As this practice has increased, laws and court decisions have begun to limit how social media can be used. For example, as reported in August 2022 by the National Conference of State Legislatures (NCSL), 26 states and Guam now prohibit employers from requiring applicants to provide their social media passwords, and 15 states and the District of Columbia apply this restriction to educational institutions (NCSL 2022a). As social media has become ever more prevalent, lawmakers likely will move to further restrict their use, especially in ways that can be seen as discriminatory.

organizations often find themselves on shaky legal ground when they interview applicants for positions. There is a common misconception that a variety of questions are "illegal." This is incorrect. The only illegal question is one that requires an applicant to reveal a disability.

It is more useful to talk about "high-risk" and "low-risk" interview or selection questions. "High-risk" questions are those that have no relevance to job duties or responsibilities. Although asking such questions is not illegal, if a "high-risk" question were to be asked of someone who is not successful in being hired or promoted, there is a strong possibility that the employer will have to explain why such a question was not indicative of an intent to discriminate. "Low-risk" questions are those that are directly relevant to job duties and responsibilities, or an applicant's experience that is relevant to the job's duties and responsibilities. Employers need to be careful in making the job-related connection between duties and responsibilities and interview questions.

Because of the potential for making employee selection decisions based on non-job-related criteria such as race or gender, employers need to be careful about what interview questions they use. The organization may be legally liable if it is found that a hiring decision was made on the basis of discriminatory factors. If the interviewer is unsure of the appropriateness of an interview question, then it should not be asked. Furthermore, the same questions should be asked of all persons being interviewed for a particular job. For example, a question regarding plans for becoming pregnant or for retirement is not appropriate for two reasons: (1) It applies only to particular candidates—in this case, female or older candidates, and (2) it delves too deeply into personal issues that likely have no bearing on the candidate's ability to perform the job.

Outside formal interviews, employers of the twenty-first century may attempt to gather information about applicants through social media such as Facebook, Twitter, and other outlets. However, employers must proceed with caution in how they use social media in their hiring processes to avoid legal challenges (see the related Current Issue sidebar "Using Social Media in the Hiring Process").

The Uniform Guidelines on Employee Selection Procedures clearly states that all parts of the hiring process must be job related and positively associated with job success. An organization's best defense against lawsuits is creating and following nondiscriminatory policies. Disseminating organizational policies serves multiple purposes, including the following:

◆   It is an initial step in educating employees in what behavior is expected and accepted by the organization. Specifying unacceptable behavior and its consequences at the onset of employment is likely to decrease future inappropriate conduct.

◆   Standard policies promote consistent employee conduct that lends itself to fair and nondiscriminatory employee treatment.

◆   Publicizing desired employee conduct is a preemptive step against litigation.

SEXUAL HARASSMENT

Increased awareness about sexual harassment came about in the second half of the twentieth century as a result of feminism and the women's movement, greater societal attention to diversity and equal accommodation in the workplace, and the growth in the number of women in the workplace. Although sexual harassment in the workplace had been occurring for a long time, it was not acknowledged as an important workplace concern until then. Not long after the passage of Title VII of the Civil Rights Act in 1964, cases alleging sexual harassment began to be filed. Courts at that time were uniformly concerned about the practice, but none found that sexual harassment was a form of sex discrimination. It took a 1986 ruling of the US Supreme Court, *Meritor Savings Bank v. Vinson*, to finally determine that Title VII prohibited sexual harassment. Exhibit 3.5 presents key court decisions from the 1980s and 1990s on sexual harassment in the workplace.

Title VII continues to be the major statute governing sexual harassment. To clarify ambiguities about what constitutes sexual harassment, the EEOC established a definition to help courts, employers, and employees understand the scope of this issue (see the accompanying Critical Concept sidebar for the EEOC definition).

Case	Key Finding and Precedent
Bundy v. Jackson, 641 F.2d 934, 24 FEP 1155, D.C. Cir. (1981)	The case extended the idea of discrimination to sexual harassment.
Meritor Savings Bank v. Vinson, Supreme Court of the United States, 40 FEP 1822 (1986)	The US Supreme Court ruled that sexual harassment can constitute unlawful sex discrimination under Title VII if the harassment is so severe as to alter the conditions of the victim's employment and create an abusive working environment.
Ellison v. Brady, United States Court of Appeals, Ninth Circuit, 924 F.2d 872 (1991)	The Supreme Court ruled that sexual harassment must be viewed from the perspective of a "reasonable woman" and not people in general; employers must take positive action to eliminate sexual harassment from the workplace.
Harris v. Forklift Systems, Inc., 114 S. Ct. 367 (1993)	An abusive work environment can be demonstrated even when the victim does not suffer serious psychological harm; the case adopted the idea that harassment occurs if a "reasonable person" would find that the behavior leads to a hostile or abusive working environment.
Burlington Industries v. Ellerth, 524 US 742 (1998)	Employers are vicariously liable for supervisors who create hostile working conditions for subordinates even if threats are not carried out and the harassed employee suffers no adverse, tangible effects. Employers may defend themselves by demonstrating that they acted quickly to prevent and correct harassment and that the harassed employee failed to utilize the company's protection.
Faragher v. Boca Raton, 524 US 775 (1998)	Employers are vicariously liable under Title VII of the Civil Rights Act of 1964 for discrimination caused by a supervisor.
Lockard v. Pizza Hut, Inc., 162 F.3d 1062 (10th Cir. 1998)	Employers can be liable when a nonemployee harasses one of their employees.
Oncale v. Sundowner Offshore Services, Inc., 523 US 75 (1998)	Same-sex harassment is actionable under Title VII.

EXHIBIT 3.5
Key Court Decisions on Sexual Harassment in the Workplace

> ⚠ **CRITICAL CONCEPT**
> EEOC Definition of *Sexual Harassment* (EEOC 2022c)

It is unlawful to harass a person (an applicant or employee) because of that person's sex. Harassment can include "sexual harassment" or unwelcome sexual advances, requests for sexual favors, and other verbal or physical harassment of a sexual nature.

Harassment does not have to be of a sexual nature, however, and can include offensive remarks about a person's sex. For example, it is illegal to harass a woman by making offensive comments about women in general.

Both the victim and the harasser can be either a woman or a man, and the victim and harasser can be the same sex.

Although the law doesn't prohibit simple teasing, offhand comments, or isolated incidents that are not very serious, harassment is illegal when it is so frequent or severe that it creates a hostile or offensive work environment or when it results in an adverse employment decision (such as the victim being fired or demoted).

The harasser can be the victim's supervisor, a supervisor in another area, a coworker, or someone who is not an employee of the employer, such as a client or customer.

quid pro quo sexual harassment
Sexual harassment that occurs when a benefit for an employee in the workplace is granted on condition of submission to sexual advances.

Two types of sexual harassment are recognized by the courts: (1) quid pro quo and (2) hostile environment. **Quid pro quo sexual harassment** occurs when a job-related benefit is made contingent on an employee's submission to sexual advances. A typical case is that of an employee at the University of Massachusetts Medical Center who was awarded $1 million in 1994 after she testified that her supervisor had forced her to engage in sex once or twice a week over a 20-month period as a condition of keeping her job (Bloomberg BNA 1994). Of greater magnitude was a class-action lawsuit, *EEOC v. Lutheran Medical Center*, on behalf of a group of female employees at Lutheran Medical Center in Brooklyn, New York. In this case, a physician engaged in inappropriate practices with female employees during employment-related exams. The EEOC ordered the hospital to pay $5.425 million and significant remedial relief on behalf of these employees. Like other sexual harassment cases, "the EEOC alleged that Lutheran knew or should have known of the sexual harassment and failed to take adequate measures to prevent such harassment" (EEOC 2003). In another case, the top official of Caritas Christi Health Care Systems—the second largest healthcare provider in New England—was forced to resign after the board voted to fire him as a result of sexual harassment accusations by at least six women (Zezima 2006).

The second type of sexual harassment is more subtle and more difficult to prove. **Hostile environment sexual harassment** occurs when the behavior of anyone in the work setting is perceived by another person as offensive and undesirable. Whereas the law is not explicit about what constitutes this type of harassment, some examples may include posting sexually explicit pictures, making sexually laden jokes, and using sexually explicit language. Courts assess the following factors in determining the legitimacy of sexual harassment claims:

hostile environment sexual harassment
Sexual harassment that interferes with a victim's work performance or creates an intimidating, hostile, or offensive working environment that affects the victim's psychological well-being.

1. The plaintiff cannot have invited the sexual advances; sexual advances must be unwelcome. Courts typically look for repetition. A plaintiff is more likely to be successful if it can be demonstrated that the harassment was not a onetime event but was persistent.

2. The harassment needs to have been severe enough to have altered the terms, conditions, and privileges of employment. Significant consequences for the employee must have occurred. The Supreme Court established several questions to help courts decide in hostile environment sexual harassment cases:

    ◆ How frequent is the discriminatory conduct?

    ◆ How severe is the discriminatory conduct?

    ◆ Is the conduct physically threatening or humiliating?

    ◆ Does the conduct interfere with the employee's work performance?

3. In determining employer liability, two questions are typically considered:

    i.   Did the employer know about the harassment, or should it have known?

    ii. Did the employer take steps to stop the behavior?

In most instances, if the employer knew about the harassment and the behavior did not stop, courts will decide that the employer did not act appropriately to curtail the behavior.

Sexual harassment charges continue to be filed with the EEOC. In 2021, the EEOC received 10,035 sexual harassment complaints and recovered $61.6 million for the people who brought the suits and others who were affected; this dollar amount does not include money from civil suits related to sexual harassment (EEOC 2022a). Although there is variation in estimates of the prevalence of sexual harassment, by any measure, it is alarmingly high. The magnitude of this problem in the workplace has been well documented, as in the following findings:

◆ A survey of 2,235 full-time and part-time female employees carried out by *Cosmopolitan* magazine found that one in three women has been sexually harassed at work. Of those who experienced harassment, 29 percent reported the issue, while 71 percent did not (Ahn and Ruiz 2015). Overall, about 75 percent of people who experience harassment do not report it, and more than half of sexual harassment claims result in no charge (Chalabi 2016).

◆ Nearly two-thirds of college students experience sexual harassment at some point during college; nearly one-third of first-year students have been the subject of harassment (Hill and Silva 2005). A study carried out by the Association of American Universities found that about 20 percent of female undergraduates are victims of sexual assault or sexual misconduct (Anderson, Svrluga, and Clement 2015).

◆ Sexual harassment is as prevalent in healthcare as in other industries, and sometimes more so. An early study indicated that nearly 75 percent of women in healthcare have been sexually harassed (Walsh and Borowski 1995). A systematic review of studies of sexual harassment against female nurses found that on average, 43.15 percent of female nurses had been victims of harassment. Harassment took multiple forms, including harassment by patients (46.59 percent), physicians (41.10 percent), patients' family (27.74 percent), and nurses (20.00 percent), as well as a variety of other coworker perpetrators (17.80 percent) (Kahsay et al. 2020).

◆ Sexual harassment in healthcare is coming to light globally; see, for example, data on sexual harassment among nurses in Turkey and Japan (Celik and Celik 2007; Hibino, Ogino, and Inagaki 2006).

◆ A survey of full-time faculty at 24 US medical schools found that 52 percent of female and 5 percent of male faculty reported being sexually harassed by a superior or colleague (Committee on Pediatric Workforce 2006).

Although sexual harassment is unfortunately common in virtually all organizations, it is particularly problematic in healthcare organizations, for two key reasons. First, sexual harassment almost always includes an important element of power and control. From a gender perspective, hospitals are unique: The majority of hospital employees are women, but those in positions of authority—physicians and administrators—are often men. Second, the nature of healthcare work entails a certain amount of intimacy among care providers. Strong, collegial relationships often form in the high-stress environment of healthcare, engendering sexual jokes and off-color humor. Such discussion can devolve into abusive, condescending, or suggestive language.

The first line of defense against sexual harassment is putting in place a sexual harassment policy. Typically, this policy includes the following elements:

◆ A definition of *sexual harassment* and a strong statement that it will not be tolerated

◆ Extensive training of all employees on the policy, with particular focus on employees who have management and supervisory authority

◆ Instructions on how to report complaints, including procedures for bypassing a supervisor if the supervisor is involved

◆ Assurances of confidentiality, protection against retaliation, and a guarantee of prompt investigation

◆ A statement that disciplinary action will be taken against harassers up to and including termination of employment

Supervisors also need to know the investigative procedures to be used when charges occur. If a complaint arises, management needs to respond immediately; launch an investigation; and, if the investigation proves the allegations true, discipline the offender according to policy.

RETALIATORY DISCHARGE

It is illegal for an employer to attempt to restrict an employee's right to file a charge of discrimination. An employer who takes any action to deter an employee from asserting a discrimination claim could be subject to a charge of **retaliatory discharge**. An important case in this regard was that of *Burlington Northern & Santa Fe Railway Co. v. White* (126 S. Ct. 2405 [2006]). In this case, Sheila White was hired to work as a forklift driver in an all-male rail yard. After several months of employment, she lodged a claim of sexual harassment and discrimination with management at Burlington Northern. In response, the company transferred White to the more difficult job of general track laborer. White filed a complaint with the EEOC, alleging that the change in her position was unlawful gender discrimination and retaliation. Burlington Northern suspended White for 37 days without pay. White filed suit under Title VII, alleging retaliation because of her transfer and later suspension. The Supreme Court unanimously determined that White's reassignment and suspension constituted retaliatory discharge discrimination.

retaliatory discharge
When an employer takes action to attempt to prevent an employee from filing a claim of discrimination against the employer, or when an employer punishes an employee for participating in a legal activity.

Employee Surveillance

Employers have an interest in monitoring employees' attendance and being on the lookout for theft because they may be held accountable for the misconduct of their employees. Privacy protections for employees are primarily found in the Fourth Amendment to the US Constitution, which limits these protections to public employees. Some courts have found that an employee of a private company has limited privacy rights against the search of a desk, office, or work area, while in other cases courts have found that private employees have some privacy rights. In *O'Connor v. Ortega* (1987), the desk and file cabinet of a state-employed physician (a public employee) were searched. Most of the Supreme Court justices agreed that the physician had a reasonable expectation of privacy in his office and that there was a reasonable expectation of privacy in the physician's desk and file cabinet. The key question here is whether the employee had a reasonable expectation of privacy. This expectation of privacy can be in a physical location (a desk or a locker) or in an electronic location (e-mail, internet usage).

Employers use electronic monitoring in the workplace to investigate various problems, including loss of productivity from such distractions as computer use for personal purposes. Use of company computer systems to send discriminatory or harassing materials can also lead to litigation if the employer fails to take proper precautionary or corrective measures. Employers may choose to undertake an employee surveillance program for a number of reasons, including the following:

◆ Ensuring and promoting safety

◆ Protecting trade secrets

◆ Enhancing productivity

◆ Preventing theft or other unlawful activity

◆ Assessing the quality and regularity of customer service

◆ Searching for drug use

◆ Limiting employer liability by detecting and recording discriminatory or illegal behavior

Monitoring techniques can be as simple and obvious as a desk search or can involve sophisticated hidden cameras and microphones. Some employers install such devices when an employee is suspected of a particular inappropriate act or when inventory has gone missing.

Surveillance of employees is widespread, and data strongly suggest that surveillance has increased as a result of many employees working from home. A study carried out by ExpressVPN (2021) concluded that

◆ While 83 percent of employers believe that there are ethical problems with employee monitoring, 78 percent of employers use monitoring software;

◆ About 33 percent of employees don't believe their online activities are being monitored by their employer, with 15 percent not believing that this was even possible;

◆ Fifty-six percent of employees feel stress and anxiety about their employer monitoring their communications;

◆ Forty-one percent constantly wonder whether they are being watched, and about 33 percent take fewer breaks because of this concern;

◆ Forty-eight percent of employees would be willing to reduce their pay if it meant not being subjected to surveillance, with 25 percent of employees willing to take a 25 percent pay cut to avoid being monitored;

◆ Thirty-seven percent of employers indicate that they have used stored recordings for terminating employees;

◆ Forty-one percent of employees admit that their recorded work calls could have gotten them fired; and

◆ Employers use stored e-mail, calls, messages, or videos to inform their performance reviews (73 percent) and to monitor the potential formation of workers' unions (46 percent).

Just where the employer's security concerns impede the employee's civil liberties and right to privacy is unclear. Certainly, the use of various monitoring techniques suggests that this line has already been crossed. Some companies are even experimenting with implanting radio frequency identification (RFID) chips in employees who are in highly sensitive positions as a way to monitor their movement and to positively identify them when necessary. It is uncertain how widespread the use of this and other technologies will be in coming years. However, given the modern world's propensity to adopt new technologies, along with its ongoing concerns about security and safety, the use of existing and emerging devices is constrained only by those who want to protect the civil liberties of society.

The Employee Polygraph Protection Act of 1988 (EPPA) was an early legislative attempt to provide direction in this area and to monitor potential for abuse. The EPPA prohibits an employer from the following practices:

◆ Requiring employees to take a lie detector test

◆ Using the results of a lie detector test

◆ Taking action against an employee for refusing to take a lie detector test or for the results of such a test

◆ Retaliating against the employee for complaining about any of these practices

The EPPA generally prohibits employers from using lie detector tests either for preemployment screening or during the course of employment. A number of people are exempt from this act, however, and may receive polygraphs, including employees suspected of involvement in an incident resulting in economic loss to the employer and prospective employees engaged in dispensing controlled substances. There are certain situations where hospitals may be exempt from the EPPA, as well as other organizations concerned with public health, defense, and national security.

DRUG TESTING

Healthcare employees have access to many controlled substances, a fact that may account for significant problems with substance abuse among healthcare employees. Some healthcare organizations test job candidates and employees for the presence of certain drugs in their urine or blood. The use of marijuana, however, has become a more complicated issue for employers and employees in the United States because of its legalization in many states. As of February 3, 2022, 37 states, 3 territories, and the District of Columbia permit marijuana for medicinal purposes. In addition, as of November 9, 2022, 21 states, 2 territories, and the District of Columbia now permit cannabis for recreational use (NCSL 2022b). Consider the challenge for a human resources manager in a healthcare system with facilities in multiple states, some of which permit recreational use of marijuana while others continue to outlaw possession of marijuana for any reason. Developing guidelines for such situations requires careful consideration.

As reported by the American Civil Liberties Union (ACLU 2022), court decisions interpreting the Fourth Amendment in regard to public employers have established a drug test as a "search." Public employers must either have a belief that an employee has used or is currently under the influence of drugs ("reasonable suspicion") or have declared an employee to be "safety sensitive" to be legally allowed to conduct a drug test. A number of states have established laws that regulate the circumstances under which an employer may test for drugs. Testing must be done confidentially, and employers must determine their next steps if the employee's results reveal illegal drug use

On the other hand, courts have given all employers a large amount of discretion in drug testing for job applicants. The basis for this latitude has been the courts' consistent determination that applicants have a lower expectation of privacy than employees do. For a detailed discussion of the legal issues involved in drug testing, see the legislative briefing kit provided by the ACLU (2022).

HIPAA COMPLIANCE

To protect the health and medical information of an individual, the US Department of Health and Human Services developed regulations under the **Health Insurance Portability and Accountability Act (HIPAA)**. The HIPAA Privacy Rule regulates the use of protected health information that is electronically transmitted or maintained by health plans, healthcare clearinghouses, and healthcare providers. The goal of the Privacy Rule is to protect the use and disclosure of protected health information.

EMPLOYMENT-AT-WILL AND PUBLIC POLICY EXCEPTIONS

The legal environment affects virtually all aspects of HRM; however, this was not always the case. Traditionally, the employee–employer relationship was guided by the **employment-at-will** principle, which assumes that both employee and employer have the right to sever the work relationship at any time without notice, for no reason or any reason, even a bad or immoral reason. For example, in the past, it was legal for an employee to be *terminated* (fired) for trying to organize a union, for being a member of a particular racial or ethnic group, or for refusing to participate in illegal activities. However, since the mid-twentieth century, the employment-at-will principle has been eroded dramatically by a variety of laws and regulations.

In the United States (except for the State of Montana, which has enacted a law to require cause for all terminations, in both public and private employment), employment is *at-will*. This means that either party to the employment relationship may terminate the relationship for any reason, without cause, and without notice.

The law has eroded employment-at-will: An exception to employment-at-will is a rule that an employer cannot terminate an employee for an illegal reason such as race, age, or a violation of public policy. For instance, an employee can claim wrongful discharge when terminated solely for reporting the employer's violation of federal occupational safety standards, refusing to commit perjury, or refusing to do any other illegal activity requested by the employer.

WHISTLE-BLOWING

Many wrongful discharge cases arise from an employer asking an employee to violate federal or state law. Courts have allowed employees to pursue such claims because there is a public interest in protecting individuals who speak up about an employer's illegal acts. Such employers are viewed as harmful to the public in general (for example, unsafe practices at nuclear reactors that can pose dangers to communities) or to employees within the company (such as locked fire and emergency exits that can result in workers' injury or death).

Health Insurance Portability and Accountability Act (HIPAA)
The 1996 federal law that protects health insurance coverage when workers lose their jobs, simplifies electronic healthcare records, and requires increased privacy of healthcare records.

employment-at-will
A principle that assumes that both employee and employer have the right to end the employment relationship at any time, for any reason.

whistle-blower
An employee who
discloses or exposes
to the government an
illegal activity in the
workplace.

A **whistle-blower** is an employee who discloses or otherwise exposes to law enforcement or a government agency any illegal activity in the workplace. Employees who "blow the whistle" on their employers are protected by the law. It is illegal for an employer to retaliate against or mistreat an employee for whistle-blowing. False claims violations are a major form of corruption that whistle-blowers have brought to the attention of authorities. Recoveries since the False Claims Act was strengthened in 1986 have totaled more than $64 billion. In 2020, the US government recovered about $2.2 billion from healthcare fraud, as reported by the US Department of Justice (DOJ 2021). Among the largest whistle-blower settlements in healthcare were the $900 million paid by Tenet Healthcare and the $1.7 billion that HCA paid between 2000 and 2003 (M. Walsh 2007).

Whistle-blowers often face an ethical and a moral dilemma when deciding whether to disclose the unpleasant information. They must consider the consequences of being deemed disloyal to their company and whether the disclosure benefits the public. An employee's decision to blow the whistle is clearly difficult, as it presents a potential career detriment, and the personal stakes are high. The laws in this area seek to alleviate such concerns.

PERSONNEL POLICIES

If the personnel policies an employer publishes in handbooks or other corporate documents imply promises of continued employment, they may restrict the employer's ability to discharge employees. Disciplinary documents prepared by inexperienced personnel may contain language that implies a promise of continued employment as well. Consider an employee who has been absent from work for several consecutive days without excuse. The employee's manager prepares a disciplinary document stating that the employee must maintain a better attendance record over the subsequent 12-month period to keep the job. This document may be interpreted as meaning that the employee can stay on the job for 12 months providing that a good attendance record is maintained. Such a provision would hamper the employer's ability to lay off or dismiss the employee for another reason. One way to avoid such an implied promise is for a manager to use language such as "Nothing contained herein alters the at-will nature of your employment or constitutes a promise of future employment." Employee handbooks and personnel policies must contain similar language in an acknowledgment page signed by the employee and placed in the employee's personnel file.

EMPLOYMENT AGREEMENTS

Another notable exception to at-will employment is the *employment agreement* with a specified term of employment. Typically, an employment agreement is in writing and is signed by both parties. However, this type of agreement is not recommended for either party.

✳ CASE EXAMPLE

To be enforceable, most courts require that noncompetition clauses protect a legitimate business interest of the employer and are reasonable in terms of geography, time, and scope. For example, a hospital that prohibits a payroll clerk from working for any hospital in the United States for three years following termination probably is not protecting its legitimate business interest, and the court will find the clause unreasonable in terms of geography, time, and scope.

In *Medical Specialists, Inc. v. Sleweon* (652 N.E.2d 517 [Ind. App. June 1995]), the plaintiff was an infectious disease specialist employed by a physician group practice. His employment agreement with the practice included a covenant not to compete within a designated geographic area. After he resigned from his position, the group practice sought to enforce the covenant. The doctor brought suit against his former employer, alleging that the covenant was unenforceable based on public policy grounds. The court ruled against the doctor because there was no evidence of a shortage of such specialists in the restricted area.

Noncompetition and nonsolicitation clauses are used by employers to protect themselves against an employee whose departure may pose a competitive risk, confidentiality breach, or product-imitation issue (see Case Example sidebar). Employers should seek legal counsel in preparing contracts with such clauses. Likewise, an employee presented with an agreement that contains these clauses should consult an attorney before signing the documents.

noncompetition and nonsolicitation clauses
Statements of agreement in a contract that prevent a departed employee from posing a competitive risk or a confidentiality breach.

TERMINATION PROCEDURES

Documentation of the circumstances surrounding a termination of employment is as important as the reason for the termination itself. Barring extreme circumstances in which the well-being of the organization is jeopardized, an employee should receive adequate notice and an explanation of the employer's dissatisfaction with the employee's attempts to remedy the problematic issues. Documentation of all incidents, requests for changes in conduct, employee evaluations, and employee responses to evaluations is the employer's responsibility. Sufficient documentation of the choice to sever an employer–employee relationship is one of the best strategies to demonstrate the fair handling of a termination and to defend against a charge of discrimination.

Although not required by law or otherwise, some employers provide employees an opportunity to correct a performance problem before termination. Under the concept of progressive discipline, an employee is made aware of the problems and the steps required to correct them. The employee usually has a reasonable amount of time to correct the problems and is made aware of the consequences of failure to do so.

Many organizations implement a termination-at-will policy that, in theory, permits the employer or the employee to sever employment relations at any time and for any reason. Although these policies allow greater employer discretion in termination matters, state and federal equal opportunity and discrimination standards supersede any private policies.

If termination is determined to be the proper course of action, the following principles must be considered:

◆ *Analyze risk before termination.* Carefully review the personnel file and examine all facts and circumstances surrounding the termination. Ensure that HR or management has investigated all valid complaints raised by the employee. Also examine the employee's personal situation or status, such as pregnancy, disability, or age.

◆ *Avoid procrastination.* Do not delay an employee's termination after satisfying the risk analysis.

◆ *Consult HR personnel.* Human resources requires advance notification of the manager's intention to terminate an individual's employment to consider the possibility of a severance agreement or the necessity of communicating the termination to other affected employees to avoid service disruption. The HR department can also process final paychecks and answer benefits questions.

◆ *Take action.* The individual who informs the employee of termination should be direct and to the point.

SEVERANCE AGREEMENTS

severance agreement
An agreement that ensures a terminated employee certain benefits from the former employer.

Some organizations use a separation or **severance agreement** at the time of termination. Such agreements often are required as a condition of an employee receiving certain benefits after leaving the job, such as severance payments, health benefits, or outplacement services (assistance finding other work).

The benefits to an employer in obtaining a severance agreement are that it is a release of legal claims and it is a covenant with the terminated employee not to sue. Because of the highly technical requirements of such a release, the employer should consult experienced human resources personnel or legal counsel.

Dismissal for Cause

In the absence of an agreement to the contrary, employers are not required to show cause to dismiss an employee. In many employment agreements, circumstances for for-cause termination are defined. Such circumstances include the following:

◆ Misconduct, including fraud, embezzlement, and commission of a criminal act

◆ Violation of corporate policy or practice

◆ Material failure to perform employment obligations

◆ Loss of license

Grievance Procedures

There are a number of ways to resolve an employee grievance. Those that will be discussed in this section are the EEO complaint process, public employees' right to due process, and alternative dispute resolution.

EEO Complaint Process

Under EEO guidelines, no employee can be discriminated against based on protected class status such as gender or race or as a result of reprisal. An employee or a class of employees who are discriminated against in this manner must first file an administrative complaint with the EEOC. Counseling, formal complaint, and appeal are all part of the EEO process. If these actions do not adequately address the situation, the employee can file suit against the employer. The EEOC website (www.eeoc.gov) is helpful on all aspects of the process.

Public Employees' Right to Due Process

Despite the many exceptions described earlier, at-will employment generally is the case for private-sector employees. The same is not true, however, for public-sector employees. Public employees who are protected by statutory entitlements enjoy certain due process rights and cannot be fired without a good reason or without notice and a hearing. Many other public employees are not so protected and are at-will employees.

When considering the discharge of a public employee, an employer must remember that specific federal and state statutes and the federal and state constitutions protect many public employees. In general, federal and many state government employees must be provided with written notice of the reasons for any proposed disciplinary action, especially termination. These employees also may be entitled to a hearing to defend themselves against termination for cause. Because of these additional rights, management should seek the assistance of HRM professionals and others when dismissing a public employee.

ALTERNATIVE DISPUTE RESOLUTION

alternative dispute resolution (ADR)
A specified conflict resolution process used in place of litigation. Often a clause in an employment contract.

Given the volume of employment litigation, some employers attempt to control the escalating costs and media attention associated with litigation by including mandatory arbitration or **alternative dispute resolution (ADR)** clauses in employment contracts. These types of clauses mandate that any disagreement or claim that arises under the terms of employment will be subject to ADR.

mediation
A nonbinding type of dispute resolution in which a neutral third party called a *mediator* attempts to assist in negotiations between the two primary parties.

There are two types of ADR: mediation and arbitration. **Mediation** is generally a nonbinding process in which opposing parties conduct semiformal settlement negotiations assisted by a neutral third-party mediator. **Arbitration**, much like a trial, is a more formal process in which both sides can present evidence and call witnesses. A neutral third-party arbitrator then makes a decision, which is binding on both parties.

OTHER EMPLOYMENT LAWS

arbitration
A binding type of dispute resolution in which both parties agree beforehand to abide by the decision of a neutral third party called an *arbitrator*.

In addition to the federal and state laws discussed earlier in this chapter, many other laws directly or indirectly affect human resources management. Managers need to be aware of these laws, how they have been interpreted by the courts, and how they affect HRM policies.

The Consumer Credit Protection Act (Title III) of 1968 prohibits an employer from discharging an employee because the employee's earnings are subject to **garnishment** and limits the amount of wages that can be withheld for garnishment in a single week. Wage garnishment occurs when an employer withholds some earnings of an employee to pay a debt resulting from a court order or other procedure. Child support payments are a common example of garnishment.

garnishment
A deduction of money from an employee's wages to pay a debt resulting from a court order or other procedure.

The Occupational Safety and Health Act of 1970 created the Occupational Safety and Health Administration (OSHA) and the National Institute for Occupational Safety and Health (NIOSH). OSHA serves two regulatory functions: setting standards and conducting inspections to ensure that employers are providing safe and healthful workplaces. NIOSH is part of the Centers for Disease Control and Prevention and conducts research and makes recommendations to prevent work-related injury and illness.

The Employee Retirement Income Security Act of 1974 (ERISA) regulates private pension plans and sets minimum standards for most voluntarily established pension and health plans. Chapter 9 on employee benefits provides further discussion of ERISA.

The Consolidated Omnibus Budget Reconciliation Act of 1986 (COBRA) is an amendment to ERISA. COBRA gives employees the right to remain on the employer's group health plan if they are fired or laid off, have their hours cut, or other such events. It also allows family members to stay on the plan if the employee dies or the employee and spouse divorce. See chapter 9 for further discussion of COBRA.

The Immigration Reform and Control Act of 1986 is intended to control unauthorized immigration to the United States and designates penalties for employers who hire people not authorized to work in the country. The act also prohibits discrimination against individuals on the basis of national origin or citizenship.

The Drug-Free Workplace Act of 1988 requires that all organizations that receive federal grants in any amount or federal contracts of $25,000 or more certify that they are providing a drug-free workplace. Drug-free-workplace certification is a precondition of receiving a federal grant, and criteria for compliance include establishing, implementing, and publicizing an explicit drug policy to all employees.

The Worker Adjustment and Retraining Notification Act of 1988 (WARN) requires employers to provide notice to employees 60 days in advance of plant closings and mass layoffs. WARN's intent is to provide workers and their families transition time to adjust to the prospective loss of employment, to seek and obtain other jobs, and, if necessary, to enter skill training or retraining.

The Uniformed Services Employment and Reemployment Rights Act of 1994 (USERRA) requires that, in most situations, employers are obligated to reemploy workers who are returning from military leave.

The Genetic Information Nondiscrimination Act of 2008 prevents an employer from using a person's genetic information in its decision to hire, fire, or promote. Executive Order 13145 offers protection against genetic discrimination to federal employees.

OTHER EMPLOYMENT ISSUES

A number of other employment issues have legal implications. Among such issues, as discussed in this section, are job-related stress, workplace violence, and workplace substance abuse.

JOB-RELATED STRESS

Especially in the healthcare industry, employers cannot allow their employees to perform job duties while suffering from extreme stress. Public health and liability problems arise for employers that do not take proactive measures in this regard. Employers should have confidential employee assistance programs available free of charge to all employees.

Workplace Violence

It is only recently that we have begun to understand the level of workplace violence against healthcare workers. An article in the *New England Journal of Medicine* provides information on this topic that is quite disturbing (Phillips 2016). Between 2011 and 2013, there were approximately 24,000 cases reported annually of workplace assaults, with nearly 75 percent of them taking place in healthcare settings. It has been estimated that healthcare workers are nearly four times as likely to require time off from work as a result of violence as they are from other injuries. In the hospital setting, a study in Minnesota reported in the same *New England Journal of Medicine* article on annual incidence of verbal assaults (39 percent) and physical assaults (13 percent). Among nurses in emergency departments, 100 percent of nurses reported verbal assault, and 82.1 percent reported physical assault in a one-year period. Among nursing home aides, 59 percent reported being verbally assaulted weekly and 16 percent on a daily basis. More than half of the aides reported that they had been physically injured by a patient. Home health care presents its own risks because of its relatively uncontrolled setting. It was reported that 61 percent of home care workers experienced workplace violence.

There is evidence that violence in the workplace has increased in recent years, possibly resulting from the stresses and uncertainty associated with the COVID-19 pandemic. Healthcare workers are particularly vulnerable. The federal government reported that healthcare workers are five times more likely to experience workplace violence than employees in all other industries (Boyle 2022). A survey carried out in early 2022 by National Nurses United (NNU 2022) found that 48 percent of nurses reported a small or significant increase in workplace violence. This represented a 119 percent increase from a year earlier (NNU 2022).

In addition to physical attacks on healthcare workers, there have been troubling reports of other forms of violence, including attacks and threats on social media. A survey of physicians in four Chicago medical schools found that 23 percent reported being attacked on social media (Pendergast et al. 2021). The alarming increase in violence resulted in the American Association of Medical Colleges (AAMC) and the National Academy of Medicine issuing a joint statement on violence against healthcare workers (AAMC 2022).

Workplace Substance Abuse

Substance abuse is the unlawful, unauthorized, or improper use of alcohol, over-the-counter drugs, or other legal or illegal products with mind-altering properties. Changes in the impaired individual's performance, appearance, and behavior are likely to be obvious. These changes have a substantial impact on the employee's ability to carry out work-related duties without endangering the individual's own safety or that of patients and coworkers.

EXHIBIT 3.6
Internet Resources for Employment Law

Resource	Website	Description
US Department of Labor (DOL)	www.dol.gov	Contains labor statistics, DOL online library, current news, listing of programs and services, and contacts
US Equal Employment Opportunity Commission (EEOC)	www.eeoc.gov	Contains information regarding filing of charges, enforcement and litigation, enforcement statistics, small business information, and the Freedom of Information Act
Government Publishing Office (GPO)	www.access.gpo.gov	Allows access to any public document offered by the federal government in print or digital format
National Labor Relations Board (NLRB)	www.nlrb.gov	Contains research, publications, and information on workplace rights
US Small Business Administration (SBA)	www.usa.gov/business	Provides guidance in all general business practices overseen by the government in some capacity
Federal Mediation and Conciliation Service (FMCS)	www.fmcs.gov	Contains information regarding dispute mediation, preventive mediation, alternative dispute resolution, arbitration services, and labor management grant

Healthcare professionals who have substance abuse or dependence problems face a unique and challenging set of circumstances, including the following:

◆ *Fear of self-reporting because of the potential loss of licensure.*

◆ *Positions of accountability and high visibility.* Consequences of addiction problems are both personal and isolating.

◆ *Access to highly addictive prescription medications.* Even when impaired professionals enter a treatment program and are highly motivated to change, their ongoing access to these medications puts them at considerable risk for relapse.

◆ *Tendency to self-treat and self-prescribe.* Health professionals may view their illness as a weakness and failure, preventing them from accepting and complying with medical advice from other professionals.

Managers, with assistance from the HR and legal departments, should discipline or dismiss employees who work while impaired.

STUDYING WORKPLACE LAWS

To accommodate the complexity of the workplace, managers must learn as much as possible about work environment regulations and should not rely on instinct alone when faced with dilemmas in areas such as discrimination, whistle-blowing, or other highly sensitive situations. Because of the intricacy and specificity of workplace regulations, no single resource exists that managers can rely on at all times. Instead, managers must acquire knowledge in specific and general areas of workplace laws. Exhibit 3.6 lists internet resources that can help in the study of employment law.

SUMMARY

Many of the laws and regulations discussed in this chapter are complex, interdependent, and often conflicting. The legal environment surrounding human resources management is under constant federal scrutiny and reform. The legal requirements imposed on an organization often shift according to industry- and state-specific regulations. Blanket policies and regulations are imposed on all employers, but there are regulations that apply specifically to segments of employers.

Mishandling any situation can harm the employer's ability to attract and retain good employees and can lead to costly litigation and negative publicity. In general, wise managers realize the convoluted nature of their job and concede to the necessity of ongoing education. Insightful managers execute thoughtful, deliberate choices. To make prudent, law-abiding decisions, an employer must know the rights of employers and employees. When dealing with employment issues, management should seek advice from experienced human resources personnel, in-house legal counsel, external legal advisers, or a combination of these experts.

For Discussion

1. Should there be a more precise definition of *reasonable accommodation* in the Americans with Disabilities Act? Why or why not?

2. Bona fide occupation qualification (BFOQ) and business necessities may be legitimate and clear. Alternatively, they may be used as a smoke screen for discrimination. Consider a job where a BFOQ may be claimed and where it is totally justifiable. Also, think of how a BFOQ may appear legitimate on the surface, but after careful due consideration, it could be used as a convenient way to discriminate in a hiring decision.

3. Why is sexual harassment so prevalent in the healthcare environment? What can be done to break this historical pattern?

4. Have federal antidiscrimination laws gone too far? Should public policy in the United States seek a return to employment-at-will?

5. What does "public policy exception to employment-at-will" mean?

6. Because employee handbooks may be used to contest a disciplinary procedure, what advice would you give to a workgroup developing an employee handbook?

7. Under what circumstances would you use a progressive discipline process? When would you choose not to use such a procedure?

8. Given the great risks to the public that can result from the work of an impaired healthcare worker, should random drug testing be used in all healthcare organizations? Why or why not?

9. Consider the case of a physician who has been practicing for 15 years and is one of the few well-established physicians in a small community. How would you respond if you learned about this physician's abuse of alcohol or drugs?

Experiential Exercises

Exercise 1

Dr. Larson grew up in a small town in North Carolina. He was intelligent and did well in college and medical school. After a fellowship in thoracic surgery, he was offered positions with good employment terms and conditions in various reputable medical practices throughout the United States.

Feeling a duty to his hometown, Dr. Larson decided to return to his community to practice medicine. He was offered and accepted employment with a multispecialty group practice. The practice paid his expenses to relocate to his hometown and required him to sign an employment agreement that contained a noncompetition provision. Because of his trusting nature, Dr. Larson did not seek an attorney's advice before signing the agreement. After several years of working at this practice, Dr. Larson fell in love with a patient who resided in another small town about 30 miles away. After this patient's recovery, Dr. Larson proposed marriage and agreed to move and work in his fiancée's hometown. He opened a private practice in this town.

After giving notice to his employer, Dr. Larson received a stern letter from the employer's counsel reminding him of his employment agreement. The agreement's noncompetition provision prevented him from working as a thoracic surgeon within a 60-mile radius of his current employer for one year after leaving employment. Given the rural nature of the community, Dr. Larson was the only thoracic surgeon within a 90-mile radius of either practice. He would have to move to the big city to practice medicine, leaving all the residents of his hometown and those of his new wife's town without a practicing thoracic surgeon.

Discuss the following issues of Dr. Larson's case:

- Given that such agreements restrict competition, under what circumstances should a court enforce a covenant not to compete?
- In general, courts will enforce a covenant not to compete if it is (1) in writing, (2) entered into at the time of employment as part of the employment contract, (3) based on reasonable consideration, (4) reasonable with respect to time and territory, and (5) not against public policy. Using this as a guide, how should the court decide in this case?

For additional information, see *Iredell Digestive Disease Clinic, P.A., v. Petrozza,* 92 N.C. App. 21, 373 S.E.2d 449 (1988), *aff'd per curiam,* 324 N.C. 327, 377 S.E.2d 750 (1989).

Exercise 2

Among those who took the US Civil Service Exam, Mariel Andrada received the highest score on the written portion. Feeling confident, she applied for a position with the city of Cary. The position required the preparation of written reports and the handling of complaints from the public, either by telephone or face-to-face. Mariel is a native of the Philippines, and English is her second language. When she was interviewed for the position, the interviewers had difficulty understanding her because of her thick Filipino accent. The city of Cary decided not to hire Mariel because the interviewers believed that her heavy accent would impede her verbal capability to respond to complaints, which was an integral part of the position.

Upon learning that she did not receive the job, Mariel appealed through a number of channels. When these appeals proved unsuccessful, she filed an action under Title VII of the Civil Rights Act. She claimed that she was discriminated against because of her accent and thus by her national origin.

Answer the following questions about this case:

1. Is the city of Cary liable under the disparate treatment theory?

2. What could the city of Cary have done to mitigate the risk of this claim?

3. What defenses are available to the city of Cary?

For helpful information on this situation, see the basis for the hypothetical case—*Fragante v. City and County of Honolulu*, 888 F.2d 591 (9th Cir. 1989).

REFERENCES

Ahn, L., and M. Ruiz. 2015. "He Said What at Work?" *Cosmopolitan*, March.

American Association of Medical Colleges (AAMC). 2022. "Joint Statement on Violence Against Health Care Workers." Press release, September 30. www.aamc.org/news-insights/press-releases/joint-statement-violence-against-health-care-workers.

American Civil Liberties Union (ACLU). 2022. "Legislative Briefing Kit: Drug Testing." Accessed October 22. www.aclu.org/other/legislative-briefing-kit-drug-testing#20.

Americans with Disabilities Act Amendments Act of 2008 (ADAAA). 2008. H.R. 3195, 110th Cong. (2008). Published June 27. www.congress.gov/bill/110th-congress/house-bill/3195/text.

Anderson, N., S. Svrluga, and S. Clement. 2015. "Survey: More than 1 in 5 Female Undergrads at Top Schools Suffer Sexual Attacks." *Washington Post*. Published September 21. www.washingtonpost.com/local/education/survey-more-than-1-in-5-female-undergrads-at-top-schools-suffer-sexual-attacks/2015/09/19/c6c80be2-5e29-11e5-b38e-06883aacba64_story.html.

Barrett, R. 2016. "Muslims File Religious Discrimination Complaint Against Ariens Co. in Brillon." Milwaukee *Journal Sentinel*. Published May 24. https://archive.jsonline.com/business/muslims-file-religious-discrimination-complaint-against-ariens-co-in-brillion-b99731823z1-380725961.html/.

Bloomberg BNA. 1994. "Medical Center Employee Awarded $1 Million in Massachusetts Suit." Employee Relations Weekly, January 31, 11–12.

Boyle, P. 2022. "Threats Against Health Care Workers Are Rising. Here's How Hospitals Are Protecting Their Staffs." American Association of Medical Colleges (AAMC). Published August 18. www.aamc.org/news-insights/threats-against-health-care-workers -are-rising-heres-how-hospitals-are-protecting-their-staffs.

Celik, Y., and S. S. Celik. 2007. "Sexual Harassment Against Nurses in Turkey." *Journal of Nursing Scholarship* 39 (2): 200–206.

Chalabi, M. 2016. "Sexual Harassment at Work: More Than Half of Claims in US Result in No Charge." *Guardian*. Published July 22. www.theguardian.com/money/2016/jul/22 /sexual-harassment-at-work-roger-ailes-fox-news/.

Committee on Pediatric Workforce. 2006. "Prevention of Sexual Harassment in the Workplace and Educational Settings." *Pediatrics* 118 (4): 1752–56. https://doi.org/10.1542 /peds.2006-1816.

ExpressVPN. 2021. "ExpressVPN Survey Reveals the Extent of Surveillance on the Remote Workforce." Updated December 1. www.expressvpn.com/blog/expressvpn-survey -surveillance-on-the-remote-workforce/.

Glynn, S. J., and D. Boesch. 2022. "Connecting the Dots: 'Women's Work' and the Wage Gap." *US Department of Labor Blog*. Published March 14. https://blog.dol.gov/2022 /03/15/connecting-the-dots-womens-work-and-the-wage-gap.

Goodman, N., M. Morris, and K. Boston. 2019. *Financial Inequality: Disability, Race and Poverty in America*. National Disability Institute. Published February. www .nationaldisabilityinstitute.org/wp-content/uploads/2019/02/disability-race-poverty -in-america.pdf.

Hibino, Y., K. Ogino, and M. Inagaki. 2006. "Sexual Harassment of Female Nurses by Patients in Japan." *Journal of Nursing Scholarship* 38 (4): 400–405.

Hill, C., and E. Silva. 2005. *Drawing the Line: Sexual Harassment on Campus*. Washington, DC: American Association of University Women Educational Foundation.

Human Rights Campaign. 2022. "Cities and Counties with Non-Discrimination Ordinances That Include Gender Identity." Accessed September 27. www.hrc.org/resources/cities -and-counties-with-non-discrimination-ordinances-that-include-gender.

Kahsay, W. G., R. Negarandeh, N. Dehghan Nayeri, and M. Hasanpour. 2020. "Sexual Harassment Against Female Nurses: A Systematic Review. *BMC Nursing* 19: article no. 58. https://doi.org/10.1186/s12912-020-00450-w.

Legal Information Institute. 2022. "Affirmative Action." Cornell Law School. Accessed October 24. www.law.cornell.edu/wex/affirmative_action.

National Conference of State Legislatures (NCSL). 2022a. "Privacy of Employee and Student Social Media Accounts." Published August 8. www.ncsl.org/research /telecommunications-and-information-technology/state-laws-prohibiting-access-to -social-media-usernames-and-passwords.aspx.

———. 2022b. "State Medical Cannabis Laws." Published November 29. https://www .ncsl.org/research/health/state-medical-marijuana-laws.aspx.

National Nurses United (NNU). 2022. "National Nurse Survey Reveals Significant Increases in Unsafe Staffing, Workplace Violence, and Moral Distress." Press release, April 14. www.nationalnursesunited.org/press/survey-reveals-increases-in-unsafe-staffing -workplace-violence-moral-distress.

Pendergast, T. R., S. Jain, N. S. Trueger, M. Gottlieb, N. C. Woitowich, and V. M. Arora. 2021. "Prevalence of Personal Attacks and Sexual Harassment of Physicians on Social Media." *JAMA Internal Medicine* 181 (4): 550–52. https://doi.org/10.1001/jamainternmed.2020 .7235.

Phillips, J. P. 2016. "Workplace Violence Against Health Care Workers in the United States." *New England Journal of Medicine* 374 (17): 1661–69.

US Bureau of Labor Statistics (BLS). 2022. "Persons with a Disability: Labor Force Characteristics—2021." News release, February 24. www.bls.gov/news.release/pdf /disabl.pdf.

US Census Bureau. 2022a. "American Community Survey (ACS)." Revised September 29. www.census.gov/programs-surveys/acs.

————. 2022b. "Disability Characteristics." Accessed August 11. https://data.census.gov /cedsci/table?q=disability&tid=ACSST5Y2020.S1810.

US Department of Justice (DOJ). 2021. "Justice Department Recovers over $2.2 Billion from False Claims Act Cases in Fiscal Year 2020." Press release no. 21-55, updated January 14. www.justice.gov/opa/pr/justice-department-recovers-over-22-billion-false -claims-act-cases-fiscal-year-2020.

US Equal Opportunity Commission (EEOC). 2022a. "Charges Alleging Sex-Based Harassment (Charges Filed with EEOC) FY 2010–FY 2021." Accessed August 11. www.eeoc.gov/statistics/charges-alleging-sex-based-harassment-charges-filed-eeoc -fy-2010-fy-2021.

————. 2022b. "Charge Statistics (Charges Filed with EEOC) FY 1997 through FY 2021." Accessed August 11. www.eeoc.gov/statistics/charge-statistics-charges-filed-eeoc-fy -1997-through-fy-2021.

————. 2022c. "Sexual Harassment." Accessed August 11. www.eeoc.gov/sexual -harassment.

————. 2003. "Hospital in New York to Pay over $5 Million to Settle Sexual Harassment by Doctor." News release, April 9. www.eeoc.gov/press/4-9-03.html (content no longer available).

————. 1978. "Uniform Guidelines for Employee Selection Procedures." *Federal Register* 43 (166): 38290–315.

Walsh, A., and S. C. Borowski. 1995. "Gender Differences in Factors Affecting Healthcare Administration Career Development." *Hospital and Health Services Administration* 40 (2): 263–77.

Walsh, M. W. 2007. "Blowing the Whistle, Many Times." *New York Times*. Published November 18. www.nytimes.com/2007/11/18/business/18whistle.html.

Wiessner, D. 2021. "EEOC, JBS Ink $55 Mln Settlement over Firing of Muslim Workers." Reuters. Published May 24. www.reuters.com/business/legal/eeoc-jbs-ink-55-mln -settlement-over-firing-muslim-workers-2021-05-24/.

Zezima, K. 2006. "Archdiocese Hospital Chief Quits After Harassment Accusations. *New York Times*, May 26, A16.

CHAPTER 4

JOB ANALYSIS AND JOB DESIGN

Sean A. Newman and Paige N. Ocker

LEARNING OBJECTIVES

After completing this chapter, you should be able to

➤ distinguish among job analyses, job descriptions, and job specifications;

➤ describe the methods by which job analyses are typically accomplished;

➤ discuss the relationship of job requirements (as developed through job analyses, job descriptions, and job specifications) to other human resources management functions;

➤ enumerate the steps involved in a typical job analysis;

➤ address the relationship between job analyses and strategic human resources management; and

➤ explain the changing nature of jobs and how jobs are being redesigned to enhance productivity.

VIGNETTE

Sunset Assisted Living is an assisted living facility in a suburb of Orlando, Florida. Since its founding in 2022, it has added 184 residents and 326 employees. However, it has not yet developed a policy manual or job descriptions. Now, some employees are arguing among themselves about who has responsibility for certain resident care functions. The new facility administrator is contemplating how best to structure her resident care positions and develop job descriptions for these positions. She has expressed frustration that the previous administrator did not address these issues before leaving for another position.

While reading this chapter, think about how the facility administrator might go about this process. What essential steps should she take and in what sequence? Whom else may she involve? How could some of these decisions affect the human resources department, the employee population, and the facility as a whole?

INTRODUCTION

In this chapter, we define *job analysis*, *job description*, and *job specification*; explore job analyses processes; and show how the results of job analysis—such as job descriptions and job specifications—relate to other human resources management functions. In addition, we emphasize that these job processes provide the organization with a foundation for making objective and legally defensible decisions in managing human resources (HR).

We also discuss how healthcare jobs have been redesigned to contribute to organizational objectives while satisfying the needs of the employees, and we review several innovative job design and work scheduling techniques to enhance job satisfaction and organizational performance.

JOBS VERSUS POSITIONS

A **job** is a group of activities and duties that entail natural units of work that are similar and related. Jobs should be clear and distinct to minimize misunderstandings and conflict and to enable employees to recognize what is expected of them. Some jobs are performed by several employees, each of whom occupies a separate position. A **position** consists of duties and responsibilities that are performed by only one employee.

For example, in a hospital, 40 registered nurses fill 40 positions, but all of them perform only one job—registered nurse. Different jobs that have similar duties and responsibilities may be grouped into a job family for purposes of recruitment, training, compensation, or advancement. For example, the nursing job family may include nursing assistants, registered nurses, the nursing supervisor, and the director of nursing services.

Healthcare organizations continually restructure and reengineer to try to become more cost effective and customer focused. They emphasize smaller scale, less hierarchy, fewer layers, and more decentralized work units. As these changes occur, managers want their employees to operate independently and flexibly to meet customer demands. The objective is to develop jobs and basic work units that are adaptable and can thrive in a world of high-velocity change.

job
A group of activities and duties that entail natural units of work that are similar and related.

position
Duties and responsibilities performed by only one employee.

JOB ANALYSIS

Job analysis is sometimes called the cornerstone of strategic human resources management because the information that analyses collect serves so many HR functions. Job analysis is the process of obtaining information about jobs by determining the job's duties, tasks, and activities.

Job analysis is critical for healthcare because it provides essential information about the level of skill and education needed and job activities that have a direct impact on patient care (Ramadevi et al. 2016). The Society for Human Resource Management (SHRM) has

job analysis
The systematic process of determining the skills, duties, tasks, activities, competencies, and knowledge required to perform particular jobs.

defined job analysis as "the process of studying a job to determine which activities and responsibilities it includes, its relative importance to other jobs, the qualifications necessary for performance of the job and the conditions under which the work is performed" (2022a, 1). Job analysis information is used in HR processes such as recruitment, selection, federal Equal Employment Opportunity (EEO) compliance, training, performance appraisal, benchmarking against other organizations, and compensation analysis. Every HR function requires knowing what the job entails and what skills are necessary to do the job well. Job analysis is a dynamic function that needs to be reviewed on a frequent basis because job duties may dramatically change as a result of economic fluctuations, modifications in care requirements, and global events such as the COVID-19 pandemic (Minton-Eversole 2020).

HR managers use this information in developing job descriptions and specifications, which in turn are used to guide employee performance and to enhance HR functions, such as recruitment and selection, development of performance appraisal criteria, and creation of content for training classes. The ultimate purpose of a job analysis is to improve organizational performance, productivity, and retention. The information used in a job analysis must be objective and verifiable so that it is of value to people who make HR decisions. Job facts are gathered, analyzed, and recorded as the job exists, not as it *should* exist. Job analysis is often performed because of changes in the nature of jobs.

job description
A detailed summary of a job's duties, tasks, responsibilities, reporting relationships, working conditions, and Fair Labor Standards Act (FLSA) exemption status.

A **job description** is a detailed summary of a job's duties, tasks, responsibilities, reporting relationships, working conditions, and Fair Labor Standards Act (FLSA) exemption status (i.e., whether an employee is subject to or exempt from overtime compensation, as discussed in chapter 3). Because no standard format for job descriptions exists, these documents vary in appearance and content from one organization to another. Most job descriptions contain the job title, a job identification section, and a duties section. They may also include a job specification section; sometimes a specification is prepared as a separate document.

A *specific* job description, as opposed to a *generic* job description, is a detailed summary of a job's duties, tasks, responsibilities, reporting relationships, and working conditions emphasizing efficiency, control, and detailed work planning. This type of description fits best with a bureaucratic organizational structure, where well-defined boundaries separate functions and levels of management. Job descriptions can help employees understand their job duties and the results they are expected to achieve and can minimize misunderstandings between employees and supervisors. Furthermore, job descriptions can serve as "advertisements" for open positions and can enhance an employer's "brand" by assisting the organization in attracting key talent.

A **job specification** describes the personal qualifications, traits, skills, background, and physical capabilities an individual must possess to perform the duties and responsibilities contained in a

 **KEY POINT**

Job analysis yields job descriptions and job specifications.

job description satisfactorily and best reflect characteristics of the organization's culture. A **job specification** typically describes the skills required to perform the job and the physical demands the job places on the employee performing it. Relevant skills include education and experience, specialized knowledge and training, licenses, and personal abilities and traits such as written and oral communication skills and manual dexterity. Physical demands are the condition of the physical work environment; workplace hazards; and the amount of walking, standing, reaching, and lifting required by the job.

Generic worker characteristics and behavior that may be important predictors of successful performance in a wide range of jobs include thoroughness, attendance, interpersonal skills, and schedule flexibility. In one study of 7,000 executives, leaders exemplified such behaviors as initiative, self-development, integrity, focus on results, and willingness to develop others (*Harvard Business Review* 2013). Job specification should try to capture these generic behaviors as well as those that are job specific. When writing job specifications, leaders should continually ask themselves what constitutes success within the position.

Exhibit 4.1 provides an example of a combined job description / job specification document for the position of staff nurse in a hospital's labor and delivery department.

Exhibit 4.2 details the job analysis process.

job specification
A description of the personal qualifications, traits, and background an individual must possess to perform the duties and responsibilities contained in a job description satisfactorily and best reflect characteristics of the organization's culture.

DATA SOURCES AND DATA COLLECTION METHODS

Conducting job analyses is primarily the responsibility of the HR department or another individual charged with this function. Although job analysts are typically responsible for the job analyses program, they usually enlist affected employees' and supervisors' cooperation. These supervisors and employees are the sources of much of the job information generated through the process.

Job information is collected in several ways, depending on why the organization wants the analysis. The organizational chart is typically reviewed to identify which jobs to include. A job analysis may be needed in the following situations:

◆ Restructuring, downsizing, merger, or rapid growth

◆ When a job's content has undergone undocumented changes, to determine whether compensation must change

◆ To document job change for recruitment, selection, training, and performance appraisal purposes

Several job analysis approaches may be used to gather data, each with specific advantages and disadvantages. Managers should consider a number of methods to collect information; it is unlikely that any one method will provide all the necessary data. Among the most popular methods of data collection are observing tasks and behaviors of jobholders,

EXHIBIT 4.1
Sample Combined
Job Description /
Job Specification
Document

JOB TITLE	Staff Nurse
DEPARTMENT	Nursing—Labor and Delivery
FLSA STATUS	Nonexempt

JOB SUMMARY

Assesses, prescribes, delegates, coordinates, and evaluates the nursing care provided. Ensures provision of quality care for selected groups of patients through utilization of nursing process, established standards of care, and policies and procedures. Administers minor medical treatments or medications (i.e., taking temperature and blood pressure, treating minor cuts and bruises) to correct or treat patient's minor health problems using first aid supplies and direction to determine need following established institutional medical department procedures. Addresses more serious clinical needs under the direction of a physician.

SUPERVISION

A. SUPERVISED BY: Unit Manager, indirectly by Charge Nurse
B. SUPERVISES: No one
C. LEADS/GUIDES: Unit Associates/Ancillary Associates in the delivery of direct patient care

JOB SPECIFICATIONS

A. EDUCATION
— Required: Graduate of an accredited school of professional nursing
— Desired: Continuing nursing education
B. EXPERIENCE
— Required: None
— Desired: Previous clinical experience
C. LICENSES, CERTIFICATIONS, AND/OR REGISTRATIONS: Current RN state license; BCLS and certifications specific to areas of clinical specialty preferred.
D. EQUIPMENT/TOOLS/WORK AIDS: PCA infusors, infusion pumps and other medical equipment, computer experience, including the ability to input and retrieve data from patients' electronic medical records.
E. SPECIALIZED KNOWLEDGE AND SKILLS: Ability to work with female patients of childbearing age and newborn patients in all specialty and subspecialty categories, both urgent and nonurgent in nature.
F. PERSONAL TRAITS, QUALITIES, AND APTITUDES: Must be able to (1) perform a variety of duties, often changing from one task to another of a different nature without loss of efficiency or composure; (2) accept responsibility for the direction, control, and planning of an activity; (3) make evaluations and decisions based on measurable or verifiable criteria; (4) work independently; (5) recognize the rights and responsibilities of patient confidentiality; (6) convey empathy and compassion to those experiencing pain or grief; (7) relate to others in a manner that creates a sense of teamwork and cooperation; and (8) communicate effectively with people from every socioeconomic background.
G. WORKING CONDITIONS: Inside environment, protected from the weather but not necessarily temperature changes. Subject to frequent exposure to infection, contagious disease, combative patients, and potentially hazardous materials and equipment. Variable noise levels.
H. PHYSICAL DEMANDS/TRAITS: Must be able to (1) perceive the nature of sounds by the ear; (2) express or exchange ideas by means of the spoken word; (3) perceive characteristics of objects through the eyes; (4) extend arms and hands in any direction; (5) seize, hold, grasp, turn, or otherwise work with hands; (6) pick, pinch, or otherwise work with the fingers; (7) perceive such attributes of objects or materials as size, shape, temperature, or texture; and (8) stoop, kneel, crouch, and crawl. Must be able to lift 50 pounds maximum, with frequent lifting, carrying, pushing, and pulling of objects weighing up to 25 pounds. Rare lifting of greater than 100 pounds. Continuous walking and standing. Must be able to identify, match, and distinguish colors.
I. Additional duties and responsibilities as assigned.

EXHIBIT 4.2
The Process of Job Analysis

Sources of Data
- Job analyst
- Employee
- Supervisor

Methods of Collecting Data
- Observations
- Interviews
- Questionnaires
- Job performance (i.e., actually performing the job)
- Employee diary method, in which jobholders record their daily activities
- Technical conference method
- Competency model technique
- Occupational Information Network (O*NET)

Job Data
- Tasks
- Duties
- Responsibilities
- Job context
- Performance standards
- Equipment used

Job Description Contents
- Tasks
- Duties
- Responsibilities
- Performance standards

Human Resources Functions
- Human resources planning
- Recruitment
- Selection
- Training and development
- Performance appraisal
- Compensation assessment
- Safety and health
- Labor relations

Job Specifications
- Skills required
- Knowledge required
- Physical demands
- Abilities required

diary method
A job analysis method in which jobholders record their daily activities.

technical conference method
A job analysis method in which job attributes are obtained from supervisors who have extensive knowledge of the job (frequently called *subject matter experts*).

competency model
A method of job analysis that identifies competencies required to do the job. These are typically divided into "can do" competencies (skills and knowledge derived from education and experience) and "will do" competencies (personality and attitudinal characteristics that reflect an individual's willingness to perform).

interviewing individuals or groups, using structured questionnaires and checklists, performing the job, reviewing employee work diaries (the **diary method**), asking job supervisors and experts (the **technical conference method**), examining the underlying personal characteristics that result in superior performance (the **competency model**), referring to the Occupational Information Network (O*NET) of the US Department of Labor, and conducting electronic or web-based job analysis.

O*NET is an internet database that includes about 20,000 occupations from the earlier printed *Dictionary of Occupational Titles* as well as an update of more than 3,500 additional occupations. The database job descriptions provide employee attributes and job characteristics, such as skills, abilities, knowledge, tasks, work activities, and experience-level requirements. The database is continually updated and is useful for a variety of HR activities, including job analysis, employee selection, career counseling, compensation analysis, and employee training.

Exhibit 4.3 shows the content model for O*NET, which uses job-oriented and worker-oriented descriptors. The model also allows occupational information to be applied across jobs, sectors, or industries and within occupations. O*NET's six-domain content

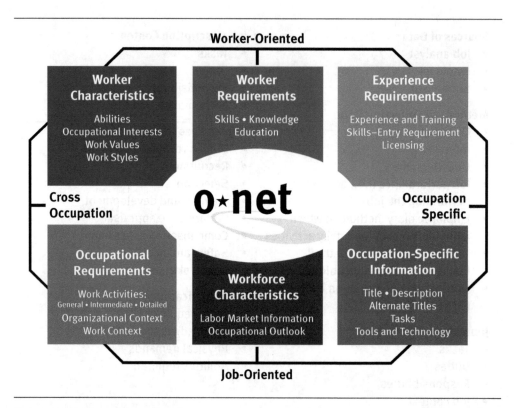

Source: O*NET Resource Center (2022).

model provides a framework for describing jobs in great detail. Not only is O*NET free to any organization, but it also provides comprehensive information on a wide variety of occupations. O*NET's website offers downloadable detailed job analysis questionnaires that can be applied to various purposes.

Healthcare organizations have been increasingly using data analytics to conduct job analysis. Algorithms will search through job postings on websites such as Indeed or LinkedIn and flag jobs for further review. HR managers then contact organizations offering jobs selected in the query to set up an interview, typically using videoconferencing platforms such as Webex or Zoom to discuss the job responsibilities. Then the knowledge, skills, abilities, and competencies are incorporated into the job analysis.

JOB ANALYSIS AND HUMAN RESOURCES

Job analysis provides the basis for tying all the HR functional areas together and for developing a sound HR program. Job requirements, as documented in descriptions and specifications, influence many HR functions. When job requirements are modified, corresponding changes must be made in other HR activities. Job analysis is the foundation of human capital strategies. Job analysis is the opportunity to understand how work functions are aligned and support the organization's missions, goals, and objectives. Job analysis is critical for forecasting future HR needs and planning for recruitment, selection, performance appraisal, compensation, training, transfer, and promotion. Job analysis information is often incorporated into HR information systems, such as Workday or Oracle, so there is a central repository of information for the organization to reference.

Job analysis is used

◆ in employee selection, and may determine whether applicants for a specific job should be required to take a particular kind of pre-employment test;

◆ to compare the relative worth of each job's contribution to the organization's overall performance;

◆ to determine training needs by comparing current employee skills to skills identified in the job analysis (training programs can then be put in place to reduce employees' skill gaps); and

◆ to formulate job descriptions and job specifications.

A major goal of job analysis is to help the organization establish the job relatedness of its selection and performance requirements. Job analysis helps employers meet their legal duties under EEO law. Section 14 C.2 of the Uniform Guidelines on Employee Selection Procedures states:

There should be a job analysis which includes an analysis of the important work behavior(s) required for successful performance. . . . Any job analysis should focus on the work behavior(s) and the tasks associated with them. (US Equal Employment Opportunity Commission [EEOC] 1978)

Any discrepancies between the knowledge, skills, and abilities demonstrated by the jobholders and the requirements contained in the job description and job specification provide clues for training needs. Career development prepares employees for advancement to jobs in which their capabilities can be used to the fullest extent possible. The formal qualifications set forth in the job specifications for higher-level jobs indicate how much more training and development are needed for employees to advance.

Job analysis is also used in recruiting. Before attempting to attract capable employees, recruiters must know the job specifications for the positions to be filled, including the knowledge, skills, and abilities required for successful job performance. The information in the job specifications is used in job postings and as a basis for attracting qualified applicants while discouraging unqualified candidates. Failure to update job specifications can result in a flood of applicants who are not qualified to perform one or more functions of the job.

The requirements in the job description are the criteria for evaluating the performance of the jobholder. The analysis may reveal, however, that certain performance criteria established for a particular job are not valid. For example, the criteria used to evaluate employee performance must be specific and job related. In healthcare, specific and job-related performance criteria may include or be based on a professional's ability to provide high-quality patient care, including medicating, feeding, and bathing activities; speak to other hospital staff concerning patient care; reduce the number of inconsistencies within electronic medical records; and follow regulatory requirements (Krijgsheld, Tummers, and Scheepers 2022). If the criteria are overly broad, vague, or not job related, employers may be charged with unfair discrimination. For example, including such subjective and questionably relevant criteria as "likable and fun to be around" or "having a bubbly personality" would be inappropriate for most situations.

Job analysis information is also important to the employee relations and labor relations functions. When employees are considered for promotion, transfer, or demotion, the job description provides a standard for comparison of talent. Regardless of whether the organization is unionized, information obtained through job analysis can often lead to more objective HR decisions.

LEGAL ASPECTS OF JOB SPECIFICATIONS

When discrimination charges arise, employers have the burden of proving that job requirements are job related or constitute a business necessity. Today, employers must be able to show that the job specifications used in selecting employees for a job are specifically associated with that job's duties. Performance standards that are used to judge employee performance for promotion, rewards, discipline, and loyalty should be job related and based on *job descriptions*. Data derived from *job analysis* in the form of a job description or job specification can have an impact on virtually every aspect of a high-performing organization and of HR management (Morgeson et al. 2016).

Today's legal environment has created a need for higher levels of specificity in job analysis and job descriptions. Employment decisions that are based on vague and non-job-related criteria are increasingly being challenged, and the challenges have mostly been successful (Dessler 2020). Managers of small healthcare organizations, where employees may perform many job tasks, must be particularly concerned about writing specific job descriptions. Many employers use internet sources such as Indeed (2022) or LinkedIn

> ⓘ **CRITICAL CONCEPT**
> Job Requirements Must Be Job Related
>
> Until 1971, job specifications used in employee selection decisions often were unrelated to the duties to be performed under the job description. A number of cases decided during the 1970s set the precedents for the laws we follow today.
>
> In the case of *Griggs v. Duke Power Company* (401 US 424 [1971]), the US Supreme Court ruled that employment practices must be job related.
>
> In *Albemarle Paper Company v. Moody* (422 US 405 [1975]), the Supreme Court found that the tests the company used for promotion perpetuated segregation and were not sufficiently job related.
>
> In *Rowe v. General Motors* (32 5 US 305 [1972]), the Supreme Court ruled that a company should have written objective standards for promotion to prevent discriminatory practices. In *US v. City of Chicago* (573 F. 2nd 416 [7th Cir. 1978]), the appeals court ruled that such objective standards should describe the job for which the person is being considered for promotion. In the *General Motors* and *Chicago* cases, these objective standards can be determined through job analysis (Nobile 1991).
>
> As a result of these landmark court decisions, organizations that do not use job analyses risk legal challenge of the validity of their hiring and promotion practices.

to facilitate writing job descriptions. After a job description is prepared and written, it is advantageous for the organization's legal counsel to review the document.

Job analysis is surrounded by several legal constraints largely because it serves as a basis for selection decisions, compensation, performance appraisals, and training. These constraints have been articulated in the Uniform Guidelines for Employee Selection Procedures and in several court decisions, as described in the nearby Critical Concept sidebar "Job Requirements Must Be Job Related." To ensure that job analysis focuses on work behaviors and associated tasks, organizations should assess job skills, knowledge, and abilities needed to perform the jobs. Then selection procedures can be developed.

Even before the Uniform Guidelines and the associated court cases discussed in the Critical Concept sidebar, labor contracts required consistent and equitable treatment of unionized employees. The information provided by job analysis is helpful to management and unions in contract negotiations and in avoiding or resolving grievances, jurisdictional disputes, and other conflicts.

WRITING JOB DESCRIPTIONS

Although HR managers consider job descriptions a valuable tool, they can encounter the following problems when using these documents:

◆ Job descriptions are often poorly written and offer little guidance to the jobholder.

◆ They are generally not updated as job duties or specifications change.

◆ They may violate the law by containing specifications that are not related to job performance.

◆ The job duties included in job descriptions are often written in vague terms.

◆ Job descriptions can limit the scope of the jobholder's activities in a rapidly changing environment.

When writing job descriptions, employers must use statements that are concise, direct, and worded simply, excluding unnecessary phrases and terms and avoiding jargon. Sentences that describe job duties typically begin with action verbs (refer back to exhibit 4.1). The word *may* is used for duties that are performed only by some workers on the job. Excellent job descriptions are of value to the employee and the employer.

Each job description typically identifies the job's most important responsibilities, and each responsibility begins with a verb that describes a specific action, such as *diagnoses, treats,* or *plans.* According to SHRM, job descriptions should be reviewed annually to ensure that the specifications are still relevant (Tyler 2013). Good job descriptions use action verbs in the present tense (e.g., *performs, administers* [rather than past tense *performed, administered*]) and inclusive language (e.g., *he/she/they, his/her/their,* and *him/her/them* [rather than just *he, his,* and *him*]). The Lesbian, Gay, Bisexual, Transgender, Queer Plus (LGBTQ+) Resource Center (2022) provides greater clarity on inclusive pronouns. Good job descriptions also avoid ambiguous words subject to interpretation (e.g., *frequently, regularly*).

Job descriptions help employees learn their job duties and remind them of the results they are expected to achieve. Descriptions can minimize the misunderstandings that occur between supervisors and subordinates regarding job requirements. Good job descriptions also establish management's right to take corrective action in the event that the duties specified are not performed or are performed at an inadequate or inappropriate level. Although the ultimate responsibility for job descriptions remains with the HR manager, the use of job description management software can facilitate the writing process (see the related "Did You Know?" sidebar).

DID YOU KNOW?
Job Description Management Software

Does writing a job description sound like a daunting task? Well, have no fear! A key trend within HR is the use of job description management software, and many organizations are taking advantage of these programs. Job description management software can assist managers in writing more inclusive job descriptions that are more likely to attract a diverse pool of applicants. One highlight of the software is its ability to analyze the "masculinity" and "femininity" of a job description and recommend or suggest more gender-neutral words. For instance, a word such as *aggressively* carries a more masculine connotation, while the word *collaboration* is perceived as more feminine in nature. Perhaps these words could be replaced with other words to avoid an overly masculine or feminine tone. Additionally, the software programs can help eliminate other types of bias, such as bias regarding race, religion, national origin, or age. Any "exclusionary" terms are pointed out, and recommendations for changes are provided. An overall readability score can be calculated, and the reading grade level can be specified. These tools can enhance employer branding and applicant engagement with the help of videos, graphics, and charts. Examples of job description management software include Ongig, JDXpert, and Textio (Luna 2017).

IDENTIFYING JOB FUNCTIONS

The job analysis process is the basic method used to identify essential job functions. An **essential job function** is one that is fundamental to successful performance of the job, while a **marginal job function** is incidental to the main function of the job—a matter of convenience, not a necessity. For example, for a nurse care manager, an essential job function would be the ability to develop treatment plans for clients with chronic diseases. A marginal job function might be the ability to drive to client sites or provide home visits or consultations. Essential job functions must be clearly delineated, not only for practical reasons but also for legal ones, in complying with the Americans with Disabilities Act (ADA), as described in the Critical Concept sidebar "What Makes a Job Function Essential?" (Recall from chapter 3 that discrimination in employment is prohibited under Title VII of the Civil Rights Act of 1964, and passage of the ADA in 1990 made discrimination based on disabilities illegal.)

essential job function
A function that is fundamental to successful performance of the job.

marginal job function
A function that is incidental to the main function of the job—a matter of convenience, not a necessity.

> ### ⓘ CRITICAL CONCEPT
> #### What Makes a Job Function Essential?
>
> The passage of the Americans with Disabilities Act (ADA) made a major impact on job analysis. Managers must now adhere to the legal mandates of the ADA when preparing job descriptions and job specifications. A key part of the ADA mandates is that a job must be described in terms of its "essential functions," which are the key elements of the job.
>
> Section 1630.2 (n) of the ADA provides three guidelines for rendering a job function essential (EEOC 1978):
>
> 1. The reason the position exists is to perform a function.
> 2. A limited number of employees are available among whom performance of the function may be distributed.
> 3. The function may be highly specialized, requiring needed expertise or abilities to complete the job.
>
> Managers who write job descriptions in terms of essential functions reduce the risk of discriminating on the basis of disability. When the essential functions of a job are defined, it is easier for the organization to accommodate an employee with a disability.

Qualified individuals with disabilities are persons who have a disability but meet the skills, education, and experience of the job requirements and can perform the essential functions with or without reasonable accommodation. As discussed in chapter 3, *reasonable accommodation* means that the employer may be required to make changes to enable a person with a disability to perform all essential functions of a particular job, whether by modifying the application process, aspects of the job itself, or the physical work environment. However, employers cannot be required to make an accommodation that imposes *undue hardship*—that is, an accommodation that is too costly or difficult for the employer to provide. (See the related Case Example sidebar, which examines the issue of reasonable accommodation in performing essential job functions.)

PERFORMING LEGALLY REQUIRED JOB ANALYSES

Other legislation requires organizations to perform thorough job analyses, including the following:

◆ The Fair Labor Standards Act categorizes employees as "exempt" or "nonexempt" based on the job analysis.

◆ The Equal Pay Act requires equal pay for equal work. When pay differences exist, job descriptions can show whether jobs are substantially different in terms of skill, effort, responsibility, and working conditions.

◆ The Civil Rights Act often requires the use of job specifications to defend against charges of discrimination in initial selection, promotion, and other HR decisions.

◆ The Occupational Safety and Health Act requires that job applicants be shown in advance descriptions of elements of a job that may endanger employee health or are considered distasteful.

These acts were all discussed in greater detail in chapter 3.

✴ CASE EXAMPLE

The issue of an organization's requirement to provide reasonable accommodation in performing the essential job functions of a neonatal intensive care unit (NICU) nurse was the focus of the case *Samper v. Providence St. Vincent Medical Center*, 675 F. 3d 1233 (2012). Plaintiff Monika Samper was a NICU nurse at Providence St. Vincent Medical Center for 11 years. Because of her fibromyalgia, Samper sought an ADA accommodation to allow her to be excused from adhering to the organization's standard attendance policy. Samper believed she should be allowed to have as many unplanned absences as she needed to cope with her condition, which could at times be debilitating. Over time, Samper's absences accumulated, putting additional stress on the available NICU nurses. After numerous performance improvement plans and coaching sessions resulted in no change in performance, Samper was dismissed. In turn, Samper sued. The US Court of Appeals affirmed the lower court's decision that regular attendance is an essential job function of a NICU nurse, and a nurse's performance is based on their ability to regularly report to work. Failure to do so could compromise patient care and put patients' lives in jeopardy. The court ruled that an allowance for unlimited absences is not a reasonable accommodation under the ADA. Because Samper could not come to work on a predictable basis, she was unqualified for the position; hence, her termination of employment was justified (Justia US Law 2022).

THE CHANGING ENVIRONMENT

Given the changes brought by globalization, technology, automation, and more recently the COVID-19 pandemic, it is even more important to frequently review and allow an appropriate level of flexibility in job descriptions. Information technology, data analytics, and automation have made it so that work functions done today may be obsolete tomorrow. In a dynamic environment wherein job demands change rapidly, job analysis data can quickly become outdated and inaccurate. Obsolete job analysis information can hinder an organization's ability to adapt to change. Ultimately, successful healthcare managers in today's world can no longer assume a static job environment. This section presents three approaches to job analysis that respond to the need for continuous change. The issue of flexibility within job descriptions is also examined.

THREE CHANGE-FORWARD APPROACHES TO JOB ANALYSIS

The first approach in responding to the need for continuous change is to adopt a future-oriented perspective on job analysis. This strategic analysis of jobs requires managers to have a clear view of how duties and tasks can be restructured to meet organizational requirements in the future. One method is to ask experts on a particular job to identify aspects of the job, the organization, and the environment that might change in the next few years and predict how those changes might affect the nature of the tasks, knowledge, skills, and abilities needed for the job in the future. By including future-oriented information in job descriptions, such as the use of telehealth, healthcare organizations can also focus employee attention on new strategic directions.

For example, if an organization decided to change its strategic focus to encourage telehealth for certain types of health needs, then job descriptions might be amended to include working with patients in person and over Zoom, Webex, or another virtual platform. Such forward-looking job descriptions would focus on what the organization aims to achieve in the future.

The second approach is to adopt a competency-based perspective on job analysis, which places emphasis on characteristics of successful performers rather than on standard job duties and tasks (SHRM 2022a). These competencies match the organization's culture and strategy and include such characteristics as interpersonal communication skills, ability to work as part of a team, decision-making capabilities, conflict resolution skills, adaptability, and self-motivation (SHRM 2022a).

Both future-oriented and competency-based approaches to change-oriented job analysis have potential impracticalities, including dependence on managers' ability to accurately predict future job needs, uncertainty that the analysis will comply with US

Equal Employment Opportunity Commission (EEOC) guidelines, and job description ambiguity resulting from basing descriptions on estimates.

A third approach is to conduct a generic job analysis. The traditional job analysis approach constrains change and flexibility by compartmentalizing and specifically defining presumably static job characteristics. It impedes cross-training employees, downward-shifting decision making, and getting employees involved in quality improvement efforts. Reducing the number of job titles and developing more generic job descriptions can provide flexibility to manage unanticipated change.

FLEXIBLE AND COMPLEX JOBS

The last item on a typical job description is often "other duties as assigned," and this phrase is increasingly becoming *the* job description. Some experts are critical of such a "cop-out" clause. It leaves open the nature of the job and may be used by unscrupulous supervisors to exploit subordinates, which can lead to legal challenges. On the other hand, proponents of this type of clause believe that it allows leaders to make the most of their workforce, as unanticipated and unforeseen circumstances and tasks may arise within the job and need to be completed (Potratz 2018). To demonstrate, this clause proved to be very beneficial during the early stages of the COVID-19 pandemic for the University of Illinois at Chicago Medical Center, as registered nurses were assigned to disinfect surfaces, remove soiled linens, and empty trash in COVID patients' rooms. Nurses were assigned these additional duties to minimize the number of staff exposed to the virus and to ration PPE articles in short supply. Such cleaning is usually not part of a nurse's job description; rather, the responsibility rests with a hospital's environmental services team (Bean 2020). However, this type of extra task was permitted through the "other duties as assigned" phrase at the end of the job description.

Generic, enlarged, flexible, complex job descriptions change the way virtually every HR function is performed. For example, in recruitment and selection, individuals who possess only the technical skills required to perform the job are not viewed as ideal candidates anymore. HR managers are also looking for broader capabilities such as competencies, intelligence, integrity, initiative, adaptability, flexibility, and an ability and willingness to develop others and work in teams.

Rapid change in healthcare makes accurate job analysis more important now and in the future. Historically, job analysis was conducted and then set aside for a time before an employer acted on its findings. Today, job requirements are in such a constant state of flux that job descriptions and specifications must be constantly reviewed to keep them relevant. Organizations that do not revise or review job descriptions and specifications may recruit new employees who do not possess the needed skills or may not provide necessary training to update employee skills.

JOB DESIGN

Job design is an outgrowth of job analysis and is the process of structuring jobs by determining the specific tasks to be performed, the methods used in performing those tasks, and how the job relates to other jobs. The goal is to maximize or enhance organizational efficiency and employee job satisfaction. The process involves changing, eliminating, modifying, and enriching duties and tasks to capture the talents of employees so that they can contribute to the organization as much as possible, develop professionally, and enhance organizational performance. Job design should simultaneously help achieve organizational objectives and recognize the capabilities and needs of those who perform the job.

Job design encompasses how a given job is defined and how it will be conducted, which involve such decisions as whether the job will be handled by an individual or by a team of employees and such determinations as how the job fits into the overall organization. Organizing tasks, duties, and responsibilities into a unit of work to achieve an objective requires conscious effort. Each job design process must acknowledge employees' unique skills and must incorporate appropriate professional guidelines or task limitations.

A recent survey of 218 professionals and managers by SHRM and *Harvard Business Review* found that being thoughtful about who is updating job design can impact how engaging the job may be. Job designed by knowledge experts and by those with higher levels of autonomy in their jobs create more enriching jobs than those who have lower levels of autonomy or have conservative life values (Parker, Andrei, and Van den Broeck 2019).

In healthcare, most professionals are constrained by which functions and tasks they may legally perform and under what type of supervision. For example, many technical functions must be performed by a physician or by another professional under direct physician supervision. Such legal constraints reduce the flexibility in designing jobs.

SPECIALIZATION IN HEALTHCARE

As a result of technological change, increased specialization, and the emergence of the hospital as the central focus of the healthcare system, approximately 700 job categories exist in the healthcare industry. The US Bureau of Labor Statistics (BLS 2022) has projected that between 2021 and 2031, healthcare jobs will increase by 13 percent, faster than any other occupation group, making it a complex effort to keep up with job analysis and design needs.

Although all the specialization in the healthcare field has increased efficiency, there are some disadvantages of specialization. If specialized work is too narrow, workers may become bored and dissatisfied because their jobs may not offer enough challenge or stimulation. They also may not develop skills to grow in the organization or identify problems that are outside their narrow area of focus. In addition, boredom and monotony lead to absenteeism and quality problems.

Healthcare executives have implemented a number of job design and redesign options to balance organizational demands for efficiency and productivity with individual needs for creativity and autonomy. Four alternative redesign approaches are (1) job enlargement and enrichment, (2) employee empowerment, (3) workgroup redesign (such as employee involvement groups and employee teams), and (4) flexible work schedules.

JOB ENLARGEMENT AND JOB ENRICHMENT

Job enlargement involves changes in the scope of a job to provide greater variety to the employee. It is a horizontal expansion of job duties with the same level of autonomy and responsibility. Such expansion can lead to higher job satisfaction and performance. For example, research by O'Laughlin and colleagues (2019) in a healthcare setting found that a job enlargement effort for advanced practice providers in a primary care clinic resulted in significant improvements in job satisfaction. Alternately, **job enrichment** is a vertical expansion of job duties that includes additional autonomy, responsibility, achievement, and recognition to provide greater challenges to the employee.

One profession that was developed in response to job enlargement and enrichment is the **multiskilled health practitioner (MSHP)**. The classic definition of *MSHP* is a "person cross-trained to provide more than one function, often in more than one discipline" (Fottler 1996, 60). These combined functions can be found in a broad spectrum of healthcare-related jobs and range in complexity from nonprofessional to professional. The functions and skills added to the worker's original job may be of a higher, lower, or parallel level. An example of such a role is a certified medical assistant. Working under the supervision of a licensed healthcare provider, medical assistants spend their time doing both administrative tasks and patient or clinical procedures.

Theories of job enrichment have long stressed that unless jobs are both horizontally and vertically enriched, little positive impact is made on motivation, productivity, and job satisfaction (Lawler 1986). Healthcare organizations use MSHPs to rotate responsibilities to relieve boredom, stimulate performance, reduce absenteeism and turnover, and provide flexibility in job assignment (Everton 2010). Staff members who are able to accomplish more than one task are more valuable to themselves and to their employers. Having people who are cross-trained and can do a variety of tasks can also help overcome temporary staffing shortages. For example, during the height of the COVID-19 pandemic, the Cleveland Clinic crossed-trained approximately 4,100 ambulatory and perioperative nurses to perform critical care procedures for COVID patients. More than 150 outpatient patient service specialists were also cross-trained to provide assistance to inpatient medical-surgical units. To enhance the success of this project, chief nursing officer Joan Kavanagh enlisted the help of local nursing school educators to assist with the cross-training efforts (Cleveland Clinic 2020).

Pressure has been mounting to revise traditional definitions of the respective roles and job duties of physicians and nonphysician clinical service providers (Beck 2014; Feyereisen et al. 2021). Physician assistants, nurse practitioners, nurses, and other providers are increasingly taking on duties once performed solely by physicians. The goal is to provide patient

job enlargement
The horizontal expansion of job duties with the same level of autonomy and responsibility.

job enrichment
The vertical expansion of job duties that includes additional autonomy, responsibility, achievement, and recognition to provide greater challenges to the employee.

multiskilled health practitioner (MSHP)
A healthcare worker who is cross-trained to serve more than one function, often in multiple disciplines.

access in geographic regions with physician shortages and to contain the costs of providing such services. The major impediment is state scope-of-practice statutes, which vary widely in terms of which practitioners are allowed to provide which services and how much autonomy nonphysician providers are allowed.

The US Veterans Health Administration (VHA) has received heavy criticism from physician groups for a proposal to let nurses with advanced training practice medicine in the VHA health system without physician supervision (Beck 2014). Not only do these groups oppose such autonomy, but they also oppose physician-led teams. Nurses have counted on outside support for the proposed changes, which they believe will facilitate timely high-quality services for many more veterans.

EMPLOYEE EMPOWERMENT

Job enlargement and enrichment approaches, such as the MSHP, formally change the jobs of employees. A less structured approach is to allow employees to initiate job changes through the concept of empowerment. *Empowerment* is allowing decisions to be made by those closest to the customers. To facilitate empowerment, organizations should provide supportive leadership and management along with a work environment that allows the employee to be successful in their role (Seibert, Wang, and Courtright 2011). Empowerment encourages employees to become innovators and managers of their own work. There are several positive outcomes from employee empowerment, including higher levels of job satisfaction, performance, and organizational commitment as well as lower turnover rates (Seibert, Wang, and Courtright 2011). To create a more positive work culture and enhance the satisfaction and stability of the certified nursing assistant (CNA) profession, some nursing home organizations have begun to involve CNAs in the decision making behind resident staffing assignments and in social event and activity planning for residents (Berridge, Tyler, and Miller 2018).

WORKGROUP REDESIGN

Exhibit 4.4 outlines the six forms of teams used in healthcare. Teams provide a forum for employees to contribute toward identifying and solving organizational problems. In healthcare, outcomes rely on professionals with diverse skills and responsibilities, making teams critical. A team can address some of the unique work challenges, such as providing around-the-clock care or managing patients with multiple care needs (Stoller 2021). For example, most hospitals have a day care team and night care team. Each team works a shift of 12 hours, with a 15-minute overlap to allow for knowledge transfer from one team to the next. When a team is working in a unit, each person has specific responsibilities for patient monitoring, which focus on patient safety and care.

In healthcare, multidisciplinary teams have helped eliminate some of the separate "silos" that healthcare professionals may have worked in and have improved patient

Type	Description
Multidisciplinary	A group staffed by a mix of specialists (nurses, physicians, and managers) formed to accomplish a specific objective. Membership on this team is usually assigned rather than voluntary.
Project team	A group formed specifically to design or promote a particular service, such as telemedicine. Members are designated by management on the basis of their ability to contribute to team success. The group normally disbands after task completion.
Self-directed team (or autonomous workgroup)	A group of highly trained individuals accountable for a whole work process that provides a service or product to an internal or external customer. Members use consensus decision making to perform job duties, solve problems, or deal with internal or external customers.
Task force team	A group formed by management to resolve a major problem. This team is responsible for developing a long-term plan for problem resolution that may include a plan for implementing the proposed solution. For example, many hospitals used task forces to develop their strategies for addressing the COVID-19 pandemic.
Process improvement team (or employee involvement group)	A group made up of experienced employees across departments or functions and charged with improving quality, decreasing waste, or enhancing productivity in processes that affect all departments. Members are normally appointed by management.
Virtual team	A group with any of the previously listed purposes that uses telecommunication or telemedicine that links geographically dispersed team members.

EXHIBIT 4.4
Types of Employee Teams in Healthcare

safety and health outcomes (Derrick 2018; see also the related Case Example sidebar). Multidisciplinary teams are often used to brainstorm the best outcomes for cancer care or other complex health conditions (Rosell et al. 2018). Other positive outcomes of being on a team include better problem solving, diverse knowledge and experience with which to address challenges, and a way to collaborate with others without having to go through bureaucratic processes to pull in resources (Moss 2018). High-performance teams also are able to develop *synergy*, in which all members of the team together produce a greater effect than the sum of all individuals' efforts. Regardless of which structure is employed, several processes have been identified with team success. These include commitment to the following:

- ◆ Shared goals

- ◆ Motivated and energetic team members

- ◆ Consensus decision making

- ◆ Open and honest communication

- ◆ Shared leadership

- ◆ Climate of trust and collaboration

- ◆ Commitment to diversity

- ◆ Acceptance of conflict and its positive resolution

A good team also requires that initial employee selection partially consider the potential employee's interpersonal skills and that extensive training be provided. The manager must also adapt to the role of leader (rather than supervisor) and must not be threatened by the growing power of the team.

 CASE EXAMPLE

Under the direction of Dr. James Brevig, Providence Regional Medical Center in Everett, Washington, managed to become one of the most elite hospitals in the United States with its unwavering commitment to high-quality patient care at a low cost. Dr. Brevig, the director of cardiac surgery, organized multidisciplinary process improvement teams with members consisting of perfusionists, cardiac surgeons, orthopedic surgeons, and other key medical staff. The goal was to lessen the number of blood transfusions needed by surgical patients because blood transfusions often result in longer hospital stays and the potential increased risk of infection and are also costly in terms of the blood itself—at the time, the average cost for a bag of blood hovered around $240. Together, the team strived to achieve a "low transfusion culture" within the hospital by having surgeons work more slowly during procedures, adjusting settings on heart bypass machines, and hiring a blood conservation coordinator. Between 2003 and 2007, patient blood transfusion rates were reduced by 25 percent, patient hospital stays were shortened by half a day, and the hospital saved approximately $4.5 million. This accomplishment would not have been possible without this collaborative team effort (Wolcott 2010; Zelinka et al. 2010).

Organizations must be aware of several obstacles to the effective functioning of teams, including overly high expectations, inappropriate compensation, lack of training, and lack of power. For example, new team members must be retrained to work outside their primary functional area, and compensation systems must be constructed to reward individuals for team achievements. New career paths to general management or higher clinical positions must be created.

Managers who feel threatened by the growing power of the team and their perception of reduced power may need further training or incentives to work with teams. Complete training would enhance skills in team leadership, goal setting, conduct of meetings, team decision making, conflict resolution, effective communication, and inclusion. Some of the most serious challenges to the effective functions of teams are posed by team members who are egotistical and narcissistic. The "Did You Know?" example from the sports world (which is rife with overblown egos) shows that it is nevertheless possible to be a true team player.

FLEXIBLE WORK SCHEDULES

The goal of flexible work schedules is to give employees greater control over their time. Various adjustments in work schedules alter the normal 40-hour workweek of five eight-hour

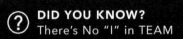

DID YOU KNOW?
There's No "I" in TEAM

Tim Duncan is a Hall of Fame basketball player who retired from the San Antonio Spurs after 19 seasons with the same team, which included five National Basketball Association (NBA) championships. Not only was his team successful over the long term, but he was as egoless as any player in the history of professional basketball. No previous or current NBA player was less of a blowhard, snob, or narcissist than Tim Duncan.

When he was an undergraduate at Wake Forest, Duncan took a psychology course during which he and two other undergrads coauthored a book chapter with their professor (Mark Leary) in a volume titled *Aversive Interpersonal Behaviors*, published in the late 1990s. Over the ensuing years, Tim internalized the lessons of that book chapter, which noted that egotistical behavior conveys to others an exaggerated perception of self that can be annoying, exasperating, and unpleasant for others. While he was the star of the Spurs, he was always the team player willing to sacrifice his own statistics and ego for the greater good of the team. His career exemplifies the concept that teams of all types do best when their members are willing to subordinate their own egos for the good of the team.

Source: Cohen (2016).

days in which everyone begins and ends their workday at the same time. Such adjustments improve organizational productivity and morale by giving employees increased control over their schedules. By allowing employees greater flexibility in work scheduling, employers can reduce some of the most common causes of tardiness and absenteeism—the time pressures of life.

Employees can adjust their work schedules to accommodate their lifestyles, to reduce pressure to meet a rigid schedule, or generally to achieve greater satisfaction. Employers can enhance their attractiveness for recruiting and retention while improving their customer service—poor service is a direct result of low levels of employee satisfaction (Chamberlain and Zhao 2019). Productivity and quality may also be enhanced through use of flexible work schedules.

In 2019, before the COVID-19 pandemic, workplace flexibility and work–life balance were already becoming important topics, with a survey by FlexJobs finding that 80 percent of its 7,200 respondents said they would be more loyal to their company if the company provided flexible work arrangements (Maurer 2019). Since the pandemic, flexible work arrangements and work–life balance have become even more important, and employers are starting to adjust (Courtney 2022). According to 2022 data collected in Fidelity's Employer-Sponsored Health & Well-Being Survey, 57 percent of organizations are focused on work–life balance (Fidelity Investments 2022). Additionally, a Deloitte survey reports that 78 percent of employees state that their employer is currently introducing or implementing new, flexible ways of working (Radin and Korba 2020).

The COVID-19 pandemic accelerated a trend of people working remotely and in flexible work arrangements. In May 2020, 48.7 million people, or 35 percent of the entire employed workforce, were working remotely from home (Coate 2021). The pandemic has changed how many companies structure work, with some allowing employees to continue working from home indefinitely, while others have shifted to "hybrid" work arrangements whereby employees may be in the office two or three days a week and work from home the other days.

In healthcare, there are clearly limits to work-from-home strategies. Many jobs must be performed on-site because they rely on caring for patients, cleaning rooms, or processing samples in labs. This raises an interesting dilemma for managers: Do you allow office staff to work remotely while members of the clinical staff have to be on-site every day? Many healthcare facilities have determined that allowing office staff to work remotely was not an equitable arrangement and have required all employees to work on-site again. Yet even for on-site work, some flexibility may be possible in schedules.

compressed workweek scheme
A work schedule redesign in which the number of days in the workweek is shortened by lengthening the number of hours worked per day.

Under the **compressed workweek scheme**, the number of days in the workweek is shortened by increasing the number of hours worked per day. The four-day 40-hour week (4/40), in which the employee works four days of 10-hour shifts and has three days off, is the most common form of compressed workweek; another variation is working seven days of 12-hour shifts over a two-week period. The compressed schedule accommodates employees' leisure-time activities and personal appointments. This schedule design still adds up to about 40 hours per week, more or less, as defined by employees' work contracts. Time worked beyond 40 hours per week would result in overtime pay for employees who are compensated on an hourly basis, meeting the stringent rules under the FLSA. The downside is that long workdays may also increase employees' and managers' exhaustion and stress. (A more detailed discussion of employee stress is presented in chapter 13, on employee well-being.)

In 2022, SHRM reported that 32 percent of employers offered some type of compressed workweek. Major reasons given for implementing compressed work schedules include enhanced staff recruitment and retention, enhanced staff time for personal appointments, and improvement in job satisfaction and morale (SHRM 2022b).

Flextime, or a schedule with flexible working hours, allows employees to choose daily starting and ending times, provided they work a certain number of hours per day or week. Typically, there is a core period during the morning and afternoon when all employees on a given shift are required to be on the job. In healthcare, flextime is most common in clerical or management functions, such as claims processing, health insurance, and human resources. Flextime is less appropriate for patient care positions because these functions must be staffed at all times.

Flexibility in work scheduling can reduce some of the traditional causes of absenteeism and turnover. It can also improve customer service by extending working hours and enhancing employee productivity (Snell and Morris 2018). In 2018, a SHRM survey found that 57 percent of companies offered flextime within core business hours and nearly a third of those allowed for flextime to be outside noncore hours (SHRM 2019).

Job sharing is an arrangement in which two part-time employees share a job that otherwise would be held by one full-time employee. Job sharers sometimes work three days a week to create an overlap day for face-to-face conferencing. Job sharing can be scheduled to conform to peaks in the daily or weekly workload. However, more time may be needed to orient, train, and develop two employees who share one role.

According to Maurer (2016), job sharing can be an important tool used to expand labor pools in healthcare. In healthcare, job sharing may work for both clinical and nonclinical positions, but a major impediment is the reluctance of managers to hire and supervise job sharers who work on a part-time basis (Schellenbarger 2016). However, it requires two individuals who are willing and able to work together to avoid problems through excellent communication and coordination of activities. Job sharing may also be something that attracts employees back into the labor market, especially those who may have retired during the pandemic. The ability to work 20 hours a week and partner with someone else on the same schedule may prove to be what is needed to expand the labor market and to combat labor shortages within the healthcare industry.

Among notable healthcare organizations that have developed physician job-sharing programs is HMO Kaiser Permanente in Northern California. This program allows two

flextime
A work schedule redesign that allows employees to choose daily starting and ending times, provided that they work a certain number of hours per day or week. Also known as *flexible working hours*.

job sharing
An arrangement in which two part-time employees share a job that otherwise would be held by one full-time employee.

physicians to share one job. Job sharing is best suited for employees who wish to work part-time and older workers who wish to phase into retirement. Job sharing can reduce absenteeism because it allows employees to have time to accommodate their personal needs even when employed. It also aids retention of valuable employees.

Job sharing may pose problems for employers, however. Among the possible concerns are the time required to orient and train a second employee and prorating of employee benefits between the two job sharers. The key to making this approach work is good communication between partners through a variety of modes of communication: phone calls, e-mails, texts, videoconferencing technology such as Zoom or Webex, voicemails, or written updates (Newman and Ford 2021). It also helps if the two partners worked in the organization together before they decided to share a job.

telecommuting
Performing work away from the office enabled by technology to communicate and collaborate with coworkers and access desktop tools.

One of the most significant work schedule innovations is telecommuting. **Telecommuting** is the act of performing work away from the office enabled by high-speed internet and communication options whereby employees can now access their entire desktop remotely using laptops, shared networks and drives, company intranets, and videoconferencing platforms. A 2021 Gallup survey found that 67 percent of all white-collar employees telecommuted, either in a hybrid work arrangement or working from home 100 percent of the time (Saad and Wigert 2021).

Employers use telecommuting to reduce costs, improve productivity, increase employee retention, boost employee morale, and enhance customer service. Telecommuting decreases overhead costs, as it eliminates or minimizes the need for office space. The two most important advantages of telecommuting are increased flexibility for employees and improved ability for organizations to attract workers who may not otherwise be available or willing to do the work. In 2022, jobs advertised as "remote" or "hybrid" were attracting seven times more applicants than those advertised as "in-person" only (Smith 2022).

Drawbacks of telecommuting may include more challenging workplace communication, a lack of employee cohesion, and employees feeling isolated. Additionally, there is the potential loss of employee creativity because of lower levels of in-person interaction, the difficulty of developing appropriate performance standards and evaluation systems, and the challenge of formulating an appropriate technology system for telecommuting. Telecommuting may also negatively affect employee–supervisor relationships (Newman, Ford, and Marshall 2020).

Telecommuting is more appropriate for companies that are not engaged in direct patient care. With that being said, while it is impossible for someone such as a nurse anesthetist to telecommute, the US Department of Health and Human Services (HHS 2020) recognizes that there are numerous other healthcare professions—such as medical billers or coders, patient service representatives, nurse care managers, and pharmaceutical company representatives—who can successfully work from home. Furthermore, evidence indicates that, when given a choice, employees prefer splitting their time between home and office, a number which has been increasing since the pandemic, with 54 percent of employees saying they would prefer to continue working from home part of the time (Saad and Wigert 2021). Siemens Healthineers (2020) has done analysis and made suggestions for how remote work in healthcare can go from something disruptive, as when COVID-19 emerged, to a permanent, productive, and safer work arrangement; the company posits that there are broad potential advantages for healthcare organizations that take time to strategically assess what gains they may capture from virtual care, which can benefit the healthcare organization and patients.

A *Wall Street Journal* article noted the following strategies that telecommuters could use to be successful in their position (Schellenbarger 2016):

◆ Be more in touch with your supervisor than others through the use of tech tools such as texts, e-mail, videoconferencing, and telephone.

◆ Prior to telecommuting, set ground rules and expectations on when and how to communicate.

◆ Agree in advance what decisions the telecommuter will make autonomously and which are too significant to make alone.

◆ Schedule weekly 20-minute one-on-one calls to update, report progress, and ask for help if needed.

◆ Schedule periodic trips to the office to build deeper relationships and trust, resolve conflicts, and gain commitment.

The bottom line is that when working remotely, the telecommuter needs to match the medium to the message, or desired outcome. The more complex the conversation, the richer and more intimate the medium should be (i.e., telephone and face-to-face communications).

Another work schedule innovation is the use of **contingent workers**. The US Department of Labor separates contingent workers into two groups: (1) independent contractors and on-call workers, who are called to work only when needed, and (2) temporary or short-term workers. Contingent workers are useful to deal with seasonal fluctuations in customer demand, to handle project-based work, to acquire skills not available among current employees, to bring in extra employees during a hiring freeze, to deal with rapid growth, and to ameliorate the effects of inadequate supply of workers in certain occupations (e.g., registered nurses).

The increasing use of contingent workers has been referred to as the "gig economy" (Sussman and Zumbrun 2016). As healthcare organizations look to fill staffing gaps, they have shifted to a contingent or "gig" workforce including travel nurses, contract physical therapists and occupational therapists, and locum tenens physicians to help fill labor shortages. Contract nurses are also frequently coming to the United States from locations around the world, with 1 in 6 nurses now being international nurses (Ehli 2022). These contingent

contingent workers
Two categories of workers defined by the US Department of Labor as (1) independent contractors and on-call workers, who are called to work only when needed, and (2) temporary or short-term workers.

staffing strategies are critical at a time when, in 2022, 35 percent of hospitals were struggling with a vacancy rate of higher than 10 percent among their nurses (NSI Nursing 2022). Additionally, given current staffing challenges, roles such as travel nurse can be lucrative. A **travel nurse** is a registered nurse who works in a short-term role at a hospital, clinic, or other healthcare facility that is experiencing a nursing shortage, making it possible to be available where the need is greatest. A travel nurse may earn about $50 per hour, and during the most critical times of the COVID-19 pandemic, some nurses we paid as much as $10,000 per week (Walker 2022). See also the accompanying Current Issue sidebar "It Pays to Be (or Hire) a Travel Nurse!"

travel nurse
A registered nurse who works in a short-term role at a hospital, clinic, or other healthcare facility that is experiencing a nursing shortage.

Contingent workers may pose managerial challenges, such as unclear management reporting relationships, lack of accountability for performance, high relative compensation, low retention rates, variable attitudes and work quality, and inadequate orientation and training. Contingent workers must be a good fit for their institutions (Boon et al. 2011). They are viewed positively by some employers but as undesirable by others. Contingent or gig workers can also introduce or present legal challenges under the FLSA for healthcare organizations. HR and leadership must make sure not to mistake or confuse these workers

---

⟹ CURRENT ISSUE
It Pays to Be (or Hire) a Travel Nurse!

Being a travel nurse has many benefits. US healthcare staffing services usually offer some form of the following to travel nurses (Ericksen 2018):

- Flexible work schedules (including three-day workweeks)
- Varying contract/assignment lengths, with opportunities to extend
- Paid travel within the United States and possibly to other countries
- Opportunity to work in a variety of nursing specialties (e.g., ICU, surgery, trauma)
- Reduced-priced or even free housing and utilities

At the same time, organizations benefit when they contract with travel nurses to fill open positions. Travel nurses can help do the following (Cornett 2022):

- Satisfy seasonal staffing needs (e.g., during winter flu season)
- Fill in-demand positions when applicant pools are too small
- Lessen organizational costs associated with benefits and payroll taxes
- Reduce the need for overtime pay
- Lower turnover costs

as employees. The IRS's Common Law Test and the Economic Realities Test can be used to determine whether a worker should be classified as a contingent worker or an actual employee.

Healthcare staffing services are the largest employers of contingent workers in healthcare. The largest healthcare staffing firm in the United States is Maxim Staffing Solutions. In 2021, Maxim staffed 35,000 external healthcare professionals at 7,500 facilities (Maxim Staffing Solutions 2022).

SUMMARY

Job analysis is the systematic process of determining the skills, duties, tasks, activities, competencies, and knowledge required to perform particular jobs. This information is relevant to the preparation of job descriptions and job specifications. Job analysis information in the form of job descriptions and job specifications provides the basic foundation for all human resources management functions.

A *job description* is an overall written summary of a particular job's duties, tasks, responsibilities, reporting relationships, working conditions, and FLSA exemption status. A *job specification* is an overall written summary of the personal qualifications, traits, and background an individual must possess to successfully perform the job.

Some combination of available job analysis methods (observation, interviews, questionnaires, job performance, diary method, technical conference method, competency model, and O*NET) should be used, because all have advantages and disadvantages. Job descriptions and job specifications, as derived from job analyses, must be done and their processes must be valid, accurate, and job related. Otherwise, the healthcare organization may face legal repercussions, particularly in the areas of employee selection, promotion, and compensation. The EEOC's Uniform Guidelines and associated court cases provide standards to help executives avoid charges of discrimination when developing documents from job analysis data.

In today's rapidly changing healthcare environment, healthcare executives should consider the potential advantage of future-oriented job analyses when change is more predictable and generic job analyses when change is less predictable. Both concepts may have legal or practical limitations that must be considered before the concepts are fully adopted.

New approaches to job design are required as healthcare organizations strive to overcome the effects of excessive specialization. Among the most significant of these effects are job redesign approaches such as the multiskilled health practitioner, employee empowerment, various team concepts, and work schedule redesign.

The healthcare field uses all the work schedule design approaches discussed here for positions that do not involve clinical care and some of them for clinical staff. Positions that involve direct patient care must be staffed 24 hours a day, seven days a week. A compressed workweek, flextime, and job sharing are the most appropriate work schedule adjustments for employees in such positions. Telecommuting may also be appropriate for nonclinical staff.

Generally speaking, work schedule redesign has affected all areas of healthcare, is still growing incrementally, and has had a positive impact on employee recruitment, retention, productivity, quality of work, client service, employee commitment, culture, public image, and return on investment. Achieving such positive outcomes requires an employer to be tuned in to the changing needs and preferences of clinical and non-clinical staff.

FOR DISCUSSION

1. Why should healthcare executives conduct a job analysis? What purpose does it serve?

2. What are job descriptions and job specifications? What is their relationship to job analysis? What do you think will happen if a healthcare organization decides not to use any job descriptions?

3. How can the existence of a high-quality job analysis make a particular human resources function, such as employee selection, less legally vulnerable?

4. Healthcare jobs are not static but change over time. What may cause a job to change over time? What implications does this change have for job analysis?

5. Describe and discuss future-oriented job analysis and generic job analysis. How may each be used to help healthcare executives cope with a rapidly changing and competitive environment? What are some potential pitfalls of each approach?

6. What are the advantages and disadvantages of using multiskilled health practitioners?

7. Refer to the work team types in exhibit 4.4. What types of work teams are most appropriate for achieving which objectives in the healthcare industry? Cite at least one successful team effort in healthcare.

8. Select one healthcare position with which you are familiar. What work schedule innovations make the most sense for this position? Why?

9. Suppose your medical office is planning to use contingent workers to fill some in-demand positions. Discuss some advantages and disadvantages of using contingent workers to staff these positions.

EXPERIENTIAL EXERCISES

EXERCISE 1

Form a team with four fellow students to make a 30-minute class presentation on the future of job analysis in the healthcare industry. All the work on this challenging project must be done by the entire team; however, your group cannot have any in-person meetings. Your virtual team must come up with ways to deal with the following issues:

- How will you organize the virtual team? Will you select a team leader? If so, based on what criteria?
- On what basis would you select team members?
- Without in-person encounters, how will you ensure that every member on the team does the assigned tasks so that a high-quality presentation is produced?

EXERCISE 2

Form a team with four or five fellow students. As a group, select one healthcare job (e.g., registered nurse, physical therapist, receptionist) with which all team members have some familiarity. Based solely on the group members' understanding of the selected job, outline the methods for conducting an analysis of the job. Draft a job description and a job specification that you believe represent the job. What future changes to the job do you think may affect your job description and job specification?

REFERENCES

Bean, M. 2020. "UIC Medical Center Asks Nurses to Clean COVID-19 Patients' Rooms." *Becker's Hospital Review*. Published March 31. www.beckershospitalreview.com /nursing/uic-medical-center-asks-nurses-to-clean-covid-19-patients-rooms.html.

Beck, M. 2014. "Battles Erupt over Filling Doctor's Shoes." *Wall Street Journal*, February 9, 161.

Berridge, C., D. Tyler, and S. Miller. 2018. "Staff Empowerment Practices and CNA Retention: Findings from a Nationally Representative Nursing Home Culture Change Survey." *Journal of Applied Gerontology* 37 (4): 419–34.

Boon, C. D., P. Denhartog, P. Boselie, and J. Paavwe. 2011. "The Relationship Between Perceptions of HR Practices and Employee Outcomes." *International Journal of Human Resource Management* 22 (11): 138–62.

Chamberlain, A., and D. Zhao. 2019. "The Key to Happy Customers? Happy Employees." *Harvard Business Review*. Published August 19. https://hbr.org/2019/08/the-key-to -happy-customers-happy-employees.

Cleveland Clinic. 2020. "COVID-19 Leads to Major Effort to Cross-Train Nurses." Published April 24. https://consultqd.clevelandclinic.org/covid-19-leads-to-major-effort-to-cross -train-nurses/.

Coate, P. 2021. "Remote Work Before, During, and After the Pandemic." *Quarterly Economics Briefing—Q4 2020*. National Counselor on Compensation Insurance (NCCI). Published January 25. www.ncci.com/SecureDocuments/QEB/QEB_Q4_2020 _RemoteWork.html.

Cohen, B. 2016. "The Golden State Warriors Have Revolutionized Basketball." *Wall Street Journal*. Published April 6. www.wsj.com/articles/the-golden-state-warriors-have -revolutionized-basketball-1459956975.

Cornett, J. E. 2022. "Why Are Hospitals Hiring Traveling Nurses?" Chron. Updated February 10. https://work.chron.com/hospitals-hiring-traveling-nurses-22729.html.

Courtney, E. 2022. "Remote Work Stats & Trends: Navigating Work from Home Jobs." FlexJobs. Accessed April 30. www.flexjobs.com/blog/post/remote-work-statistics/.

Derrick, H. 2018. "Interdisciplinary Healthcare Teams." *SPNHA Review* 14 (1): 8.

Dessler, G. 2020. *Human Resources Management*, 16th ed. Upper Saddle River, NJ: Pearson Education.

Ehli, N. 2022. "Short-Staffed and COVID-Battered, U.S. Hospitals Are Hiring More Foreign Nurses." National Public Radio (NPR). Published January 6. www.npr.org/sections /health-shots/2022/01/06/1069369625/short-staffed-and-covid-battered-u-s -hospitals-are-hiring-more-foreign-nurses.

Ericksen, K. 2018. "Top 10 Benefits of Being a Traveling Nurse." *Nursing Blog* (Rasmussen University). Published March 6. www.rasmussen.edu/degrees/nursing/blog/10 -benefits-of-being-traveling-nurse/.

Everton, W. 2010. "Keeping Your Best and Brightest Workers." *Nonprofit World* 28 (6): 12–13.

Feyereisen, S., M. McConnell, C. Thomas, and N. Puro. 2021. "Physician Dominance in the 21st Century: Examining the Rise of Non-Physician Autonomy Through Prevailing Theoretical Lenses." *Sociology of Health and Illness* 43 (8): 1867–86.

Fidelity Investments. 2022. "New Research from Fidelity and Business Group on Health Finds Employers Answering the Call for Help: Focusing on Mental and Physical Health and Work/Life Balance as Employees Return to the Office." Press release, March 31. https://fidelityinvestments2020news.q4web.com/press-releases/news-details /2022/New-Research-From-Fidelity-and-Business-Group-on-Health-Finds-Employers -Answering-the-Call-for-Help-Focusing-on-Mental-and-Physical-Health--WorkLife -Balance-as-Employees-Return-to-the-Office/default.aspx.

Fottler, M. 1996. "The Role and Impact of Multiskilled Health Practitioners in the Health Services Industry. *Hospital and Health Services Administration* 41 (1): 55–75.

Harvard Business Review. 2013. "Women in the Workplace: A Research Roundup." *Harvard Business Review* 91 (9): 86–89.

Indeed. 2022. "How to Write a Job Description." Updated July 11. www.indeed.com/hire /how-to-write-a-job-description.

Justia US Law. 2022. "Samper v. Providence St. Vincent Medical, No. 10-35811 (9th Cir. 2012)." https://law.justia.com/cases/federal/appellate-courts/ca9/10-35811/10 -35811-2012-04-11.html.

Krijgsheld, M., L. Tummers, and F. Scheepers. 2022. "Job Performance in Healthcare: A Systematic Review." *BMC Health Services Research* 22: article no. 149. Published February 4. https://doi.org/10.1186/s12913-021-07357-5.

Lawler, E. E. 1986. *High Involvement Management*. San Francisco: Jossey-Bass.

Lesbian, Gay, Bisexual, Transgender, Queer Plus (LGBTQ+) Resource Center. 2022. "Gender Pronouns." University of Wisconsin–Milwaukee. https://uwm.edu/lgbtrc/support /gender-pronouns/.

Luna, J. 2017. "5 New Tools to Help You Write More Diverse Job Descriptions." *Writing Job Descriptions* (blog), Ongig. Published April 26. https://blog.ongig.com/writing-job -descriptions/diversity-tools/.

Maurer, R. 2019. "Flexible Work Critical to Retention, Survey Finds." Society for Human Resource Management. Published September 10. www.shrm.org/resourcesandtools /hr-topics/talent-acquisition/pages/flexible-work-critical-retention.aspx.

———. 2016. "Flexible Work Options in Health Care Can Result in a Win-Win." Published June 19. www.shrm.org/hr-today/news/hr-news/pages/flexible-work-health-care .aspx.

Maxim Staffing Solutions. 2022. "Medical Staffing." Accessed June 11. www.maximstaffing .com/medical-staffing/.

Minton-Eversole, T. 2020. "Updating Job Descriptions During the Pandemic." Society for Human Resource Management. *HR Magazine*. Published November 23. www.shrm.org /hr-today/news/hr-magazine/winter2020/pages/updating-job-descriptions-during -the-pandemic.aspx.

Morgeson, F. P., M. Spitzmuller, A. S. Garza, and M. A. Campion. 2016. "Pay Attention! The Liabilities of Respondent Experience and Carelessness When Making Job Analysis Judgments." *Journal of Management* 42 (7): 1904–33.

Moss, D. 2018. "11 Ways to Build Stronger Teams." *Book Blog* (Society for Human Resource Management). Published March 28. www.shrm.org/hr-today/news/hr-magazine/book -blog/pages/11-ways-to-build-stronger-teams.aspx.

Newman, S. A., and R. C. Ford. 2021. "Five Steps to Leading Your Team in the Virtual COVID-19 Workplace." *Organizational Dynamics* 50 (1): article no. 100802. https://doi .org/10.1016/j.orgdyn.2020.100802.

Newman, S. A., R. C. Ford, and G. W. Marshall. 2020. "Virtual Team Leader Communication: Employee Perception and Organizational Reality." *International Journal of Business Communication* 57 (4): 452–73.

Nobile, R. J. 1991. "The Law of Performance Appraisals." Personnel 35 (1): 1–2.

NSI Nursing Solutions. 2022. *2022 NSI National Health Care Retention & RN Staffing Report*. Published March. www.nsinursingsolutions.com/Documents/Library/NSI _National_Health_Care_Retention_Report.pdf.

O'Laughlin, D. J., J. A. Bold, D. R. Schroeder, and P. M. Casey. 2019. "Professional Satisfaction of Advanced Practice Providers in Primary Care Specialties." *Journal of Healthcare Management* 64 (5): 279–90.

O*NET Resource Center. 2022. "The O*NET Content Model." Accessed June 10. www.onetcenter.org/content.html.

Parker, S., D. Andrei, and A. Van den Broeck. 2019. "Why Managers Design Jobs to Be More Boring Than They Need to Be." Society for Human Resource Management. Published June 12. www.shrm.org/resourcesandtools/hr-topics/organizational-and-employee-development/pages/why-managers-design-jobs-to-be-more-boring-than-they-need-to-be.aspx.

Potratz, A. 2018. "Avoiding Headaches with the 'Other Duties as Assigned' Provision." Business Journals. Published March 7. www.bizjournals.com/bizjournals/how-to/human-resources/2018/03/avoiding-headaches-with-the-other-duties-as.html.

Radin, J., and C. Korba. 2020. "COVID-19 as a Catalyst: The Future of Work and the Workplace in Healthcare." *Deloitte Insights*. Published November 12. www2.deloitte.com/us/en/insights/industry/health-care/health-care-workforce-trends.html.

Ramadevi, D., A. Gunasekaran, M. Roy, B. K. Rai, and S. A. Senthilkumar. 2016. "Human Resource Management in a Healthcare Environment: Framework and Case Study." *Industrial and Commercial Training* 48 (8): 387–93.

Rosell, L., N. Alexandersson, O. Hagberg, and M. Nilbert. 2018. "Benefits, Barriers and Opinions on Multidisciplinary Team Meetings: A Survey in Swedish Cancer Care." *BMC Health Services Research* 18 (1): 1–10.

Saad, L., and B. Wigert. 2021. "Remote Work Persisting and Trending Permanent." Gallup. Published October 13. https://news.gallup.com/poll/355907/remote-work-persisting-trending-permanent.aspx.

Schellenbarger, S. 2016. "Win Over a Remote Boss." *Wall Street Journal*, March 16, D1, D3.

Seibert, S. E., G. Wang, and S. H. Courtright. 2011. "Antecedents and Consequences of Psychological and Team Empowerment in Organizations: A Meta-Analytic Review." *Journal of Applied Psychology* 96 (5): 981.

Seimens Healthineers. 2022. "Our Response to COVID-19." Accessed October 2. www
.siemens-healthineers.com/covid-19.

Smith, M. 2022. "Flexible Jobs Are Attracting 7 Times More Applicants Than In-Person
Roles." CNBC. Published March 4. www.cnbc.com/2022/03/04/flexible-jobs-are
-attracting-7-times-more-applicants-than-in-person-jobs.html.

Snell, S. A., and S. Morris. 2018. *Managing Human Resources*, 18th ed. Boston: Cengage
Learning.

Society for Human Resource Management (SHRM). 2022a. "Performing Job Analysis."
Accessed April 15. www.shrm.org/resourcesandtools/tools-and-samples/toolkits
/pages/performingjobanalysis.aspx.

———. 2022b. "SHRM Opposes Bill Mandating 32-Hour Workweek in California." Press
release, April 13. www.shrm.org/about-shrm/press-room/press-releases/pages/shrm
-opposes-bill-mandating-32-hour-workweek-in-california.aspx.

———. 2019. *Leave and Flexible Working: SHRM Employee Benefits 2019*. Published June.
www.shrm.org/hr-today/trends-and-forecasting/research-and-surveys/Documents
/SHRM%20Employee%20Benefits%202019%20Leave%20and%20Flexible%20
Working.pdf.

Stoller, James K. 2021. "Building Teams in Health Care." *Chest* 159 (6): 2392–98.

Sussman, A. C., and J. Zumbrun. 2016. "Gig Economy Spreads Broadly." *Wall Street Journal*, March 26, A1–A2.

Tyler, K. 2013. "The Basic Job Description Is the Foundation of Nearly Every HR Function."
HR Magazine. Published January 1. www.shrm.org/hr-today/news/hr-magazine/pages
/0113-job-descriptions.aspx.

US Bureau of Labor Statistics (BLS). 2022. "Occupational Outlook Handbook: Healthcare
Occupations." Updated September 8. www.bls.gov/ooh/healthcare/home.htm.

US Department of Health and Human Services (HHS). 2020. *Securely Teleworking in
Healthcare*. Report no. 202003260918. Published March 26. www.hhs.gov/sites
/default/files/securely-teleworking-healthcare.pdf.

US Equal Employment Opportunity Commission (EEOC). 1978. "Uniform Guidelines for Employee Selection Procedures." *Federal Register* 43 (166): 38290–315.

Walker, A. 2022. "What Does a Travel Nurse Do & How Can You Make the Most Money as a Travel Nurse?" Nurse.org. Published October 1. https://nurse.org/articles/how-to -make-the-most-money-as-a-travel-nurse/.

Wolcott, J. 2010. "Providence in Everett Enjoys National Attention for Its High-Quality, Low-Cost Health Care Model." Herald*Net*. Published February 2. www.heraldnet.com /business/providence-in-everett-enjoys-national-attention-for-its-high-quality-low -cost-health-care-model/.

Zelinka, E., J. Brevig, J. McDonald, and R. Jin. 2010. "The Perfusionist's Role in a Collaborative Multidisciplinary Approach to Blood Transfusion Reduction Cardiac Surgery." *Journal of Extra-Corporeal Technology* 42 (1): 45–51.

CHAPTER 5

RECRUITMENT, SELECTION, AND RETENTION

Gabriella "Gabbi" J. Maris and Bruce J. Fried

Joan Hampton is director of a nationally known home health care agency that is currently recruiting for a nurse manager. The nurse manager job involves supervising other nursing and ancillary staff, managing the scheduling process, coordinating nursing activities with other home health services, providing direct service, and ensuring compliance with policies, procedures, and regulatory requirements. Following are the major job requirements:

- Current and unencumbered state license to practice as a registered nurse
- Three years' experience as a registered nurse, at least one of which must involve full-time experience in providing direct patient care in the home health setting; one year supervisory or management experience preferred
- Current cardiopulmonary resuscitation (CPR) certification
- Ability to assess patient status and identify requirements relative to age-specific needs
- Excellent verbal and written communication skills
- Strong interpersonal skills and ability to work in teams
- Knowledge of federal and state rules and regulations, Joint Commission standards, and other regulatory requirements
- Strong fiscal planning and human resources management skills

Sandra Goodman has been with the home health agency for five years and has proven to be a diligent, hardworking, and reliable employee. For the past 15 months, she has held the temporary position of nurse manager and has done well. She sets high standards for herself, has become an expert in the agency's reporting and billing procedures, and understands regulatory requirements and the agency's financial operations. Sandra has applied for the permanent position of nurse manager, for which she has many of the qualifications.

Along with Sandra, Michaela Roberts is being considered for the position. Michaela has seven years of experience in home health care and three years of experience as an emergency department nurse. However, she has no supervisory experience and limited financial skills. Several nurses in the agency interviewed and liked Michaela and recommended her.

Joan is inclined to offer the job to Sandra because of her experience and because she could step into the position with little training. However, several nurses have come to Joan indicating that they will quit if Sandra is offered and accepts the job: Although Sandra has performed well in the temporary nurse manager role, she has an autocratic personality and management style that have alienated many of the nurses. She has been known to lose her temper and insult the staff for failure to follow procedures.

Whereas the other nurses support hiring Michaela, Joan believes that she does not have the time to properly orient and train her for the position. Michaela is bright and indicates a willingness and aptitude to learn, but Joan is much more comfortable and secure with Sandra. However, she is also concerned with morale problems and turnover if she decides to hire Sandra. What advice would you give Joan, and why?

INTRODUCTION

Staffing an organization can be defined as "getting the right people into the right positions in a timely manner." Yet while this definition is correct, staffing also involves determining where to find applicants, defining criteria for selecting the most appropriate applicant, and doing all we can to keep people—retain them—in the organization. Thus, *recruitment* refers to various methods to generate a pool of applicants. *Selection* involves choice: Who among applicants should be chosen for a particular position? *Retention* refers to keeping people in the organization after they have been hired.

We address these three important processes—recruitment, selection, and retention—in a single chapter because they are integrally interrelated and also related to other human resources management (HRM) functions. These human resources (HR) practices are highly interdependent. For example:

◆ The success of recruitment efforts determines in part how selective an organization can be in hiring. An organization can be more selective when a relatively large supply of qualified applicants apply.

◆ Developing a recruitment plan that seeks to generate a pool of qualified applicants depends first and foremost on the existence of an accurate, current, and comprehensive job description.

◆ When an organization selects the applicant who is the best fit for the position, it may have a higher likelihood of retaining the individual. A poor selection process may lead to a misalignment of goals between the organization and individual, which could result in dissatisfaction and turnover.

◆ Employee retention may be enhanced by the effectiveness of an organization's orientation and socialization processes.

As with all HRM functions, organizations must be cognizant of legal considerations when developing and implementing recruitment and selection procedures. For example, it is illegal under Title VII of the Civil Rights Act to discriminate in hiring based on race, gender, and other characteristics, and those involved in employee selection need to be diligent in ensuring that these factors do not bias hiring decisions. (Chapter 3 on legal issues includes a detailed description of Title VII; chapter 11 discusses diversity, inclusion, and belonging in the workplace.)

RECRUITMENT

Recruitment refers to the means by which organizations attract qualified individuals on a timely basis and in sufficient numbers and encourage them to apply for jobs. In starting

recruitment
The means by which organizations attract qualified individuals on a timely basis and in sufficient numbers and encourage them to apply for jobs.

a recruitment effort, organizations should be clear about the nature of the job and the desired qualifications. They may also consider additional questions, such as the following:

- Should we recruit and promote from within, or should we focus on recruiting external applicants—or both?

- Should we consider alternative approaches to filling jobs with full-time employees, such as outsourcing, flexible staffing, and hiring part-time or temporary employees?

- How important is it for employees to fit in with the culture of the organization? Should we seek applicants who *fit* the current culture or those who would *add* to the current culture?

An organization's recruitment success depends on many factors, including the attractiveness and reputation of the organization and the job; the community and the labor market in which it is located; unemployment and the nature of the economy; the organization's work climate and culture; managerial attitudes and behavior; and workload.

Recruitment can be challenging for many organizations and specific jobs. This task has been worsened by the COVID-19 pandemic. In a 2021 poll, 65 percent of executives indicated being "very" or "extremely" concerned that they could recruit candidates following the discovery of the highly contagious Omicron variant of the virus (Maurer 2022). The labor market experienced unprecedented turnover and numbers of open job positions, making recruitment an obstacle for human resources departments in various industries across the United States (Maurer 2021).

In the next section, we look at how individuals make choices about seeking jobs and accepting job offers. These are extremely personal decisions, dependent on a multitude of factors. However, there are some common factors that recruiters need to be aware of.

FACTORS THAT INFLUENCE JOB CHOICE

Accepting a job offer is a big decision with possibly lifelong implications. What do potential employees look for in a job? After an individual is offered a position, how does that person make the decision to accept or reject the offer? Applicants are certainly concerned with compensation, benefits, and opportunities for career mobility and promotion. They may also consider the availability of other positions and the competitiveness of the job market.

Applicants are sensitive to the attitudes and behaviors of the recruiter or whoever is their first contact with the organization. First impressions are potent, because the sense of whether one fits in with the organization is often decided at this stage. Early negative first impressions may be difficult to reverse. Applicants are more likely to accept positions in organizations that share their values and style.

These considerations lead to the important issue of how organizations communicate their values to potential job applicants. The examples that follow indicate how organizations communicate their values and why they should be considered an "employer of choice." Consider the following recruitment message for WakeMed, a large health system in Raleigh, North Carolina:

At WakeMed Health & Hospitals, we are guided by a simple—yet powerful—mission: to improve the health and well-being of our community by providing outstanding and compassionate care to all. To deliver on this mission, WakeMed employs the "best minds and the biggest hearts" in the business. Our team includes over 8,500 experienced registered nurses, technologists, medical professionals, support staff, and a medical staff of more than 1,200 physicians and advanced practice providers who are dedicated to putting patients first. When it comes to culture and benefits, we recognize that when we take good care of our employees, our employees can take even better care of our patients. We proudly offer competitive salaries that reflect background, experience and special skills. Our benefits programs are designed to give you and your family the support you need for today while planning for a successful tomorrow. We promote diversity in the workplace, provide equal employment opportunity for all qualified applicants, and we participate in E-verify. We think it's pretty simple—we care for our employees and our employees care for the community. (WakeMed 2022)

The Cleveland Clinic focuses on joining "a culture that encourages excellence":

Healthcare is evolving, and Cleveland Clinic is transforming healthcare—pushing the limits and paving the way to establish new practices and set new standards. We believe in moving away from the physician-centric model of care and instead putting the patient at the center of everything we do. We are developing the most innovative patient experiences with our constant investment in continuing education and leadership development programs. (Cleveland Clinic 2022)

On the Mayo Clinic's recruitment website home page, one powerful sentence stands alone: "Imagine a job could change your life." Farther down the page, under its clickable "Physicians & Scientists" header, Mayo Clinic goes on to state:

At Mayo Clinic, you are a colleague of some of the most talented, experienced physicians in the world. You work with patients, conditions, and cases that most doctors will never encounter in their professional lives. In our physician-led environment, you will discover a culture of teamwork, professionalism and mutual respect where the needs of the patient always come first. (Mayo Clinic 2022)

Emory Healthcare promotes itself to prospective employees in this simple but powerful message about "The Emory Difference":

> You'll be joining a workforce of 25,000 individuals strong—and a health care system recognized for its commitment to our employees. Time and time again, our community turns us to deliver exceptional care. In fact, nearly half of the physicians recognized in the 2020 "Top Doctors" issue of *Atlanta Magazine* are physicians who are part of the Emory Healthcare Network, Emory medical staff, or faculty of Emory University School of Medicine. We're proud to have more Top Doctors recognized than any other Atlanta health system. (Emory Healthcare 2022)

Kaiser Permanente emphasizes the value that each individual member of its workforce provides:

> Fiercely committed to our members, our mission, our communities, and each other, every single member of the Kaiser Permanente team is essential to our success. Together, our more than 280,000 dedicated professionals work to advance Kaiser Permanente's commitment to delivering a healthier tomorrow. Driven by passion, we strive to take Kaiser Permanente to the next level. With the wellness of our patients and our communities at heart, we work to revolutionize health and care in America and around the world. (Kaiser Permanente 2022b)

Organizations promote themselves as good places to work by appealing to a variety of employee needs, interests, and values. Understanding the factors that affect job choice is central to developing effective recruitment strategies. It is valuable to distinguish between individual characteristics and job characteristics.

individual characteristics
Personal considerations that influence a person's job decision.

Individual characteristics are personal considerations that influence a person's job decision. The factors that lead a family physician to accept employment with a rural health center may be distinct from those that lead a nurse to accept employment with an urban teaching hospital. Life and career stage may affect the relative importance of these factors. **Job characteristics** may include such job-related decision-making factors as flexibility, compensation, hours, challenge and responsibility, advancement opportunities, job security, geographic location, and employee benefits. It is difficult for an organization to create the "perfect" job for all because no two individuals are the same in their individual characteristics and job preferences (see the related Critical Concept sidebar "The 'Perfect' Job").

job characteristics
Job-related decision-making factors such as flexibility, compensation, hours, challenge and responsibility, advancement opportunities, job security, geographic location, and employee benefits.

Compensation and benefits (discussed more fully in chapters 8 and 9) are often key elements in an individual's decision to accept a position. For some healthcare positions, compensation is complicated by differential pay rates, hiring or signing bonuses, incentive pay, and relocation assistance. *Hot-skill premiums*—temporary pay premiums added to base pay for employees with in-demand skills—have become particularly common in

> ## ⚠ CRITICAL CONCEPT
> ### The "Perfect" Job
>
> Is there a "perfect" job? Rarely. When a person accepts a job, they usually must make compromises and trade-offs. For example, the organization may not be able to meet an applicant's initial expectations for pay, but professional development and career opportunities may offset the lower salary enough to make the job seem worth accepting. A parent concerned about childcare responsibilities may reject an offer of an otherwise ideal job because the two-hour daily commute places undue stress on the child and parent. Employers and applicants must be aware of the multiple factors that go into a job acceptance decision and the weight placed on each of these factors.

healthcare, although premiums usually remain in place even after market pressures ease. These premiums may be structured in a number of ways, including incorporating the premium into the individual's salary, providing a hiring or annual bonus, and slotting an employee into a higher salary range than is usually warranted for that job (Berthiaume and Culpepper 2008; Mercer 2014). Skill premiums have been highly utilized to recruit nurses during the COVID-19 pandemic. Healthcare administrators have been required to offer nurses increased pay as many have quit their jobs to become *travel nurses* (registered nurses [RNs] who work in a short-term role at a hospital or other healthcare facility that is experiencing a nursing shortage), whereby they can earn significantly more money (Walker 2022). Advertised pay rates for travel nurses increased by 67 percent from January 2020 to January 2022 (Vesoulis and Abrams 2022). As nurses observe this trend, more leave their jobs to become travel nurses, and thus the cycle continues. It is unclear how or when this cycle will end. (See the accompanying Current Issue sidebar "Travel Nurses and the COVID-19 Pandemic." See also the previous discussion in chapter 4, including its Current Issue sidebar "It Pays to Be (or Hire) a Travel Nurse!")

The relative importance of compensation to employees is complex. Under certain circumstances, employees may leave an organization for another to obtain only a small incremental increase in compensation. In other cases, employees may stay with an organization even when offered a generous improvement in compensation by another organization.

The amount of challenge and responsibility inherent in a particular job is frequently a key job choice factor; professionals typically seek positions that put their training to best use. Many applicants value jobs with advancement and professional development opportunities; however, there are often limited opportunities for clinical staff to advance while continuing to do clinical work. Advancement opportunities for technically trained

CURRENT ISSUE
Travel Nurses and the COVID-19 Pandemic

As the demand for nurses increased during the COVID-19 pandemic, hospitals began to rely more heavily on utilizing travel nurses. During this time, travel nurse salaries increased by 200 percent, to an average hourly rate of $154 per hour, which calculates to an annual salary of roughly $320,320. In comparison, the average staff RN salary was $52.95 per hour, or $110,144 annually (NSI Nursing Solutions 2022). When hospitals are forced to pay these higher premiums, they have less money available to increase wages for staff RNs. Many frustrated staff RNs then leave their roles to become travel nurses, and the cycle continues (Vesoulis and Abrams 2022). To lower costs, hospitals must decrease their use of travel nurses; eliminating 20 travel nurses will save the average hospital $4,203,680. However, only 22.7 percent of the hospitals surveyed indicated they would do so (NSI Nursing Solutions 2022).

individuals may be limited to management positions. For some individuals, taking on management responsibilities may lead to feelings of loss of their professional identity. In addition, clinically trained people often do not have the required management skills to work in a managerial capacity. The clinical nurse specialist (CNS) position is an example of how nursing has sought to retain nurses in clinical positions while offering career growth and professional development (see "Did You Know?" sidebar).

Job security is a traditional determinant of job choice. The healthcare and business environment can be characterized by great uncertainty during organizational change including mergers, acquisitions, and downsizing. Fear regarding job security was once limited largely to blue-collar workers, but professionals and managers may also feel at risk.

Research shows that flexibility is now the most sought-after benefit for job seekers. This finding is largely a result of the need for increased flexibility that was caused by the COVID-19 pandemic. Many workers experienced flexibility in scheduling or the ability to work from home and are now seeking jobs where they can continue to experience these benefits. Thus, many employers are now using flexibility as a way to attract job applicants (Maurer 2022).

Geographic location and other lifestyle concerns may be highly important to applicants, particularly for individuals in dual-income families, in which the potential for spouse employment may play a significant role in acceptance decisions.

Employee benefits continue to grow in importance in job acceptance. In some highly competitive fields, many companies have moved beyond traditional benefits, such as health insurance and vacation pay, into such areas as membership in country clubs or health clubs, on-site day care, and financial counseling. Exhibit 5.1 illustrates how three hypothetical job applicants may assess the relative importance of particular job features. Although the table oversimplifies the job choice process, it shows how personal preferences and life circumstances may affect job choice. The first column briefly describes each applicant. The second column states each applicant's minimum standards for acceptance along five dimensions: pay, benefits, advancement opportunities, travel requirements, and the ability to work from home. These five dimensions are sometimes categorized as *noncompensatory standards*. That is, no other element of the job can compensate if these standards are not met; they are deal breakers. Column 3 is a description of a hypothetical job being considered by the job applicant. After looking at the minimum standards for job acceptance (column 2), consider how each of the three applicants would assess the acceptability of the particular job. For example, person 2 views health insurance as an absolute requirement for acceptance, and person 3, who does not like to travel and considers working from home very important, will be unlikely to accept a job that requires substantial travel and only limited opportunity for working at home, regardless of anything else.

? DID YOU KNOW?
Clinical Nurse Specialists

Clinical nurse specialists (CNSs) are advanced practice nurses (APNs) who hold a master's or doctoral degree in a specialized area of nursing practice. Their area of clinical expertise may be in

- a population (e.g., pediatrics, geriatrics, women's health),
- a setting (e.g., critical care, emergency room),
- a disease or medical subspecialty (e.g., diabetes, oncology),
- a type of care (e.g., psychiatric, rehabilitation), or
- a type of health problem (e.g., pain, wounds, stress).

In addition to the conventional nursing responsibilities that focus on helping patients prevent or resolve illness, a CNS's scope of practice includes diagnosing and treating diseases, injuries, and disabilities within the individual's field of expertise. Clinical nurse specialists provide direct patient care, serve as expert consultants for nursing staff, and take an active role in improving healthcare delivery systems. Research has demonstrated that the work of clinical nurse specialists has been associated with reduced hospital costs and length of stay, reduced frequency of emergency room visits, and fewer complications among hospitalized patients.

Source: Adapted from National Association of Clinical Nurse Specialists (2022).

EXHIBIT **5.1**
Three Hypothetical
Applicants

Applicant	Minimum Standards for Job Acceptance	Job Description
Person 1:		*Job:* Provider relations coordinator
23 years old, single	*Pay:* At least $55,000	*Pay:* $60,000
	Benefits: Health insurance; retirement savings plan	*Benefits:* Health and dental insurance with relatively high deductible; optional vision insurance; basic and supplementary life insurance; short- and long-term disability coverage; retirement savings plan with employer matching
	Advancement opportunities: Very important	*Advancement opportunities:* Recruitment done internally and externally
	Travel requirements: Unimportant	*Travel requirements:* Average 25 percent travel
	Work from home: Unimportant	*Work from home:* Fully remote position
Person 2:		*Job:* Healthcare consultant
Sole wage earner for large family	*Pay:* At least $85,000	*Pay:* $80,000
	Benefits: Health and dental insurance; optional vision insurance; basic and supplementary life insurance; short- and long-term disability coverage; retirement savings plan with employer matching	*Benefits:* Health, dental, and vision insurance with low deductibles and copays; basic and supplementary life insurance; short- and long-term disability coverage; retirement savings plan with employer matching
	Advancement opportunities: Very important	*Advancement opportunities:* Strong history of promotions within one year
	Travel requirements: Prefers not to travel more than 25 percent of the time	*Travel requirements:* Average 50 percent travel
	Work from home: Flexibility occasionally needed	*Work from home:* Must be on-site when not traveling
Person 3:		*Job:* Academic medical center research assistant for multisite clinical trial
Spouse of high-wage earner	*Pay:* At least $35,000	*Pay:* $45,000
	Benefits: Unimportant	*Benefits:* Health and dental, and voluntary vision insurance; basic and supplementary life insurance; short- and long-term disability coverage; retirement savings plan with employer matching
	Advancement opportunities: Unimportant	*Advancement opportunities:* None
	Travel requirements: Difficulty traveling more than one week per year	*Travel requirements:* Three days per quarter to meet with other research site personnel
	Work from home: Very important	*Work from home:* Option to work remotely two days per week

The Recruitment Process

The human resources plan should provide a foundation of information for recruitment. A human resources plan includes specific information about the organization's strategies, the range of jobs required by the organization, core organizational values, and recruitment and hiring practices. Those involved in recruitment and selection must have a thorough understanding of the position that needs to be filled, the position's required competencies, and its relationship to other positions in the organization. A recruitment effort should begin with a job analysis that provides information about the job and required qualifications. (Job analysis and job design are discussed in chapter 4).

Recruitment requires an assessment of the external environment, specifically information about the supply of potential applicants, and a market analysis that provides information about compensation and benefits for people who hold similar jobs in other organizations. Many organizations obtain this information through wage and salary surveys. It is also important to review the results of previous recruitment efforts. Have they been successful? What have been the major obstacles faced in identifying and hiring qualified applicants? External recruitment sources, such as colleges, competing organizations, professional associations, and social media, should be assessed to determine whether they have yielded successful candidates in the past. Logistical issues may also be examined, such as the timing of a recruitment effort; for some positions, seasonal factors are relevant, such as the time of graduation from nursing school.

As part of planning for recruitment and reviewing past recruitment efforts, additional questions include the geographic scope of the search. Will this job require an international search, or will the local labor market suffice? Or is it possible to recruit an individual from inside the organization, or a previous job applicant? For internal searches, an updated **human resources information system (HRIS)** can provide helpful information. Many systems include information described in exhibit 5.2. A **skills inventory** database maintains information on current employees' performance records, skills and certifications, educational background, training completed, seminars attended, work history, and other job-related data. Such a database is useful for many HR functions, including broadening the pool of applicants and succession planning. (Succession planning, discussed in chapter 6, is particularly critical for higher-level employees.) Some organizations use **personnel replacement charts**, which show the current position and promotability for each position's potential replacement. In addition, former employees who left under favorable conditions are increasingly a source of recruitment, making up 4.5 percent of all new company hires in 2021. These "boomerang" employees who come back after time away bring unique strengths to an organization, such as a familiarity with organization processes and culture that makes *onboarding* (orienting and training) them less expensive (Vozza 2022). Boomerang employees may send an implicit message to current employees about the desirability of the work environment. Some may return after pursuing opportunities that broadened

human resources information system (HRIS) An integrated information system designed to provide managers with information for human resources decision making.

skills inventory A manual or electronic system designed to keep track of employees' experiences, education, skills, knowledge, abilities, and other characteristics.

personnel replacement charts Lists of key personnel in an organization and their possible replacements in the organization, including information about their current performance and promotability.

HRIS Data	Uses in Recruitment
Skills and knowledge inventory	Identifies potential internal candidates
Previous applicants	Identifies potential external candidates
Recruitment source information: • Yield ratios • Cost • Cost per applicant • Cost per hire	Helps in the analysis of cost effectiveness of recruitment sources
Applicant tracking	Provides an automated method for labor-intensive recruitment tasks
Employee performance and retention information	Provides information on the success of recruitment sources used in the past

their skill sets or industry knowledge, taking time away because of personal circumstances, or having been part of pandemic firings (Vozza 2022). Organizations should also maintain records of applicants who were not hired in the past because they may be qualified for positions that arise in the future.

Recruitment and selection can be costly, and we often do not consider the wide range of expenses associated with hiring. For a single position, the cost may be equivalent to, and in some cases may exceed, the position's annual salary. As a result, it is important to measure the efficiency of the recruitment process. Exhibit 5.3 shows measures for assessing the effectiveness and efficiency of the recruitment process. Each of these measures varies depending on the job, and a good HRIS and cost-accounting system can help the organization understand the major costs associated with recruitment and selection.

internal recruitment
An approach to employee recruitment that emphasizes identifying and recruiting applicants who are already members of the organization.

external recruitment
An approach to employee recruitment that emphasizes identifying and recruiting applicants outside the organization.

RECRUITMENT SOURCES

An initial step in the recruitment process is *applicant sourcing*—specifying where qualified applicants are located. **Internal recruitment** refers to promotion or transfers from within the organization. **External recruitment** regards applicants from outside the organization. Each source of applicants has its advantages and disadvantages, as shown in exhibit 5.4. Internal recruitment may be advantageous because candidates are generally already known to the organization; managers are familiar with the applicant's past performance and future potential. Internal applicants are also familiar with the organization and culture and therefore may not require as much start-up time or onboarding as external applicants. Internal hiring may also build morale because it signals to other employees that there are opportunities for advancement.

Type of Cost	Expenses
Cost per hire	Advertising, agency fees, employee referral bonuses, recruitment fairs and travel, and sign-on bonuses
	Staff time: salary; benefits; and overhead costs for employees to review applications, set up interviews, conduct interviews, check references, and make and confirm an offer
	Processing costs: opening a new file, medical examination, drug screening, and credential checking
	Travel and lodging for applicants
	Background checks
	Drug-testing expenses
	Travel and expenses (for applicant and recruiter)
	Prehire health screenings
	Immigration expenses
	Relocation expenses
	Orientation and training
	Note: Cost-per-hire measures can be calculated for all referral sources or by individual referral source.
Application rate	Ratio of referral factor: number of candidates to number of openings
	Applicants per posting
	Qualified applicants per posting
	Protected class (group of individuals protected under a particular law) applicants per posting
	Number of internal candidates, number of qualified internal candidates
	Number of external candidates, number of qualified external candidates
Time to hire	Time between job requisition and first interview
	Time between job requisition and offer
	Time between offer and acceptance
	Time between job requisition and starting work

EXHIBIT 5.3
Measures of Recruitment Effectiveness and Efficiency

(continued)

Exhibit 5.3
Measures of
Recruitment
Effectiveness and
Efficiency
(continued)

Type of Cost	Expenses
Recruitment source effectiveness	Offers by recruitment source
	Hires by recruitment source
	Employee performance (using performance evaluation information and promotion rates)
	Employee retention by recruitment source
	Offer acceptance rate (overall and by recruitment source)
	Percent of accepted hires who stay in position
Quality of hire	Number of high-quality applications received
	Recruitment tools, technology/AI to identify high-quality applicants
Interview-to-hire ratio	Number of applicants interviewed to number of applicants hired for position
Offer acceptance rate	Percent of candidates offered position who accept position
	Timeliness of offers by company
	Competitiveness of offers by company
Time in process step	Amount of time spent in each step of hiring process
	Identification of bottlenecks, waste in process steps, including application process
Application drop-off rate	Number of applicants who begin application but do not finish it
Recruiter effectiveness	Response time
	Time to fill
	Cost per hire
	Acceptance rate
	Employee performance
	Retention
Miscellaneous	Materials and other special or unplanned expenses
	Reference checking
	New employee orientation

Sources: Adapted from Fitz-enz and Davison (2002); Industry Today (2022); Society for Human Resource Management (SHRM 2015).

Recruiting Internal Candidates	
Advantages	**Disadvantages**
May improve employee morale and encourage valued employees to stay with the organization	May cause morale problems among those not selected
Permits greater assessment of applicant abilities; candidate is a known entity	May deny the organization fresh talent and new ideas if it depends too heavily on internal recruitment
Draws from pool of applicants who have a good understanding of the organization	May require strong training and management development activities
May be faster, and may involve lower cost for certain jobs	May manifest the Peter Principle (employees may be promoted to their highest level of competence and then be promoted to and remain at a level at which they are incompetent)
Provides good motivation for employee performance	
May reinforce employees' sense of job security	May cause ripple effect in vacancies

Recruiting External Candidates	
Advantages	**Disadvantages**
Brings new ideas into the organization	May cause morale problems for internal candidates who were not selected
May be less expensive than training internal candidates	May be difficult to obtain reliable information about applicant
Draws candidates who come without prior negative relationships with others in the organization and without involvement in organizational politics	May identify candidate who has technical skills but does not fit the culture of the organization
	May require longer adjustment and socialization for new employee compared with internal candidate

Exhibit 5.4
Advantages and Disadvantages of Internal and External Recruitment

Peter Principle
The theory that employees in an organization will be promoted to their highest level of competence and then be promoted to and remain at a level at which they are incompetent.

One possible negative result of internal recruitment is that technically skilled employees who are promoted to management positions may lack management skills. Such promotion exemplifies the classic **Peter Principle**, a common phenomenon in which successful employees continue to be promoted until they reach one position above their level of competence (Peter and Hull 1969). The principle also notes that on reaching one's level of incompetence, it is likely that the individual will not be fired, and thus the tendency is for others to work around this person (Asghar 2014), which leads to organizational inefficiency.

The Peter Principle, named after educator Laurence Johnston Peter, who popularized the theory, can be avoided with careful employee selection and training procedures. Exhibit 5.5 provides an example of the Peter Principle in a scenario to consider and discuss.

Internal recruitment may also cause disarray in the organization. A promotion may create a *ripple effect*—one individual moves into another position, leaving a vacancy; this vacancy, in turn, is filled by someone else, who causes another vacancy, and so forth.

An advantage of external recruitment is that candidates from outside the organization may bring new ideas. The organization can specifically target candidates with the skills needed rather than settle for an internal candidate who may know the organization but lack the required skills and knowledge for the position. External applicants tend to be unencumbered by political alliances and internal conflict and therefore may be easier to bring into a difficult political environment than an internal applicant. This lack of complication is often one of the reasons for selecting a new chief executive officer from outside the organization.

Some applicants are not easy to characterize as internal or external—for example, those who have worked for the organization in a temporary or part-time capacity. This practice is common in nursing, where travel nurses or agency nurses may apply or be recruited for full-time positions.

EXHIBIT 5.5

An Example of the Peter Principle

Consider the following scenario:

Miranda had been a labor and delivery nurse for four years. She took initiative, trained incoming nurses, had great patient satisfaction, and demonstrated high commitment to her job. Miranda was largely regarded as the strongest member of the labor and delivery nursing team, so, when the unit was looking for a nurse manager, Miranda's name was naturally brought up. After discussion with leadership, Miranda expressed some hesitancy about leaving direct patient care but ultimately accepted the new role. Miranda excelled as a nurse manager, and it was only a matter of months before she was asked to become the nurse coordinator at the organization's nearby community hospital. Again, Miranda hesitated but ultimately took the role after persuasion from leadership. After eight months in the role, it became clear that Miranda was not a good fit for this position, as she lacked many of the management competencies needed to manage all of nursing. Miranda was no longer performing well and was ultimately unhappy in the role, and so she left the organization.

"How did we get to this point?" members of leadership asked as they sat in a meeting to discuss a new plan for the role. "Not only have we lost our nurse coordinator and now must rehire for that role, but we've also lost our best labor and delivery nurse."

How much of Miranda's poor performance as a nurse coordinator is the responsibility of leadership? What are the organizational consequences of Miranda's resignation? In the future, how should the organization go about filling this role to avoid a similar outcome?

Current employees sometimes refer friends and acquaintances for positions in an organization. **Employee referral** is an excellent source of applicants because the referring employee knows the organization and can do an initial screening of the applicant. Employee referral can be a powerful recruitment strategy, yielding employees who are more likely to be extended an offer, accept an offer, remain in the position longer, and have better job performance (Gautier and Munasinghe 2020). Additionally, referral pools of candidates have become more diverse over time, according to a Glassdoor survey reported by Miles (2022). Use of referral programs may help organizations achieve their diversity recruiting initiatives (Miles 2022). Employee referral programs are becoming increasingly popular in healthcare. For example, Kaiser Permanente offers cash rewards for employee referrals for selected positions and has a webpage devoted to employee referrals (Kaiser Permanente 2022a). According to Todd Davis, a recruiting consultant with a large California physician group, "Peer referrals are the most powerful recruiting tool. When I get a referral in-house I know the candidate is going to have the skills and the interest, because a colleague has already made the contact" (Zappe 2006, 30). Some employee referral programs give financial rewards to employees if the new hire remains with the organization for a defined period.

> *employee referral*
> An approach to recruitment in which current employees help identify promising applicants.

Employment agencies or executive search firms may be used to recruit applicants. These organizations help firms with recruitment and provide assistance for people seeking jobs. Agencies may specialize in particular types of searches and typically work either on a commission or on a flat-fee basis.

THE RECRUITING MESSAGE IN RECRUITMENT AND SELECTION

The major objective of the recruitment and selection process is to ensure that the right applicant will accept the job offer. Effective recruitment messages ensure that applicants understand the job and its qualifications. Overall, the following four types of information should be communicated:

1. *Applicant qualifications*: education, experience, credentials, and any other qualifications, within legal constraints

2. *Job basics*: title, responsibilities, compensation, benefits, location, and other pertinent working conditions (e.g., night work, travel, promotion potential)

3. *Application process*: deadline, resume, cover letter, transcripts, references, and submission instructions

4. *Organization and department basics*: name and type of organization, department, and other information about the work environment

The recruiting message should be presentable in a flexible online format because more than half of US adults use the internet in their job searching (see the related "Did You Know?" sidebar).

THE REALISTIC JOB PREVIEW

realistic job preview
A process in which applicants are given a true picture of a job, including its strengths and weaknesses, through verbal information, discussions with job incumbents, employee shadowing, and other methods.

A **realistic job preview** refers to the process of giving applicants a true picture of a job, including its strengths and weaknesses. This preview may include verbal information, discussions with job incumbents, employee shadowing, and other methods. Use of realistic job previews is related to higher performance and lower attrition from the recruitment process, lower initial expectations, lower voluntary turnover, and lower turnover overall. The use of realistic job previews in healthcare is growing and has been shown to be an evidence-based retention strategy (Gilmartin, Aponte, and Nokes 2013). Some employers have begun using virtual reality (VR) to give applicants an even more realistic job preview. VR can allow applicants to practice job tasks, meet potential coworkers, and experience the physical workspace without physically entering the office. This method has been particularly helpful for remote hiring during the COVID-19 pandemic, as it simulates an on-site feel for the prospective employee (Grensing-Pophal 2022).

EVALUATING THE EFFECTIVENESS OF RECRUITMENT

Recruitment can be expensive, so it is important to evaluate the effectiveness of recruitment efforts to reduce wasteful spending. The evaluation process depends on reliable and comprehensive applicant data, a well-functioning HRIS, applicant quality and disposition, and recruitment costs. Common measures of a recruitment function's success include the following:

◆ *Quantity and quality of applicants.* Effective recruitment yields a sufficiently large number of candidates who meet the minimum requirements.

◆ *Overall recruitment cost and cost per applicant.* This calculation helps determine the cost-effectiveness of recruitment methods.

◆ *Diversity of applicants.* Attracting applicants who represent the diversity of the service population is frequently a recruitment goal.

◆ *Recruitment time or time-to-fill.* The more time spent on proper recruitment, the greater the chance that the ideal candidate will emerge. However, a lengthy recruitment process frequently results in greater costs, disruption of service or work, and potential dissatisfaction among current employees who must fill in for the vacant position.

SELECTION

Selection refers to the process of evaluating job applicants with the goal of identifying the best person for a position. Employee selection is largely a matter of predicting which applicant is most likely to achieve success. *Success* may be defined as not only proficiency in the job but also longevity in the position.

Selection must be distinguished from simple hiring. In selection, a careful analysis of an applicant's qualifications is performed. However, job offers are sometimes extended with little or no systematic evaluation of applicants—a common example is hiring an individual based on political or personal connections, where non-job-related factors supersede objective measures of suitability. There are also circumstances when a position must be filled quickly or when there is a labor shortage in a particular area. In these cases, an organization may simply hire whoever meets the minimum qualifications. In organizations in remote or otherwise undesirable locations, applicant availability may be the key criterion for selection.

selection
The process of evaluating job applicants with the goal of identifying the best person for a position.

THE QUESTION OF FIT

person–job fit
The traditional foundation for human resource selection, in which a successful applicant possesses the knowledge, skills, and abilities required for the job.

Selection processes seek primarily to ensure **person–job fit**. The goal of selection is simply to determine whether the applicant has the competencies to do the job. An accurate job description provides the foundation for beginning the process of evaluating the qualifications of applicants.

In many circumstances, an organization may be interested in more than technical qualifications. There may also be interest in how well a potential employee will fit into the organization, which could include teamwork and community, relationships with coworkers, customer service attitudes and skills, and work-related values. **Person–organization fit** can be critical to job success. Person–organization fit is almost always more difficult to assess than technical skills, and it is sometimes impractical to hire on this basis, particularly when recruitment for difficult-to-fill positions may generate only a few applicants. It is important to point out the potential for bias in hiring for person-organization fit. If an organization only hires those who fit the current culture, they may unfairly favor applicants who are similar to themselves and those around them.

person–organization fit
An approach to employee selection that emphasizes the extent to which an applicant's attitudes, behaviors, values, and beliefs align with the culture, norms, and values of the organization.

Decision makers should discuss the appropriate balance between person–job and person–organization fit, depending on the position. Hiring a nurse on a psychiatric unit requires a high level of person–organization fit because nurses must interact closely with staff and patients, and fitting into the therapeutic setting is critical to success, whereas person–organization fit may be less important in hiring a medical data-entry clerk, whose work may entail relatively little interaction with others. It is becoming more popular for organizations to seek "cultural add" as opposed to "cultural fit," with the emphasis placed on what the individual can *add* to the organization's culture (see Debate Point sidebar for further exploration of this idea). There are also situations in which employers want to purposely hire people who do not fit the current norms, such as when the culture is dysfunctional and the organization wants to bring in people with new ideas and approaches to improve it.

SELECTION TOOLS

selection tools
Information-gathering methods used in employee selection to obtain job-related information about applicants.

To help make hiring decisions, employers use **selection tools**—information-gathering methods used to obtain job-related information about applicants. These methods include application forms, criminal records checks, psychological tests, interviews, employment verification, drug screening, educational background, reference checks, verification of professional certifications, motor vehicle records checks, social media checks, and credit history.

A **critical incidents analysis** is useful for uncovering the hidden or less formal aspects of job performance. The process starts with identifying examples of excellent and poor performance by current or potential jobholders. Examples may be drawn from the experience of current jobholders and from the insights of individuals knowledgeable about the job. For a new job in an organization, we may need to ask people knowledgeable about job

(X) DEBATE POINT

The idea of fit in hiring may be important to facilitate teamwork and positive working relationships. However, is there a risk that too much fit can be negative? If we only want people in our organization who are like us, is there the possibility that the organization may become stagnant and miss opportunities for improvement? Furthermore, can the idea of fit really be a disguise for simple prejudice bias? It has been suggested that *cultural fit* is "an incredibly vague term, often based on gut instinct. The biggest problem is that while we invoke cultural fit as a reason to hire someone, it is far more common to use it to not hire someone" (Wharton School, University of Pennsylvania 2015). Another writer noted that in many organizations, the idea of fit "has gone rogue"—interviews with 120 decision makers found that many were using subjective personal criteria rather than screening for individuals who could succeed in the organization's culture (Rivera 2015). More recently, hiring for *cultural add* has been suggested as an alternative to cultural fit. Cultural add can be explained as "[flipping] Culture Fit on its head. Instead of seeing difference as a weakness, it encourages seeing the value. Culture Add is asking 'What can this person bring to the table?' as opposed to 'Does this person fit the mould?'" (Kinkaid 2022). Is it better to focus on culture fit or culture add in hiring? Under what circumstances might it be helpful to hire people who specifically do not fit the current "norms" or culture of the organization? Does hiring for "fit" prevent diversity of thought and, if so, does focusing on cultural "add" effectively mitigate this shortcoming?

expectations to obtain examples of poor and excellent performance. After these behaviors are collected, they are grouped into job dimensions. Measures may then be developed for each dimension. The critical incidents approach involves the following four steps:

1. Identify people knowledgeable about the job.
2. Generate critical incidents that represent positive and negative performance.
3. Identify key job dimensions based on these incidents.
4. Develop selection tools to assess applicants on these dimensions.

Exhibit 5.6 provides examples of three critical incidents and the job dimensions in which each incident is grouped. This exercise yields a thorough understanding of the job's

critical incidents analysis
A process of generating lists of good and poor examples of job performance and translating them into employee selection criteria; this process helps uncover less formal—but important—aspects of performance.

technical requirements, formal qualifications, and informal but critical aspects of success-ful performance.

REFERENCE CHECKS

Most organizations rely on certain sources for checking applicants' background. These sources include information from references, criminal records, driving records, social media,

Job	Critical Incident	Job Dimensions
Physician, orthopedics department	In an administrative staff meeting to review plans for the coming year, this physician exhibited strongly condescending and rude behaviors toward other team members.	• Ability to work in teams • Respect for other professionals
Nurse, emergency department	After a school bus accident, the emergency department was overwhelmed with children and frightened parents. This nurse effectively and appropriately managed communication with parents and obtained assistance from elsewhere in the hospital.	• Creativity and resourcefulness • Leadership • Ability to work effectively under crisis conditions • Strong interpersonal skills
Medical director, public health department	The local media reported an outbreak of salmonella that resulted in one child being hospitalized. The outbreak was traced to a fast-food restaurant that had been inspected by health department personnel less than one week earlier. The health department was blamed for not preventing the outbreak. This medical director conducted a thorough internal investigation and found that it was an isolated incident caused by mishandling of food on a single occasion. She communicated effectively at a press conference, defending the health department and assuring the public of the safety of local eating establishments.	• Effective crisis manager • Strong communication and media skills • Strong sense of public accountability

and credit checks. The usefulness of reference checks is questionable. Agreement among people who provide a reference for the same applicant may be low. This discrepancy may be explained by the reluctance to provide negative feedback and the possibility that raters may be evaluating different aspects of job performance. It is also not clear that information provided in references is predictive of future performance. The following explanations have been suggested for the poor predictive power of reference checks:

◆   Many measures used in reference checks have low reliability; where reliability is low, validity is also low.

◆   Individuals who provide references frequently only use a restricted range of scores—typically high—in evaluating applicants. If almost all reference checks are positive, they are likely to be poor predictors of job performance.

◆   In many instances, applicants preselect the people who provide the references and are highly likely to select only those who will provide a positive reference.

How can the validity and usefulness of reference checks be improved? Research in this area offers the following conclusions (Gatewood, Barrick, and Feild 2018):

◆   The most recent employer tends to provide the most accurate evaluation of an individual's work.

◆   Reference givers are more likely to provide an honest assessment if they have had adequate time to observe the applicant.

◆   References tend to be more valid if the applicant is the same gender, ethnicity, and nationality as the reference giver.

◆   Reference checks are likely to be valid when the old and new jobs are similar in content.

Reference checks are widely used, but their usefulness is decreasing. Some organizations advise their employees to provide only minimal information about former employees, such as job title and dates of employment, to reduce the liability of the referring organization to lawsuits from the hiring organization (through charges of negligent hiring) or the applicant (through claims of defamation of character). Exhibit 5.7 provides some basic guidelines for the appropriate use of references.

A less formal way to glean information about these applicants is to examine them via social media, as many organizations are now doing. (See the accompanying Did You Know? sidebar "Employers, Candidates, and the Internet"; also refer back to the chapter 3 section "Employee Screening and Selection Procedures" and its Current Issue sidebar "Using Social Media in the Hiring Process" for discussion of the legal concerns in this regard.)

EXHIBIT 5.7
Guidelines for the
Appropriate Use of
Reference Checks

1. Ask for and obtain only job-related information.
2. Do not ask for information that may be deemed illegal.
3. Secure written permission from applicants to contact their references; this permission may be included on the application form.
4. Make sure that individuals who check references are trained in how to interview them, probe for additional information, and accurately record reference information.
5. Record reference information in writing.
6. Use the reference-checking process to confirm information provided by the applicant and to identify gaps in the employment record.
7. Consider using preemployment information services, particularly for sensitive positions.

JOB INTERVIEWS

A job interview is used for virtually all positions, largely because information from the application, references, and other documentation is usually incomplete. Interviews are sometimes given the greatest weight in hiring decisions but may present problems with reliability and validity, such as the following:

- Because applicants are not usually given interview questions in advance, they may not have the opportunity to prepare answers that would showcase their abilities.

- Questions may not be standardized, and interviewers might ask different questions of people applying for the same position.

- Some types of interview questions that are designed to get a general sense of an applicant's personality may be irrelevant to the role and responsibilities of the job, such as, "If you were a flavor of ice cream, what flavor would you be and why?"

- Where multiple interviewers are used, their questions, interview style, and interpretation and scoring of answers may vary.

- Untrained interviewers may ask questions that may lead to legal difficulties for the organization, such as inquiries about disabilities or plans for marriage, starting a family, or retirement.

Even with these shortcomings, the interview can be an effective and efficient method of acquiring information about applicants (see the Critical Concept sidebar "A Successful Interview Process"). Furthermore, it can be a valuable recruitment tool because it allows the interviewer to highlight the positive features of the organization and the job.

DID YOU KNOW?
Employers, Candidates, and the Internet

In a Harris Poll survey of 1,005 hiring managers, 71 percent indicated that social media screenings are an effective preemployment screening method (Karami 2020). Additionally, 67 percent indicated that they use social media to research job candidates, and 55 percent reported not hiring a candidate as a result of something found in the social media screening (Karami 2020).

In a 2017 CareerBuilder survey (Salm 2017), the following were top reasons for not hiring a candidate following a social media screening:

- Candidate posted provocative or inappropriate photographs, videos, or information: 39 percent
- Candidate posted information about them drinking or using drugs: 38 percent
- Candidate made discriminatory comments related to race, gender, or religion: 32 percent
- Candidate criticized their previous company or a fellow employee: 30 percent
- Candidate lied about qualifications: 27 percent
- Candidate had poor communication skills: 27 percent
- Candidate was linked to criminal behavior: 26 percent
- Candidate shared confidential information from previous employers: 23 percent
- Candidate's screen name was unprofessional: 22 percent
- Candidate lied about an absence: 17 percent
- Candidate posted too frequently: 17 percent

Yet in the internet age, a job candidate who does not appear to use social media at all may attract attention in another way, making prospective employers wonder whether the candidate is hiding something. In the Harris Poll, 21 percent of hiring managers said they would not be likely to consider an applicant who had no social media presence (Karami 2020).

unstructured interview
An interview technique in which questions are usually open-ended and guided by applicant answers and interviewer preferences.

Job interviews can be unstructured or structured. An **unstructured interview** is an interview technique in which questions are usually open-ended and guided by applicant answers and interviewer preferences. It is not actually unstructured per se (i.e., lacking any structure) but rather is not standardized and has a less formal structure than the structured interview. Unstructured interviews may be subjective and can be less reliable than structured

> ⚠ **CRITICAL CONCEPT**
> A Successful Interview Process
>
> The job interview is a common method of assessing applicants. To be used successfully, interviews should
>
> - focus on assessing applicants' ability to carry out the essential functions of the job;
> - be planned in advance;
> - use questions that all interviewers have agreed are important, relevant, and job-related;
> - not include questions that may lead to legal difficulties, such as inquiries regarding religion or marital status;
> - use the same set of questions for all applicants for the same position;
> - allow time for the interviewee to ask questions;
> - include a planned time immediately after each interview to score and assess applicants; and
> - be conducted by individuals trained in interviewing techniques.
>
> To be sure that interview questions obtain the information sought and are phrased in an understandable manner, questions should optimally be pretested prior to their use in an actual interview.

structured interview
An interview technique in which questions and related constructs (and sometimes, preferred answers) are developed in advance.

situational interview question
A type of interview question in which applicants are asked how they would handle specific situations that may arise on the job.

behavioral interview question
A type of interview question in which applicants are asked to relate how they handled a specific type of job situation in their past experience.

interviews. However, their flexibility may help interviewers probe for unique information about applicants that could be overlooked using a structured interview format.

In a **structured interview**, questions are clearly job related and based on the results of a thorough job analysis (as described in chapter 4). Situational, behavioral, job-knowledge, and worker-requirement questions are most commonly posed during a structured interview. The same structured interview is typically used for all applicants for a particular position.

A **situational interview question** asks applicants to describe how they would handle a hypothetical work scenario. A **behavioral interview question** asks candidates how they have previously handled a situation that is similar to a situation they may encounter on the job. Following is a scenario and related situational and behavioral questions. The applicant characteristics being assessed are the ability to handle a stressful situation, ability to deal appropriately with the public, and professionalism.

Scenario: You are the administrator of an emergency department at a medium-sized community hospital. It is 8:30 p.m. and you receive a call from the clerk responsible for check-in. There has been an influx of patients for reasons that are unclear. Patients must wait up to five hours to be seen by a physician, and their anger and frustration increase as they wait. The lobby is filling up as patients wait to be seen, allowing for no social distancing.

Situational interview questions: As the administrator, how would you handle this situation? What would you do first? Who are the most critical people or groups that you would need to consider? What are their particular interests and concerns? How and what would you communicate to them?

Behavioral interview questions: Think about a situation on your last job in which you were faced with upset patients or customers. What was the situation? What did you do? What was the outcome?

A **job-knowledge interview question** assesses whether applicants have the knowledge needed to do the job. For example, an applicant interviewing for the position of operating room nurse may be asked such questions as the following:

♦ What are three things you should always ask a patient before surgery?

♦ How would you prepare a patient for an appendectomy?

♦ How would you prepare the operating room for a patient with a latex allergy?

A **worker-requirement interview question** seeks to determine whether the candidates are able and willing to work under the specific conditions of the job. For example, applicants for a consulting position may be asked whether they are able and willing to travel for a designated portion of their work.

Whatever interview format is used, interviews must be conducted with the following guidelines in mind:

1. Prepare yourself in advance. For an unstructured interview, learn the job requirements so that you can formulate appropriate questions. For a structured interview, become familiar with the questions to be asked. Review materials or information about the applicant as well.

2. Before the interview, make sure that the physical environment in which the interview will take place is organized, clean, well lit, and a comfortable temperature. (If the interview is being conducted through an online video platform rather than in person, see exhibit 5.8, which provides tips for a successful virtual interview.)

3. As the interview begins, describe the job and invite questions about it.

4. Put the applicant at ease, and convey an interest in the person. A purposely stressful interview is not desirable, as other reliable and ethical methods can

job-knowledge interview question
A type of interview question asked to assess whether applicants have the knowledge needed to do the job.

worker-requirement interview question
A type of interview question asked to determine whether applicants are able and willing to work under the specific conditions of the job.

be used to assess an applicant's ability to handle stress. A stressful interview reflects poorly on the organization.

5. Recognize that interviewing may not be everyone's greatest strength. If the applicant fails to answer an important part of a question, ask a follow-up question to get the information you are seeking.

6. Do not come to premature conclusions—positive or negative—about the applicant, particularly in unstructured interviews.

7. Listen carefully, and ask for clarity if the applicant's responses are vague.

8. Observe and take notes on relevant aspects of the applicant's dress, mannerisms, and affect, such as motivation, attitude, expressed interest in the job, and comfort with the interview process.

9. Provide an opportunity for the applicant to ask questions throughout the interview, at the end, or both.

10. Do not talk excessively. Remember that an interview is an opportunity to hear from the applicant.

11. Do not ask questions that are unethical or that put the organization in a legally vulnerable position (see exhibit 5.9 and also refer to chapter 3).

12. Explain the selection process that comes after the interview. This explanation includes informing applicants when they should expect to receive the results of their job application and interview, how this information will be communicated, and the process by which applicants can inquire with questions about the job or the disposition of their application.

13. Evaluate the applicant as soon as possible after the interview.

APPLICATIONS AND RESUMES

Application forms and resumes contain useful information about applicants. The major drawback to these selection tools is that they may misrepresent an applicant's qualifications. *Resume inflation* occurs when applicants misrepresent any aspect of their background or qualifications.

Several methods can be used to improve the usefulness and quality of application forms. First, create an addendum to the application that asks applicants to provide information specific to the open position. Second, include a statement on the form that requires

EXHIBIT 5.8
Tips for a
Successful Virtual
Interview

The COVID-19 pandemic required many organizations to conduct interviews virtually on a video platform, such as Zoom, rather than in person. This may be a trend that continues far into the future because of the convenience of virtual interviewing, with fewer scheduling barriers and no travel needed.

For both the interviewer and the interviewee, the following are some tips for a successful virtual interview:

- Set up your equipment in a quiet, well-lit room. Avoid backgrounds that are distracting or cluttered; use a background filter if necessary.
- Test your video and audio well before the start of the interview. Ensure that your voice can be heard clearly through the microphone.
- Secure a stable internet connection. Have the interviewer's phone number or email nearby in case you become disconnected and need to notify them.
- Place the camera at eye level. Place books or boxes underneath your computer to raise it to that level, if necessary.
- When speaking, look not just into the camera but through the camera. This replicates the feeling of maintaining eye contact and exudes confidence. Do not just look at the other person's video.

the applicant to indicate that all the information reported is accurate; the applicant should then be required to sign or initial this statement. Third, ensure that questions that may lead to legal difficulties (e.g., marital status, height, weight) are excluded from the form.

ABILITY AND APTITUDE TESTS

Some organizations use **ability and aptitude tests** that assess such applicant traits as personality type, honesty, integrity, cognitive reasoning, and fine motor coordination. Organizations need to be sure that the traits measured in these tests are relevant to the particular job. Debate continues about the validity of many of these tests.

ASSESSMENT CENTERS

An **assessment center** is a multidimensional method of evaluating applicants. Applicants are assessed using various methods, including interviews, work simulations, leaderless group discussions, and role playing. Assessment centers set up situations wherein individuals perform activities similar to those they may encounter in a job. Some companies establish assessment centers to determine how well current employees will handle new jobs or assignments.

ability and aptitude tests
A wide range of employment tests that evaluate applicants along dimensions relevant to the job; for example, personality type, honesty, integrity, cognitive reasoning, and fine motor coordination.

assessment center
Physical location where testing is done, or a series of assessment procedures that are administered, professionally scored, and reported to hiring personnel, to evaluate applicants or assess employees' developmental needs.

Exhibit 5.9
Inappropriate
and Appropriate
Interview
Questions

Personal and Marital Status

Inappropriate	Appropriate
How tall are you? *(but acceptable if a safety requirement)*	*(When it is part of the job)* Are you able to lift 50 pounds and carry it 20 yards?
How much do you weigh? *(but acceptable if a safety requirement)*	*Note: After hiring, inquiring about marital status for tax and insurance forms is allowed.*
That's a beautiful ring! Who's the lucky person?	
Do you live alone or with someone else?	
Do you smoke?	

Parental Status and Family Responsibilities

Inappropriate	Appropriate
Are you pregnant?	This job requires overtime occasionally. Would you be able and willing to work overtime as necessary?
Do you plan to have children?	
How many children do you have?	Travel is an important part of this job. Would you be willing to travel as needed?
What are your childcare arrangements?	Would you be willing to relocate if necessary?
	Note: After hiring, inquiring about dependent information for tax and insurance forms is allowed.

Age

Inappropriate	Appropriate
How old are you?	Do you meet the legal minimum age for the hours or working conditions of this position?
In what year were you born?	
When did you graduate from high school or college?	*Note: This question may be asked to verify compliance with state or federal labor laws.*
What year will you reach retirement age?	*Note: After hiring, verifying legal minimum age with a birth certificate or other form of identification and asking for age on insurance forms are permissible.*

National Origin

Inappropriate	Appropriate
Where were you born?	Are you authorized to work in the United States?
Where are your parents from?	May we verify that you are a legal US resident, or may we have a copy of your work visa status?
What is your heritage?	
What is your native tongue?	To meet the bilingual requirement as posted for this job, can you read, write, and speak Spanish fluently?
What languages do you know? *(too general to be appropriate)*	*(appropriate as relevant to the job)*

EXHIBIT 5.9
Inappropriate
and Appropriate
Interview
Questions
(continued)

Race or Skin Color

Inappropriate	Appropriate
What is your racial background?	This organization is an equal opportunity employer. Race is required information only for affirmative action programs. If you wish to be considered for these programs, will you tell me which racial category you identify with?
Are you a member of a minority group?	
You look so tan. Have you been out in the sun?	

Religion or Creed

Inappropriate	Appropriate
What religion do you follow?	What days are you available to work?
Do you attend a house of worship regularly?	Are you able to work the hours of our required schedule?
Which religious holidays would you need to be taking off from work?	
A lot of people in the department are Catholic. Are you?	

Disability

Inappropriate	Appropriate
Do you have any disabilities?	*(When it is part of the job)* Are you able to lift 50 pounds and carry it 20 yards?
How does your condition affect your abilities?	*(When it is part of the job)* Are you able to kneel?
Have you had recent illnesses or hospitalizations?	Are you able to perform the essential functions of this job with or without reasonable accommodations?
What is your medical history?	
or Please fill out this medical history document.	
When was your last physical exam?	*Note: After hiring, asking about the person's medical history on insurance forms is allowed.*
Are you HIV-positive?	

Criminal Record

Inappropriate	Appropriate
Have you ever been arrested?	*Note: Questions about convictions by civil or military courts are appropriate if accompanied by a disclaimer that the answers will not necessarily cause loss of job opportunity. Generally, employers can ask only about convictions and not arrests (except for jobs in law enforcement and security clearance) when the answers are relevant to job performance.*
Have you ever spent a night in jail?	

(continued)

Exhibit 5.9
Inappropriate
and Appropriate
Interview
Questions
(continued)

	Affiliations	
Inappropriate		**Appropriate**
To what clubs or associations do you belong?		Do you belong to any professional or trade groups or other organizations that you consider relevant to your ability to perform this job?

Note: Questions listed in this table are generally not illegal, with the exception of questions about disability status (illegal under the Americans with Disabilities Act as Amended). For example, it is not illegal to ask an applicant's date of birth, but it is illegal to deny employment to an applicant solely because the person is 40 years of age or older—unless age is a bona fide occupational qualification. In this case, the question is not illegal, but a discriminatory motive for asking is illegal. An unknown or ambiguous motive is what makes any question with discriminatory implications inappropriate. If an individual is denied employment, having been asked such questions can lead the applicant to claim that the selection decision was made on the basis of age, gender, or another characteristic on which it is illegal to discriminate.

RETENTION

The demand for healthcare workers is increasing and will continue for the foreseeable future. Among the most commonly cited reasons for this increased demand are population growth, the aging of the population, improved diagnostic techniques that enable earlier detection of disease, and heightened consumer demand for a full range of diagnostic and therapeutic technologies. Chronic workforce shortages will continue to characterize the health system, although the extent of many health workforce shortages varies by health profession and geographic factors.

Among the most critical employee groups in the healthcare workforce is registered nurses. According to US Bureau of Labor Statistics (BLS 2022) projections, the number of employed registered nurses is expected to grow by 6 percent, from about 3.1 million nurses in 2021 to about 3.3 million nurses in 2031, with about 203,200 RN job openings each year, on average, largely because of individuals changing to other occupations or retiring. Nursing labor markets are local, and there will likely be considerable geographic variation in the extent to which the supply of nurses meets demand. Major cities such as Washington, DC, tend to have below-average RN employment, while higher-than-average RN employment rates are found in some smaller metropolitan areas, including Rochester, Minnesota; Bloomsburg-Berwick, Pennsylvania; Morgantown, West Virginia; Durham–Chapel Hill, North Carolina; and Ann Arbor, Michigan. Highly populated areas tend to experience the greatest nursing shortages, as the number of nurses graduating each year is not large enough to keep up with demand for healthcare services within most large cities (NurseJournal Staff 2022). Therefore, assuming increased demand for RNs, certain regions are likely to experience shortfalls in the supply of nurses.

CRITICAL CONCEPT
Why People Leave Jobs

People leave jobs for many reasons. Some reasons may be addressed by managers, while others may be out of managers' control. Among the most common reason for people leaving jobs is dissatisfaction with their supervisor. It is often said that "people leave their boss, not their job." Even with an effective retention program in place—including good pay—retention may be jeopardized by a manager who alienates employees through inappropriate behavior and interactions. When designing a retention initiative, it is key to ensure that supervisors exercise their authority and interact with staff appropriately.

These broad societal factors are largely out of the control of individual healthcare organizations, and each organization has its own mission, service profile, and workforce requirements. Each organization also faces its unique external environment, reputation, labor market, and competitors. These local conditions, more than national trends, substantially influence workforce needs and worker vacancy rates. These vacancy rates, in turn, highlight the need for organizations to do a better job at recruiting, selecting, and retaining staff. In this section, we explain our concern with turnover, enumerate the costs associated with turnover, discuss the factors that contribute to turnover (see the Critical Concept sidebar "Why People Leave Jobs"), and explore the methods proven to improve retention. Although we use the nursing shortage as a basis to explore the turnover and retention issue, we are aware also of the shortages in other healthcare professions, such as among radiologic technicians, primary care physicians, and pharmacists. The lessons in our discussion, however, are applicable to other professions as well.

DISTINGUISHING TURNOVER FROM RETENTION

It is important to make a distinction between the separate, although related, concepts of **turnover** (departures from an organization) and **retention** (maintaining employee employment with an organization). Many organizations view retention as the inverse of turnover and, as a result, miss out on critical trends that are happening within their systems. The **turnover rate** is a simple ratio that provides only a summary of the gross movement in and out of the organization during a specific time frame (usually one year). Rates may also be narrowed to certain types of turnover, such as voluntary turnover, or calculated for a

turnover
Employee departures from an organization.

retention
Maintaining employee employment with an organization.

turnover rate
A ratio providing a summary of the gross movement in and out of the organization during a specific time frame.

retention rate
The percentage of specific individuals or cohorts that enter and exit the organization.

particular department or discipline. The **retention rate**, on the other hand, is the percentage of specific individuals or cohorts that enter and exit the organization. The key distinction is that retention views an individual or a group as an entity; therefore, retention allows for a more thorough examination of how the loss of one individual or cohort influences retention strategies and productivity.

For example, an organization that experiences a slight decline in turnover (say, from 20 percent to 18 percent) over a five-year period may think that it is doing well in addressing its retention problem. However, during that same five-year time span, the retention rate of individuals who have between 5 and 15 years of service declined (say, from 70 percent to 35 percent). These rates may indicate that the organization has difficulty retaining experienced employees and needs to explore and implement new retention strategies. Alternatively, the organization may discover that while its turnover rate decreased, the retention rate among physical therapists dramatically declined. In other words, the overall turnover rate may mask severe retention problems. Overall, organizations need to thoroughly examine both turnover and retention rates to successfully deal with the challenge of staff shortages.

TRENDS AND FACTORS IN NURSE TURNOVER

In examining nurse turnover, researchers have sought to understand the trends in turnover as well as the factors associated with turnover. The demand for healthcare workers has increased, but the quality of their work life has decreased. This issue has been amplified during the COVID-19 pandemic. The turnover rate for staff nurses in 2021 was 27.1 percent, an 8.4 percent increase from 2020. For the first time in the history of the Nursing Solutions survey, the RN turnover rate was higher than the hospital average turnover rate, which in 2021 was 25.9 percent. Nurses working in surgical services experienced the lowest turnover rate (18.8 percent), while nurses in step-down (30.2 percent), telemetry (30.2 percent), and emergency (29.7 percent) experienced the highest; certified nursing assistant (CNA) turnover also was among the highest in nursing, at 35.5 percent (NSI Nursing Solutions 2022).

Particularly worrisome to many nurse leaders is the disturbingly high rate of turnover of newly licensed and newly hired RNs. According to the Nursing Solutions survey, 31 percent of newly hired RNs left their job in their first year in 2021 (NSI Nursing Solutions 2022). This statistic has drawn attention to the need for careful attention to assessing work environments, measuring turnover, and improving onboarding processes.

Whereas turnover certainly affects patient care, it also represents a significant cost to hospitals. The costs associated with employee termination, recruitment, selection, hiring, and training are substantial. It is estimated that the average cost of each RN turnover is $46,131, and a mere 1 percent increase in RN turnover costs the average hospital $262,289 per year (NSI Nursing Solutions 2022).

Compared with hospitals, nursing homes face exceedingly high levels of nursing turnover. Information from a study published in *Health Affairs* revealed a stunning median turnover rate of 94 percent among all employees in skilled nursing care centers in the United States in 2017 and 2018 (Spanko 2021). Among RNs, the mean turnover rate was an alarming 140.7 percent. Among direct care staff, CNAs had the largest mean turnover rate at 129.1 percent; licensed practical nurses (LPNs) experienced a median turnover rate of 114.1 percent (Spanko 2021). During the COVID-19 pandemic, some short-term and long-term care facilities were forced to close because of lack of staffing. Such closures impacted patient care in several ways, including creating additional patient flow and capacity challenges for hospitals that could not discharge patients to long-term care facilities (Chatterjee 2022). The situation is similarly challenging for home care agencies. A 2022 survey of home health and home care professionals found that 80 percent of respondents identified staffing as their greatest challenge not related to COVID-19; further, 32 percent indicated that retention was their top staffing concern (Filbin 2022).

STUDIES ON NURSING TURNOVER

Dissatisfaction has been cited as a key reason for turnover and departure from the nursing profession in the twenty-first century. In a worldwide study, nurses surveyed in the United States had the highest rate of job dissatisfaction—41 percent, four times higher than the dissatisfaction score of the professional workforce in general (Aiken et al. 2001; Albaugh 2003). Oft-cited reasons for dissatisfaction include work schedules; lack of opportunities for advancement; work environment; lack of independence at work; inadequate wages; issues associated with professional status; poor, unresponsive, and unsupportive management; work overload; high patient-to-nurse ratios; inadequate staffing; and lack of respect and appreciation from management (McHugh et al. 2011; Vaidya 2013). These issues have been compounded by the COVID-19 pandemic, as nurses have experienced increased unprecedented stressors and burnout. A 2021 survey found that only 32 percent of nurses were "very" or "completely" satisfied with their job, as opposed to 52 percent before the pandemic (Davis 2021). The most commonly reported reasons for poor nurse retention surround stressful work environments, poor leadership, inadequate staffing, burnout, and inadequate compensation (Advisory Board 2021). For other reasons for nurse turnover, see the related "Did You Know?" sidebar.

Length of work shift may also affect nurse retention. A 2012 study found that nurses who worked 10 hour or longer shifts were two and a half times more likely to report burnout and dissatisfaction with their job than those who worked shifts less than 10 hours (AMN Healthcare 2018). A survey conducted by Medscape found that while a substantial proportion of nurses had regrets about their choice of profession, 60 percent of APNs, 56 percent of RNs, and 48 percent of LPNs would choose their profession again (Peckham 2015).

DID YOU KNOW?
Top Reasons for Nurse Turnover

A McKinsey & Company survey of 400 frontline nurses found the following factors associated with nurse turnover to be most important (Berlin et al. 2021):

1. Insufficient staffing levels (59 percent)
2. Demanding nature/intensity of workload (56 percent)
3. Emotional toll of job (54 percent)
4. Don't feel listened to or supported at work (51 percent)
5. Physical toll of job (50 percent)
6. Family needs and/or other competing life demands (46 percent)
7. Seeking higher paid position (43 percent)
8. Insufficient personal protective equipment (42 percent)
9. Retirement (38 percent)
10. Too much uncertainty or lack of control (37 percent)
11. Lack of respect from some patients or their families (30 percent)
12. Don't feel prepared or trained sufficiently (26 percent)
13. Fear of COVID-19 infection for self or family (23 percent)
14. Don't see an appealing professional development pathway (21 percent)

Turnover has an adverse effect on organizational performance and quality of care. Numerous studies have documented the relationship between a shortage of registered nurses, increased nurse workload, and quality of care (Cimiotti et al. 2012; Needleman et al. 2011; Tubbs-Cooley et al. 2013). Nurses tend to agree that shortages affect the quality of care. Buerhaus and colleagues (2005) found that three-quarters of RNs believe that nursing shortages lead to problems in the quality of care, quality of their work lives, and the amount of time nurses can spend with patients. These concerns have been present among nurses for many years. An earlier well-cited survey conducted by the American Nurses Association (ANA 2001) found that 75 percent of nurses felt that the quality of nursing care had declined. Among respondents who claimed that quality has suffered, more than 92 percent cited inadequate staffing as the reason, and 80 percent indicated nurse dissatisfaction. The ANA survey also reported that more than 54 percent of respondents would not recommend the profession to their children or friends. Confirming evidence from earlier studies, Aiken and colleagues (2001) argued that low nurse-to-patient ratios are strongly related to higher levels of dissatisfaction and emotional exhaustion. These studies highlight the connections among nurse dissatisfaction, turnover, and quality of care that had had existed long before the COVID-19 pandemic, which then exacerbated the situation.

RETENTION STRATEGIES

Many of the factors associated with effective recruitment are also applicable to retention because a person's reasons for accepting an employment offer and for staying with that employer are often similar. Retention strategies are a necessary follow-up to recruitment. With the opportunities available to nurses in other organizations and work roles, retention strategies are as essential as compensation and training.

Organizations can somewhat control turnover, but their influence is limited. The market profoundly affects the movement of employees, and retention strategies have not achieved the consistent success once anticipated. Each organization needs to develop its own retention strategies and tailor them to the particular circumstances of the institution.

The following generic retention strategies have proved effective:

◆ Selecting the right employees.

◆ Improving orientation and onboarding processes by creating a "buddy" program and otherwise helping new employees establish professional and personal relationships with colleagues.

◆ Offering competitive compensation. Compensation comes in many forms, including signing bonuses, premium and differential pay, forgivable loans, bonuses during employment, and extensive benefits.

◆ Structuring jobs so that they are more appealing and satisfying by carefully assigning and grouping tasks, providing employees with sufficient autonomy, allowing flexible work hours and scheduling, enhancing the collegiality of the work environment, and instituting work policies that are respectful of individual needs.

◆ Putting in place a strong management and supervisory team. The idea that people quit their bosses, not their jobs, is especially true in nursing, as nurses sometimes leave because of poor working relationships with their managers or other healthcare professionals.

◆ Making opportunities for career growth available.

◆ Providing adequate staffing to control patient care workloads.

◆ Monitoring turnover to identify specific root causes, including identifying managers whose departments have high turnover rates.

◆ Developing and implementing ways to retain valued employees.

◆ Attempting to reverse a nurse's decision to leave an organization.

An evidence-based protocol was developed that identifies key factors related to decreasing turnover (Gess, Manojlovic, and Warner 2008). This protocol emphasizes approaches that improve organizational commitment among nurses, focusing on facilitating autonomy, improving communication, and offering rewards and recognition to nursing staff. Specific retention goals include encouraging staff members to seek learning experiences, encouraging and supporting creative freedom in practice, supporting a participative management structure with shared governance, acknowledging work and providing positive feedback, listening to what nurses are saying about patient care, implementing shared governance models, and increasing communication. The American Nurses Credentialing Center (ANCC) established the **Magnet Recognition Program** to acknowledge and reward healthcare organizations that demonstrate and provide excellent nursing care. Designated Magnet hospitals are characterized by fewer hierarchical structures, decentralized decision making, flexibility in scheduling, positive nurse–physician relationships, and nursing leadership that supports and invests in nurses' career development (ANCC 2022). Magnet hospitals have been found to have better patient outcomes and higher levels of patient satisfaction (McHugh et al. 2011). Compared with other hospitals, Magnet institutions have lower turnover and higher job satisfaction among nurses (Huerta 2003; Upenieks 2002). These findings suggest that becoming a Magnet healthcare organization has the potential to increase nurse satisfaction and improve retention (Drenkard 2010).

Magnet Recognition Program
A program established by the American Nurses Credentialing Center to acknowledge and reward healthcare organizations that demonstrate and provide excellent nursing care.

INTERNATIONAL RECRUITMENT AND MIGRATION

Recruiting health professionals from other countries can help address the US health workforce shortage. In the United States, about 25 percent of physicians were born and educated in other countries, and about 5.4 percent of nurses were educated overseas, according to the American Association of International Healthcare Recruitment (AAIHR 2022). Because of demand for their skills, US physicians and nurses have had opportunities to seek employment internationally since the late twentieth century, and professionals trained abroad are important parts of healthcare systems in many countries (see the Current Issue sidebar "Push and Pull Factors in Physician and Nurse Migration").

The implications of international migration of physicians and nurses are a source of increasing debate. While physicians and nurses who migrate to other countries can benefit from better working conditions or salaries in their destinations, their movement can exacerbate inequalities in the worldwide distribution of healthcare workers. Developing countries whose citizen doctors leave lose their investments in education and training, income tax revenue, and potential for national growth, and their population's health may

CURRENT ISSUE
Push and Pull Factors in Physician and Nurse Migration

Physician and nurse migration are often discussed in terms of push and pull factors. *Push factors* motivate physicians and nurses to leave their home countries, while *pull factors* cause them to choose particular receiving countries.

Push factors include low compensation, poor working conditions, political instability and insecurity, inadequate housing and social services, and lack of educational opportunities and professional development.

Pull factors include opportunities for professional training and career advancement, personal development, better job opportunities, a stable political environment, and higher wages.

Source: Li, Nie, and Li (2014).

be adversely affected. In nations where healthcare workforce shortages are already severe, the need to replace professionals who emigrate depletes the system's resources, claiming funds that normally go toward fighting diseases and promoting public health. These factors only worsen existing healthcare disparities between developed and developing countries.

Recruitment of workers from abroad has important ethical implications, but thus far there has been little guidance for developing appropriate policies. An exception is the United Kingdom, which is one of the few major receiving countries to develop a specific policy to guide the recruitment of internationally trained physicians and nurses. Its National Health Service (NHS) has created the Code of Practice on International Recruitment, which includes the following provisions (Buchan 2007):

- ◆ Developing countries should not be targeted for active recruitment by the NHS unless the government of that country formally agrees.

- ◆ NHS employers should use only recruitment agencies that have agreed to comply with the Code of Practice.

- ◆ NHS employers should consider regional collaboration in international recruitment activities.

- ◆ Staff recruited from abroad should have the same legal protections as other employees.

- ◆ Staff recruited from abroad should have the same access to further training as other employees.

The movement of international medical and nursing graduates into the US healthcare system raises several important issues for managers and leaders. Managers must be aware of issues of ethical recruitment, regulation and visas, credentialing, and adaptation. All these areas must be considered to maximize the success of recruitment and incorporation of international professionals and minimize migration's negative effects on sending countries.

SUMMARY

Recruiting, selecting, and retaining employees continue to be important HRM functions, especially in such a competitive, pressurized environment as healthcare. Healthcare organizations and their HR departments face enormous challenges. They need to seek employees who (1) have specialized skills but are flexible enough to fill in for other positions, (2) bring in expertise and are able to work in groups whose members are not all experts, (3) are strongly motivated yet comfortable with relatively flat organizational structures in which traditional upward mobility may be difficult, and (4) have diverse backgrounds and skill sets while fitting the job and the organizational values. HR professionals need to develop innovative strategies to improve retention.

FOR DISCUSSION

1. Given two equally qualified applicants—one from inside and one from outside the organization—how would you decide which one to hire? What are the pros and cons of each?

2. Some healthcare organizations are unable to pay market rates for certain positions, such as increased pay for travel nurses. What advice would you give such an organization about possible recruitment and retention strategies?

3. The use of work references is increasingly viewed as unreliable. How can employers legally and ethically obtain information about an applicant's past performance? What measures can best verify information contained in a job application or resume?

4. What are the advantages and disadvantages of recruiting through the internet? What advice would you give to a hospital that is considering using the internet for recruitment?

5. It has often been stated that "people leave their boss, not their job." What does this statement mean, and why is it important?

EXPERIENTIAL EXERCISES

EXERCISE 1

Note: This case was developed in collaboration with Caroline LeGarde Shafa, vice president of operations at Sibley Memorial Hospital in Washington, DC.

Grayson County Regional Health Center is a private, not-for-profit, 225-bed acute care hospital located in a rural community in a southeastern state. The hospital provides a broad range of inpatient and outpatient services, including cardiology, obstetrics, gynecology, general surgery, internal medicine, urology, family medicine, dermatology, pediatrics, psychiatry, radiology, nephrology, ophthalmology, occupational medicine, and rehabilitation services. The center offers 24-hour emergency care. The center is built on a 96-acre site, and its service area includes Grayson County and parts of three neighboring rural counties.

In the last 20 years, the region has suffered severe economic setbacks. Most of the textile industry has moved out of the region because of outsourcing, and the town itself has fallen into disrepair. An increasing proportion of the population—33 percent of children and 22 percent of the elderly—lives below the poverty line. The county has a civilian labor force of 27,568 and currently has an unemployment rate of 13 percent. The county's infant mortality rate is 2 percent.

The center has 85 physicians, representing 29 subspecialties, on staff. It has affiliation relationships with two academic health centers—one about 90 miles away, and the other 100 miles away. The center employs more than 800 people, is fully accredited by The Joint Commission, and is certified to participate in Centers for Medicare & Medicaid Services (CMS) programs. The center is governed by an 18-member board of trustees, which includes the chief of the medical staff, the immediate past chief of the medical staff, the chief executive officer, and 13 members selected by the board from the community at large.

The center has strong community ties. Its staff members participate in community health screenings, health education programs, and health fairs. It serves as the meeting place for many support groups. Although it has been under financial stress for the last five years, it continues to have strong support in the community.

The employee turnover rate at the center is 40 percent. Over the last few years, the turnover rate for nurses has ranged from 15 to 50 percent. Physician recruitment and retention are also major concerns. Currently, only one radiologist is practicing in Grayson County, and there is a shortage of physicians in all specialties.

The center relies heavily on Medicaid and Medicare revenue, leaving the hospital in a difficult financial condition. It is unable to pay market rates for nurses and other professionals, so nursing units are understaffed and nurses feel overworked and underpaid.

The quality of patient care may also be decreasing. A local newspaper article reported that patients at the center were often left on stretchers in the hallway for long periods, staff members were unresponsive to patient and family concerns, and crying in the hallways is not unusual.

Nurses and other professional groups report poor communication between senior management and employees. Bad relationships between middle managers and frontline staff are also a problem in some departments. This situation became particularly difficult two years ago when the center embarked on a large building project. Employees could not understand how the center could afford to build new facilities but was unable to pay market rates to its staff.

The nursing turnover problem at the center has reached crisis proportions. Recent exit interview surveys indicate that financial concerns are the major reason for leaving. The center has tried numerous strategies, including improving the work environment by adding amenities (such as lower prices in the cafeteria) and training middle managers. For a short time 18 months ago, nurse salaries matched market rates, but the center fell behind again shortly thereafter. The RN vacancy rate currently is 18 percent.

As a consultant to the center, you are expected to make recommendations to address the nursing shortage. Specifically, you have been asked to develop short-term strategies to cope with the current crisis and long-term strategies to improve the overall recruitment and retention picture. Consider the following questions:

- How will you identify the most important reasons for the current shortage?
- How will you develop short-term and long-term strategies?

Exercise 2

What do you look for in a job? In a group, consider the following questions:

1. What do you look for in an organization, besides a job for which you are qualified and that provides an acceptable level of compensation and benefits?

2. What aspects of an organization might make you consider turning down an otherwise good job offer?

3. What is meant by *organizational culture* and why does it play a role in the employee selection process? Which do you think should be of greater focus in hiring: cultural fit or cultural add? Why?

4. When considering a job offer, people often look at organizational culture to see if it is consistent with their own values. How do you find out about the culture of an organization?

REFERENCES

Advisory Board. 2021. "The Top 5 Reasons Why Nurses Quit Their Jobs." Published March 11. www.advisory.com/daily-briefing/2021/03/11/nurse-burnout.

Aiken, L. H., S. P. Clarke, D. M. Sloane, J. A. Sochalski, R. Busse, H. Clarke, P. Giovannetti, J. Hunt, A. M. Rafferty, and J. Shamian. 2001. "Nurses' Report on Hospital Care in Five Countries." *Health Affairs* 20 (3): 43–53.

Albaugh, J. 2003. "Keeping Nurses in Nursing: The Profession's Challenge for Today." *Urologic Nursing* 23 (3): 193–99.

American Association of International Healthcare Recruitment (AAIHR). 2022. "What Is a Foreign-Educated Healthcare Professional?" Accessed May 3. https://aaihr.org/what-is-a-foreign-educated-healthcare-professional/.

American Nurses Association (ANA). 2001. *Analysis of American Nurses Association Staffing Survey.* Silver Spring, MD: ANA.

American Nurses Credentialing Center (ANCC). 2022. "ANCC Magnet Recognition Program." Accessed June 14. www.nursingworld.org/organizational-programs/magnet/.

AMN Healthcare. 2018. "Rise in Healthcare Overtime Threatens Patient Safety and Nurse Turnover." Published August 22. www.amnhealthcare.com/amn-insights/news/rise-in-healthcare-overtime/.

Asghar, R. 2014. "Incompetence Rains, er, Reigns: What the Peter Principle Means Today." *Forbes*. Published August 14. www.forbes.com/sites/robasghar/2014/08/14/incompetence-rains-er-reigns-what-the-peter-principle-means-today/?sh=51c5e1b88759.

Berlin, G., M. Lapointe, M. Murphy, and M. Viscardi. 2021. "Nursing in 2021: Retaining the Healthcare Workforce When We Need It Most." McKinsey & Company. Published May 11. www.mckinsey.com/industries/healthcare-systems-and-services/our-insights/nursing-in-2021-retaining-the-healthcare-workforce-when-we-need-it-most.

Berthiaume, J., and L. Culpepper. 2008. "'Hot Skills': Most Popular Compensation Strategies for Technical Expertise." Society for Human Resource Management. Published

January 14. www.shrm.org/resourcesandtools/hr-topics/compensation/pages/popularcompensationstrategies.aspx.

Buchan, J. 2007. "International Recruitment of Nurses: Policy and Practice in the United Kingdom." *Health Services Research* 42 (3 Pt 2): 1321–35.

Buerhaus, P. I., K. Donelan, B. T. Ulrich, L. Norman, M. Williams, and R. Dittus. 2005. "Hospital RNs' and CNOs' Perceptions of the Impact of the Nursing Shortage on the Quality of Care." *Nursing Economics* 23 (5): 214–21.

Chatterjee, R. 2022. "The Pandemic Pummeled Long-Term Care—It May Not Recover Quickly, Experts Warn." National Public Radio (NPR). Published February 22. www.npr.org/sections/health-shots/2022/02/22/1081901906/the-pandemic-pummeled-long-term-care-it-may-not-recover-quickly-experts-warn.

Cimiotti, J. P., L. H. Aiken, D. M. Sloane, and E. S. Wu. 2012. "Nurse Staffing, Burnout, and Health Care–Associated Infection." *American Journal of Infection Control* 40 (6): 486–90.

Cleveland Clinic. 2022. "Provider Recruitment." Accessed June 14. https://my.clevelandclinic.org/professionals/provider-recruitment.

Davis, C. 2021. "New Survey Reveals the Significant Impact of COVID-19 on Nurse Satisfaction Levels." *Health Leaders*. Published December 3. www.healthleadersmedia.com/nursing/new-survey-reveals-significant-impact-covid-19-nurse-satisfaction-levels.

Drenkard, K. 2010. "Going for the Gold: The Value of Attaining Magnet Recognition." *American Nurse Today*. Published March. www.americannursetoday.com/going-for-the-gold-the-value-of-attaining-magnet-recognition/.

Emory Healthcare. 2022. "Find Your Career." Accessed May 15. www.emoryhealthcare.org/careers/index.html.

Filbin, P. 2022. "'Perfect Storm' of Staffing Challenges Continues to Batter Home-Based Care Operators." *Home Health Care News*. Published March 2. https://homehealthcarenews.com/2022/03/perfect-storm-of-staffing-challenges-continues-to-batter-home-based-care-operators/

Fitz-enz, J., and B. Davison. 2002. *How to Measure Human Resources Management*. New York: McGraw-Hill.

Gatewood, R. D., M. R. Barrick, and H. S. Feild. 2018. *Human Resource Selection,* 9th ed. New York: Wessex.

Gautier, K., and L. Munasinghe. 2020. "Build a Stronger Employee Referral Program." *Harvard Business Review.* Published May 26. https://hbr.org/2020/05/build-a-stronger-employee-referral-program.

Gess, E., M. Manojlovic, and S. Warner. 2008. "An Evidence-Based Protocol for Nurse Retention." *Journal of Nursing Administration* 38 (10): 441–47.

Gilmartin, M. J., P. C. Aponte, and K. Nokes. 2013. "Time for Realistic Job Previews in Nursing as a Recruitment and Retention Tool. *Journal for Nurses in Professional Development* 29 (5): 220–27.

Grensing-Pophal, L. 2022. "Using Virtual Reality for Remote Hiring." Society for Human Resource Management (SHRM). Published February 1. www.shrm.org/resourcesandtools/hr-topics/technology/pages/using-virtual-reality-remote-hiring.aspx.

Huerta, S. 2003. "Recruitment and Retention: The Magnet Perspective." *Journal of Illinois Nursing* 100 (4): 4–6.

Industry Today. 2022. "Top Recruitment Metrics in 2022." *Industry Today.* Published March 18. https://industrytoday.com/top-recruitment-metrics-in-2022/.

Kaiser Permanente. 2022a. "Northern California Employee Referral Program Overview." Accessed June 8. https://erp.kaiserpermanentejobs.org/ncal/howtorefer.aspx.

———. 2022b. "Working Here." Accessed May 15. www.kaiserpermanentejobs.org/working-here.

Karami, S. 2020. "71% of Hiring Decision-Makers Agree Social Media Is Effective for Screening Applicants." PRWeb. Published October 14. www.prweb.com/releases/71_of_hiring_decision_makers_agree_social_media_is_effective_for_screening_applicants/prweb17467312.htm.

Kinkaid, B. 2022. "Down with Culture Fit! Long Live Culture Add!" *Vitamin T* (blog), Vitamin Talent. Published February 7. https://vitamintalent.com/blog/down-with-culture-fit-long-live-culture-add.

Li, H., W. Nie, and J. Li. 2014. "The Benefits and Caveats of International Nurse Migration." *International Journal of Nursing Sciences* 1 (3): 314–17.

Maurer, R. 2022. "Employers Are Responding to Job Candidates' Changing Expectations." Society for Human Resource Management (SHRM). Published January 22. www.shrm.org/hr-today/news/all-things-work/Pages/employers-respond-to-job-candidates-changing-expectations.aspx.

———. 2021. "Recruiters Will Continue to Adapt in 2022." Society for Human Resource Management (SHRM). Published November 9. www.shrm.org/resourcesandtools/hr-topics/talent-acquisition/pages/recruiters-will-continue-adapt-in-2022.aspx.

Mayo Clinic. 2022. "Life-Changing Careers." Accessed October 4. https://jobs.mayoclinic.org.

McHugh, M. D., A. Kutney-Lee, J. P. Cimiotti, D. M. Sloand, and L. H. Aiken. 2011. "Nurses' Widespread Job Dissatisfaction, Burnout, and Frustration with Health Benefits Signal Problems for Patient Care." *Health Affairs* 30 (2): 202–10.

Mercer. 2014. *2014 Mercer/Gartner IT Jobs and Skills: Building the IT Workforce of the Future: Survey Report*. Published September. www.mercer.com/content/dam/mercer/attachments/global/Talent/workforce-rewards/mercer-2014-gartner-it-jobs-and-skills.pdf.

Miles, M. 2022. "How to Grow Your Team Better, Faster with an Employee Referral Program." BetterUp. Published January 10. www.betterup.com/blog/employee-referral-program.

National Association of Clinical Nurse Specialists (NACNS). 2022. "What Is a CNS?" Accessed October 4. www.nacns.org/about-us/what-is-a-cns.

Needleman, J., P. Buerhaus, V. Pankratz, C. L. Leibson, S. R. Stevens, and M. Harris. 2011. "Nurse Staffing and Inpatient Hospital Mortality." *New England Journal of Medicine* 364 (11): 1037–45.

NSI Nursing Solutions. 2022. *2022 NSI National Health Care Retention & RN Staffing Report*. Published March. www.nsinursingsolutions.com/Documents/Library/NSI_National_Health_Care_Retention_Report.pdf.

NurseJournal Staff. 2022. "The U.S. Nursing Shortage: A State-by-State Breakdown." *NurseJournal.* Published September 29. https://nursejournal.org/articles/the-us-nursing-shortage-state-by-state-breakdown/.

Peckham, C. 2015. "Nurses Tell All! Salaries, Benefits, and Whether They'd Do It Again." Medscape. Published November 17. www.medscape.com/viewarticle/854372_6.

Peter, L. J., and R. Hull. 1969. *The Peter Principle.* William Morrow.

Rivera, L. A. 2015. "Guess Who Doesn't Fit In at Work." *New York Times.* Published May 30. www.nytimes.com/2015/05/31/opinion/sunday/guess-who-doesnt-fit-in-at-work.html.

Salm, L. 2017. "70% of Employers are Snooping Candidates' Social Media Profiles." Published June 15. www.careerbuilder.com/advice/social-media-survey-2017.

Smith, A. 2015. "Searching for Work in the Digital Era." Pew Research Center. Published November 19. www.pewinternet.org/2015/11/19/searching-for-work-in-the-digital-era/.

Society for Human Resource Management (SHRM). 2015. "Cost-Per-Hire: What External and Internal Costs Should Be Included in a Cost-Per-Hire Calculation?" Published March 26. www.shrm.org/resourcesandtools/tools-and-samples/hr-qa/pages/costperhirecalculation.aspx.

Spanko, A. 2021. "Nursing Homes Have 94% Staff Turnover Rate—With Even Higher Churn at Low-Rated Facilities." *Skilled Nursing News.* Published March 2. https://skillednursingnews.com/2021/03/nursing-homes-have-94-staff-turnover-rate-with-even-higher-churn-at-low-rated-facilities/.

Tubbs-Cooley, H. L., J. P. Cimiotti, J. H. Silber, D. M. Sloane, and L. H. Aiken. 2013. "An Observational Study of Nurse Staffing Ratios and Hospital Readmission Among Children Admitted for Common Conditions." *BMJ Quality and Safety* 22 (9): 735–42.

Upenieks, V. 2002. "Assessing Differences in Job Satisfaction of Nurses in Magnet and Nonmagnet Hospitals." *Journal of Nursing Administration* 32 (11): 564–76.

US Bureau of Labor Statistics (BLS). 2022. "Occupational Outlook Handbook: Registered Nurses." Modified September 8. www.bls.gov/ooh/healthcare/registered-nurses.htm.

Vaidya, A. 2013. "Top 5 Drivers of Nurse Dissatisfaction." *Becker's Hospital Review*. Published January 18. www.beckershospitalreview.com/hospital-management -administration/top-5-drivers-of-nurse-dissatisfaction.html.

Vesoulis, A., and A. Abrams. 2022. "Contract Nurse Agencies Are Making Big Money in the Age of COVID-19: Are They 'Exploiting' the Pandemic?" *Time*. Published February 23. https://time.com/6149467/congress-travel-nurse-pay/.

Vozza, S. 2022. "Why You Should Welcome Back Boomerang Employees." Society for Human Resource Management (SHRM). Published February 9. www.shrm.org /resourcesandtools/hr-topics/people-managers/pages/boomerang-employees.aspx.

WakeMed. 2022. "Careers." Accessed March 24. www.wakemed.org/careers/.

Walker, A. 2022. "What Does a Travel Nurse Do & How Can You Make the Most Money as a Travel Nurse?" Nurse.org. Published October 1. https://nurse.org/articles/how-to -make-the-most-money-as-a-travel-nurse/.

Wharton School, University of Pennsylvania. 2015. "Is Cultural Fit a Qualification for Hiring or a Disguise for Bias?" Knowledge@Wharton. Published July 16. https://knowledge .wharton.upenn.edu/article/cultural-fit-a-qualification-for-hiring-or-a-disguise-for -bias/.

Zappe, J. 2006. "The State of Recruitment and Staffing: Be Aggressive, or Be Gone." *Workforce Management*, February 27, 29–31.

Zielinski, D. 2019. "Blue-Collar Workers More Likely to Search for Jobs on Their Smartphones." Society for Human Resources Management (SHRM). Published June 3. www .shrm.org/resourcesandtools/hr-topics/talent-acquisition/pages/blue-collar-workers -search-for-jobs-smartphones.aspx.

CHAPTER 6

ORGANIZATIONAL AND EMPLOYEE DEVELOPMENT

Carla Jackie Sampson and Julene Campion

After completing this chapter, you should be able to

➤ understand and articulate the role of organizational development and its contribution to the achievement of the strategic goals and priorities;

➤ describe the significance of aligning the organization's mission, values, and competencies with the organization's performance and productivity initiatives;

➤ describe culture and discuss the impact on employee engagement;

➤ recognize the importance of leadership development in the organization's long-term success; and

➤ describe the elements of employee training, including opportunities for career progression and skills development in support of achieving the organization's strategic priorities.

VIGNETTE

Evergreen, a health system located in the Northeast with 24,000 employees, was founded more than 100 years ago with a mission of providing exceptional healthcare to the people of the communities it serves. Shonda, the CEO, recently joined the organization and introduced a new strategic plan and key initiatives. Brian, the chief human resources officer (CHRO), met with Shonda to discuss her vision and the changes required to achieve it. During her conversation with Brian, Shonda focused on critical organizational and employee development (OED) initiatives, which included the following:

1. Align performance and productivity initiatives with the organization's strategic goals.
2. Create a culture that reinforces the organization's mission, vision, values, and competencies and enhances employee engagement.
3. Design a best-in-class employee training and development program that is aligned with the long-term success of the organization and supportive of all levels of employees.

The CEO asked the CHRO to develop a strategic plan resulting in the achievement of these key OED initiatives.

INTRODUCTION

For many healthcare organizations, the vision and mission serve as a critical compass. Exemplary healthcare organizations have clear alignment among their mission, vision, values, competencies, and strategic goals and priorities. Periodic review and revision of these factors are necessary to execute an organization's strategy successfully. A healthcare organization's strategic plan should engage, enable, and align all employees. *Organizational and employee development (OED)* is an emerging discipline within human resources that aligns, integrates, synchronizes, and prioritizes the organization's strategic goals and key initiatives with all other functions of an organization, as described by the Society for Human Resource Management (SHRM 2022b).

To achieve their strategic goals, healthcare organizations often strive to become more market-driven, customer friendly, innovative, and adaptive. **Organizational development (OD)** can help an organization achieve these goals. The primary function of OD is to increase an organization's effectiveness through planned interventions related to the organization's processes and people, resulting in improved productivity, return on investment, and employee satisfaction. OD usually involves applying behavioral science knowledge to improve an organization's effectiveness through employee empowerment, employee engagement, and problem-solving skills (Van Vulpen 2022). **Employee development (ED)** is an organization's effort to encourage professional growth in its employees. ED may include elements of mentoring, coaching, sponsoring, stretch assignments, special projects, continued education, and formal leadership development programs. The most successful OED programs are designed to align the organization's vision and mission with the strategic plan through a series of interventions. In OED, an **intervention** is a series of activities and events designed to help an organization become more productive and effective.

Facilitating change requires both OD and training. OD provides a systematic learning and development strategy aligned with organizational goals and may include training, but it is not limited to training. **Training** is the acquisition of knowledge, skills, abilities, and competencies needed to perform a particular job. Whereas training focuses on the individual, OD focuses on the whole organization. Effective OD and training require a high level of management and staff engagement and commitment for success.

For example, many healthcare organizations focus on the three key priorities of (1) the patient experience, (2) the financial health or profit margin of the system, and (3) the recruitment and retention of an engaged and diverse workforce. One of the changes currently in progress is the shift from the traditional brick-and-mortar setting to a telehealth model. This shift aligns with all three of these priorities because it provides patients with easier access to care, reduces the expenses related to leased and owned buildings, and widens the talent pool to those living in areas outside the geographic area. However, there is potential for failure without planned interventions to support these significant changes. Provider adoption of telehealth services could fail if there is no appropriate education,

organizational development (OD)
An organization's endeavor to increase its effectiveness through planned interventions related to the organization's processes and people.

employee development (ED)
An organization's effort to encourage professional growth in its employees, which may include elements of mentoring, coaching, sponsoring, stretch assignments, special projects, continued education, and formal leadership development programs.

intervention
A series of activities and events designed to help an organization become more productive and effective.

training
The acquisition of knowledge, skills, abilities, and competencies needed to perform a particular job.

technical support, and infrastructure. Revenue could be negatively impacted if patients do not use the telehealth options and instead seek care elsewhere. Employee engagement could also be negatively affected if employees working remotely do not feel connected to their supervisor or team. Creating a culture of trust, empowerment, and accountability is also critically important.

The activation of an intervention can mitigate these risks by

- identifying opportunities to enhance the patient experience in a digital environment proactively,

- educating providers on new protocols for telehealth visits,

- supporting the transition from an on-site work environment to a remote environment, and

- developing leadership programs that build trust and ensure accountability while enhancing employee engagement.

OED DEPARTMENTS OR OUTSOURCING: WHO DOES THE WORK?

Centralizing OED services is ideal. However, in several hospitals and health systems, the training and education function is administered by many educators in unrelated departments across the facility. In this case, the organization should assign a coordinator of educational services to ensure that training and other instructional programs are not duplicated, the offerings are necessary, and the educational process is consistent throughout, including the design, facilitation, and participant-tracking elements.

Outsourcing the OD function may be appropriate on some occasions—for example, if the staff is small or lacks an OD expert. Hiring an outside firm to create or conduct engagement surveys may also provide baseline data and ensure confidentiality. Because of the variety of training subjects related to the operations of a healthcare organization (see exhibit 6.1), it is easy to see how outsourcing may be necessary. However, employees with experience in and knowledge of the topic may be able to serve as effective facilitators or instructors in place of OD staff, and to hardwire the processes and policies that support employee engagement. Several helpful societies and networks (see "Did You Know?" sidebar) can help in-house employees improve their OD skills.

ORGANIZATIONAL DEVELOPMENT AND CULTURE

A unifying mission statement, values that resonate with the mission, and competencies together create a shared sense of purpose while communicating the expected skills and behaviors and shaping the organization's culture. According to SHRM (2022c), *culture*

Management-Mandated Topics	Position-Specific Topics	Intervention Topics
Antiharassment	Patient safety	Customer service
Diversity and inclusion	Leadership	Building high-performing teams
Disaster preparedness	Understanding organ donation	Dealing with difficult people
Quality improvement	Patient-centered care	Coaching for excellence
New-employee orientation	In-service	Embracing change

EXHIBIT 6.1
Topics and Dimensions of Training

DID YOU KNOW?
Helpful Societies and Networks for OD

The Society for Human Resources Management (SHRM; www.shrm.org) has a robust organizational development and learning area. The site also contains information on student organizations and memberships. SHRM produces *HR Magazine* and various human resources publications.

The American Society for Health Care Human Resources Administration (ASHHRA; https://ashhra.org) was established in 1964 and focuses on content and resources for HR leaders in the healthcare sector.

The Association for Talent and Development (ATD; www.td.org) is dedicated to workplace learning and training professionals. ATD publishes the monthly *T+D* magazine, with best practices, trends, and new technology.

The Organization Development (OD) Network (www.odnetwork.org) is an international professional association of organization development practitioners. OD Network's listserv features trends, best practices, and networking opportunities.

---

consists of shared beliefs and values established by leaders and then communicated and reinforced through various methods, ultimately shaping employee perceptions, behaviors, and understanding. The culture frames the daily experiences of how and when information is communicated, the level of autonomy and the decision-making model, the conflict management style, the levels of trust and respect, and inclusion or sense of belonging.

Transforming the culture to align with the strategic plan is an important responsibility of OD. One of the foundations of the culture transformation process is identifying and communicating the organization's values. OD works cross-functionally with leaders throughout the organization to shape the values that will identify and govern the desired culture and then develop a change management plan that ensures that those cultural values are disseminated and understood throughout the organization. This rollout of cultural values is a critical milestone in any organization's culture change journey. Once articulated, these values become the organization's shared vocabulary, identifying people's behaviors and attitudes toward their work and one another.

Creating a sense of common purpose and alignment governed by a set of universally understood values and corresponding behaviors enables an organization to readily adapt to a changing environment and execute the organizational strategy. Cultural values provide a framework for employee action that does not require immediate supervision. Organizations become nimbler with streamlined decision making and clear, two-way communication channels. Having clear communication and employees empowered to act within the cultural values framework can develop a resilient culture. One of the best ways to test the health of an organization's culture is through the periodic measurement of employee engagement.

EMPLOYEE ENGAGEMENT

employee engagement
A measure of the employees' positive and negative perceptions of the organization that have a direct impact on retention, job satisfaction, and job performance.

One of the major objectives of OD is **employee engagement**, which is a measure of the employees' positive and negative perceptions of the organization that have a direct impact on retention, job satisfaction, and willingness to learn and perform at work. Engaged employees are willing to go above and beyond job expectations. Engaged employees demonstrate higher levels of performance, commitment, and loyalty, resulting in improved financial performance for their organizations (Buhlman and Lee 2019; Gallup 2022). On the other hand, employees with low engagement just meet the minimum job expectations and feel disconnected from the organization, which may affect morale (see the related Critical Concept" sidebar "The Link Between Employee Engagement and Organizational Effectiveness"). By emphasizing shared manager and personal responsibility, coupled with intrinsic motivation, it is possible to increase employee engagement dramatically. However, various factors in an organization affect employee on-the-job behaviors beyond their skills, knowledge, and abilities, including quality of life at work, the nature of the job, relationships with colleagues and managers, opportunities for advancement, rewards and recognition, and company practices (SHRM 2022a).

A poorly managed employee engagement process can have a negative impact on the organization's culture. The basic premise is that if you ask your employees to tell you what they really think, you had better be prepared to do something about it. Otherwise, you have done more harm than good. Engagement surveys that allow for transparency throughout the process enable OD to create a culture defined by the maxim, "This is what you told us needs to be improved, and this is what we are going to do about it." Engagement improves when employees feel they are being heard and the organization is willing to use their input

> **⚠ CRITICAL CONCEPT**
> The Link Between Employee Engagement and Organizational Effectiveness
>
> A recent study by the Gallup Organization provides insightful information about the linkages between employee engagement and key metrics of organizational effectiveness (Gallup 2022). In a large study of multiple companies across several industries, Gallup found significant differences in outcomes between high-engagement and low-engagement work units.
>
> Compared with low-engagement work units, high-engagement work units were found to have the following:
>
> - 10 percent higher levels of customer loyalty and engagement
> - 18 percent higher levels of sales productivity
> - 23 percent higher profitability
> - 28 percent less theft
> - 41 percent fewer quality defects
> - 43 percent lower turnover in low-turnover organizations and 18 percent lower turnover in high-turnover organizations
> - 58 percent fewer patient safety incidents
> - 64 percent fewer occupational safety incidents
> - 81 percent less absenteeism

to improve the workplace experience. Various OD interventions are available to assess and develop employee engagement. A few of these and their major considerations are described in exhibit 6.2. An intervention may deploy these tools sequentially.

After they have been undertaken, employee engagement measurements and follow-up actions become integral to the health of the organizational culture. The engagement process builds credibility within the organization through implementing a change management process predicated on employee feedback. The employee engagement process requires that leaders at all levels be willing to implement the changes recommended by their teams. This idea that "they are listening to us" creates a culture wherein employees are more connected and committed to the organization and its goals. When engagement aligns with strategy, organizational outcomes improve. Healthcare organizations are including employee engagement results in their overall strategic goals and aligning incentive compensation for supervisors and managers with those results. Having a tangible measure of employee engagement gives OD a critical role in helping a healthcare organization achieve its strategic goals (see the related Case Example sidebar).

EXHIBIT 6.2
Employee
Engagement
Interventions

Tool	Description	Benefits and Points to Consider
Online survey	Questionnaire distributed to all employees or departments as necessary	Encourages candor because responses are anonymous
		Can be regularly and systematically administered
		Easy to compile findings and communicate to managers and employees
		May be viewed as a public relations gimmick
		Follow-through to employees may be more challenging to demonstrate
Focus group	Small group of employees assembled to answer questions from a moderator	Useful way to explore themes that were previously generated (from surveys)
		Can provide more context for management
		Can explore extent of some sentiments
Feedback and quality circles	Groups of employees who voluntarily meet regularly with their supervisors to discuss and investigate problems, initiate solutions, or take other actions	Efforts at improvement are tangible for employees and build management credibility
		Can effect culture change because employees probe issues and generate solutions themselves
		May help employees feel more empowered to act
		Difficult when staffing shortages prevail
		Employees with low engagement may not participate
Team building	Social or team activities to facilitate collaboration	May receive insufficient participation for success from employees with low engagement who may not view these activities as helpful
		Off-site collaboration may not translate to workplace collaboration

---

(✱) **CASE EXAMPLE**

Like many U.S healthcare systems, a large integrated health system located in the US Mid-Atlantic region experienced urgent and unprecedented challenges during the early months of the COVID-19 pandemic. These challenges related to ever-changing patient protocols, concerns for healthcare providers' personal safety, staffing shortages, and increased employee burnout. The OD department developed a series of two-minute *pulse surveys* to measure and monitor these areas of concern. The pulse surveys, deployed multiple times in 2020, each consisted of five multiple-choice questions and one open-ended question. The results were quickly analyzed, and a change management plan was developed to address employee concerns.

In 2021, the organization developed a new engagement strategy, which consisted of deploying a comprehensive engagement survey each November and a pulse survey each May. The OD department moved the system away from the previous methodology of developing complex action plans to improve engagement scores. Instead, they introduced a new approach whereby the manager and employees determined the *One Thing* they would work on together to improve the employee experience. Each leader reviewed the survey results with their team to collectively determine the One Thing the team would choose to work on for that year. The team and leader distilled their One Thing into a simple statement that could be easily understood and articulated. For example:

> *Team's One Thing: To work more effectively while prioritizing our mental and physical health and well-being.*

To support the process the teams would use to improve their One Thing, they developed the following three shared commitments. For example:

1. *Take more meetings as walk and talks (W&T) or spend more time away from the keyboard (AFK)—can be time to read, stretch, ride a bike, volunteer, or play with a pet.*
2. *Plan time to W&T or AFK as a group and spend time together (outside as weather permits) more often.*
3. *Role model W&T, AFK, and DC (direct connections, usually in person). Invite others to join us in our commitments.*

After the commitments were developed, the teams would revisit them at each team meeting or *huddle* (short meeting, typically at the beginning of the day) to reaffirm them. The ongoing pulse surveys became the yardstick against which progress could be tracked and processes refined.

EMPLOYEE DEVELOPMENT

Many organizations have mandatory training for all employees. Some positions have specific training requirements that may involve licensing, certification, and renewals. For example, healthcare personnel may need to obtain a certain number of training hours per year to maintain professional licensure. Training may also be required for an organization to maintain its accreditation (see the related Critical Concept sidebar "Training and Accreditation").

Little opportunity to advance and a lack of training and development were among the top reasons for dissatisfaction cited among millennial or Generation Y (born 1981–1996) and Generation Z (born 1997–2010) employees (Deloitte Global 2022). Development and advancement options contribute to an attractive place to work, demonstrating the organization's commitment to employee career progression. Organizations that provide development opportunities prepare employees to assume greater responsibility or more challenging work or projects. Employee development can also equip staff with new skills and competencies to work cross-functionally, spark creativity, and tap into hidden talent (Rinne 2022).

Whether it is used as a response to an intervention or as a method for achieving strategic or retention goals, employee development is a significant component of the work of OD. Training can also be a strategic tool for success because it can diagnose the organization's problems and identify the elements that are working well, using employees as the measurement. When effective, it can generate before-and-after data to show the effects of change.

> ### ⚠ CRITICAL CONCEPT
> Training and Accreditation
>
> Healthcare organizations undergo an accreditation process every few years to ensure patient safety and quality of services. The Joint Commission is the major accrediting organization in the healthcare industry, and its qualifying process requires healthcare professionals and staff to have education and training. Organizational development is integral to the qualifying process, as it provides the tracking and documentation to meet The Joint Commission's standards for quality and patient safety, which for hospitals and some other types of healthcare organization also reflect the requirements of the Centers for Medicare & Medicaid Services (CMS).
>
> The Joint Commission's website (www.jointcommission.org) is a rich resource of information on standards and performance improvement measures in healthcare, which often drive training and education for those who seek to meet or maintain certification and strive for excellence.

EMPLOYEE ONBOARDING

Formal **onboarding** is the process of integrating newly hired employees into the organization. Onboarding includes *orientation* and opportunities to learn about the new organization and its culture, mission, and values. **Orientation** is the completion of new-hire forms and other routine tasks (SHRM 2022d). Onboarding helps new employees compare their expectations for a future with the organization to reality. If there is no formal process, the employee will go through an informal process of indoctrination by other employees. Onboarding by peers can be valuable, but it is not sufficient. With only informal onboarding, the new employee may receive inaccurate, incomplete, or biased information.

In onboarding, the organization answers many employee-centered questions and is provided with an opportunity to explain and educate about workplace structure, policies, practices, standards, and expectations. The employee should be exposed to a balance of job-specific and organization-related information. Exhibit 6.3 lists areas commonly covered in new-employee onboarding.

New employees usually decide within six months of employment whether to stay, and employee onboarding gives organizations the opportunity to get the relationship off to a good start. High-quality onboarding thus is crucial to the successful transition of new

onboarding
The process of integrating newly hired employees into the organization.

orientation
The completion of new-hire forms and other routine tasks for new employees.

EXHIBIT 6.3
Onboarding Content

Employee-Centered Information	Organization-Specific Information
Facilities: badges/name tags; location of restrooms, parking, security, first aid, water fountains, food services/cafeteria	Overview of organization: introduction, history, culture, customs/traditions, organizational structure, mission, vision, and values
Details of job duties: work hours, job description, performance criteria	Safety: precautions, accident-reporting procedures
Compensation: pay rates, deductions, overtime, holiday pay	Policies: privacy of information, guidelines, constraints, internet use, telecommuting
Benefits: insurance, holidays, leave, retirement	Procedures, rules, and resources for reporting discrimination or illegal activities
Online portals/channels, intranet	
Department tour: workspace/office, entrances/exits, supervisor's location	Employee relations: reporting sick leave, probationary period length and activity limitations, expectations and disciplinary practices, grievance process
Career planning: development opportunities, resources for growth	Community activities and sponsored events

hires into contributing organizational members (see the related Critical Concept sidebar "Onboarding and Orientation Best-Practice Ideas").

ONBOARDING LOGISTICS

Onboarding programs may last one or two days in some organizations; in others, it may be a series of events over several months. In healthcare workplaces, feeling the impact of an unfilled position, management wants to initiate the new hire quickly and speed up the learning curve. Therefore, onboarding programs use fast-paced training techniques.

One of the best approaches to orienting a new employee is breaking up the onboarding into brief sessions over days or weeks. The employee remembers much more when given bites of information that can be thoroughly digested while adjusting to the new work surroundings. Because the employee stays connected to the work process during orientation,

---

⚠ CRITICAL CONCEPT
Onboarding and Orientation Best-Practice Ideas

Many organizations have successfully revamped their onboarding processes. A typical new employee orientation at the University of Michigan Medical Center consists of individual registration, photo identification, and paperwork. There is an introduction to the university's policy, culture, and values. This session includes time with refreshments for new employees, during which they may talk to peers. Such an onboarding feature gives new employees the opportunity to "meet and greet" university-sponsored business partners (University of Michigan 2022).

Some employers are offering a company "road map" whereby new employees explore the company's culture and history while engaging in key relationships with coworkers and managers. Organizations that engage in formal onboarding with step-by-step programs teach new employees their roles and company norms (Vozza 2016). Other companies may engage new employees with personal questions or send welcome packages.

Another innovative strategy involves a personalized method that can include some combination of the following, tailored to a new employee's needs: videos on an employee's working day; online training videos; a guide to employee success; an explanation of the importance of the employee's role; and guidelines for appropriate communication within the workplace (Indeed 2022).

the new hire may be more satisfied and more likely to stay with the organization long term. This orientation style benefits the organization as well.

DEPARTMENT ONBOARDING

Onboarding responsibility may be distributed throughout the organization; however, to be successful, it must also have accountability. Supervisors represent the front line of onboarding and training because they are in the best position to affect engagement and retention (Chopra-McGowan 2022). They should be responsible for explaining the work tasks and responsibilities, as well as outlining performance expectations and making introductions to the other members of the team. Peers should also be encouraged to provide information to newcomers. Peers are best positioned to share information about the work team, sources of support, and where to find or request tools and supplies (SHRM 2022d). Some organizations assign a mentor or "buddy" to work with new hires.

LEADERSHIP DEVELOPMENT

Leadership development helps organizations grow and thrive amid the rapidly changing environment. Without effective leaders, the organization risks inefficient allocation of resources, conflicting business and clinical priorities, and miscommunication, which can all damage the organization. Leadership development processes help the organization identify and prepare rising leaders and retain those already in these positions. These processes should equip leaders with continuous access to the tools, support, and training necessary to empower and motivate their teams.

Leadership development training might include the following:

- Change management

- Communication

- Conflict resolution

- Enterprise risk management

- Time management

- Strategic planning

- Coaching and mentoring

- Financial management

SUCCESSION PLANNING

succession planning
The process of identifying and developing employees for potential promotion or transfer into positions that are critical to operations.

Succession planning is the process of identifying and developing employees for potential promotion or transfer into positions that are critical to operations; it ensures that the vitality of an organization continues. The succession planning process is outlined in exhibit 6.4.

The goal of succession planning is to prepare for the inevitable movement of people through transfers, promotions, turnover, and retirements. Such movement creates holes in the hierarchy that need to be filled by qualified replacements. Such voids can be minimized by having a succession plan ready when needed.

In many organizations, succession planning focuses only on top executive positions. However, it is just as important to include plans for key positions in middle and lower management. An organization facing a wave of professionals close to retirement or voluntary separation and no plan for their replacement faces a serious threat.

EXHIBIT 6.4
The Succession
Planning Process

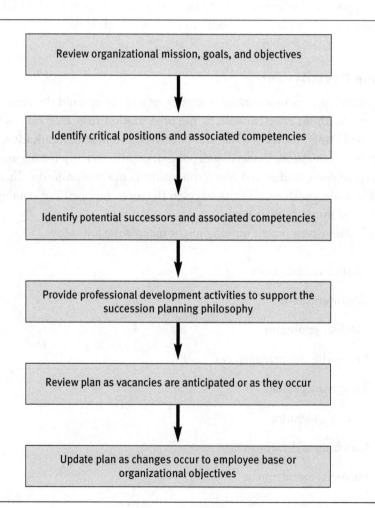

Review organizational mission, goals, and objectives

↓

Identify critical positions and associated competencies

↓

Identify potential successors and associated competencies

↓

Provide professional development activities to support the succession planning philosophy

↓

Review plan as vacancies are anticipated or as they occur

↓

Update plan as changes occur to employee base or organizational objectives

Because of the fluidity of positions and people in organizations, it is crucial to understand that such planning must be reviewed and revised frequently. A critical step in the succession planning model is forecasting demand for key positions and identifying skill gaps among current staff. Skills that are critical today may be different from those that will be needed in the future. After future needs are determined, managers must identify and develop high-potential internal candidates through internal and external training, cross-functional experiences, and job rotation. Encouraging career advancement within the organization can improve company loyalty and employee engagement.

Succession planning should yield the following outcomes:

◆ Adjustment to labor market conditions

◆ Adjustment to demographic characteristics of the employee base and community served

◆ Identification of potential vacancies in critical positions

◆ Identification of potential successors who can fill the positions with additional development

◆ Improvement of employee engagement and retention

◆ Enhancement of the employer brand

◆ Enhancement of workplace sustainability

COACHING AND MENTORING

Coaching and mentoring programs are complements to leadership and employee development. The coaching process includes relationship building, which instills confidence and helps employees engage, develop, and learn. This new confidence improves their performance and creates a positive working environment for all employees. Effective coaching requires a manager to be clear, collaborative, and communicative while helping employees set and accomplish their own development goals, giving timely feedback, and providing recognition.

Mentoring is not the same as coaching. The relationship between a mentor and mentee is based on advice and direction given to the mentee, while coaching is about support. Formal mentoring requires actionable and measurable goals, as advised by the Association for Talent Development (ATD 2022a). A mentorship program can benefit professionals at every career stage and also helps create a positive work environment. Mentoring is seen more often for a senior employee to advise a junior or less-experienced employee on their skills as well as professional and career development. (For other mentoring models, see the accompanying "Did You Know?" sidebar, and "The Special Role of Mentors and Mentoring" in chapter 7.)

? **DID YOU KNOW?**
Many Models for Mentoring

Besides the traditional one-on-one mentoring described in this chapter, there are many other models and techniques for mentoring, including the following (ATD 2022a):

Group Mentoring: One or several mentors work with a group of mentees.
Peer Mentoring: Employees in the same role or department pair up to support each other.
E-Mentoring: The mentorship relationship is conducted virtually.
Reverse Mentoring: The junior employee mentors a more senior professional.
Speed Mentoring: This model, borrowed from "speed dating," involves a series of brief, one-on-one conversations with a set of mentors, which may be part of an event or industry meeting.

THE TRAINING DESIGN PROCESS

To ensure that organizational learning is effective, an organization should take a systematic approach. Consistency of planning, execution, and metrics gives credibility and power to the OD process.

Changes in technology and advances in healthcare influence an organization's operations and processes, making new training programs, education, and training design necessary. Quality assurance reports may help the OD department identify areas in which deficiencies exist and training is needed. Another information source for OD to mine in search of organizational skill gaps and process improvement opportunities is the organization's patient satisfaction survey database. Best-in-class health systems routinely survey patients to ascertain satisfaction across a broad spectrum of potential patient interaction "touch points." These satisfaction surveys ask patients to rate their experiences on a five- or ten-point scale, responding to statements and questions such as the following:

◆   My provider was on time for my scheduled appointment.

◆   My provider listened to my concerns.

◆   My provider asked me questions about my symptoms.

◆   Based on your experience, how likely are you to refer a friend or family member to this practice?

The Affordable Care Act requires that patient satisfaction survey scores be considered when healthcare systems request Medicare and Medicaid reimbursement. Therefore, OD's ability to identify training opportunities that improve the patient experience directly impacts the organization's financial bottom line.

Several models for training design exist, and all these models meet the primary objective of an effective training initiative—for the information to be transferable or applicable to the participant's work. After all, who wants to train just for the sake of training? In today's business climate, no organization or department can afford to be frivolous—at least not if it wants to survive or thrive. The models are a subset of a larger design structure commonly referred to as **instructional systems design (ISD)**. ISD provides an organized, systems approach to training.

The most ubiquitous design is the **ADDIE model** (analysis, design, development, implementation, and evaluation). ADDIE ensures that the how, what, why, where, who, and when of training are addressed. The ADDIE approach constantly evaluates the training initiative, ensuring that it is compatible with and effective in the changing workplace. Exhibit 6.5 depicts the five ADDIE steps central to good training design. The design plan must be detailed and include updated timelines, but it must also be flexible enough to change with organizational requirements. The organizational structure should facilitate, not detract from, the success of a training initiative.

Decisions about the training method and the involved personnel should follow a systematic assessment of the initiative. For example, it may be tempting to decide who the facilitator will be before assessing the need for training. This action may jeopardize the effectiveness of the training. It may add pressure to the process, reducing the purpose of the training to "make it fit" the facilitator rather than provide value. The needs assessment and design phase should drive the training initiative. Sometimes a needs assessment reveals that training is not the proper remedy for the problem—for example, lack of employee motivation or poor staff morale cannot be rectified by training. To mitigate the risk associated with poorly prepared trainers, many organizations are adopting a "train the trainer" process. "Train the trainer" relies on the expertise of subject matter experts, often from outside the organization, who train and certify the organization's trainers or training teams. This way, when the subject matter experts depart, the organization retains the training competency on-site with a cadre of credentialed trainers.

ANALYSIS

Step one of the training design processes is *analysis*, in which facts are collected to determine what kind of intervention is necessary. **Needs assessment** is a tool that the design team can use to determine whether gaps exist between the desired and actual levels of performance, according to organizational requirements or performance standards. One of the most effective methods for determining the gap between what *is* and what *should be*

---

instructional systems design (ISD)
An organized, systems approach to training.

ADDIE model
Analysis, design, development, implementation, and evaluation; a systems approach to training.

needs assessment
A tool used to determine whether gaps exist between the desired and actual performance levels, according to organizational requirements or performance standards.

Exhibit 6.5
Training Design
Process Overview

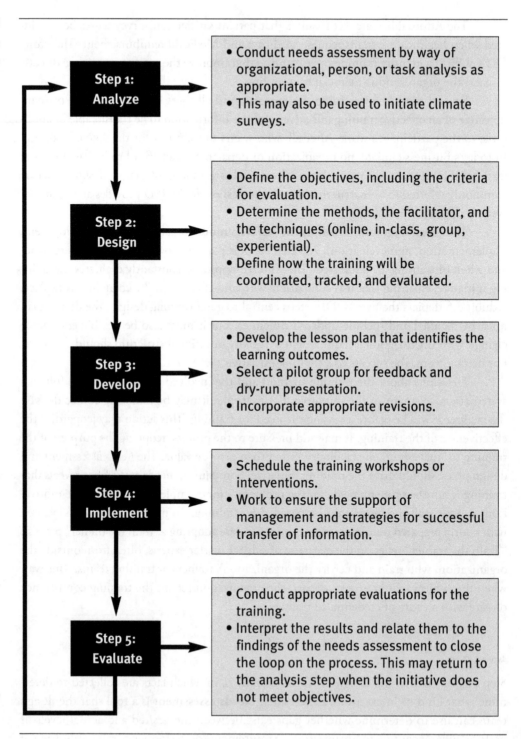

Step 1: Analyze	• Conduct needs assessment by way of organizational, person, or task analysis as appropriate. • This may also be used to initiate climate surveys.
Step 2: Design	• Define the objectives, including the criteria for evaluation. • Determine the methods, the facilitator, and the techniques (online, in-class, group, experiential). • Define how the training will be coordinated, tracked, and evaluated.
Step 3: Develop	• Develop the lesson plan that identifies the learning outcomes. • Select a pilot group for feedback and dry-run presentation. • Incorporate appropriate revisions.
Step 4: Implement	• Schedule the training workshops or interventions. • Work to ensure the support of management and strategies for successful transfer of information.
Step 5: Evaluate	• Conduct appropriate evaluations for the training. • Interpret the results and relate them to the findings of the needs assessment to close the loop on the process. This may return to the analysis step when the initiative does not meet objectives.

is the classic Marvin Weisbord (1978) Six-Box Model. The six boxes (purpose, structure, rewards, helpful mechanisms, relationships, and leadership) are intended to be considered within the larger context of the environmental demands. Relying on information from each of the six boxes, the model seeks to assist practitioners in determining the fit between (1) the organization and the environment and (2) the organization and the individual. Incorporating these six areas into the survey design will help identify gaps, which may be appropriate for intervention consideration.

Developing a high-quality needs assessment tool is crucial because the tool will gather data that help the training designer decide on the best type of intervention. That intervention will affect the issue being studied, such as patient safety, personnel issues such as turnover and grievances, or organization-wide productivity and knowledge.

Learning needs can be determined by

- reviewing organizational records and reports, supervisors' evaluations and recommendations, and critical incident reports;

- directly observing workers;

- conducting surveys;

- checking professional standards;

- brainstorming;

- testing workers;

- reading existing literature; and

- holding focus groups.

TRAINING DESIGN

Step two of the training design process is the **training design** itself, in which the grand plan is established, timelines are set, and the overall project outline is created. It is important to develop options to keep the plan flexible.

The critical tasks in step two are to

- accurately outline the objectives,

- communicate them to all involved, and

- ensure that they are thoroughly understood.

training design
The unifying thread of all training modes, in which the grand plan is established, timelines are set, and the overall project outline is created.

KEY POINT

The number one question of people who attend training is *What's in it for me?* This question must always be at the forefront of training design.

At this point, it is also wise to consider the answer to the number one question of people who complete training: *What's in it for me?* This question must always be at the forefront of training design because it reminds the designer that participants must be kept engaged. Engagement comes, in part, from the lessons and experiences participants take away from the training.

TRAINING DEVELOPMENT

training development
The step of the training design process in which the training materials, including the curriculum and learning outcomes, take shape; also includes a dry run and feedback.

Step three of the design process is **training development**, in which the training materials, including the curriculum and learning outcomes, take shape. Training development also includes a dry run; feedback on the test run determines whether revisions or midcourse corrections are needed.

Training has evolved from the days when presenters dumped massive amounts of information on participants (the "sit and soak" method). Today's trainer is a facilitator of ideas and thought who involves participants so that their transformation can begin during the sessions. During step three, the curriculum is molded and sharpened to guide and enhance the facilitation.

TRAINING IMPLEMENTATION

training implementation
The step of the training design process in which rollout occurs and evaluation data are collected for analysis.

Step four of training design is **training implementation**, in which the workshops or interventions are rolled out, and evaluation data are collected for analysis. At this time, the plan's built-in flexibility enables design revisions to be made if user or participant feedback dictates. To help employees and supervisors manage their time appropriately, organizations should make the training schedule available early and hold multiple sessions on varied days and times to accommodate individual needs.

TRAINING EVALUATION

training evaluation
The step of the training design process in which the information collected after implementation is reviewed to determine whether objectives were met.

Step five is **training evaluation**, in which the information collected after implementation is reviewed to determine whether objectives were met.

Managers should strive to use evaluation metrics because such information could clear the way for executive buy-in and long-term budget approval. The traditional framework for training evaluation is based on four increasingly challenging criteria (Kirkpatrick 2010a, 2010b):

1. *Course reactions*—extent to which trainees like the program based on its usefulness, quality, and instructor skills.

2. *Training learning*—extent to which employees understand and retain principles, facts, and techniques.

3. *Behavior change*—changes in job-related behaviors or performance that can be attributed to training.

4. *Organizational results*—extent to which tangible outcomes such as productivity, costs, and improved clinical service quality that can be attributed to training are realized by the organization.

Training reactions may reflect the degree to which staff liked the program as opposed to how much they learned, which can have an impact on their job performance. Trainee learning may have been understood but not transferred to enhancement of job performance (Ketter 2011). The goal, which is often not attained, is to facilitate staff willingness to progress from knowing to doing.

While the third and fourth criteria—behavior change and organizational results—are most useful for evaluation, they pose significant challenges in identifying and utilizing appropriate tools for measuring data. For example, return on investment (ROI) is an important business aspect for the training program and whether the financial benefits outweigh the financial costs. One possible approach to address this problem is to use more sophisticated

---

CRITICAL CONCEPT
Pretest and Posttest Method of Training Evaluation

One of the most common ways to evaluate training effectiveness is the pretest and posttest method. This evaluation is done before and after training, using a questionnaire that asks respondents to rate certain aspects of the training. The questionnaire may be designed using a Likert response or a simple yes–no construction. Either way, this method presents information revealing differences in knowledge and skills before and after training.

Having a control group take the pretest and posttest without going through the training is recommended to make the evaluation much clearer and establish support for training.

measures, including pre- and posttest results using a control group (see the Critical Concept sidebar "Pretest and Posttest Method of Training Evaluation").

If the evaluation shows that OD fell short of the training objectives and that the training did not address or improve the situation at hand, the design process goes back to step one, analysis. Because objectives sometimes shift with organizational changes, it is not uncommon for the design process to be repeated. Many OD teams run the cycle on their training programs often to maintain quality and ensure that the objectives continue to be met.

TRAINING DELIVERY MODES

Many training delivery modes for training exist today: in-class, e-learning, online asynchronous (self-paced and student-centered), online synchronous (live and scheduled), mobile learning, instant messaging, videoconferencing, and webinars. As a result of evolving technology and stagnant travel budgets, many healthcare organizations are using social networking and various social media such as blogs, wikis, huddles, and discussion groups to foster informal learning.

The use of social media connects people so they can solve work-related issues. Information technology (IT) can also change the training focus from addressing skill deficits to assisting employees in doing their jobs better. The social media approach means that this help is available on demand, and rapidly changing needs may make it difficult to specify.

E-learning is a method for online training using technology-based methods such as employee intranets, and the internet. The benefits of e-learning are numerous and include reduced costs, greater convenience and flexibility, and improved retention rates.

A version of e-learning is live virtual instruction that uses a web-based platform to deliver live, instructor-led training to geographically dispersed learners. Such training can be provided in shorter blocks of time (e.g., 60-minute modules) as opposed to several days. The result is greater convenience and cost savings.

Webinars deliver on-demand training through live or recorded broadcasts on the internet. This medium allows the presenters and the training participants to sit in their own offices or be in other cities or countries than that of the presenter. Organizations that have multiple locations often use webinars to reduce their training costs.

Educators are trending toward greater use of electronic media to deliver training. A fast-growing technological innovation is **mobile learning**, sometimes called *m-learning*. Through mobile learning, educational content is delivered through smartphones, tablets, or laptops. Content is easy to access, and delivery is flexible enough to accommodate just about any schedule.

The right technologies facilitate flexible learning opportunities crucial for employees who work in fast-paced and demanding environments. Allowing employees to access training and development materials on their personal mobile devices puts the power and

webinars
Seminars posted on the internet, either conducted live or recorded and broadcast.

mobile learning
Educational delivered through mobile devices such as smartphones, tablets, or laptops.

accountability for ongoing skill development in the employee's hands while also allowing HR leadership the ability to track compliance and identify individual and collective strengths and areas for improvement.

Instant messaging (IM) and chatbots provide avenues for training in real time; they offer quick responses to employees' real-time on-the-job needs. IM allows human users to exchange short written messages. *Chatbots* are computer programs designed to mimic human actions, sometimes in the guise of a character, to create a more user-friendly experience for the person seeking the information.

Virtual reality (VR) uses several technologies to replicate the entire real-life work environment (rather than just several aspects, as do the types of simulations described later in this chapter for off-the-job training and in chapter 5 for giving applicants a realistic job preview). VR immerses a participant in a computer-generated three-dimensional environment that changes in response to the person's hand and body movements.

TRAINING METHODS

The training method should match a given situation appropriately. Selecting the proper method optimizes the quality and usefulness of the training and increases the likelihood of accomplishing the education objective—for the information to be transferable or applicable to the work of the participant. Sometimes the best method is a combination of two or three techniques. On-the-job training is conducted while the employee is at the workplace, but other training may take place "off the job"—that is, away from the workplace and outside working hours. (These two types and examples of training methods within each of them are listed in exhibit 6.6 and described in the two sections that follow.) Each type of training has its own benefits, and both types face implementation challenges, as the following discussion shows.

ON-THE-JOB TRAINING

On-the-job training encompasses a number of methods, as described in the paragraphs that follow.

Cross-training educates team members about other members' jobs so that they may be capable of performing them when a team member is absent or is assigned another job, or has left the organization. If effectively implemented, cross-training will improve individual and organizational flexibility while enhancing employee morale and interdepartmental relations.

Diversity and bias training consists of programs designed to teach employees about specific cultural and gender differences and how to respond to them in the workplace. Such training

KEY POINT

The main objective of training is for the information to be transferable or applicable to the participant's work.

EXHIBIT 6.6
Training Types and
Methods

On the Job	Off the Job
Cross-training	Lectures
Diversity and bias training	Group discussion
Customer service training	Role playing
Ethics training	Case studies
Shadowing	Simulation
Coaching	Game-based learning

is particularly important in the healthcare industry, which is both diverse and heavily dependent on the use of team structures. (Chapter 11 provides a detailed discussion of diversity, inclusion, and belonging in the workplace.) To be meaningful, diversity training programs need to include content about unconscious bias and exhibit cultural sensitivity toward all groups—including white males, who have traditionally resisted such training because they believed it was directed at or against them. Making the link between diversity and belonging may be more effective in engaging staff with diverse backgrounds than simply training, which often has focused mainly on debunking ethnic stereotypes.

Customer service training is the development of customer service skills, particularly for staff members who have direct patient and client contact. Such skills can determine the success and very survival of healthcare organizations—affecting employee satisfaction and retention, customer satisfaction and loyalty, and organization performance (Fottler, Ford, and Heaton 2010).

Ethics training is often an overlooked area for staff enhancement in organizational development. For such training to be effective, it must make the translation from the organizational guidelines to actual organizational behavior. Unethical behaviors may take many forms, including unsafe work practices, bullying, intimidating others, stealing from the employer, or failing to report unethical behavior in others. All these behaviors have a negative impact on employee engagement and productivity. Without ethics training, employees may not readily see some behaviors as unethical. Moreover, incidents of unethical behavior are often not reported because of staff concern about negative repercussions, especially if the offender is in a higher position in the organization. Training techniques that focus on both recognizing and addressing such behaviors may be helpful; such techniques should cover communication techniques for how to challenge inappropriate behavior effectively, role playing (discussed in greater detail in the "Off-the-Job Training" section that follows), and feedback on performance, all of which can increase skills and confidence levels (Edmonson and Zelonka 2019).

Shadowing is used to show an employee what a colleague or a supervisor does on a daily basis. Common shadowing activities include attending meetings, sitting in on decision-making sessions, and observing the coworker on the job. This method works best when knowledge must be transferred quickly such as from a departing employee to a trainee, or when a position is complex. The effectiveness of the method depends on the ability of the person being shadowed and the willingness of the participant.

In *coaching* the employee receives highly individualized correction, feedback, and timely information to improve performance as discussed earlier in this chapter.

OFF-THE-JOB TRAINING

Some on-the-job training is effective, but most training happens off the job so that employees can concentrate fully on learning.

Lectures are usually verbal presentations by instructors. They are effective for large groups and when the dissemination of information is the goal. *Group discussion*, which may also include a lecture, lets participants inject their ideas and thoughts into the training. The lecture format is effective for small groups and when idea generation is needed, but the discussions need to be well facilitated to ensure that the group stays on track.

Role playing is applicable and transferable to the workplace because it involves creating a realistic scenario in which the participants take on roles and practice developing the skill sets necessary to accomplish a certain task. Role playing is an excellent way to teach coaching, giving and receiving feedback, and conflict resolution skills.

Use of *case studies* builds practicality and workplace transferability into the training experience. A written description of a real-world incident is presented to a group for discussion and formulation of solutions. The case study method lets group members practice critical thinking, communication, decision making, and negotiation.

Simulation is another efficient means of providing practical experience to participants. During a simulation, participants are briefed about either a fictitious workplace or their real organization. Participants are divided into groups to discuss and decide what they would do about the problem, and then each group evaluates the work of the other groups. Simulation is an excellent teaching tool within departments—for example, for training emergency department employees in disaster response and management.

Game-based learning is another method for skill development. In this type of training, participants achieve the learning outcomes by playing the game. Game-based learning is a cost-effective method to encourage learner involvement, create social connections, and stimulate interest while enhancing the participant's knowledge and performance. Games may also result in better knowledge retention, memorable learning, and a more enjoyable learning atmosphere than typical learning methods. A related concept is *gamification*, in which some gaming elements—such as rewards, levels, badges, leaderboards, and challenges—are applied as incentives to change behavior and achieve learning outcomes (O'Donnell 2020). For example, onboarding, employee engagement, leadership, and compliance training can be gamified as challenges or award points to encourage participation.

IMPLEMENTATION CHALLENGES

A well-conceived training program will fail if management cannot convince participants of its merits. Participants must believe that the program has value and will help them achieve their personal and professional goals if it is to succeed. But implementation may fail for many other reasons as well. First, participants may be action-oriented and believe that they are too busy to devote time to the program. Second, finding qualified instructors who are familiar with organizational philosophy, strategies, and goals may be a challenge. Third, training may involve unwanted change, which in turn may result in resistance. Fourth, employees may think that they are already well acquainted with the position requirements and believe there is no need for additional training. Finally, the support of top management is required for any training program to succeed. Such support needs to be demonstrated by what managers do (i.e., reward participants) much more than what they say (i.e., that they think it is a good idea).

THE FUTURE OF ORGANIZATIONAL AND EMPLOYEE DEVELOPMENT

The COVID-19 pandemic underscored just how critical OED is to an organization's success (see the Current Issue sidebar "'The Great Resignation' as a Wake-Up Call"). What will the future bring to OED? How will workplace learning look in the ever-shifting business climate? In this time of extreme competition and globalization, organizations rely on strategies that develop highly skilled workers who are then expected to drive productivity and quality. This practice will likely remain constant. Historically, OD departments have been the first departments to be eliminated, but this practice has become less common as organizations rely more on strategic training to drive performance.

  One trend is to brand OED as the talent management function. *Talent management* encompasses all that is done to recruit, retain, develop, reward, and promote people, and it takes a strategic approach to these activities. Talent management assumes that the organization is only as good as its talent—that is, its people.

  As staffing becomes more and more challenging in healthcare, HR leaders and talent development professionals must find ways to engage employees efficiently and effectively. **Microlearning**—presentation of new information in small chunks (segments of ten minutes or less)—is one way to do that. Microlearning can be presented in video format, but it can also be experienced through listening to a podcast, participating in a game, or engaging via social media (ATD 2022b).

  Another trend leverages the growth of technology, particularly online meeting platforms, social and electronic media (m-Learning and e-learning), and **MOOCs** (massive open online courses), often available without a fee (MOOC.org 2022). These technology-based learning methods allow presenters and participants to be in different places and for

microlearning
A training and development method that presents new information in small chunks (segments of ten minutes or less).

MOOCs
Free online courses on a variety of topics that are available to anyone worldwide to enroll. MOOCs stands for *massive open online courses*.

CURRENT ISSUE
"The Great Resignation" as a Wake-Up Call

The ramifications of the COVID-19 pandemic continue to ripple through the global workplace. People who lived in big cities moved to less populated suburbs if they had the financial means and the ability to work remotely. Many people who were allowed to work from home found that after two years of working in a home office, they had little desire to return to the corporate office full-time. Unfortunately, many workers were furloughed or fired as businesses shut down either by mandate or of their own volition. For many workers, especially those sidelined by closures, the pandemic offered the first opportunity in a lifetime to truly step back and assess their work–life balance. This reckoning led to what has been termed "The Great Resignation."

The pandemic tipped the balance of power between the organization and the employee away from the employer. Many people used the experience to reassess their professional goals and aspirations and decided that their current position was not fulfilling. That so many people arrived at that conclusion should serve as a bellwether for HR professionals. The question that emerges is, "Why did it take a pandemic for us to realize what was happening to our employees?"

By late 2022, there were indications that many workers who resigned from their jobs during the pandemic have had second thoughts. But they nevertheless will not be content to return to prepandemic conditions in the workplace. Thus now more than ever, OED is crucial to an organization's success and, perhaps, to an organization's survival. American workers have expressed themselves and expect to be treated with respect and dignity. The fundamentals of organizational and employee development we have been discussing in this chapter are the basic "blocking and tackling" which, when done well, can make an organization resilient enough to withstand even a once-in-a-generation upheaval like a pandemic.

learning to be asynchronous and on demand. These developments are well suited to an increasingly remote and hybrid work environment.

A final trend is to make employee development self-directed and easily accessible. As organizational structures become flat, the traditional image of career "ladders" becomes less applicable as career pathways meander across the organization. Allowing employees to pick and choose which transferable skills and competencies they would like to add to their career portfolio, using free on-demand options, gives them ownership of their career development and ultimately benefits the organization (Rinne 2022).

SUMMARY

Organizational and employee development is part of the changing healthcare landscape. The challenge is to remain flexible enough to respond to the changing needs of the organization and its employees. Finding training methods that help build a productive, highly functioning workforce is not easy, but adaptability, innovation, and continual pursuit of best practices can ensure sustainable results. An organization can more easily adapt to the constantly shifting environment when its OD department and executive management are strategic partners. Together, their combined perspective can better anticipate their organization's development needs.

FOR DISCUSSION

1. Describe an example of a successful new-employee onboarding. Why are employee needs and organizational needs both important to consider?

2. Why is it important to engage senior management early in the OD process?

3. What types of ethical challenges have you observed in the work or school setting? Can these challenges be addressed by ethics training? How can the effectiveness of such training be maximized?

4. Why is employee engagement important? How can such engagement be enhanced in a healthcare organization?

5. Research your current organization's mission, vision, cultural values, and competencies. Evaluate how well they align with and support the strategic plan.

6. Develop three to five questions to ask employees to test their knowledge and understanding of how their role contributes to the achievement of the strategic priorities.

7. Research the elements of a best-in-class employee engagement program and survey; describe how you would adapt it for your organization.

8. Identify a systematic change required in your organization to achieve the organization's strategic priorities and conduct a needs assessment and a supporting ADDIE.

EXPERIENTIAL EXERCISES

EXERCISE 1

Argosy Medical Center, a 400-bed critical care facility, has been in operation for more than 18 years. Its mission is to provide healthcare services of the highest standard of excellence and ensure patient satisfaction.

In the past, staff members were excited to be part of the Argosy family, and patients noticed this attitude and enthusiasm. Argosy became the hospital of choice because patients felt that the staff genuinely cared about them, which made their experience positive regardless of their health status. In their exit surveys, patients gave the hospital high ratings, and they frequently wrote glowing comments about the staff's genuine concern.

In the last couple of years, however, Argosy's employees seem to have lost their passion, and patient complaints about poor customer service have increased. Management has attributed its employees' attitude to higher workloads and burnout. Employees are now required to attend a refresher course each year to keep them motivated and in tune with the hospital's mission and to reenergize them about their work.

The course includes a review of the hospital's values, its mission, and the standards of service everyone is expected to follow. Because the course lasts only one hour, participants do not get to interact, ask questions, or give feedback. Since the refresher course was implemented, employees have not been surveyed for their feedback or insights. Because staff members are constantly busy, they have had no opportunity to discuss the decline in employee morale and the poor customer service. Everyone is aware of the problem, but no time has been put aside to address it, other than the yearly course reminding staff to provide good customer service regardless of the situation.

Argosy's CEO has summoned you, the director of the OD department, to come up with a way to address the problem.

- What interventions would you recommend? Come up with two options.
- Defend your preferred option to the CEO and include a timeline for your plan.

EXERCISE 2

Health Valley Hospital provides comprehensive services, including cancer, heart, trauma, and emergency services. It has 2,300 full-time employees. For eight years, Health Valley has had a decentralized philosophy of training and organizational development. Almost every department has its own trainer or educator. The HR department also has an education component, called Education Services, that provides training on general topics, including new-employee orientation, customer service, leadership/management, and staff development. Education Services does not provide training on topics such as nursing education, patient safety, emergency medical services, or disaster preparedness. Because so many separate training units exist at Health Valley, each training unit tracks its own educational information. With the constant interruptions and emergencies inherent in the hospital environment, this tracking function sometimes is pushed to the low end of daily priorities.

Health Valley's CEO has heard so much about all the education that occurs within the organization that he wants to highlight it to the hospital's board of directors. The CEO immediately sends a memo to the HR department asking for all sorts of education-related information, including a listing of all education and training activities, detailing each activity's title, objectives, and outcomes; how it meets organizational objectives; and the names of the educator or facilitator and the employees who attended.

Because the training information is not housed in a central location, this CEO request is a major undertaking. Each training unit tracks the information in its own format, including spreadsheets, handwritten lists, electronic databases, and file folders. The only way for this request to be handled successfully is for all the involved units to work together collaboratively and quickly to do the following:

1. Contact the education, training, or OD department in a local hospital or healthcare facility. Interview the head of the department to gain insight into how the training and tracking function is handled (centralized or decentralized, for example). Ask what works well and not so well and listen for improvements they would like to make.

2. Formulate a short-term plan for responding to the CEO's request.

3. Design a long-term plan for addressing the problem and preventing it from happening again.

Consider the following questions:

- How should the information be gathered and stored so that it is readily available next time?
- How is having a centralized recording system valuable?

EXERCISE 3

Using the ADDIE model discussed in this chapter, design a training program that addresses the customer service expectations of walk-in patients in the emergency department. Include an evaluation process that answers the following questions:

- What method will you use to evaluate the knowledge transfer?
- How will you know whether you met your training objectives?

EXERCISE 4

Your healthcare facility has asked you to explore succession planning as a possible strategy for organizational sustainability. To get started, research two organizations that have adopted a succession planning strategy and compare their programs and outcomes. How will you apply what you have learned from this research to your recommendation for your own facility?

REFERENCES

Association for Talent Development (ATD). 2022a. "What Is Mentoring?" Accessed August 13. www.td.org/talent-development-glossary-terms/what-is-mentoring.

————. 2022b. "What Is Microlearning?" Accessed August 13. www.td.org/talent -development-glossary-terms/what-is-microlearning.

Buhlman, N. W., and T. H. Lee. 2019. "When Patient Experience and Employee Engagement Both Improve, Hospital's Ratings and Profits Climb." *Harvard Business Review*. Published May 8. https://hbr.org/2019/05/when-patient-experience-and-employee -engagement-both-improve-hospitals-ratings-and-profits-climb.

Chopra-McGowan, A. 2022. "Effective Employee Development Starts with Managers." *Harvard Business Review*. Published March 1. https://hbr.org/2022/03/effective -employee-development-starts-with-managers.

Deloitte Global. 2022. *The Deloitte Global 2022 Gen Z and Millennial Survey*. Deloitte Touche Tomatsu. Accessed August 20. www2.deloitte.com/content/dam/Deloitte/global /Documents/deloitte-2022-genz-millennial-survey.pdf.

Edmonson, C., and C. Zelonka. 2019. "Our Own Worst Enemies: The Nurse Bullying Epidemic." *Nursing Administration Quarterly* 43 (3):274.

Fottler, M., R. C. Ford, and C. P. Heaton. 2010. *Achieving Service Excellence in Healthcare Management*. Chicago: Health Administration Press.

Gallup. 2022. "What Is Employee Engagement and How Do You Improve It?"

Accessed June 21. www.gallup.com/workplace/285674/improve-employee-engagement -workplace.aspx.

Indeed. 2022. "Onboarding Employees: New Trends for 2022." Accessed June 21. www
.indeed.com/hire/c/info/onboarding-employees-trends?gclid.

Ketter, P. 2011. "Creative Institutional Design Equals Successful Learning Transfer." *T+D*
65 (7): 10.

Kirkpatrick, D. L. 2010a. "Evaluation of Training." In *Training and Development Handbook*, edited by R. L. Craig, 301–19. New York: McGraw-Hill.

———. 2010b. "The Four Levels Are Still Relevant." *T+D* 64 (9): 16.

MOOC.org. 2022. "About MOOCs." edX. Accessed August 13. www.mooc.org/.

O'Donnell, R. 2020. "The Year Ahead in Learning Technology." Society for Human
Resource Management. Published February 11. www.shrm.org/resourcesandtools/hr
-topics/technology/pages/learning-technology-trends-2020.aspx.

Rinne, A. 2022. "Stop Offering Career Ladders: Start Offering Career Portfolios." *Harvard
Business Review*. Published August 10. https://hbr.org/2022/08/stop-offering-career
-ladders-start-offering-career-portfolios.

Society for Human Resource Management (SHRM). 2022a. "Developing and Sustaining
Employee Engagement." Accessed August 12. www.shrm.org/resourcesandtools/tools
-and-samples/toolkits/pages/sustainingemployeeengagement.aspx.

———. 2022b. "Introduction to the Human Resources Discipline of Organizational and
Employee Development." Accessed June 21. www.shrm.org/resourcesandtools/tools
-and-samples/toolkits/pages/introorganizationalandemployeedevelopment.aspx.

———. 2022c. "Understanding and Developing Organizational Culture." Accessed June
21. www.shrm.org/ResourcesAndTools/tools-and-samples/toolkits/Pages/understan
dinganddevelopingorganizationalculture.aspx.

———. 2022d. "Understanding Employee Onboarding." Accessed August 13. www.shrm
.org/resourcesandtools/tools-and-samples/toolkits/pages/understanding-employee
-onboarding.aspx.

University of Michigan. 2022. "New Employee Orientation." Accessed June 21. https://hr
.umich.edu/working-u-m/my-employment/new-employee-orientation.

Van Vulpen, E. 2022. "What Is Organizational Development? A Complete Guide." Academy to Innovate HR (AHIR). Accessed June 21. www.aihr.com/blog/organizational-development/.

Vozza, S. 2016. "8 Creative Onboarding Practices That Take Employees Outside." Fast Company. Published August 11. www.fastcompany.com/3062694/8-creative-onboarding-practices-that-take-employees-outside.

Weisbord, M. 1978. *Organizational Diagnosis: A Workbook of Theory and Practice*. New York: Basic Books.

CHAPTER 7

PERFORMANCE MANAGEMENT

Bruce J. Fried

LEARNING OBJECTIVES

After completing this chapter, you should be able to

➤ define *performance management* and describe the key components of a performance management system;

➤ describe the purposes and approach of a performance review;

➤ discuss the reasons that organizations engage in performance management;

➤ identify the characteristics of good rating criteria for performance appraisal;

➤ distinguish between rating errors and political factors as sources of distortion in performance appraisal; and

➤ explain the steps required in planning for and conducting a successful performance management interview with an employee.

JOAN AND ABIGAIL

Joan is an administrative assistant in a hospital department of general surgery. She reports to the business manager, Abigail. Joan has been in her position for two years, and today is the assigned day for her annual review. The forty-minute meeting has been scheduled for 9:00 a.m. When Joan enters Abigail's office, Abigail says, "Please sit down. We'll have to keep this short because I'm bogged down with budget work that did not get done yesterday. I think we can get through this in the next fifteen minutes. Is that okay with you?" Joan agrees.

Abigail continues, "As you recall, we use a rating scale here, and like all other employees, you'll be rated on ten criteria. You are rated on a five-point scale, ranging from unsatisfactory to excellent. I'll go through areas of concern. First, there is Timeliness. I'm rating you down from last year, where you received a 4, for 'very good.' This time, I've given you a 3, which is 'satisfactory.' Two weeks ago, you were ten minutes late for my meeting with the department's budget committee. Before you get all upset about this, I know that you had to take your little girl to the doctor that morning and that you warned me that you'd be late. But, Joan, you have to do a better job separating your personal life from your work life."

Joan replies, "I believe this was the only time in the past year that I was late for work, and I don't know why I'm being rated down for the whole year because of one event."

"Well, we're running short on time, so let's move onto something else," Abigail responds. "I received a complaint, when was it, a few months ago, from one of our accounting technicians that there were some errors in an Excel spreadsheet you had prepared on revenues, and it took him over an hour to reenter the data. In your last review, I gave you a rating of 3 for Accuracy. But I've got to mark you down to a 2, for 'poor,' this time around."

Joan is getting visibly upset at this point, and responds, "Last year at my review, we discussed my role in preparing these spreadsheets, and I reminded you that this was definitely not in my job description, nor was I asked anything about my Excel skills during the job interview. I said that I'd be willing to take this on if you would provide me with sufficient training. You said that you would do this, but it never happened. I've been doing my best, but I literally have had no one to help me and review my work."

"Oh, yes, I vaguely remember something about this," Abigail replies. "But you should have been more assertive about demanding this or we wouldn't be in this predicament now and you would not have created extra work for the accounting department. It's unfair for you to pass on shoddy work for others to fix. It's not their job description to fix your work."

Abigail fails to notice Joan's stunned expression because she has started looking through some papers on her desk. "Joan, I've got to cut this short," Abigail says. "Everything else on your review is fine. In fact, I've moved you from a 3 to a 4 on Courtesy. Everyone likes you; you're agreeable to taking on additional tasks and staying late. But you've got to work on your time management and accuracy in your work. Please sign your review, which indicates that I shared and discussed this with you. Thank you for coming by this morning."

BOB AND CAROLYN

Bob has been a laboratory technician in a medical group practice for two years. When he took the job, he reviewed his job description and uses it to plan and evaluate his performance. Since he started employment, he has come to work on time, had few absences, and feels that he is doing a good job. He has received only a few minor complaints from his supervisor and occasionally from a physician in the practice. Bob believes he is always responsive to complaints and takes corrective action when there is a problem. In fact, he helped improve the functioning of the lab by making several suggestions to reduce the time it takes to get results back to providers. His coworkers respect him because he is willing to voice many of their concerns about the workload and understaffing of the lab.

Bob's supervisor, Carolyn, is busy and has little time to discuss job performance. Bob understands, and he has always believed that "no news is good news." He was told a month ago that the practice would start doing regular annual performance reviews. Carolyn scheduled a time for a review but canceled it one hour before they were supposed to meet. She gave no reason. They had difficulty finding an alternate time, but eventually Carolyn found a 20-minute slot during which they were both available.

After the review, Bob stepped out of Carolyn's office, and (as one coworker reported) he was shaking and was clearly upset. When he discussed the meeting with a coworker, Bob noted that he was commended for his excellent attendance and punctuality. His supervisor was happy with the quality and accuracy of his work. However, when discussing Bob's attitude, Carolyn described Bob as aggressive, insubordinate, and pushy and accused him of involving himself in things that were none of his business. When Bob asked for examples, Carolyn indicated that he should keep to his job responsibilities and not get involved in the management of the lab. She also accused Bob of "abusing the use of the phone, wasting money, and endangering patients." While Bob acknowledged that he frequently had to phone his babysitter because of problems with child care, he explained that these calls never interfered with his efficiency or effectiveness. Nevertheless, Carolyn suggested that Bob consider leaving the practice, indicating that he "didn't fit in with the way we do things here." At the end of the review, Carolyn told Bob that he would be ineligible for any pay increase this year because of his attitude and other behaviors.

SILAS AND SCOUT

Silas graduated from a health management program almost two years ago and has been working as an administrative resident in a large health system. The health system includes ten hospitals and more than 50 affiliated network healthcare organizations including medical group practices, long-term care facilities, and specialized treatment centers. Silas reports to Scout, who is director of network relations for the health system. They have a regular check-in monthly, although Scout has an open-door policy and encourages Silas to bring issues or questions to her as they arise.

It is March 2, and time for their monthly 8:00 a.m. check-in. The meeting is scheduled for one hour. After entering her office, Silas says, "Thank you for meeting with me." Scout's response is similar to her response in earlier check-in sessions: "Good morning. How can I make your job easier and more productive and meaningful?" Silas responds, "All seems to be going well. You recall that last time we met, you suggested I spend additional time with two new medical practices that have recently joined our network. I have done so, and I have found myself spending one to two full days every week with these practices, given their need for onboarding into the network and our procedures and guidelines. In particular, I've been providing them with detailed instructions on implementing our quality improvement procedures and discussing operational concerns, metrics, and numerous other issues. It feels like it's beginning to get in the way of other duties that I have in the health system."

Scout responds, "Thank you for your work with these medical practices. I've received very positive responses from the physicians in those practices about your approach and professionalism. However, I understand that this may be interfering with your other work. Let me suggest that I assign someone from our quality improvement group to work with you on onboarding these practices. I am thinking in particular of Angela, who just completed a large project with one of our hospitals and has about a week before starting their next project. You can discuss with them how you would like to divide your work, but they would also benefit from working with these practices because they will eventually be doing substantial QI work with our medical practices." Silas agrees with this and believes he could better manage his overall workload if he could share some of the onboarding work with Angela.

Scout then moves on to another issue. "I know that you've been stretched pretty thin lately, and we'll try to get this fixed. I want to follow up with you about submission of your monthly network revenue reports. I need these three days before my meetings with the senior management team so that I can review them and distribute the information prior to the meeting. This is the second month in a row where I did not get the reports until a day before the meeting. The senior management team depends on these reports each month, and they are critical to monitoring and evaluating the work of our network members." Silas acknowledges that he knew he'd been late with the reports. "The first time the delay was due to my own negligence and poor planning. Another project had taken up more time than I expected. I've since reorganized my time, and I think I've got a better system for managing my time. This past month the problem was that several of our network partners had just finished implementing a new information system. There was a delay in their getting the information to me and from there, things just cascaded badly." Scout responds, "Thank you for clarifying this. I know about the new information system and some of the problems that this created. I think the interoperability issues have been resolved. In the future, please just keep me informed if you expect to face a delay again. I can plan for this if necessary. But when it happened earlier, I felt a bit blindsided, and it made our department look disorganized. Again, thank you for taking on so much work. I know that it is often difficult to have so many projects going all at once."

Scout thanks Silas for coming in for the check-in, concluding, "You're doing great work for the health system amid a lot of pressure and change. And please stop by any time if any issues arise. Otherwise, we'll meet again next month."

INTRODUCTION

The ultimate goal of human resources management (HRM) is to align the work of individuals and teams with the goals of the organization. In this chapter we discuss *performance management*—the component of HRM that seeks to coordinate all efforts involved in improving employee performance. We describe the essential components of performance management and the potential for pitfalls in the process. The focus of performance management is to work with employees to continuously monitor, review, and improve performance.

We occasionally use the terms *performance appraisal* and *performance management* interchangeably. Each term, however, has a unique meaning. **Performance appraisal** involves methods of assessing the level of employee performance and refers mainly to the collection of information about employee performance and discussion of that information with the employee. **Performance management** is a much broader term that encompasses all the activities supervisors carry out to manage and improve employee performance, including not only appraisal but also supervision, rewards, and training. Broadly speaking, performance management is "a continuous process of identifying, measuring, and developing the performance of individuals and workgroups and aligning performance with the strategic goals of the organization" (Aguinis 2019).

Performance management includes the following managerial responsibilities and activities:

- ◆ Setting performance goals with employees

- ◆ Monitoring employees' progress toward their goals

- ◆ Designing strategies with employees to make and sustain improvement

- ◆ Providing ongoing feedback and coaching

As with all human resources functions, performance management is the responsibility of all managers. While the formal human resources department often plays a role in ensuring that performance management activities are carried out, doing the actual work of performance management is the role of the manager.

Exhibit 7.1 illustrates how the various performance management functions interrelate. Employee performance and productivity are at the forefront in healthcare organizations. The Joint Commission requires accredited healthcare organizations to assess, track, and improve the competence of all employees (Joint Commission 2021). Eligibility for the prestigious Baldrige National Quality Award includes specific criteria related to the workforce, including workforce engagement, performance management, and career development (Baldrige Performance Excellence Program 2021). These bodies monitor healthcare organizations' performance management systems because they recognize the importance of high-functioning individuals and teams.

---

performance appraisal
Methods of assessing the level of employee performance.

---

performance management
All the activities supervisors carry out to manage and improve employee performance; includes appraisal, supervision, rewards, and training.

Human Resources Management (HRM) Function	How Performance Management Information Affects HRM Function	How HRM Function Affects Performance Management
Job analysis	Information about employee performance may require that jobs and responsibilities are restructured.	Accurate information about job responsibilities is key to developing criteria for evaluating employee performance.
Diversity, equity, and inclusion	Employee performance information provides guidance to promote the success of traditionally underrepresented groups	Ensuring the success of diversity initiatives requires that organizations have effective methods of onboarding, orientation, and coaching.
Recruitment and selection	Employee performance information provides managers with insight about the effectiveness of alternative sources of recruitment and the effectiveness of selection criteria and procedures.	Ability to recruit and select employees may affect the types of criteria and standards developed to evaluate employee performance.
Training and development	Performance management procedures provide information on employees' training and development needs; performance information provides information to assess training effectiveness.	Performance evaluation tools may be designed and used to assess the impact of training programs.
Compensation	Performance management information provides managers with information to help them design a performance-based compensation system.	A fair and equitable compensation system may lead to higher levels of employee performance.

EXHIBIT 7.1
Performance Management Linkages with Other Human Resources Functions

Performance management serves two overall purposes. First, performance management serves a developmental function aimed at helping employees and teams improve their performance. This function involves a number of activities, including working with employees to set goals, providing ongoing feedback to employees on their performance, identifying training needs, and ensuring that training initiatives are accessible, meaningful, and relevant to the individual's job. Second, performance management may be used for administrative purposes. Administrative functions include using performance management as a tool to make and document personnel decisions (e.g., promotion, discipline, termination), ensuring adherence to legal requirements, evaluating the effectiveness of training activities, and providing input into compensation decisions.

These two purposes—developmental and administrative—may sometimes be in conflict. For example, unlike the supervisor in the "Joan and Abigail" vignette at the beginning of the chapter, who displayed indifference and then blindsided her employee with criticism during a too-brief review, a good manager should be interested in coaching an employee to help the employee identify and overcome obstacles to success. To do this, the manager may ask the employee to be honest about the positive aspects of their performance as well as areas needing improvement. However, if the performance management process also has an impact on compensation decisions (an administrative use of performance management), the employee may be reluctant to identify performance problems if they suspect that acknowledging problems may have a negative impact on their pay. This concern brings up the age-old problem of linking performance with compensation and is discussed further in chapter 8.

PERCEPTIONS OF AND MISUNDERSTANDINGS ABOUT PERFORMANCE MANAGEMENT

As noted earlier, one common issue surrounding performance management is distinguishing between performance appraisal and performance management. *Performance appraisal* refers essentially to obtaining information about employee performance and providing that information to the employee. *Performance management* encompasses a much broader set of activities associated with facilitating employee performance. It is best understood as "an ongoing conversation about performance and how supervisors and the organization can provide additional support when needed" (Aguinis and Burgi-Tian 2021). Performance management uses information about past performance to develop strategies for improving individual, team, and organizational performance. Like other organizations, the consulting and business services firm Deloitte has taken on an expansive role for performance management, well beyond simply obtaining performance information (see the accompanying Case Example for a summary of the performance management approach that Deloitte uses).

Yet another key factor distinguishing performance appraisal and performance management is that the responsibility for performance management lies not only with the

---

(✱) CASE EXAMPLE

Deloitte provides an excellent prototype for the broad scope and meaningfulness of performance management. Its focus is on two key dimensions: (1) engaging and motivating people, and (2) collecting and using reliable assessments of individual performance. Contrary to trends that place paramount emphasis on metrics, the Deloitte model is "analog"—that is, using conversations and recognizing that conversations can be as powerful as numbers. This is not to say that Deloitte has abandoned metrics. Rather, data are used extensively, but the data are drawn from multiple sources and perspectives; Deloitte has recognized that "data only tell part of the story. We need to let our people, their managers, and their counselors tell the rest" (Orlando and Bank 2016).

The Deloitte model consists of five key features: (1) frequent and future-focused check-ins with employees; (2) "performance snapshots" consisting of a four-question instrument to capture a team leader's assessment of team member performance; (3) the Team Pulse Survey, a ten-question survey used to help team leaders understand the team experience; (4) quarterly leadership panel reviews to customize career development plans for employees; and (5) career coaches to provide advice and mentorship to employees. As noted by a Deloitte leader, "We're still learning the power of the new system, understanding the right cadence for everything; it puts the focus on development of our people, and that is really the goal of a performance management system—how [to] get our people performing at a higher level" (Orlando and Bank 2016).

---

manager but also with the employee, team members, and, in some instances, individuals who work with the employee on only a temporary basis but whose perspective is valued in terms of the individual's performance. In today's organizations, it is not unusual for individuals to work on multiple projects or programs, and while employees may have a formal supervisor, they may have informal accountabilities to other managers. This is referred to as a *matrix* structure. A hospital social worker, for example, may have a formal social work supervisor but may also work on clinical teams wherein the team leader may be a physician or a leader from any number of other disciplines, depending on the content of the work. In evaluating an individual's performance in a matrix structure, it is often necessary to obtain input from a range of individuals beyond the formal manager. In fact, it is desirable to encourage employees to think and work beyond their particular "silo." Casciaro, Edmondson, and Jang (2019) suggest that encouraging people to connect with expertise throughout the organization enhances learning and improves organizational performance. Performance management systems that involve individuals outside the immediate workgroup can facilitate this learning. By contrast, in a traditional performance appraisal system, the formal manager is typically the only individual responsible for the process. Opportunities to learn and develop are likely to be missed.

While we understand the importance of taking a broad perspective on employee performance management, most organizations unfortunately are limited in their approach. One of the most common mistakes managers make is to focus performance management simply on the annual performance review, which typically includes documentation of an employee's performance for the year and perhaps an interview. There is nothing inherently wrong with the annual review, but it represents only a fraction of the actual scope of performance management. In fact, if the only feedback that an employee ever receives is during the annual review, it is likely that the annual review discussion will be filled with emotional tension, conflict, and dishonesty, leading to heated disagreements. Furthermore, these negative outcomes may be exacerbated when the annual review is the sole basis for compensation decisions. The key point is that performance management should be an ongoing process that occurs on a daily basis. The annual review is only one component of that process. An effective manager provides feedback continuously and addresses and manages performance problems when they occur. Just as we think about our health daily, not just during an annual physical exam, we should address performance issues—both positive and negative—as they arise and not wait for the official review time. The Mercer organization carries out periodic surveys of human resource issues globally. The accompanying Current Issue sidebar "Mercer's 2019 Global Performance Management Study" presents a summary of key findings from a recent survey (Mercer 2019).

There is also a false perception that performance management is not relevant to all members of the organization. Performance management is relevant across the organization, from lower-level employees to senior managers, and even to individuals outside of the formal organizational structure, such as board members (National Council of Nonprofits 2022). However, there is a mistaken belief that performance management is intended mainly for lower-level employees and that the higher an employee moves in the organization, the less important performance management becomes. This perception may be based on the belief that performance management is sometimes seen as a threatening and even punitive process that is often carried out in a condescending or demeaning manner—which, unfortunately, in many cases is true. In particular, the dreaded "annual review" may be more likely to stimulate fear and defensiveness than a collaborative effort aimed at performance improvement. There is a belief among some people that one of the benefits of moving up in the organization is exemption from such an insulting procedure as performance management. This view may also be based on the assumption that higher-level employees do not need supervision in the same manner that lower-level employees do. Indeed, evidence indicates that performance management does not reach all levels of the organization. Studies have repeatedly found that both supervisors and employees view performance management negatively, with many people questioning its fairness and viewing the process of conducting

CURRENT ISSUE
Mercer's 2019 Global Performance Management Study

The Mercer organization carries out a periodic global survey of performance management. The 2019 study found that only 2 percent of companies felt that their approach to performance management delivered exceptional value (Mercer 2019). Seventy percent of companies indicated the need to improve the linkage between performance management and other workforce-related processes, including employee development, promotions, and succession planning. Between 2013 and 2019, it was found that organizations declined in their use of key elements of performance management, including goal setting with employees, conducting year-end discussions, and completing performance evaluations. In the area of defined job competencies, healthcare organizations were more likely than other organizations to have technical competencies, likely a reflection of the technical expertise required in many healthcare jobs. However, the study found that healthcare providers are less likely than other employers to have performance-related conversations with employees. In healthcare organizations, 70 percent felt that they needed to improve the link between performance management and such functions as employee development, promotions, and succession planning (Mercer 2019).

The Mercer report concluded with "four truths" about performance management. First, goal clarity is of utmost importance in working toward employee improvement. Because of rapid change, employee goals should be set so that employees understand how they contribute to the business. Second, effective coaching is central to improvement, and managers need to be both empathetic and action oriented. Third, while about 15 percent of companies have eliminated numerical ratings, Mercer cautions against completely abandoning ratings because employees need to know where they stand in the organization. Fourth, Mercer emphasizes the need for an "integrated people strategy" whereby employee performance management is integrated with other key functions (Mercer 2019).

performance management interviews as a distasteful and emotionally taxing chore (Holzer et al. 2019).

While employees and managers are certainly supportive of efforts to improve individual, team, and organizational performance, there has been persistent cynicism about the usefulness of traditional performance management procedures. A study of executive-level compensation carried out by the Society for Human Resource Management (SHRM) found that workers perceived a lack of fairness in compensation policies and that highly paid executives were not held to the same performance standards as lower-level employees. Employees often lack a sense of transparency about the performance review process and the criteria on which they are evaluated (Buckingham and Goodall 2015). This perception of inequity is confirmed by research showing that appraisals of senior executives are often done in an inconsistent and haphazard manner (Longnecker and Fink 2017; Longnecker and Gioia 1992; Lucas 2022). However, it is important for performance management to begin at the senior level of the organization, which includes boards objectively evaluating senior executives' performance.

Such an approach communicates the value of performance management to others in the organization, increasing the likelihood that the process will be taken seriously by people at other levels of the organization. The American College of Healthcare Executives (ACHE 2021) has developed a detailed inventory of competencies for healthcare managers, which could easily be adapted into an assessment tool for managers at multiple levels. The American Hospital Association (AHA) also provides detailed guidance for evaluating the hospital CEO (Giella 2017). Similarly, the AHA provides detailed guidance for hospital boards of trustees to help them evaluate the engagement and performance of hospital boards (Lorsbach 2022).

There is, in sum, considerable cynicism about performance management. This cynicism grows out of a perception that aspects of performance management are distasteful, subjective, and uncomfortable. Managers are often ill at ease about sitting down and discussing concerns with employees, and employees may resent the paternalism and condescension that often accompany such discussions. This cynicism is clearly based on the fact that performance appraisals are sometimes punitive in tone, and, particularly when closely tied to employee compensation, have high emotional content.

Related to the high emotional content in performance appraisals is the concern that appraisals often do not achieve their goal of improving accountability. Rather, they serve merely to motivate employees to "cover their bases"—that is, to hide mistakes and problems. Performance management unfortunately has a history of being implemented without clear and objective performance standards and measures, along with a misguided focus on past performance rather than looking toward the future. Many leaders are coming to understand what human resources (HR) leaders have been advocating for many years: Annual reviews should be replaced by ongoing coaching and mentorship, and collaborative planning between managers and employees. The former senior vice president of People Operations for Google stated that "performance management as practiced by most organizations has become a rule-based, bureaucratic process, existing as an end in itself rather than actually shaping performance. Employees hate it. Managers hate it. Even HR departments hate it" (Bock 2015, 152). There has even been a call to abolish performance reviews (see the Current Issue sidebar "Get Rid of the Performance Review?"). We will return to other issues that can be pitfalls for performance management. First, however,

CURRENT ISSUE
Get Rid of the Performance Review?

Various writers in the twenty-first century have commented on the inadequacy of traditional methods of performance appraisal. Some have noted that not only are they often ineffective, but they also may be harmful to employees and the organization overall. In well-publicized articles in *The Wall Street Journal*, Culbert (2008, 2010) advocates abolishing the performance review. He suggests that participants in performance reviews work at cross-purposes. The manager wishes to discuss performance improvement, while the employee is most concerned with compensation. This conflict limits communication, creates unnecessary tension, and has a negative impact on morale. Further, the link between performance and pay is bogus. He states that market forces and the organization's budget, not performance, are the primary determinants of compensation. Likewise, he adds, the claim of objectivity is false, as evidenced by the fact that many employees' performance reviews change substantially when they change managers.

Culbert also claims that performance reviews are often based on a "one size fits all" model, which is inappropriate because each job has its own demands and requirements. He also presents the argument that performance reviews impede rather than support employee growth because employees who ask for help may be viewed as incompetent and lacking in confidence. Teamwork is hindered because reviews typically focus on the individual rather than the team. The author offers an alternative to performance reviews: performance *previews*.

A performance preview enables managers to guide and assist subordinates to improve their performance. Both manager and employee are accountable for improved performance. Using a preview model, the manager and the employee collaboratively address problems. This approach "welds fates together" and asserts that it is "the boss's responsibility to find a way to work well with an imperfect individual, not to convince the individual there are critical flaws that need immediate correcting" (Culbert 2008). If an employee fails to improve or perform to expectations, it is the failure of the manager, not solely of the employee.

More recently, Trost (2017) provided a detailed critique of performance appraisals in which he criticized the design and intent of performance appraisal. He questions, for example, who the "customer" is for performance appraisal. Typically, the customer may be senior managers, supervisors, or the human resources department. He questions why the employee is not considered the customer and how the performance appraisal process would be altered if it focused on employee needs.

At the 2021 SHRM Annual Conference and Expo, attendees learned from survey results that after receiving the annual performance review, 18 percent of women reported crying, while 25 percent of men reported doing so. Thirty-four percent of millennials (people born 1981–1996) said the annual review has driven them to tears. Fifty-seven percent of all the individuals surveyed reported that the annual review made them feel as though they were in competition with coworkers. Presenters noted that the traditional annual review tends to promote favoritism, inconsistency, and a variety of biases. They affirmed that the annual review tends to increase confrontation. They made a number of recommendations, which are also addressed in this chapter (Janove 2021):

1. Initiate more frequent conversations about performance.
2. Adopt a less cumbersome and more welcoming approach.
3. Separate the review from any discussion of compensation.
4. Train managers on coaching techniques to help them get away from being the traditional "boss."
5. Include 360-degree feedback.

it is helpful to address the substance of performance management, the criteria we use to evaluate an employee's performance.

In this chapter, we focus on improving performance management processes. As summarized by Lin and Kellough (2019), we will address the following concerns in the course of the chapter: flawed performance standards or measures; lack of valid information about an employee's performance; inadequate time to conduct an effective appraisal; inadequate or nonexistent training on how to conduct an appraisal; lack of authority on the part of the supervisor; inadequate support from senior management; a history of inflated performance appraisals, making honest appraisal difficult; use of a forced distribution or quota model for rating performance; and concerns with documentation.

DOING PERFORMANCE MANAGEMENT WELL

Despite the widespread criticism of performance management, it remains a vitally important set of activities. Performance management has an impact on virtually all aspects of an organization and the employee's work. Decisions about promotions, compensation, training, discipline, and a host of other factors require a valid and well-implemented performance management system.

Every organization has its own approach to performance management, but there are common themes and approaches that are applicable to any model of performance management. These themes are the importance of criteria for evaluating performance; the necessity of collecting useful information about these criteria; and the importance of training managers to implement performance management as it is intended, including the need for managers to be aware of common errors in evaluating employees. Each of these themes is discussed in the sections that follow.

ESTABLISHING APPRAISAL CRITERIA

performance standards
Indicators of what a job is meant to accomplish, how performance is measured, and what the expected levels of job performance are.

As with all areas of human resources management, an effective performance management system must begin with clear job expectations, responsibilities, and **performance standards**. The process of establishing appraisal criteria begins with the job description (discussed in depth in chapter 4). In today's organizations, job descriptions tend to be dynamic and change frequently because of a variety of factors, including modifications in what a particular job's responsibilities entail, the manner in which departments and teams organized, and the technology being used. The important point is that we should not take for granted that the job description is accurate and current. Just as we need to review the job description prior to recruiting someone to fill a vacant position, the job description must be reviewed as we revamp our performance management system. Otherwise, the performance management process can easily lead to misunderstanding (e.g., "I didn't think that was part of my job!").

Managers and employees need to communicate clearly, agree on the content of the job, and have a shared understanding of job expectations. A key part of this process is agreeing on specific, measurable criteria by which performance will be evaluated and the measures by which these criteria will be evaluated. Evaluation criteria should always be matched to the job description and performance expectations. Criteria development is a challenging task and requires sincere and open employee–manager collaboration. Evaluation criteria must be agreed on well in advance of any type of feedback process, such as periodic performance reviews. More simply, employees should not be surprised in a performance review to hear about the criteria used to assess their performance.

 KEY POINT

> An effective performance management system depends on accurate job descriptions with clear expectations. They need to be communicated clearly to the employee along with the criteria and measures that will be used to assess the employee's performance.

In developing criteria for evaluating an employee's performance, it is important to remember that all jobs ultimately exist to meet organizational goals. In other words, criteria for evaluating an individual employee should have meaning and strategic relevance to the organization as a whole. For example, if improving the level of patient satisfaction is an important organizational goal, it is reasonable to expect that performance criteria for clinical and other staff should be related to patient relations. In fact, if we consider that internal customer relations is also important, customer relations becomes relevant even for employees who do not interact directly with patients.

The first critical issue in developing evaluation criteria is that individual performance appraisal criteria are an extension of criteria used to evaluate the performance of the organization overall. Criteria based on strategic relevance also help justify the need for training to close gaps between employees' current skills and needed competencies to help accomplish organizational objectives.

Second, criteria for evaluating employee performance should be comprehensive, be meaningful, and consider the full range of an employee's major functions as defined in the job description. Managers may, however, fall into the trap of evaluating an employee based on only a limited range of job responsibilities. The problem of **criterion deficiency** emerges when a manager focuses on a single performance criterion to the exclusion of other important, but perhaps less easily quantifiable, performance dimensions (Muchinsky 2006). Managers may tend to focus on an aspect of work that is easily measurable but omit equally important but less easily measurable qualities. For example, counting the number of visits made by a home care nurse is relatively simple. However, if we are concerned with the quality of these visits and the nature of patients seen by the nurse, it is certainly desirable to assess the quality of care provided during those visits as well as the case mix and challenges faced in conducting these home visits.

criterion deficiency
A focus on a single performance criterion to the exclusion of other important but perhaps less quantifiable performance dimensions.

Third, employees should not be evaluated on factors that are clearly outside their control. **Criterion contamination** refers to the influence that factors out of the employee's control may have on performance (Muchinsky 2006). In healthcare, this problem is particularly pervasive because of the complexity of patient care and the interdependence of the factors that affect quality and clinical outcomes. Clinicians, for example, may have little control over patient volume or the speed with which laboratory test results are reported. Therefore, appraisal criteria should include only items over which the employee has control.

Fourth, criteria for evaluating employees should be reliable and valid. **Reliability** refers to the consistency with which a manager rates an employee in successive ratings (assuming consistent performance) or the consistency with which two or more managers rate an employee's performance given comparable information. One of the biggest complaints from employees is lack of fairness in how they are evaluated. Criteria reliability can be improved by selecting objective criteria and by training managers to apply the criteria in an acceptable and systematic manner.

Reliability can be improved if there is a system in place to *calibrate* (adjust or standardize) managers' ratings. The purpose of calibration is to make certain that managers are rating their subordinates according to the defined criteria and avoiding inconsistent ratings, such as those that result from excessive leniency or strictness. Accomplishing calibration among raters is not easy, and it involves developing clear guidelines for rating employees and training managers in their use.

These guidelines may seem straightforward and easy to implement, but in today's world, and certainly for most jobs in healthcare, there are both objective and subjective elements. In a review of performance management processes, Cappelli and Conyon (2018) argue that "jobs are too complex to be governed by simple contracts that require performance to be defined and measured in simple ways." While we ideally should focus evaluations on objective measures of performance, we also need to consider important but more subjective measures of performance. For these more subjective elements, dialogue between managers and employees is critical so that there is agreement on both the importance of these elements and the manner in which an employee will be evaluated.

Validity is the extent to which appraisal criteria actually measure the performance dimension of interest. For example, if we are interested in measuring a nurse's ability to carry out nursing responsibilities during emergency medical procedures, simply measuring the nurse's knowledge of these responsibilities may be inadequate. It would be important to have methods to actually observe and assess the nurse's success in carrying out these procedures. Such assessment may be accomplished through observation of a real emergency situation or a simulated situation that requires the application of these procedures.

Having clear criteria for evaluation is the first step in developing accurate and useful appraisals. However, even with such criteria in place, there are numerous opportunities for managers to inaccurately rate employees. Known as **rating errors**, managers' distortions of performance ratings—positive or negative—reduce the accuracy and usefulness of appraisals.

Distortions are often related to the attitudes and disposition of the manager. The following eight rating errors are most commonly made:

1. *Distributional.* These errors come from raters' tendency to use only a selected part of the rating scale. There are three forms of distributional errors:

    A. *Leniency:* A rater may be biased in favor of giving positive ratings, not necessarily because it is justified by high performance levels but often to avoid conflict and confrontation with an employee.

    B. *Strictness:* This is a characteristic of raters who are overly critical of performance and accordingly may be viewed as unfair when compared with other raters. Strictness is at the opposite end of the distributional error spectrum from leniency.

    C. *Central tendency:* Like lenient raters, some raters try to avoid conflict and confrontation by essentially rating everyone average, or in the middle of a rating scale, instead of honestly evaluating their actual performance.

2. *Halo effect.* These errors occur when a manager rates an employee high on all evaluation criteria, without distinguishing between components of the employee's work. That is, a manager who is particularly fond of a particular employee may rate that person high on all aspects of performance without identifying differences in performance among work tasks and responsibilities. The opposite, known as the *horn effect*, may also occur: Managers who have a difficult relationship with an employee may rate that employee low on all aspects of performance, regardless of actual job performance. (The names of the two effects allude to an angel's halo and a devil's horns.)

3. *Personal bias.* Related to the halo/horn effect, personal bias may lead a manager to rate an employee higher or lower than deserved because of the rater's personal like or dislike of the employee. Personal bias may be *explicit* (conscious and purposeful) or *implicit* (unconscious). The issue of implicit bias is pervasive in management and is addressed specifically in chapter 11.

4. *Similar-to-me errors.* These errors occur when a rater evaluates those who are similar to them more highly than those who are not like them (Grant 2018). Earlier research showed this bias to be strongest when a manager and an employee share demographic characteristics, such as race and age group (Snell and Morris 2018).

5. *Spillover effect* or *past-record anchoring.* Evidence has been found that managers tend to be positively biased toward employees whom they have previously evaluated in a positive manner (Breuer, Nicken, and Sliwka 2013).

6. *Contrast effect.* These errors occur when raters compare employees with one another rather than use objective standards for job performance. The forced distribution ranking system (discussed later in this chapter) deliberately uses this strategy in assessing employees.

7. *Temporal errors.* This type of error occurs as a result of how performance-related information is selected. *Recency errors* occur when a manager evaluates an employee based largely on recent events—which may be positive or negative—rather than on performance during an entire evaluation period. (This is what happened to Joan in the "Abigail and Joan" vignette that opened the chapter.) The recency effect may also come into play when a manager sees improvement in an employee and, rather than evaluate the employee on established criteria, the manager compares current with past performance, leading to rating inflation. In other words, managers may inflate a performance rating based on the magnitude of improvement rather than on objective measures of performance.

8. *Inaccurate information or preparation.* For many jobs, managers need to spend time identifying and soliciting information from individuals who work closely with the employee. A biased performance evaluation may result if managers fail to obtain relevant information about an employee's performance. This issue is particularly critical for employees who work on multiple teams, whereby the employee's performance may not be easily seen by the formal manager.

In addition to conscious and unconscious biases that may affect the appraisal process, the reality of politics in organizations can distort an otherwise well-designed performance management process. Pressures from within the organization may induce a manager to inflate, deflate, or completely avoid doing a performance review. Managers may realize that they will have to continue working with the employee, and a review that is less than completely positive may harm their relationship and upset workplace climate and productivity. In such instances, a manager may inflate an appraisal to eliminate the potential for conflict and discord.

A manager may also falsely inflate an appraisal to enable an employee to receive a merit increase or other financial reward. Although unwarranted inflation of ratings destroys the intent of both performance management and the compensation system (discussed further in chapter 8), managers may choose to err on the side of generosity toward the employee. This practice raises a fundamental problem with pay-for-performance systems—namely, that the appraisal process may become biased when compensation enters the equation.

Similarly, managers may artificially deflate an appraisal to shock an employee into improving or to teach a rebellious employee a lesson. No evidence exists that such treatments are effective, but there is the risk that in their position of power, managers may "weaponize" the appraisal process. Managers may also artificially deflate an appraisal to speed up the discipline or termination process. This possibility raises the issue of ensuring ongoing documentation of employee performance—both positive and negative. If managers evaluate their employees on a regular basis, there should be no need to exaggerate negative aspects of an employee's performance should the need for discipline or termination of employment arise. Exhibit 7.2 summarizes these and other political distortions of the appraisal process.

COLLECTING JOB PERFORMANCE DATA

As discussed earlier, employee performance information is collected for both developmental and administrative purposes. Traditional performance appraisal methods involve the supervisor observing and recording the employee's performance using a format provided by the organization. Ideally, the supervisor communicates to the employee the criteria and measures used to assess performance. These criteria may be outcome, output, or behavioral measures. Outcomes, for example, may include the impact or quality of an

EXHIBIT 7.2
Political Pressures to Distort a Performance Review

Reasons Managers May Inflate an Appraisal	Reasons Managers May Deflate an Appraisal
To maximize merit increases for an employee, particularly when the merit ceiling is considered low	To shock an employee into higher performance
To avoid hanging "dirty laundry" out in public (in case the appraisal information is viewed by outsiders)	To teach a rebellious employee a lesson
To avoid creating a written record of poor performance that would become a permanent part of the individual's personnel file	To send a message to an employee suggesting that the employee should think about leaving the organization
To avoid confrontation with an employee with whom the manager recently had difficulties	To build a strongly documented record of poor performance that may speed up the termination process
To give a break to a subordinate who has shown improvements	
To promote an undesirable employee "up and out" of the organization	

Source: Adapted from Longenecker, Sims, and Gioia (1987).

employee's work. For an individual working in an academic medical center, an outcome may be the number of publications in refereed journals or the individual's record in acquiring National Institutes of Health research grants. Clinical outcomes might include the percentage of hypertensive patients who have controlled blood pressure. Output measures might include the number of patients seen over a period of time. Behavioral measures may include a range of topics, including communication skills, teamwork, and patient relations. Given the complexity of many jobs, however, it is often impossible for a single supervisor to accurately assess each employee's performance along multiple dimensions. For example, in the example of an organization with a matrix structure described earlier, there are circumstances wherein an employee may spend a significant amount of time working on a project that may be managed by someone other than the employee's supervisor. The supervisor may not have the opportunity to observe and assess the employee's performance. In response to such situations, various alternative approaches to performance data collection have been developed.

A **self-appraisal** is an evaluation done by the employee being evaluated (see "Did You Know?" sidebar). It is generally done prior to the formal appraisal conducted by the manager and is typically done for developmental purposes. Self-appraisals can also broaden managers' understanding of employees and their jobs and improve managers' understanding of the factors associated with employees' performance. Self-appraisals may also be used to identify areas of potential disagreement between employee and manager to facilitate more meaningful discussion. This approach is particularly useful when a manager seeks employee involvement in the appraisal process, and is an important component of employee engagement.

An important challenge in performance management is evaluating a manager's effectiveness as a supervisor of others. That person's manager may be incapable of validly assessing this individual's supervisory effectiveness. In this instance, employees may be asked to evaluate their supervisor's performance. This process can be useful to help managers develop their supervisory skills. Referred to as **subordinate appraisal**, this approach can identify areas in which managers lack self-awareness and help improve managerial effectiveness. However, from the subordinates' perspective, providing information on their supervisor's performance may be viewed as risky because of fear that managers may retaliate against them if they perceive anything negative in the evaluation. Thus, such appraisals should be done anonymously; if anonymity cannot be preserved, the appraisal is unlikely to provide valid information. Subordinate appraisal is most likely to be useful in organizations with a healthy and open organizational climate.

A **team-based appraisal** evaluates the work of a team and is typically done as a supplement to individual appraisal. An organization that measures and rewards team accomplishments signals that it places a high value on teamwork. Organizations may link team performance with pay, although team-based compensation is not a necessary component

self-appraisal
An evaluation done by an employee on the employee's own performance, usually in conjunction with the manager's performance appraisal.

subordinate appraisal
A performance evaluation of a manager by the manager's subordinates.

team-based appraisal
Evaluation of the work of teams; used under the assumption that service or product quality is largely the result of team, not individual, efforts.

DID YOU KNOW?
Differences in Self-Ratings

When doing self-appraisals, there is a common perception that people will tend to exaggerate their level of performance. However, the situation is more complex. In some circumstances, for example, women tend to be less confident than men (Bordalo et al. 2019) and less likely to self-promote or ask for a promotion (Bosquet, Combes, and García-Peñalosa 2019; Exley and Kessler 2021; Hospido, Laeven, and Lamo 2022). Such situations may result in lower self-appraisal ratings relative to men. Although it turns out that people do exaggerate their performance level in many circumstances, it has been found that high-performing employees tend to provide more accurate self-assessments than lower-performing employees. In addition, cultural differences play a role in self-appraisals. In cultures that stress individual achievement (such as the United States), individual efforts and outcomes are emphasized, and self-appraisals tend to be exaggerated. In collectivist cultures emphasizing harmony and solidarity (such as India), employees may be less willing to draw attention to themselves and may report more modest self-appraisals (Varma, Budhwar, and DeNisi 2008).

team-based compensation
Rewards given to individual members of a team in recognition of the team's performance.

of team-based appraisal. In fact, **team-based compensation** may exacerbate anxieties and frustrations if the team experiences the **free rider syndrome**, a problem affecting teams in which one or more members benefit from team rewards without putting forth corresponding effort.

If team-based appraisals are used, there must be agreement on appraisal criteria, including the mix of behavior-based, output-based, and outcome-based criteria. Team members may also assess the performance of other team members. This approach reinforces to employees that the organization values responsible team behavior and **team citizenship**; it may also increase team cohesion and enhance communication. How team members are involved in appraisals needs to be addressed: Are all members involved in appraising every other member? Who should provide feedback to members? While this approach may help build teams, it could also result in alienation and conflict if feedback is provided in a divisive manner. Therefore, those involved in providing feedback should be trained in interviewing and feedback techniques.

Team-based appraisals remain relatively rare. A 2016 survey of 218 human resources management leaders found that 90 percent of respondents used individual performance information, while only 15 percent included team evaluations, and less than 5 percent

free rider syndrome
A problem affecting teams in which one or more members benefit from team rewards without putting forth corresponding effort.

team citizenship
Employee behaviors and attitudes that are respectful of team norms and expectations.

incorporated team development strategies into their performance management processes (*Human Resource Executive* 2016). Thus, while much attention has been focused on the importance of teamwork, performance management processes remain focused on the individual. As stated by a director of human resources in a large healthcare system, "There is an acknowledgement that we do much of our work in teams, cross-functionally, but the system we use for performance management hasn't kept up with reality. It can only handle the direct reporting relationship" (*Human Resource Executive* 2016).

Recognition that managers may have incomplete information about an employee's performance led to the development of tools to obtain information from multiple sources. **Multisource appraisal**—also known as *360-degree feedback* or *multirater assessment*—recognizes that for many jobs, reliance on only one source of performance information is inadequate. The basis of multisource appraisal is that an employee's performance cannot be comprehensively assessed unless perspectives are obtained from others within, and sometimes outside, the organization. These sources may include the employee's supervisor, peers, subordinates, clients, and other internal and external customers. Typically, multisource appraisal is done for developmental purposes, and it must be designed and administered with great care. Benefits and limitations or risks of multisource appraisal are summarized in exhibit 7.3.

Information about employee performance can be based on individual traits and characteristics, behaviors, and results or outcomes. Selection of a particular type of information depends largely on the nature of the job. Performance in these three dimensions can be quantified using the methods explored in the following sections. Each approach has its strengths and shortcomings and is useful for particular types of jobs and circumstances.

Ranking

Ranking is a simple method of appraisal in which managers list employees in order from best to worst on some overall measure of employee performance. Ranking is typically employed for administrative purposes, such as for making personnel decisions (e.g., pay increases, promotions, and layoffs). Although it is useful for such purposes, ranking lacks the precision of other methods. Ranking is disadvantageous because it

- ◆ focuses only on a summary rating of work performance and may not take into account the complexity of jobs;

- ◆ becomes cumbersome with large numbers of employees and may force appraisers to artificially distinguish among employees;

- ◆ lists employees in order of their performance but does not indicate the relative differences in employees' contribution to the organization; and

- ◆ provides no guidance on specific deficiencies in employee performance and therefore is not useful in helping employees improve.

multisource appraisal
A form of performance evaluation in which many individuals—such as supervisors, subordinates, other coworkers, customers, and patients—provide a richer description of an employee's performance than may be obtained from a single rater. Also referred to as *360-degree feedback* or *multirater assessment*.

ranking
A method of appraisal in which managers list employees in order from best to worst on an overall measure of employee performance.

One type of ranking that has come under a great deal of criticism is the process of **forced distribution**, also known as *forced ranking* or *stack ranking*. With forced distribution models, employees are compared with other employees, not evaluated on their own performance. Managers are instructed to assign a defined percentage of employee performance evaluations into predetermined performance categories, similar to grading students on a curve.

For example, managers may be directed to designate 15 percent of employees as high performers, 20 percent as moderately high, 30 percent as average, 20 percent as low average, and 15 percent as poor. Although largely out of favor, the forced distribution approach has been justified in a number of ways, including the following (Giumetti, Schroeder, and Switzer 2015):

forced distribution
A performance evaluation method in which managers are required to assign a defined percentage of employees to particular predetermined performance categories. Also called *forced ranking* or *stack ranking*.

◆ It minimizes leniency by requiring managers to assign a set proportion of employees into designated performance levels.

◆ It brings discipline to the appraisal process.

◆ Because it is a comparative process, it may be used for such purposes as promotion and compensation decisions, job assignments, and layoffs.

◆ It encourages managers to provide employees with honest feedback and helps minimize rater bias.

◆ It can help reinforce a norm of intolerance for low performance.

◆ It can help organizations focus on important performance criteria.

Although these objectives may be met by using a forced distribution approach, they may corrupt the entire purpose of performance management, which is to obtain honest information that can be used for employee development and improvement. Managers may also be uncomfortable with the expectation that a defined percentage of their employees must be classified as "poor." The implicit assumption is that the percentage ranked lowest are "bad" employees and perform at a level potentially requiring discipline or dismissal. In fact, one can have a high-performing work unit where all employees are excellent; forced distribution, however, requires that managers sort their employees into high- and low-performing groups. Where there are critical staff shortages, this technique may have marginal utility. That is, rather than firing employees who have been designated as low performers, investing in training and development may yield more positive results.

The most controversial use of forced distribution was developed by Jack Welch, former chief executive officer of General Electric (Welch and Byrne 2003). Known as the "20-70-10 plan," this scenario requires managers to assign employees to one of three groups. This approach requires that the lowest 10 percent of employees be told to improve or eventually

Exhibit 7.3
Multisource
Appraisal Benefits
and Limitations or
Risks

Benefits	Limitations or Risks
Emphasizes performance dimensions valued by the organization	People providing feedback must have a high level of trust in the organization, the managers, and the appraisal process.
Provides the employee with richer and more useful information than may be obtained from an appraisal conducted by a single supervisor	Employees must be assured of anonymity, which is difficult in small organizations or where a manager has a small span of control.
Explicitly recognizes the importance of focusing on internal and external customers	A psychologically safe environment is needed for multisource appraisal to work.
Aligns with team development goals and initiatives	Employees may use the appraisal as a means of retribution.
Contributes to employee involvement and development	Information obtained from multiple sources may be difficult to integrate or combine.
Minimizes bias because it includes multiple perspectives	Feedback must be done by a trained individual in a positive manner that encourages insight and growth.

be fired. This approach is hotly debated (see Debate Point sidebar). One study of human resources executives, half of whom worked in organizations that use forced distribution, reported that this approach resulted in lower productivity, inequity, and skepticism, and negatively affected employee engagement, morale, trust in management, and collaboration (Pfeffer and Sutton 2006). Lawsuits have been filed at such companies as Ford Motor Company and Goodyear that have challenged the legality of forced distribution, claiming that the process discriminates against older workers. Ford abandoned forced distribution in 2001 and settled two class-action cases for about $10.5 million (Bates 2003). In 2013, Microsoft abandoned forced distribution, in large part because of its negative impact on developing high-performing teams, as well as legal challenges claiming that the ranking process was discriminatory (Olson 2013).

Forced distribution models may have a negative impact on motivation, particularly among employees who were not assigned to the highest-performing group. According to expectancy theory, people are motivated when feel there is a linkage between the effort (E) they put into their work and their performance (P), and between their performance (P) and rewards (R). For example, if a student feels that no matter how hard they study (E) for an exam, they are likely not to pass (P), then they would perceive no reward (R) to be gained from making the effort to study. Using expectancy theory, Chattopadhyay (2019) studied the $E \rightarrow P \rightarrow R$ relationships among employees working under a forced distribution system and compared their motivation with that of employees working under a normal appraisal system. The study found that the individuals in the forced distribution model lacked the expectation that effort would lead to performance and that higher levels of performance would lead to greater rewards. In essence, they lacked the expectation that there would be a "return on investment" of their effort.

Graphic Rating Scale

A **graphic rating scale** is a rating scale that uses points along a continuum and measures employee traits or behaviors. Despite its shortcomings, this method is popular because scales are easy to construct and, with limitations, can be applied to many types of jobs. Such scales measure a series of dimensions through anchor points (such as a scale of 1 to 6) that indicate levels of performance. As the example in exhibit 7.4 shows, both traits and behaviors may be assessed. Note that many of the items included in the exhibit may be prone to subjective judgment and misinterpretation; as discussed in the next paragraph, this is a major criticism of graphic rating scales.

Among the drawbacks of graphic rating scales is that scale items may be overly general and not specific to the requirements of a particular job. Critical job-specific items may be absent from a graphic rating scale that is applied uniformly across the organization. In their most basic form, graphic rating scales may also be highly subjective. Without

graphic rating scale
An employee performance rating scale that uses points along a continuum and measures traits or behaviors. Such a scale may be prone to subjective judgment and misinterpretation.

(X) DEBATE POINT

Forced distribution, or forced ranking, was developed in part as a response to managers being overly lenient with employees and not applying effective performance expectations. Where it has been used, this approach has shown some effectiveness in forcing managers to better distribute their rankings and, ideally, to rate employees more honestly. Although this approach has been largely but not entirely discarded, are there aspects to forced distribution that should be maintained? Are there certain types of organizations in which forced distribution is more useful than in others? And are there some types of organizations where forced distribution is clearly destructive to the goals and perhaps culture of the organization? Understanding that there are always trade-offs in the use of certain practices, are there situations where the benefits of forced ranking outweigh the costs? What would those situations be?

specifically identifying the metrics used to develop ratings, graphic rating scales can have low reliability because managers may differ in the definition of criteria and the basis on which to rate a particular employee. When used without adequate discussion and coaching, employees may lack information about areas needing improvement and how to improve their performance. Managers themselves may find these scales awkward to use because they may not see these scales as relevant to the employee's job. Managers may be particularly uncomfortable when subjective and ill-defined performance ratings are linked with employee compensation.

Perhaps the most important drawback of graphic rating scales is that they typically do not weight behaviors and traits according to their importance to a particular job. For

EXHIBIT 7.4

Example of a Graphic Rating Scale

Rater: Please answer the following questions about the employee.

Question	Scale					
1. How would you rate this person's pace of work?	1 slow	2	3	4	5	6 fast
2. What level of effort does this person expend?	1 below capacity	2	3	4	5	6 full capacity
3. What is the quality of this person' work?	1 poor	2	3	4	5	6 good
4. How would you describe this person's degree of flexibility?	1 rigid	2	3	4	5	6 flexible
5. How would you rate this person's openness to new ideas?	1 closed	2	3	4	5	6 open
6. How much supervision does this person need?	1 a lot	2	3	4	5	6 a little
7. How readily does this person offer to help out by doing work outside the normal scope of the person's work?	1 seldom	2	3	4	5	6 often
8. How well does this person get along with coworkers?	1 not well	2	3	4	5	6 very well

example, pace of work (item 1 in exhibit 7.4) may be crucial to the job of some employees but unimportant to others. Another risk is using a one-size-fits-all approach to criteria—sometimes a scale is borrowed from another organization or adapted for another position without considering how the scale applies to the particular job or organization.

Behavioral Anchored Rating Scale

Graphic rating scales can be improved by the use of a **behavioral anchored rating scale (BARS)**, which provides specific behavioral descriptions, or "anchor" statements, descriptive of particular levels of employee performance for each important job dimension. Exhibit 7.5 is an example of a BARS that measures the performance of a clinical trials coordinator. Note that the scale assesses the four dimensions of leadership, communication, delivery of results, and teamwork, all of which are highly relevant to the work of a clinical trials coordinator. In some instances, the behavioral measures are relatively easy to observe (e.g., delivery of results), while in other instances, the measures may be a bit more subjective (e.g., teamwork). Using BARS, a manager can explain the reason behind the ratings rather than vaguely state "unacceptable" or "average" in response to the performance criteria. With BARS, managers can explicitly describe their expectations for improved performance.

Developing a BARS is not a simple matter. Ideally, a BARS is established through the joint efforts of a manager and an employee. It requires a firm understanding of the job as well as agreement on both the most important job dimensions and the behavioral anchors associated with each job dimension.

Behavioral anchored rating scales provide a number of advantages over other appraisal methods. They may be more acceptable to both managers and employees because they focus on observable job dimensions and behaviors of direct relevance to the job, which reduces the potential for rating errors and bias. Response categories are also more clearly defined. That is, actual behaviors are used instead of vague adjectives, such as *good* and *fair*. BARS can minimize employee defensiveness and conflict with the manager by basing appraisal on observable behaviors. Finally, BARS provides a foundation for identifying areas for training and development (see the Current Issue sidebar "Using a BARS to Improve Surgical Safety").

Among the disadvantages of using a BARS is the amount of time, effort, and expense that may be required for its development. Use of this approach is most justifiable when a large number of jobholders are performing the same job (e.g., nurses, transporters). Use of a BARS is most appropriate for jobs whose major components consist of physically observable behaviors.

A variation of the BARS is the **behavioral observation scale**, an approach whereby the rater indicates the frequency with which the employee exhibits specified desirable behaviors that have been identified through job analysis and discussions with managers and supervisors. Exhibit 7.6 is an example of a behavioral observation scale for a patient relations representative. As seen in the exhibit, six desirable behaviors for this job are identified, and

behavioral anchored rating scale (BARS) A performance measurement scale that identifies the key dimensions of a job and specifies observable behaviors descriptive of particular levels of performance for each job dimension.

behavioral observation scale A performance measurement system that asks the rater to indicate the frequency with which the employee exhibits specified desirable behaviors.

EXHIBIT 7.5
Example of
a Behavioral
Anchored Rating
Scale for a Clinical
Trials Coordinator

Task Dimension	Scale	Definition
Leadership	4	Identifies alternative methods that enhance productivity and quality and that eliminate unnecessary steps
	3	Takes the initiative to bring attention to productivity problems
	2	Has difficulty with change and providing support for the required change
	1	Uses inappropriate interpersonal skills and creates unproductive working relationships
Communication	4	Communicates openly, completely, and straightforwardly with management, peers, and coworkers
	3	Listens and seeks intent of communication
	2	Has difficulty expressing decisions, plans, and actions
	1	Is unable to communicate accurately with team members
Delivery of results	4	Completes 90 to 100 percent of all projects within specified time frame and budget and according to standards
	3	Completes 75 to 90 percent of all projects within specified time frame and budget and according to standards
	2	Completes 50 to 75 percent of projects within specified time frame and budget; sometimes produces substandard work
	1	Completes less than 50 percent of projects within specified time frame and budget; frequently produces substandard work
Teamwork	4	Contributes positively to problem definition and takes responsibility for outcomes
	3	Respects suggestions and viewpoints of others
	2	Has trouble interacting with others and understanding individual differences
	1	Does not contribute positively to team functioning

> **CURRENT ISSUE**
> Using a BARS to Improve Surgical Safety
>
> The World Health Organization (WHO) developed a behaviorally anchored rating scale (BARS) to evaluate the use of the Surgical Safety Checklist developed by WHO. Five domains are included in the instrument, known as WHOBARS, with each domain associated with a specific aspect of behavior, communication, or verification critical to the success of the checklist. WHOBARS was created for use in research and assessment of surgical team performance to compare differences among institutions and as a tool to measure improvement after an intervention focused on improving the use of the checklist (Devcich et al. 2016). A follow-up study found that WHOBARS demonstrated high reliability as a method of evaluating how well surgical teams adhere to surgical checklist protocols (Medvedev et al. 2019).

the rater indicates the frequency with which the patient relations representative observed each behavior. As with the BARS, there must be a clear understanding of the job and those behaviors most reflective of high levels of performance. Managers and employees must agree on the behaviors expected of the employee.

Critical Incident Approach

Critical incidents refer to workplace occurrences and employee behaviors that are outstanding or substandard. Using the **critical incident approach**, managers keep a record of unusually favorable or unfavorable occurrences in an employee's work. These incidents may then be used in performance feedback sessions and can supplement and enrich other methods, such as graphic rating scales. A strength of this method is that it provides a richly descriptive record of an employee's performance and can be useful in subsequent discussions with the employee. The method may also increase the perception of fairness in that managers are required to tangibly justify ratings with observable evidence. The approach requires that the manager closely and continuously monitor employee performance, which is not always feasible, although linking the critical incident method with multisource appraisal raises the possibility that incidents may be observed and recorded by other individuals in the organization.

critical incident approach
A performance management method in which a manager collects employee performance information by keeping a record of favorable or unfavorable occurrences in an employee's work.

Exhibit 7.6
Example of
a Behavioral
Observation
Scale for a
Patient Relations
Representative

	Almost Never				Almost Always
1. Responds to patient or family concerns within 24 hours	1	2	3	4	5
2. Conducts investigations into complaints effectively	1	2	3	4	5
3. Communicates results of investigations to relevant parties	1	2	3	4	5
4. Follows up with patient or family after investigation	1	2	3	4	5
5. Identifies and analyzes both immediate and distant causes of patient complaints	1	2	3	4	5
6. Makes useful and practical recommendations for improvement based on results of investigation	1	2	3	4	5

Documentation of critical incidents need not be lengthy, but it should be tied to an important performance dimension. The following hypothetical example describes a critical incident for a mental health case manager:

In speaking with her client—an individual with a severe mental disorder—the case manager discovered that the client was about to be evicted from her apartment for nonpayment of rent. She was able to work with the client and the landlord to develop a payment plan and to negotiate successfully with the landlord to have much-needed repairs in the apartment done. She followed up with the client weekly regarding payment to the landlord and the home repairs, and positive outcomes have been achieved in rent payment, home repairs, and the client's emotional stability.

This incident provides an excellent illustration of the case manager's creativity and skills in negotiation and communication, all of which are important performance dimensions for a case manager.

A weakness of the method is that the incidents collected may be viewed out of context and in some cases may create a false impression of a pattern where none exists. In instances where unfavorable incidents are recorded and discussed, the employee may feel defensive when those collected incidents are brought up, particularly if they had been previously resolved and, from the employee's point of view, there would seem to be no reason to "rehash" them. The manager should steer the discussion to emphasize what was learned from those incidents and how the employee has applied (or can apply) that learning to improve subsequent job performance.

Management by Objectives

Performance management methods discussed to this point have focused largely on employee behaviors. Behaviors are important, but productivity and actual outcomes are critical. Here we discuss a performance management method that emphasizes linking organization-wide goals with individual employee goals (for our purposes, we will use the terms *objectives* and *goals* interchangeably). The process involves setting organizational goals, establishing corresponding departmental goals, discussing departmental goals with employees, setting individual goals with employees, assessing individual achievement of these goals, and providing feedback and coaching to help employees improve their performance. Individual goals are usually outcome driven, such as improving patient satisfaction scores, successful implementation of a new program, or improved patient outcomes. They may also be behavioral, such as improving the manner in which team members work together. Two key aspects of this goal-setting process are that goals are (1) aligned and supportive of organizational objectives, and (2) set collaboratively by the employee and the manager. This outcome-driven appraisal process may be referred to by other terms, such as *management by results*, but the general principle may be summarized by the term **management by objectives (MBO)**.

Achievement of individual goals becomes the standard by which each employee's performance is assessed. As with all forms of performance management, monitoring and feedback should be an ongoing process, which enables employees to assess their own progress and provides managers with an opportunity to coach and mentor their subordinates. Key strengths of this method include the following:

- ◆ Ensures that employee goals support departmental and organizational goals

- ◆ Facilitates agreement between manager and employee about goals and metrics for measuring goal achievement

- ◆ Provides a clear basis for managers to provide ongoing objective feedback and coaching to improve employee performance

MBO is most effective when managers and employees understand that senior management supports and is committed to it. MBO requires managers to obtain substantial training in setting goals, giving feedback, and coaching. Although goal setting is central to MBO, the process by which goals are set is also highly important.

management by objectives (MBO)
A performance management method that involves setting performance goals for employees, coaching them to help them achieve their goals, and reviewing progress over a specified period.

KEY POINT

Goal setting is an important aspect of employee supervision. For goal setting to be effective, goals must be clear, measurable, realistic, and developed in collaboration with the employee. Employees must also be given the tools to succeed, including appropriate training and coaching.

Depending on the job, organizations may use a variety of results-oriented methods such as MBO. These approaches are most useful when the work yields objectively measurable outcomes. Variations of MBO are most commonly used for senior executives, for whom objectively measurable bottom-line concerns may be paramount, as well as salespeople and, beyond the field of healthcare, sports teams and individual athletes. The approach may be combined with other performance appraisal methods, particularly for jobs in which both the manner in which work is done (that is, behaviors) and outcomes are critical and measurable.

Performance Review Interview

A performance review interview provides an opportunity for a supervisor and an employee to reflect on the employee's performance and plan for the future (see Critical Concept sidebar "The Contents of a Performance Review Interview"). In most organizations, performance reviews are formally conducted on an annual basis and may include discussions about personnel decisions, such as a promotion, change in compensation, disciplinary action, transfer, or recommendations for training. As noted throughout this chapter, supervisors should provide employees with feedback on a continuous basis, not just at review time, and supervisors and employees should come into the annual performance review interview with a view toward developing improvement strategies and problem solving. The annual review is not a time to deliver surprises to employees. The performance review should be reserved for the following actions:

◆ Providing employees with the opportunity to discuss performance and performance standards

◆ Addressing employee strengths and weaknesses

◆ Identifying and recommending strategies for improvement

◆ Discussing personnel decisions, such as compensation, promotion, and termination

◆ Defining a variety of regulatory requirements that deal with employee performance and discussing compliance methods

The administrative purposes of the performance review interview commonly revolve around decisions regarding promotion, compensation, or termination. To defend against charges of discrimination, organizations should maintain accurate and current information on employee performance. For example, if disciplinary action is required, it is essential that managers have a record of behaviors that may warrant such action.

The developmental role of the performance review interview includes improving employee performance, identifying strengths and weaknesses, suggesting training opportunities, and providing advice on career development.

Among the many challenges in performance management is addressing both administrative and developmental needs. It may be unrealistic to expect an employee to focus on individual development while waiting for information about a raise. A common practice is to separate the performance review interview from the process of informing employees about compensation decisions, perhaps providing the latter information several weeks after the formal review. (Compensation is discussed in detail in chapter 8.) Because performance management has historically focused on evaluation and performance measurement, relatively little attention has been given to its role in improvement, yet the ultimate objective of performance management is to improve employee performance.

A key step in the improvement process is to provide performance information to the employee. Many managers are reluctant to provide feedback because they fear confrontation and conflict, which are real concerns, given many employees' negative past experiences with performance management. In discussing performance with an employee who has shown performance concerns, it is essential for the manager to diagnose and understand the sources of a performance problem. We typically think of performance problems as being

---

⚠ CRITICAL CONCEPT
The Contents of a Performance Review Interview

The formal performance review is a time to reflect on past performance and plan for the future. Employee and manager can discuss problems and suggest solutions. There should be no surprises during this discussion. Although suggestions for improvement should certainly be discussed, critical information about performance should have been communicated earlier, close to the time at which the particular performance issue happened. Discussing compensation at a separate meeting is advisable so the interview can center on improvement and not money.

rooted in ability or motivation. Where abilities are lacking, then engaging the employee in a discussion of training and development opportunities is appropriate. In other instances, motivation may be a concern, and this issue may be related to the organization's reward and incentive system. There may also be distracting personal circumstances, including emotional challenges faced by the employee. Finally, performance problems may be rooted in organizational factors, such as relationships with team members and supervisors, the manner in which a job is designed and work distributed, and the quality of supervision. There may be a combination of factors at play, which is why performance interviews need to be interactive so that the employee can provide information to help a manager identify the sources of performance obstacles.

SMART Goals

Critical to achieving performance improvement is goal-setting. Many managers use the SMART acronym as a guide. Goals should be

Specific,

Measurable,

Achievable,

Relevant, and

Time-bound.

For example, consider a common, yet often unmet, New Year's resolution: "to be healthier." Without specificity, the goal setter lacks criteria by which it will be possible to judge whether the individual has become healthier. "To lose ten pounds" is a better goal: It is specific and clearly measurable.

Goals should be challenging but achievable. Whether a goal of losing ten pounds is achievable depends to a great extent on individual circumstances. An already lean person may not be capable of losing ten pounds, nor would doing so be likely to improve such a person's health. For such an individual, a more achievable and relevant goal might be "to take regular walks" to improve cardiovascular health and overall fitness.

A time frame for achieving the goal should be set to keep the goal relevant and motivate the individual. For example, we could further revise the original goal to "to lose ten pounds within five months." We have now revised our original and likely-to-be-neglected goal, "to be healthier," to a goal that is SMART and more likely to be achieved: to lose ten pounds within five months, which would translate to just two pounds per month. It would be up to the individual to determine whether the weight loss would be accomplished through a decrease in calorie consumption, an increase in exercise, or a combination of the two. For the lean individual in the previous example, changing the goal from the general one "to take regular walks" to the specific one "to walk at least one mile three times a week" would make it easier to tell whether this ongoing goal had been achieved each week.

The SMART guideline for goal setting has broad applications. In the workplace, it can be used as an effective tool for performance management. Managers and employees can use SMART goals to define and set clear expectations about job performance and performance improvement. SMART goals can be used to create accountability and can serve as a specific, objective basis for future feedback and performance review.

Managers and employees can also use SMART goals as a guide to designing strategies for improvement. For example, if a nurse in a clinic has a goal to "in three months, reduce the time a patient waits to have blood pressure taken to within 15 minutes of arrival," the nurse can work with the manager to develop a plan for achieving it. The manager and the nurse may determine that the intake system requires modifications to achieve this goal; the two can then develop a plan to make the needed changes. This approach to goal setting yields goals that motivate, rather than defeat, employees. Further, it promotes performance improvement that is relevant to the organization.

In keeping with SMART goals, the following ten guidelines can help make a performance management interview useful and valuable:

1. *Provide feedback and coaching on an ongoing basis.* This is the most important of all guidelines for discussing performance with employees. Managers should review employees' performance regularly, not just during the formal review process. Giving continuous feedback is a key managerial responsibility. By providing ongoing feedback, the manager preempts any surprises at the formal appraisal. The "Joan and Abigail" and "Bob and Carolyn" vignettes at the beginning of this chapter illustrate (among other things) the problems faced when feedback does not occur on a regular basis.

2. *Evaluate the frequency and content of formal performance reviews.* The frequency of formal appraisals varies according to an employee's performance and longevity in the organization. For an average performer, more frequent interviews may be necessary to ensure that improvement goals are on track. For marginal or poor performers, formal interviews may need to be held monthly (or perhaps more often) to provide an opportunity for closer coaching and, if necessary, disciplinary action.

   For a high performer, an annual interview (with ongoing informal feedback) may be sufficient. Such an interview may focus on reinforcing existing levels of performance and discuss employee development and promotion possibilities. For top performers, turning the interview into a "stay interview" can be very effective (Bergeron 2022). A *stay interview* is "a conversation with a high-performing employee with the goal of discovering what they like about their role, and what they would like to change. Stay interviews are an opportunity to both uncover what motivates that employee and to also build trust with them as a manager" (Heinz 2022). Stay interviews have been particularly pertinent during the COVID-19 pandemic, when organizations witnessed unprecedented high levels of voluntary turnover.

3. *Prepare for the interview.* Prior to the interview, the manager should have a set of goals, be equipped with data, have a strategy for presenting performance information, be able to anticipate the employee's reactions, and be prepared to engage the employee in planning and problem solving. The interview should be held in an appropriate location, and the manager should bring relevant supporting information for reference. Some people recommend holding the interview in a neutral location rather than in the manager's office to lessen the emotional content often present in such situations.

4. *Use multiple sources of information.* Performance information from several sources is useful, especially in situations where the job is highly complex and involves interactions with individuals inside and outside the organization. In these situations, the manager may be unable to adequately observe all aspects of an employee's work.

5. *Encourage employee participation.* Employee self-assessment is commonly part of the performance management process. Employees may have great insight into their own performance concerns, and these concerns may not always be apparent to the manager. The appraisal environment should be beneficial to employees, not punitive. A positive environment may be difficult to create, given many employees' negative perceptions of the performance review process. Employee participation is vital because each employee must assume accountability for improvement, and the first step to being accountable is understanding what needs to be done and helping develop strategies toward that effort. Improvement should be viewed as a partnership between the manager and the employee.

6. *Focus on future performance and problem solving.* Reviewing past performance is important, but the emphasis should be on setting goals for the future and generating specific strategies for meeting those goals. In many cases, employees will identify factors outside their control that may contribute to lower-than-expected levels of performance. Discussion of these factors

is appropriate during a review session. Follow-up sessions should also be scheduled as needed.

7. *Focus on employee behavior and results, not personal traits.* In almost all cases, the purpose of performance feedback is to help employees improve their work, not to change the person. The review session is not the time to try to change an employee's values, personality, motivation, or fit with the organization. If these factors are problems, they should have been considered during the selection process or during the period under review. Instead, the manager should focus on behaviors and outcomes and seek to engage the employee in productive discussion. Doling out condescending criticisms and reciting a litany of the employee's problems are rarely useful tactics and are likely to generate employee defensiveness and resentment, which will create further obstacles to improvement.

8. *Reinforce positive performance.* One of the most effective ways a manager can ally with an employee is to ensure that the interview focuses on all aspects of performance, not just the negative. Rewarding and reinforcing positive performance is essential to productive human relationships. Employees need to hear what they are doing right or they will become demoralized and less able to improve in problem areas.

9. *Ensure that performance management is supported by senior managers.* The best way to destroy any effort at implementing a performance management system is for word to get out that senior management is either unsupportive of or ambivalent about the process. Senior management must assert and communicate that performance management is important to meeting organizational goals and that it must be done at all levels of the workforce. If this message is absent, weak, or ambiguous, the performance management system will fade away or become a meaningless bureaucratic exercise.

10. *Plan follow-up activities and pay attention to expected outcomes and timetables.* Given the complex and hectic nature of organizations, it is easy to lose focus on the important but not urgent aspects of work. If plans are put into place, they should be accompanied by timetables, expectations, and concrete follow-up. Without follow-up, the integrity of the performance management process will be jeopardized.

Every manager seeks employees who are highly motivated and productive. This goal is challenging for a number of reasons. Employee motivation is in itself a complex phenomenon and is influenced by many factors outside the manager's control. Cause-and-effect relationships are not always clear: Managerial interventions may not always yield the performance improvements we are seeking. For instance, compensation clearly has some motivational potential for most employees, but money is not an effective motivator in all circumstances. In healthcare organizations with small margins, the possibility of monetary rewards tends to be limited, and managers—working with HR—must be creative in offering other kinds of benefits (see chapter 9 on employee benefits).

Training Managers to Implement Performance Management

In addition to using valid and reliable evaluation criteria, the most important strategy for overcoming implementation problems with performance management is manager training. The objective of such training is to increase each manager's consistency in using the techniques required by the system. Training increases managers' familiarity with the performance management system, including its purpose and guidelines for use. In this way, variations among managers and rating errors may be minimized.

To reduce their potential for errors, managers need to be aware of their own potential for making rating errors and learn strategies to identify their predisposition toward making certain types of errors. Self-awareness may also be improved through training in implicit bias, which has benefits beyond performance management. For example, managers may reduce the number of distributional errors they make by improving their awareness of the appraisal tool and their understanding of the objective standards used to evaluate performance. Again, the success of training efforts is contingent on the existence of valid and reliable assessment instruments and clear performance standards.

While acknowledging much of the bad press that performance management has received, we have focused in this chapter on key aspects of performance management that need to be incorporated into any performance management system. Many organizations have discarded traditional methods of performance management and replaced them with more proactive systems that are viewed as adding value to the organization (Buckingham and Goodall 2015). Although we have discussed the benefits of such approaches as management by objectives and multisource appraisal, we also caution the reader about the limitations and risks associated with these and other methods.

The Special Role of Mentors and Mentoring

Traditional discussions of performance management do not usually encompass the role of mentors and mentoring. The mentoring process has been seen as largely removed from the day-to-day work of an organization, and mentors may be external to the organization where they do not have formal authority over the individual or their work. However, mentors can have a profound impact on an employee's performance, their work, and their career progress. Furthermore, there are increasing numbers of organizations that have developed formal mentoring initiatives and integrated them into the life of the organization. This development has been spurred in part by diversity and inclusion initiatives that have sought to improve the recruitment, retention, and development of employees from underrepresented groups.

The term *mentor* refers to an "experienced individual" who "imparts knowledge, expertise and wisdom to a less experienced person" (D'Angelo 2022). Mentors may be formally assigned by the organization within the structure of a formal mentoring program. Alternatively, mentor–mentee relationships may develop informally and involve internal or external mentors. It is common for people to have more than one mentor at a single point in time, and for mentor relationships to come and go over a person's career. For the individual mentee, there are advantages to internal and external mentors. An internal mentor can potentially help an individual navigate the complexities and uncertainties of organizational politics and provide helpful short- and long-term guidance. External mentors may provide a broader perspective and offer guidance that transcends the individual's immediate employment circumstances.

Many organizations now have internal mentoring programs. Such programs may serve multiple purposes, including providing on-the-job training, facilitating succession planning, reinforcing diversity and inclusion efforts, showing employees that the organization cares about their welfare and careers, and adding value to the organization by developing their employees and maximizing retention (Gurchiek 2022).

SUMMARY

In the twenty-first century, an important transition has taken place: Many organizations have moved from conducting performance appraisals to implementing more comprehensive performance management systems. Historically, performance appraisal focused primarily on judging employee behavior. The process was viewed as negative and punitive and was generally dreaded by managers and employees.

Performance *management*, rather than appraisal, implies an improvement-focused process in which efforts are made to assess performance and develop specific collaborative strategies to enhance it. Recognizing that employee performance depends on an employee's skills and motivation plus facilitative factors in the work environment, managers should develop improvement strategies that may include training, work process redesign, and other behavioral or environmental changes.

An important aspect of performance management is the development of relevant appraisal criteria for the employee's position—criteria that are aligned with and supportive of the goals of the organization. Appraisal data may be gathered through a variety of mechanisms, including the employee, subordinates, team members, other coworkers, and even customers, clients, or patients. Methods for organizing these data may involve a ranking, a graphic rating scale, a behavioral anchored rating scale, a behavioral observation scale, a critical incidents record, or achievement of outcomes or objectives. The choice of approach depends on the job, the organization's goals, and, perhaps most important, the organization's culture, particularly its readiness to face performance issues honestly and openly.

FOR DISCUSSION

1. What is the distinction between performance appraisal and performance management?

2. Why does The Joint Commission require hospitals and other healthcare organizations to have a performance management system?

3. What is the relationship between performance management and continuous quality improvement?

4. What are the advantages and disadvantages of including discussions of compensation during a performance management interview?

5. What is the difference between performance appraisal rating errors and political factors that influence the accuracy of performance appraisal information?

6. How does a manager decide how often to conduct formal performance management interviews?

7. Why does employee participation in the performance management process matter?

8. Why would a manager consider obtaining information from others about a particular employee's performance?

EXPERIENTIAL EXERCISES

EXERCISE 1

Summit River Nursing Home (SRNH) is a 60-bed nursing home that serves a suburban community in the Midwest. The facility provides a broad range of services to its residents, including recreational activities, a clinical laboratory, dental services, dietary and housekeeping services, mental health and nursing services, occupational and physical therapies, pharmacy services, social services, and diagnostic X-ray services.

The facility has a good reputation in the community and is well staffed. Each nursing home resident receives at least two hours of direct nursing care every day. Licensed practical nurses administer medications and perform certain treatment procedures. Certified nursing assistants perform most of the direct patient care. A dietary service supervisor and a registered dietitian manage the daily operations of the food service department.

Activity coordinators provide nonmedical care designed to improve cognitive and physical capabilities. Two social workers work with residents, families, and other organizations; an important part of their role is to ease the adjustment of residents and their families to the long-term care environment. They also help identify residents' specific medical and emotional needs and provide support and referral services. Environmental service workers maintain the facility with a goal of providing a clean and safe facility for the residents. Housekeeping staff also have considerable contact with residents on a day-to-day basis. SRNH has contractual relationships with a dental practice, physical therapists, a pharmacist, a psychologist, and a multispecialty physician practice. The management team at SRNH consists of an administrator, a finance director, a human resources director, a director of nursing, and administrative support personnel.

Recently, concerns about quality have emerged at the nursing home. Several instances of communication breakdown among staff have occurred, as have several instances of medication error. A resident satisfaction survey also revealed problems of which management had been unaware. Some of the problems concern contract staff members who have not been included in the organization's performance management process.

After discussions between management and employees, it was determined that a team atmosphere among staff was lacking. Each member of the management team was asked to develop a strategy to improve the level of teamwork in the facility. The human resources director agreed to take action in the following three ways:

1. Ensure that all job descriptions address teamwork and that these changes are discussed with employees.

2. Develop and implement a team-building training program for all employees, including contract staff.

3. Revise the performance management approach so that it focuses on teamwork in addition to individual skills and accomplishments.

The first two strategies were relatively easy to complete. Job descriptions were revised, and supervisors met with employees to discuss the changes. With the assistance of an outside consultant, a training program was implemented to teach employees communication and conflict management skills. Several, but not all, contract employees attended the training program.

The third strategy, revision of the performance management approach, posed some difficulties. The current performance management system is traditional, using a 12-item graphic rating scale (some with behavioral descriptions) that measures aspects of work such as attitude, quality of performance, productivity, attention to detail, job knowledge, reliability, and availability. The form also provides room for comments by supervisors and employees. This rating approach was found to be incapable of addressing the team components of the jobs. An additional problem is that several staff members are on contract and are not fully integrated into the organization. These staff members currently are not included in the organization's performance management process.

The human resources director wants to modify the performance management process to achieve two goals. First, the system should include methods for assessing and improving team performance. Second, the system should include contract employees, many of whom work for a limited period and may only work on a part-time or as-needed basis.

You are a consultant to the human resources director. Your job is to address these two goals. Consider the following questions:

- How would you proceed with the task of modifying the performance management process?
- What specific strategies do you think should be considered?
- Whom would you involve in developing the process?
- What obstacles do you see in implementing your approach? How would you overcome these obstacles?

EXERCISE 2

Various articles are cited in this chapter that critique performance management. There are countless other critiques written by researchers, human resources management associations, managers, and consultants. Review the critiques that currently appear, using such search terms as "criticisms of performance management." Extract the key ideas and recommendations from four critiques. Compare and contrast the critiques in terms of the nature of the criticism, the evidence presented in support of the criticism, and recommendations for change.

EXERCISE 3

As noted in this chapter, performance management is not simply the responsibility of the human resources department. However, HR departments typically play a role in ensuring compliance with HR policies. This role includes making sure that managers or supervisors have carried out performance management functions. For this exercise, interview one or two HR managers (these may be vice presidents, directors, or HR leaders identified by another title) and pose the following questions. Be sure to probe to obtain more information:

1. What is the role of the HR department in ensuring that performance management functions are carried out?
2. What are the goals of performance management in this organization?

3. What is the approach of performance management in this organization? Is there a defined protocol, and are there forms or other structures and processes?

4. What obstacles have you encountered in implementing performance management in this organization?

5. How would you evaluate the success of implementing performance management in this organization?

REFERENCES

Aguinis, H. 2019. *Performance Management for Dummies*. New York: John Wiley.

Aguinis, H., and J. Burgi-Tian. 2021. "Talent Management Challenges During COVID-19 and Beyond: Performance Management to the Rescue." *Business Research Quarterly* 24 (3): 233–40.

American College of Healthcare Executives (ACHE). 2021. *ACHE Healthcare Executive 2021 Competencies Assessment Tool*. Chicago: ACHE. www.ache.org/-/media/ache/career -resource-center/cat_2021.pdf21.

Baldrige Performance Excellence Program. 2021. *Baldrige Excellence Builder*. Publication no. T1663. Published January. www.nist.gov/system/files/documents/2021/01 /29/2021-2022-baldrige-excellence-builder.pdf.

Bates, S. 2003. "Forced Distribution." *HR Magazine*. Published June 1. www.shrm.org/hr -today/news/hr-magazine/pages/0603bates.aspx.

Bergeron, P. 2022. "Stay Interviews Can Be an Antidote to Exit Interviews." Published February 23. www.shrm.org/resourcesandtools/hr-topics/employee-relations/pages /stay-interviews-can-be-an-antidote-to-exit-interviews.aspx.

Bock, L. 2015. *Work Rules!* New York: Twelve.

Bordalo, P., K. Coffman, N. Gennaioli, and A. Shleifer. 2019. "Beliefs About Gender." *American Economic Review* 109 (3): 739–73.

Bosquet, C., P. P. Combes, and C. García-Peñalosa. 2019. "Gender and Promotions: Evidence from Academic Economists in France." *Scandinavian Journal of Economics* 121 (3): 1020–53.

Breuer, K., P. Nicken, and D. Sliwka. 2013. "Social Ties and Subjective Performance Evaluations: An Empirical Investigation." *Review of Management Science* 7 (2): 141–57.

Buckingham, M., and A. Goodall. 2015. "Reinventing Performance Management." *Harvard Business Review* 93 (4): 40–50.

Cappelli, P., and M. J. Conyon. 2018. "What Do Performance Appraisals Do?" *ILR Review* 71 (1): 88–116.

Casciaro, T., A. C. Edmondson, and S. Jang. 2019. "Cross-Silo Leadership." *Harvard Business Review,* May–June, 130–39.

Chattopadhyay, R. 2019. "Impact of Forced Distribution System of Performance Evaluation on Organizational Citizenship Behaviour." *Global Business Review* 20 (3): 826–37.

Culbert, S. A. 2010. "Yes, Everyone Really Does Hate Performance Reviews." *Wall Street Journal*, April 11.

———. 2008. "Get Rid of the Performance Review!" *Wall Street Journal,* October 20.

D'Angelo, M. 2022. "How to Find a Mentor." *Business News Daily*. Updated August 5. www.businessnewsdaily.com/6248-how-to-find-mentor.html.

Devcich, D., J. Weller, S. J. Mitchell, S. McLaughlin, L. Barker, J. W. Rudolph, D. B. Raemer, M. Zammert, S. J. Singer, J. Torrie, C. M. A. Frampton, and A. F. Merry. 2016. "A Behaviourally Anchored Rating Scale for Evaluating the Use of the WHO Surgical Safety Checklist: Development and Initial Evaluation of the WHOBARS." *BMJ Quality and Safety* 25: 778–86.

Exley, C. L., and J. B. Kessler. 2021. *The Gender Gap in Self-Promotion*. Working Paper w26345. National Bureau of Economic Research (NBER). Revised May. www.nber.org /system/files/working_papers/w26345/w26345.pdf.

Giella, T. 2017. *The CEO Performance Appraisal*. American Hospital Association (AHA) Trustee Services. Published October. https://trustees.aha.org/sites/default/files /trustees/the-ceo-performance-appraisal.pdf.

Giumetti, G., A. Schroeder, and F. Switzer III. 2015. "Forced Ranking Rating Systems: When Does 'Rank and Yank' Lead to Adverse Impact?" *Journal of Applied Psychology* 100 (1): 180–93.

Grant, G. 2018. "Similar-to-Me Bias: How Gender Affects Workplace Recognition." *Forbes*. Published August 7. www.forbes.com/sites/georginagrant/2018/08/07/similar-to-me-bias-how-gender-affects-workplace-recognition.

Gurchiek, K. 2022. "Looking for a Mentor? Authors Offer Advice on Creating a Mentoring Program." Society for Human Resource Management (SHRM). Published January 28. www.shrm.org/resourcesandtools/hr-topics/organizational-and-employee-development/pages/looking-for-a-mentor-experts-offer-advice-to-students-emerging-professionals.aspx.

Heinz, K. 2022. "What Is a Stay Interview? 13 Questions to Ask." Built In. Updated September 23. https://builtin.com/recruiting/stay-interview.

Holzer, M., A. Ballard, M. Kim, P. Shuyang, and D. Felix. 2019. "Obstacles and Opportunities for Sustaining Performance Management Systems." *International Journal of Public Administration* 42 (2): 132–43.

Hospido, L., L. Laeven, and A. Lamo. 2022. "The Gender Promotion Gap: Evidence from Central Banking." *Review of Economics and Statistics* 104 (5): 981–96.

Human Resource Executive. 2016. *Seeking Agility in Performance Management*. Palm Beach Garden, FL: LRP Media Group.

Janove, J. 2021. "Get Rid of Performance Reviews." Society for Human Resource Management (SHRM). Published November 9. www.shrm.org/resourcesandtools/hr-topics/employee-relations/humanity-into-hr/pages/get-rid-of-performance-reviews.aspx.

Joint Commission. 2021. *All Accreditation Programs Survey Activity Guide January 2021*. Published January 20. www.jointcommission.org/-/media/tjc/documents/accred-and-cert/survey-process-and-survey-activity-guide/2021/2021-all-programs-organization-sag.pdf.

Lin, Y. C., and J. E. Kellough. 2019. "Performance Appraisal in the Public Sector: Examining Supervisors' Perceptions." *Public Personnel Management* 48 (2): 179–202.

Longenecker, C. O., and L. Fink. 2017. "Lessons for Improving Your Formal Performance Appraisal Process." *Strategic HR Review* 16 (1): 32–38.

Longenecker, C. O., and A. Gioia. 1992. "The Executive Appraisal Paradox." *Academy of Management Executive* 6 (2): 18–28.

Longenecker, C. O., H. P. Sims, and D. A. Gioia. 1987. "Behind the Mask: The Politics of Employee Appraisal." *Academy of Management Executive* 1 (3): 183–93.

Lorsbach, B. H. 2022. "Assessing the Engagement and Effectiveness of Boards." American Hospital Association (AHA) Trustee Services. Accessed October 8. https://trustees .aha.org/assessing-engagement-and-effectiveness-boards.

Lucas, S. 2022. "Why Your Performance Review Won't Work for Senior Employees." *Evil HR Lady* (blog), Cornerstone. Accessed October 31. www.cornerstoneondemand.com /resources/article/why-your-performance-review-wont-work-senior-employees/.

Medvedev, O. N., A. F. Merry, C. Skilton, D. A. Gargiulo, S. J. Mitchell, and J. M. Weller. 2019. "Examining Reliability of WHOBARS: A Tool to Measure the Quality of Administration of WHO Surgical Safety Checklist Using Generalisability Theory with Surgical Teams from Three New Zealand Hospitals." *BMJ Open* 9 (1): e022625. https://doi.org /10.1136/bmjopen-2018-022625.

Mercer. 2019. *Performance Transformation in the Future of Work: Four Truths and Three Predictions Based on Insights from Mercer's 2019 Global Performance Management Study*. Report no. 6009949c-GB. New York: Mercer/MarshMcLennan. www.mercer.us /content/dam/mercer/attachments/private/us-2019-performance-transformation-in -the-future-of-work.pdf.

Muchinsky, P. M. 2006. *Psychology Applied to Work*, 8th ed. Belmont, CA: Thomson Wadsworth.

National Council of Nonprofits. 2022. "Self-Assessments of Nonprofit Boards." Accessed October 8. www.councilofnonprofits.org/tools-resources/self-assessments-nonprofit -boards.

Olson, E. G. 2013. "Microsoft, GE, and the Futility of Ranking Employees." *Fortune*. Published November 18. http://fortune.com/2013/11/18/Microsoft-ge-and-the-futility-of -ranking-employees/.

Orlando, J., and E. Bank. 2016. "A New Approach to Performance Management at Deloitte." *People & Strategy* 39 (2): 42–44.

Pfeffer, J., and R. I. Sutton. 2006. *Hard Facts, Dangerous Half-Truths, and Total Nonsense: Profiting from Evidence-Based Management*. Boston: Harvard Business School Press.

Snell, S., and S. Morris. 2018. *Managing Human Resources*, 18th ed. Boston: Cengage Learning.

Trost, A. 2017. *The End of Performance Appraisal*. New York: Springer.

Varma, A., P. S. Budhwar, and A. DeNisi. 2008. *Performance Management Systems: A Global Perspective*. New York: Routledge.

Welch, J., and J. A. Byrne. 2003. *Jack: Straight from the Gut*. New York: Warner Business Books.

CHAPTER 8

COMPENSATION PRACTICES, PLANNING, AND CHALLENGES

Bruce J. Fried, Brigid K. Grabert, and John Cashion

LEARNING OBJECTIVES

After completing this chapter, you should be able to

➤ describe the purposes of compensation and compensation policy in healthcare organizations;

➤ distinguish between extrinsic reward and intrinsic reward and the value of each to employees;

➤ explain the concept of balancing internal equity and external competitiveness in compensation;

➤ describe the challenges and problems faced in designing and implementing pay-for-performance plans;

➤ discern how particular practice settings affect physician income and physician compensation strategies; and

➤ describe value-based payment trends and the role of the Affordable Care Act in increasing the use of such models.

VIGNETTE

The Foster Clinic is a large multispecialty group practice located in a city with a population of 50,000 in a county with 200,000 residents. The clinic provides care to patients throughout the county and several adjacent counties. In addition to its main office, the Foster Clinic also has offices in three communities in adjacent counties. The practice employs 15 physicians in internal medicine, five in orthopedics, seven in family practice, one in neurology, three in podiatry, two in general surgery, three in obstetrics/gynecology, three in gastroenterology, three in cardiology, one in pulmonology, one in rheumatology, and three in pediatrics. There is also a hospitalist on staff.

The clinic also employs several nurse practitioners, physician assistants, and others. There is a laboratory in the clinic and a radiology practice within a half mile of the main office. The practice has a nonphysician executive director and a management team consisting of a medical director, associate directors, and a cadre of administrative and information technology (IT) support.

In the past year, the clinic has begun to run into financial difficulties due in large part to reduced reimbursements and a growing number of patients who became unemployed and lost their health insurance. A consulting group was brought in to examine options for improving the practice's financial position. After three weeks of study, the consultants concluded that patient volume needed to increase, and in particular the practice needed to target patients with good health insurance. The group also recommended that the practice stay open several additional evenings a week and weekends.

The consulting group has recommended that the clinic move from a largely salary-based compensation system to a system that more explicitly links compensation with volume of patients seen and revenue generated. The team presented its recommendations to the physicians. The physicians expressed great support for increasing the clinic's hours and in fact had been expanding access in similar ways in recent years. However, the suggested compensation system was not as popular. Every physician in the practice objected to the plan, although physicians varied considerably on what they found objectionable. The management team must now evaluate the compensation plan, listen to physician concerns, and develop a financial compensation plan that is acceptable to its medical staff.

INTRODUCTION

How is individual compensation determined? Exhibit 8.1 summarizes the multiple factors that potentially affect an individual's compensation and which affect one another: the organization, the job, the external environment, and the employee. This chapter examines the interrelationships among these factors.

Organizational issues include both formal and informal factors. By formal factors, we consider policies and procedures that are officially established by the organization, such as compensation policies, including the organization's values and how the organization assesses the worth of jobs. In healthcare, for example, procedure-based physicians, such as surgeons, tend to earn significantly more than other physicians. This disparity is attributable to a number of factors, including the income that procedure-based physicians generate for the organization relative to other workers, as well as supply and demand issues. The organization's ability to pay is an important factor as well. For example, a local public health department generally has fewer resources at its disposal than a private for-profit hospital. Therefore, salaries for individuals performing the same job may differ substantially between organizations. Unionization also plays a significant role in compensation; in general, employees who belong to a labor union tend to earn more than those who are not unionized. Considering compensation, the organization's values may refer to formally espoused beliefs in equity and fairness in how rewards are allocated. However, informally, the organization as a whole or individuals within the organization may violate these values. Thus, informal factors—such as organizational politics, prejudice, favoritism, nepotism, and sexism—may certainly play a role in determining compensation, even though they should not. The key point is that both formal and informal factors may affect an individual's compensation.

While compensation is affected by those organizational factors, the job itself is a key factor in determining compensation—so much so that it is treated as a separate factor in the model presented in exhibit 8.1. Organizations use a variety of approaches toward placing a monetary value on jobs. Ideally, organizations would engage in careful job analysis and generate accurate and current job descriptions. Using this information, organizations would then evaluate jobs and establish salaries based on the jobs' value to the organization. In reality, as discussed later in this chapter, organizations often rely more on the labor market in determining salaries. To remain competitive, they may pay people more than the assessed value resulting from the job evaluation process. If the job is part of a unionized collective bargaining unit, compensation will be affected, typically in a positive direction for the worker.

The external environment has a major impact on compensation. The external environment includes laws, such as federal and state minimum wage laws and various laws and regulations related to employee benefits. Geographic factors are also a key external determinant of compensation, affecting the cost of living and subsequently the level of compensation required to attract employees. Some organizations use compensation surveys to assess the competitiveness of local labor markets. In healthcare, several companies carry out periodic compensation surveys. Insurance coverage and unionization level are other elements of the external environment that must be taken into consideration.

Finally, employees themselves influence compensation, through individual characteristics such as their job performance, seniority, experience, perceived potential to contribute to the organization, and political influence.

Factors that may lead to job satisfaction and good performance include interest in the work, competent supervision, flexibility, growth and earning potential, and personal reward. Although money is not everything, it is a significant motivator and a frequent measure of the value that an employer places on its employees. Pay is a crucial issue to employers and employees, and thus the way a compensation system is set up is extremely important.

A **compensation system** consists of all the tangible rewards (i.e., money, goods, and services) that employees receive for the work they put forth. Note that we do not include other rewards—that is, intangible but often more potent rewards than compensation. When satisfied and motivated people describe their work, they may say, "My work is very *rewarding.*" Yet rarely, if ever, are people referring to salary when they make such a statement. Rather, they are likely referring to the positive feelings they get from a job. A physical therapist may feel rewarded when a stroke patient regains mobility; a health insurance navigator may feel rewarded by having successfully enrolled members of an immigrant family in a health insurance plan; and a physician working in a hospice may feel rewarded by observing the way family members support one another as a relative nears the end of life. In fact, people may forgo a certain amount of material compensation in the interest of doing work they find meaningful—yes, rewarding. For example, a physician may choose to work in a federally qualified health center, forgoing a significantly higher salary that could be gained from working in a private practice. For now, however, we will leave behind the substantial role played by intangible rewards, although we will occasionally refer back to this idea as we discuss the more common usage of *rewards*, which generally refers to money and other material benefits.

We use the term **total compensation** to refer to direct and indirect compensation. *Direct compensation* refers to wages, salaries, commissions, and bonuses paid to individuals in exchange for their work. It includes base pay, short-term and long-term incentives, stock options, and other forms of payment. Note that this definition does not use the term *employees* because people sometimes work for an organization who are not technically employees. In healthcare, physicians are the classic example of a group that often are not hospital employees but are nevertheless paid for the work they do in a hospital. *Indirect compensation* consists of all other material rewards, including benefits (such as health insurance, retirement plans, membership in fitness clubs, employee discounts), employer contributions to Social Security, paid time off (such as vacation and sick time), and training opportunities. Total compensation is a key factor in the success of employee recruitment and retention (as discussed in chapter 5).

---

compensation system
Money, goods, and services provided to employees in return for employees' work.

---

total compensation
All aspects of direct and indirect rewards given to employees, including money, benefits (such as health insurance and retirement plans), paid time off (such as vacation and sick time), and stock options.

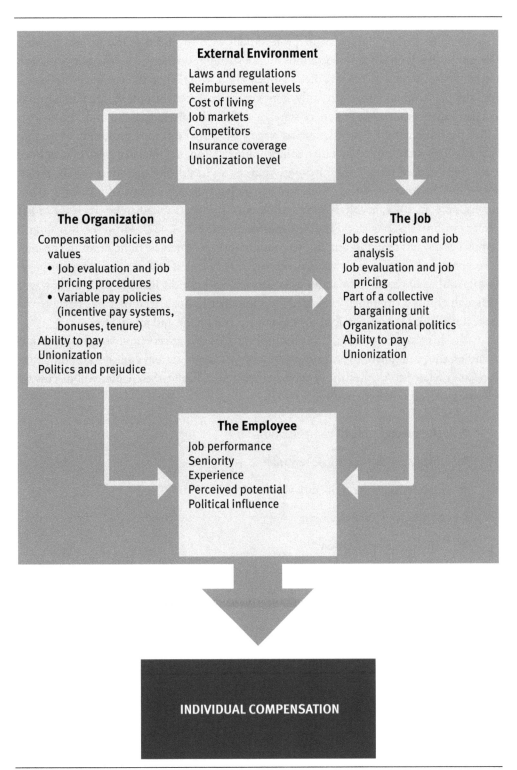

EXHIBIT 8.1
Factors Affecting
Individual
Compensation

External Environment
Laws and regulations
Reimbursement levels
Cost of living
Job markets
Competitors
Insurance coverage
Unionization level

The Organization
Compensation policies and
values
• Job evaluation and job
  pricing procedures
• Variable pay policies
  (incentive pay systems,
  bonuses, tenure)
Ability to pay
Unionization
Politics and prejudice

The Job
Job description and job
  analysis
Job evaluation and job
  pricing
Part of a collective
  bargaining unit
Organizational politics
Ability to pay
Unionization

The Employee
Job performance
Seniority
Experience
Perceived potential
Political influence

INDIVIDUAL COMPENSATION

Healthcare presents complexities that are not often encountered in other sectors. First, many healthcare employees are professionals with advanced education and training. The employees' professional associations exert a strong influence over their compensation, and employees routinely compare their compensation with that of others in their profession. For example, hospital nurses can easily compare their salaries with nurses in other hospitals in a particular community, region, or state, or with national averages. Second, shortages of skilled professionals drive up salaries and wages, allowing healthcare professionals to enjoy relatively high mobility and lucrative compensation. Third, the financial value of healthcare work is influenced heavily by third-party payers, so healthcare providers cannot always determine the price of services and may not be paid the actual cost of providing them. For example, in 2021, hospital-based audiologists were paid a median hourly wage of $50 (American Speech-Language-Hearing Association [ASHA] 2022). However, if insurance companies pay less than this amount per hour of service, it may be difficult for the hospital to compensate its audiologists with market wages. However, if an insurance company pays a hospital only $40 per hour for audiologist services, how can the hospital pay market wages? Although this is a simplified example, it is clear that limits placed by third-party payers make it difficult for organizations to respond to rising wage and salary levels.

In this chapter, we address the multiple factors that affect employee compensation, including the structure of the organization's compensation system and specific compensation issues related to the healthcare environment. Specifically, the chapter will discuss the following aspects of compensation:

- The strategic role of compensation
- Intrinsic versus extrinsic rewards
- Determining the monetary value of jobs
- Methods of job evaluation
- Variable compensation
- Pay for performance
- Special considerations for compensating physicians
- Payment methods and practice settings
- Future directions for physician compensation

THE STRATEGIC ROLE OF COMPENSATION

We often think of healthcare professionals as being motivated largely by a desire to serve and help others. Although such altruism certainly influences nurses, physicians, and other healthcare workers, they are also influenced to work for and stay with an organization by financial rewards. A fair and competitive compensation system is essential because professional shortages occur in cycles, leaving organizations to compete with one another for a limited supply of employees (see the Current Issue sidebar "Trends Affecting Hospital Employee Compensation").

A compensation system must be approached strategically and have multiple goals, including

◆ rewarding employee performance,

◆ achieving internal equity or fairness within the organization,

◆ competing within relevant labor markets,

◆ aligning employee behavior and performance with organizational goals,

◆ attracting and retaining high-performing employees,

◆ keeping the compensation budget within organizational financial constraints, and

◆ complying with legal requirements.

INTRINSIC VERSUS EXTRINSIC REWARDS

Compensation is one type of reward for people—but it is not the only mechanism by which people are rewarded. **Extrinsic rewards** are tangible and may be in the form of direct

extrinsic rewards
Tangible aspects of compensation, such as pay and benefits.

CURRENT ISSUE
Trends Affecting Hospital Employee Compensation

In late 2021, *Becker's Hospital Review* published an article identifying five major trends affecting employee compensation in hospitals (Plescia 2021). First, staffing shortages have forced hospitals to pay increasingly more for staff. Second, there has been an increase in the number of overtime hours worked by hospital employees, requiring hospitals to pay more than 50 percent more for overtime work. Third, turnover rates have increased, largely as a result of burnout. In 2021, it was estimated that the average cost of turnover for a bedside nurse was about $40,000. Fourth, turnover and shortages have put hospitals in the difficult position of having to use more expensive agency staff, such as travel nurses, as well as temporary employees. Fifth, largely related to COVID-19, hospitals have had to pay more in wages and bonuses to retain employees.

monetary compensation (wages or salaries) and stock options as well as indirect compensation in the form of benefits, such as health insurance; and paid time off, such as vacation pay. The costs of indirect compensation are not trivial; healthcare organizations spend an additional 20 to 35 percent of salary costs on a variety of benefits. **Intrinsic rewards** are intangible; for example, recognition from a supervisor for completing an assignment or an expression of thanks from a patient.

Managers must pay attention to rewards that may not require fiscal resources. Encouraging employees, establishing a collegial practice environment, setting consistent performance objectives, and conducting periodic performance assessments are all strategies that cost more in time and commitment than in direct money expenditures but are nevertheless valued by employees.

COMPENSATION DECISIONS AND DILEMMAS

We expect a great deal from compensation systems. However, these goals are often in conflict with each other. A common conflict is between fairness in compensation and the need to offer competitive salaries. Offering competitive salaries may upset the organization's **internal equity**—that is, the pay relationships among jobs in an organization and the extent to which workers are compensated fairly. Registered nurse anesthetists are a case in point. According to the US Bureau of Labor Statistics (2022), the national median annual salary for nurse anesthetists in 2021 was $195,610. Given the growth in demand, coupled with shortages, hospitals may need to pay premium wages to attract nurse anesthetists. Experienced nurses who have been with the hospital for several years may find that newly hired (and perhaps less experienced) nurses may earn salaries greater than theirs. These nurses may very well feel they are being treated unfairly unless their salaries are also raised. One tangible option for these nurses is to find employment elsewhere and take advantage of the increase in compensation. The hospital also has a choice: increase wages for all nurse anesthetists (which may cause resentment among other nurses!) or live with morale issues and the potential for turnover.

When developing a compensation policy, the organization must first decide whether to pay above, below, or at prevailing rates. This may be an explicit decision based on the organization's ability to pay, as well as local labor market considerations. For certain jobs in high demand, the organization may be forced to pay above market rates to successfully attract applicants. Second, the organization must identify which employee characteristics and behaviors will be rewarded. Choosing which behaviors and other factors to reward signals what the organization values. For example, an organization may wish to reward employees who exhibit a high level of customer service, when in reality annual raises may be based more on cost of living increases or longevity in the organization. On the other hand, employee retention issues may be so important to an

---

intrinsic rewards
Intangible aspects of compensation, such as public recognition; praise from a supervisor; and feelings of accomplishment, recognition, or belonging to an organization.

---

internal equity
The pay relationships among jobs in an organization and the extent to which workers are compensated fairly.

organization that giving retention bonuses is more critical than giving bonuses based on service quality.

Developing and improving compensation systems is a never-ending challenge. Changes in the marketplace, trends in healthcare professions, and redirection of organizational goals and objectives add up to mean that compensation policies and plans are seldom stable.

INTERNAL EQUITY AND EXTERNAL COMPETITIVENESS

An organization must maintain a balance between internal equity and external competitiveness in its compensation system. **Equity theory** is a useful and well-tested framework for understanding the impact of perceived equity and inequity on employee motivation and performance (Adams 1963). *Equity* is the perceived fairness of the relationship between what a person contributes to an organization (inputs) and what that person receives in return (outcomes). Examples of inputs include education, seniority, skills, effort, loyalty, and experience. Outcomes include pay, benefits, job satisfaction, opportunities for growth, and recognition. Equity theory suggests that employees calculate the ratio of their outcomes to their inputs. Then they compare their own ratio to those of other people. The basic idea of equity theory is shown in exhibit 8.2.

Employees compare themselves with people in the same organization or with people who hold similar jobs in other organizations. For example, operating room nurses may compare their own ratio with the ratios of

♦ other operating room nurses in the same hospital,

♦ other nurses performing different tasks,

♦ other types of staff members, and

♦ nurses who perform similar work in other organizations.

equity theory
The theory that the perceived fairness of the relationship between what an employee contributes to an organization and what the employee receives in return affects the employee's motivation and performance.

Perception	Individual Ratio		"Referent" Other Ratio
Equity	Outcomes / Inputs	=	Outcomes / Inputs
Overpayment Inequity	Outcomes / Inputs	>	Outcomes / Inputs
Underpayment Inequity	Outcomes / Inputs	<	Outcomes / Inputs

EXHIBIT 8.2
Equity Theory

Through this comparison, employees develop a belief that they are being treated either equitably or inequitably. Feelings of inequity create discomfort, and people naturally seek to restore a sense of equity (see related Critical Concept sidebar "How Employees Try to Restore Equity in the Workplace") or leave the organization or field for a more equitable situation. Employees' tendency to evaluate fairness in the workplace is common in all organizations. These comparisons may be highly subjective and based on limited or inaccurate information. Regardless of the basis of these assessments, managers must understand and deal with these perceptions.

As discussed earlier in the example of nurse anesthetists, equity issues are particularly troublesome because of shortages in certain healthcare professions. Newly graduated nurses, for example, may be hired at a salary level that approaches the compensation of experienced nurses. The seasoned employee is faced with several choices: Accept the situation, seek additional compensation, change jobs within the organization, take on additional responsibilities, or move to another organization to achieve the financial benefits of being newly hired. In some markets, job hopping is a common method for increasing compensation.

---

① CRITICAL CONCEPT
How Employees Try to Restore Equity in the Workplace

Employees who perceive inequity may attempt to create an equitable situation by increasing their outcomes or decreasing their inputs. Employees can seek to increase their outcomes by working harder and as a result may obtain additional compensation or a promotion. Note that working harder may also increase the inputs side of the ratio. Employees can also seek to increase their outcomes by organizing other employees, possibly in the form of unionization, and by engaging in illegal activities, such as theft or false reporting of hours worked.

Inputs can be decreased through working fewer hours—coming in late, leaving early, being absent—and by putting forth less effort. Employees may also attempt to restore a sense of equity by changing their perceptions of the inputs or outcomes of others. For example, an employee may convince themself that the employee they compare themself with has more experience and is therefore entitled to a higher level of compensation. Similarly, an employee may conclude that while their salary may be lower than someone else's, working conditions are much better at their own organization than at the other workplace. In other instances, an employee may simply change their frame of reference by changing the person with whom they compare themself.

THE QUARTILE STRATEGY FOR PAY POSITIONING

While organizations seek to ensure internal equity, they must also be externally competitive by providing compensation that matches or exceeds salaries given to employees who perform similar jobs in other organizations. If an organization's compensation is not competitive, the organization risks turnover and staff shortages, particularly in geographic areas where the supply of certain professionals is scarce.

When confronting a tight labor market, organizations, explicitly or otherwise, formulate strategies to position themselves. Pay positioning strategies typically follow a *quartile strategy*, in which a salary range is subdivided into four equal parts, or *quartiles*. Most employers seek to position themselves in the second quartile (the middle of the market) or higher. By choosing a second-quartile position, organizations can control costs but still attract and retain employees.

An employer that uses a first-quartile strategy chooses to pay below market compensation. Employers may take this position because of a lack of funds or to take advantage of a surplus of workers. A major disadvantage of using a first-quartile strategy is high turnover. Also, if the labor supply tightens, the organization may have difficulty attracting and retaining workers. A low-quartile position may also have quality-of-care ramifications.

Mohr and colleagues (2004) studied nursing homes in the lowest tier—facilities in which greater than 85 percent of the residents were on Medicaid and which had correspondingly fewer resources to hire staff—and found that economic constraints lead to lower staffing intensity (care hours per patient day), use of lesser-trained staff, and ultimately lower quality of care. To address concerns about quality of care in nursing homes, the Centers for Medicare & Medicaid Services (CMS) developed a Nursing Home Compare website (now Care Compare) and created a five-star rating system based on staffing ratios, state health inspections, and quality measures for nursing homes certified by Medicare and Medicaid (Boccuti, Casillas, and Neuman 2015; Medicare.gov 2022).

A third-quartile strategy, in which employees are paid at above market value, is more aggressive than a first- or second-quartile strategy. A third-quartile strategy may be used to ensure that a sufficient number of employees with the required capabilities are attracted and retained; it also allows an organization to be more selective. A third-quartile strategy may also be used to build a new organization or service line that requires employees with highly specialized and scarce skill sets. A fourth-quartile strategy is one in which the employer's compensation level is, on average, higher than 75 to 100 percent of the salaries of other employers.

There are several situations wherein certain employees may be paid at or below market rates while other employees are paid substantially above market rates. First, this variation may result from the supply and demand for particular skills and competencies. For example, a rural hospital may find that to attract an operating room nurse, it must offer a salary above that of other employers in the labor market for that job—and the labor market can in fact be a particular region, the state, or even the whole nation. For other positions in that same hospital, wages may be closer to the prevailing wage rate. The key point is that organizations feel great pressure to attract employees and, within their financial constraints, are pushed to offer salaries that are highly competitive.

A second reason for variations in compensation across the organization is that salaries generally include a range, and this range may include salary points that are both below and above market rates for that position. Where an individual's salary falls within that range is typically related to such factors as experience, years in the organization, and performance. Thus, an individual just starting out may be paid at the lower end of the range, possibly below the market rate, while a more experienced person may be paid above average levels for this position.

DETERMINING THE MONETARY VALUE OF JOBS

How do organizations decide how much a job is worth in monetary terms? In some instances, organizations simply look at the market and pay prevailing wages for a particular job, especially in tight labor markets, where wage and salary surveys may be the dominant method used to set compensation levels, at least for certain jobs. In these situations, salary decisions may be based almost exclusively on labor market information.

job evaluation
A formal process designed to determine the monetary value of a job based on job descriptions and specifications.

A more systematic approach is **job evaluation**, a formal process designed to determine the monetary value of jobs in an organization. Compensation is determined by using precise information about jobs, including tasks performed, knowledge and skill requirements, supervisory responsibilities, and other factors. Jobs are "priced" relative to other jobs in the same organization. For job evaluation to be fair and useful, it is essential that there be accurate and current job descriptions.

The premise of a job evaluation is that jobs that require greater qualifications, involve more responsibility, and entail more complex duties should pay more than jobs with lower knowledge and skill requirements or more straightforward tasks. A **benchmark job**, which is a well-understood job with relatively stable knowledge, skills, and abilities, is used to establish the basis on which other comparable jobs are evaluated.

benchmark job
A well-understood job with relatively stable knowledge, skills, and abilities; it is used to anchor pay scales for comparable jobs.

METHODS OF JOB EVALUATION

Numerous methods of job evaluation exist, each with its own advantages and drawbacks. Six of these methods will be discussed in the sections that follow: (1) ranking, (2) job classification systems, (3) pay bands and broadbanding, (4) point system, (5) factor comparison, and (6) market pricing.

RANKING

The simplest job evaluation method is ranking—listing jobs in order of their value to an organization. The entire job, rather than individual components of the job such as skill requirements, is considered. Because individual judgment is used, ranking can be highly subjective. Managers may have difficulty assigning ranks, particularly when there are many jobs in an organization.

JOB CLASSIFICATION SYSTEMS

In a **job classification system,** jobs are classified into job groups based on predetermined characteristics, such as educational requirements, level of responsibility, working conditions, supervisory responsibilities, and knowledge requirements. A job is then assigned a compensation level based on its classification. This approach is most common in the public sector. For example, the federal government's General Schedule (GS) consists of 15 grades, with GS-1 at the lowest level and GS-15 at the highest level. Within each grade are ten steps, which account for variations in compensation related to longevity in the position and other factors. In the GS system, each job is classified into a grade based on knowledge requirements, responsibilities, physical effort, and working conditions. Each grade is associated with a salary range, which varies by geographic location to account for cost-of-living differences. Like ranking, job classification systems may entail considerable subjectivity and are vulnerable to manipulation. Jobs can be misclassified, or perceived as misclassified, because of faulty assumptions made by the job analyst. (For an example of how the GS system works, see FederalPay.org 2022).

> *job classification system*
> A method of categorizing jobs based on predetermined job requirements wherein each job grade is associated with a salary range.

Job classification systems may also pose problems when applied to healthcare systems with multiple organizations because two jobs with the same title may require different responsibilities in different settings. For example, a registered nurse in a skilled nursing facility performs duties substantially different from those performed by a registered nurse in an outpatient surgery center. If a job classification system places these two jobs in the same category, the resulting compensation may not reflect differences between the jobs.

PAY BANDS AND BROADBANDING

A **pay band** is a salary range for a particular job category. A pay band typically includes a salary range, which includes a minimum, midpoint, and maximum for the job category. An individual's salary is set somewhere within that pay band, depending on the person's experience, time in the organization, or other factors as determined by the organization.

> *pay band*
> A salary range for a particular job category.

Some organizations have narrow pay bands, and the salary range for a job is small. Employees move up through a range by years of service, performance, or some other factor. In such situations, an employee can quickly reach the top of the pay range, leaving no room for any additional raise in salary. Narrow bands provide little flexibility in compensation. If the employer wishes to provide additional compensation to an employee who assumes new responsibilities or learns new skills, the employer's main options are promotion or job reclassification, which can be difficult to accomplish.

Broadbanding was a response to the constraints imposed by narrow pay bands. Broadbanding was first developed in the 1980s by the US Navy and was subsequently adopted by companies looking for new ways of managing and rewarding their employees. Broadbanding widens pay bands so that the compensation potential for a particular job is broader, lengthening the spread between the low end and high end of salary bands. A broadband is a large salary range that spans pay opportunities formerly covered by several separate, small salary ranges.

For example, the following pay range for a job with a midpoint of $15.00 per hour is based on a 30 percent range:

Maximum = Midpoint × 1.15	Minimum = Midpoint × 0.85
Maximum = $15.00 × 1.15= $17.25	Minimum = $15.00 × 0.85 = $12.75

Note that in this situation it would be relatively easy for an employee to max out and no longer have the ability to improve their salary, except by taking another position within the organization (assuming they are able to find one for which they qualify) or by quitting and looking for the same or a similar job elsewhere. As noted by the Society for Human Resource Management (SHRM 2022), organizations that are seeking greater flexibility might consider broadening the pay band, with perhaps a 40 percent range in hourly pay, as follows:

Maximum = Midpoint × 1.20	Minimum = Midpoint × 0.80
Maximum = $15.00 × 1.20 = $18.00	Minimum = $15.00 × 0.80 = $12.00

It is possible, in fact, to have much broader bands, and this is particularly the case among executive employees, where that range spread can be 80 percent to 200 percent of the midpoint. For example, a salary band with a midpoint of $50,000 per year may include a range from $40,000 to $100,000 (Salary.com 2019).

Numerous jobs can be included within a single band. A major advantage of broadbanding is that it provides greater flexibility when managing an employee's compensation. Compensation can be changed without the necessity of changing job titles or reclassifying jobs. Individuals can also be moved between jobs without concern for dramatic changes in salary. For example, an employee may be reluctant to move into another position because of the possibility of a salary decrease. With broadbanding, jobs may be in the same broad salary band, allowing for stability in salary. Employees can also be more easily rewarded for taking on new responsibilities or obtaining new skills. Throughout its history, there has been considerable debate about the merits of broadbanding and the challenges in implementing this approach to compensation (see the Critical Concept sidebar "Advantages and Concerns with Broadbanding").

Point System

A **point system** is a common job evaluation tool. The premise of point systems is that organizations do not compensate people for jobs but pay for specific valued aspects of the job. These are referred to as **compensable factors**. Examples of compensable factors include knowledge and skills required to do the job, experience requirements, accountability, supervisory responsibilities, and working conditions. Each compensable factor is assigned a maximum number of points, and points are assigned to a job based on the extent to which the job contains each compensable factor. Points in turn are associated with compensation levels and pay ranges. Exhibit 8.3 provides a hypothetical example of a point system to evaluate jobs. In this organization, eight compensable factors were identified, and each job in the organization is evaluated based on those factors. Points are totaled for each job, and the point total corresponds with a particular level of compensation. It is important to remember that there is no universal point system that is applied to all organizations. Each organization defines its own set of compensable factors and the points allocated to the degrees within each factor. In the organization represented in exhibit 8.3, the highest (5th) degree of skill is the most highly valued compensable factor in the organization, yielding 110 potential points.

Exhibit 8.4 shows how the organization represented in exhibit 8.3 might apply the compensable factor of autonomy. At the lowest level of autonomy (1st degree, assigned 0 points), the job does not allow any alteration in the manner in which work is accomplished. Consider the case of an assembly line worker whose job is completely routinized, with no reason or opportunity for the worker to exercise any type of discretion or flexibility. This job would likely be classified as 1st degree in its level of autonomy, at least for the traditional assembly-line job where workers have little or no say in the speed of work or the ability to point out errors. A job classified as having some level of autonomy—2nd degree—is one in which the jobholder follows detailed instructions but may be required to make limited decisions based on previously identified exceptions. A hospital billing clerk would likely fit into this category. A nurse's aide may fall into the 3rd degree level of autonomy, whereby detailed instructions are provided on how to accomplish the work, but independent initiative and judgment are required because of the multiple factors that affect patient care. A registered nurse would likely be considered a job with substantial autonomy—4th degree—in which there are standard protocols of care but in which substantial independent judgment is required to deal with variations among patients and other uncertainties. Finally, the highest level of autonomy, the 5th degree, may be best illustrated by a hospital director, for whom

point system
A method in which jobs are assigned points based on compensable factors predetermined by the organization. Points are then translated into salary levels.

compensable factors
Fundamental elements of a job, such as knowledge, skills, experience, accountability, supervisory responsibility, and working conditions, that are used as a basis for assigning points to a job and establishing compensation levels within a point system.

① CRITICAL CONCEPT
Advantages and Concerns with Broadbanding

Interest in broadbanding has waxed and waned over the years, but the idea of providing managers with greater flexibility in establishing wages is consistent with trends toward flatter, less hierarchical organizations and the use of flexible jobs that may be adapted to changing circumstances. Such approaches to job design enable organizations to respond quickly to competitive pressures and changes in the environment. With broadbanding, employees can more easily shift responsibilities as market and organizational requirements change.

Broadbanding offers other advantages, including the following:

- It emphasizes career development over job promotion by enabling companies with fewer promotional opportunities to reward employees for obtaining new skills and responsibilities.
- Authority for compensation decisions is largely decentralized to operating managers. Managers find it easier to gain approval for changes in compensation because broadbanding enables them to reward employees without going through the many justifications that traditional classification systems require.
- The broader pay bands give managers greater flexibility to recognize and reward diverse levels of individual contribution.

Because of these advantages, broadbanding is particularly useful for smaller and less hierarchical organizations.

The most difficult aspect of implementing broadbanding is helping employees think differently about how they are paid. Pay grades have long been used to determine status, titles, and eligibility for perks, and it can be difficult for employees to let go of this preconception. Broadbanding may also place less emphasis on external market rates as salaries change. There are control concerns as salaries may increase, significantly creating potential budget issues.

Broadbanding also implies fewer upward promotion opportunities. With a smaller number of pay bands, promotions to a higher grade level will occur less frequently than before. Employees must assume significantly greater job responsibilities to warrant placement in a higher band.

Factors	1st Degree	2nd Degree	3rd Degree	4th Degree	5th Degree
Knowledge	19	33	47	63	100
Skill	20	49	73	80	110
Autonomy	0	15	60	80	90
Supervisory responsibilities	0	10	16	25	30
Responsibility for work process	0	8	16	22	30
Physical demands	10	20	30	44	55
Mental demands	10	25	44	55	65
Unavoidable hazards	5	11	15	20	26

EXHIBIT 8.3
Job Evaluation Using a Point System

Compensable Factor: Autonomy

1st degree	Position receives regular supervision and work directions. No latitude given to alter work methods. (5 points)
2nd degree	Position receives regular supervision and work directions. Position has considerable latitude to select work methods. (15 points)
3rd degree	Position receives broad work supervision and direction. Position has complete latitude to accomplish work goals and objectives. (60 points)
4th degree	Position has complete latitude to accomplish work goals and objectives with little or no supervision or direction. (80 points)
5th degree	Position has complete latitude to accomplish and/or develop strategic goals and objectives for the organization. (90 points)

EXHIBIT 8.4
Compensable Factor Point Allocation Example

job-specific goals clearly must be met but the methods of accomplishing them are largely under the control of the jobholder.

As noted, the organization in our example places the highest value on skill, giving it the greatest number of potential points. The organization can apply this system to every job, assigning points based on these factors (although there are some preconditions, as described in the related Did You Know? sidebar). Points are then translated into monetary terms, such as hourly wages or annual salaries. For example, a job that has been assigned 506 points (the maximum that may be achieved) may be worth $50 per hour. A job that falls between 450 and 475 points may be allotted an hourly wage of $45 per hour. Note that a point value can also be translated into a wage range. For example, a job that has been assigned 250 points may have a pay range from $23 to $30 per hour. Using ranges lets the organization tailor salaries to other factors, such as individual performance or tenure in the organization.

The point system can be ineffective and misleading if objective and current information about the particular job being evaluated is unavailable. Therefore, it is essential that a thorough job analysis be conducted so that those involved in evaluating the job have clear and unambiguous information about the job.

A key value of point systems is that they aim to ensure internal equity in an organization's compensation. That is, all jobs are evaluated based on the same compensable factors. However, a major drawback of a point system is that it does not account for variations in the labor market. For example, the jobs of medical transcriptionist and nursing assistant may have the same number of points, but if nursing assistants are in much greater demand

---

? DID YOU KNOW?
Preconditions for Using a Point System

A point system of job evaluation can be an effective and efficient way to assign wages in an organization. However, to implement a point system, several preconditions must be met:

- Compensable factors must be acceptable to all parties.
- Compensable factors must validly distinguish among jobs.
- Compensable factors must be relevant to the jobs under analysis.
- Jobs must vary on the compensable factors selected so that meaningful differences in jobs can be identified.
- Compensable factors must be measurable.
- Compensable factors must be independent of one another.
- Job evaluation and market pay rates must be reconciled. For example, there are circumstances in which the market demands a level of pay higher than the formal job evaluation process would warrant, often because of scarcity and high demand for the job.

in a particular community, the organization may need to pay them appreciably more than the point total would warrant. Making such an exception would enable the organization to be externally competitive for nursing assistants, but at the same time, it would create a situation of internal inequity. As discussed earlier in the chapter, the conflict between internal equity and external competitiveness is a constant challenge for many organizations. Similarly, consider the case of an experienced dietitian who has been working for a hospital for 15 years, at present earning an annual salary of $70,000. If dieticians are in short supply in the community, the hospital may need to hire a new graduate at a salary close to (or above) $70,000. Most organizations value experience, but where the labor market demands a higher wage, the need to fill a position becomes more critical than experience. In turn, the experienced dietitian may choose to leave the organization and work somewhere else where they can earn more.

FACTOR COMPARISON

The **factor comparison method** combines features of the ranking and point system methods. It differs from point systems in that compensable factors for a job are evaluated against compensable factor scores for benchmark jobs in the organization. The compensable factors usually include skill, mental effort, physical effort, responsibilities, and working conditions.

factor comparison method
A method of job evaluation in which compensable factors for one position are evaluated against those factors in a benchmark job.

MARKET PRICING

The job evaluation approaches discussed thus far focus on ensuring equity in the workplace. However, compensation in healthcare organizations often depends largely on labor supply, and **market pricing** often determines compensation. Because of scarcities in many of the health professions, market pricing of jobs often supersedes formal job evaluation methods.

Employers learn about area wages largely from salary surveys carried out by the following:

market pricing
A method of setting salaries based on market factors (supply and demand).

- American Hospital Association (www.aha.org)

- Financial Executives International (www.financialexecutives.org)

- Heidrick and Struggles International (www.heidrick.com/en)

- Society for Human Resource Management (https://shrm.org)

- US Bureau of Labor Statistics (www.bls.gov)

Websites such as Salary.com (www.salary.com) can also provide salary information.

VARIABLE COMPENSATION

In addition to base compensation, many organizations have an additional part of total compensation that varies. Variable compensation is most commonly used to reward employee behaviors or outcomes or organizational or team performance. There are many types of variable compensation, including team-based incentives and skills-based or knowledge-based pay.

TEAM-BASED INCENTIVES

Healthcare work is largely carried out by teams of people, and success is almost always the result of collective effort. To reflect this effort, managers consider numerous approaches to rewarding team performance.

team-based incentives
Variable compensation schemes based on the performance of a team. An individual's salary may be determined in part by the performance of the team.

Team-based incentives can be used to boost productivity and performance, improve quality and customer service, and increase retention. However, the use of team-based incentives is often constrained by the need to also reward individual performance. Among the challenges faced in team-based incentive compensation is whether to provide the same financial reward for each member. If there are differences in individual contributions to team performance, should rewards vary among team members?

For example, a care delivery team made up of an obstetrician, a case manager, a social worker, and a nurse's aide may be rewarded for delivering more infants, experiencing minimal adverse events, and achieving high patient satisfaction scores. What level of reward should be assigned to the team? Will inequities in rewards cause some team members to work less in achieving team objectives? These are only a few of the questions that must be addressed before implementing a team-based compensation system (see the related Critical Concept sidebar "Bundled Payments").

SKILLS-BASED OR KNOWLEDGE-BASED PAY

In some instances, organizations wish to reward employees who obtain additional skills or competencies. In a **skills-based or knowledge-based compensation system**, employees may be given supplementary pay if they acquire additional work-related skills or knowledge. The reward structure of this approach is based on the range, depth, and types of skills that employees acquire. These new skills or areas of knowledge may not be central to the individual's current job but may make the employee more adaptable and thus more valuable to the organization. Examples would be increasing an employee's salary after the employee completes an advanced degree or obtains certification in a new procedure. Such systems encourage employees to learn and develop new skill sets.

skills-based or knowledge-based compensation system
A compensation system in which employees are financially rewarded for mastering new skills or acquiring new knowledge.

> ⚠ **CRITICAL CONCEPT**
> Bundled Payments
>
> A *bundled payment*, also called an *episode-based payment*, is a single payment made to a team of providers or a healthcare facility, or both, to cover the entire cost of an episode of care. These payments are based on the expected cost of the condition, with adjustment for individual patient characteristics and diagnosis, and the providers take on the financial risk of costs that exceed the bundled payment. A joint replacement is a common example of a procedure using a bundled payment structure. The bundled payment is thought to encourage coordination between providers for a single episode of care and to improve quality (Friedberg et al. 2018). One 2020 meta-analysis, however, suggests that these positive effects are currently limited to a select number of procedures (Agarwal et al. 2020).

PAY FOR PERFORMANCE

A **pay-for-performance system** is built on the principles that good work deserves to be rewarded and that pay based on good work produces improved performance. In a pay-for-performance system, employees are financially rewarded based on their achievement of preestablished goals. In healthcare, there are two general types of pay-for-performance systems: productivity-focused pay for performance and quality-focused pay for performance.

PRODUCTIVITY-FOCUSED PAY FOR PERFORMANCE

Productivity-focused pay for performance links financial incentives to employees' productivity. Fee-for-service physician payment is a direct form of payment based on productivity. Many organizations use physician payment schemes containing some form of productivity-focused pay for performance. Despite the growing use of value-based care and other reforms, fee-for-service remains the dominant form of payment for physician services, with an average of 70.8 percent of physician practice revenue received through fee-for service (Rama 2017).

Productivity-focused pay programs may be structured in a variety of ways. A *piece-rate incentive* rewards employees for each unit of output produced, whether the unit is a product or a service. The *commission* system, most common in sales, is structured so that

pay-for-performance system
A compensation system that rewards employees based on their job performance; managers evaluate their employees' work according to preestablished goals, standards, or company values.

productivity-focused pay for performance
A compensation system that ties financial incentives to individual employee productivity.

employees receive a percentage of their gross receipts. A *bonus* is a onetime financial reward to recognize individual or organizational performance.

A *profit-sharing plan* enables employees to share in the organization's profits, and a *gain-sharing plan* allocates to employees a portion of the gains made by the organization as a result of increased efficiency or productivity. The gain-sharing approach has manifested itself in a number of forms, such as the Scanlon Plan, the Rucker Plan, and Improshare (Gordon 2022; Greenberg 2022). Regardless of program structure, with productivity-focused pay for performance, rewards are tied to the accomplishment of goals.

QUALITY-FOCUSED PAY FOR PERFORMANCE

The second type of pay for performance in healthcare is **quality-focused pay for performance.** The goal of this approach is to encourage the delivery of high-quality healthcare services. Pay-for-quality programs reward activities and practices that are likely to improve healthcare outcomes, including doing more prevention screenings, ensuring up-to-date patient vaccinations, investing in information technology designed to reduce medical errors, and following evidence-based clinical guidelines. By improving outcomes, quality-focused pay-for-performance programs hope to produce healthier and more satisfied patients and ultimately reduce costs.

As the Affordable Care Act (ACA) encourages transition to value-based payments, with a focus on quality measures, it is useful to examine the role that physician practice executives play in the implementation of these programs. *Practice executives* are administrators responsible for negotiating quality targets and incentives with health plans. They are responsible for implementing pay-for-performance programs in their respective organizations. (See the related Current Issue sidebar on medical homes and accountable care organizations [ACOs]).

Bokhour and colleagues (2006) interviewed practice executives from 69 physician organizations in Massachusetts. These practice executives were responsible for implementing pay-for-performance programs that affect more than 5,000 primary care physicians. The findings of this study shed light on concerns about successful implementation of such programs (Bokhour et al. 2006):

◆ Practice executives indicated that quality-oriented incentives were better aligned with physicians' inherent desires to provide high-quality care than were productivity- or utilization-oriented incentives.

◆ Practice executives did not unanimously agree that financial incentives motivated individuals to achieve quality improvement goals.

> **⚠ CRITICAL CONCEPT**
> Medical Homes and Accountable Care Organizations
>
> Since the passage of the Affordable Care Act (ACA) in 2010, there has been an emphasis on shifting from the volume-based metrics of the fee-for-service (FFS) model to a value-based payment model. The value-based payment model is designed to reduce growing healthcare costs while incentivizing provider behaviors that promote quality of care rather than being based exclusively on amount of services provided. The law created an Innovation Center within CMS to test new payment models in Medicare, Medicaid, and the Children's Health Insurance Program (CHIP) in an effort to increase quality of healthcare and decrease costs. These new models include the *patient-centered medical home*, also known as the *primary care medical home* (PCMH), and the *accountable care organization* (ACO). The PCMH is a model that focuses on primary care provision, keeping the patient at the center of focus. The model aims to deliver better-coordinated and comprehensive primary care, including the provision of preventive and mental health care, acute care, and chronic care. The PCMH model uses a team-based strategy for care delivery, often including providers throughout a community, and incorporates the use of healthcare information technology to better share patient information across providers and demonstrate greater responsiveness to patients' preferences for accessible services; it also has a system-level commitment to quality and quality improvement (Agency for Healthcare Research and Quality [AHRQ] 2022). ACOs were developed to coordinate care across the healthcare needs spectrum, not just in primary care, with the goal of increasing quality and decreasing costs. With better coordination, ACOs work to decrease waste in the provision of medical care to their patients by preventing such unnecessary care as duplicate tests and avoiding medical errors (CMS 2022a).

- ◆ Physicians were concerned that some quality measures were outside of their scope of control. For example, measures for achieving a certain level of preventive screenings relied on patient cooperation.

- ◆ Physicians indicated that data recording and reporting were often inaccurate or did not represent a true measure of quality.

- ◆ The method of monetary distribution affects the rewards' power to motivate change. For example, distributing rewards equally to all physicians is much less motivating than distributing rewards based on each physician's performance. The latter method, however, was sometimes found to be unfair in cases where several physicians were involved in the treatment of a particular patient but only one of them got credit toward program measures.

◆   Some organizations recognize that delivery of quality care depends not only on physicians but also on the active participation of all members of the practice. These organizations retain program rewards and reinvest them in infrastructure that facilitates delivery of quality care, rather than distributing them to individuals.

CRITICISMS OF PAY FOR PERFORMANCE

A number of criticisms have been made of pay for performance. A major argument against pay for performance is that pay-for-performance systems require a valid method of assessing employee performance—and this is an area in which many organizations fall short (Kumar 2015). Others argue that there is a tendency for some organizations to implement pay for performance inconsistently—that is, to abandon it when there are fewer financial resources available (Fisher 2016). In the healthcare environment, the evidence is mixed about the impact of paying physicians for quality, in large part because the science of measuring quality is still in its infancy (Rice 2015). An extreme problem is that pay-for-performance schemes may lead employees to engage in ethically questionable or illegal activities to achieve performance goals (Stout 2014). Because compensation is linked to goal achievement, pay for performance may also encourage employees to set goals that are easily achievable. As a result, pay for performance may hamper improvement efforts and discourage risk-taking and innovation.

Healthcare providers often assess quality by analyzing three types of measures—structural, process, and outcome (Agency for Healthcare Research and Quality [AHRQ] 2015). *Structural measures* focus on the organization's capacity and skill, including measures such as patient-to-provider ratio or the proportion of providers who have achieved board certification. *Process measures* focus on steps taken (or not taken) by providers during clinical encounters which are correlated with patient outcomes. Process measures often emphasize preventative measures, such as whether a patient is screened in a timely manner or immunized. *Outcome measures* focus on the ultimate result of the clinical encounter and include metrics such as mortality and readmission rates. When incorporating these measures into a compensation plan, an employer must consider trade-offs among data reliability, completeness, and timeliness. For example, process measures are often immediately available and reliable (e.g., a screening was or was not done), but they do not guarantee positive outcomes. Likewise, outcome measures are complete and final, but they may require considerable lag time or fail to explain confounding factors causing the ultimate result.

In designing pay-for-performance systems, it is important to recognize that any incentive system will lead to anticipated and unanticipated (and sometimes negative) consequences. For example, paying primary care physicians for seeing more patients may have the effect of lowering the level of quality provided to patients. Similarly, paying a physician based on the quality of patient outcomes may give the physician an incentive to see only relatively healthy patients who are more likely to have positive health outcomes than patients with complex medical conditions. People respond to incentives, and it is important to anticipate possible responses to these incentives prior to implementing an incentive system.

SPECIAL CONSIDERATIONS FOR COMPENSATING PHYSICIANS

Depending on the practice settings, physicians are subject to a variety of compensation methods. Before World War II (1939–1945), most physicians were general practitioners who delivered care in independent practices on a fee-for-service (FFS) basis. This practice changed radically after the war, with an explosion of medical subspecialties nurtured by battlefield needs, the rise of care within hospitals instead of at home, and the advent of employer-based medical insurance. As soon as patients were no longer directly responsible for the cost of care, payers of the services (employers or government) and providers of care were no longer obliged to justify costs to consumers. The result was a system that paid physicians whatever they requested, without validating the need and appropriateness of services or costs. Eventually payers developed *managed care* practices, which shifted attention to payment mechanisms as a means to modify clinical behavior and ultimately lower costs.

Managed care was created largely in response to wide variations in treatment for the same condition. For example, two adjacent communities, with similar populations and demographics, may have dramatically different rates of a particular type of surgery. Where scientific justification cannot account for such differences, it is natural to examine the incentive systems that motivate physician behavior.

One approach to changing physician incentives is **capitation**. Under capitation, a physician or physician group is paid a fixed monthly fee, called a *capitated fee*, for each patient on the roster. The fee is intended to cover professional services required to care for each patient. Providers under capitation are typically paid an established *per member per month* (PMPM) rate for each covered patient. The challenge for the practitioner is to provide these services within the limits of the total monthly payment. Any funds left over after delivering care belong to the physician. It is expected that in any given month, the care for some patients will cost more than the capitated fee but that many other patients will not cost the physician anything. The goal is for the physician to make a profit each month while providing the appropriate care for all patients who need care. Thus, capitation is seen as providing an incentive for physicians to perform the appropriate level of care without generating excess costs. However, because physicians keep the unused portion of the monthly fee as profit, some may be tempted to provide less than the optimal amount

capitation
A method of paying for health services in which a provider is paid a prepaid amount for each patient, regardless of the amount of health services provided.

solo practice
An approach to providing medical services in which a physician works as a single, office-based practitioner.

group practice
The general name for many types of physician practices wherein two or more physicians have established a legal entity to deliver care together. Group members typically share premises, personnel, and other resources.

independent practice association (IPA)
A corporation formed by a collection of physician practices, often including solo and group practitioners, that join forces to take advantage of economies of scale for contracting, business services, or ancillary services.

staff-model HMO
A setup in which physicians and health professionals are salaried employees of a health maintenance organization (HMO), and the clinics or health centers in which they practice are owned by the HMO.

of care. Another concern with capitation is patients with preexisting medical conditions. Physicians worry that the cost to care for such patients will eat up their capitation payments, even though the conditions existed before the current physicians got involved. Medical group bankruptcies were not uncommon in the 1990s because of their inability to adapt and manage within the constraints of capitation. As a result, other physician compensation approaches have surfaced, as described in the next section.

PAYMENT METHODS AND PRACTICE SETTINGS

Physicians practice in a variety of settings, and each setting is characterized by particular payment methods. The five most common setups are (1) office practices, (2) the staff model in health maintenance organizations (HMOs), (3) hospital-based physicians, (4) locum tenens practices, and (5) physician managers. The ACA has encouraged more collaborative practice models, such as the ACO and the PCMH, both of which were discussed in sidebars earlier in this chapter.

OFFICE PRACTICE

Three broad categories of office practice are solo practice, group practice, and independent practice association. A **solo practice** consists of one physician, who works as a single, office-based practitioner. Solo practitioners often employ nonphysician staff, such as a billing specialist or office manager. A **group practice** is composed of two or more physicians who have established a legal entity to deliver care together. An **independent practice association (IPA)** usually consists of a collection of practices, often including solo and group practitioners, that join forces to take advantage of economies of scale for contracting, business services, or ancillary services (such as laboratory services).

For solo and group practice physicians, the dominant reimbursement modes are pure fee-for-service and salary plus incentive. Over the years, the fees paid to physicians by private and government payers have been significantly reduced. As fees are lowered, physicians have an incentive to increase volume to reach their target income; consequently, service utilization has increased. However, trends to increasingly tie payment to meeting quality measures may serve to shift away from purely volume-driven care provision.

IPAs may seek risk contracts from a payer, particularly if the IPA is large and well integrated. IPAs are often paid from a discounted FFS schedule with an incentive program that adds money to the total reimbursement for the group. Such groups actively monitor utilization internally, usually comparing it with national standards and scientifically validated treatment guidelines. Physicians who deviate significantly from these norms are either reeducated by their peers or asked to leave the group.

While staff-model HMOs aim to improve quality of care by using salaried providers, the structure of the HMO restricts patients to accessing care within the HMO network. Another model introduced to provide higher-quality care is the accountable care organization (ACO), which allows patients more flexibility to see providers of their choice, as they are not required to seek care within the ACO. The Affordable Care Act (ACA) established the Medicare Shared Savings Program, in which providers can voluntarily participate by using an ACO model to care for their Medicare patient population. These ACOs aim to provide high-quality coordinated care for their Medicare fee-for-service patient population and meet set quality, financial, and reporting targets. If the ACOs meet these targets and comply with ACO requirements, they can share in any generated cost savings with CMS. As of January 2022, there were 483 Shared Savings Program ACOs in the United States, serving more than 11 million Medicare beneficiaries (CMS 2022b). A recent study of the Shared Savings Program ACO program found average net savings of $190 per beneficiary without reducing quality (Zhu et al. 2021).

STAFF MODEL

Some medical groups or HMOs employ physicians on a straight salary basis or **staff-model HMO**—a model common in the late 1970s and early 1980s but less so today. The staff model is considered a closed-panel HMO, where patients obtain services through a limited number of providers who are salaried HMO employees (Centers for Disease Control and Prevention [CDC] 2022). A strength of this model is that physicians are not distracted by concerns about generating revenue. They are able to focus on practicing medicine. On the other hand, they do not have the monetary incentive many other payment arrangements provide.

This model presents several drawbacks. One in particular is the difficulty in recruiting physicians who want to be employees. Some directors of staff-model HMOs were frustrated by the difficulty in motivating salaried physicians to extend themselves beyond prescribed hours

 KEY POINT

In independent practice associations (IPAs), incentives are designed to encourage the group to perform at a high level, but regardless of the success in reaching these goals, the physicians are paid for each service provided.

and tasks. (For another model that emphasizes quality of care but provides greater flexibility, see the Current Issue sidebar "The ACA and the Medicare Shared Savings Program ACO Model.")

Hospital-Based Physicians

A growing group of physicians—hospitalists, pathologists, radiologists, and anesthesiologists, among others—practice almost exclusively within the confines of nonacademic hospitals. Many physicians are directly employed by hospitals and receive a straight salary. Sometimes physicians form professional corporations that contract with hospitals for services. For instance, a hospital may contract to have services provided by a group of emergency medicine physicians. This group will staff the emergency room, be paid on a contractual basis, and maybe even take over the administration of the unit. The same model can apply to other specialties. The doctors are not employees of the hospital but are independent contractors.

The arrangement is somewhat different for hospital-based physicians working in academic tertiary care medical centers. A large percentage of physicians in an academic setting are in training as residents or fellows. Their salaries are paid in large measure from Medicare reimbursements received by the medical center for the purpose of supporting graduate medical education. Thus, their salaries are not linked to their clinical performance or the numbers of patients they see or procedures they perform. For staff or faculty physicians, salary is also the rule, although clinical activity is often figured into their compensation.

The mission of the academic physician may be summarized as a combination of teaching, research, and patient care. Because reimbursements to hospitals have decreased, academic physicians often perform additional clinical work. A **faculty practice plan** is a group practice that comprises the faculty of the medical center. Salaries in academic medicine are invariably lower than those in the private-practice sector.

Some physicians in the academic setting focus entirely on research and may see no patients at all. Many of them derive the bulk of their salaries from grants they secure from outside agencies; the remainder may come from the university. The longevity of researchers in this environment often depends on their ability to successfully secure external grants.

faculty practice plan
A group practice that comprises the faculty of a medical center; it was created as a way to leverage the billings generated by faculty into some sort of shared distributions.

Locum Tenens Practices

A **locum tenens physician** is a temporarily employed physician; locum tenens physicians are typically paid a fixed amount for services provided. *Locum tenens* is a Latin phrase meaning "to hold the place of; to substitute for" (LocumTenens.com 2022). The twenty-first-century trend toward use of locum tenens physicians has been linked to physician shortages, the growth in the number of partially retired physicians, lifestyle considerations that new physicians favor, and the increase in female physicians, who may be more likely to seek flexible jobs to help balance career and family duties (Dudley, McLaughlin, and Lee 2022). The use

locum tenens physician
A temporarily employed physician; typically paid a fixed amount for services provided.

of locum tenens physicians is likely to increase because of the flexibility this system affords to the physician and the organization. A 2022 survey found that 88 percent of healthcare facilities had used locum tenens physicians or other locum tenens providers within the past year (AMN Healthcare 2022). For some physicians, locum tenens arrangements become permanent, providing greater work flexibility.

PHYSICIAN MANAGERS

A growing number of physicians are employed as managers in such roles as medical director, consultant, and administrator. Many are employed by organizations that want to better understand and control the resources they devote to employee healthcare benefits. Physician managers are attuned to the unique problems of their employer and are able to help benefits coordinators and human resources administrators address complex employee health coverage issues. They also serve as liaisons between the benefits coordinators or human resources personnel and external vendors such as health plans, provider groups, and ancillary providers.

FUTURE DIRECTIONS FOR PHYSICIAN COMPENSATION

There is considerable uncertainty about the future of physician compensation (see the related Debate Point sidebar). However, given the ongoing concern with quality and value, the following are trends that are likely to continue:

◆ *Physician reimbursement will likely continue to be increasingly linked to quality metrics of performance.* In 2019, CMS set goals for all Medicare Part A/B beneficiaries and for 50 percent of Medicaid beneficiaries to be enrolled in accountable care plans by 2025 (CMS 2021).

◆ *Complementary and integrative health services will likely continue to be used.* Americans on the whole spend about $30.2 billion out of pocket per year on complementary health approaches, including massage therapy, acupuncture, and the use of natural products such as fish oil (National Institutes of Health 2016). The number of adults using massage, chiropractic, and acupuncture therapy without health insurance coverage for these services increased from 2002 to 2012, and those with coverage for these services mainly had only partial coverage (Nahin, Barnes, and Stussman 2016).

◆ *Employers will likely continue to reduce their role as the primary source of health insurance for their employees.* The Affordable Care Act placed consumers on the individual market for health insurance in the role of selecting their healthcare plans, and as more employers opt out of traditional health insurance provision for their employees, more people may enter the individual insurance market and will become accountable for making healthcare choices. As long as the ACA remains in place, certified federal navigators and nonprofits will continue to help consumers understand these decisions, along with information provided online from the federal marketplace and other sources. Other employers still providing health insurance for their employees are increasingly opting to use high-deductible health plans and health savings accounts to encourage their employees to take greater responsibility for their healthcare utilization and expenses. The theory behind this option is that patients will be more conscious of the cost of healthcare if they are expending their own financial resources—rather than those of a third party—to pay for health services.

Ⓧ DEBATE POINT

How does an organization measure physician productivity? It is becoming increasingly common to link physician compensation to productivity. But measuring physician productivity is often a challenge. Consider the following questions:

- If a patient new to the practice is counted at a higher value than a returning patient, what defines a *new* patient? Someone who has never been seen before? Someone who has not been seen within a given time frame? Someone who has not been seen for a nonacute visit?

- For a procedure-based specialty, such as gastroenterology, does the physician who performs the procedure get full credit, or should partial credit go to the physician who has seen the patient most frequently over the past year?

- For an obstetric practice, should the physician who performs a greater number of vaginal deliveries (which take more time but are less invasive to the mother) receive more credit than the physician who performs a greater number of cesarean section operations (which produce higher revenue)?

- How are other activities and factors—such as seniority, the number of call days taken, and service on hospital or medical society committees—accounted for and valued? Are they counted as part of physician productivity?

- How should meeting quality benchmarks be counted in the measurement of a physician's productivity?

SUMMARY

Healthcare is in the midst of continuous change in compensation systems. Perhaps the most important and enduring trend is the focus on performance as a basis for compensation. This trend extends to hospitals and individual physicians.

Although pay-for-performance systems are increasingly popular, it is essential to understand the consequences of pay-for-performance arrangements. The unanticipated consequences, some of which are negative, are often not understood until after a system has been in place for some time.

FOR DISCUSSION

1. Suppose you are a manager at a low-budget healthcare setting, such as a local health department. How will you recruit new staff and motivate current employees when competitors in the area are able to pay 30 to 40 percent more than your organization can?

2. Suppose you are a staff nurse in a hospital that uses an incentive compensation system. Do you have an obligation to disclose the nature of the compensation arrangement to patients? If so, how should this information be communicated, and by whom?

3. Suppose you are a physician belonging to an ACO; however, you are still primarily paid through fee-for-service reimbursement. Can you identify competing incentives that may be present and explain how you would approach such a dilemma?

4. What warnings would you give to a team designing an incentive system?

5. How will you design a team-based compensation system to prevent potential "free riders" on the team from taking advantage of the system?

6. What effect has managed care had on designing physician compensation models?

7. For a four-person surgical group practice, what kind of formula may be devised to fairly and consistently measure and reward productivity? What changes may be needed if one surgeon decides to perform more office work and less surgery?

EXPERIENTIAL EXERCISES

EXERCISE 1

Mapleton Family Medicine is a physician group practice located in a small city (population 150,000) in the Midwest. Mapleton's eight physicians include family physicians, internists, and pediatricians. The practice is owned by two of the physicians; the other six physicians are currently salaried. The owners are concerned with productivity and quality in the practice. There is a relatively long waiting time for appointments, and a recent chart review revealed that the percentage of children who are up-to-date with immunizations has dropped. Also, anecdotal evidence suggests that at-risk people are not routinely receiving flu and pneumonia vaccinations. Many patients have complained about having to wait up to 90 minutes in the waiting room. At this time, however, the practice is not in a position to hire another physician.

Each physician in the practice currently sees an average of 25 patients per day. The owners want this number increased to 30 patients per day without sacrificing quality of care. To reach this goal, they are thinking of moving to an incentive system, whereby physicians have a base salary equivalent to 75 percent of their current salary and have the opportunity to earn up to 125 percent of their base salary if they meet defined volume and quality goals. Although the owners have not completely thought this system through, they want to set 30 patients per day as a base and, through the incentive system, encourage physicians to see, on average, up to 35 patients per day.

In terms of quality, the owners have considered the following three measures:

1. Patient satisfaction surveys

2. Child-immunization audit data

3. Patient waiting times

Quality goals will be set biannually for each physician. The expectation is that physicians who achieve the goals will earn their full salary (assuming patient volume is adequate), and quality measures above their goals will result in bonuses according to a pay schedule.

You have been brought in to advise the owners on their proposed compensation plan. You will need to first answer in your own mind the following questions:

• Do you see any potential negative consequences of this plan based on the information provided? If so, how would you address these concerns?
• How do you think the physicians in the practice would react to this plan? Should they be involved in developing the plan, and if so, how should they be involved?
• What advice will you give the owners before they proceed?

EXERCISE 2

Compare two organizations' approaches to setting salary levels. First, identify two healthcare organizations that are similar in mission and size. For example, you may select two medical group practices, two medium-sized community hospitals, or two nursing homes of similar size. You may choose two organizations in the same geographic area and labor market or two in different markets.

Next, identify and interview the senior human resources management executive or the individual who best understands the compensation philosophy, system, design, and decision-making process. The goal of this exercise is to identify the organization's compensation strategy, including its approach to balancing competing compensation objectives.

Summarize the compensation philosophy, policy, and practices in each organization and write a report on the similarities and differences between the two compensation systems.

Use the following questions to guide your compensation comparison:

1. What is the policy of the organization on compensating employees at market rates? Is there an explicit policy to pay below market, at market, or above market? Does the approach vary by the type of employee and the particular labor market?

2. Does the organization have a specific strategy for attracting, recruiting, and retaining employees in difficult-to-fill positions? If so, for which positions has this been an issue? What strategies have been used in these circumstances?

3. How does the organization evaluate or "price" jobs? Does it conduct a formal job evaluation process? If so, how often and under what circumstances? Are there certain jobs where the market dictates salary, rather than the salary being the result of a job evaluation process?

4. Does the organization face any of the following problems? If so, how does the organization address them?

    - Wage compression

    - Employees "topping out" of their salary range

    - High prevalence of employee departures because of compensation-related factors

    - Perceptions among employees that aspects of the compensation system are unfair

REFERENCES

Adams, J. S. 1963. "Toward an Understanding of Inequity." *Journal of Abnormal and Social Psychology* 67 (5): 422–36.

Agarwal, R., J. M. Liao, A. Gupta, and A. S. Navathe. 2020. "The Impact of Bundled Payment on Health Care Spending, Utilization, and Quality: A Systematic Review." *Health Affairs* 39 (1):50–57.

Agency for Healthcare Research and Quality. 2022. "Defining the PCMH." Reviewed August. www.ahrq.gov/ncepcr/tools/pcmh/defining/index.html.

———. 2015. "Types of Health Care Quality Measures." Reviewed July 15. www.ahrq.gov/talkingquality/measures/types.html.

American Speech-Language-Hearing Association (ASHA). 2022. *ASHA 2021 Audiology Survey*. Published April 7. www.asha.org/siteassets/surveys/2021-audiology-survey-hourly-wages.pdf.

AMN Healthcare. 2022. *2022 Survey of Locum Tenens Staffing Trends: Moving Toward a More Flexible Physician Workforce*. Dallas, TX: AMN Healthcare.

Boccuti, C., G. Casillas, and T. Neuman. 2015. "Reading the Stars: Nursing Home Quality Star Ratings, Nationally and by State." Kaiser Family Foundation. Published May 14. http://kff.org/report-section/reading-the-stars-nursing-home-quality-star-ratings-nationally-and-by-state-issue-brief/.

Bokhour, B. G., J. F. Burgess Jr., J. M. Hook, B. White, D. Berlowitz, M. R. Guldin, M. Meterko, and G. J. Young. 2006. "Incentive Implementation in Physician Practices: A Qualitative Study of Practice Executive Perspectives on Pay for Performance." *Medical Care Research and Review* 63 (1): 73S–95S.

Centers for Disease Control and Prevention (CDC). 2022. "Health, United States, 2020–2021: Health Maintenance Organization (HMO)." National Center for Health Statistics. Reviewed August 12. www.cdc.gov/nchs/hus/sources-definitions/hmo.htm.

Centers for Medicare and Medicaid Services (CMS). 2022a. "Accountable Care Organizations (ACOs): General Information." Updated October 3. https://innovation.cms.gov/innovation-models/aco.

———. 2022b. "Medicare Shared Savings Program Continues to Grow and Deliver High-Quality, Person-Centered Care Through Accountable Care Organizations." Press release, January 26. www.cms.gov/newsroom/press-releases/medicare-shared-savings-program-continues-grow-and-deliver-high-quality-person-centered-care-through.

———. 2021. "Health Care Payment Learning and Action Network." Updated September 21. https://innovation.cms.gov/initiatives/Health-Care-Payment-Learning-and-Action-Network/.

Dudley, J., S. McLaughlin, and T. H. Lee. 2022. "Why So Many Women Physicians Are Quitting." *Harvard Business Review*. Published January 19. https://hbr.org/2022/01/why-so-many-women-physicians-are-quitting.

FederalPay.org. 2022. "General Schedule Payscale." Accessed October 10. www.federalpay.org/.

Fisher, A. 2016. "Why Performance Bonuses and Merit Raises Don't Work." *Fortune*. Published February 24. http://fortune.com/2016/02/24/salary-bonuses-merit-raises-effectiveness/.

Friedberg, M. W., P. G. Chen, M. Simmons, T. Sherry, P. Mendel, L. Raaen, J. Ryan, P. Orr, C. Vargo, L. Carlasare, C. Botts, and K. Blake. 2018. *Effects of Health Care Payment Models on Physician Practice in the United States*. Santa Monica, CA: RAND Corporation. www.rand.org/pubs/research_reports/RR2667.html.

Gordon, J. 2022. "What Is a Gain Sharing Plan?" The Business Professor. Updated April 16. https://thebusinessprofessor.com/en_US/employment-law/gain-sharing-plan-definition.

Greenberg, A. 2022. "What Is Gainsharing and Can It Improve Employee Performance?" ContractRecruiter.com. Published April 19. www.contractrecruiter.com/gainsharing-improve-employee-performance/.

Kumar, S. 2015. "Five Reasons Merit-Based Pay Hurts Average Workers." *Fortune*. Published July 24. http://fortune.com/2015/07/24/5-reasons-merit-based-pay-hurts-average-workers/.

LocumTenens.com. 2022. "About Locum Tenens Physician Staffing." Accessed October 13. www.locumtenens.com/about-us/what-is-locum-tenens/.

Medicare.gov. 2022. "Find & Compare Nursing Homes, Hospitals & Other Providers Near You." Accessed October 29. www.medicare.gov/care-compare/.

Mohr, V., J. Zinn, J. Angelelli, J. M. Teno, and S. C. Miller. 2004. "Driven to Tiers: Socioeconomic and Racial Disparities in the Quality of Nursing Home Care." *Milbank Quarterly* 82 (2): 227–56.

Nahin, R. L., P. M. Barnes, and B. J. Stussman. 2016. *Insurance Coverage for Complementary Health Approaches Among Adult Users: United States, 2002 and 2012*. NCHS Data Brief No. 235. Published January. Hyattsville, MD: National Center for Health Statistics.

National Institutes of Health. 2016. "Paying for Complementary and Integrative Health Approaches." National Center for Complementary and Integrative Health (NCCIH) Pub. No. D331. Updated June. https://nccih.nih.gov/health/financial.

Plescia, M. 2021. "5 Trends in Employee Compensation." *Becker's Hospital Review*. Published November 3. www.beckershospitalreview.com/compensation-issues/5-trends-in-employee-compensation.html.

Rama, A. 2017. *Payment and Delivery in 2016: The Prevalence of Medical Homes, Accountable Care Organizations, and Payment Methods Reported by Physicians*. AMA Economic Health Policy Research report no. 2017-4. American Medical Association (AMA). Published October. www.ama-assn.org/sites/ama-assn.org/files/corp/media-browser/public/health-policy/prp-medical-home-aco-payment.pdf.

Rice, S. 2015. "Physician Quality Pay Not Paying Off." *Modern Healthcare*. Published May 30. www.modernhealthcare.com/article/20150530/MAGAZINE/305309979.

Salary.com. 2019. "What Is Broadbanding in Compensation?" *Salary.com* (blog). Published May 16. www.salary.com/blog/what-is-broadbanding-in-compensation/.

Society for Human Resource Management (SHRM). 2022. "How to Establish Salary Ranges." Accessed May 1. www.shrm.org/resourcesandtools/tools-and-samples/how-to-guides/pages/howtoestablishsalaryranges.aspx.

Stout, L. A. 2014. "Killing Conscience: The Unintended Behavioral Consequences of 'Pay for Performance.'" *Journal of Corporation Law* 39 (3): 525–61.

US Bureau of Labor Statistics (BLS). 2022. "Occupational Outlook Handbook: Nurse Anesthetists, Nurse Midwives, and Nurse Practitioners; Pay." Updated September 8. www.bls.gov/ooh/healthcare/nurse-anesthetists-nurse-midwives-and-nurse-practitioners.htm#tab-5.

Zhu, M., R. S. Saunders, D. Muhlestein, W. K. Bleser, and M. B. McClellan. 2021. "The Medicare Shared Savings Program in 2020: Positive Movement (and Uncertainty) During a Pandemic." *Health Affairs Blog*. Published October 14. www.healthaffairs.org/do/10.1377/forefront.20211008.785640/.

CHAPTER 9

EMPLOYEE BENEFITS

Melissa G. McCraw and Dolores G. Clement

LEARNING OBJECTIVES

After completing this chapter, you should be able to

➤ discuss the history and trends of employee benefits management;

➤ explain the rationale and tax implications of offering benefits in addition to compensation and why benefits are critical to the recruitment and retention of healthcare staff;

➤ describe a variety of benefits that may be offered with employment and relate the management implications of offering each;

➤ relate the knowledge of employee benefits to selected human resources management issues and systems development; and

➤ make suggestions for the design and communication of benefit plans.

Doris Cannon is a nurse employed by Metropolitan Hospital, a county hospital in the Pacific Northwest. She recently graduated from college, and this is her first job with benefits. She has rent and student loans to pay, so she is developing a budget and needs to watch her expenses. While she was in college, she was covered by her parents' healthcare insurance, so she never really worried about paying for healthcare. She is still covered on her parents' plan and knows she can stay on that plan until the end of the month in which she turns 26. Doris wonders if there is a more affordable option offered. She has only 30 days to enroll in one of her employer's plan offerings and thus needs to make a decision soon. How can she decide what the best option is for her from a cost standpoint? How can she find out more about the provisions of each of these plans? Aside from the cost of premiums, what are some of the other factors that she should consider as she makes her decision?

INTRODUCTION

Benefits are a competitive lever in recruiting, hiring, and retaining employees. Employment benefits provide additional compensatory value to individuals and their families by providing time off, insurance against uncertain events, and additional targeted services. The success of any healthcare organization requires a concerted investment in human capital for many reasons. Demand for experienced healthcare providers has never been greater, while competition for clinical staff, including physicians, has intensified. Nonclinical staff members are in great demand as well. The labor shortage is compounded by the fact that there are more applicants to most medical, nursing, and allied health schools than spots available. Replacement and turnover costs far exceed the cost of investing wisely in human capital.

In most healthcare organizations, labor costs are the single largest line item in the operating budget. An increase in labor cost is often related to the cost of employer-sponsored benefits as many benefits are based on a percentage of employees' salaries. Thus, the cost of benefits can be a significant line item in any operating budget

As discussed in chapter 8, *total compensation* encompasses all aspects of direct and indirect rewards given to employees. The employee's base salary is the key aspect of the direct rewards, but indirect rewards can carry significant additional value in the form of the benefits package. An employer may help articulate this fact in several ways, including the following:

◆ Including a section on pay stubs that notes the employer-paid portion of health insurance

◆ Providing benefits calculation tools on the company website or intranet

◆ Producing customized benefits statements during the annual open enrollment process

◆ Using social media to communicate benefits through a patient portal or interactive applications

◆ Incorporating total compensation in offer letters and negotiations

Whereas chapter 8 addressed the broader topic of designing compensation systems and included much discussion related to the direct rewards, such as determining the monetary value of jobs and payment methods, this chapter focuses on the indirect rewards in its detailed discussion of benefits.

A 2021 survey of healthcare CEOs by the American College of Healthcare Executives (ACHE 2022) found that personnel shortages were the top issue confronting hospitals. Financial challenges, patient safety and quality, access to care, and patient satisfaction were also in the top ten (ACHE 2022). Significant workforce shortages are exacerbated by the aging workforce, clinicians leaving their professions or patient-facing roles as a result of burnout, and the rate of growth in healthcare jobs. As discussed earlier in chapter 5, offering a comprehensive benefits structure is an increasingly important recruitment and retention tool. (The accompanying Critical Concept sidebar "Employers of Choice Offer Competitive Benefits" in this chapter also emphasizes this point.) The use of the internet and social media makes researching potential employers virtually effortless. Candidates and employees can access detailed information about employers online and are often well versed in companies' available benefits, even before receiving an offer.

The US Bureau of Labor Statistics (BLS 2022a) estimated that the cost of employee benefits accounts for approximately 31.0 percent of total compensation for civilian workers and 38.3 percent for state and local government employees.

Because of the importance of benefits to the entire employee compensation package, many tasks involved in the design, communication, and monitoring of benefit plans are the responsibility of human resources (HR) personnel. Knowledge of the organization, the market, and the needs of the workforce is crucial in deciding what benefits to offer. Beyond benefits that are mandated, what other benefits should be offered? To what extent should benefits be offered to particular classifications of employees? To what extent should trends in the economy and the industry at large affect changes to company benefits offerings?

This chapter presents an overview of the most common employee benefits, describes a variety of benefits that may be offered and their tax implications, explains the role of government in benefits management, and discusses key issues in the design and management of benefit plans.

CRITICAL CONCEPT
Employers of Choice Offer Competitive Benefits

The pressure to offer a competitive benefits package is significant in healthcare. This importance is illustrated in part by the weight that is placed on compensation and benefits packages by organizations that are recognized as "employers of choice." Benefits are an important factor in an applicant's decision of whether to accept employment. In addition, offering a comprehensive benefits package is considered an empirical domain of evidence for designation by the American Nurses Credentialing Center (ANCC) as a Magnet healthcare system, one of the most prestigious distinctions healthcare organizations can receive for nursing excellence (ANCC 2019).

BRIEF HISTORICAL BACKGROUND

Retirement benefit programs in the United States can be traced back to the Plymouth Colony settlers' military retirement program of 1636, according to the Employee Benefit Research Institute (EBRI 2013). Beyond retirement plans, health coverage benefit programs across industries are a development of the late nineteenth and early twentieth centuries. In the late 1800s, industries began to employ physicians because of the increasing potential for worker injury in a country that was undergoing industrialization. The railroad, mining, and lumber industries offered extensive medical services, which were necessary because workers were helping expand into areas in the West where care was not available. Companies retained a doctor and made mandatory deductions from workers' salaries to cover the cost of the medical services or the salary of the physician (Starr 1982). The rise in industrialization also led to the creation of disability insurance in the late 1800s. Although coverage was not tied to employment at that time, individuals could purchase coverage that served as assurance that they would still have income in the event of a disability.

Coverage of workers in the railroad, mining, and lumber industries was the stimulus for Justin Ford Kimball to create Baylor University's hospital prepayment plan in 1929; this plan was the precursor to Blue Cross. The initial arrangement was simple and direct between the university hospital and teachers in the Dallas area (Cunningham and Cunningham 1997). This prepayment plan (which allowed up to 21 days of care in the hospital for 50 cents per month) was different from any type of conventional insurance. Prepayments were made directly to the hospital that was providing the care, with no third-party involvement.

SOCIAL SECURITY ACT

The Great Depression, which began in 1929, shed light on the financial problems of the aged, ill, and disabled populations. These concerns led to the passage of the Social Security Act in 1935 and the federal government's involvement in providing retirement income protection. By mandating salary withholding starting in 1935 as a contribution to the trust fund for Social Security, a precedent was set, and other benefits coverage began to expand. Social Security provided some retirement benefits and included coverage of categorical programs but not medical coverage for people who were older or poor. Amendments to the Social Security Act in 1956 and 1964 added income protection for people with disabilities, along with health insurance under Medicare for Americans aged 65 or older and people with disabilities and under Medicaid for low-income people (EBRI 2013; Medicaid.gov 2022).

EMPLOYER-SPONSORED BENEFITS

The wage freeze during World War II (1939–1945) allowed companies to offer benefits in lieu of wage increases. Employers benefited from the federal exemption from tax liability of defined benefits. Subsequent legislation that permitted tax-preferential treatments incentivized employers to offer more private, voluntary benefits. Over time, providing benefits became less affordable.

Federal and state governments regulate and carefully monitor the tax treatment and administration of benefits. Since the 1950s, much legislation has established guidelines to protect individuals and employers in administering employment-related benefits; the legislation also monitors public and private benefit plans. Exhibit 9.1 lists federal legislation that affects benefits administration. Employers are responsible for ensuring that they are in compliance with all the rules and regulations that govern their employees' benefits. The following section illustrates the regulatory compliance expected of employers, using four examples of the most far-reaching legislation, including the Patient Protection and Affordable Care Act of 2010, more commonly known simply as the Affordable Care Act (ACA).

EXHIBIT 9.1
Legislation and Regulations That Affect Employee Benefits Administration

Legislation or Regulation	Major Accomplishment	Legal Citation	Web Address
Patient Protection and Affordable Care Act of 2010	Provides access to quality healthcare coverage for all Americans; also establishes minimum standards of coverage required by employer-based plans, mandated benefits, removal of lifetime coverage limits and limits on coverage of preexisting conditions, access to preventive care with no out-of-pocket expenses, and a healthcare marketplace for individual purchasing of healthcare insurance	Public Law 111-148	www.congress.gov/111/plaws/publ148/PLAW-111publ148.pdf
Supreme Court Case *Obergefell v. Hodges*	Requires all 50 states and the District of Columbia to perform and recognize same-sex marriages on the same terms and conditions as the marriages of opposite-sex couples	576 US644 (2015)	www.supremecourt.gov/opinions/14pdf/14-556_3204.pdf
Respect for Marriage Act	Requires the US federal government and all US states and territories to recognize the validity of same-sex and interracial civil marriages in the United States	Public Law No: 117-228 (12/13/2022)	www.congress.gov/bill/117th-congress/house-bill/8404

Legislation or Regulation	Major Accomplishment	Legal Citation	Web Address
Tax Cuts and Jobs Act of 2017	Eliminated the tax penalty for not having insurance coverage or exemption, as required under the individual mandate of the ACA	Public Law 115-97	www.congress .gov/bill/115th -congress/ house-bill/1/text
Economic Growth and Tax Relief Reconciliation Act (EGTRRA) of 2001	Provides greater flexibility and increased contributions and deductibility limits for various defined contribution plans; also expanded portability rules for retirement plans	Public Law 107-16	www.congress .gov/107/plaws /publ16/PLAW -107publ16.htm
Government Accounting Standards Board (GASB) Statements No. 43 and No. 45	Require government employers to book the accrued cost of future retiree benefits as a current liability; similar to FASB 106 provisions for publicly traded companies; began in 2007 on a phased-in basis	N/A	www.gasb.org /project_pages /opeb_summary .pdf
Health Insurance Portability and Accountability Act (HIPAA) of 1996	Provides for the elimination of waiting periods when participants move between group health plans; provides regulations for privacy and security of health-related information within a company that has access to such information and regulations for how an employer may use, store, and transmit such protected information	Public Law 104-191	www.aspe.hhs .gov/admnsimp /pl104191.htm
Newborns' and Mothers' Health Protection Act (NMHPA) of 1996	Requires that group health plans that offer maternity coverage pay for at least a 48-hour hospital stay following childbirth (96-hour stay in the case of Cesarean section)	S. Rept. 104-326	www.congress .gov/congressional -report/104th -congress/senate -report/326/1

EXHIBIT 9.1
Legislation and Regulations That Affect Employee Benefits Administration
(continued)

(continued)

EXHIBIT 9.1
Legislation and
Regulations
That Affect
Employee Benefits
Administration
(continued)

Legislation or Regulation	Major Accomplishment	Legal Citation	Web Address
Mental Health Parity Act (MHPA) of 1996	Provides that large group health plans cannot impose annual or lifetime dollar limits on mental health benefits that are less favorable than any such limits imposed on medical/surgical benefits	Public Law 104–204	www.govinfo.gov /content/pkg /PLAW -104publ204 /html/PLAW -104publ204.htm
Women's Health and Cancer Rights Act (WHCRA) of 1998	Provides protections to patients with group or individual health plans who choose to have breast reconstruction in connection with a mastectomy	Public Law 105-277	www.govinfo.gov /content/pkg /PLAW -105publ277 /html/PLAW -105publ277.htm
Employee Retirement Income Security Act of 1974 (ERISA)	Establishes minimum standards by which many pension and health plans in private industry are governed; requires plans to provide participants with plan information about plan features and funding; provides fiduciary responsibilities for plan managers; requires plans to establish grievance and appeal processes; gives participants the right to sue for benefits and breaches of fiduciary duty	Public Law 93-406	www.govinfo.gov /content/pkg /STATUTE-88/pdf /STATUTE-88 -Pg829.pdf
Medicare Prescription Drug Improvement and Modernization Act (MMA) of 2003	Introduced Medicare Part D, prescription drug coverage, and Medicare Advantage products; allows greater choice of coverage as private insurance companies can provide coverage through preferred provider organizations (PPOs), fee-for-service, medical savings accounts, and other special-needs plans directly to the Medicare population	Public Law 108-173	www.congress .gov/bill/108th -congress/house -bill/1

Legislation or Regulation	Major Accomplishment	Legal Citation	Web Address
Pension Protection Act (PPA) of 2006	Provides additional protection against employers that underfund defined benefit retirement plans by giving additional premiums, closing loopholes, raising caps on minimum employer contributions, and requiring measurement of funding levels; also provides additional enhancements in the defined contribution plans; allows for easier implementation of automatic enrollment in deferred savings plans, ensuring that participants have greater access to their financial investments and to professional advice	Public Law 109-280	www.govinfo.gov /content/pkg /PLAW-109publ 280/pdf/PLAW -109publ280.pdf
Consolidated Omnibus Budget Reconciliation Act (COBRA) of 1985	Provides qualifying employees and their families the right to continue to participate in employer-sponsored health coverage for a limited time after certain qualifying changes in family status, such as the loss of a job	Public Law 99-272	www.ssa.gov /policy/docs/ssb /v49n8/v49n8p22 .pdf
Uniformed Services Employment and Reemployment Rights Act (USERRA) of 1994	Provides continuous employment and benefits for soldiers who are deployed while employed	38 USC § 4301	www.osc.gov /Services/Pages /USERRA.aspx

EXHIBIT 9.1
Legislation and Regulations That Affect Employee Benefits Administration *(continued)*

MAJOR FEDERAL LEGISLATION

Four major federal laws that affect benefit coverage and administration are the Employee Retirement Income Security Act of 1974 (ERISA), the Consolidated Omnibus Budget Reconciliation Act of 1985 (COBRA), the Health Insurance Portability and Accountability Act of 1996 (HIPAA), and the Affordable Care Act (ACA). Each of these acts has specific implications for benefits management. Communicating the worth of benefits is essential in making benefits play a part in recruitment and retention.

ERISA

ERISA is a federal law administered by the US Department of Labor to establish minimum standards by which many pension and health plans in private industry are governed. Most nongovernmental companies in the United States are covered by ERISA, but state and federal agencies are not. The types of protection mandated by ERISA are primarily administrative in nature. For example, employers must maintain plan documents in accordance with applicable federal laws and ensure that definitions for plan eligibility are not discriminatory. ERISA also includes expectations for the fiduciary aspects of administration, requiring plan administrators to appropriately manage the assets of the plan, develop a process for plan participants to obtain benefits or benefits information, and inform participants of the right to sue for the company's breach of fiduciary responsibility. The organization must also file annual tax returns after an external audit of the plan has been conducted.

COBRA

Over the years, ERISA has been amended so that health plans include greater protections for employees. For example, COBRA provides qualifying employees and their families the right to continue to participate in employer-sponsored health coverage for a limited time after certain qualifying changes in family status, such as the loss of a job. Often, directly buying individual medical insurance is much more expensive for an employee, but COBRA helps employees and their families by guaranteeing them continued access to the employer's healthcare plan at the current group rate. The employee pays the full healthcare premium, which is often less expensive than buying an individual policy.

COBRA covers any employer-sponsored group health plan that had 20 or more employees on more than 50 percent of typical business days in the previous calendar year (US Department of Labor 2022a). In addition, COBRA requires companies to provide timely notification to all covered beneficiaries in the event that a qualified family status change would make those individuals eligible for COBRA. Hefty penalties can be assessed for failure to adhere to these timely notification guidelines.

HIPAA

HIPAA was enacted in 1996 to protect employees and their families who have preexisting medical conditions or who could suffer health coverage discrimination because of health-related factors (US Department of Labor 2022d). For example, under HIPAA, an individual who changes employers may have no waiting period for coverage of preexisting illness if the break in coverage from the prior employer is fewer than 63 days. In addition, the confidentiality of protected health information (PHI) is specifically outlined in HIPAA. The ACA further expanded patient protections that began with HIPAA.

HIPAA is intended to balance access to claims information or other medical information with the need for an employer to make revenue-driven decisions. When employers access claims information to make decisions about offering coverage, they must respect individual privacy requirements. For example, employers cannot make coverage decisions that would have an adverse impact on individuals, such as eliminating coverage for a specific diagnosis because a number of employees have that diagnosis.

In many healthcare organizations, enforcing HIPAA is the responsibility of a compliance officer. Computerized health records are also protected by HIPAA, as is the disclosure of medical information by staff. The provisions of HIPAA were expanded with inclusion in the Newborns' and Mothers' Health Protection Act, the Mental Health Parity Act, and the Women's Health and Cancer Rights Act. Audits of compliance can be conducted, and failure to follow the provisions of ERISA, COBRA, or HIPAA can subject the employer to serious financial penalties.

ACA

The ACA was passed and signed into law by President Barack Obama on March 23, 2010. This landmark legislation was gradually phased in, though there were delays in the implementation of many provisions. The intent of the ACA was to expand health coverage to millions of uninsured Americans, expand the Medicaid program to cover all adults with income below 138 percent of the federal poverty line, lower healthcare costs, and reduce inefficiencies in the healthcare system. The ACA also mandated that employers could not discriminate against employees by denying coverage because of preexisting conditions.

The ACA affects the administration of employer-sponsored plans through coverage mandates, minimum essential coverage, and removal of coverage limits for preexisting conditions and waiting periods for employer plans. The act also mandates coverage of adult children up to age 26 regardless of their student, marital, or residency status. Employers with more than 50 employees must be in compliance with these regulations in their plans if the plan is not a "grandfathered" plan. The ACA also established public and private healthcare exchanges for the purchase of health insurance. The public exchanges are operated by each state, or the states can defer to the federally run exchange in lieu of running their own exchange. Private exchanges are commonly operated by large consulting firms to provide controlled access to exchanges by employer-sponsored plans. Employer-sponsored plans must also provide access to healthcare benefits to all full-time employees. Individuals without access to an employer-sponsored plan may qualify for a subsidy for purchase of individual health insurance. The US Internal Revenue Service (IRS) has defined *full-time employees* as those working more than 30 hours a week (IRS 2022c). This regulation has become an employment concern for many employers that have high utilization of a part-time workforce, such as schools, tourism, and retail.

Since its passage, the ACA has faced a number of legal challenges—culminating in the US Supreme Court's dismissal in 2021 of a challenge mounted by the former Trump administration and Republican leaders of several states—and many failed attempts to overturn the act, yet it remains largely intact and continues to provide affordable healthcare coverage to millions of Americans. In coming years, Congress may even build on the ACA to cover more people and provide permanent financial relief to families.

MANDATORY BENEFITS

The following sections describe the employee benefits that are mandated by law and those that are voluntary. The tax implications of each benefit are also discussed.

SOCIAL SECURITY AND MEDICARE PART A

The Federal Insurance Contributions Act (FICA) authorizes a payroll tax that funds Social Security, disability, and Medicare Part A. FICA requires Social Security payroll taxes to be collected from the employee and matched by the employer. In 2022, the FICA employee contribution was 6.2 percent of wages, up to a taxable wage base of $147,700 (IRS 2022g). For 2023, the FICA employee contribution was set at 6.2 percent, up to a taxable wage base of $160,200 (Social Security Administration 2022). The Medicare rate for 2022 and 2023 was 1.45 percent of wages, with no wage limit (IRS 2022g; Social Security Administration 2022). Employers must match each of these amounts and send the total withheld and matched amounts to the federal government. After the taxable wage total is made, only the Medicare Part A deduction with the employer match is sent. The taxable wage base is determined annually by the IRS and is subject to change.

UNEMPLOYMENT COMPENSATION

Unemployment compensation, also called unemployment insurance, is mandatory for employers and varies by state. The intention of unemployment compensation is to protect employees who have lost their jobs under certain circumstances, such as being laid off. Voluntary separation and termination for cause that is well documented are typically not covered.

The premium amount for unemployment insurance is calculated based on the types of positions in the organization and the experience of the company with reductions in force. For example, an organization with a high proportion of professional staff, such as a hospital, would likely pay more than one with a lower-paid workforce, such as a sales force, because the amount of salary to supplement for a professional is likely to be higher in the event of a layoff.

WORKERS' COMPENSATION

Workers' compensation legislation was passed to protect employers from possible litigation for workplace injuries and to provide wages and benefits, including medical expenses, to employees who are injured on the job. Federal employees are covered by four disability programs administered by the Office of Workers' Compensation Programs (US Department of Labor 2022e). Each state has its own rules governing its workers' compensation program. Most states mandate that employers have insurance coverage, although some states provide their own workers' compensation funds to which employers can contribute. Many organizations choose to self-insure workers' compensation to save costs, and this strategy can be successful if managed well. In a healthcare setting, workers' compensation claims may result from injuries incurred from events such as lifting patients, being stuck by needles, and being exposed to disease. Increased emphasis on employee safety and improved training specific to common workplace hazards has helped healthcare organizations reduce workers' compensation expenses.

Events outside employers' control, such as the COVID-19 pandemic, can negate efforts to reduce workers' compensation expenses. The National Council on Compensation Insurance (NCCI) estimates that COVID-19 claims have the potential to result in workers' compensation claims exceeding $500 million over the duration of the pandemic. About 70 percent of claims filed represented the healthcare sector (Rosin, Mayen, and Fernes 2021). However, NCCI estimates for pandemic-related workers' compensation claims are based on their activities in 36 states and the District of Columbia. A nationwide estimate (i.e., adding claims from the remaining states of California, Delaware, Massachusetts, Michigan, Minnesota, New Jersey, New York, North Dakota, Ohio, Pennsylvania, Washington, Wisconsin, and Wyoming) may easily exceed $1 billion.

VOLUNTARY BENEFITS

Most benefits that employers provide are offered voluntarily—that is, they are not mandated by law—and as such can differ from one employer to another. Administration of some

---

⊛ CASE EXAMPLE

A registered nurse may choose to seek employment at another medical center for a modest gain in hourly rate without realizing that the benefits offered by the new employer are not as robust as those given by the current employer. In this example, the healthcare organization will have to recruit and orient a new registered nurse, when in fact the resignation might have been prevented if the individual had fully understood the value of the employer's benefits package.

vacation leave
The number of days an individual employee is eligible to take for vacation with pay, based on the individual's years of service and employee category.

sick leave
A policy that allows employees to get paid during time off as a result of illness, injury, or medical appointments.

personal leave
A policy that allows employees to get paid time off without having to specify the reason.

voluntary benefits may need to follow established rules and guidelines or reporting requirements; if so, the employer is responsible for ensuring compliance. Some voluntary benefits are entirely taxable, some are tax-exempt, and others are tax-deferred. The following sections discuss the most common voluntary benefits offered by employers. (See also the accompanying Case Example sidebar underscoring the importance of a competitive benefits package as part of a retention strategy.)

LEAVE BENEFITS

Vacation leave is fully taxable when taken. Employers establish vacation eligibility according to employee category—salaried or hourly. Length of service usually determines the number of vacation days with pay that can be accrued and carried over from year to year. Employers must account for accrued vacation liability, meaning that an employer has to be sure it can cover the cost of every employee's vacation time earned.

Sick leave allows employees to get paid during time off as a result of illness, injury, or medical appointments. As with vacation leave, employers establish sick and illness leave policies according to category of employee.

Personal leave—paid time off that an employee may take without having to specify the reason—is a form of employee benefit offered by some employers in addition to vacation leave and sick leave. It is typically used for doctor's appointments, child illness, jury duty, or mental health days.

Paid time off (PTO) is an increasingly common offering, especially in healthcare organizations, that combines vacation leave, sick leave, personal leave, and sometimes holidays, into one total bank of available paid time away from work. This system allows employees to determine how they would like to use their time and may be more attractive for healthy employees because they are in effect offered more vacation time.

Family and medical leave is covered by the Family and Medical Leave Act (FMLA), which applies to employers with more than 50 employees. Under the FMLA, employers must offer up to 12 weeks of unpaid leave per year for maternity or other medical needs to eligible employees (US Department of Labor 2022b, 2022c). Employees can take advantage of this benefit if they have worked at least one year and have put in 1,250 hours of service in the 12 months before the requested leave (US Department of Labor 2022c). Individual employers may choose to pay for this leave, but that is left to their discretion.

Reasons given for an FMLA leave include the birth or adoption of a child, taking care of a family member with a serious illness, or an employee's own illness or injury. Family and medical leave can be taken on an intermittent basis. It is important for employers to track employees' unpaid leave because the 12-month period in which it can be taken can be based on either a *fixed-year basis* (e.g., calendar or fiscal year) or *rolling basis* (e.g., 12 months since the first day of leave). The employer covered by the FMLA must stipulate the basis or standards for the benefit. For example, the employer may request a medical certificate if the employee requests the leave for a medical purpose.

HEALTH INSURANCE

Employer-sponsored health insurance is one of the most expensive items in an employer's budget because of the escalating costs of healthcare. Although health insurance remains a voluntary benefit, employers, particularly larger organizations, are mandated to offer this benefit or pay a penalty under the ACA. Employers that provide health insurance can deduct their expenditures from pretax earnings. Employees usually are offered a choice of private health insurance plans, including traditional and managed care options; the offer also extends to employees' dependents, such as their spouses and children (see also the Critical Concept sidebar "Health Benefits for Healthcare Workers"). Exhibit 9.2 summarizes various types of health insurance plans.

Benefits designed to provide protections and services related to dental care, vision care, disability, and life insurance are typically categorized under "other health and welfare benefits," which are discussed in the next section.

Some employers opt to self-insure, negotiating with a private health insurance company to administer benefits to employers through an administrative services contract. Self-insured employers may extend coverage to dependents. The federal legalization of same-sex marriages in 2015 mandated employers to cover same-sex spouses and legal dependents (IRS 2022e).

paid time off (PTO)
The number of paid days or hours off work for which an individual employee is eligible; it does not distinguish absences between vacation leave, sick leave, and personal leave.

family and medical leave
Unpaid time off for maternity, for employee extended illness or injury, or for the employee to care for a family member with serious illness.

> ⚠ **CRITICAL CONCEPT**
> Health Benefits for Healthcare Workers
>
> Health benefits coverage presents a unique challenge for healthcare organizations. Healthcare workers tend to use more health services than employees in other industries because of their medical knowledge and their proximity to services, and the cost of providing them care is affected by the contracts that third parties, such as managed care companies and insurance companies, have negotiated to pay providers and facilities.

Type	What Is Covered?	Advantages	Disadvantages
Full service	First-dollar coverage provided on all medical and hospital services up to a predetermined maximum	Members receive coverage for extensive medical and preventive care, both inpatient and outpatient	Expensive for employer because of high claims costs

Complexity involved as the plans may pay physician claims and hospital claims differently |
| Comprehensive | Cost sharing of medical expenses at a predetermined percentage of claims (coinsurance), after an up-front deductible, up to a predetermined out-of-pocket maximum above which the plan pays 100 percent of claims | Introduced cost sharing with the member and other cost-control features, such as second surgical opinion, preadmission review, and full coverage for diagnostic tests | All cost-control incentives are written on the front of the claim

Provides no incentive to reduce overutilization and use of high-cost providers |
| Preferred provider organization (PPO) | Claims incurred at providers that participate in the insurance carriers' PPO network are paid at a higher level than claims incurred at nonparticipating providers | Claims costs are reduced because of negotiated discounts with the insurance carriers when members use a participating provider | Potentially substantial cost differential if care is sought at a nonparticipating medical provider

Members must first determine whether their provider is participating in the network |

Type	What Is Covered?	Advantages	Disadvantages
Health maintenance organization (HMO)	Only claims incurred at providers that participate in the insurance carriers' HMO network are covered; all specialty care is directed through the member's gatekeeper or primary care physician, with referrals to the appropriate provider	Primary care physicians are paid by the insurance company to be gatekeepers; this keeps costs down as gatekeepers can manage the care received from a specialist and ensures that the specialists are part of the participating network	More limited network size, making it more difficult for members to find participating physicians All care must be directed through the gatekeeper, creating additional visits or time necessary to provide access to specialists
High-deductible health plan (HDHP)	Medical care for the member is not paid until a high deductible is met, typically greater than $2,000; after this deductible is met, claims are paid at a predetermined cost-sharing percentage; usually provided as part of a consumer-driven health plan and supplemented with health reimbursement accounts or health savings accounts	Members are encouraged to understand the costs of medical care as they must meet a high deductible before the employer plan will pay for claims Usually, preventive care is excluded from the deductible, thus encouraging wellness	Members must pay high-deductible amount out of their own pocket before coverage can begin; members may not have budgeted for these amounts Providers must get billed amounts from patients instead of insurers Greater risk for nonpayment

EXHIBIT 9.2
Types of Health Insurance Plans *(continued)*

Self-insured healthcare is attractive for many healthcare organizations because it typically allows greater flexibility in plan design. For example, the plan can be designed to encourage staff to use the employer's providers and facilities by providing financial incentives such as lower copayments and lower out-of-pocket expenses. Such a design can positively affect the cost of administering the health plan because the revenue generated may pay for the cost of paying claims. Self-insured organizations are not obligated to offer state-mandated health benefits. Large employers are more likely to self-insure if the organization can predict insurance costs from their employees' prior experience and have the funding to self-insure and handle fluctuations in expenses.

OTHER HEALTH AND WELFARE BENEFITS

Employers who want to attract top-quality people in a competitive marketplace may choose to offer a variety of additional health and welfare benefits. As described in the sections that follow, these benefits may include some combination of mental health coverage, wellness and fitness programs, dental and vision coverage, prescription drug benefits, flexible spending accounts, long-term and short-term disability insurance, long-term care insurance, life insurance, and other voluntary benefits. Exhibit 9.3 summarizes selected types of these additional health and welfare benefits.

Mental Health Coverage

Under the Mental Health Parity Act, mental illness is considered a medical condition. Thus, employers are required to provide the same level of coverage for mental illness as they would for a physical condition (Centers for Medicare & Medicaid Services [CMS] 2022). The COVID-19 pandemic affected employer voluntary medical benefits such as telehealth and mental health services, leading many employers to cover them in the same way as other physical conditions. Mental health benefits seem especially relevant to healthcare workers. Surveys from McKinsey's Center for Societal Benefit Through Healthcare found that about 70 percent of employers surveyed in late 2020 planned to invest in mental health resources by starting, continuing, or expanding benefits in 2021 (Coe et al. 2021). To contain costs for mental health, an employer can elect to carve out mental health and use a special behavioral health company to focus on mental health needs (see the Critical Concept sidebar "Employee Assistance Programs"). Because behavioral health companies are niche providers, they can provide economies of scale that may not be possible with a larger health insurer.

Benefit	What Does It Do?	Who Pays?	Who Determines the Amount?	Types of Plans	
Mental health	Covers programs relating to the diagnosis and treatment of mental health and substance abuse	Generally included in employer-provided health insurance	Employer may choose to offer multiple plans and must be treated with equivalence to medical/surgical benefits with respect to annual and lifetime limits: may include financial requirements and treatment limitations	Same as health plan	**EXHIBIT 9.3** Selected Types of Other Health and Welfare Benefits
Wellness and fitness	Covers programs and activities designed to promote safety and good health among employees	Generally funded by employer; however, employee must participate or engage in activities to earn rewards	Employer determines program rewards or disincentives	Physical fitness programs; smoking cessation; health risk appraisals; biometric screenings; weight loss programs; stress reduction programs	
Dental	Covers a percentage of dental care up to an annual maximum	Employer and employee; generally a greater percentage of the cost is borne by the employee	Employer may choose to offer multiple plans from which employees may choose, or the employer provides a single plan	Dental indemnity; dental PPO*; dental HMO[†]; direct dental	

(continued)

			Who Deter-mines the	
Benefit	**What Does It Do?**	**Who Pays?**	**Amount?**	**Types of Plans**
Vision	Covers a pre-determined amount of expenses for exams, frames, lenses, and con-tacts, among others, during a specified period (annually or biannually)	May be included in health insurance or provided as a voluntary supplemental coverage	Employer may choose to offer multiple plans from which employ-ees may choose, or the employer pro-vides a single plan	Vision PPO; Vision HMO
Prescription drug coverage	Covers some amount of the cost of prescription medications	May be included in health insur-ance or as a separate rider to the health insurance policy	Employer may choose to offer multiple plans from which employ-ees may choose, or the employer pro-vides a single plan	Two-tier coverage; three-tier coverage; four-tier cov-erage; cover-age after deductible
Flexible spending account (FSA)	Allows employ-ees to deduct a fixed, pretax amount from their paycheck over the plan year either for out-of-pocket medical expenses or for dependent care for a child aged 14 or younger or an adult because of age or mental disability	Employee elects the specific pay-roll amount; employer has the ability to provide a matching dol-lar amount	Employee estimates expenses in the respective category for the next plan year; must be elected each year, and any monies remaining after the plan year are forfeited to employer	Medical care; dependent care

EXHIBIT **9.3**
Selected Types of
Other Health and
Welfare Benefits
(continued)

Benefit	What Does It Do?	Who Pays?	Who Determines the Amount?	Types of Plans
Disability	Provides a level of income to the employee after a predetermined period out of work due to illness, injury, or disease	Employer provides a basic level of coverage; employees may choose to purchase supplemental coverage	Employer chooses the level of the basic coverage; employees may elect varying levels of supplemental coverage	Short-term disability; basic long-term disability; supplemental long-term disability
Long-term care insurance	Pays some or all long-term care costs, thereby preventing depletion of the policyholder's assets	Usually funded by employee, can be provided by employer	Employer may choose to offer multiple options within a set number of plans	Medicare; Medicaid; private long-term care insurance; group long-term care insurance; accelerated death benefits from life insurance
Life insurance	Provides a death benefit for the covered person, payable to a predesignated beneficiary	Employer provides a basic level of life insurance; employees may elect to purchase supplemental coverage on themselves, spouse, and/or children	Employer chooses the level of the basic coverage; employees may elect varying levels of supplemental coverage	Group term life; group universal life; group variable life; group variable universal life

EXHIBIT 9.3
Selected Types of Other Health and Welfare Benefits
(continued)

(continued)

Exhibit 9.3
Selected Types of
Other Health and
Welfare Benefits
(continued)

Benefit	What Does It Do?	Who Pays?	Who Determines the Amount?	Types of Plans
Health savings account (HSA)	Allows employees enrolled in a high-deductible health plan to accrue funds in a tax-advantaged medical savings account	Employee or employer can make contributions either through pretax payroll deduction or direct to the financial institution: claimed as a deduction to gross income on taxes	Amounts deposited within the plan year must not exceed IRS statutory limit	Health plan only
Health reimbursement account	Reimburses an employee through an employer-funded account for the employee's medical expenses	Must be funded by employer only	Employer provides funding for the account based on its own criteria—no plan requirements	Health plan only

*PPO: preferred provider organization
†HMO: health maintenance organization

Wellness and Fitness Programs

More and more workplace initiatives are focusing on wellness and fitness, especially in healthcare organizations. Multiple studies indicate the effectiveness of workplace wellness programs with engaged employees. Employer-sponsored wellness and fitness programs can contribute to a healthier and more productive workforce, though evidence to support their cost-effectiveness and their effects on healthcare spending and utilization is mixed (Jones, Molitor, and Reif 2019; Mattke et al. 2013; Song and Baicker 2019). Use of incentives to boost employee engagement appears to be an important factor (see the related Current Issue sidebar "Rewarding Healthful Behavior").

CRITICAL CONCEPT
Employee Assistance Programs

An employee assistance program (EAP) is effective in controlling mental health costs if such a program is used as a gatekeeper to access mental-health-related services. EAPs typically offer a finite number of counseling and therapy sessions with professionals in the field, and all proceedings are confidential. Some employers allow managers to mandate referral to the EAP to address concerns about an employee's mental health. Regardless of how employees access EAPs, use of the services in these programs is typically more cost-effective than use of a psychiatrist under a healthcare benefit.

CURRENT ISSUE
Rewarding Healthful Behavior

The healthcare industry has shown renewed interest in providing incentives to employees to improve their health and reduce risky behaviors. Many healthcare organizations and insurance companies ask employees to complete personal health assessments to determine current and future risks based on family medical history. Others provide special payments to staff for positive health and lifestyle factors such as the following:

- Having normal blood pressure
- Not smoking
- Maintaining a healthy body mass index

The future will bring increased focus on disease prevention and fitness for duty among healthcare workers. This emphasis is expected to stem the escalating costs of healthcare, encourage better management of chronic diseases, reduce injuries, and increase productivity. HIPAA stipulates that employers may offer these incentives to employees only if the incentive is based on participation and not on the results of the test or assessment.

Wellness programs may be easier to implement in healthcare than in other industries for several reasons:

1. Many healthcare organizations require preemployment health assessments based on the physical requirements of a position.

2. Healthcare organizations typically have numerous content experts and other resources on-site.

3. Healthcare workers are typically more sophisticated consumers of wellness and preventive programs than are workers in other fields.

Still, many healthcare employees do not take advantage of services such as free flu shots. The low percentage of healthcare workers who got a flu shot caused organizations such as The Joint Commission and the Centers for Disease Control and Prevention (CDC) to bring the matter to the forefront for healthcare administrators. The Joint Commission previously required hospitals and health systems to meet 90 percent influenza vaccination compliance and identify the reasons that healthcare staff do not get flu shots. Although that requirement has been relaxed, the Joint Commission will continue to review that organizations have a goal to improve influenza vaccination rates and have processes in place to increase participation (Joint Commission 2022). The CDC (2022a, 2022b) also requires hospitals and other types of healthcare facilities to report their rates of vaccination for healthcare workers, volunteers, and students. In response to these requirements, most healthcare organizations have mandated that employees be vaccinated or be required to wear masks when they have contact with patients. Organizations also are making an effort to ensure that influenza shots are offered more conveniently during all shift times.

Dental and Vision Coverage

Dental insurance is sometimes offered to employees and their dependents as an addition to health insurance, although many employees expect this coverage. The cost associated with dental care is rising at a rate similar to the cost of other healthcare. An option for a self-insured healthcare organization that is affiliated with a dental school is to contract directly with the school to provide dental care.

Vision coverage is typically an add-on to the health insurance benefit. Vision plans typically include basic coverage for an annual eye exam and contact lenses or glasses. A vision network frequently provides better coverage at a more affordable price.

Prescription Drug Benefits

Prescription drug benefits may be part of health insurance coverage. Medication coverage is costly to the organization and to the employee even with the use of a drug formulary (a list of approved medications). Costs will continue to rise with continued acceptance of bioengineered drugs and other new lifesaving treatments. The use of a pharmacy network can control costs if the formulary is carefully constructed to encourage employees to use less-costly prescriptions, such as generic drugs. The use of pharmacy benefit management companies has also helped reduce pharmaceutical costs. These companies perform the normal reviews of drug utilizations, manage the formulary, and negotiate the costs of drugs with pharmaceutical firms; thus, they can leverage the overall expense of providing the benefit.

Flexible Spending Accounts

Flexible spending accounts (FSAs) allow employees to set aside, via payroll deduction, a tax-deferred amount that can be used to offset qualified expenses for medical care or dependent care. An FSA is a "use-it-or-lose-it" benefit because it presents a risk to the program participant who does not accurately calculate the amount of unpaid medical or dependent care expenses that will be incurred in the year ahead. The guidelines for medical and dependent care accounts differ. Medical FSAs can be used for qualified medical, dental, and vision expenses. The IRS determines the maximum amount employees can contribute to their FSA each year. In 2022, limits allowed for a maximum contribution of $2,850 and a maximum carryover amount of $570 (Miller 2021).

The IRS has defined guidelines for what is considered a qualified expense (e.g., many cosmetic procedures are not qualified) and permits employers to decide whether to allow reimbursements for the cost of over-the-counter products. More and more employers are contracting with companies that provide an FSA debit card that can be used for qualified expenses. This method typically allows reimbursement of medical expenses, including over-the-counter products, without requiring cumbersome paperwork or determination of whether the expense qualifies.

Unlike medical FSAs, for which the maximum amount of deferred income is determined by the ACA, the maximum for dependent care FSAs is determined by the IRS (2021; see also Miller 2021). In 2021, IRS regulations allowed $10,500 per household (IRS 2022d). Unlike for a medical spending account, the employee can be reimbursed for expenses only up to the amount that has actually been tax-deferred via payroll deduction (see the Current Issue sidebar "Employer Limits to FSAs"). Medical and dependent care FSAs are popular with employers because a lower taxable wage base means less FICA tax paid by employer and employee. Further, an FSA's use-it-or-lose-it provision means that

flexible spending accounts (FSAs) Accounts that allow employees to set aside, via payroll deduction, a tax-deferred amount that can be used to offset qualified expenses for medical care or dependent care.

CURRENT ISSUE
Employer Limits to FSAs

Employers tend to be conservative with setting the maximum amount employees are allowed to defer to an FSA because an employee can submit expenses at any time in the plan year and the employer must reimburse the employee regardless of the amount that has been deferred already. For example, an employer could set $2,850 as the maximum annual medical FSA limit. A participating employee who elected to defer the maximum could present the employer in January with receipts that total $2,850 and then quit in February—long before the maximum has been deducted from the employee's paychecks. Because of this risk, employers should carefully consider their likely exposure when determining the maximum deferral allowed.

the employer can keep the funds that are deferred but are not processed for reimbursement. Employers can also charge administrative fees for allowing staff to use FSAs, thereby offsetting the costs of processing.

Long-Term Disability Insurance

long-term disability (LTD) insurance
A welfare benefit designed to provide employees with income if they become disabled and cannot work.

Long-term disability (LTD) insurance is considered a welfare benefit because it is designed to provide employees with income (typically a fixed percentage of predisability earnings) if they become disabled and cannot work. Because of the nature of their work, healthcare employees have a higher risk of disability than workers in many other industries; thus, providing this benefit may provide a competitive advantage for a healthcare organization. Physicians and nurses specifically ask about LTD coverage when comparing benefit packages between healthcare organizations. LTD insurance typically becomes active after an employee has been unable to work for 90 to 180 days or more; however, this feature of the plan can be decided by the employer (BLS 2022b).

One manner of providing LTD insurance is through a specialty-specific plan. This type of insurance is particularly popular among physicians because the definition of a *disability* is that the injured person can no longer perform the duties of the specialty that the person was practicing at the time of the injury. Thus, under this definition, a surgeon who can no longer see clearly enough to perform surgery is considered disabled and as such can collect disability pay to supplement other incomes—say, as a general practitioner. While popular with employees, specialty-specific plans are costly, and few insurers offer them as an option.

Short-Term Disability Insurance

Short-term disability insurance is an optional benefit for which the employee must pay—either for the entire cost or a significant portion of the premium. This insurance may be an employer-paid benefit, usually in conjunction with PTO benefits, with benefits determined according to employee tenure and salary level. With short-term disability insurance, an employee is covered from the time that the illness, condition, or disability starts to the time that the eligibility period for long-term disability has been satisfied. Preexisting conditions may be taken into consideration in the approval process to enroll in this type of insurance. Most plans provide 50 to 60 percent of salary to those who receive short-term disability.

> **short-term disability insurance**
> An optional benefit for which the employee must pay, in which an employee is covered from the time that an illness, a condition, or a disability starts to the time that the eligibility period for long-term disability has been satisfied.

Long-Term Care Insurance

Long-term care (LTC) insurance usually covers the cost of nursing homes, home health care, and assisted living. This insurance is an attractive benefit for older employees as they face decisions about how to care for their parents and plan for their own future. LTC insurance can include a daily allowance for care at a nursing or assisted living facility as well as in-home care. Some plans allow employees to buy inflation protection and extend coverage beyond their employment. However, because of the risks and losses, and the failed attempt to have LTC included in the ACA, the number of insurance companies that offer LTC plans has decreased significantly, and those that do offer coverage may limit it because of the relatively low profit margin for employer-sponsored programs compared to individual policies. The National Association of Insurance Commissioners (NAIC 2019) reports that less than one-half of 1 percent of all employers offer LTC insurance. The Congressional Research Service (CRS 2020) reports that in 2018, only 6.6 million individuals had an LTC insurance policy—less than 3 percent of the US population aged 18 or older. Along with lack of availability, the high cost of the premiums serves as a major deterrent for most people.

> **long-term care (LTC) insurance**
> Insurance to help cover the cost of nursing homes, home care, and assisted living for older adults.

Life Insurance

Life insurance is frequently a base benefit offered by employers in all industries. A number of types exist, as shown in exhibit 9.4.

Term group life insurance provided by the employer allows employers to leverage the size of their organization to purchase a more affordable plan. Although all staff who meet eligibility requirements are offered this group insurance, they are no longer covered after they leave the organization.

By contrast, an attractive feature of an *employee-sponsored life insurance* plan is its portability—an employee can purchase it at the group rate even after resigning from the organization. Such portability is offered through a *universal life insurance* program, which is more expensive for the employer because its benefits extend beyond employment.

Insurance Type	What Does It Do?
Term	Covers all benefited employees, provided as a flat amount or multiple of salary from the date of eligibility through the length of employment.
Supplemental term	Covers employees, their spouse, and/or their dependent children; purchased by the employee.
Permanent	Accrues a cash value over time and never expires.
Ordinary	Converts to permanent life insurance as the employee contributes to the policy over the span of employment.
Variable	Charges premiums that are level over time, but the benefits relate to the value of the assets behind the contract at the time the benefits are made payable.
Universal	Provides a term amount of coverage and an accumulating cash value with flexible premium amounts and timing schedules.
Variable universal	Provides a guaranteed death benefit with the flexibility of universal premium schedules and the additional investment value of the assets of a variable life insurance policy.
Corporate owned	Is permanent life insurance purchased for key executives but owned by the organization; at the time of the insured's death, the employer will take the value of what was paid in premiums and pay a death benefit to the executive's beneficiaries.
Split dollar	Consists of varying forms of permanent life insurance purchased for key executives or company owners; the two parties split the premium payments and/or the death benefit.
Paid up	Is paid in such a way that all or part of the life coverage is fully paid up when the employee retires; as the premium is paid, the amounts of group term coverage are decreased as the paid-up amount increases; this type is no longer commonly used.

Supplemental life insurance is an optional benefit that many companies allow employees to purchase on behalf of their spouse and children. The ability to buy supplemental insurance at a group rate can be an attractive benefit for some employees. However, portable policies are typically favored, because the employee can convert an employer-sponsored plan into an individual plan upon termination or resignation from the company.

Other Voluntary Benefits

Two other types of voluntary benefits are *health savings accounts (HSAs)* and *health reimbursement accounts.*

An HSA is available to taxpayers in the United States who are enrolled in a high-deductible health plan. It allows employees to accrue funds in a tax-advantaged medical savings account. The employee, the employer, or both can make contributions to this plan. Contributions can be either withheld through pretax payroll deduction or made directly to the financial institution and then claimed as a deduction to gross income on taxes. Amounts deposited within the plan year must not exceed the statutory limit set by the IRS (2022f). HSA funds may be used to pay not only medical expenses but also health insurance premiums, and funds may be rolled over into the next plan year; amounts in the account are portable when employees leave employment.

A health reimbursement account pays back an employee through an employer-funded account for the employee's medical expenses. The employer provides funding for the account based on its own criteria. Funds may be used to pay individual health insurance premiums, and funds may be rolled over into the next plan year; amounts may be portable when employees leave employment, but there are potential tax implications.

RETIREMENT PLANS

A retirement plan is often a cornerstone of a comprehensive benefits plan. The type of plan offered and the amount that the employer contributes can be valuable recruitment tools. Careful plan design can also create incentives that support retention strategies. Many organizations provide a base contribution to such plans and offer a vehicle for employees to save for their own retirement. The two main types of retirement plans are the *defined benefit plan* and the *defined contribution plan*. Exhibit 9.5 enumerates the differences between these two types and presents a hybrid of the two.

The IRS categorizes retirement plans as *qualified* or *nonqualified*. Savings plans that allow staff to contribute to their own retirement are called *tax-deferred plans*. Each of these five types of plans is explained in the sections that follow.

EXHIBIT 9.5
Categories of
Retirement Plans

Retirement Plan Category	What Is It?	Types	Advantages	Disadvantages
Defined benefit	Provides a retirement benefit payable to the employee on attainment of age and years of service, based on a percentage of salary during working years; usually payable monthly for the lifetime of retiree and/or spouse	Final average salary Career average salary Dollars times years of service	Benefits based on years on the job, encouraging long-term service Benefits based on salary, usually at the highest level	Not as portable as defined contribution plan Cannot borrow against the plan Assets not directly allocated to the participant until retirement Employer must fund account based on future amounts payable Payable to retiree in either a qualified joint and survivor annuity or a life annuity
Defined contribution	Employer provides a contribution to an account based on the employee's current salary/earnings, employee can draw on the account after retirement with reduced tax liability	Profit sharing (401k, 401a) Employee stock option plans Money purchase plans Tax-deferred savings	Employee generally allowed to direct the investments Assets are allocated to employee so the balance is available at any time At end of employment, assets are transferable to other accounts Can be paid out in lump sum or in installments over a period of time	Final balance in account is based on the performance of the market and the selected investments No guaranteed benefits

Retirement Plan Category	What Is It?	Types	Advantages	Disadvantages
Hybrid	Combines aspects of both defined benefit and defined contribution plans	Cash balance Floor offset Pension equity	Balance in account is available to employee	Complex and not easily understood Although the account "balance" is available, it may not be in real dollars but may be an actuarially estimated value

EXHIBIT 9.5
Categories of Retirement Plans *(continued)*

Defined Benefit Plans

A **defined benefit plan** is a group plan, not an individual account. The contribution amount that the employer must make to such a plan is determined based on the number of participants and their ages, salaries, and projected retirement dates. In theory, the funds contributed to a defined benefit plan should be sufficient to fund all retirees each year. Upon retirement, the actual monetary benefit that the employee receives is determined through a formula and is based on the individual's years of service and salary preceding retirement. Many state-sponsored retirement plans are defined benefit plans. Other benefits of employment may continue with the payment of a cash benefit.

Defined Contribution Plans

With a **defined contribution plan**, the employer contributes an amount to an employee's individual retirement account. The employer determines the rate of this contribution and decides how to calculate it. Contribution amounts can vary and may be based on such factors as salary, years of service, or a combination of age and years of service. Using age and years of service as a basis for contribution can help attract midcareer employees because the employer can contribute more to their accounts than to the plans of newer and younger staff for whom retirement may not be a current priority.

In addition, the employer can choose the vendor companies and may approve and restrict investment options for employees within these choices. Employees then determine which vendor to use and how to allocate investments (e.g., higher or lower risk levels). The amount an employee receives on retirement is dependent on the value that the employee initially established, managed, and grew over the years. The IRS

defined benefit plan
A type of retirement plan that provides a retirement benefit payable to the employee on attainment of age and years of service, based on a percentage of salary during working years; usually payable monthly for the lifetime of retiree and/or spouse.

defined contribution plan
A type of retirement plan in which the employer provides a contribution to an account based on the employee's current salary/earnings, and the employee can draw on the account after retirement with reduced tax liability.

determines the limits on the maximum allowable employer contributions, and these limits are adjusted annually.

Qualified Retirement Plan

A **qualified retirement plan** has strict eligibility and vesting requirements and strict taxable limits. For example, at least 70 percent of employees who are not highly compensated must be eligible to participate in a qualified plan. A *highly compensated* employee is defined by the IRS (2022a) as an owner of more than 5 percent of the interest in the company or who, in the preceding year, received more than $135,000 (in 2022; limit is set by the IRS annually) in compensation. Plans that are covered by ERISA must undergo periodic nondiscrimination testing to ensure that this requirement is met.

Qualified retirement plans receive more tax benefits than nonqualified plans do, and typically the employee and employer are not taxed until the time a distribution is made. Most qualified plans allow employees to withdraw monies for hardships such as loss of home or excessive medical bills, or to pay college education expenses for their children. The employee is taxed for a hardship withdrawal and is charged a penalty for early (before retirement age) withdrawal.

Nonqualified Retirement Plan

A **nonqualified retirement plan** is typically designed to meet the needs of key executives and is not subject to as many government regulations as a qualified plan is. This condition allows nonqualified plans to exceed some of the limits of qualified plans.

Because nonqualified plans do not come with as many restrictions as qualified plans, they are perceived as carrying a risk of forfeiture, as creditors may *attach* to the plan assets—that is, if money is owed, it can legally be deducted from a nonqualified plan if the creditor sues for collection.

Tax-Deferred Plans

A **tax-deferred plan** is a savings plan that allows staff to contribute to their own retirement. Deferred compensation results in reduced tax liability for the employer and the employee, which makes such a plan popular. Many organizations encourage employees to participate in tax-deferred plans by matching the contributions employees make to their retirement accounts. Some organizations also include contributions to such plans as a part of annual performance reviews, increasing the employer-matched amount based on performance.

Media coverage has touted the advantage of Roth 401(k), Roth 403(b), and other nonqualified salary deferral options. Employees and employers should research the potential

qualified retirement plan
A type of retirement plan with strict eligibility and vesting requirements and strict taxable limits, in which employees receive more tax benefits than from nonqualified plans; typically the employee and employer are not taxed until the time a distribution is made.

nonqualified retirement plan
A type of retirement plan typically designed to meet the needs of key executives; not subject to as many government regulations as a qualified plan is.

tax-deferred plan
A savings plan that allows staff to contribute to their own retirement.

effects of nonqualified plans before deciding to participate. The total amount that can be deferred is determined by the IRS and varies annually. Further, the IRS determines the maximum allowable contributions and maximum salary (i.e., $305,000 in 2022) to which not-for-profit companies can contribute (IRS 2022b). If an employer offers multiple options, it must consider the total of all contributions. Limits are set based on aggregation of all plans offered and the actual amount of contribution by plan.

OTHER VOLUNTARY BENEFITS

Other voluntary benefits may include programs that are offered through the employer that require participating employees to pay for the premiums or services. These programs can include benefits such as auto, home, or pet insurance; cancer or other specific disease coverage; supplemental hospitalization and disability payments; group legal services; and concierge services. Many healthcare organizations also offer staff uniform allowances, extensive educational and professional growth opportunities, and tuition reimbursement. Further, organizations should consider on-site child care, a benefit offer that can make a health system more competitive from a recruitment and retention standpoint. Assistance with adult day care is another optional benefit that may be attractive to employees caring for older adults.

Perquisites, commonly called *perks*, are benefits that may be offered to executives. Such perks may include car allowances, cell phones, club memberships, or equipment for a home office. Other executive-level benefits may include cash bonuses and awards, stock options, and severance packages for full or early contract termination. Many of these benefits are taxable, and organizations should review their tax implications carefully.

DESIGNING A BENEFITS PLAN

Many factors must be considered when designing a benefits structure that meets the needs of the organization, including demographics, cost considerations, the self-insurance option, managerial implications, and communication.

DEMOGRAPHICS

In the current US work environment, employees from multiple generations are working side by side more than ever before. With such a mixture of employees, employers must be aware of generational differences when designing a benefits package. For example, older employees may be more interested in retirement plans and life insurance, whereas younger employees may place greater value on paid time off, student loan repayment, and frequent bonuses. Organizations need to be aware of these differences and consider offering a range of options for all employees. An organization can learn about these preferences by analyzing market data and getting employee input through opinion surveys or focus groups.

The demographics of the employee population can be a key determinant in benefits package design. For example, there are age-related concerns that affect employees such as chronic illness and related screening and prevention services. Therefore, workforce demographics may affect the timing of regular cancer screenings that are built into designed plans. Economic trends may also affect benefit distributions. When economic downturns occur, some older employees may defer retirement.

COST CONSIDERATIONS

Benefits program designers should know the budget allocated for the benefits program so that they can plan accordingly or find possible funding sources. Employees are typically aware of and care about the insurance premiums they pay out of pocket and the annual increases of those payments. Many employers pass cost increases on to employees by raising the amount deducted from employees' paychecks for health insurance coverage. This cost-shifting can cause controversy if employees are paying more than the employer is or if salary raises do not absorb the cost of the benefit increases. Cost-containment strategies could include raising out-of-pocket expenses for those who do not use the healthcare organization's facilities and providers or increasing copayments and deductibles. Another effective cost-control strategy is to provide employees an incentive to waive coverage if they can show proof of coverage through their spouse or if they can arrange for retiree health coverage from a former employer.

Outsourcing benefits administration may be another cost-saving option. However, the employer may lose the ability to customize the benefits package for its employees and may encounter employee dissatisfaction if the customer service provided by the benefits administrator is less than ideal.

Another cost-control strategy is to use *cafeteria plans*, also called *section 125 plans* for the section of the Internal Revenue Code that authorizes the method (IRS 2022f). Cafeteria plans are popular with employers and employees. Employees can use pretax payroll deductions for certain qualifying costs such as insurance premiums, certain medical expenses not covered by the employer, and expenses associated with dependent care. Employees can also reduce their overall tax liability and thus increase their take-home pay. Cafeteria plans are also advantageous for employers because the employer match to FICA taxes is reduced, which can save them large amounts of money. In addition, some states reduce the employer's liability for workers' compensation.

 **KEY POINT**

A benefits program can help attract and retain employees in a competitive market, so it must be well designed and cost-effective.

SELF-INSURANCE OPTION

In designing a benefits program, employers may choose to self-insure certain benefits rather than fully insure with a third party. **Self-insurance** means that the employer takes the risk to appropriately budget, underwrite, and administer a customized benefit rather than contract for a standard plan. A self-insured plan typically allows the employer greater flexibility in plan design. Self-insured health and dental plans can be structured to incentivize employees to seek care for themselves and their families at the facilities of the healthcare organization.

If an organization chooses to self-insure, contracting with a third party for stop-loss insurance is a wise move. **Stop-loss insurance** mitigates the risk to the employer if there are large claims in a given plan year. For example, if the employer purchases $200,000 of stop-loss insurance, then that amount is the most that the employer will pay for a given claim; all costs beyond this stop-loss amount are absorbed by the insurance vendor.

self-insurance
An insurance design wherein the employer budgets, underwrites, and administers a customized benefit rather than contracts for a standard plan.

stop-loss insurance
A kind of insurance that mitigates the risk to the employer in the event that there are large claims in a given plan year.

MANAGERIAL IMPLICATIONS

Given the complexities, legalities, and fiduciary requirements associated with all the benefits described in this chapter, it is advisable to assign experienced and qualified benefits professionals to the task of designing or assisting in a benefits program. In particular, certified employee benefits specialists are extremely valuable to this process. Experienced benefits professionals are familiar with the requirements for accounting, audits, tax filing, and other implications of benefits administration. Further, it is helpful to have the benefits staff collaborate with the budget staff so that accurate projections of changes in plan designs or premiums can be reflected in the organizational budget.

COMMUNICATION

Communication is key to the administration of a successful benefits plan. Plan administrators should use every opportunity to keep employees abreast of benefits offered. For example, employers should provide employees with regular information and updates about their total compensation, including the value of employer-sponsored benefits and salaries. During open enrollment periods, employers should circulate detailed information because this is an opportune time to explain the benefits structure. Also, employers should always include a disclaimer that employer-sponsored benefits are subject to change so that staff understand the possibility that some benefits may be eliminated or reduced in the future, based on economic or other operational exigencies. See exhibit 9.6 for a list of resources related to employee benefits.

Exhibit 9.6
Resources for
Additional
Information on
Employee Benefits

Who?	Where?	What?
Benefits Link	www.benefitslink.com/index.html	Portal to news, analysis, opinions, and government documents about employee benefit plans
Centers for Medicare & Medicaid Services (CMS)	www.cms.gov	Access to research, guidance, statistics, resources, and tools related to Medicare, Medicaid, and Children's Health Insurance Program (CHIP) programs sponsored by the federal government
Employee Benefit News (EBN)	www.benefitnews.com	Media resource that provides comprehensive, high-quality news on the benefits industry
Federal Register	www.govinfo.gov/app/collection/FR	Official daily publication for federal rules, proposed rules, and notices as well as executive orders and other presidential documents
Internal Revenue Service (IRS)		
Forms and publications	www.irs.gov/forms-instructions	Quick access to all published forms and publications of the IRS
Frequently asked questions	www.irs.gov/faqs	General questions and answers regarding tax regulations
International Foundation of Employee Benefit Plans (IFEBP)	www.ifebp.org	Nonprofit organization that is an objective and independent source of employee benefits, compensation, and financial literacy education and information
Pension Benefit Guaranty Corporation (PBGC)	www.pbgc.gov	Federal corporation created by the Employee Retirement Income Security Act (ERISA) of 1974 that protects the pensions of private, single-employer, and multiemployer defined benefit pension plans of US workers
US Department of Labor Employee Benefits Security Administration (EBSA)	www.dol.gov/agencies/ebsa	Guidance and recent changes in labor laws and regulations as they pertain to employer-sponsored pensions, health plans, and other employee benefits

SUMMARY

In the competitive healthcare arena, employers are challenged to offer as comprehensive a benefits package as possible that will attract and retain healthcare workers at all stages of their careers. Employers are further challenged to provide these benefits cost-effectively with careful consideration to designing a structure that will meet the diverse needs of their employees. Attention must be paid to the complex federal guidelines that govern many benefits programs so that compliance standards and fiduciary responsibility are met.

FOR DISCUSSION

1. What role do benefits play in the concept of *total compensation*?

2. How did the Social Security Act change the way retirement benefits were viewed?

3. In designing a benefits plan, what are the most important considerations for an employer?

4. Employers are finding it more difficult to support health insurance coverage as a benefit, as it has become more costly than the tax savings for offering it. Is employer-based health insurance on its way out, and if so, is it more or less practical to maintain it as a benefit in a healthcare organization?

5. How has the Affordable Care Act (ACA) affected the healthcare benefits offered to Americans, as well as the cost of healthcare? What are the pros and cons of offering health insurance or letting employees go to a health insurance exchange for coverage? Note organizational, market, policy, and financial implications in your response.

EXPERIENTIAL EXERCISE

The purpose of this exercise is to give readers an opportunity to analyze the benefits provided by a healthcare organization. Begin this exercise by visiting the website of a local hospital to see how much information about benefits is posted online. Then visit or call the organization's HR department and obtain answers to the following questions:

- How are benefits communicated to employees at this hospital?
- What benefits are offered to full-time, part-time, and hourly employees?
- Do physicians receive the same benefits as other employees?
- What perquisites (perks) are offered to executives?

- How many total employees are in the HR department, and how many are assigned to handle benefits administration? How many of the staff are certified employee benefits specialists?
- Are there any benefits that the organization is considering but not currently offering? If yes, what are they and how were they identified? If no, what benefits may be added if the organization can afford to do so?
- How have recent health reforms affected the employer from both a benefits design and a cost perspective?

After visiting the department, write a summary of what was found. In writing the summary, assess how comprehensive the benefits package is for employees and how well it is communicated.

REFERENCES

American College of Healthcare Executives (ACHE). 2022. "Top Issues Confronting Hospitals in 2021." Published February 4. www.ache.org/learning-center/research/about-the-field/top-issues-confronting-hospitals/top-issues-confronting-hospitals-in-2021.

American Nurses Credentialing Center (ANCC). 2019. *2019 Magnet Application Manual*. Silver Spring, MD: ANCC.

Centers for Disease Control and Prevention (CDC). 2022a. "HCP Influenza Vaccination Summary Reporting FAQs." National Healthcare Safety Network (NHSN). Updated October 17. www.cdc.gov/nhsn/faqs/vaccination/faq-influenza-vaccination-summary-reporting.html.

———. 2022b. *The National Healthcare Safety Network (NHSN) Manual: Healthcare Personnel Safety Component Protocol; Healthcare Personnel Vaccination Module; Influenza Vaccination Summary*. NHSN. Reviewed August 22. www.cdc.gov/nhsn/pdfs/hps-manual/vaccination/hps-flu-vaccine-protocol-508.pdf.

Centers for Medicare & Medicaid Services (CMS). 2022. "The Mental Health Parity and Addiction Equity Act (MHPAEA)." Accessed June 17. www.cms.gov/cciio/programs-and-initiatives/other-insurance-protections/mhpaea_factsheet.html.

Coe, E., J. Cordina, K. Enomoto, A. Mandel, and J. Stueland. 2021. "National Surveys Reveal Disconnect Between Employees and Employers Around Mental Health Need."

McKinsey & Company. Published April 21. www.mckinsey.com/industries/healthcare
-systems-and-services/our-insights/national-surveys-reveal-disconnect-between
-employees-and-employers-around-mental-health-need.

Congressional Research Service (CRS). 2020. *Long-Term Care Insurance: Overview.*
Report no. IF11614. Published August 6. https://crsreports.congress.gov/product/pdf
/IF/IF11614.

Cunningham, R., III, and R. M. Cunningham Jr. 1997. *The Blues: A History of the Blue Cross
and Blue Shield System.* DeKalb: Northern Illinois University Press.

Employee Benefit Research Institute (EBRI). 2013. *EBRI Databook on Employee Benefits.*
Washington, DC: EBRI.

Internal Revenue Service (IRS). 2022a. "Definitions." Updated September 23. www.irs
.gov/retirement-plans/plan-participant-employee/definitions.

———. 2022b. "401k Plans—Deferrals and Matching When Compensation Exceeds the
Annual Limit." Updated September 22. www.irs.gov/retirement-plans/401k-plans
-deferrals-and-matching-when-compensation-exceeds-the-annual-limit.

———. 2022c. "Identifying Full-Time Employees." Updated September 29. https://
irs.gov/affordable-care-act/employers/identifying-full-time-employees.

———. 2022d. "Publication 503 (2021), Child and Dependent Care Expenses." Updated
January 5. www.irs.gov/publications/p503.

———. 2022e. "Rev. Rul. 2013-17." Accessed October 14. www.irs.gov/pub/irs-drop/rr
-13-17.pdf.

———. 2022f. "Sections 125 and 223—Cafeteria Plans, Flexible Spending Arrangements,
and Health Savings Accounts—Elections and Reimbursements for Same-Sex Spouses
Following the *Windsor* Supreme Court Decision." Notice 2014-1. Accessed October 14.
www.irs.gov/pub/irs-drop/n-14-01.pdf.

———. 2022g. "Topic No. 751 Social Security and Medicare Withholding Rates." Updated
August 29. www.irs.gov/taxtopics/tc751.

———. 2021. *26 CFR 601.602: Tax Forms and Instructions.* Rev. Proc. 2021-45. Published
November 10. www.irs.gov/pub/irs-drop/rp-21-45.pdf.

Joint Commission. 2022. "R3 Report Issue 3: Influenza Vaccination." Accessed November 1. www.jointcommission.org/standards/r3-report/r3-report-issue-3---influenza-vaccination/#.Y1xVRC1h1No.

Jones, D., D. Molitor, and J. Reif. 2019. "What Do Workplace Wellness Programs Do? Evidence from the Illinois Workplace Wellness Study." *Quarterly Journal of Economics* 134 (4) 1747–91. https://academic.oup.com/qje/article/134/4/1747/5550759.

Mattke, R., L. Hangsheng, J. P. Caloyeras, C. Y. Huang, K. R. Van Busem, D. Khodyakov, and V. Shier. 2013. *Workplace Wellness Programs Study*. Santa Monica, CA: RAND Corporation.

Medicaid.gov. 2022. "Program History." Accessed October 15. www.medicaid.gov/about-us/program-history/index.html.

Miller, S. 2021. "Health FSA Contribution Cap Rises to $2,850." Society for Human Resource Management (SHRM). Published November 11. www.shrm.org/resourcesandtools/hr-topics/benefits/pages/2022-fsa-contribution-cap-and-other-colas.aspx.

National Association of Insurance Commissioners (NAIC). 2019. *CIPR Program: The State of Long-Term Care Insurance*. Published December. https://content.naic.org/sites/default/files/inline-files/2019_CIPR_LTCI%20Brief.pdf.

Rosin, B., V. Mayen, and K. Fernes. 2021. "COVID-19 and Workers Compensation—What We Know Now." National Council on Compensation Insurance (NCCI). Published June 23. www.ncci.com/Articles/Pages/Insights-COVID-19-WorkersComp-What-We-Know-Now.aspx.

Social Security Administration. 2022. "Contribution and Benefit Bases, 1937–2023." Accessed October 13. www.socialsecurity.gov/OACT/COLA/cbb.html#Series.

Song, Z., and K. Baicker. 2019. "Effect of a Workplace Wellness Program on Employee Health and Economic Outcomes: A Randomized Clinical Trial." *JAMA* 321 (15): 1491–1501. https://jamanetwork.com/journals/jama/fullarticle/2730614.

Starr, P. 1982. *The Social Transformation of American Medicine*. New York: Basic Books.

US Bureau of Labor Statistics 2022a. "Employer Costs for Employee Compensation—June 2022." News release, September 20. www.bls.gov/news.release/pdf/ecec.pdf.

————. 2022b. "National Compensation Survey: Glossary of Employee Benefit Terms September 2022; Overview." Updated September 22. www.bls.gov/ncs/ebs/national -compensation-survey-glossary-of-employee-benefit-terms.htm.

US Department of Labor. 2022a. "Continuation of Health Coverage—COBRA." Accessed October 14. www.dol.gov/general/topic/health-plans/cobra.

————. 2022b. "Family and Medical Leave Act." Accessed October 14. www.dol.gov /agencies/whd/fmla.

————. 2022c. "Family and Medical Leave (FMLA)." Accessed October 14. www.dol.gov /general/topic/benefits-leave/fmla.

————. 2022d. "Portability of Health Coverage." Accessed October 14. www.dol.gov /general/topic/health-plans/portability.

————. 2022e. "Workers' Compensation Programs." Accessed October 14. www.dol.gov /general/topic/workcomp.

CHAPTER 10

ORGANIZED LABOR

Carla Jackie Sampson, Bruce Fried, and Donna Malvey

After completing this chapter, you should be able to

➤ understand the relationship between organized labor and management in healthcare;

➤ distinguish among the phases of the labor relations process;

➤ describe the evolving role of unions in the healthcare workforce;

➤ examine legislative and judicial rulings that affect the management of organized labor in healthcare settings;

➤ review emerging healthcare labor trends, including the impact of social media on the labor–management relationship.

VIGNETTE

The chief executive officer (CEO) of a midsize urban hospital was late one Friday evening, so he took a shortcut that caused him to walk by the employee lounge. He walked inside and shook his head. With all the problems of budget cuts and trying to make ends meet, he realized that little money had been available for the upkeep of nonpatient areas such as the employee lounge. The carpet was dirty and worn, the coffee mugs were chipped, the wallpaper was torn, and the refrigerator groaned as it cycled on and off. The CEO decided enough was enough. The employees had worked hard and should, at minimum, have an inviting and pleasant employee lounge.

He marched back to his office and called the chief operating officer (COO) to instruct her to create a weekend miracle by calling in the work crews to update and refurbish the employee lounge. He ordered new carpets, new wallpaper, and new furniture and appliances, and he wanted it all done by Monday. The CEO told the COO, "I keep telling the employees how much I appreciate their help, especially in these financially tight times, but now I am going to show them. And be sure to replace those old, chipped coffee mugs." Early on Monday morning, the CEO walked by the employee lounge. It looked terrific, and someone had already made coffee. He made a note to himself to tell the COO what a great job she had done.

When he got to his office, he found the union steward sitting on the couch. "I need to have a word with you," the union steward said. He had several words, as it turned out: He said that the CEO had violated the collective bargaining contract and that refurbishing the employee lounge should have been discussed with the union. The union steward spent 20 minutes complaining about violations and procedures.

After the union steward left, the CEO called the COO and told her to put the lounge back the way it was, including the chipped coffee mugs. Then the CEO muttered to himself, "That is the last time I try to do anything nice for anyone around here. I have learned my lesson."

INTRODUCTION

Tension has marked the relationship between unions and management since the earliest days of unionization. Despite a few notable periods when unions and management have identified common interests and found common ground, an adversarial tone has characterized the relationship. Analyses from Bloomberg Law indicate that more than 207,000 healthcare workers were covered under more than 400 labor agreements that were set to expire in 2022 (Wallender, Kullgren, and Reed 2022). Coupled with an ongoing labor shortage, labor–management tensions appeared likely to escalate. Since the healthcare industry must operate reliably in the face of constant unpredictable change, the relationship between union employees and management is more important than ever.

In the response to the COVID-19 pandemic, many workforce issues took center stage. Safety of the working environment, shortages of personal protective equipment (PPE), short-staffing, and temporary layoffs increased tensions among employees, especially among nurses. Managers must stay abreast of the needs of their employees and find creative ways to problem solve to ease workplace tensions and promote a positive labor relations program in the workplace.

Mounting tensions among employees lead to a rise in union activity when employee demands for proper working conditions, wages, and benefits go unheard. To secure union membership, a union organizing drive can extend over many months, and during this time, management has ample opportunity to engage in union avoidance strategies. Management may express its disapproval of unionization and inform employees about the disadvantages of unionization. However, some management activities are illegal. The National Labor Relations Act (NLRA) establishes guidelines for fair labor practices during a union organizing drive. For example, it is illegal for management to threaten employees involved in a unionization effort. Management may not intimidate or unjustifiably discipline union organizers. Spying on union meetings is also prohibited.

In the sections that follow, union activity will be discussed, including trends in membership, the labor relations process, and important legislative and judicial rulings related to union activity. The chapter concludes with a discussion of recent developments related to unionization in the healthcare industry and guidelines for management.

First, we must define some basic terms. A **union** is an organization formed by employees to act as a single unit when dealing with management about workplace issues, hence the term *organized labor*. Unions are not present in every organization because employees must authorize a union to represent them. Management may view unions as threats because they are often perceived to interfere with management's ability to make and implement decisions. When a union is present, management may no longer unilaterally make certain decisions about the terms and conditions of work. Instead, management must negotiate many decisions with the union. Similarly, employees may no longer communicate

union
An organization formed by employees to act as a single unit when dealing with management about workplace issues.

directly with management about work issues but must go through their union representative instead. Thus, the union functions as an intermediary, a practice that is relatively expensive to maintain for both parties. Employees pay union dues, and management incurs additional costs for such things as contract negotiations and any increases in salaries and benefits negotiated by the union. The **labor relations process** occurs when management (as the representative for the employer) and the union (as the exclusive bargaining representative for the employees) jointly determine and administer the rules of the workplace.

*labor relations
process*
The process whereby
management and the
union jointly decide on
and administer terms
and conditions of
employment.

Labor costs in healthcare generally account for 70 to 80 percent of expenditures, and as a result, controlling labor costs is critically important. Thus, if a union negotiates even a minor wage or benefit increase, it can result in a significant increase in total costs. Management in the twentieth century considered this potential expense a strong incentive to keep unions out of the organization (Scott and Seers 1996). However, given the trends of unionization in healthcare, managers in the twenty-first century are increasingly forced to work with unions (see the accompanying Critical Concept sidebar "Trends in Union Membership"). This chapter examines the phenomenon of healthcare unionization and provides direction for managing with organized labor. In addition, the chapter explores behaviors and strategies that comprise the labor–management relationship; explains the processes of organizing, negotiating, and administering contracts; discusses developments in healthcare unionization; and considers the effect of labor laws, amendments, and rulings on human resources (HR) strategies and goals.

⚠ **CRITICAL CONCEPT**
Trends in Union Membership

According to the US Bureau of Labor Statistics (BLS 2022b), the union membership rate has steadily decreased, from 20.1 percent of the workforce in 1983, the first year for which comparable union data are available, to 10.3 percent in 2021 (BLS 2022b). In 2021, the total number of employees belonging to a union was approximately 14.0 million. Unions have recently been more successful in organizing workers in the public sector than in the private sector and in healthcare rather than in other industries. The union rate for government or public-sector workers has held steady since 1983 and stood at 33.9 percent in 2021, while the rate for private-industry workers has fallen to 6.1 percent, or about half over the same period (BLS 2022b). In the public sector, local government workers had the highest union membership rate—41.7 percent in 2020 (BLS 2021). This group reflects several heavily unionized occupations such as teachers, firefighters, and police officers.

Managing effectively with organized labor requires the development and maintenance of a positive labor relations program. A productive and positive labor–management relationship can be accomplished only through integration with other HR functions. For example, employees expect management to provide a work environment that is clean and safe from workplace hazards and health-related concerns, including communicable diseases such as AIDS and hepatitis B, or workplace violence in general (Occupational Health and Safety Administration 2022). If management allows the environment to deteriorate, then union organizers are likely to focus on these issues. In addition, the labor relations process occurs across all levels of the organization and involves all levels of management. For example, senior management may develop objectives and strategies regarding wage rates and staffing ratios while midlevel managers and frontline supervisors will implement these objectives.

An effective labor relations program in healthcare requires an understanding of the processes of organizing, negotiating, and administering contracts with a union and specific knowledge of emerging healthcare labor trends. A productive and positive labor–management relationship requires a commitment to compromise by both parties; the alternative is often an adversarial relationship. However, just because a union has won the right to represent employees does not mean that management has to accept all of its terms. All parties—management, unions, and employees—have a vested interest in the success and survival of the organization; yet they also may have conflicting interests. For example, unions may seek to improve employee benefits, while management, faced with budget cutbacks and declining reimbursements, will resist such improvements because of concerns about containing costs. Thus, the challenge for management is working with the union to reconcile differences fairly and consistently.

Exhibit 10.1 shows that the labor–management relationship may reflect a range of possible behaviors and strategies, from the most positive or collaborative (in which management and the union share common goals oriented toward the organization's success) to the most negative or oppositional. Even if the relationship is neutral and both parties cooperate to maintain the status quo, various factors can cause the relationship to shift in either direction. For instance, corporate restructuring, such as a merger, may create uncertainty for the union and management and, as a result, may reposition their relationship. However, the direction in which the relationship moves will depend largely on the knowledge and understanding of the labor relations process on both sides.

OVERVIEW OF UNIONIZATION

Union membership has been declining steadily for decades. From the 1950s to the 1970s, union membership represented 25 to 30 percent of the US workforce; during the 1980s and 1990s, organized labor's influence and bargaining power declined and weakened as the nature of US industries shifted from factories and traditional union strongholds to services

Exhibit 10.1

Ranges of the Labor–Management Relationship in Healthcare

Positive	Neutral	Negative
Management and union have joint collaboration on the rules of the workplace	Management and union have a fairly neutral relationship	Management and union have a mostly adversarial and unstable relationship
Management and union have a positive relationship, with both parties focusing on the success and survival of the organization	Management–union relationship is neither oppositional nor supportive	Contract administration is predominantly oppositional and self-serving
Management and union proactively respond to external threats	Management and union focus on maintaining status quo	Management and union tend to be reactive to external threats

and technologies (Fottler et al. 1999). This trend appears to have continued, as evidenced by the fact that organized labor has been unable to make any net gains in membership despite downward pressure on wages, increasing healthcare insurance costs, and outsourcing of service and manufacturing jobs overseas.

Overall, the proportion of wage and salary workers who were union members was 10.3 percent in 2021, slipping from 10.8 percent in 2020, but returning to the 2019 proportion. The slight increase in 2020 is attributed to the decrease in nonunionized workers compared with unionized workers. The total number of union members in 2021 was 14.0 million, a decrease from 14.6 million in 2014, as reported by the US Bureau of Labor Statistics (BLS 2022b).

The healthcare workforce comprises an estimated 18.2 million workers (and is growing; see "Did You Know?" sidebar), representing one of the largest pools of unorganized workers in the United States and a prime target for union organizers. Approximately 7.1 percent of the healthcare workforce was affiliated with union membership in 2020 (BLS 2021). Of the approximately 9 million people employed in healthcare practitioner and technical occupations in 2021, only 11.7 percent were union members (BLS 2021). Among about 4.6 million people employed in healthcare support occupations in 2021, an even smaller proportion—8.3 percent—were union members (BLS 2021).

Labor experts believe that healthcare unions represent one of the few areas in which organized labor has been showing some energy. For example, nurses were overextended during the pandemic, and many left the profession. The remaining nurses are demanding increased wages and mandatory staffing ratios as healthcare organizations still show negative margins and experience supply chain delays (Pattani 2021). Amid these tensions,

DID YOU KNOW?
Fastest-Growing Occupations

Projections by the US Bureau of Labor Statistics (BLS 2022a) for 2031 indicate that nurse practitioner is the fastest-growing health occupation, representing an increase of 5.3 percent from the 2021 level. Physical and occupational therapist assistants and home health and personal care aides also are projected to experience greater growth rates than other healthcare occupations.

healthcare unions have invested heavily in membership recruitment and helping members gain influence in response.

THE LABOR RELATIONS PROCESS

In an attempt to protect workers' rights to unionize, the US Congress in 1935 passed the **National Labor Relations Act (NLRA)**, which serves as the legal framework for the labor relations process in the United States. Although the NLRA has been amended over the years, it remains the only legislation that governs federal labor relations. The law contains significant provisions intended to protect workers' rights to form and join unions and to engage in collective bargaining. The law also defines unfair labor practices, which restrict both unions and employers from interfering with the labor relations process. The NLRA delegates to the National Labor Relations Board (NLRB) the responsibility for overseeing implementation of the NLRA and for investigating and remedying unfair labor practices. NLRB rulemaking occurs on a case-by-case basis.

Key participants in the labor relations process include the following:

◆ Management officials, who serve as surrogates for the owners or employers of the organization

◆ Union officials, who are usually elected by members

◆ The government, which participates through executive, legislative, and judicial branches at federal, state, and local levels

◆ Third-party neutrals such as mediators and arbitrators

The labor relations process encompasses three phases that are equally essential: the recognition phase, the negotiation phase, and the administration phase.

National Labor Relations Act (NLRA) The legal framework for the labor relations process in the United States; it contains significant provisions intended to protect workers' rights to form and join unions and to engage in collective bargaining, and it defines unfair labor practices.

RECOGNITION PHASE

During the recognition phase, unions attempt to organize employees and gain representation through either voluntary recognition of the union or a representation election, which certifies that the union has the authority to act on behalf of employees in negotiating a collective bargaining agreement. In rare cases, the NLRB may direct an employer to recognize and bargain with the union if evidence exists that a fair and impartial election would be impossible. Since the 1990s, management strategies and tactics have become more aggressive during the recognition phase as management has endeavored to keep unions from representing employees. For example, management may institute unfair labor practices such as filing for bankruptcy, illegally firing union supporters, and relocating. Although unions may file grievances with the NLRB over these practices and the use of illegal or union-busting tactics, legal resolution usually occurs years after the fact and long after union elections have been held. Thus, both unions and management understand that the battle lines are drawn in the recognition phase, and both sides will be fervently engaged in shoring up support.

The desire to unionize is related to three key issues: wages, benefits, and employee perceptions about the workplace. To obtain information on employees' desire to unionize, management relies on signals or indicators in the workplace. Exhibit 10.2 summarizes some of the behaviors that may indicate organizing activities or the potential for organizing employees. For example, a high turnover rate is a characteristic of many healthcare institutions: The US hospital turnover rate was 25.9 percent in 2021 (NSI Nursing Solutions 2022). However, when employees leave their jobs for a local competitor, management must investigate the underlying reasons for turnover. Even simple issues, such as an increase in requests for information on policies and procedures, can indicate problems and should not be discounted.

EXHIBIT 10.2
Warning Indicators for Healthcare Organizations

Item	Increase or Decrease	Comment
Turnover—especially to competitors	Increase	Turnover in healthcare organizations typically is much higher than in organizations in other industries because of enhanced mobility from licensing and standardization; however, if employees move to competing organizations in the local area, such movement may indicate dissatisfaction rather than career opportunities.

EXHIBIT 10.2
Warning Indicators
for Healthcare
Organizations
(continued)

Item	Increase or Decrease	Comment
Employee-generated incidents	Increase	Staff members fight among themselves; theft or damage to organization's property occurs; insubordination related to routine requests by supervisors occurs.
Grievances	Increase	More grievances are being filed with the human resources (HR) office compared with informal settlements by supervisors and employees.
Communication	Decrease	Staff members are reluctant to provide feedback and generally become quiet when management enters the room; suggestion boxes are empty and employees are less willing to avail themselves of the "open door" system or other mechanisms to express dissatisfaction or describe problems.
HR office informational requests	Increase	Employees express interest in policies, procedures, and other matters related to the terms and conditions of employment, and they want this information in writing; verbal responses no longer satisfy them.
Offsite meetings	Increase	Employees appear to be congregating more at off-site premises.
Grapevine activity	Increase	Rumors increase in number and intensity.
Absenteeism and/or tardiness	Increase	Employees are engaging in union-organizing activities prior to and during work hours.
Social media activity	Increase	Employee posts about the employer on social media platforms trend negative.

KEY POINT

Many people believe that the primary reason for joining a union is to increase wages and benefits. However, money is only one factor in unionization. Key reasons for joining a union are recognition, protection from humiliation, hope-lessness, lack of control, job insecurity, broken promises made by management, and the need to have one's interests represented to management.

During the recognition phase, the union solicits signed **authorization cards** that designate the union to act as the employees' collective bargaining representative. When at least 30 percent of employees in the bargaining unit have signed cards, the union requests that the employer voluntarily recognize the union. Voluntary recognition is rarely granted by employers and occurs infrequently in healthcare organizations. When employers refuse voluntary recognition of the union, the union is then eligible to petition the NLRB for a representation election. In response to the petition, the NLRB verifies the authenticity of the signatures collected by the union, determines the appropriate **bargaining unit**, and sets a date for a secret-ballot election. Healthcare workers represent a significant number of all workers participating in NLRB elections.

authorization cards
Documentation cards signed by individual employees that indicate a desire to designate the union to act as the employees' collective bargaining representative.

bargaining unit
A group of employees recognized by the National Labor Relations Board to be an appropriate body for collective bargaining under the National Labor Relations Act.

A bargaining unit is a group of employees recognized by the NLRB to be an appropriate body for collective bargaining. The NLRB determines which employees are eligible to be in a bargaining unit and thereby eligible to vote in the election. The NLRB permits a total of eight bargaining units in healthcare settings. (The history of this determination is provided later in this chapter.) Although the NLRB has modified its criteria over the years, it has not changed its outlook on managerial or supervisory employees, who are ineligible for membership in a bargaining unit. In a landmark 2006 ruling, the NLRB clarified and set forth guidelines for determining whether an individual is a supervisor under the NLRA. The NLRB ruled that charge nurses were supervisors, thereby making them and certain other nurses like them ineligible for bargaining-unit representation. This ruling represented an opportunity to reclassify many nurses as members of management and thereby potentially decrease the union's ability to recruit new members.

Generally, the union election is scheduled to occur on workplace premises during work hours. The union is permitted to conduct a preelection campaign in accordance with solicitation rules that are outlined for both unions and management. During the campaign, management may not make threats or announce reprisals regarding the outcome of the election, such as telling nurses that people will be laid off if the union is elected or that people will get pay raises if the union loses. Management also may not directly ask employees about their attitudes or voting intentions or those of other employees. Management is allowed, however, to conduct *captive-audience speeches*, which are meetings during work time to inform employees about what certifying a union will mean for the organization and to persuade employees to give management another chance.

To win the election and be certified by the NLRB as representing the bargaining unit, the union must achieve a simple majority or 50 percent plus 1 of those voting. When the union wins the election, it assumes the duties of the exclusive bargaining agent for all employees in the unit, including those employees who did not vote in favor of the union. The union may lose the right to represent employees in the bargaining unit through a **decertification** election. Unions have a legal obligation of **fair representation**—they must evenhandedly represent all bargaining-unit employees, both union members and nonmembers alike.

NEGOTIATION PHASE

After winning the certification election, the union will begin to negotiate a contract on behalf of the employees in the bargaining unit. Federal labor laws encourage **collective bargaining** on the theory that employees and their employers are best able to reach agreement on issues such as wages, hours, and conditions of employment through negotiating their differences. The NLRA (Section 8 [d], 1935) defines *collective bargaining* as follows:

> The performance of the mutual obligation of the employer and the representative of the employees to meet at reasonable times and confer in good faith with respect to wages, hours and terms and conditions of employment or the negotiation of an agreement, or any question arising thereunder, and the execution of a written contract incorporating any agreement reached requested by either party to agree to a proposal or require the making of a concession.

The NLRA requires an employer to recognize and bargain in good faith with a certified union, but it does not force the employer to agree with the union or make any concessions. The key to satisfying the duty to bargain in good faith is approaching the bargaining table with an open mind and negotiating with the intention of reaching final agreement.

Bargaining issues have evolved over the years as the result of NLRB and court decisions. Those issues are categorized as illegal, mandatory, or voluntary (permissive). Illegal subjects, such as age-discrimination employment clauses, may not be considered for bargaining. **Mandatory bargaining issues** must be addressed if they are introduced by one of the parties for negotiation. There are more than 60 mandatory issues, including wages and benefits, hours of work, grievance procedures, and vacations. Voluntary, or permissive, bargaining may or may not be addressed. Examples of **voluntary bargaining issues** include strike insurance and benefits for retired employees.

Prior to bargaining, management will formulate a range of positions for each issue, which is similar to an opening offer, followed by a series of benchmarks that represent expected levels of settlement. Management must calculate a resistance point beyond which it will cease negotiations. Two experts in negotiations from Harvard University (Fisher and

---

decertification
A National Labor Relations Board procedure available for employees when they believe, usually as a result of an election, that the union no longer represents the interests of the majority of the bargaining unit.

fair representation
A union's legal obligation to evenhandedly represent all bargaining-unit employees, both union members and nonmembers alike.

collective bargaining
An activity whereby union and management officials attempt to resolve conflicting interests in a manner that will sustain and possibly enrich their continuing relationships.

mandatory bargaining issues
Topics related to wages, hours, and other conditions of employment that must be negotiated as part of collective bargaining if raised by the union or management.

Ury 1981) developed a widely accepted and utilized principled method of negotiation based on the merits or principles of the issues. The following four basic points guide this method:

1. *People.* Separate the people from the problem.

2. *Interests.* Focus on interests, not the positions that people hold.

3. *Options.* Generate a variety of alternative possibilities.

4. *Criteria.* Insist that solutions be evaluated using objective standards.

According to this method, management will formulate a *best alternative to a negotiated agreement* (BATNA) for each issue. In this manner, negotiators evaluate whether the type of agreement that can be reached is better than no agreement at all. By considering mutual options for gain, the negotiator offers a more flexible approach toward bargaining and increases the likelihood of achieving creative and acceptable solutions.

Collective bargaining is a laborious and time-consuming endeavor. Bargaining requires not only listening to others but also attempting to understand the motivation behind the dialogue. Successful negotiators make every effort to understand fully what true interests underlie bargaining positions and why they are so fiercely held. Also, negotiators are receptive to any signals that are being communicated, including nonverbal communication such as body language (Fisher and Ury 1981).

Bargaining, as depicted in exhibit 10.3, can be conceptualized as a continuum of bargaining behaviors and strategies. At one end of the continuum is **integrative bargaining**, which seeks win–win solutions that are acceptable to both parties. This type of bargaining requires trust and cooperation of both parties. At the opposite end is **concessionary bargaining**, in which the employer asks the union to eliminate, limit, or reduce wages and other commitments in response to financial constraints. This type of "winner takes all" bargaining is likely to occur when the organization is in financial jeopardy and is struggling to survive. In the center is **distributive bargaining**, which is a win some–lose some type of bargaining in which each party gives up something to gain something else. This type of bargaining is likely when negotiations are contentious and full of conflict.

Even when both parties negotiate in good faith and fulfill the covenants of the NLRA, agreement still may not be reached. When this happens, the parties are said to have reached an **impasse**.

A variety of techniques may be used to resolve an impasse. As discussed in chapter 3, these techniques may involve third parties and include *mediation*, in which a neutral mediator evaluates the dispute and issues nonbinding recommendations. If either party rejects the mediator's recommendations, *arbitration* is an alternative. An *arbitrator*, similar to a mediator, is a neutral third party, but an arbitrator's decisions are legally binding. For example, arbitrators may recommend that either party's position be accepted as a final

Integrative Bargaining (win–win)	Distributive Bargaining (win some–lose some)	Concessionary Bargaining (winner takes all)

EXHIBIT 10.3
Collective Bargaining Continuum

offer, or they can attempt to split the differences between the two parties' positions. (For more on these distinctions, see the Critical Concept sidebar "Mediation and Arbitration.")

If these techniques of mediation or arbitration fail to resolve the impasse, employers or the union can initiate work stoppages that may take the form of a lockout or strike. A **lockout** occurs when the employer shuts down operations either during or prior to a dispute. A **strike**, on the other hand, is employee initiated. Lockouts or strikes can occur during negotiations and also during the life of the contract. Special provisions for work stoppages in healthcare settings are discussed later in this chapter.

No-strike and no-lockout clauses can be negotiated in the collective bargaining agreement. No-strike clauses essentially prohibit strikes, either unconditionally or with conditions. An *unconditional no-strike clause* means that the union and its members will not engage in either a strike or a work slowdown while the contract is in effect. A *conditional no-strike clause* bans strikes and slowdowns except in certain situations and under specific conditions, which are delineated in detail in the agreement. Comparable clauses for lockouts exist for employers.

impasse
A deadlock in negotiating between management and union officials over terms and conditions of employment.

lockout
An act by an employer when it shuts down operations during or before a labor dispute.

strike
A temporary stoppage of work by a group of employees for the purposes of expressing a grievance or forcing a demand.

> **⚠ CRITICAL CONCEPT**
> Mediation and Arbitration
>
> *Mediation* is typically used to help management and labor reach agreement on a contract by presenting the disagreement to a neutral third party called a *mediator*. Mediation is voluntary, and there is no legal requirement for either side to come to agreement based on the mediator's advice.
>
> *Arbitration* involves submitting a dispute to a neutral third party called an *arbitrator*, whose decision is legally binding on each of the parties. *Rights arbitration* is used when there is a disagreement or conflict over the interpretation of a union contract. *Interest arbitration* may be used to resolve an impasse during contract negotiations. In any kind of arbitration, both sides must agree on the person named as arbitrator (or, when more than one person, the arbitration panel) and agree to abide by the arbitrator's decision.

ADMINISTRATION PHASE

When an agreement between the union and the employer is reached, it must be recorded in writing and executed in *good faith*, which means that the terms and conditions of the agreement must be applied and enforced. This agreement includes wages and salaries; disciplinary, grievance, and arbitration procedures; and other issues. The right to discharge, suspend, or discipline is clearly enunciated in contractual clauses and in the adoption of rules and procedures that may or may not be incorporated in the agreement.

The heart of administering the collective bargaining agreement is the grievance procedure. This procedure is a useful and productive management tool that allows implementation and interpretation of the contract. A **grievance** must be well defined and restricted to violations of the terms and conditions of the agreement. However, other conditions may give rise to a grievance, including violations of the law or company rules, a change in working conditions or past company practices, or violations of health and safety standards.

The grievance process usually contains a series of steps. These steps are generally stated in the contract negotiated between labor and management. The first step always involves the presentation of the grievance by the employee (or representative) to the immediate supervisor. If the grievance is not resolved at this step, broader action is taken. Because most grievances involve an action taken by the immediate supervisor, the second step necessarily must occur outside the department and at a higher level, usually involving the employee (or representative) and a department head or other administrator. The written grievance will document the events as the employee perceived them, cite the appropriate contract provisions that allegedly have been violated, and indicate the desired resolution or settlement prospects.

If the grievance remains unresolved at this point, a third step becomes necessary that involves an in-house review by top management. A grievance that remains unresolved after the third step may go to arbitration if provided for in the contract and if the union is in agreement. Grievances must follow **due process**—the procedural aspect of disciplinary cases, such as following time limits prescribed in the labor agreement, providing union representation, and notifying an employee of a specific offense in writing.

An *arbitration hearing* permits each side an opportunity to present its case. Similar to a court hearing, witnesses, cross-examinations, transcripts, and legal counsel may be used. As with a court hearing, the nature of arbitration is adversarial. Thus, cases may be lost because of poor preparation and presentation. Generally, the courts will enforce an arbitrator's decision unless it is shown to be unreasonable, unsound, or capricious relative to the issues under consideration. Also, if an arbitrator has exceeded the given authority or issued an order that violates existing state or federal law, the decision may be *vacated* (declared invalid). Consistent and fair adjudication of grievances is the hallmark of a sound labor–management relationship.

In healthcare settings, the strike is the most severe form of a labor–management dispute. A critical part of negotiation planning is an honest assessment of strike potential. This assessment involves identifying strike issues that are likely to be critical for all parties.

grievance
Any employee's concern over a perceived violation of the labor agreement that is submitted to the grievance procedure for eventual resolution.

due process
The procedural aspect of disciplinary cases under a labor agreement.

Although estimating the effect of possible strikes, including economic pressures from lost wages and revenues, is essential, the key to a successful strike from the perspective of the union is to impose enough pressure on management to expedite movement toward a compromise. Pressure may be psychological or economic. In healthcare settings, the real losers in a strike are the patients and their families. During a strike, patients may be denied services or forced to postpone treatment, be relocated to another institution, or even be discharged prematurely.

Management must be aware of critical factors that affect its ability and willingness to withstand a strike. When attempting to estimate the impact of these factors, managers will evaluate several key indicators, including revenue losses, timing of the strike, and availability of replacements for striking workers (but regarding the latter, see the Critical Concept sidebar "Rolling Strike"). Management must also contemplate factors that affect the union, such as whether the union will provide striking employees with strike benefits and, if so, for how long. Both parties must also consider the impact of outside assistance to avoid or settle a strike.

A REVIEW OF LEGISLATIVE AND JUDICIAL RULINGS

Exhibit 10.4 summarizes important legislative and judicial rulings and their effect on healthcare settings. As the exhibit indicates, in the twenty-first century, significant rulings have centered primarily on organizing issues, mostly involving physicians and nurses and their eligibility for inclusion in bargaining units. In 2004, the focus shifted to financial issues such as changes to the Fair Labor Standards Act (described in chapter 3), which exempted most nurses from overtime pay. Unions were also affected by changes to the **Labor Management Reporting and Disclosure Act of 1959**. Stricter reporting was required that aimed at increased transparency and accountability for how unions spend dues money (*Harvard Law Review* 2004).

Labor Management Reporting and Disclosure Act of 1959
A US labor law that regulates labor unions' internal affairs and their officials' relationships with employers.

> **① CRITICAL CONCEPT**
> Rolling Strike
>
> During a strike, it is legal for employers to hire replacement workers. In response to this management practice, a union may implement a *rolling strike* in situations where the union's members work at multiple locations. A rolling strike is one in which one work site at a time is targeted for a walkout, with the particular work site changing each day. This calculated unpredictability of the strike location makes it difficult for management to hire replacement workers.

Exhibit 10.4
Summary of
Important
Legislative and
Judicial Rulings

Year	Legislation or Judicial Ruling	Effect on Healthcare Organizations
1947	Taft-Hartley amendments to National Labor Relations Act (NLRA)	Exempted not-for-profit hospitals from NLRA coverage, including collective bargaining
1962	Executive Order #10988	Permitted federally supported hospitals to bargain collectively
1974	Healthcare amendments to NLRA	Extended NLRA coverage to private, not-for-profit hospitals and healthcare institutions; special provisions for strikes, pickets, and impasses
1976	National Labor Relations Board (NLRB) ruling: Cedars–Sinai Medical Center, Los Angeles	Ruled that medical residents, interns, and fellows (house staff) are students and excluded from collective bargaining
1989/1991	NLRB ruling / Supreme Court affirmation on multiple bargaining units: PL 93-360	Expanded the number of bargaining units in acute care hospitals from three to eight
1999	NLRB ruling: Boston Medical Center	Reversed Cedars–Sinai Medical Center decision and ruled that house staff are employees, not students, and can therefore be included in collective bargaining
2001	Supreme Court decision regarding nurse supervisors: *NLRB v. Kentucky River Community Care, Inc.*	Ruled that registered nurses who use independent judgment in directing employees are supervisors, a decision expected to limit unions' ability to organize nurses
2003	US Department of Labor (19 C.F.R. pts 403 and 408)	Adopted a rule that increases union financial reporting requirements to provide for transparency of union financial structures and accountability of how unions spend their dues
2004	Part 541 of the Fair Labor Standards Act	Resulted in US Department of Labor issuing new rules that make most nurses ineligible for overtime pay

Year	Legislation or Judicial Ruling	Effect on Healthcare Organizations
2006	NLRB ruling: Oakwood Heritage Hospital, Taylor, Michigan	Addressed supervisory status in response to the Supreme Court's decision in the *Kentucky River* case; issued guidelines for determining whether an individual is a supervisor under the NLRA; and reclassified certain nurses (i.e., charge nurses) as management and thus ineligible to join unions, a decision expected to reduce potential for union recruitment, and one that could permit employers to challenge existing contracts and remove nurses from bargaining units
2011	NLRB decision that allowed much smaller groups (no more than 10 workers) to unionize	Led to a growing number of unionization efforts at smaller healthcare entities, such as blood drive centers and emergency care centers
2011–2013	*Specialty Healthcare*, 357 NLRB No. 83, in which the NLRB redefined the "appropriate unit" standard to allow for smaller bargaining units; ruling later appealed, and in 2013, US Court of Appeals for the Sixth Circuit granted right to enforce original ruling	Permitted bargaining units that consist of one department or one classification (e.g., certified nursing assistants) rather than "wall-to-wall" units; ruling not applicable to employers that are acute care hospitals
2014–2015	NLRB ruling on expedited elections	Changed the process for filing and processing petitions for union representation of employees, essentially shortened the required time between filing a petition and holding an election, and was expected to tilt NLRB election procedures in favor of unions
2019	NLRB ruling on expedited elections	Modified the 2014 expedited rule by lengthening the time between petition filing and election, to assure that expedited elections are efficient and fair
2019	NLRB ruling: Prime Healthcare Paradise Valley, LLC	Ruling prohibits mandatory arbitration policies that limit employees' right to file complaints with the NLRB. Ruling applies to both unionized and nonunionized settings.

EXHIBIT 10.4
Summary of Important Legislative and Judicial Rulings *(continued)*

Much attention has been directed toward organizing issues; specifically, the determination of who is considered a supervisor. A supervisor, after all, is excluded from the bargaining unit. By definition, a manager cannot be a member of a labor union. However, as organization structures have grown increasingly flat and less hierarchical, many jobs have expanded to include a managerial or supervisory component. Accordingly, determining who is considered a supervisor has become challenging, especially with regard to health professionals who operate with some autonomy (Von Bergen 2006). Particularly significant for healthcare is the case of *NLRB v. Kentucky River Community Care, Inc.*, in which the US Supreme Court criticized the NLRB's lack of clarity in its interpretation of the term *independent judgment* to determine supervisory status. Subsequently, the NLRB adjusted its definition of supervisory status. In 2019, the NLRB determined unanimously that boilerplate or standard arbitration agreements are insufficient for employers to restrict employees from filing complaints with the NLRB.

The **Taft-Hartley Act** amended the NLRA in 1947 and is often referred to as "pro-management" legislation. The primary intent of its amendments was to strike a balance in the NLRA because most of its protections and rights applied to workers, and employers needed a means for redress. In other words, whereas the original NLRA protects workers and unions, the Taft-Hartley Act protects employers (see the related Critical Concept sidebar "The Closed Shop, Open Shop, and Union Shop"). Taft-Hartley also gave states federal permission to enact **right-to-work laws**, which essentially prohibit employees from being forced to join unions as a condition of employment. As of mid-2022, 27 states, mostly in the South and West, had enacted such laws (National Council of State Legislatures 2022). Unions oppose right-to-work laws in part because under the NLRA, unions are responsible for representing all employees in the bargaining unit, even those members who choose not to join the union and consequently pay no union dues. Non-union members of the bargaining unit are often referred to as "free riders" because they acquire all the benefits of union membership without any cost. Meanwhile, proponents of right-to-work laws maintain that no one should be forced to join a private organization, especially if that organization is using dues money to support causes that contravene an individual's moral or religious beliefs.

As enacted in 1935, the NLRA did not exempt healthcare employees explicitly, but court interpretations tended to exclude healthcare workers from its regulations. Taft-Hartley had a significant effect on healthcare workers because it specifically excluded from the definition of *employer* private, not-for-profit hospitals and healthcare institutions. However, the NLRB asserted jurisdiction over proprietary (i.e., for-profit) hospitals and nursing homes. The **1974 Health Care Amendments to the Taft-Hartley Act**, Public Law 93-360, brought the private, not-for-profit healthcare industry within the jurisdiction of federal labor law. With passage of the 1974 Health Care Amendments, approximately 2 million additional

---

Taft-Hartley Act
Law that amended the National Labor Relations Act in 1947; it protects employers and gives states permission to enact right-to-work laws.

right-to-work laws
Laws that prohibit union membership (and related union security clauses) as a condition of employment, in accordance with point 14(b) of the National Labor Relations Act.

1974 Health Care Amendments to the Taft-Hartley Act
Legislation that made approximately 2 million additional healthcare workers eligible for union representation and provided stringent protections regarding work stoppages to safeguard patient care.

> ### ⚠ CRITICAL CONCEPT
> #### The Closed Shop, Open Shop, and Union Shop
>
> The *closed shop* is an arrangement whereby an employer is permitted to hire only union members. This arrangement is illegal under the Taft-Hartley Act amendments. Under *open shop* provisions, no employee is required to join or contribute money to a labor union as a condition of employment. A *union shop* is an arrangement whereby an employee must join the union after starting work. This arrangement is not permitted in "right-to-work" states. Conversely, a *yellow dog contract* is one in which employees agree not to join a union as a condition of getting hired by an employer that opposes unionization. Under the National Labor Relations Act, such an arrangement is illegal.

healthcare workers became eligible for union representation (Stickler 1990). However, these amendments provided stringent protections regarding work stoppages to safeguard patient care. Exhibit 10.5 summarizes the provisions for strikes and **picketing** and impasse resolution requirements. In drafting the 1974 amendments, the congressional committee specifically included a ten-day strike and picket notice provision, a requirement that had not been applied to other industries. The committee did so to ensure that healthcare institutions would have sufficient advance notice of a strike.

picketing
Outside patrolling by union members of any employer's premises for the purpose of achieving a specific objective.

The reprisals for violating the ten-day notice are substantial. For example, workers engaged in work stoppage in violation of the strike notice lose their status as employees and are subsequently unprotected by NLRA provisions. The amendments also provide exceptions to the requirements for unions to give advance notice of a work stoppage. If the employer has committed a flagrant or serious, unfair labor practice, then notices are not required. In addition, the employer may not use the ten-day notice period to essentially undermine the bargaining relationship that otherwise exists. For example, the facility can receive supplies, but it is not free to stockpile supplies for an unduly extended period. Similarly, the facility cannot bring in large numbers of personnel from other facilities for the purpose of replacing striking workers (Kruger and Metzger 2002).

In 1989, an NLRB ruling established eight units for the purpose of collective bargaining in acute care hospitals. The American Hospital Association (AHA) strongly opposed the 1989 NLRB ruling because the AHA thought that it would lead to a proliferation of unions in hospitals. The AHA appealed to the US Supreme Court. The Supreme Court affirmed the NLRB's ruling in 1991. The eight collective bargaining units include the following:

1974 Healthcare Amendments to the Taft-Hartley Act	General National Labor Relations Act Provisions
30-day "reasonable" time to picket following which a representation petition must be filed by the union with the National Labor Relations Board (NLRB).	Similar requirement
90-day notice for modifying an existing collective bargaining agreement.	60-day requirement
60-day notice to the Federal Mediation and Conciliation Service (FMCS) of impending expiration of existing collective bargaining agreement.	30-day requirement
Following FMCS notification, the contract must remain in effect for 60 days without any strikes or lockouts.	30-day requirement
30-day notice of a dispute must be given to FMCS and appropriate state agency during initial negotiations.	No similar requirement
The director of FMCS is authorized to appoint a board of inquiry in the event of a threatened or actual work stoppage.	No similar authority
10-day written notice to employer and FMCS of strikes or pickets required of healthcare unions. [*Note: This notice cannot occur before either (1) the end of the 90-day notice to modify the existing contract or (2) the 30-day notice in the case of an impasse during negotiations of the new contract.*]	No similar requirement
Section 19 provides for an alternate—a contribution to designated 501(c)(3) charities—for the payment of union dues for persons with religious convictions against making such payments.	No similar requirement

1. Physicians
2. Nurses:
   — Registered nurses
   — Graduate nurses
   — Non–nursing department nurses
   — Nurse anesthetists
   — Nurse instructors
   — Nurse practitioners

3. All professionals, except for registered nurses and physicians:
   — Audiologists
   — Chemists
   — Counselors
   — Dietitians
   — Educational programmers
   — Educators
   — Medical artists
   — Nuclear physicists
   — Pharmacists
   — Social workers
   — Technologists
   — Therapists
   — Utilization review coordinators
4. Technical employees:
   — Infant-care technicians
   — Laboratory technicians
   — Licensed practical nurses
   — Operating room technicians
   — Orthopedic technicians
   — Physical therapy assistants
   — Psychiatric technicians
   — Respiratory therapy technicians
   — Surgical assistants
   — X-ray technicians
5. Business office clerical employees
6. Skilled maintenance employees
7. Guards
8. All other nonprofessional employees

As with all bargaining unit determinations, supervisors are excluded from union membership.

DEVELOPMENTS IN ORGANIZING HEALTHCARE WORKERS

A number of developments have taken place in the process of organizing healthcare workers. In the sections that follow, we examine how these developments have affected four key groups: (1) unions, (2) physicians, (3) house staff and medical students, and (4) nurses. We also take a look at how the internet and social media have contributed to these developments.

UNIONS

The union landscape shifted dramatically in 2005, when the Service Employees International Union (SEIU) ended its relationship with the American Federation of Labor and Congress of Industrial Organizations (AFL–CIO) because of a failure to pursue aggressive strategies to recruit new members (see also "Did You Know?" sidebar on the AFL–CIO). The SEIU subsequently aligned itself with the Change to Win federation, joining six other former AFL–CIO affiliates that similarly chose to sever ties with the AFL-CIO. The SEIU action reduced the AFL–CIO membership of 13 million at that time by about a third. Currently, the SEIU has about 2 million members (SEIU 2022a).

In 2007, the SEIU announced the formation of a separate national healthcare union—SEIU Healthcare—that focuses exclusively on healthcare workers. It is the largest healthcare union in the United States, with a membership of 1.1 million workers (SEIU 2022b). It has been visible in its support of efforts to expand nurse–patient ratios and efforts to organize physicians. In addition to its focus on hospital, nursing, and long-term care workers, SEIU Healthcare targets employees in ambulatory surgery centers, laboratories, clinics, and other healthcare areas. The local unions of SEIU Healthcare have been visibly active in recruitment and bargaining, leveraging worker experiences during the COVID-19 pandemic (see, e.g., SEIU Local 521 2022).

In 2009, the National Union of Healthcare Workers (NUHW) formed in response to troublesome practices regarding the management of healthcare unions. After a split from the SEIU over organizing philosophy, the NUHW aims to maintain complete transparency in establishing better working conditions and giving its members a stronger voice in the workplace. In 2013, the NUHW teamed up with the California Nurses Association (CNA), which represented 85,000 nurses in 2013 and proved to be a politically large partner for the NUHW (Maher 2013). The NUHW represented more than 16,000 healthcare workers in 2022, compared with about 1.1 million represented by the SEIU Healthcare arm (NUHW 2022; SEIU 2022b).

DID YOU KNOW?
The AFL–CIO

The AFL–CIO is not a union but is a federation of many unions. It resulted from the merger of the American Federation of Labor and the Congress of Industrial Organizations. The AFL–CIO is composed of 55 national and international unions and includes about 12.5 million workers (AFL–CIO 2022). It is a powerful voice in lobbying, voter registration, and political education.

In 2009, National Nurses United (NNU) became the largest union representing registered nurses (NNU 2022a). It united three of the largest and most powerful nurse unions: CNA, United American Nurses / National Nurses Organizing Committee (UAN/ NNOC), and the Massachusetts Nurses Association (MNA). The AFL–CIO is affiliated with the NNOC—an affiliation that was extended to the NNU. In 2022, members of the New York State Nurses Association voted to join the NNU, bringing the NNU's total membership to nearly 225,000 nurses (NNU 2022b). The consolidation of these unions likely means more activism, especially recruiting nationwide.

PHYSICIANS

Historically, physicians resisted union organizing for various professional and philosophical reasons. In fact, much of the American Medical Association (AMA) membership views unionism as antithetical to professionalism and unions as economic devices that extract benefits for their members at the expense of patient trust and confidence. Organizing physicians also presents legal challenges because the majority of physicians are independent contractors and thus are technically ineligible for union membership. Only *employed* physicians, including those employed in academic settings, are authorized to bargain collectively. Physicians who practice as independent contractors are restricted from collective bargaining by the Sherman Antitrust Act of 1890, which prohibits all business combinations that restrain free trade. Therefore, these physicians cannot legally talk with one another about price of service. Subsequently, independent contractors who engage in collective bargaining with entities such as health plans and insurers risk exposure to federal antitrust suits (Bowling, Richman, and Schulman 2022).

Nonetheless, the growth of managed care in the 1990s provided a powerful incentive for the rise of the physician union movement in the United States. The vast majority of physician complaints and efforts to unionize derived from corporate interference in medical decision making and coercive practices of managed care organizations (Anawis 2002; Luepke 1999). At its annual meeting in June 1999, the AMA House of Delegates approved a controversial resolution, creating a national bargaining unit for physicians. The bargaining unit—Physicians for Responsible Negotiations (PRN)—permitted employed physicians to bargain with health plans and insurers. The resolution was controversial because the AMA, which traditionally opposed physician unions, reversed its position. In so doing, the AMA recognized collective bargaining as an acceptable professional mechanism for interacting with government and other third-party payers. Federal and state legislation also was proposed in support of amending antitrust laws to permit independent physicians to unionize. However, this legislation did not gain widespread support and was subsequently abandoned.

The PRN struggled for survival and recruited few members. In 2002, the AMA reduced its financial support for the PRN, only guaranteeing the union's survival through the year 2003. In March 2004, the AMA, with little press attention, severed its relationship with the PRN. In June 2004, the PRN partnered with SEIU and its two other affiliated doctors' unions—the Doctors Council and the National Physicians Alliance. This affiliation represented the largest collection of unionized physicians in the United States, including approximately 20,000 salaried and private-practice physicians and medical residents and interns (Michels 2004; Romano 2004). Although little evidence exists to explain why the PRN was not well supported by physicians, the loosening of managed care was likely a dominant factor. Increases in consumer choice and open access effectively reduced many of the physician complaints and problems that previously sustained interest in unionizing.

With the passage of the Affordable Care Act (ACA) in 2010 and the establishment of accountable care organizations (ACOs), along with a recent trend toward employing physicians, physician unions are resurfacing because physicians are increasingly becoming employees rather than self-employed (see chapter 2 for a discussion of this trend). In 2012, approximately 50 percent of physicians were already employed by large healthcare entities. As of 2022, approximately 75 percent of all physicians are employed, either by health systems or by other corporations (Dailey 2022). In addition, these numbers may have a generational component because younger physicians appear to be willing to give up income for a better quality of life, which means more regular working hours and less responsibility for patients after hours. The trend toward increased employment of physicians, particularly by insurers and private equity companies, opens up possibilities for physicians at the bargaining table.

HOUSE STAFF AND MEDICAL STUDENTS

In 1999, the NLRB ruled that house staff at Boston Medical Center were employees, not students. The impact of this ruling is that *house staff* (medical residents, interns, and fellows) in private hospitals are now legally entitled to bargain collectively. This determination was a reversal of a 1976 ruling for Cedars–Sinai Medical Center in Los Angeles in which house staff were classified as students (NLRB 1999; Yacht 2000). About 15 percent of house staff in the United States are unionized as of 2022 (Weiner 2022). Some are represented by the Committee of Interns and Residents (CIR, part of the SEIU) or the Union of American Physicians and Dentists, while others have created their own collective organizations. Opponents of house staff unionization suggest that union activity will create adversarial relationships between house staff and their instructors. For example, unions can negotiate resident promotions and fight against disciplinary actions and dismissal of poorly performing house staff. Other resistance is related to the potential for costly wage increases and the threat of strikes if agreement is not reached. However, proponents of unionized house staff argue that this movement has the potential to improve house staff compensation and working conditions—particularly the grueling schedules. Prounion supporters suggest that a union may improve quality and the patient experience by protecting diverse young doctors from bias, discrimination, and mistreatment by giving them a grievance process (Weiner 2022). In 2022, the Committee of Interns and Residents represented about 22,000 house staff in California, Florida, Massachusetts, New Jersey, New Mexico, New York, Vermont, and the District of Columbia (CIR 2022).

NURSES

Nurses are mainly employed in hospitals, where they represent the largest service and thus a significant labor cost. Nurses play a key role in patient care, providing care 24 hours a day, seven days a week. Historically, nurses have struggled with the conflict among their obligation to patients, their profession, and union representation. According to the American Nurses Association (ANA 2022), approximately 4.3 million registered nurses (RNs) work in the United States. Yet despite uneven salary levels across the profession and widespread, persistent discontent with working conditions, the majority of these nurses are not unionized. Approximately 20 percent of RNs and 10 percent of LPNs/LVNs are union members (Nurse. org 2022). In addition, because of a 2006 NLRB landmark ruling concerning supervisory status, many nurses are no longer eligible for union membership (refer back to exhibit 10.4).

Unlike physicians, whose workplace problems and needs are often addressed without the help of unions, nurses have a different experience. Nurse–management relationships are often strained. National nurse shortages and pressures on hospitals to trim labor costs have increased nursing workloads and hours and thus the potential for nurses to commit errors during long shifts. In the early twenty-first century in Massachusetts, work hours were a contentious nursing issue that led to work stoppages and strike threats during contract negotiations. Patient care issues appear to have motivated many nurses to unionize. Nurses often speak out in protest against cost-reducing measures that negatively affect patient care (Malvey 2010).

Today, nurse activism is ongoing and widespread. From informational pickets and protests to threats of strikes, nurses appear prepared to take action to ensure patient safety, adequate staffing, and better wages and benefits, especially after their experiences during the COVID-19 pandemic. Nurses report exhaustion after having worked overtime, and units remain understaffed because of unfilled positions. For example, in April 2022, 5,000 nurses affiliated with Stanford Health Care and the Lucile Packard Children's Hospital in California staged a one-week strike for better mental health support and wages, and staffing levels to match patient acuity (Mensich 2022). At Saint Vincent Hospital in Massachusetts, 800 nurses were on strike from March to December 2021—for 301 days. These nurses wanted to protect patients from unsafe understaffing conditions at the facility, which they had reported more than 600 times during the year leading up to the strike (Pietrewicz 2021). During the strike, the hospital hired about 100 nonunion nurses and cut back on the services it offered, including reducing inpatient capacity from 380 to 300 beds and discontinuing outpatient cardiac rehabilitation and wound care. In addition, the hospital eliminated ten inpatient psychiatric beds—half the usual capacity—as well as two of eight surgical units (Pietrewicz 2021). When the unionized nurses' contracts were ratified in

January 2022, the new agreement that would extend to December 2025 included wage increases, manageable workloads, and clear rules to govern workplace violence (Gooch 2022). Nurses remain committed to their patients and their profession, and this commitment often requires activism to be heard.

By joining and becoming active in unions, nurses are exercising their voice and using tools of unionism, including election petitions, contract negotiations, and work stoppages such as sick-outs and strikes. Nurses are capturing the public's attention and using their influence to obtain community support. However, aggressive activism has yielded mixed results. Nurses' efforts to influence patient safety and quality-of-care legislation have been successful at the state level but not at the federal level. For example, in 1999, California enacted the first law that established mandatory minimum nurse-to-patient staffing ratios. This law, in effect, requires hospitals to reduce nurse workloads and improve patient safety by guaranteeing minimum specific nurse-to-patient ratios for acute-care, acute-psychiatric, and specialty hospitals. It also serves as a framework for mandates in other states and at the federal level. Massachusetts followed suit in 2014 to enact minimum nurse-to-patient staffing ratios for the intensive care unit.

Similarly, nursing unions have achieved success at the state level with mandatory overtime legislation. State laws that prohibit or limit mandatory overtime have been enacted in 18 states: Alaska, California, Connecticut, Illinois, Maine, Maryland, Massachusetts, Minnesota, Missouri, New Hampshire, New Jersey, New York, Oregon, Pennsylvania, Rhode Island, Texas, Washington, and West Virginia (Deering 2022). However, corresponding federal legislation has not been enacted despite heavy union opposition to mandatory overtime. Nursing unions also failed to stop revisions to the Fair Labor Standards Act, which effectively exempts most nurses from overtime pay (as shown earlier in exhibit 10.4).

Nurses are among the most stressed workers. In a 2022 American Nurses Foundation survey of 12,894 of nurses in various settings across the United States, 65 percent of acute care nurses reported feeling burned out. Ninety percent of respondents reported that they had had or may have had direct exposure to a patient who had tested positive for COVID-19 (American Nurses Foundation 2022). The survey also reported the following:

◆ Two-thirds (66 percent) of the nurses had experienced bullying at work.

◆ Three-quarters (75 percent) reported feeling stress, exhaustion, or frustration.

◆ A large majority (89 percent) were working at organizations with severe staffing shortages.

◆ More than half (60 percent) of nurses aged 35 or younger had experienced severe stress, violence, or a traumatic event as a result of COVID-19.

◆ Less than one-fifth (19 percent) of nurses aged 35 or younger responded that they felt that their organizations cared about their well-being.

These and other surveys and reports show several tensions that may negatively affect the labor–management relationship and that may signal heightened labor activity in the future. Overall, nurses have become increasingly assertive in having their voices heard through unionization, and the emergence of large and powerful nursing unions indicates that nurses will continue to be heard in the workplace. Priority issues for nurses center on workload, mandatory overtime, staffing cuts, floating to unfamiliar areas, workplace safety, and benefits such as wages and pensions (Philbrick and Abelson 2021; Spetz and Given 2003). Chapter 13 contains a detailed discussion of the issues that can lead to stress and burnout and presents strategies for addressing employee well-being.

THE IMPACT OF THE INTERNET AND SOCIAL MEDIA

The NLRB has been very consistent in its support of employees using social media to address work-related issues and to share information with other employees, whether or not the employees are union members: On its website, the NLRB (2022) advises:

> Even if you are not in a union, federal law gives you the right to band together with coworkers to improve your lives at work—including joining together in cyberspace, as on Facebook. Using social media can be a form of "protected concerted" activity. You have the right to address work-related issues and share information about pay, benefits, and working conditions with coworkers on Facebook, YouTube, and other social media. But just individually griping about some aspect of work is not "concerted activity": what you say must have some relation to group action, or seek to initiate, induce, or prepare for group action, or bring a group complaint to the attention of management.

However, social media activity is not protected if an employee uses social media to say things about one's employer "that are egregiously offensive or knowingly and deliberately false, or if you publicly disparage your employer's products or services without relating your complaints to any labor controversy" (NLRB 2022).

The role of the internet in union organizing and solicitation campaigns and in collective bargaining and contract administration is receiving increasing attention. The internet has become an influential tool for unions, as it has for many other causes. Union websites offer current information on union activities and developments and promote membership benefits. Because unions must observe specific rules about visiting work premises to solicit during union recognition campaigns, the internet, social media, and videoconferencing tools offer unprecedented opportunities to communicate with employees without time and place restrictions.

With e-mail, social networking websites, podcasts, and blogs, unions utilize communication channels that can reach prospective members without alerting their employers.

Some websites, such as the CNA's, offer sample contracts for nurses to use in bargaining with employers. Similarly, employers have the ability to disseminate information via the internet. Furthermore, some websites and blogs are dedicated to sharing negative information about unions, such as the number of complaints of unfair labor practices filed against unions for coercive or intimidating behavior shown toward employees. Enhanced communication also means transparency, and social media offer both employers and unions unprecedented insight and information regarding each other's efforts.

MANAGEMENT GUIDELINES

Remember the following key points about labor relations:

1. *Whether a healthcare organization is union or nonunion, it should have a policy on unionism, and this policy should be communicated to current and prospective employees.* A positive labor–management relationship begins with the screening process. All prospective employees should be given information about the institution's position toward unions and its goals and strategies of fair and consistent dealings with unions. Employee handbooks and orientation represent other opportunities to communicate management's commitment to provide equitable treatment to all employees concerning wages, benefits, hours, and conditions of employment. Furthermore, management must also communicate that each employee is important and deserves respect, and that adequate funds and management time have been designated to maintain effective employee relations.

2. *Management not only must have effective policies and procedures for selection of new employees but also must ensure proper fit of personnel with specific jobs.* Job analyses, job descriptions, job evaluations, and fair wage and salary programs are essential in establishing a fair work environment. Management must not make promises that cannot be fulfilled; at the same time, it should strive to do whatever is possible to improve employee relations. Monitoring employee attitudes through confidential surveys is essential; otherwise, management is dependent on the union for communicating worker problems or changes in attitudes.

3. *Management must fulfill its roles and responsibilities to employees by providing necessary training, especially for frontline supervisors who are instrumental in determining how policies are implemented and in serving as liaisons between management and employees.* If supervisors are not properly trained, grievances are less likely to be settled quickly and are more likely to escalate into substantive formal disputes. Training is especially critical in healthcare settings

because of constant, rapid changes in technology, and workplace safety issues. Management's commitment to training must be consistent with fair and honest treatment of employees. Similarly, if management fails to establish objective performance policies and does not ensure that they are followed routinely, then the labor–management relationship will be adversely affected. Employees may perceive inequities and unfairness and experience problems of declining morale and productivity because rewards are not matched with performance.

4. *Inconsistent and unfair application of disciplinary policies and procedures can create unnecessary grievance problems.* At a minimum, the principle of just cause should guide the disciplinary process. When employees file grievances, they expect prompt attention to their requests. Delay in responding to complaints or ignoring them sends a clear signal to employees that management does not care about their problems and thus cannot be trusted. Furthermore, management's credibility with employees will then deteriorate, creating an imbalance that leads employees to perceive that the union's position is the more honest one.

5. *Each phase of the labor-relations process is interrelated and can affect the outcome of other phases.* For example, if the union is able to obtain representation through voluntary recognition, then the negotiations for a collective bargaining agreement will likely be less adversarial than if a representation election is called. Similarly, if the negotiations for a collective bargaining agreement are contentious, difficulties may occur in administering the contract. Thus, having a full understanding of each phase and its potential to enhance or impede the overall process of labor relations is essential.

Summary

Managing with organized labor is challenging. Even though unionism has been declining nationally for decades, the relatively unorganized healthcare workforce has continued to grow and has become a serious target for unions, particularly during the pandemic. Because union membership and election activity have increased in healthcare settings, managers must devote high-level attention to the application and maintenance of a positive labor relations program that integrates human resources functions and includes social media networking sites and other Internet-based communication tools.

The rise of claims of unfair labor practices and the increase in threats of strikes, walkouts, and other work stoppages suggest that the labor–management relationship in healthcare is strained. Pressure from the shrinking economy and healthcare reform have led to widespread layoffs and reimbursement cuts. The growth in the number of employed physicians could mean significantly more pressure on employers at the bargaining table and rising costs to meet physicians' demands. The dissatisfaction expressed by nurses and their willingness to organize cannot be ignored. Management must be prepared to deal with these challenges.

FOR DISCUSSION

1. Why should management have a policy on unionism? What purpose does such a policy serve?

2. Describe the three phases of the labor relations process. Why are all phases equally important?

3. What are some of the behaviors that may indicate to managers that organizing activities are occurring? Why?

4. How is union activity likely to be affected by changes in the health system? Which particular changes are likely to affect unionization and union–management relations?

5. Given the changing role of physicians as employees rather than independent contractors, is it desirable for them to organize and join unions? What are the potential positive and negative consequences of physicians joining unions?

EXPERIENTIAL EXERCISES

EXERCISE 1

Think of a healthcare facility in your community with which you are familiar. Then, based on your knowledge of the organization, respond to the following questions, and summarize your thoughts in a paper one to two pages long.

1. What are your impressions of nurses' satisfaction and the issues that concern them?

2. Are the nurses union members?

3. If they are union members, what factors led them to unionize?

4. If the nurses are not union members, do you think these nurses are likely or unlikely to join a labor union in the future? Why, or why not?

5. What would be the benefits of joining a union? What would be the risks?

EXERCISE 2

Unions and management have goals with which they concur and others where there may be disagreements. For example, in a healthcare setting, both unions and management would likely have an interest in the organization providing high-quality services. On the other hand, management may disagree with the union with respect to investment in employee development; the union may have an interest in seeing greater resources spent on training and development, while management may have an interest in reducing costs and perceive this investment as low priority. Consider the list of goal areas in the following table, and for each goal area, indicate the likely interests of union and management. After you complete the table, answer the following questions:

- Which goals are similar?
- Which goals have the potential for conflict?

Goal Areas	Union Goals	Management Goals
Survival		
Growth		
Profitability		
Competitiveness		
Recruitment and retention of employees		
Employee well-being		
Motivation of employees		
Flexibility		
Decision making		
Effective use of human resources		
Communication		

EXERCISE 3

This exercise is a team project. With guidance from your course instructor, identify a local healthcare organization and its senior human resources executive. This could be a vice president for human resources, director of human resources, or similar title. Arrange for your team to interview this individual, focusing on the theme of unions and unionization. Your goal is to learn about the organization's history with unions (it may or may not be unionized) and its beliefs and attitudes toward unions. Use the following questions as a guide. However, be sure to probe (tactfully) and engage in a productive discussion. After completing the interview, your team should write a summary, two to three pages long, of the interview.

Suggested questions:

1. Is this organization unionized? (If yes, then proceed with the questions that follow. If no, skip questions 2–7 and go on to questions 8–15.)

2. Which employee groups are unionized? What is the name of the union or unions?

3. What is the history of unionization and how long have unions been present in the organization? What factors in your opinion led to the success of a union organizing drive?

4. What impact have unions had on any aspect of the organization—positive or negative?

5. How would you describe the relationship between the union (or unions) and management?

6. Have there been particular difficulties in working with the union(s)?

7. What is the labor relations process like in the organization? Please describe the unionization campaign, collective bargaining, and contract administration.

8. Would you please describe successful and unsuccessful unionization efforts that have taken place in this organization?

9. What is the prevailing attitude toward unions among senior management?

10. What actions, if any, has the organization made to prevent unionization? This may include, for example, efforts to improve relationships with employees and ensure that working conditions and salaries are viewed positively by employees.

11. What are the major complaints or concerns among employees? You may focus on one group, such as nurses, or address the question more generally.

12. What mechanisms does the organization have to monitor employee morale and emerging concerns? Does the hospital have a formal grievance procedure? If so, is it effective?

13. Does the organization have a formal or informal employee forum to allow employees to voice their concerns? If so, how effective is it at gauging employee concerns?

14. How do employees react to the way that management responds to employee concerns? If possible, please provide an example of how an employee concern was addressed in a positive and productive manner.

15. How do you think the organization could address concerns more effectively?

REFERENCES

American Federation of Labor and Congress of Industrial Organizations (AFL–CIO). 2022. "About Us." Accessed August 12. https://aflcio.org/about.

American Nurses Association (ANA). 2022. "Nurses in the Workforce." Accessed October 27. www.nursingworld.org/practice-policy/workforce/.

American Nurses Foundation. 2022. *COVID-19 Two-Year Impact Assessment Survey: Younger Nurses Disproportionally Impacted by Pandemic Compared to Older Nurses; Intent to Leave and Staff Shortages Reach Critical Levels.* Pulse on the Nation's Nurses Survey Series. Published March 1. www.nursingworld.org/~492857/contentassets /872ebb13c63f44f6b11a1bd0c74907c9/covid-19-two-year-impact-assessment-written -report-final.pdf.

Anawis, M. A. 2002. "The Ethics of Physician Unionization: What Will Happen If Your Doctor Becomes a Teamster?" *DePaul Journal of Health Care Law* 6 (1): 83–110.

Bowling, D., B. D. Richman, and K. A. Schulman. 2022. "The Rise and Potential of Physician Unions." *JAMA* 328 (7): 617–18.

Committee of Interns and Residents (CIR). 2022. "About Us." Accessed October 17. www .cirseiu.org/who-we-are/.

Dailey, E. 2022. "Physician Employment Is Changing: What Does That Mean for the Industry?" Advisory Board. Published April 27. www.advisory.com/daily-briefing/2022/04 /27/physician-employment.

Deering, M. 2022. "Understanding Mandatory Overtime for Nurses: Which States Enforce Mandatory Overtime?" *Nurse Journal.* Updated August 29. https://nursejournal.org /resources/mandatory-overtime-for-nurses/.

Fisher, R., and W. Ury. 1981. "Getting to Yes—Negotiating an Agreement Without Giving In." In *Harvard Negotiation Project*, edited by B. Patton, 21–53. Boston: Houghton Mifflin.

Fottler, M. D., R. A. Johnson, K. J. McGlown, and E. W. Ford. 1999. "Attitudes of Organized Labor Officials Toward Health Care Issues: An Exploratory Survey of Alabama Labor Officials." *Health Care Management Review* 24 (2): 71–82.

Gooch, K. 2022. "Saint Vincent Nurses Ratify Contract, End Longest Nurses Strike in Massachusetts History." *Becker's Hospital Review*. Published January 4. www.beckers hospitalreview.com/hr/saint-vincent-nurses-ratify-contract-end-longest-nurses-strike -in-massachusetts-history.html

Harvard Law Review. 2004. "Labor Law: Department of Labor Increases Union Financial Reporting Requirements." *Harvard Law Review* 117 (5): 1734–40.

Kruger, K. F., and N. Metzger. 2002. *When Health Care Employees Strike: A Guide for Planning and Action*. San Francisco: Jossey-Bass.

Luepke, E. 1999. "White Coat, Blue Collar: Physician Unionization and Managed Care." *Annals of Health Law* 8: 275–98.

Maher, K. 2013. "Health-Care Unions Will Join Forces." *Wall Street Journal*, January 3.

Malvey, D. 2010. "Unionization in Healthcare: Background and Trends." *Journal of Healthcare Management* 55 (3): 154–57.

Mensich, H. 2022. "Stanford Nurses Ratify Deal, Ending Weeklong Strike." Healthcare Dive. Published May 3. www.healthcaredive.com/news/stanford-nurses-hospital -strike-ends-ratified-agreement/623043/.

Michels, T. J. 2004. "Three Doctors' Unions Form Partnership to Unite Resident, Salaried, and Private Practice Physicians." SEIU Press Release. www.seiu.org/media /pressreleases (content no longer available).

National Council of State Legislatures. 2022. "Right-to-Work Resources." Accessed October 27. www.ncsl.org/research/labor-and-employment/right-to-work-laws-and-bills .aspx.

National Labor Relations Board (NLRB). 2022. "About NLRB: Social Media." Accessed October 17. www.nlrb.gov/about-nlrb/rights-we-protect/the-law/employees/social-media.

———. 1999. Boston Medical Center Corp., 330 N.L.R.B. 152 (N.L.R.B-BD 1999).

National Nurses United (NNU). 2022a. "About National Nurses United." Accessed October 27. www.nationalnursesunited.org/about.

———. 2022b. "New York State Nurses Association and National Nurses United Announce Historic Affiliation to Grow National Movement of Nurses to Advance Interests of Patients, RNs." Press release, October 20. www.nationalnursesunited.org/press/new-york-state-nurses-association-and-national-nurses-united-announce-historic-affiliation.

National Union of Healthcare Workers (NUHW). 2022. "About NUHW." Accessed October 27. https://nuhw.org/about/.

NSI Nursing Solutions. 2022. *2022 National Healthcare Retention & RN Staffing Report*. Published March. www.nsinursingsolutions.com/Documents/Library/NSI_National_Health_Care_Retention_Report.pdf.

Nurse.org. 2022. "Should I Join a Nurses Union? Pros and Cons." Published January 20. https://nurse.org/articles/pros-and-cons-nursing-unions/.

Occupational Health and Safety Administration (OSHA). 2022. "Employer Responsibilities." Accessed August 7. www.osha.gov/as/opa/worker/employer-responsibility.html.

Pattani, A. 2021. "Health Workers Unions See Surge in Interest Amid Covid." Kaiser Health News. Published January 12. https://khn.org/news/article/health-workers-unions-see-surge-in-interest-amid-covid/.

Philbrick, I. P., and R. Abelson. 2021. "Health Care Unions Find a Voice in the Pandemic." *New York Times*. Published January 28. www.nytimes.com/2021/01/28/health/covid-health-workers-unions.html.

Pietrewicz, A. 2021. "Worcester's St. Vincent Hospital Says It Will Scale Back Services Due to Ongoing Nurses Strike." GBH. Published July 28. www.wgbh.org/news/local-news /2021/07/28/worcesters-st-vincent-hospital-says-it-will-scale-back-services-due-to -ongoing-nurses-strike.

Romano, M. 2004. "Labor Union Didn't Work." *Modern Healthcare* 34 (22): 32–34.

Scott, C., and A. Seers. 1996. "Determinants of Union Election Outcomes in the Non-Hospital Health Care Industry." *Journal of Labor Research* 17 (4): 701–15.

SEIU Local 521. 2022. "COVID-19: Protecting Our Healthcare Workers and Patients." Accessed October 27. www.seiu521.org/protecthealthcareworkers/.

Service Employees International Union (SEIU). 2022a. "Members." Accessed October 27. www.seiu.org/members.

———. 2022b. "What Type of Work Do SEIU Members Do?" Accessed October 27. www .seiu.org/cards/these-fast-facts-will-tell-you-how-were-organized.

Spetz, J., and R. Given. 2003. "The Future of the Nurse Shortage: Will Wage Increases Close the Gap?" *Health Affairs* 22 (6): 199–206.

Stickler, K. B. 1990. "Union Organizing Will Be Divisive and Costly." *Hospitals* 64 (13): 68–70.

US Bureau of Labor Statistics (BLS). 2022a. "Employment Projections: Fastest Growing Occupations; Table 1.3 Fastest Growing Occupations, 2021 and Projected 2031." Updated September 8. www.bls.gov/emp/tables/fastest-growing-occupations.htm.

———. 2022b. "Union Members—2021." News release, January 20. www.bls.gov/news .release/pdf/union2.pdf.

———. 2021. "A Look at Union Membership Rates Across Industries in 2020." Published February 25. www.bls.gov/opub/ted/2021/a-look-at-union-membership-rates-across -industries-in-2020.htm.

Von Bergen, J. M. 2006. "Testing Unions' Clout: Pivotal Cases: For Some Employees, Their Union Status Hinges on an NLRB Decision That Will Define the Word Supervisor." *Philadelphia Inquirer*, August 10.

Wallender, A., I. Kullgren, and A. Reed. 2022. "Health-Care Strike Risk Runs High as Hundreds of Labor Deals End." Bloomberg Law. Published January 24. https://news .bloomberglaw.com/daily-labor-report/health-care-strike-risk-runs-high-as-hundreds -of-labor-deals-end.

Weiner, S. 2022. "Thousands of Medical Residents Are Unionizing: Here's What That Means for Doctors, Hospitals, and the Patients They Serve." *AAMC News*. Published June 7. www.aamc.org/news-insights/thousands-medical-residents-are-unionizing -here-s-what-means-doctors-hospitals-and-patients-they.

Yacht, A. C. 2000. "Unionization of House Officers: The Experience at One Medical Center." *New England Journal of Medicine* 342 (6): 429–31.

CHAPTER 11

DIVERSITY, INCLUSION, AND BELONGING IN THE WORKPLACE

Carla Jackie Sampson, Bruce J. Fried, and Jeffrey Simms

LEARNING OBJECTIVES

After completing this chapter, you should be able to

➤ understand the definitions of and distinctions between diversity, inclusion, and belonging;

➤ recognize the factors associated with creating an inclusive environment;

➤ recognize the importance of diversity, inclusion, and belonging in healthcare;

➤ value the diversity of patients and coworkers; and

➤ develop strategies for recruiting and retaining a diverse team.

Jack is in a senior leadership position at a medium-sized, inpatient medical center in a rural area in the southeastern part of the United States. At the last board of trustees meeting, Jack mentioned that he has a few key administrative position vacancies in his department and that he is beginning the process of posting and hiring for these positions. After the meeting, the only Black trustee on the board approached Jack and asked for about 15 minutes of his time. Jack has always respected this trustee and graciously agreed to meet with him. During the brief conversation, the trustee commended Jack on his leadership of the hospital but wanted to share some opportunities for improvement with him. In a thoughtful manner, he posed two questions to Jack and asked him not to immediately respond, but to take some days to ponder the questions:

1. Have you ever thought about why a hospital this size has only one underrepresented minority trustee?
2. From a demographic perspective, do you believe that the clinical and administrative team of the hospital represents the patients you serve daily?

He thanked Jack for his time and said he looked forward to seeing him at the next board meeting.

This conversation with the trustee stayed with Jack for the next several days, and he decided to research the questions raised by the trustee. He discovered through board of trustee meeting minutes that there had been limited discussion around the topic of diversity and inclusion, and when he asked the president of the medical center about it, the response was, "We are proud of the fact that we've worked very hard to ensure that our board of trustees has a Black trustee."

Jack then asked the human resources team to pull a report of the full-time employees at the hospital, including information about race and ethnicity. Internally, Jack was struggling with the fact that he has been in leadership with this hospital for more than ten years and he hadn't given much thought to the racial and ethnic composition of the medical center's employees. The data revealed that 98 percent of the physicians employed by the hospital are white males; 95 percent of the nurses working at the hospital are white females; 100 percent of the administrative leadership team, including the president, are white males; and the chief nursing officer is a white female. As Jack continued to review the data, he noticed that 90 percent of the nursing assistants, custodians, and food service staff are either Black or Latine. Troubled by these findings, Jack raised many questions in his mind and considered if, how, and when to broach this issue with his colleagues and board members. He immediately began looking for resources related to diversity and inclusion in healthcare organizations.

INTRODUCTION

Patients who enter the US health system represent the diversity of the population in the country. By *diversity*, we refer not only to race and ethnicity but also to age, socioeconomic status, political perspective, and geographic location, to name just a few dimensions. A report published by the US Census Bureau (Vespa, Armstrong, and Medina 2020) examines the nation's demographic turning points and provides population projections from 2020 to 2060. The Census Bureau projects that by the year 2045, more than half the people living in the United States are likely to be part of a minoritized race or ethnic group. By 2028, the percentage of foreign-born US citizens and residents will be at the highest level since 1850, and immigration is projected to be the largest driver of population growth by 2030. In 2020, 50 percent of children in the United States were single-race non-Hispanic white, while by 2060, this percentage will decrease to only 36 percent. The population of people who are of two or more races will grow the fastest among all races/ethnicities. The United States will also face continuing aging of the population. By 2040, older adults (aged 65 and older) are projected to outnumber children—that is, those aged 17 or younger.

In 2012, the American College of Healthcare Executives, American Hospital Association, Association of American Medical Colleges, Catholic Health Association of the United States, and National Association of Public Hospitals and Health Systems announced a joint call to action for the elimination of healthcare disparities. "Addressing disparities is no longer just about morality, ethics and social justice: It is essential for performance excellence and improved community health," these groups declared (Institute for Diversity in Health Management and Health Research and Educational Trust 2012). In 2019, this call became more urgent, with many more national associations, states, and local authorities joining in. Racism was declared a public health emergency as the disproportionate impact of COVID-19 on minoritized communities added to the evidence about health disparities.

Diversity is critical to the quality of and access to health services, and not solely for concerns about equity and fairness in hiring and career advancement practices. Therefore, to improve health status and outcomes, health systems and providers need to be intentional regarding their efforts to improve diversity and inclusion.

PERSPECTIVES ON DIVERSITY

Views of diversity have evolved through the years, and each perspective has its own set of rationales. A classic review of these paradigms was presented by Thomas and Ely (1996), who noted, at the time, that there had been three stages of diversity. It is important to note that many, if not most, organizations show characteristics of all these paradigms.

As *diversity* first entered the lexicon of management, emphasis was initially placed on preventing discrimination against specific groups; Thomas and Ely (1996) refer to this perspective as the "discrimination-and-fairness paradigm." Among organizations using this paradigm, it is common to see mentoring and career development programs, particularly for women and people of color, as well as strategies aimed at recruiting and retaining under-represented groups. Many, if not most, organizations continue to engage in these types of activities and may also be pressured by legal obligations.

Whereas the "discrimination-and-fairness paradigm" sought to favor assimilation and discounting of differences among people, the second perspective on diversity celebrated differences. Referred to by Thomas and Ely (1996) as the "access-and-legitimacy paradigm," organizations with this perspective began to see value in differences and in fact saw differences as a way of reaching previously ignored consumer groups and new markets. From a marketing perspective, many organizations segmented their products and services for specific groups. Employing representatives of those groups would enable the organization to gain insight into the preferences of such groups and tap into new markets. This perspective provides the foundation of the "business case" for diversity. On the face of it, this perspective makes sense, but it also creates the risk of pigeonholing people into particular roles. For example, a typical refrain might be, "Let's ask Maria [a Latina] about what Latinos prefer in this product offering." Or in a healthcare setting, "Let's get input from Cynthia, who can give us the women's perspective on the best way to bring women with substance abuse problems into treatment." The access-and-legitimacy paradigm provides an important perspective, but it may be viewed as only using people to the extent that they are seen to represent the preferences of a demographic group, and thus may likely be perceived as exploitative. This paradigm also ignores within-group differences in culture and preferences, and *intersectionality* (which is explored in the next section) as well as personal preference and experiences.

Thomas and Ely (1996) articulate what they refer to as "The Emerging Paradigm: Connecting Diversity to Work Perspectives." In this third perspective, having a diverse workforce can enable an organization to obtain new perspectives and to learn—above and beyond the specific demographic insights of employees. As discussed later, all people view the world through a particular "frame," and what may be apparent to one person may not be so obvious to others (Thomas and Ely 1996). Diversity brings people together with distinct frames and adds to the collective ability to see things in more than one way. The point is that having people with contrasting views of the world will almost always bring in alternative ways of looking at situations. While it is often difficult to predict just where these unique insights will emerge, having a diverse group of employees increases the chances of the organization being able to innovate and learn.

Looking back, Ely and Thomas (2020) admit that just having a diverse workforce does not unlock the benefits of innovation or improved organizational outcomes. They contend that hiring for diversity does not necessarily redistribute power within the organization. That is, while many organizations have achieved numerical diversity goals, women and minorities have remained largely underrepresented at senior decision-making levels. Ely and Thomas (2020) call the emerging paradigm the "add diversity and stir" approach.

In retrospect, since we have not made the expected progress we need to add the concept of *inclusion*—that is, creating an environment where we not only "have the numbers" to demonstrate our commitment to diversity but also respond to the need to create and sustain an environment that welcomes and encourages the diverse perspectives brought by these employees. Creating such an environment also signals to potential employees that the organization is a good place to work for underrepresented groups, which in turn assists in recruitment and retention.

Finally, neglecting to create an inclusive environment risks our not being able to attract whole segments of highly trained employees who can provide healthcare or manage operations. In labor markets where many organizations have difficulty attracting talent—underrepresented or otherwise—hospitals and other healthcare organizations cannot afford to miss such opportunities. Failure to recruit the most talented employees may mean the difference between being a provider and employer of choice or losing ground to competitors (Adams 2022).

DEFINITION OF *DIVERSITY*

The definition of **diversity** continues to evolve. For years the word was used as a descriptor limited mostly to race and ethnicity, and to things that we can see readily. Today, the definition has become increasingly broader in scope and includes employee attributes such as age, gender, race, variations in work style, personal and social characteristics, and how these dimensions of diversity intersect to shape the individual—that is, **intersectionality**. In an article in *Becker's Hospital Review*, Jayanthi (2016) describes generational perspectives on the understanding of diversity. For baby boomers (people born from 1945 through 1964), the concept of diversity has always included gender, status, sexual orientation, and religion, and this viewpoint is reflective of their background and the era in which they came of age. Millennials (people born from 1982 through 2004) build on this foundational lens for diversity and expand it to include differing experiences, identities, and perspectives. "This newer, all-inclusive definition of diversity is perpetuated by the millennial generation who tend to define diversity in the context of experiences, opinions and thoughts, while older generations focus on religion, demographics and representation," Jayanthi (2016) points out. For example, millennials in the United States would describe their personal and professional networks as being more racially and ethnically inclusive than those of their parents, which has caused millennials to widen the diversity lens beyond the earlier, more limited descriptors. Exhibit 11.1 displays a sampling of the multiple dimensions of diversity. This list is not all-inclusive, but it provides a framework for viewing diversity beyond race and ethnicity. The ever-evolving definition of *diversity* continues to emphasize how important it is for individuals, businesses, and organizations—especially health systems and providers—to embrace diversity, inclusion, and belonging.

diversity
The collective and individual mixture of differences based on aspects of identity that include the qualities, experiences, and work styles that make individuals unique. Diversity attributes are broad and may refer to age, language, generation, class, country of origin, physical or cognitive abilities, race, religion, disability status, ethnicity, and many other attributes.

intersectionality
The aspects of social identity such as race, gender, gender identity, and class that overlap and create connected systems of privilege or discrimination.

Diversity includes, but is not limited to . . .		
Race	Sexual orientation	Age
Ethnicity	Political views	Economic class
Religion	Values	Geographic region
Gender	Physical abilities	Education
Gender identity	Country of origin	Language
Marital status	Cognitive styles	

inclusion
The manner and
extent to which
diverse members of
an organization are
accepted and are
fully integrated into
the organization.
Inclusion describes
the intentional and
ongoing activities that
foster engagement
with diversity and
diverse members,
and create supportive
cultures for all people,
particularly for those
who have been
minoritized.

belonging
The goal of diversity
and inclusion
initiatives so that
all views, beliefs,
and values are
acknowledged,
respected, and
integrated.

The idea of diversity has also expanded to include the critical role of **inclusion**. Diversity encompasses the many ways people differ, including gender, race, sexual identity, and age, while inclusion ensures the functionality of a diverse group or organization. In other words, inclusion goes beyond mere numbers to include an organizational culture that is accepting and encouraging of diverse perspectives. A culture of inclusion is necessary to achieve the benefits of gaining knowledge and valuable perspectives. However, inclusion requires consistent strategic engagement to create the environment that fully supports people who are not members of majority groups so that they feel that they belong. A sense of **belonging** is the goal of diversity and inclusion initiatives so that all views, beliefs, and values are acknowledged, respected, and integrated. These are critical ingredients to building a respectful, productive, and supportive work culture, and thus belonging is what employees perceive about inclusion. Exhibit 11.2 illustrates the interrelationship of diversity, inclusion, and belonging.

An inclusive environment provides processes that allow everyone to be a part of the network of information and opportunities in the organization. For example, an organization can increase the number of underrepresented minority employees through its recruitment approaches as developed by the human resources team. But if that same organization does not foster an environment of inclusion, it will struggle with both recruitment and retention. Inclusive organizations have cultures that encourage full participation of all members without fear of unwarranted criticism. An inclusive organization is best able to take advantage of the unique contributions of its members. Organizations attain reputations for how people are accepted and managed, and these views are often difficult to change. Recruitment and retention are addressed later in this chapter.

As implied in the opening vignette, the senior leader of his organization, Jack, is confronted with evidence that the leadership team, hospital staff, and board of trustees for this facility are not representative of the community that the organization is serving. As Jack develops a strategy for addressing this issue, it is crucial for him to communicate the *value* of diversity and to ensure that those on his team understand that they all have a part to play in improving the diversity of the organization and developing an inclusive culture. This is not just a task for the human resources team. It requires that leadership styles align

Belonging = The Goal
What employees feel

Diversity = The Data
Number of diverse people (however defined) in the organization

Inclusion = The Actions
Organizational choice to purse deliberate initiatives to create supportive culture

EXHIBIT 11.2
Interrelationship of Diversity, Inclusion, and Belonging

themselves with the processes that will promote a sustainably diverse and inclusive work environment that can lead to a sense of belonging throughout the organization. It is also critical that Jack and his colleagues appreciate the shortcomings of the organization and how they may affect its effectiveness and competitiveness.

In his attempt to communicate these messages to managers in the organization, Jack might consider a classic exercise adapted from the Teaching Tolerance Project, developed by the Southern Poverty Law Center, as a starting point. It is based on the premise that as individuals develop a broader understanding of diversity, they become better able to see opportunities for improvement, as described later in this chapter.

The Valuing Differences approach considers the individual's values, culture, background, and life experiences. Note that life experience includes voluntary and involuntary direct exposures. That experience plays an important developmental role that shapes, for example, problem-solving and leadership skills (Gafni 2021). As indicated in exhibit 11.3,

Country of origin	Values
Geographic region	Gender
History and ancestral heritage	Sexual orientation
Neighborhood where we grew up	Education
Neighborhood where we live now	Occupation
Family	Ethnicity
Religion	Culture and cultural traditions
Physical abilities	Socioeconomic class
Age	Language

EXHIBIT 11.3
Your Worldview: Some Factors That Make Up Your FRAME

Source: Adapted from Southern Poverty Law Center (2017).

EXHIBIT 11.4
Remembering and
Using Your FRAME

F Figure out the facts. Not just what is apparent to you, but all the facts. Seek more information, ask questions, and listen.

R Reflect on reality. Is it my reality or their reality? Am I looking at this through my FRAME or trying to see it through their FRAME?

A Acknowledge an open mind. Think about your expectations and whether they are appropriate. Are you making assumptions based on your FRAME?

M Maintain an open mind. Just because someone else's FRAME differs from yours does not make them wrong. What can you learn from them? What can they learn from you? What do you have in common?

E Expand your experiences. Explore, expose yourself, and encounter differences; develop cultural humility.

Source: Adapted from Southern Poverty Law Center (2017).

a wide variety of factors may affect the way we view the world. Then, using the FRAME acronym (see exhibit 11.4), the approach encourages people to apply what they know as their own frame to overcome biases and appreciate the perspectives of other people's frames.

DIVERSITY, INCLUSION, AND THE TEAM ENVIRONMENT

Many organizations have instituted formal processes and procedures to encourage a diverse workforce. Some of these efforts are driven by legal requirements to ensure that the organization is compliant with a variety of equal employment opportunity laws, such as the Civil Rights Act and the Americans with Disabilities Act as Amended. However, it is important to ensure that these efforts are not thwarted by a culture that does not foster the development and growth of all employees. For example, an organization might challenge itself with the following questions:

◆ Why are we successful in hiring underrepresented minority and lesbian, gay, bisexual, transgender, or queer/questioning (LGBTQ) employees but having difficulty retaining those same individuals?

◆ How is information about opportunities for advancement circulated in our organization?

◆ Is there a formal posting of advancement opportunities, or are they directed by leadership via private, informal networks?

◆ Are middle managers trained in managing a diverse workforce?

Teams are an integral part of healthcare organizations, and as their use continues to increase, the creation of an inclusive culture is particularly critical. Edmondson and Roloff (2009) address diversity and inclusion in reference to the concept of **psychological safety**. They make the powerful case that psychological safety is a key factor determining an organization's ability to achieve belonging for diverse employees. They define *psychological safety* as the "belief that one will not be rejected or humiliated in a particular setting or role, and describes a climate in which people feel free to express work-relevant thoughts and feelings" (Edmondson and Roloff 2009, 48). A lack of psychological safety in organizations often results in employees feeling marginalized because of their differing opinion, perspective, or experience. This marginalization in turn limits the input of people who could otherwise have made contributions informed by other perspectives, or, using the FRAME language, people who see the world through different frames. Thus, psychological safety is critical to belonging.

    Consider the case of Betty, the administrative manager for a large ambulatory care center that is affiliated with a large academic medical center. As a part of the strategic plan for the health system, senior leaders are proposing that all ambulatory care centers in the system will start offering patients weekend hours. As Betty reviews this proposal, she is concerned because her religious practices discourage working on the Sabbath. In a recent departmental leadership meeting, Betty's director expressed his thoughts about the need for everyone to make sacrifices regarding this strategic plan and his expectation that no one will express concerns about this expansion of service hours because it is a revenue issue. Betty in turn is given the implicit message that it is "not okay" to question this new policy because of the apparent strong support for it by senior management. Betty may be afraid of being ostracized by her colleagues, criticized for not being a "team player," or simply being told that the policy is rigid and that everyone needs to make sacrifices. In fact, there might be a solution to Betty's problem with that policy that can meet the objectives of the policy while also respecting her religious practices. However, without a climate of psychological safety, such options may never be explored because Betty is too afraid to speak up and thus leadership remains oblivious to the problem. The ambulatory care center where she works could benefit from hiring a chief diversity officer (see "Did You Know?" sidebar).

psychological safety
Belief that one will not be rejected or humiliated in a particular setting or role; also an atmosphere in which people feel free to express work-relevant thoughts and feelings.

CHANGING THE CULTURE

As noted earlier in this chapter, based on projected population growth, US minorities soon will no longer be in the minority. By 2045, more than half of all Americans will belong to a group other than non-Hispanic white, and by 2060, about 20 percent of the US population will be foreign born (Vespa, Armstrong, and Medina 2020). This continued growth in diverse populations means that hospital administrators, healthcare providers, health policymakers, and caregivers should be attentive to these demographic

> **? DID YOU KNOW?**
> **Chief Diversity Officer**
>
> According to a 2012 report written by the Institute for Diversity in Health Management and the Association of American Medical Colleges entitled *The Role of the Chief Diversity Officer in Academic Health Centers*, many companies and organizations have created a senior-level position known as the *chief diversity officer* to drive all strategic efforts around diversity and inclusion (Institute for Diversity in Health Management and Association of American Medical Colleges 2012). These efforts can be successful only to the extent that the chief diversity officer is empowered to effect culture change throughout all levels of the organization, with ready access to the necessary resources to support these initiatives.

shifts and their implications for many aspects of healthcare. Organizations that focus solely on attracting and retaining diverse teams limit the value that diversity adds to the organization. Companies must look closely at their organizational culture to identify how the diversity that has been created in the organization can be included and so support belonging and learning, development, and innovation as a consequence (see also the related Current Issue sidebar "Diversity Enhances Performance, but Should That Be the Rationale?").

Each organization is unique and faces its own challenges related to diversity and inclusion. However, there are key practices that should likely be used by all organizations to monitor their progress in improving diversity and assessing the impact of improved processes that may have been put in place. For example, organizations should regularly monitor organizational climate and employee demographic statistics to determine whether there are practices that impede improvements in diversity. Where discriminatory hiring and promotion practices are found, organizations must act quickly and with transparency to dismantle those processes and structures. Although biases may not be purposely discriminatory (and from a legal perspective, the motivation behind discriminatory practices may not be relevant), they may have a negative effect on diversity, inclusion, and belonging. It is important to note that discriminatory practices are not good business practices. For example, an organization that restricts its hiring to graduates of specific academic institutions or professional associations may limit its ability to recruit a diverse and *qualified* applicant pool.

There are a number of professional associations devoted to support of minority and special-interest professionals in the United States, including the following:

- National Association of Health Services Executives (www.nahse.org)

- National Association of Latino Healthcare Executives (www.nalhe.org)

- AHA Institute for Diversity and Health Equity (https://ifdhe.aha.org)

- Asian Healthcare Leaders Community, within the American College of Healthcare Executives (www.ache.org/membership/communities-forums-and-networks/asian-healthcare-leaders-community)

- LGBTQ Community, within the American College of Healthcare Executives (www.ache.org/membership/communities-forums-and-networks/lgbt-community)

Healthcare leaders must understand that the work to create an inclusive and supportive organizational culture should be regarded as a long journey. There may be resistance to these ideas and questions about the relevance of this work. Some people may think of diversity as being only about race and having representative numbers. However, at its core, the concept of diversity and inclusion is about equity. *Equity* is a deliberative process that demands

- consideration of the needs of diverse people *and* consideration of their histories of subjugation and deprivation;

- redistribution of resources;

- redistribution of power; and

- creation of opportunities.

CURRENT ISSUE
Diversity Enhances Performance, but Should That Be the Rationale?

McKinsey & Company, a global management consulting firm, found that organizations that exhibit gender and ethnic diversity are, respectively, 15 percent and 35 percent more likely to outperform those that don't (Parsi 2017). However, single-minded pursuit of diversity goals to enhance the organizational competencies for innovation, design thinking, or creative problem solving found in diverse organizations could exploit diverse employees (Ely and Thomas 2020). Organizations must create the conditions in which these employees can thrive and have processes and leaders that support diversity and inclusion.

Expressed this way, the resistance to diversity and inclusion initiatives that organizations often experience becomes clearer. Some individuals may not understand the need for change and be unwilling to engage with these efforts. Others may feel threatened by the potential to lose access to power or privileges. Leaders must approach this work with grace, humility, and curiosity: Mistakes will be made, and they present opportunities to listen, learn, and grow. Key components in the change management strategy are trust and transparency. Leaders must repeatedly communicate their vision for the new organization and the role each person in the organization will play to achieve success. This communication must be grounded in organizational values and share not only the expectations for interactions in the inclusive culture but also the behaviors that will not be tolerated. Only then can the shifts in prevailing attitudes and behaviors transform the organizational culture to be inclusive.

APPROACHES TO DEVELOPING AN INCLUSIVE ORGANIZATIONAL CULTURE

A key element in promoting a culture of inclusion and belonging is the role of the leader (Sampson 2022). Although there is a vast body of literature on leadership competencies, including models of desirable leader behaviors, leader traits, and servant leadership, only recently have *inclusive* leadership models and competencies begun to appear. At its essence, *inclusive leadership* means "cherishing the points of differences and treasuring the dissimilar perspectives and lenses each person brings" (Sampson 2022, 335; see also Bourke and Titus 2020). Inclusive leadership entails developing trust and creating room and space for people who may otherwise feel marginalized. Among the multiple and interrelated competencies around inclusive leadership are: developing interpersonal trust; developing human capital by providing support for diverse team members; seriously and honestly considering diverse perspectives and resolving conflicts, and being adaptive in one's work by taking into consideration the unique challenges of each situation (Tapia and Polonskaia 2020). These unique challenges involve understanding a complex array of interrelated factors including the organizational culture, existing power dynamics, traditions (both functional and dysfunctional), personalities, and—perhaps of greatest importance (and the most difficult)—employees' beliefs about the organization's commitment to inclusion and belonging. That is, leaders may have their own views of how their organization is perceived (often erroneously positive!) that may, unfortunately, be far from the truth. An inclusive approach to leadership is quite different from traditional approaches to leadership that have tended to apply rigid models to prescribe appropriate management behavior.

Moving an organization's culture to be more attuned to the needs and interests of diverse populations is not considered to be a necessarily expensive proposition (see "Did You Know?" sidebar for information on a helpful toolkit). However, such transformations require support from all parts of the organization and employees at all organizational levels.

In addition, nonemployees also have a role to play in effecting a new organizational culture. For example, physicians are generally not employees of a healthcare organization in the traditional sense. However, their attitudes and behaviors can have a profound impact on attitudes, communication, and encouragement of diverse perspectives. The progression toward creating a diverse and inclusive culture requires consistent support from all areas of the organization. All departments should be offered the opportunity to provide input and be involved in the transformation of the organization. Following are four basic steps that can be taken to begin this process:

1. ***Create a civility and respect value statement.*** Developing a statement that emphasizes commitment to civility and respect is a simple step that will have a powerful impact on the organization. The organization should provide an opportunity for all stakeholders to contribute to the preparation of this statement. Allowing this level of input is integral to the impact of this statement. After the value statement has been finalized, it should be posted in common areas throughout the building, as well as on the website.

2. ***Develop a diversity and inclusion council.*** Providing an opportunity for employees to be involved in the strategic direction of the organization in regard to diversity and inclusion is important, and creating a diversity and inclusion council or steering committee has proven to be a successful best practice. The council should have a direct report to the senior leadership team and provide direction regarding diversity initiatives.

3. ***Create employee resource groups.*** Employee resource groups (ERGs) provide underrepresented employees or employees with shared interests a safe space to share their experiences within the organization. ERGs can help build an inclusive culture and boost employee engagement as well as belonging. Like diversity and inclusion councils, ERGs should have the backing of senior leadership to be effective. However, ERG membership is voluntary, and the primary purpose should be to provide a support system for employees.

4. ***Offer educational workshops on unconscious biases and training on diversity and inclusion.*** Organizations that have invested in providing opportunities for employees and other stakeholders to participate in diversity and inclusion training or workshops are creating a culture that embraces diversity and inclusion. National organizations that provide training and facilitate diversity workshops include the Office of Equity, Diversity, and Inclusion at the National Institutes of Health (www.edi.nih.gov/training); the National Coalition Building Institute (http://ncbi.org); and the National Diversity Council (www.nationaldiversitycouncil.org).

The AHA Institute for Diversity and Health Equity has developed *Equity of Care: A Toolkit for Eliminating Health Care Disparities* (AHA 2015). This initiative encourages organizations to reduce disparities through four steps: (1) collect relevant data on race, ethnicity, and language preferences; (2) increase cultural competency training; (3) increase diversity in leadership and governance; and (4) strengthen community partnerships (AHA Institute for Diversity and Health Equity 2022). More than 1,700 hospitals and health systems have joined the AHA's #123forEquity pledge campaign (AHA Institute for Diversity and Health Equity 2022).

Organizational transformations are difficult and time-consuming. Cultures are not created overnight, and changing a culture is not a trivial exercise. Several prominent health organizations, however, have made significant progress in representing best practice in diversity and inclusion initiatives. A summary of three selected initiatives follows:

1. *Mayo Clinic: Committed to continuous progress.* Providing culturally appropriate care requires the organization to reflect the population that it serves. At Mayo Clinic, initiatives are set to improve inclusiveness and participation throughout the organization and are aligned to the organization's overall strategic goals. Leaders are working to increase the number of female and underrepresented leaders, staff, and students. There are several Mayo Employee Resource Groups (MERGS) sponsored by senior executives. MERGs include spaces for employees who identify as African descendant, Filipino, LGBTI, veteran, Iranian, Indian, and "eMERGing leaders," to name just a few (Mayo Clinic 2022).

2. *Robert Wood Johnson University Hospital: Mirroring the multicultural community of New Brunswick, New Jersey, for leadership and governance.* Robert Wood Johnson created a data-driven plan for diversity and inclusion in 2012. Initiatives addressed enhancing diversity of the board and bringing diversity to leadership by establishing a mentoring program for employees with senior leaders and employee resource groups, conducting an analysis of the succession planning program, and linking executive compensation to diversity goals. Within three years, the proportion of minorities on the leadership team had increased from 4 percent to 32 percent (Livingston 2018).

3. ***Henry Ford Health System: Translating workforce DEI to better patient care.*** Evidenced by its diverse senior leadership team and board of trustees, Henry Ford Health System (HFHS) has DEI initiatives include hiring practices that prioritize the local community; training opportunities to recognize unconscious bias and improve cross-cultural communication; and building health system policies to prioritize equity. HFHS links engagement and inclusion via ERGs for shared interests along several dimensions of diversity (Henry Ford Health 2022).

SUMMARY

In a society growing increasingly diverse, the need to attract and retain a workforce that reflects this diversity is a continuing challenge. It is imperative to understand that diversity goals are not simply important for purposes of fairness and social justice, although these are certainly important ideals. Diversity and inclusion make sense for purposes of organizational effectiveness, quality, and competitiveness. A diverse workforce helps us better understand the needs of populations and ultimately address population health concerns. A diverse workforce also brings into the organization novel ideas and new ways of looking at problems and challenges. However, efforts to attract and retain diverse employees fail when their views, beliefs, and values are othered or they sense that they are merely tolerated. For these reasons, it is incumbent on all healthcare leaders to build inclusive and supportive work cultures that reflect principles of diversity, inclusion, and belonging.

FOR DISCUSSION

1. Select two dimensions of diversity. Why are they important elements for improving the quality of care in a healthcare organization?

2. How can the presence of an inclusive culture improve recruitment and retention efforts?

3. How does one distinguish between legal requirements for nondiscrimination, as discussed in chapter 3, and inclusion and belonging?

4. In trying to assess a healthcare organization's culture regarding diversity, inclusion, and belonging, what would you or another prospective employee look for as evidence of an inclusive culture?

5. What are some of the competencies required of an inclusive leader?

6. Consider an organization in which you have worked. How would you describe that organization's culture regarding diversity, inclusion, and belonging? What evidence would you bring to bear in making this assessment?

EXPERIENTIAL EXERCISES

EXERCISE 1

As described in this chapter, some organizations have chief diversity officers, whose job is to monitor and improve the diversity and inclusive character of the organization. In other organizations, this role may be carried out elsewhere in the organization, such as the human resources department. For this exercise, identify that individual in a particular healthcare organization who has responsibility for improving its diversity and inclusiveness. Conduct an interview with this person to identify the major diversity and inclusion issues facing the organization. Suggested questions include the following:

- Does the workforce in this organization resemble the patients being served in terms of race, ethnicity, language, religion, and other dimensions of diversity?
- Does the organization monitor employee attitudes about inclusion? If so, how is this done? Can you tell me of a time when information about employee attitudes led to an intervention or organizational change?
- Does the organization provide training on managing in a diverse environment and dealing with diverse groups of patients? If so, how is the impact of that training measured? Has it proven to be effective?
- Are underrepresented minorities present throughout the organizational hierarchy? Is there a system for assertively supporting the professional development and promotion of members of minority groups?
- Does this organization routinely collect information about turnover by demographic group or other dimensions of diversity? If so, have significant patterns emerged in the likelihood of members of certain groups voluntarily leaving the organization?
- What do you see as the major challenges in creating a diverse and inclusive culture in this organization? What steps has the organization taken to meet these challenges, and how would you assess their level of success?

EXERCISE 2

Conduct a survey of your class member colleagues to discover their definitions of an inclusive organization. Ask respondents to also provide examples or indicators of both a highly inclusive and a less inclusive organization.

Adams, B. 2022. "Make Your Employer Brand Stand Out in the Talent Marketplace." *Harvard Business Review*. Published February 8. https://hbr.org/2022/02/make-your -employer-brand-stand-out-in-the-talent-marketplace.

REFERENCES

AHA Institute for Diversity and Health Equity. 2022. "American Hospital Association #123forEquity Campaign to Eliminate Health Care Disparities." Accessed November 6. https://ifdhe.aha.org/123forequity.

American Hospital Association (AHA). 2015. *Equity of Care: A Toolkit for Eliminating Health Care Disparities*. Published January. www.hpoe.org/Reports-HPOE/equity-of-care -toolkit.pdf.

Bourke, J., and A. Titus. 2020. "The Key to Inclusive Leadership." *Harvard Business Review*. Published March 6. https://hbr.org/2020/03/the-key-to-inclusive-leadership.

Edmondson, A., and K. Roloff. 2009. "Diversity Through Psychological Safety." *Rotman Magazine*, September, 47–51.

Ely, R. J., and D. A. Thomas. 2020. "Getting Serious About Diversity: Enough Already with the Business Case." *Harvard Business Review*. Published November. https:// hbr.org/2020/11/getting-serious-about-diversity-enough-already-with-the-business -case.

Gafni, N. 2021. "Do Your DE&I Efforts Consider Age, Class, and Lived Experience?" *Harvard Business Review*. Published July 1. https://hbr.org/2021/07/do-your-dei-efforts -consider-age-class-and-lived-experience.

Henry Ford Health. 2020. "Henry Ford's Accomplishments, Commitment to Diversity Recognized Again in National Rankings." Published May 13. www.henryford.com/news /2020/05/diversity-accomplishments-recognized-once-again-in-national-rankings.

Institute for Diversity in Health Management and Association of American Medical Colleges. 2012. *The Role of the Chief Diversity Officer in Academic Health Centers*. Published November. https://store.aamc.org/downloadable/download/sample/sample _id/222/.

Institute for Diversity in Health Management and Health Research and Educational Trust. 2012. *Diversity and Disparities: A Benchmark Study of U.S. Hospitals*. Published June. www.hpoe.org/diversity-disparities.

Jayanthi, A. 2016. "The New Look of Diversity in Healthcare: Where We Are and Where We're Headed." *Becker's Hospital Review*. Updated July 22. www.beckershospitalreview.com/hospital-management-administration/the-new-look-of-diversity-in-healthcare-where-we-are-and-where-we-re-headed.html.

Livingston, S. 2018. "Fostering Diversity for the Next Generation of Healthcare Leaders." *Modern Healthcare*. Published October 13. www.modernhealthcare.com/article/20181013/NEWS/181019970/fostering-diversity-for-the-next-generation-of-healthcare-leaders.

Mayo Clinic. 2022. "Mayo Employee Resource Groups (MERGs)." Published October 20. www.mayoclinic.org/equity-inclusion-diversity/our-employees/mergs.

Parsi, N. 2017. "Workplace Diversity and Inclusion Gets Innovative." *HR Magazine*, February, 39–45.

Sampson, C. J. 2022. "Inclusive Leadership." In *Leadership in Healthcare: Essential Values and Skills*, 4th ed., edited by C. Dye, 331–46. Chicago: Health Administration Press.

Southern Poverty Law Center. 2017. "Valuing Differences: Discovering your FRAME." Accessed May 6. www.tolerance.org/sites/default/files/general/tt_valuing_differences%5b1%5d. pdf (content no longer available).

Tapia, A., and A. Polonskaia. 2020. *The 5 Disciplines of Inclusive Leaders: Unleashing the Power of All of Us*. Oakland, CA: Berrett-Koehler Publishers.

Thomas, D. A., and R. J. Ely. 1996. "Making Differences Matter: A New Paradigm for Managing Diversity." *Harvard Business Review* 74 (5): 79–90.

Vespa, J., D. M. Armstrong, and L. Medina. 2020. *Demographic Turning Points for the United States: Population Projections for 2020 to 2060*. Report no. P25-1144. Washington, DC: US Department of Commerce, Economics and Statistics Administration, US Census Bureau. Revised February. www.census.gov/content/dam/Census/library/publications/2020/demo/p25-1144.pdf.

CHAPTER 12

APPLYING QUALITY IMPROVEMENT AND IMPLEMENTATION SCIENCE IN HUMAN RESOURCES PRACTICES

Hillary K. Hecht and Bruce J. Fried

After completing this chapter, you should be able to

➤ describe the role of quality improvement in healthcare;

➤ name quality improvement methods, including key features and tools;

➤ describe the role of implementation science in healthcare;

➤ name implementation science methods, including key frameworks; and

➤ discuss human resources management considerations for implementing, staffing, and sustaining a quality improvement effort.

Vignette

The Bright Eyes Clinic has recently hired Imani into a leadership role as its third oph-thalmology clinic manager in the past four years. In her first week, she speaks privately with multiple staff members in the clinic, who share some concerns about managing patient scheduling.

Technician Concerns: "Listen, Imani, it's the fault of the doctors," says a frus-trated technician. "We are running an ophthalmology clinic in a large academic medical center, and the clinicians treat clinic staff as if it's their own private practice. Each doctor wants things done one particular way, different from the other doctors, and at any one time, each of us technicians is prepping patients for three or four different doctors with opposite preferences. All the doctors insist on scheduling their patients for eight in the morning, so of course the patients are upset when they're not seen until ten or eleven o'clock. Where are the schedulers? Don't they realize that the way they schedule patients is a recipe for patient frustration, or patients leaving the clinic without being seen? Oh, and ask me and I'll tell you how many times a doctor doesn't even show up in the clinic until nine o'clock."

Physician Concerns: Imani introduces some of these concerns in her conversation with a physician later that week. "Is that what the technicians are saying about us?" the physician responds. "Listen, we deal with some pretty complex cases, and if this means that patients have to wait a bit longer, then the patient business associates should be aware of this and communicate better with patients in the waiting room. That's their job, right? And you know, we also have a residency program, and training residents also takes time. We all have particular specialties, so of course we each have our own preferences for how patients are prepped. I know the technicians would like it if all the patients were the same so they could standardize their work, but this isn't clinically appropriate for our patients' needs. We all want to best support patients with what they need from their visits here, and we have different perspectives on patients' highest priorities. I just don't know how to make scheduling easier for our patients and staff, and to help our technicians' jobs be clearer while still having our patients ready for the care they need when we join them in the exam rooms."

Staff Concerns: Imani talks with administrative staff members, one of whom says, "As a patient business associate, it's my job to register patients, deal with insurance and payment issues, answer phones, and calm down unhappy and frustrated patients, doctors, and technicians. My job is constant multitasking and emotional management, and because I've been here for eight years, I know how this clinic functions—or doesn't function. I do my best to communicate with patients and all clinic staff. I try to treat our patients with respect and dignity, which is hard when I am almost constantly respond-ing to some urgent crisis. On the positive side, I will say that everyone who works here is committed to our patients and continuing our tradition of providing high-quality care. There are some changes I am ready to make, but for some parts of this job, I'm not even sure what change would make it better or easier."

    Imani's Response: From her experience and education, Imani realizes that she is dealing with a number of process issues, and she has decided to implement a quality improvement initiative to review and change clinic processes toward an ultimate *goal of improving patient and staff satisfaction*. Her first tasks are to create a project plan, then to communicate her approach to everyone in the clinic. Next, Imani will need to determine the composition of the quality improvement team and recruit her teammates to join her efforts, a job that she will find particularly challenging given the clinic's difficult history and interpersonal frustrations.

INTRODUCTION

This chapter builds on previous chapters in this text, which describe the link between effective strategic human resources (HR) management practices and desirable organizational outcomes, including quality, efficiency, profitability, productivity, and growth. This chapter focuses on how HR practices can support quality improvement (QI) initiatives, and how healthcare organizations can use implementation science (IS) methods to achieve quality goals. Healthcare organizations pursuing QI strategies must critically review and modify their HR practices to ensure that HR practices support quality goals.

The QI model is built on twin pillars of (1) information and measurement, and (2) stakeholder engagement. These pillars include a workforce focused on defining and addressing quality problems, including the process of designing, implementing, and evaluating workflow changes. As the QI movement has progressed, much attention has been given to the accuracy and precision of measurement, yet the human participant side of QI has not received as much attention as the measurement side.

This chapter offers guidance to recruit and train a workforce to engage successfully in QI activities, where workplace culture can effectively encourage staff to sustain meaningful organizational changes. Among the goals of this chapter is to help QI projects move toward parity between measurement and human engagement foci.

WHAT IS QUALITY IMPROVEMENT (QI)?

Within clinical practice, QI is concerned with better patient outcomes and achieving a specific outcome or threshold that balances being affordable, accurate, and easy. This approach allows QI to focus locally and quickly on how best to achieve the agreed-on quality in a specific setting.

Imagine a three-circle Venn diagram balancing overlapping characteristics of affordable, accurate, and easy, which Panepinto (2013) has illustrated as "cheap," "good," and "fast." The center, mutually overlapping part of the diagram is not possible to achieve in a QI project! Quality improvement can choose up to two priorities, whereby *affordable and accurate* would take a long time to achieve; *affordable and easy* would make fewer improvements to the quality of care; and *easy and accurate* would cost more resources to achieve. QI projects will choose among these three realistic priorities based on resources and goals.

 **KEY POINT**

> Quality improvement (QI) methods and strategies cannot meet their full potential without attending to the human workforce factors that make them possible.

What Is Implementation Science (IS)?

Once we know from scientific methods which things work and *how* they work, implementation science helps us measure out how to allow those things to happen in the real world. IS offers a menu of theories and frameworks to help one understand the focused effort it takes to translate evidence-based practices into clinical settings where care is provided (Bauer et al. 2015). Yet, as reported by Bauer and colleagues (2015), on average, only half of all best practices get implemented into clinical practice. For those that do, it takes on average 17 years for evidence-based practices to be incorporated into regular, routine healthcare practice!

Healthcare organizations vary in their strategies and objectives, but it is safe to say that all healthcare organizations are concerned with the quality of care they provide to their patients and with the safety of their patients. Both quality and safety affect patient care, costs to patients and the system, and patient and employee satisfaction. These dimensions create incentives for organizations to evolve and make changes toward providing higher-quality care. As a result, measuring and improving quality are imperative processes for healthcare providers, whether they are individual physicians, group practices, hospitals, or other organizations that provide health services. In this chapter, we discuss *quality improvement* and *implementation science* as two related approaches to address some of the measurable outcomes that health organizations care most about.

Why Do Healthcare Organizations Care About Quality?

Three key reasons that healthcare organizations care about quality are the following:

1. *Moral and ethical obligation.* Healthcare organizations provide high-quality services, products, and procedures to their patients because it is the right thing to do, morally obligatory. Most healthcare organizations employ people from multiple disciplines and training, many of which have a *professional code of ethics.* These codes can help guide professionals in making decisions in their field and staying true to the underlying goals of their field's purpose. (See the related Case Example sidebar.) Healthcare organizations may have a shared vision, values, or mission statement that brings together their goals and aligns all disciplines toward a collaborative mission. In these statements, an organization may lay out aspirational goals about the quality of care it intends to provide and how it might do so.

2. *Patient health outcomes and patient safety.* Healthcare organizations exist to provide healthcare to patients. In doing so, care goals may be established, and keeping patients safe is a big part of working toward those health goals. Striving for high-quality care can help patients reach their health goals, and

also not create new health concerns, illnesses, or injuries during the process of receiving care.

3. *Healthcare organizations' financial incentives.* One way care providers have ensured their financial stability has been by increasing the volume of services that they provide. As discussed in chapter 8, there has been a shift from payments based on *volume* to payments based on *value.* Focusing on quality of care helps providers center efficient, high-value care toward patients' goals. The prevalence of accountable care organizations (ACOs) as a payment structure is one of many efforts to prevent unnecessary care and reduce medical errors (Centers for Medicare & Medicaid Services [CMS] 2022). ACOs are moving in the direction of explicitly rewarding care quality, and commercial payers are encouraging healthcare organizations to participate in QI efforts (Watkins 2014). This focus on high-quality, lower-cost care comes with enticing financial incentives for providers and healthcare organizations.

Beyond organizations' moral obligation to provide high-quality health services, the financial position of a healthcare organization is increasingly affected by quality and patient safety. For example, the Physician Quality Reporting System applies a "negative payment adjustment" to physicians and members of group practices who did not provide sufficient information on their quality measures for services covered under Medicare Part B. Looking forward, attentiveness to quality and value is driving the evolution of healthcare models and arguments for healthcare spending in the United States.

DEFINING QUALITY

At the most basic level, *quality* refers to ensuring that every patient receives the appropriate care at the appropriate time. The Institute of Medicine (IOM; since 2015 known as the National Academy of Medicine), a longtime leader in patient safety and quality, provides a more formal definition, defining **quality** as "the degree to which health services for individuals and populations increase the likelihood of desired health outcomes and are consistent with current professional knowledge" (IOM 1990, 5). Still, the practical meaning of *quality* varies, depending on one's perspective, role, and personal values. For example, a patient with diabetes may prioritize creating food habits that are simple and stress-free to implement in their busy workdays, with some tolerance for diabetic symptoms in exchange for less time spent monitoring their disease. Their primary care provider might prioritize their A1C indicator measure as staying consistently below a designated threshold with regular measurement. The clinic administrator may be most concerned with preventing emergency visits and how accurately insurance claims are filed during regularly scheduled office visits. Each of these quality outcomes may align and all support the same behaviors toward the

quality
The degree to which health services for individuals and populations increase the likelihood of desired health outcomes and are consistent with current professional knowledge.

> ### ✳ CASE EXAMPLE
>
> Consider the healthcare field of social work in the United States. The National Association of Social Workers (NASW) has a disciplinary code of ethics (which you can read in full online; see NASW 2022). This code is based on values of service, social justice, dignity and worth of the person, importance of human relationships, integrity, and competence. When studying to join their profession, social workers practice using this code of ethics to provide care and services to their clients, and they learn how to apply this code to interacting with their colleagues and the broader community. To work as a licensed social worker, practitioners are asked to professionally abide by this code of ethics and use it to guide their decision making. In healthcare organizations, social workers may find that their disciplinary code of ethics aligns with and sometimes conflicts with the mission or values statements made by their employer. In hospital settings, ethics committees are typically available to provide counsel for difficult decision making when it is unclear how to move forward and implement an ethical decision-making process, or when providers from different disciplines come to different conclusions about the course of patient care.

same goals, or they may take different approaches or prioritize different measurable goals. Overall, *quality* is often an inherent goal in the mission of healthcare organizations and is the responsibility of everyone in the healthcare workforce.

The concept of quality naturally extends into the realm of patient safety. **Patient safety** covers a wide array of issues and may be summarized as "freedom from accidental or preventable injuries produced by medical care" (Agency for Healthcare Research and Quality [AHRQ] 2022). Because accidents can result in errors that derail healthcare improvement efforts, the National Academy of Medicine considers patient safety "indistinguishable from the delivery of quality health care" (IOM 2004).

Avedis Donabedian is often identified as the individual responsible for developing a systematic framework for understanding and addressing quality in healthcare (Donabedian 1980). The Donabedian model defines *quality* on the basis of three dimensions: structure, process, and outcome. *Structure* refers to "the relatively stable characteristics of the providers of care, of the tools and resources they have at their disposal, and of the physical and organizational settings in which they work" (Donabedian 1980, 81). Elements of structure include such things as hospitals, the healthcare workforce, financial resources, and medical equipment. *Process* refers to the "set of activities that go on within or between practitioners and patients" (Donabedian 1980, 80), or the processes involved in providing healthcare services. Finally, *outcome* refers to "a change in a patient's current and future health status

patient safety
Freedom from accidental, erroneous, or preventable injuries and adverse effects produced by medical care.

that can be attributed to antecedent healthcare" (Donabedian 1980, 83). Outcomes are the end result of care and may be measured at the individual, organizational, or population level.

Donabedian also addresses the relationships among the three dimensions of quality. To some degree, this relationship is linear: Structure determines process, which in turn affects outcomes. However, these relationships are more complex. Outcomes, for example, often depend on factors outside the control of the healthcare system. Indeed, although quality may be assessed purely in terms of patient outcomes, from a practical standpoint, an organization wishing to improve patient outcomes must trace quality back to fundamental dimensions of process and structure. The approach of the quality improvement movement seeks to improve quality by first understanding the complexity of any single measure of quality and its antecedents. Put another way, a key goal of any quality improvement effort is to understand the root causes of deficiencies in quality.

QUALITY AND QUALITY IMPROVEMENT

In the landmark 2001 report *Crossing the Quality Chasm*, the IOM identified six key characteristics of a high-quality healthcare system (IOM 2001):

1. It is *safe*—for everyone, all the time.

2. It is *effective*—it provides the best care, based on evidence, to improve outcomes.

3. It is *patient centered*—it maintains respect for patient values, preferences, and autonomy.

4. It is *timely*—patients are not subjected to long waits.

5. It is *efficient*—patients receive high value for money spent.

6. It is *equitable*—patients are treated fairly, without discrimination.

Failure in one or more of these areas threatens care quality, limits potential benefits to patients, and can result in harm or death.

The current approach to quality has evolved from an earlier quality assurance model, which addressed quality from a largely reactive perspective and often was viewed as policing and punitive in nature. Where errors or defects appeared, the central question from quality assurance was typically associated with blame: "Whose fault was this?" QI, by contrast, addresses quality issues from both prospective and retrospective perspectives, with the emphasis on systems and processes rather than malicious intent. A central question in the QI era is "How can we improve our processes—the system—to improve outcomes of value to our organization?" Rather than emphasizing the individual's role in a quality issue, attention is given to the system and the intended goals. Much of the QI movement is driven by an understanding that "every system is perfectly designed to get the results it gets" (Batalden and Davidoff 2007a, 1060).

QI extends beyond the quality assurance approach of finding errors to include understanding and improving processes in which errors can occur. QI distinguishes itself from quality assurance by its systems approach of responding to factors in the environment, processes, and culture that led to the problem at hand. It is well understood that the healthcare environment is dynamic, and healthcare organizations encounter new challenges on a continuous basis. Fittingly, QI is a continuous process that may include multiple rapid cycles of ongoing improvement. Thus, QI as used in healthcare is often referred to more specifically as *continuous quality improvement* (CQI). In these ways, QI is a harm reduction tool whereby collaborative design helps build processes in which it is harder to make errors, or easier to catch and respond to errors that do occur in patient care delivery. A distinguishing feature of QI today is that it generally includes the use of one of several formal methodologies to achieve specified organizational goals.

Across all QI methods, several key themes have emerged, notably the role of data and evidence in analyzing problems and then designing and testing changes. Of equal focus is the role of people and teams that collaborate in designing, testing, and analyzing changes toward a shared quality goal. QI efforts rely on people in many types of roles and can be driven by frontline employees' or management's goals. Frontline employees work most closely with a problem, are often directly affected by this problem in their day-to-day work, and may have a deep understanding about the detailed circumstances in which the problem is occurring. Managerial and administrative employees may have leadership and budgetary authority to commit appropriate resources to responding to the problem. A rich understanding of a quality problem may be gained by collaboration among employees at multiple organizational levels and disciplines. This analysis can then lead to timely and accurate analysis of the quality issue, development of improvement strategies, and measurement of their impact. Multidisciplinary, multilevel teams are essential to fully understanding a problem and navigating toward an intended outcome.

KEY QUALITY ISSUES

The first step in QI typically involves analyzing the situation and diagnosing specific problems to address. We can measure quality through each of six characteristics identified in the previous section (*safe, effective, patient-centered, timely, efficient,* and *equitable*). When developing measures of these quality characteristics, or domains, we categorize whether we are measuring (1) structural quality, (2) process quality, or (3) outcomes. *Structural quality* refers to the resources and administration delegated to support high-quality care, which can be adjusted by adding resources, changing types of resources available, and modifying the qualifications or volume of administrative support to a QI initiative (Donabedian

1980). *Process quality* includes culture and cooperation—that is, the steps that members of an organization take to get something done (Kunkel, Rosenqvist, and Westerling 2007). Processes may be formally or informally inscribed in organizational culture and may range from a simple set of steps to complex decision trees with many steps, supplies, and people involved. *Outcome quality* refers to goal achievement and how closely the achieved result matches the intended results (Donabedian 1980).

When we measure within the domain of *effectiveness* (corresponding to the second of the six characteristics listed in the previous paragraph), we can parse distinct types of ineffectiveness related to utilization of healthcare services, each of which impacts patient safety and care quality. Utilization challenges may include overuse, underuse, and misuse of care provided. Each of these types of problems has distinct causes and implications.

Overuse refers to situations in which a patient receives a drug or treatment without medical justification. Examples of overuse include treating people with antibiotics for simple infections or failing to follow effective options that cost less or cause fewer adverse side effects. Overuse is typically a result of process issues. Examples include treating a routine ear infection with antibiotics, using an expensive magnetic resonance imaging (MRI) scan to make a diagnosis that could be achieved using a less-expensive imaging exam, or duplicating a diagnostic test because of poor care coordination. Often less costly, equally effective solutions to a common healthcare need are available. Overuse raises costs for patients (as well as insurers) while subjecting them to increased, unnecessary health risks compared with the lower-cost diagnostic or treatment options. Estimates of the cost of unnecessary expenditures range from 10 percent to a staggering 30 percent of total healthcare spending (Brownlee, Saini, and Cassel 2014). In other words, "more" treatment is not necessarily linked to better health outcomes in healthcare. When approaching a problem to treat, clarifying what the intended outcome is and then exploring the most effective options to achieve that outcome can mitigate overuse in healthcare.

In contrast to overuse, **underuse** refers to situations where providers fail to provide patients with medically necessary care or do not adhere to evidence-based guidelines. Examples include failure to provide beta-blockers to patients with coronary artery disease and failure to vaccinate older adult patients against pneumonia. The Agency for Healthcare Research and Quality (AHRQ 2013) reported that in 2009, Americans failed to receive 30 percent of the care they needed to treat or prevent medical conditions. The growth of the evidence-based medicine movement, in which providers are expected to follow specific guidelines, reflects the process nature of the underuse issue, though it can also cause health outcome consequences. Although process-related solutions can be highly effective, underuse can also be traced to structural issues, such as inadequate access to highly qualified healthcare providers, or lack of understanding about preventive treatment options. It can also be traced to issues beyond the control of healthcare providers, such as structural lack of health insurance, or unsafe living conditions. Therefore, when measuring underuse, we might simultaneously be measuring by proxy equitable outcomes in healthcare quality.

overuse
A situation that occurs when a drug or treatment is given without medical justification. Examples of overuse include treating people with antibiotics for simple infections or failing to follow effective options that cost less or cause fewer side effects.

underuse
A situation that occurs when providers fail to provide patients with medically necessary care or do not adhere to evidence-based guidelines. Examples include failure to provide beta-blockers to patients with coronary artery disease or failure to vaccinate older adult patients against pneumonia.

Finally, **misuse** refers to incorrect diagnoses, medical errors, and other preventable conditions. Misuse occurs when care is provided incorrectly or when patients receive the wrong care altogether. Misuse typically either harms patients or prevents them from experiencing the full benefit of a treatment. In *To Err Is Human* (IOM 1999), the IOM broke the silence regarding medical errors, estimating that they cause up to 98,000 deaths each year. Examples of misuse include treating a patient with an antibiotic for which the patient has a known allergy, not taking precautions to prevent hospital-acquired infections, and operating on the wrong side of a patient. Misuse is almost always the result of a process issue. Misuse is particularly troubling because it often has serious health consequences for patients that are almost entirely preventable. Electronic health records (EHRs) represent one approach to improving care coordination and minimizing the misuse of healthcare services by coordinating documentation, and flagging reminders for providers to confirm information before proceeding with care. Process solutions can prevent avoidable, unintended misuse of care.

misuse
A situation that occurs when care is provided incorrectly or when patients receive the wrong care altogether. Misuse typically either harms patients or prevents them from experiencing the full benefit of a treatment.

HISTORY OF QUALITY IMPROVEMENT

Quality improvement has been defined as the "combined and unceasing efforts of everyone—healthcare professionals, patients and their families, researchers, payers, planners, and educators—to make the changes that will lead to better patient outcomes (health), better system performance (care) and better professional development" (Batalden and Davidoff 2007b, 2).

The QI approach embraced by the healthcare industry grew out of QI applications from the Japanese manufacturing industry. Although quality control was first emphasized within US production efforts during World War II (1939–1945), the quality focus deteriorated when the war ended. Disenchanted by the decision to abandon quality control programs, prominent quality experts Joseph Juran and W. Edwards Deming accepted an invitation to help restructure Japanese production methods after World War II (Quality Gurus 2018a, 2018b). Instead of relying on product inspection as a quality metric, Juran and Deming focused on improving all organizational processes. As a result, Japanese goods made significant gains on the international market, and Japan continued to develop into a quality leader.

In the 1980s, strategies from the Japanese QI approach, a philosophy called "companywide quality control," began to extend into US organizations in manufacturing and military industries. The US Naval Air Systems Command adopted a Japanese-style management approach in the early 1980s, coining the term *total quality management* (TQM). US Fortune 500 companies began to follow suit, learning from leading quality experts in Japan. The US Congress finally brought the quality focus to the US healthcare industries with the establishment of the Agency for Health Care Policy and Research (now the Agency for Healthcare Research and Quality, or AHRQ) in 1989. As QI gained prominence within healthcare contexts, not-for-profit organizations arose in the years that accelerated improvement, including the Institute for Healthcare Improvement (IHI) in 1991 and the National Patient Safety Foundation in 1996. Since the founding of these organizations, and the popular reports *To Err Is Human* (IOM 1999) and *Crossing the Quality Chasm* (IOM 2001), the healthcare industry has firmly embraced and promoted the quality movement.

QUALITY AND PROCESS IMPROVEMENT

Continuous quality improvement (CQI) is an overarching strategy that includes a "structured organizational process for involving personnel in planning and executing a continuous flow of improvements to provide quality health care that meets or exceeds expectations" (Johnson and Sollecito 2020, 3). CQI carries with it the belief that existing operations and processes always have room for improvement and that quality gains are always possible. Organizations may adopt CQI principles for one or more particular reasons: (1) to achieve process improvement; (2) to gain a competitive advantage in the marketplace; or (3) to conform to regulations and requirements. Regardless of the motivation, CQI supports the overall mission of healthcare organizations and offers benefits for patients as well as the organization.

Given the similarities between the definitions and principles of CQI, TQM, and QI, these terms are often used interchangeably. As described in the next section, there are differences among these approaches. However, the approaches also have many parallel components, including the use of a series of steps to support the development and testing of changes in an organization. In general, the methods assume that errors result from poor processes and that many errors are preventable.

COMMON QUALITY IMPROVEMENT STRATEGIES

Quality improvement may be carried out through a number of strategies, each with its own methodology and benefits. These strategies include TQM, the Model for Improvement (MFI), Six Sigma, and Lean, each of which will be briefly introduced in this section. In concluding the section, we will examine the common themes and tools found throughout these quality improvement strategies.

TOTAL QUALITY MANAGEMENT (TQM)

TQM draws on behavioral science, economic theory, and process analysis to guide improvements. TQM arose fairly early in the evolution of QI and does not include a single formal framework. The American Society for Quality (ASQ 2022) defines TQM as a "management system for a customer-focused organization that involves all employees in continual improvement. It uses strategy, data, and effective communications to integrate the quality discipline into the culture and activities of the organization."

The principles of TQM include the following:

Customer focus. TQM emphasizes that the customer determines the level of quality required and thus whether QI efforts are successful and worthwhile.

Total employee involvement. TQM stresses that organizations should encourage employee participation in QI efforts. Employee commitment depends on psychological safety, empowerment, and the proper environment.

Process-centered thinking. TQM promotes *process thinking*, in which the steps of a process are defined, and performance measures are continuously monitored to detect variation.

Integrated system. TQM focuses on the horizontal processes interconnecting organizational functions and roles.

Strategic and systematic approach. TQM encourages the formulation of a strategic plan that integrates quality as a core component.

Continuous improvement. TQM emphasizes that organizations should remain analytical and creative to find ways to become more competitive and effective at meeting goals.

Fact-based decision making. TQM requires organizations to collect and analyze data to support decision making and assess the effectiveness of improvement strategies.

Communication. TQM expects communication to support employee morale and motivation.

MODEL FOR IMPROVEMENT (MFI)

The Model for Improvement (MFI) consists of three fundamental questions followed by multiple Plan-Do-Study-Act (PDSA) cycles. The MFI is the preferred model of the Institute for Healthcare Improvement and is commonly used in healthcare (IHI 2022). The MFI developed from studies of innovation demonstrating that discovery, learning, and intervention cannot be reduced to a linear model. As a result, the MFI calls for gradual development and testing of change in the system. This process is accomplished through numerous rapid tests of minor changes through PDSA cycles. Ultimately, the MFI guides improvement efforts and offers an efficient trial-and-learning methodology (Langley et al. 2009). The MFI can be divided into a planning stage and a testing stage with the following elements:

◆ Planning stage

Goals of the effort. Set specific, measurable aims.

Ways to measure improvement. Determine which quantitative measures will be used to evaluate changes.

Changes to be made. Select changes based on feedback from those involved with the operation, internal data, or success stories of others.

◆ Testing stage: PDSA methodology

Plan—Develop a plan and implement the change gradually.

Do—Implement the change and collect data for analysis.

Study—Analyze the change. Compare the results to the expectations.

Act—Decide how to move forward. Determine whether the change is feasible or needs to be altered. Depending on the extent of alteration needed, either go back to the planning stage or continue with additional PDSA cycles.

As presented in a toolkit published by AHRQ (2020), the PDSA diagram first outlines MFI's three questions as (1) "What are we trying to accomplish?" (2) "How will we know that a change is an improvement?" and (3) "What changes can we make that will result in improvement?" This set of questions leads into a cycle of PDSA behaviors which then revisits the three questions for ongoing improvements in a continuous process.

SIX SIGMA

Developed by Motorola in the late 1980s, Six Sigma draws on TQM principles while focusing on identifying and eliminating the causes of errors by minimizing variation in processes. The term *Six Sigma* is derived from the Greek letter sigma and six standard deviations from the mean of normally distributed data, as illustrated by a bell curve. Statistically, the objective of the Six Sigma method is to reduce variations in output whereby a process produces fewer than 3.4 defects per 1 million opportunities (Lin 2021).

In addition to its set of tools and improvement methods, Six Sigma also developed an infrastructure of individuals with formal credentials in training to use Six Sigma methods ("champions," "black belts," "green belts," etc.). Over time, Six Sigma has evolved into multiple distinct methodologies for use in specific circumstances. The two most common of these methodologies are DMAIC (define, measure, analyze, improve, control) and DMADV (define, measure, analyze, design, verify). Specifically, DMAIC is intended to be used with existing processes, while DMADV is intended to be used when developing new processes. Although the frameworks include several steps, each step can be broken down to include additional tools and methods.

Key elements of the DMAIC framework are as follows:

Define process improvement goals consistent with customer demands and organizational strategies.

Measure the current process (focus on defects) and develop a baseline for future comparison.

Analyze the process to identify all relevant factors and verify cause-and-effect relationships. Identify the key root cause of unacceptable variation.

Improve or optimize the process on the basis of the analysis. Implement a solution and standardize the process.

Control the process to sustain future gains. Create a plan to ensure that any variances are corrected before they result in defects.

The DMADV framework is as follows:

Define the project goals and customer requirements.

Measure and determine customer needs and specifications; benchmark against competitors and industry.

Analyze the process options.

Design the process to meet the customer needs.

Verify the design performance and capability to meet customer needs.

Lean

Growing out of the Toyota Production System in the early 1990s, the Lean manufacturing strategy is based on a set of five production principles that encourage continuous improvement through waste reduction. Waste reduction efforts are supported by demand-flow manufacturing, where goods and services are delivered only in direct response to customer requests. Overall, Lean aims to reduce production time, lower inventory needs, increase productivity, and allow for more efficient use of capital equipment (Langley et al. 2009). The Lean approach includes the following five steps (Lean Enterprise Institute 2022):

1. *Customer's perspective.* Specify value from the customer's perspective.

2. *Value stream.* Identify all steps in the value stream (i.e., the process) and eliminate steps that do not create value for the customer.

3. *Flow.* Ensure that value-creating steps occur in tight sequence so that the product or service flows smoothly toward the customer.

4. *Pull.* Ensure that the flow of work occurs in response to customer demand (i.e., it is "pulled" by customer demand rather than "pushed" by the organization onto the customer).

5. *Perfection.* Repeat steps 1 through 4 until a state of perfection is reached, where perfect value is created without waste.

COMMON THEMES AND TOOLS

The methodologies just discussed are by no means the only QI methods used in healthcare or other industries. No single methodology has developed the reputation of being better than the others; in fact, many organizations use hybrid models. For example, some organizations characterize their QI approach as "Lean Six Sigma," incorporating ideas from the Lean principles as well as Six Sigma's DMAIC framework. The Joint Commission has combined Lean, Six Sigma, and *change management*—"a systematic approach that prepares an organization to accept, implement, and sustain the improved processes that result from the application of Lean and Six Sigma tools"—into a QI methodology it calls Robust Process Improvement (Joint Commission Resources 2022). The MFI also shares some Lean concepts.

The differences among the methods are often more in terms of style than substance. For example, some methods focus on reducing variation, while others emphasize waste reduction; some methods promote gradual incremental change, while others promote larger fundamental changes. Regardless of the QI method used, all have the same general purpose—to provide a structured approach for evaluating processes and guiding improvement efforts.

Common features across methods can be organized into several underlying themes. First, each QI method emphasizes the importance of planning. In the planning stage, organizations evaluate current performance, identify areas for improvement, and set specific improvement goals. The second theme includes organizing and coordinating QI efforts. In this stage, organizations implement the plan developed in the previous stage. QI methods all emphasize actively managing the QI process. QI methods also examine organizations as systems and appreciate the assumption that most quality issues are a result of dysfunctional *processes* rather than incompetent people. As noted in the opening vignette, the ophthalmology clinic employs a competent and dedicated staff, but they are working under competing priorities, so their processes have led to misunderstandings and frustrations for patients and staff. QI methods all seek to understand an organization's processes, which may initially be obscured. Finally, the third theme refers to sustaining change. This stage includes scaling up the change to other parts of the organization, fine-tuning and adapting the change as necessary, and ingraining QI principles into the organizational culture.

Important to QI methods is the use of measures that are valid and meaningful. Measures may be simple, cheap, and clear to observe, such as the number of minutes a patient spends in the waiting room, the rate of infections per all inpatients, and number of times medication was erroneously dispensed. Measuring feelings, such as patient and employee satisfaction, is harder to do yet may be very meaningful to the organization and relevant to its goal outcomes.

Finally, QI methods value participation of appropriate individuals at all organizational levels, including patients, family members, staff, and internal customers in the organization. As a result, QI methods emphasize presenting quality-related information in a form that is accessible and meaningful to people with diverse skills and perspectives. Aligning all members of a QI process on goals, outcomes, and measures in language that everyone can understand will support collaborative efforts to the shared goal.

DEFINING *IMPLEMENTATION SCIENCE*

Implementation science (IS) is a relatively new, complex discipline that is most concerned with *how* evidence-based practices actually work in the "real world"—that is, outside controlled trial contexts—and the contextual factors necessary for these practices to succeed. Implementation scientists often collaborate on interdisciplinary teams and use rigorous research methods to test various features of what makes an evidence-based practice succeed or not in particular circumstances. *Implementation* refers to the process of putting a plan or evidence-based practice into effect. IS builds off *effectiveness research*, basic and clinical science that show why certain practices or clinical interventions are effective toward patient health outcomes. For example, an effectiveness research study might measure which dose is the best dose of a new medication in patients with certain characteristics, and a subsequent implementation science research study would then determine the contexts and criteria to get that best dose to the patient in a clinical setting so that patients can take the medication as prescribed.

HISTORY OF IMPLEMENTATION SCIENCE: A DISCIPLINE

Implementation science partners with *dissemination science*, which promotes knowledge sharing and incorporation of existing known findings. IS has a goal to increase uptake of evidence-based practice beyond what is effective about the clinical intervention itself (Bauer and Kirchner 2020). As a discipline, IS was formalized during the 1970s and 1980s in the United States, in attempts to implement national best practices around public health initiatives and standardize measures of success (Lobb and Colditz 2013). IS discipline grew into a useful approach in the 1990s to research the gap that the IOM identified between health policies and health practices, figuring out how to apply existing evidence-based practices toward improving health outcomes and reducing health disparities.

Like QI, IS is structured through models and frameworks as a wide, complex set of tools with which to structure research questions and compare outcomes. IS overlaps with emerging fields including improvement science, knowledge translation, delivery science, and program science (UW Implementation Science Resource Hub 2022b). Like many of its peer fields, IS aims to bridge the knowledge-to-action gap and help practitioners use known best practices in their work. Comparably to QI, IS relies on the right people with the right tools in place to implement and evaluate the success of an organizational change.

POPULAR IS FRAMEWORKS

Implementation science organizes its frameworks into (1) process models, (2) determinant frameworks, (3) classic theories, (4) implementation theories, (5) evaluation frameworks, and (6) hybrid determinant and process theories (UW Implementation Science Resource Hub 2022a). Any given implementation research project may use a combination of theories from any of these six categories. Defining a clear research question is a first step for researchers to choose the most appropriate tools to use to answer that question. There are even decision-making tools online to help researchers compare and choose the best framework to apply to their research project. Unlike QI, which has a narrow set of tools and frameworks used to achieve changes and goals of patient care, IS has a broad array of tools, frameworks, methods, and measures with which to achieve its goals. Part of the expertise that implementation scientists bring to their work is the knowledge of and ability to recommend the best framework for a given research question or implementation goal. Exhibit 12.1 compares QI and IS strategies.

Enola Proctor is a leader in implementation science research. Grounded in social work and public health disciplines, Proctor's research helps measure meaningful outcomes of implementing the best practices in delivering healthcare (Council on Social Work Education 2022). Proctor's outcomes model fits within the evaluation frameworks category of IS, which aims to name and make useful the outcomes of implementation research. Proctor's outcomes model organizes measurable outcomes into (1) *implementation outcomes*, which include acceptability, adoption, appropriateness, cost, feasibility, fidelity, and penetration; (2) *service outcomes*, which include efficiency, safety, effectiveness, equity, patient-centeredness, and timeliness; and (3) *client outcomes*, which include satisfaction, function, and symptomatology (Proctor et al. 2011). In an implementation study, all outcomes may be named,

	Quality Improvement (QI)	Implementation Science (IS)
Context	**Practice**	**Research**
Documentation	Process and outcomes often documented internally within an organization	Process and outcomes often reported in peer-reviewed journal manuscripts
Participants' privacy	Institutional Review Board (IRB) approval may not be required if the goals are for clinical practice, not for research	IRB approval required for human subjects' participation in interventions implemented
Methods	Uses strategies from manufacturing and production disciplines to rapidly and cyclically iterate on improvements	Uses quantitative and qualitative measures derived from a wide menu of frameworks and theories
Goals	Improving a specific quality measure in a targeted setting	Understanding how and why practices do or do not experience uptake, and the contextual factors influencing uptake of evidence-based practices

EXHIBIT 12.1
Comparing QI and IS Strategies

though likely a few key outcomes will be the focus of the study. Each of these outcomes has specific definitions and validated measures to capture in a healthcare setting. Proctor continues to drive forward the field of implementation science by refining IS frameworks, leading the Implementation Research Institute within the National Institute of Mental Health, and advising the World Health Organization.

THE ROLE OF HUMAN RESOURCES IN IMPROVEMENT STRATEGIES

The central focus of this chapter is the key role of individuals and teams in the QI and IS processes. Successful launch and sustainment of QI or IS methods clearly require support and meaningful participation from stakeholders at every level of the organization. To conduct a QI or IS project, a clinical setting needs information (data), access, resources (supplies, infrastructure), *and* human participation to achieve a change. Within HR, we recognize the importance of matching people with motivation, knowledge, skills, and capacity to fully participate in a QI or IS project. HR or project managers will be tasked with budgeting project time and money for team member training and orientation, time for monitoring and evaluation, and time for team members to reflect together and plan for sustained change. The effectiveness of the QI process or IS research frequently depends on team members collaborating and the team's ability to make an impact on the broader healthcare system (Health Resources and Services Administration 2022). If the team is not working well together for any reason, then whatever human capital may be present on the team will not be used to its fullest extent.

The rationale for using teams in QI efforts is clear: Employees in many functional roles may have the best insights into what is causing a problem and the feasibility of alternative changes. Because they will be most directly tasked with implementing changes, these staff can attest to the cases in which this problem arises and which previous solutions have been tried. Because so many quality problems in healthcare are complex and have multiple causes, quality issues require a team approach, wherein team members can collectively share knowledge, interpret data, and generate change options. The composition of QI or IS teams should ideally reflect the complexity and disciplinary diversity of the problems to be addressed. Membership frequently includes representation of individuals at multiple organizational levels because changes always require understanding by people at diverse levels in the organization.

What are the consequences of failing to engage employees and teams in QI efforts? At the most basic level, the opportunity to obtain and utilize the profound knowledge possessed by employees is lost. This profound knowledge includes an understanding of how a particular system operates and how multiple subsystems interact, which can be crucial to professional development of individual team members and historical knowledge within the organization. All QI efforts seek to build knowledge—to learn. Absent the perspectives of those possessing profound knowledge about the system, all that remains may be observations and data that are disconnected from how the system actually operates.

Teams vary in their effectiveness, and a team can intentionally evolve into a well-oiled machine. In fact, however, teams have more reasons to fail than to succeed. Exhibit 12.2 provides a cynical list of factors that may jeopardize a well-intentioned QI or IS effort. This recipe for failure is provided to make the point that each stage of a QI or IS effort depends on effective teams. Teams in fact play a significant role in all aspects of healthcare and are particularly central to providing safe care.

HUMAN RESOURCE PRACTICES AND TEAM EFFECTIVENESS

As a central element in an organization's mix of strategies, QI must be supported by a set of well-aligned HR strategies. You have started to develop many HR strategies as you have worked through previous chapters of this textbook. Exhibit 12.3 summarizes key questions to consider in evaluating the alignment of HR practices with QI initiatives toward a goal of team effectiveness.

To ensure that your QI or IS effort *will* fail, combine the following action ingredients:

- Don't think too much about who should be on a QI or IS team; just throw it together, based on whoever happens to be in the room or hallway when you start. Be sure to restrict participation only to managers and policy administrators who are not involved in the day-to-day of implementing the change.
- Choose ineffective team leaders, and don't give them any clear direction or training. They can "build the plane as they fly it."
- Don't bother with training the team members, either.
- Always assume that team members are committed to the QI or IS mission without developing strategies to develop and assess team member engagement or motivation.
- Let team members know that they will face severe personal consequences if any error is made. Only perfect outcomes will be tolerated.
- Do not provide necessary resources for the team.
- Do not provide adequate time during work hours for the team to meet. If they are dedicated, they will figure it out during their personal time.
- Host ad-hoc, infrequent meetings at times and locations that are inconvenient for most members of the team.
- Don't disseminate a meeting agenda ahead of time that would enable team members to adequately prepare for it. Team members should only be contributing through impromptu improvising.
- Make sure that the meeting space is small, dimly lit, poorly ventilated, chilly, and lacking enough chairs for every team member. If any equipment is needed, call IT after the meeting has started and make everyone wait until it is delivered before continuing. Never provide food or beverages.
- Present data in a form that is inaccessible or confusing to team members.
- Invite a senior team member to dominate team discussions.
- Always discount contributions of team members with fewer years of formal academic training.
- Do not have any mechanisms to recognize individual contributions or team achievements.
- Do not encourage sustained senior management support for QI or efforts. A onetime thumbs-up will do.
- Do not provide time and a framework for teams to debrief on and improve their own team processes.

Let the mixture simmer and stew indefinitely, or turn up the heat suddenly for a spectacular flambé. Either way, your QI or IS failure will be guaranteed.

EXHIBIT 12.2
Recipe for Failure in Quality Improvement or Implementation Science

EXHIBIT 12.3
Considerations
for Quality
Improvement
Initiatives

HR Practices	HR Checklist to Prepare for Quality Improvement (QI) Initiatives (Answers to Questions Should Be Yes)
Job design and job descriptions	Are collaborative skills, competencies, and teamwork expectations included in job descriptions? Are expectations about participation in quality improvement activities addressed in job descriptions?
Employee recruitment and selection	In recruitment efforts, is the opportunity to participate in QI activities presented as a valuable part of the job and career development? Are multiple people involved in interviewing applicants to help assess team-related competencies? Do these interviews allow candidates opportunities to learn more about the people they would be collaborating with on a QI team?
Training	Do employees receive training that is directly applicable to the organization's QI methodology, such as teamwork and measurement skills? Do employees have a voice in defining what training they want and need over time? Does the organization provide resources and time for training?
Communication and culture	Is the organization sufficiently resourced and flexible to support open lines of communication, both vertically and horizontally? Do all employees, especially the most marginalized, feel it is safe to express their views? Are employees, particularly those in roles with power, coached on how to solicit and respond to colleagues in roles with less status, power, or prestige? Are employees given concrete examples of how all roles are valuable and respected at the organization?
Performance management	Is engagement in QI activities included as a key measure of employees' performance? Are employees informed that their participation in QI activities will be an element in their individual evaluation? Are employees given ongoing feedback on their work in teams and QI teams specifically?
Reward systems	Are there methods to reward team citizenship and participation in QI activities? Are there incentives and mechanisms to reward teams for their performance and successes? Are rewards for individual and team performance meaningful to these individuals and team members? Do recipients want to receive the rewards they are given? Are they able to receive and utilize their rewards? Are they able to suggest which rewards they prefer?
Management style and organizational structure	Do managers model management styles that are consistent with QI philosophy? Does the organization support decentralized decision making? When QI team members face difficulties collaborating, or an issue arises in their work, do they know how to escalate their concerns—that is, do they know which managers or leaders they can ask for support? Do managers understand the importance of psychological safety to sustaining a QI-focused culture?
HR systems	Does the organization have metrics to evaluate its own effectiveness and efficiency? Does the organization employ QI methodologies to improve its own HR systems? Do employees know that they are allowed to flag potential HR problems? Do they know how and to whom they should communicate these concerns?

What makes a team effective? Antecedents of team effectiveness can be assessed at several organizational levels. First, antecedents of team effectiveness can be evaluated at the individual level. As the saying goes, "The whole is only as good as the sum of its parts." Thus, the characteristics of team members will greatly influence the effectiveness of the team as a whole. People who form QI teams should keep this in mind when selecting, evaluating, and training employees. Individual-level factors include job descriptions that specify that team participation is a central job function, the selection of highly qualified employees who can work effectively in specific roles on teams, performance management and appraisal methods that include teamwork as a key job requirement, reward systems that motivate participation in team activities, and training of employees in the use of QI methods.

Second, antecedents of team effectiveness can be evaluated at the team level. One can build a car out of high-quality parts, but if the parts do not fit together well or if they are assembled incorrectly, the car may not run safely. Likewise, the relationships between individuals on a team will affect the effectiveness of the team as a whole. QI project leaders shall consider **team composition**, including factors such as horizontal, vertical, social demographic, and cultural diversity; team leadership; psychological safety; potential team conflict; and communication. These interpersonal connections can be developed as part of team formation and incentivized throughout the QI project. Considering previous existing relationships and which team members are meeting for the first time through this project may help guide how structured team cohesion activities should be. **Learning collaboratives** are cooperatives whereby people on multiple QI teams come together to learn from the successes (or shortcomings) of others in similar organizations working on related QI projects. These collaboratives also represent an opportunity to spread advancements throughout the broader healthcare system.

Finally, antecedents of team effectiveness can be evaluated at the organizational level. Even a well-made car will not work without fuel, and performance will suffer on poor roads. Similarly, higher-level organizational factors shape the environment in which a team operates. These organizational factors include the support of senior management, the availability of resources (money, time, supplies, infrastructure, personnel) to carry out QI functions, an organizational culture that supports QI, and training in QI and related areas. Resources are particularly critical for QI success. For example, if the organization does not provide sufficient resources to support QI functions, a team manager has three options for recourse: (1) lobby senior management for greater resource support, (2) find a way to provide the necessary support within the department using existing resources and flexibility, or (3) restructure the expectations of what is feasible given existing resources. By understanding factors at the contextual, organizational level that support team effectiveness, managers and human resources officers can better inform their decisions and actions to more effectively foster team effectiveness.

Among the central tenets of QI is the identification of system- and process-level problems rather than individual deficiencies. Even where an individual error may have led

team composition
The size of the team, the combination of existing skills and disciplinary backgrounds and knowledge sets of team members, and other factors relevant to the particular tasks the team is facing. For example, a team may include stakeholders external to the organization, such as suppliers and patients.

learning collaboratives
Cooperatives whereby people on multiple quality improvement (QI) teams come together to learn from the successes and challenges (or shortcomings) of others in similar organizations working on related QI projects.

root cause analysis
A structured approach to analyzing adverse events by identifying underlying factors that increase the probability of errors. This structure might include asking *why* consecutively to understand the deepest cause for a process or action.

to a medication error or another threat to patient safety, **root cause analysis** will often identify processes that inadequately protected the organization and patients from human error. Root cause analysis is a structured approach to analyzing adverse events by identifying underlying factors that increase the probability of errors (AHRQ 2019). Human mistakes are thus recast in a QI culture from blaming the individual to critically evaluating the organization's processes. This observation leads us to the construct of *psychological safety*, defined as "a shared belief held by members of a team that the team is safe for interpersonal risk taking" (Edmondson 1999, 354). In the context of QI, interpersonal risk taking can be extended to include acknowledging errors, contributing to discussions of organizational processes without fear of being denigrated by others, and having the freedom to contribute information that may be contrary to the majority opinion. In fact, the need for psychological safety extends into the larger organization; that is, an organization focused on quality must establish an environment wherein all employees are encouraged to speak, be heard, be taken seriously, and be respected.

The issue of psychological safety is particularly critical in QI teams that bring people together from multiple disciplines and organizational levels. Edmondson and Roloff (2009) note the many challenges faced in creating a psychologically safe environment when multiple dimensions of diversity are present. In a clinical setting, a psychologically safe environment is one in which a certified nursing assistant is comfortable expressing a view contrary to that of a physician, and all degrees, credentials, and perspectives are respected regardless of power relationships. Remember also that psychological safety is a subjective phenomenon. While a manager may feel confident in having created an open and amicable environment, employees' perceptions may be quite different—and perception among the team members with the least power, status, or privilege is what encourages or limits openness.

process analysis
Breaking down organizational processes to identify bottlenecks, blockages, inefficiencies, and waste in an effort to understand how a process operates and how it may be improved.

Among the key features of all QI efforts is **process analysis**—that is, breaking down organizational processes to identify bottlenecks, blockages, inefficiencies, and waste. Process analysis can provide an improved understanding of how a process operates and how a process may be improved. A *fishbone diagram* (also referred to as an *Ishikawa* or *cause-and-effect diagram*) is frequently employed to identify causes of defects or variation in processes and outputs. Exhibit 12.4 shows the basic structure of a fishbone diagram. Participants involved in process analysis first identify causes under broad categories, which may vary according to the particular situation. As causes are entered, subcauses may then be discovered, leading eventually to an actionable set of causes and subcauses. Typically, causes are grouped into such categories as people, materials, machines, and methods. The goal is to identify those causes through an iterative process of working toward root causes (sometimes referred to as the *5 Whys*). As one considers root causes, team members may move from a blame-oriented perspective to one that focuses on the underlying causes of quality and safety problems.

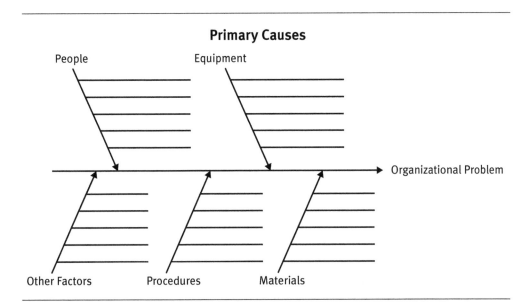

EXHIBIT 12.4
Using a Fishbone Diagram to Determine Problem Causation

SUMMARY

This chapter introduced quality improvement and implementation science as they interact with HR practices in healthcare settings. We discussed common QI and IS methods and discussed HR practices related to the effectiveness of QI teams. The quality movement in healthcare remains in full force, and like any team-based effort, QI must be actively supported throughout the organization to provide high-quality healthcare.

Developing a successful team capable of carrying out a QI effort may be a laudable organizational success, even if desired outcomes take time to occur. When measuring change, teams must be sure that sufficient time has passed for the change to have an effect and be measurably different, and then evaluate the sustainability of the changes. Ensuring that the outcomes measured align with the original intent of the improvement problem identified can reassure team members that they have responded to and changed what they set out to do.

Striving for ongoing process improvement can help improve patient outcomes, make for a more enjoyable and satisfying workplace, and support the financial and cultural health of the organization, aligning the goals of all stakeholders in a healthcare system.

FOR DISCUSSION

1. What are some goals and objectives of healthcare organizations? Spend one minute jotting down every possible goal you can think of, from the perspective of administrators, clinicians, staff, patients, and insurers.

2. Why is the success of quality improvement dependent on appropriate human resources management? Where do HR practices align with QI efforts?

3. Name a problem for which you would use QI methods. Name a research question for which you would use IS methods. What do they have in common? Where do they diverge?

4. How does QI influence health equity? How does IS influence health equity?

5. Early in the section titled "Quality and Quality Improvement," the following famous quotation is cited: "Every system is perfectly designed to get the results it gets." How is the quotation applicable to human resources management?

6. Think about a time when you made a mistake recently. (It's OK! We all make mistakes.) What would you have changed about the circumstances of your situation that would have lessened the negative consequences of that mistake? What could you do, or what process could you put in place, so that the same mistake doesn't happen again? Are there any other people who could help you prevent that mistake from happening again? How could they help?

7. Have you ever learned something new, or gained new evidence that has influenced how you do something in your own life? How did you know how to apply that knowledge to fit in with your current practices and habits? Did you find any parts of implementing that new evidence in your life that were challenges, or "barriers," to taking the new evidence into consideration? What did you do in response to those barriers?

8. Reflecting on the HR skills you have been building throughout this textbook, which tools will you reach for when you are asked to participate on a QI team? What HR skills will you use to form a QI team?

9. Consider a quality-oriented healthcare organization wishing to hire people who are inclined toward working on QI projects. In addition to the technical skills required for the job, what other applicant criteria should be measured when screening and selecting candidates for the job?

10. Recall from the vignette at the beginning of this chapter that Imani is developing a QI initiative at the Bright Eyes Clinic to improve patient and staff satisfaction at the ophthalmology clinic. Imani is considering what components she will need for a successful team. Name at least four roles or positions that should be included

on the team. Name at least five skills that a team member should bring to the collaboration. Name at least two knowledge topics that should be invited into the team composition.

When Imani is selecting team members who will cumulatively fulfill the criteria you named, she can also consider diversity of tenure at Bright Eyes Clinic, diversity of motivations to contribute, and each individual member's willingness to learn and participate. How would you introduce team members to one another to highlight the strength, knowledge, and skills that they bring to the team? Imani will ask all team members who participate to also engage their colleagues outside this QI team in the team's focused QI efforts.

Help Imani with her QI project. Name the problem that Imani is trying to respond to. Fill out the fishbone diagram as Imani for this problem. What outstanding questions do you need to ask of the team that you have previously formed? What subcauses of Imani's problem can you start to diagnose using this tool? What HR responses do you need to address these problems?

EXPERIENTIAL EXERCISES

EXERCISE 1

Think about the next step in your career. This might be a specific job you are looking for in the field you are studying or a specific healthcare organization for which you aspire to work. Look for a job in your intended field that includes at least one of the strategies described in the section "Common Quality Improvement Strategies": TQM, MFI, Six Sigma, Lean. Answer the following questions about that job:

- What is the title of the position?
- What credentials or trainings are listed as "must-haves" in the job description? What are additional "nice-to-haves" or optional skills?
- From the job description, can you tell how this role performs on a QI team?
- From the job description, can you tell how this role collaborates with colleagues in other disciplines?

Thinking about this job, spend 90 seconds brainstorming on the following three questions:

1. How would you choose which of the four QI strategies to use in the workplace?
2. Under what circumstances might you opt for one of the other three or some other strategy instead of the one you chose?
3. If you were on the job tomorrow, how would you learn more about that strategy to use it at work?

In your previous work and school life, think about a team that you have been a part of. It could be a sports team, a group project for a class, a work team, or another situation in which you collaborated with people to achieve a goal. Answer the following questions:

- What are three key features about your team that helped you achieve your goal?
- Or, if you did not achieve your goal, what are at least two barriers your team encountered that prevented you from achieving your goal?
- What else would you have wanted or needed to help your team achieve its goal, or to make the process of achieving your goal smoother?
- If you were to be on the job you chose at the beginning of this exercise tomorrow, how would you bring what you learned from this team experience to that job?

EXERCISE 2

This adapted case example was originally drafted by Jenna Green and Will Haithcock. Questions to discuss for the exercise follow the case example.

Prairie Regional Medical Center (PRMC) is a 245-bed hospital that offers a comprehensive range of inpatient and outpatient medical services to residents of central Kansas in the midwestern United States. The medical staff of PRMC consists of more than 125 physicians and dentists representing a number of specialties, and PRMC is one of the largest employers in the area. PRMC is fully accredited for all services surveyed by The Joint Commission.

Felix, a 68-year-old patient, presented to PRMC with a peptic ulcer and underwent abdominal surgery (a diagnostic laparotomy). He was admitted to the patient tower for an anticipated four-day monitoring and recovery stay after his surgery, which was performed without any complications. Other than the recent operation, Felix has been in relatively good health and has been feeling well. Felix's medical history includes diabetes, and five years ago, he began wearing hearing aids in both ears.

Jessie, a registered nurse, was assigned to Felix's care during his recovery. He would be able to monitor and care for Felix for his entire recovery because Jessie works a unique schedule of five days on, five days off. Jessie negotiated this specific schedule when he took a promotion to join PRMC's surgical inpatient department three years ago, after five years of working in PRMC's emergency medicine trauma center. Jessie requested to work five consecutive 12-hour days from 7:00 a.m. to 7:00 p.m. in order to share childcare responsibilities with his husband, and recently Jessie has also been caring for his aging parents during his time outside work.

By day 3 of Felix's recovery, Felix and his family began to observe and comment that communicating with Jessie had become more difficult compared with the previous two days. Jessie was responding with an annoyed tone to Felix and his family's questions and noticeably yawned three or four times each time he came in for routine checks. Felix's wife, who had been visiting Felix for a few hours each day, noticed that Jessie had begun to take markedly longer to respond to Felix's call lights than the previous days, even though Felix was making comparable requests. Later that evening before shift change, Jessie took Felix's vitals as he had done the previous two days to prepare for the night shift. Everything appeared normal, so he returned to his other patients on the floor for his final check-in before heading home to his family.

On day 4, Jessie returned to his shift at 7:00 a.m. to find that Felix's status was declining. He had a temperature of 102 degrees Fahrenheit, his blood pressure was low, and he had difficulty breathing. Jessie tried to quickly get caught up with what he had missed for each of his patients throughout the night but began nervously fidgeting when someone mentioned that Felix's temperature spike likely occurred during the previous day shift and was missed by the nursing staff. Jessie knew that he was the last person to sign off on Felix's chart before the night-shift transition and could not help but feel an overwhelming sense of guilt and personal responsibility that he could have prevented Felix's current discomfort.

Jessie now acted through a rush of anxious adrenaline, as he knew he needed to quickly get to the root cause of what had happened. He retraced his steps throughout his entire course of care the previous day, and then he realized: Amid his fatigue and distractions during yesterday's continuously busy patient response, Jessie had forgotten to come in prior to his last vitals check to remove Felix's hearing aids. As recommended, Jessie had taken Felix's tympanic temperature (via the ears), though inadvertently, Jessie had done this with both hearing aids still in. Jessie knows from his training that the standard recommendation is to remove hearing aids and wait 10 minutes before taking a temperature, and Jessie had been following this protocol during all vital checks in each of the other 15 times he had done so since Felix arrived. When Jessie realized his mistake, he hurried to find his new nurse manager, Ellis, on duty. Jessie knew he had a duty and an obligation to be transparent with any and all concerns, and that protocol required he report this mistake to Ellis as soon as he could. Jessie wasn't sure whether his mistake caused Felix's decline, but Ellis needed to be aware of it. After all, Jessie thought, "I'm human, I make mistakes. We all do sometimes."

Jessie was incredibly nervous about explaining to Ellis what had happened because he knew that Ellis was skeptical of Jessie's work schedule and Jessie's ability to perform safely during many long consecutive shifts. Ellis had joined the team last year and was pushing the whole unit to take more continuous quality improvement initiatives while managing difficult nurse staffing shortages on most shifts. Jessie had already been working his current schedule with high praise from patients and previous managers when Ellis joined the team, so Ellis agreed to continue this schedule while monitoring Jessie's ongoing performance with that schedule. Ellis is open to hearing all staff's concerns about when they work best and what she can do to set them each up for success, so she wanted to support Jessie in remaining in a shift that works for his family life and allows him to support the unit as best he can. Ellis and Jessie had a brief chat in between patients about what happened and how to care for Felix going forward. Ellis asked Jessie to think about what safeguards he can put in place to ensure that this never happens again and reminded him that she will be following the process of documenting this incident with the Patient Relations team and will include Jessie in conversations about consequential actions to ensure patient safety. Jessie went back to continue to care for all his patients on the floor, with support from other members of the team to take over caring for Felix for the rest of the week.

Ellis then met with Ji-Yoo, who is the surgical unit liaison on PRMC's Patient Relations team, to document this incident and discuss response strategy. Ellis had simultaneously set forth an investigation to determine how the infection had been missed and when it was acknowledged and treated under their care. The investigation revealed that the temperature spike should have been detected under Jessie's care, so Ellis and Ji-Yoo went to check in on Felix and his family.

Felix's wife sounded worried and exasperated, sighing that Jessie had seemed visibly drowsy and distracted that third day—yawning, checking his watch, and rubbing his eyes. She went on say that Jessie's mood was much less cooperative the day before, and she was really worried about knowing what was going on with Felix and didn't know how to learn from Jessie what she could do to support her husband. Holding her husband's hand, Felix's wife shared with Ellis and Ji-Yoo that she didn't know what she would do if he didn't get better right away and asked what her options were to escalate reporting about this incident so that it never happened to anyone else, while pleading with Ellis and Ji-Yoo to get the best care for her husband during the rest of his stay.

Ellis and Ji-Yoo reconvened in an office to talk through the rest of the process and next steps. Ellis wondered out loud how a mistake of this gravity would impact Jessie's continued employment at PRMC, and what type of management he would need, or if he would able to provide high-quality care going forward. Ellis confirmed to Ji-Yoo that this was the first documented complaint against Jessie since joining the surgical unit, and generally he receives positive reviews from his patients and colleagues. In his whole eight-year tenure at PRMC, Jessie mostly received high praise from all previous supervisors, which is part of why previous supervisors were so flexible to accommodate Jessie's scheduling and family needs, outside typical PRMC scheduling practices. Ji-Yoo prompted Ellis to reflect on Jessie's recent performance and how this schedule seemed to be working for him lately. Ellis thought back about Jessie appearing more distracted lately and looking visibly exhausted and frustrated by the last few days of his days of his rotation, while he usually seemed upbeat and enthusiastic on the first few days of his rotation. Ellis asked Ji-Yoo about the unit and departmental consequences of this adverse event and how it might affect her ability to advocate for her staff and staffing resources with hospital administrators over the next year. They talked through the resulting situation that because Felix would now likely have a longer inpatient stay because of his extended need for recovery, his Medicare insurance would no longer reimburse PRMC for Felix's care, so the hospital would have to assume these costs. Given this large financial consequence, Ellis and Ji-Yoo discussed employment consequences for Jessie and how Ellis could best manage her team going forward.

QUESTIONS FOR EXPERIENTIAL EXERCISE 2

1. Ellis is considering how much Jessie's scheduled shift may have contributed to the mistake. From Ellis's perspective, write out a script to have a private conversation with Jessie about his ongoing schedule. What scheduling concerns would you bring up? How might you approach scheduling with a new nurse whom you don't yet know?

2. Later in the week, as he was recovering, Felix and his wife asked Ellis what Jessie's employment consequences would be after such a mistake. If you were Ellis, how would you respond to them?

3. An independent PRMC QI team is made aware of this situation. If you were a member of the QI team, what five questions would you ask of Jessie and the clinical team to decide how to structure your response to this concern? Write them out.

4. Draft a research question that could test how to implement a procedure to prevent this scenario from happening again. What HR practices are you taking into consideration?

REFERENCES

Agency for Healthcare Research and Quality (AHRQ). 2022. "Glossary: Patient Safety." Accessed October 18. https://psnet.ahrq.gov/glossary-0?f%5B0%5D=glossary_az _content_title%3AP.

———. 2020. "Health Literacy Universal Precautions Toolkit, 2nd Edition: Plan-Do-Study-Act (PDSA) Directions and Examples." Updated September. www.ahrq.gov/health -literacy/improve/precautions/tool2b.html.

———. 2019. "Root Cause Analysis." Published September 7. https://psnet.ahrq.gov /primer/root-cause-analysis.

————. 2013. *2012 National Healthcare Quality Report*. AHRQ Publication No. 13-0002. Rockville, MD: Agency for Healthcare Research and Quality.

American Society for Quality (ASQ). 2022. "History of Total Quality Management." Accessed October 18. https://asq.org/quality-resources/total-quality-management /tqm-history.

Batalden, P., and F. Davidoff. 2007a. "Teaching Quality Improvement: The Devil Is in the Details." *Journal of the American Medical Association* 298 (9): 1059–61.

————. 2007b. "What Is 'Quality Improvement' and How Can It Transform Healthcare?" *BMJ Quality and Safety* 16 (1): 2–3.

Bauer, M. S., L. Damschroder, H. Hagedorn, J. Smith, and A. M. Kilbourne. 2015. "An Introduction to Implementation Science for the Non-Specialist." *BMC Psychology* 3 (1): 1–12. https://doi.org/10.1186/s40359-015-0089-9.

Bauer, M. S., and J. Kirchner. 2020. "Implementation Science: What Is It and Why Should I Care?" *Psychiatry Research* 283: article no. 112376. https://doi.org/10.1016/j.psychres .2019.04.025.

Brownlee, S., V. Saini, and C. Cassel. 2014. "When Less Is More: Issues of Overuse in Health Care." *Health Affairs* Blog. Published April 25. www.healthaffairs.org/do/10 .1377/forefront.20140425.038647.

Centers for Medicare & Medicaid Services (CMS). 2022. "Accountable Care Organizations (ACOs): General Information." Updated October 3. https://innovation.cms.gov /innovation-models/aco.

Council on Social Work Education (CWSE). 2022. "Dr. Enola Proctor." Accessed October 18. www.cswe.org/about-cswe/awards/2021-awardees/dr-enola-proctor/.

Donabedian, A. 1980. *Explorations in Quality Assessment and Monitoring: The Definition of Quality and Approaches to Its Assessment*. Chicago: Health Administration Press.

Edmondson, A. 1999. "Psychological Safety and Learning Behavior in Work Teams." *Administrative Science Quarterly* 44 (2): 350–83.

Edmondson, A., and K. Roloff. 2009. "Diversity Through Psychological Safety." *Rotman Magazine*, September, 47–51.

Health Resources and Services Administration (HRSA). 2022. *Improvement Teams*. Accessed June 15. www.hrsa.gov/quality/toolbox/508pdfs/improvementteams.pdf.

Institute for Healthcare Improvement (IHI). 2022. "Science of Improvement: Testing Changes." Accessed October 18. www.ihi.org/resources/Pages/HowtoImprove/Scien ceofImprovementTestingChanges.aspx.

Institute of Medicine (IOM). 2004. *Patient Safety: Achieving a New Standard for Care.* Washington, DC: National Academies Press.

———. 2001. *Crossing the Quality Chasm: A New Health System for the 21st Century.* Washington, DC: National Academies Press.

———. 1999. *To Err Is Human: Building a Safer Health System.* Washington, DC: National Academies Press.

———. 1990. *Medicare: A Strategy for Quality Assurance, Volume 1.* Edited by K. N. Lohr. Washington, DC: National Academies Press.

Johnson, J. K., and W. A. Sollecito. 2020. *McLaughlin & Kaluzny's Continuous Quality Improvement in Health Care,* 5th ed. Burlington MA: Jones & Bartlett.

Joint Commission Resources. 2022. "High Reliability in Health Care Is Possible." Accessed October 19. www.jcrinc.com/products-and-services/high-reliability#846cf7cab3a04c9 8bc7ed0e4fad978ad_5d7162ccd81e4a51a786ef44f7aa3b78.

Kunkel, S., U. Rosenqvist, and R. Westerling. 2007. "The Structure of Quality Systems Is Important to the Process and Outcome: An Empirical Study of 386 Hospital Depart-ments in Sweden." *BMC Health Services Research* 7: article no. 104. https://doi.org/10 .1186/1472-6963-7-104.

Langley, G. L., R. D. Moen, K. M. Nolan, T. W. Nolan, C. L. Norman, and L. P. Provost. 2009. *The Improvement Guide: A Practical Approach to Enhancing Organizational Per-formance,* 2nd ed. San Francisco: Jossey-Bass.

Lean Enterprise Institute. 2022. "Lean Thinking and Practice." Accessed June 15. www .lean.org/lexicon-terms/lean-thinking-and-practice/.

Lin, M. 2021. "Which Is Better for Engaging Health Care Staff: Lean or Six Sigma?" Virginia Mason Institute. Updated February 1. www.virginiamasoninstitute.org/2016/02/better -engaging-health-care-staff-lean-six-sigma/.

Lobb, R., and G. A. Colditz. 2013. "Implementation Science and Its Application to Popula- tion Health." *Annual Review of Public Health* 34: 235. https://doi.org/10.1146/annurev -publhealth-031912-114444.

National Association of Social Workers (NASW). 2022. "Read the Code of Ethics." Accessed October 18. www.socialworkers.org/About/Ethics/Code-of-Ethics/Code-of -Ethics-English.

Panepinto, L. 2013. "Art by Venn Diagrams." Muddy Colors. Published October 3. www .muddycolors.com/2013/10/art-by-venn-diagrams/.

Proctor, E., H. Silmere, R. Raghavan, P. Hovmand, G. Aarons, R. Griffey, and M. Hensley. 2011. "Outcomes for Implementation Research: Conceptual Distinctions, Measurement Challenges, and Research Agenda." *Administration and Policy in Mental Health* 38: 65–76. https://doi.org/10.1007/s10488-010-0319-7.

Quality Gurus. 2018a."Edwards Deming—Life Story and Teachings." Published January 20. www.qualitygurus.com/w-edwards-deming/.

———. 2018b. "Life and Works of Quality Guru Joseph Juran." Published January 20. www.qualitygurus.com/joseph-juran/.

UW Implementation Science Resource Hub. 2022a. "Pick a Theory, Models, or Frame- work." University of Washington. Accessed October 18. https://impsciuw.org /implementation-science/research/frameworks/.

———. 2022b. "What Is Implementation Science?" University of Washington. Accessed October 18. https://impsciuw.org/implementation-science/learn/implementation -science-overview/.

Watkins, R. W. 2014. "Understanding Quality Improvement Is More Important Now Than Ever Before." *North Carolina Medical Journal* 75 (3): 220–23.

CHAPTER 13

EMPLOYEE WELL-BEING

Amanda Raffenaud and Tina Yeung

LEARNING OBJECTIVES

After completing this chapter, you should be able to

➤ differentiate between healthy levels of stress and dysfunctional stress in the workplace;

➤ discuss burnout concepts as related to health professions;

➤ describe methods of recognizing stress and burnout in oneself and work colleagues;

➤ identify burnout risk factors at administrative, professional, and organizational levels;

➤ discuss specific burnout concerns for physicians, nurses, medical students and residents, healthcare executives, and other healthcare professions; and

➤ discuss strategies to address stress and burnout in a healthcare organization.

VIGNETTE

It is now two years into the COVID-19 pandemic. Peter Donovan, assistant vice president of patient experience at Northwest Health Systems, has just reviewed the latest Hospital Consumer Assessment of Healthcare Providers and Systems (HCAPS) report from his team. The quarterly report showed that scores for communication with doctors and nurses and the responsiveness of hospital staff dropped by 10 points compared with last quarter's results and from the same quarter one year ago. Peter is very concerned about this drop in the quality of patients' reported experience, but he knows that the challenges brought on by the pandemic have impacted his hospital's staff, particularly among intensive care unit (ICU) nurses. Peter consults Isla Walker, the ICU charge nurse. Isla tells Peter that the nurses were "just stretched too thin." Nurses have been through a lot over these last two years. Staffing shortages, witnessing so many patients dying from COVID, the lack of personal protective equipment (PPE), the long hours, and the stress of endangering their family members all have taken a toll on the nurse workforce. Even more, nurses have expressed to Isla that many of them have considered leaving the nursing profession. Many nurses no longer find joy in their work. Isla also has expressed concern about the limited resources to support her nurses. After their discussion, Peter reaches out to Fabian Warner, the director of human resources, to fill him in on his conversation with Isla. It turns out that Fabian is aware of the issue and recognizes that staff members at all levels and units are stressed and burned out. What should the leadership team do to address these concerns?

INTRODUCTION

The healthcare workforce has consistently been forced to navigate one constant phenomenon: change. From a global pandemic and increased workforce shortages to a growing emphasis on telehealth and digital medicine, healthcare employees are continually expected to deliver care amid significant change. So much uncertainty and so many unknowns create a persistent and worsening problem: increased levels of stress and burnout among healthcare professionals. Stress and burnout affect healthcare workers at all organizational levels, including clinical and administrative employees. In the United States, burnout among healthcare employees is now recognized as a national public health issue (Terry and Matthews 2021). Organizational leaders must include employee well-being as a key strategic priority. In this chapter, we address the topic of stress and burnout, including the causes, risk factors, and impacts; assessment of stress and burnout; and opportunities for healthcare leaders to engage in employee wellness practices.

STRESS AND BURNOUT

Stress and burnout constitute a significant health and safety challenge, impacting from 35 percent to 60 percent of the US workforce (Melnyk et al. 2022). Workplace stress is common in all industries but is particularly prevalent in healthcare. Even before a global pandemic, healthcare providers reported high levels of stress at work. Worsening practice conditions, including workforce shortages (see accompanying Current Issue sidebar) and inconsistent management support, have exacerbated the issue (Merz 2021).

WHAT IS STRESS?

Stress is a common facet of life and is usually experienced by everyone at some point. **Healthy stress** is generally positive and may be a short-term experience of bodily or mental tension that allows an individual to stay alert and focused while developing resilience. A healthy level of this stress may be beneficial for motivation and productivity. However, it becomes problematic and dysfunctional when stress is ongoing or excessive. **Dysfunctional stress**, also known as *negative stress*, is an ongoing experience of bodily or mental tension that can lead to physical and mental disorders, including anxiety, depression, and burnout (Maslach, Schaufeli, and Leiter 2001; Portoghese et al. 2017). Both employees and organizations face significant consequences when employees experience dysfunctional stress.

The fact that we need some healthy stress to perform but too much stress is problematic suggests that there is a dynamic relationship between stress and performance. Optimal healthy stress levels vary with the individual and over time. Within that zone of tolerance, stress can improve productivity. However, beyond that zone, the prolonged heightened anxiety accompanying dysfunctional stress decreases performance (Kent et al. 2020).

healthy stress
A short-term experience of bodily or mental tension that allows an individual to stay alert and focused while building resilience.

dysfunctional stress
An ongoing experience of bodily or mental tension that can lead to physical and mental disorders, including anxiety, depression, and burnout. Also known as *negative stress*.

CURRENT ISSUE
Healthcare Workforce Shortage

Even before the COVID-19 pandemic, the US healthcare system faced a workforce shortage, especially in nursing. The nursing workforce is aging; many nurses are nearing retirement, and there are not enough nurses on the pathway to replace the outgoing nurses. Reasons include the shortage of nurse faculty, maxed-out classroom space, and limited clinical training sites. In 2019, more than 80,000 qualified nursing school applicants were turned away (Hughes 2022).

The pandemic has only exacerbated the healthcare workforce shortage. About one in five healthcare workers have left their job since the pandemic started in 2020. The US Bureau of Labor Statistics estimates that the healthcare sector has lost nearly half a million workers since February 2020 (Yong 2021). Many healthcare workers opted to leave their profession. Others had no choice because they contracted long COVID and can no longer work. In spring 2020, during the early stages of the pandemic, healthcare workers were overwhelmed by the number of victims and the stopgap measures adopted to manage the deceased across the country. Those who stayed and continued to care for patients were often overworked and cared for sicker non-COVID patients who had delayed seeking care. There were instances of healthcare workers being mistreated or even attacked by COVID patients or their families who demanded unproven treatments. Reports also surfaced that some workers were poorly treated or compensated by their employers (Yong 2021).

WHAT IS BURNOUT?

burnout
A cumulative negative response to prolonged occupational stress such as excessive demands on energy, strength, or resources.

Burnout is a cumulative negative response to prolonged occupational stress, such as excessive demands on energy, strength, or resources (Freudenberger 1974; Portoghese et al. 2017; Reith 2018). Herbert Freudenberger, a clinical psychologist, first studied burnout in 1974. He noticed that frequent volunteering at a New York City healthcare clinic led to the volunteer staff's emotional depletion and development of psychosomatic symptoms (Freudenberger 1974). The World Health Organization (WHO 2019) describes burnout as a syndrome characterized by "1) feelings of energy depletion or exhaustion; 2) increased mental distance from one's job, or feelings of negativism or cynicism related to one's job; and 3) reduced professional efficacy."

Burnout is often associated with increased job demands paired with a decrease in the necessary resources to complete one's job (Portoghese et al. 2017). In today's healthcare workforce, employees and leaders must understand how to recognize signs of stress and burnout to pursue employee wellness.

RECOGNIZING STRESS AND BURNOUT IN ONESELF AND COLLEAGUES

Recognizing stress and burnout requires much self-awareness and authenticity from employees and leaders. To honestly assess one's internal well-being and current work conditions or that of colleagues is paramount in managing stress and preventing burnout. With these conditions properly managed, leaders can then implement strategies to promote employee well-being (discussed later in the chapter).

Recognizing Stress

Identifying dysfunctional stress levels within the workplace usually begins with noticing one or more symptoms of interpersonal or relationship issues or mental or physical health issues, such as depression, anxiety, sleep disturbances, negative self-talk, physical pain, or heart problems (PsychCentral 2022). Employees can combat stress with self-awareness and leadership support before it progresses to burnout.

Recognizing Burnout

Damaging levels of stress may lead to burnout. Recognizing burnout, for oneself or colleagues, occurs when noticing its symptoms, such as fatigue, malaise, frustration, cynicism, and inefficacy (Reith 2018). Further, as leaders at all levels notice these symptoms, they must begin to address dysfunctional levels of stress and burnout. Both healthcare practitioners and leaders should be familiar with the 12 stages of burnout (Kraft 2006). Although these stages are not necessarily sequential or even incurred by every individual experiencing burnout, recognizing these stages is key to promoting employee wellness. The 12 stages are the following:

1. Compulsion to prove oneself

2. Working harder

3. Neglecting one's own needs

4. Displacement of conflicts

5. Revision of values

6. Denial of emerging problems

7. Withdrawal

8. Noticeable behavior changes

9. Depersonalization

10. Inner emptiness

11. Depression

12. Burnout syndrome

The duration of any one stage can vary, and employees may experience multiple stages simultaneously (Kraft 2006). Leaders can also use burnout stages and burnout inventories (discussed later) to better guide their understanding while measuring employee burnout.

As reported by WHO (2019), the eleventh edition of the International Classification of Diseases (ICD-11) characterizes burnout as an "occupational phenomenon" related to unsuccessful management of "chronic workplace stress." Healthcare leaders should implement ongoing conversations about stress and burnout with individual employees and teams at large that are separate from the performance review process. Conversations between employees and leaders should address job demands, working hours, levels of support, workplace relationships with colleagues, and overall job satisfaction or dissatisfaction (PsychCentral 2022). When stress and burnout risk factors are recognized, leaders can implement strategies to reduce these conditions to support employee well-being.

BURNOUT RISK FACTORS

risk factor
Something that increases risk or susceptibility.

Healthcare professionals face tremendous pressure in their work environment, which frequently leads to burnout. A **risk factor** is something that increases risk or susceptibility. Workers routinely face many stressors that can serve as risk factors for burnout, including competing job demands, staffing shortages, supply shortages, difficult relationships with colleagues and leaders, and patient incivility. The chronic exposure to daily stress among healthcare workers is not new, but the COVID-19 pandemic has exposed the systemic problem in the US healthcare system. Therefore, from a systemwide perspective, we can divide the risk factors for burnout into three broad categories: administrative, professional, and organizational. These categories are further explained in the three sections that follow.

administrative risk factors
Multiple documentation requirements that increase healthcare practitioners' susceptibility to stress and burnout.

ADMINISTRATIVE RISK FACTORS

Administrative risk factors describe the sheer volume of tasks required of clinical practitioners. These include addressing documentation requirements in the electronic health record (EHR), maintaining compliance to meet regulatory reporting required by the organization and various external agencies, and ensuring that documentation is completed for reimbursement from payers.

While the EHR has changed the healthcare industry by making data available to inform clinical and managerial decisions, it has made achieving a work–life balance more difficult. Healthcare professionals can now conveniently (and may be expected to) log into their EHR and work from home. Clinicians may feel like they cannot sign off until they have documented their patient encounters (Ofri 2019). Information technology–related stress is becoming more pervasive as the US healthcare system becomes increasingly more digitally connected (Gardner et al. 2019).

PROFESSIONAL RISK FACTORS

In healthcare, **professional risk factors** are inherent in the work. Healthcare workers are exposed daily to suffering, leading to what is known as *compassion fatigue* (Durate, Pinto-Gouveia, and Cruz 2016). Other professional risk factors include staffing shortages leading to unmanageable patient loads, loss of autonomy and control, and devaluation of the role and profession as a result of a "top-down" approaches to leadership (Dillon et al. 2019).

professional risk factors
Inherent risks attributable to the nature of one's work.

ORGANIZATIONAL RISK FACTORS

Organizational risk factors that lead to burnout in healthcare include 12-hour shift work structures, organizational performance targets, lack of support staff, and inadequate support from management or leadership. Shift work is used extensively in healthcare, especially in hospital settings. However, 12-hour shift work structures have been documented to place additional strain on employees, leading to work–family conflict and decreased perceived health (Jacobsen and Fjeldbraaten 2018).

Further, healthcare leaders focus intensely on initiatives required to meet performance metrics (Dillon et al. 2019). Often, this focus places an undue burden on healthcare professionals and increases their stress as they not only are responsible for the care of their patients but also have to meet these metrics. Finally, as healthcare organizations operate with leaner budgets and increasingly challenging and complex patient needs, practitioners are expected to do more work with fewer support staff (Dillon et al. 2019; Raffenaud et al. 2020). As we have seen, these systemwide risk factors can lead to health professional burnout. It is important to understand these concerns for healthcare professionals.

organizational risk factors
Results of organizational operational decision making that increase healthcare workers' susceptibility to stress and burnout.

CONCERNS FOR HEALTHCARE PROFESSIONALS

Regardless of their role, healthcare professionals of all types are facing unprecedented stress and burnout. This section focuses on specific concerns and the prevalence of burnout among healthcare workers, specifically physicians, nurses, medical students/residents, and healthcare executives.

Physicians

By 2030, it is predicted that the demand for physicians will outstrip the supply, and there will be a shortage of up to 121,300 physicians in the United States (Zhang et al. 2020). The aging population, population growth, new technologies, and the increased number of people insured under the Affordable Care Act (ACA) are some of the factors contributing to the increased demand for physician services. Even before the pandemic, physician burnout was a problem. More than half the physicians in the United States experience burnout (Dyrbye et al. 2017; Reith 2018). Emergency medicine, family medicine, general internal medicine, and neurology are among the physician specialties at the highest risk of experiencing burnout (Dyrbye et al. 2017). A survey of 6,800 physicians conducted by the American Medical Association (AMA) and the Mayo Clinic sought to evaluate the prevalence of physician burnout compared with the general population from 2011 to 2014. This research found that physicians displayed higher rates of emotional exhaustion (43 percent of physicians versus 25 percent of the general public), depersonalization (23 percent versus 14 percent), and overall burnout (50 percent versus 29 percent) over a three-year span (Vassar 2016).

Moreover, the current body of literature also indicates a correlation between physician burnout and various demographic factors, including sex, age, relationship status, age of dependent children, and spousal/partner occupation. Female physicians, younger physicians (i.e., those aged 54 or younger), those who have children (aged 20 or younger), and those with spouses/partners who are not physicians are all more likely to experience symptoms of burnout than other physicians (Dyrbye et al. 2017). Perhaps the most alarming finding is the high rate of suicide among physicians by gender compared with the general public—40 percent higher for male physicians and 130 percent higher for female physicians (Moss 2019).

Nurses

Workplace-induced stress among nurses has been documented dating back to 1960. The nurse's role is stressed-filled "based upon the physical labor, human suffering, work hours, staffing, and interpersonal relationships that are central to the work nurses do" (Jennings 2008, 137). Further, studies dating back to 1999 surveying more than 10,000 registered inpatient nurses and a 2007 survey of approximately 68,000 registered nurses found that 43 percent experienced a high degree of emotional exhaustion. Emotional exhaustion was reported by 35 percent of hospital nurses, 37 percent of nursing home nurses, and 22 percent of nurses working in other settings (Dyrbye et al. 2017). In a study of nurses in managerial and executive positions, Raffenaud and colleagues (2020) found that nurse managers and nurse executives experienced greater work–family conflict compared with staff nurses. Because nursing makes up the largest healthcare profession in the United States, there is a need to dedicate resources to mitigate and support nurses experiencing stress and burnout (Zhang et al. 2018).

MEDICAL STUDENTS AND RESIDENTS

Medical students and *residents*, who are physicians in training, also experience burnout. Contributing factors include work–life imbalance, discrimination, and feeling unappreciated. A 2014 study of medical residents and program directors at a large tertiary academic medical center across all specialties measured burnout among residents. With a 61 percent response rate (307 out of 504), the study found that 69 percent of those responding met the criteria for burnout and 17 percent screened positive for depression (Holmes et al. 2017; Reith 2018). Burnout among this population of caregivers has been associated with negative behaviors during schooling and training and increased rates of stress, dishonest actions, and alcohol abuse (Dyrbye et al. 2017; Jackson et al. 2016). Medical students and residents are our future physician workforce. Thus, as with other practitioners, solutions are needed for medical students and residents to allow them to complete their training and start their careers on the right path.

HEALTHCARE EXECUTIVES

Healthcare executives navigate an increasingly challenging and complex healthcare system that requires a focus on cost, delivery, operations, and outcomes (WittKieffer 2019). Further, healthcare executives are charged with cultivating a resilient workforce while also anticipating the unexpected, such as the COVID-19 pandemic. Healthcare executives are required to identify and address changing healthcare regulations, shifting reimbursement mechanisms, changing economic and environmental factors, and other elements that impact the health of their community. Over time, the weight of such obligations can become mentally taxing.

WittKieffer, a global executive search firm, surveyed more than 9,000 healthcare top-level executives to understand the causes and impact of burnout among healthcare executives. Seventy-nine percent (343 healthcare executives) indicated that executives do experience burnout and that it negatively impacts their organization. Further, healthcare executives indicated that their organizations need to do better at preventing and reducing burnout (WittKieffer 2019).

As healthcare continues to evolve, healthcare leaders have a responsibility to create a culture that recognizes and reduces burnout among their workforce, but it is just as important for healthcare executives to practice self-care to prevent burnout. The pressure on executives to balance multiple demands has substantial consequences for their organization, their workforce, their patients, and the community.

EXTERNAL FACTORS CONTRIBUTING TO BURNOUT

As detailed in the two sections that follow, two key external factors contributing to burnout in the healthcare field are technology and the COVID-19 pandemic. Unlike risk factors (i.e., administrative, professional, and organizational), which are inherently intrinsic to working in healthcare as clinicians and nonclinicians, external factors can also contribute to burnout among healthcare workers.

TECHNOLOGY FACTORS

Increased use of technology in healthcare has undoubtedly improved patient care. However, the diffusion of technology has also been met with some resistance by healthcare professionals. Technology may be viewed as increasing documentation burden, information overload, frequent interruptions, and changes in physician–patient interactions (National Academies of Sciences, Engineering, and Medicine 2019; Shanafelt et al. 2016; Yates 2020). Research on the relationship between the use of health information technology (HIT) and burnout suggests that EHRs may be seen as cumbersome and a means to fulfill regulatory and billing requirements rather than improve healthcare delivery. Practitioners may also have negative perceptions of EHR functionality and usability. Another contributing factor to burnout is the amount of time a practitioner spends in the EHR after normal working hours, referred to by some observers as "pajama time" (Poon, Rosenbloom, Zheng 2021).

COVID-19 PANDEMIC

The impact of the COVID-19 pandemic was unprecedented, unexpected, and uncontrolled by the US healthcare system. Since the start of the pandemic, approximately 20 percent of all healthcare workers have left their jobs (Yong 2021). Healthcare systems were forced to respond quickly and pivot from normal day-to-day operations. Many nonclinical healthcare employees have also had to pivot during the COVID-19 pandemic. Some shifted to *telecommuting*—working from home—to slow the spread of the virus. At the same time, many providers also began offering *telehealth services*—virtual office visits to their patients.

On the front lines, the healthcare system initially lacked adequate PPE to meet the increased demand, and many employees had to work extralong shifts. More important, when healthcare workers returned home after their shifts, many feared exposing their loved ones to COVID and had to self-isolate (Hoffman 2020; Shreffler, Petrey, and Huecker 2020). As a consequence, many experienced high levels of stress.

A 2020 study of healthcare workers caring for COVID-19 patients revealed that many of these workers experienced symptoms of depression (50 percent), anxiety (44.6 percent), insomnia (34 percent), and distress (71.5 percent) (Lai et al. 2020). As Hoffman (2020) warns, these mounting psychological struggles can hinder healthcare workers' ability to maintain their focus to continue caring for all patients. Further, the likelihood of frontline healthcare workers developing posttraumatic stress disorder (PTSD) because of the pandemic is an issue that will confront the United States and other nations.

ORGANIZATIONAL STRATEGIES TO REDUCE STRESS AND BURNOUT

To prevent and reduce stress and burnout, it is necessary to first recognize the underlying factors leading to burnout. The Maslach Burnout Inventory, developed by Christina Maslach, is the most widely used instrument to measure burnout. It assesses three dimensions associated with burnout: emotional exhaustion, depersonalization (i.e., disengagement), and a diminished sense of personal accomplishment (Maslach and Jackson 1981; Rotenstein et al. 2018).

Marchalik and Shanafelt (2020) argue that to reduce and prevent stress and burnout, healthcare organizations need to focus on the process rather than simply on metrics. Rather than reporting scores or ranking, healthcare organizations should consider focusing on implementing and measuring the impact of process improvement measures. The American Nurses Credentialing Center's Magnet Recognition Program is an example of focusing on processes of work. Instead of reporting on satisfaction scores, the program measures evidence of investments, such as a regular survey of nursing staff, the presence of a confidential feedback process for nurses to provide input, and attention to nurse leadership development, among others. Focusing on processes rather than simply reporting numbers allows healthcare organizations to address key drivers of burnout (Marchalik and Shanafelt 2020).

Equally important as focusing on process improvement is the need to dedicate resources to creating an organizational culture of employee well-being that acknowledges the profound impact that stress and burnout can have on the workforce. The National Academies of Sciences, Engineering, and Medicine (2019) propose six goals to promote and maintain a positive work environment where clinicians and nonclinicians experience a safe, healthy, and supportive atmosphere while fostering ethical and meaningful practice. The six goals are summarized as follows:

1. Create a positive work environment to prevent and reduce burnout, foster professional well-being, and promote high-quality care.

2. Create a positive learning environment for students and trainees that supports professional development and the well-being of students and trainees early in their professional training.

3. Reduce administrative burden on clinicians resulting from laws, rules, and regulations stemming from healthcare policy.

4. Adopt technology solutions that support clinicians in providing high-quality patient care.

5. Reduce barriers and stigmas associated with clinicians obtaining emotional and mental support needed to prevent and reduce burnout symptoms.

6. Invest in research to produce evidence-based strategies to promote clinical professional well-being.

Two promising strategies in the effort to reduce stress and burnout are (1) building workforce resilience and (2) finding and recognizing joy in work, as described in the sections that follow.

BUILDING WORKFORCE RESILIENCE

In the cover story for the May/June 2022 issue of *Healthcare Executive* magazine, "The Path of Most Resilience: Building a Strong and Fulfilled Healthcare Workforce," several healthcare leaders were interviewed, and many ideas and recommendations were shared for building a resilient workforce. A key recommendation was a commitment to a "people-first" culture (Van Dyke 2022, 10). Accordingly, the path to building a resilient workforce needs to focus on five pillars: (1) creating a workforce strategic plan, (2) prioritizing schedule flexibility and coverage, (3) developing an innovative recruitment and development strategy, (4) recognizing and valuing employees, and (5) promoting a high "say-do" ratio culture among leadership. These pillars are summarized in exhibit 13.1.

FINDING AND RECOGNIZING JOY IN WORK

The Institute for Healthcare Improvement (IHI) developed a framework and strategies to achieve the goal of "Joy in Work." *Joy* as defined by IHI should be an asset leveraged and nurtured by healthcare leadership: "Joy in work is more than just the absence of burnout or an issue of individual wellness; it is a system property" (Perlo et al. 2017). Consequently, organizations have a responsibility to reduce stress and burnout and should consider adopting IHI's framework for "Improving Joy in Work." The following steps can help build an organizational culture that is focused on creating jobs and reducing dysfunctional stress and burnout (Perlo et al. 2017):

Step 1. Ask your staff, "What matters to you?"

Step 2. Identify unique impediments to joy in work in the local context. Identify barriers (i.e., processes, issues, or circumstances) to what matters in meeting professional, social, and psychological needs within the workplace.

Pillar	Related Action
Workforce Strategic Plan	Complete a two- to three-year strategic analysis of current and future staffing in both clinical and nonclinical areas to include the following: • Number of current openings • Number of projected retirements • Labor market dynamics
Schedule Flexibility and Coverage	Plan to include remote or hybrid (on-site and remote) options, an in-house staffing agency, and the ability for nursing staff to choose their shifts.
Innovative Recruitment and Development	Offer free training in exchange for a commitment of employment after graduation, and partner with local nursing programs to offer experiential learning opportunities to nursing students. Offer courses on management of stress and conflict in the workplace, critical thinking, and other nonclinical courses to prepare nursing students for expected workplace stressors. Dedicate resources to peer-based coaching and mentoring within the organization.
Employee Recognition and Support	Recognize employees through a special event (e.g., nurses week). Offer monetary and nonmonetary awards as a show of appreciation. Bolster wellness programs such as relaxation rooms. Increase social support.
Leadership High "Say-Do" Ratio	Embrace transparency, integrity, and honesty in employee interactions, backing up words with leadership actions.

EXHIBIT 13.1
Five Pillars of Workforce Resilience

Source: Adapted from Van Dyke (2022).

Step 3. Commit to a systems approach to making joy in work a shared responsibility at all levels of the organization. Leaders work together to help remove the identified impediments to sustain joy.

Step 4. Use improvement science to test approaches to improving joy in work in the organization. Improvement science can help leaders accelerate improvement to create a more joyful and productive place to work.

The Joy in Medicine Health System Recognition program was created by the American Medical Association (AMA 2022) to recognize committed or already engaged organizations that sought to prevent burnout and improve physician satisfaction. Healthcare systems with 100 or more physicians or advanced practice providers are eligible to apply. The objectives of the program are to do the following:

◆ Provide a road map to healthcare leaders in their pursuit of employee well-being.

◆ Unite the healthcare community focused on building a culture of joy in medicine.

◆ Build awareness of solutions that promote joy and help spur investment within healthcare systems to reduce physician burnout.

To be recognized by the program, the following six competency areas must have been demonstrated (AMA 2022):

1. **Commitment:** Establish a well-being committee or well-being office.

2. **Assessment:** Monitor physician burnout using an assessment tool.

3. **Efficiency of practice environment:** Measure time spent in the EHR after work hours.

4. **Leadership:** Promote leadership development.

5. **Teamwork:** Measure teamwork metrics.

6. **Support:** Establish peer support programs.

SUMMARY

The reality brought on by the COVID-19 pandemic made it clear that healthcare organizations need to focus on the well-being of their people. Healthcare workforce burnout in the United States is a critical problem, and the pandemic has only made this issue more urgent. Employee well-being must be a priority focus area in the healthcare industry. Understanding and recognizing the risk factors associated with burnout is essential for protecting employees, patients, organizations, and the healthcare system at large. Healthcare leaders play a unique role in addressing burnout among clinical and nonclinical employees. Healthcare leaders need to build a resilient workforce that supports employees and promotes workplace wellness. By focusing on the process, healthcare leaders can assess what programs and policies are needed to cultivate employee well-being, thereby preventing and reducing the onset of burnout symptoms. Consequently, a commitment to employee well-being will benefit clinicians, patients, healthcare executives, and the healthcare organization.

FOR DISCUSSION

1. Define the two key types of stress.

2. What are some signs and symptoms that would be cause for concern for stress and burnout among your coworkers?

3. Compare and contrast the specific burnout concerns for physicians, nurses, medical students and residents, and healthcare executives.

4. Describe external factors that contribute to burnout.

5. Why is "joy" described as an asset, and why is it important to prevent burnout?

6. Discuss strategies healthcare organizations can implement to address stress and burnout among their workforce.

EXPERIENTIAL EXERCISES

EXERCISE 1

This chapter emphasized the importance of creating a resilient workforce. In healthcare, workers anticipate a somewhat high-stress work environment, but no one anticipated the sheer strain and burnout that the COVID-19 pandemic has caused on our frontline healthcare workers. The pandemic brought to light how ill prepared our healthcare system was when confronted with a pandemic.

This exercise has three parts:

1. Consider your current organization and review its policies and programs on providing emotional and well-being support to employees. What types of programs are available to employees? How much emphasis does your organization place on employee well-being?

2. Research other organizations that are known to have great support programs for their employees. Summarize these programs and the support provided to their employees.

3. Given what you learned about your organization and the organization you researched, what new programs and support would you make available at your organization?

Exercise 2

Develop an infographic to create awareness for burnout. Make sure that the infographic includes potential action steps and available support programs.

References

American Medical Association (AMA). 2022. "Joy in Medicine Health System Recognition Program." Accessed September 30. www.ama-assn.org/practice-management /sustainability/joy-medicine-health-system-recognition-program.

Dillon, E., M. Tai-Seale, A. Meehan, V. Martin, R. Nordgren, T. Lee, T. Nauenberg, and D. Frosh. 2019. "Frontline Perspectives on Physician Burnout and Strategies to Improve Well-Being: Interviews with Physicians and Health System Leaders." *Journal of General Internal Medicine* 35 (1): 261–67.

Durate, J., J. Pinto-Gouveia, and B. Cruz. 2016. "Relationships Between Nurses' Empathy, Self-Compassion and Dimensions of Professional Quality of Life: A Cross-Sectional Study." *International Journal of Nursing Studies* 60: 1–11.

Dyrbye, L. N., T. D. Shanafelt, C. A. Sinsky, P. F. Cipriano, J. Bhatt, A. Ommaya, C. P. West, and D. Meyers. 2017. *Burnout Among Health Care Professionals: A Call to Explore and Address This Underrecognized Threat to Safe, High-Quality Care.* NAM Perspectives Discussion Paper. National Academy of Medicine. Published July 5. https://iuhcpe.org/file _manager/1501524077-Burnout-Among-Health-Care-Professionals-A-Call-to-Explore -and-Address-This-Underrecognized-Threat.pdf.

Freudenberger, H. 1974. "Staff Burn-Out." *Journal of Social Issues* 30 (1): 159–65.

Gardner, R., E. Cooper, J. Haskell, D. Harris, S. Poplau, P. Kroth, and M. Linzer. 2019. "Physician Stress and Burnout: The Impact of Health Information Technology." *Journal of the American Medical Informatics Association* 26 (2): 106–14.

Hoffman, J. 2020. "I Can't Turn My Brain Off: PTSD and Burnout Threaten Medical Workers." *New York Times*. Published May 16. www.nytimes.com/2020/05/16/health/coronavirus-ptsd-medical-workers.html.

Holmes, E. G., A. Connolly, K. T. Putnam, K. M. Penaskovic, C. R. Denniston, L. H. Clark, D. R. Rubinow, and S. Meltzer-Brody. 2017. "Taking Care of Our Own: A Multispecialty Study of Resident and Program Director Perspectives on Contributors to Burnout and Potential Interventions." *Academic Psychiatry* 41 (2): 159–66.

Hughes, S. 2022. "AHA Letter Re: Challenges Facing America's Health Care Workforce as the U.S. Enters Third Year of COVID-19 Pandemic." American Hospital Association. Published March 1. www.aha.org/lettercomment/2022-03-01-aha-provides-information-congress-re-challenges-facing-americas-health.

Jackson, E. R., T. D. Shanafelt, O. Hasan, D. V. Satele, and L. N. Dyrbye. 2016. "Burnout and Alcohol Abuse/Dependence Among U.S. Medical Students." *Academic Medicine* 91 (9): 1251–56.

Jacobsen, D. I., and E. M. Fjeldbraaten. 2018. "Shift Work and Sickness Absence—The Mediating Roles of Work–Home Conflict and Perceived Health." *Human Resource Management* 57 (5): 1145–57.

Jennings, B. M. 2008. "Work Stress and Burnout Among Nurses: Role of the Work Environment and Working Conditions." In *Patient Safety and Quality: An Evidence-Based Handbook for Nurses*, vol. 2, ed. R. G. Hughes, 137–48. Rockville, MD: Agency for Healthcare Research and Quality.

Kent, J., M. Thornton, A. Fong, E. Hall, S. Fitzgibbons, and J. Sava. 2020. "Acute Provider Stress in High Stakes Medical Care: Implications for Trauma Surgeons." *Journal of Trauma and Acute Care Surgery* 88 (3): 440–45.

Kraft, U. 2006. "Burned Out." *Scientific American Mind* 17 (3): 28–33.

Lai, J., S. Ma, Y. Wang, Z. Cai, J. Hu, N. Wei, J. Wu, H. Du, T. Chen, R. Li, H. Tan, L. Kang, L. Yao, M. Huang, H. Wang, G. Wang, Z. Liu, and S. Hu. 2020. "Factors Associated with

Mental Health Outcomes Among Health Care Workers Exposed to Coronavirus Disease 2019." *JAMA Network Open* 3 (3): e203976. https://doi.org/10.1001/jamanetworkopen .2020.3976.

Marchalik, D., and T. Shanafelt. 2020. "Addressing Burnout Among Health Care Professionals by Focusing on Process Rather Than Metrics." *JAMA Health Forum* 1 (9): e201161. https://doi.org/ 10.1001/jamahealthforum.2020.1161.

Maslach, C., and S. E. Jackson. 1981. "The Measurement of Experienced Burnout." *Journal of Organizational Behavior* 2 (2): 99–113.

Maslach, C., W. B. Schaufeli, and M. P. Leiter. 2001. "Job Burnout." *Annual Review of Psychology* 52: 397–422.

Melnyk, B. M., A. P. Hsieh, A. Tan, A. M. Teall, D. Weberg, J. Jun, K. Gawlik, and J. Hoyinh. 2022. "Associations Among Nurses' Mental/Physical Health, Lifestyle Behaviors, Shift Length, and Workplace Wellness Support During COVID-19." *Nursing Administration Quarterly* 46 (1): 5–18.

Merz, S. 2021. "Behavioral Health in the Pandemic: Making the Shift from Mental Illness to Mental Well-Being." *Frontiers of Health Services Management* 38 (1): 338.

Moss, J. 2019. "Burnout Is About Your Workplace, Not Your People." *Harvard Business Review*. Published December 11. https://hbr.org/2019/12/ burnout-is-about-your -workplace-not-your-people.

National Academies of Sciences, Engineering, and Medicine. 2019. *Taking Action Against Clinician Burnout: A Systems Approach to Professional Well-Being*. Washington, DC: National Academies Press.

Ofri, D. 2019. "The Business of Healthcare Depends on Exploiting Doctors and Nurses." *New York Times*. Published June 8. www.nytimes. com/2019/06/08/opinion/sunday /hospitals-doctors-nurses-burnout.html.

Perlo, J., B. Balik, S. Swensen, A. Kabcenell, J. Landsman, and D. Feeley. 2017. *IHI Framework for Improving Joy in Work*. Cambridge, MA: Institute for Healthcare Improvement.

Poon, Eric G., S. T. Rosenbloom, and K. Zheng. 2021. "Health Information Technology and Clinician Burnout: Current Understanding, Emerging Solutions, and Future Directions." *Journal of the American Medical Informatics Association* 28 (5): 895–98.

Portoghese, I., M. Galletta, A. Burdorf, P. Cocco, E. D'Aloja, and M. Campagna. 2017. "Role Stress and Emotional Exhaustion Among Health Care Workers." *Journal of Occupational and Environmental Medicine* 59 (10): e187–93.

PsychCentral. 2022. "Recognizing and Dealing with Stress." Reviewed July 13. https://psychcentral.com/lib/recognizing-and-dealing-with-stress#1.

Raffenaud, A., L. Unruh, M. Fottler, A. X. Liu, and D. Andrews. 2020. "A Comparative Analysis of Work–Family Conflict Among Staff, Managerial, and Executive Nurses." *Nursing Outlook* 68 (2): 231–41.

Reith, T. P. 2018. "Burnout in United States Healthcare Professionals: A Narrative Review." *Cureus.* Published December 4. www.cureus.com/articles/16398-burnout-in-united-states-healthcare-professionals-a-narrative-review.

Rotenstein, L. S., M. Torre, M. A. Ramos, R. C. Rosales, C. Guille, S. Sen, and D. A. Mata. 2018. "Prevalence of Burnout Among Physicians." *Journal of the American Medical Association* 320 (11): 1131–50.

Shanafelt, T. D., L. N. Dyrbye, C. P. West, and C. A. Sinsky. 2016. "Potential Impact of Burnout on the US Physician Workforce." *Mayo Clinic Proceedings* 91 (11): 1667–68.

Shreffler, J., J. Petrey, and M. Huecker. 2020. "The Impact of COVID-19 on Healthcare Worker Wellness: A Scoping Review." *Western Journal of Emergency Medicine* 21 (5):1059.

Terry, D., and D. P. Matthews. 2021. "Technology-Assisted Supplemental Work Among Rural Medical Providers: Impact on Burnout, Stress, and Job Satisfaction." *Journal of Healthcare Management* 66 (6): 451–58.

Van Dyke, M. 2022. "The Path of Most Resilience: Building a Strong and Fulfilled Healthcare Workforce." *Healthcare Executive* 37 (3): 9–15. https://healthcareexecutive.org/-/media/ache/healthcare-executives/mj22/he_mj22_downloadedition.pdf.

Vassar, L. 2016. "How Physician Burnout Compares to General Working Population." American Medical Association. Published January 27. www.ama-assn.org/practice -management/physician-health/how-physician-burnout-compares-general-working -population.

WittKieffer. 2019. *The Impact of Burnout on Healthcare Executives*. Oak Brook, IL: Witt- Kieffer. www.wittkieffer.com/webfoo/wp-content/uploads/Burnout-Survey-Report _2019_Final_New-Logo.pdf.

World Health Organization (WHO). 2019. "Burn-out—An 'Occupational Phenomenon': International Classification of Diseases." Published May 28. www.who.int/mental _health/evidence/burn-out/en/.

Yates, S. 2020. "Physician Stress and Burnout." *American Journal of Medicine* 133 (2): 160–64.

Yong, E. 2021. "Why Health-Care Workers Are Quitting in Droves." *Atlantic.* Published November 16. www.theatlantic.com/health/archive/2021/11/the-mass-exodus-of -americas-health-care-workers/620713/?msclkid=778871bad13311ecb7e217d81ca0b 68f.

Zhang, X., D. Lin, H. Pforsich, and V. W. Lin. 2020. "Physician Workforce in the United States of America: Forecasting Nationwide Shortages." *Human Resources for Health* 18 (1): 1–9.

Zhang, X., D. Tai, H. Pforsich, and V. W. Lin. 2018. "United States Registered Nurse Work- force Report Card and Shortage Forecast: A Revisit." *American Journal of Medical Qual- ity* 33 (3): 229–36.

GLOSSARY

1974 Health Care Amendments to the Taft-Hartley Act Legislation that made approximately 2 million additional healthcare workers eligible for union representation and provided stringent protections regarding work stoppages to safeguard patient care.

ability and aptitude tests A wide range of employment tests that evaluate applicants along dimensions relevant to the job; for example, personality type, honesty, integrity, cognitive reasoning, and fine motor coordination.

academic progression Efforts to promote the advanced education of the nursing workforce, including LPN to RN, RN to BSN, and BSN to MSN or other graduate nursing degree.

ADDIE model Analysis, design, development, implementation, and evaluation; a systems approach to training.

administrative risk factors Multiple documentation requirements that increase healthcare practitioners' susceptibility to stress and burnout.

affirmative action A set of procedures designed to eliminate and prevent unlawful discrimination among applicants, including taking race, gender, ethnicity, disability, and veteran status into consideration in an attempt to promote equal opportunity; often used in hiring practices.

Age Discrimination in Employment Act (ADEA) Federal law passed in 1967 that prohibits employment discrimination against employees and applicants aged 40 or older.

alternative dispute resolution (ADR) A specified conflict resolution process used in place of litigation. Often a clause in an employment contract.

Americans with Disabilities Act (ADA) The federal civil rights law passed in 1990 that prohibits discrimination based on disabilities.

arbitration A binding type of dispute resolution in which both parties agree beforehand to abide by the decision of a neutral third party called an *arbitrator*.

assessment center Physical location where testing is done, or a series of assessment procedures that are administered, professionally scored, and reported to hiring personnel, to evaluate applicants or assess employees' developmental needs.

authorization cards Documentation cards signed by individual employees that indicate a desire to designate the union to act as the employees' collective bargaining representative.

bargaining unit A group of employees recognized by the National Labor Relations Board to be an appropriate body for collective bargaining under the National Labor Relations Act.

behavioral anchored rating scale (BARS) A performance measurement scale that identifies the key job dimensions of a job and specifies observable behaviors descriptive of particular levels of performance for each job dimension.

behavioral interview question A type of interview question in which applicants are asked to relate how they handled a specific type of job situation in their past experience.

behavioral observation scale A performance measurement system that asks the rater to indicate the frequency with which the employee exhibits specified desirable behaviors.

belonging The goal of diversity and inclusion initiatives so that all views, beliefs, and values are acknowledged, respected, and integrated.

benchmark job A well-understood job with relatively stable knowledge, skills, and abilities; it is used to anchor pay scales for comparable jobs.

bona fide occupational qualification (BFOQ) A specific employment qualification that requires some kind of discrimination because the job requires someone of a particular age, gender, race, or other characteristic.

branding The organization's corporate image or culture.

broadbanding A method of classifying jobs using fewer but wider pay grades (salary ranges) than traditional compensation systems do.

burnout A cumulative negative response to prolonged occupational stress such as excessive demands on energy, strength, or resources.

business strategy A set of strategic alternatives from which an organization chooses to compete in a particular industry or market most effectively.

capitation A method of paying for health services in which a provider is paid a prepaid amount for each patient, regardless of the amount of health services provided.

collective bargaining An activity whereby union and management officials attempt to resolve conflicting interests in a manner that will sustain and possibly enrich their continuing relationships.

compensable factors Fundamental elements of a job, such as knowledge, skills, experience, accountability, supervisory responsibility, and working conditions, that are used as a basis for assigning points to a job and establishing compensation levels within a point system.

compensation strategy The set of rewards that organizations provide to staff in exchange for their performance of various organizational tasks and jobs.

compensation system Money, goods, and services provided to employees in return for employees' work.

compensatory damages Payment to compensate a claimant in a court decision for loss, injury, or harm suffered by another's breach of duty.

competency model A method of job analysis that identifies competencies required to do the job. These are typically divided into "can do" competencies (skills and knowledge derived from education and experience) and "will do" competencies (personality and attitudinal characteristics that reflect an individual's willingness to perform).

compressed workweek scheme A work schedule redesign in which the number of days in the workweek is shortened by lengthening the number of hours worked per day.

concessionary bargaining A type of bargaining in which the employer asks the union to eliminate, limit, or reduce wages and other commitments in response to financial constraints.

contingent workers Two categories of workers defined by the US Department of Labor as (1) independent contractors and on-call workers, who are called to work only when needed, and (2) temporary or short-term workers.

corporate strategy A set of strategic alternatives from which an organization chooses as it manages its operations simultaneously across several industries and markets.

criterion contamination The influence that factors outside the employee's control have on performance.

criterion deficiency A focus on a single performance criterion to the exclusion of other important but perhaps less quantifiable performance dimensions.

critical incident approach A performance management method in which a manager collects employee performance information by keeping a record of unusually favorable or unfavorable occurrences in an employee's work.

critical incidents analysis A process of generating lists of good and poor examples of job performance and translating them into employee selection criteria; this process helps uncover less formal—but important—aspects of performance.

decertification A National Labor Relations Board procedure available for employees when they believe, usually as a result of an election, that the union no longer represents the interests of the majority of the bargaining unit.

defined benefit plan A type of retirement plan that provides a retirement benefit payable to the employee on attainment of age and years of service, based on a percentage of salary during working years; usually payable monthly for the lifetime of retiree and/or spouse.

defined contribution plan A type of retirement plan in which the employer provides a contribution to an account based on the employee's current salary/earnings, and the employee can draw on the account after retirement with reduced tax liability.

developmental strategy A set of methods that facilitate the enhancement of an organization's human resources' quality.

diary method A job analysis method in which jobholders record their daily activities.

disparate impact The result of a practice that may appear to be neutral but has a discriminatory effect.

disparate treatment When employees are treated differently because of race, color, religion, gender, national origin, age, disability, or other protected class category.

distributive bargaining A win some–lose some type of bargaining between the union and the employer in which each party gives up something to gain something else.

diversity The collective and individual mixture of differences based on aspects of identity that include the qualities, experiences, and work styles that make individuals unique. Diversity attributes are broad and may refer to age, language, generation, class, country of origin, physical or cognitive abilities, race, religion, disability status, ethnicity, and many other attributes.

due process The procedural aspect of disciplinary cases under a labor agreement.

dysfunctional stress An ongoing experience of bodily or mental tension that can lead to physical and mental disorders, including anxiety, depression, and burnout. Also known as *negative stress*.

employee development (ED) An organization's effort to encourage professional growth in its employees, which may include elements of mentoring, coaching, sponsoring, stretch assignments, special projects, continued education, and formal leadership development programs.

employee engagement A measure of the employees' positive and negative perceptions of the organization that have a direct impact on retention, job satisfaction, and job performance.

employee referral An approach to recruitment in which current employees help identify promising applicants.

employment-at-will A principle that assumes that both employee and employer have the right to end the employment relationship at any time, for any reason.

environmental assessment A crucial element of strategic human resources management in which an organization reviews the changes in the legal and regulatory climate, economic conditions, and labor market realities to understand current opportunities and threats.

Equal Employment Opportunity Commission *See* US Equal Employment Opportunity Commission (EEOC).

equity theory The theory that the perceived fairness of the relationship between what an employee contributes to an organization and what the employee receives in return affects the employee's motivation and performance.

essential job function A function that is fundamental to successful performance of the job.

evidence-based HRM Human resource management decisions based on critical thinking applied to available data, internal business metrics, or results of research studies.

external recruitment An approach to employee recruitment that emphasizes identifying and recruiting applicants outside the organization.

extrinsic rewards Tangible aspects of compensation, such as pay and benefits.

factor comparison method A method of job evaluation in which compensable factors for one position are evaluated against those factors in a benchmark job.

faculty practice plan A group practice that comprises the faculty of a medical center; it was created as a way to leverage the billings generated by faculty into some sort of shared distributions.

Fair Labor Standards Act (FLSA) The 1938 law that establishes a federal minimum wage; establishes a standard 40-hour workweek; and contains provisions for work performed beyond the standard workweek. It also sets limits on child labor.

fair representation A union's legal obligation to evenhandedly represent all bargaining-unit employees, both union members and nonmembers alike.

family and medical leave Unpaid time off for maternity, for employee extended illness or injury, or for the employee to care for a family member with serious illness.

flexible spending accounts (FSAs) Accounts that allow employees to tax defer, via payroll deduction, an amount that can be used to offset qualified expenses for medical care or dependent care.

flextime A work schedule redesign that allows employees to choose daily starting and ending times, provided that they work a certain number of hours per day or week. Also known as *flexible working hours*.

forced distribution A performance evaluation method in which managers are required to assign a defined percentage of employees to particular predetermined performance categories. Also called *forced ranking* or *stack ranking*.

free rider syndrome A problem affecting teams in which one or more members benefit from team rewards without putting forth corresponding effort.

functional strategies Strategies that consider how the organization will manage each of its major functions, such as marketing, finance, and human resources.

functional training Training that produces personnel who can perform tasks but who may not know the theory behind the practice.

garnishment A deduction of money from an employee's wages to pay a debt resulting from a court order or other procedure.

graphic rating scale An employee performance rating scale that uses points along a continuum and measures traits or behaviors. Such a scale may be prone to subjective judgment and misinterpretation.

grievance Any employee's concern over a perceived violation of the labor agreement that is submitted to the grievance procedure for eventual resolution.

group practice The general name for many types of physician practices wherein two or more physicians have established a legal entity to deliver care together. Group members typically share premises, personnel, and other resources.

Health Insurance Portability and Accountability Act (HIPAA) The 1996 federal law that protects health insurance coverage when workers lose their jobs, simplifies electronic healthcare records, and requires increased privacy of healthcare records.

healthy stress A short-term experience of bodily or mental tension that allows an individual to stay alert and focused while building resilience.

hostile environment sexual harassment Sexual harassment that interferes with a victim's work performance or creates an intimidating, hostile, or offensive working environment that affects the victim's psychological well-being.

HR metrics Measures of human resources outcomes and performance.

human resources information system (HRIS) An integrated information system designed to provide managers with information for human resources decision making.

human resources management (HRM) The processes (recruitment, selection, training and development, performance management, compensation, and employee relations) performed within the organization or external to it and more informal management of employees performed by all administrators.

impaired practitioner A healthcare professional who is unable to carry out their professional duties with reasonable skill and safety because of a physical or mental illness, including deterioration through aging, loss of motor skill, or excessive use of drugs and alcohol.

impasse A deadlock in negotiating between management and union officials over terms and conditions of employment.

inclusion The manner and extent to which diverse members of an organization are accepted and are fully integrated into the organization. Inclusion describes the intentional and ongoing activities that foster engagement with diversity and diverse members, and create supportive cultures for all people, particularly for those who have been minoritized.

independent practice association (IPA) A corporation formed by a collection of physician practices, often including solo and group practitioners, that join forces to take advantage of economies of scale for contracting, business services, or ancillary services.

individual characteristics Personal considerations that influence a person's job decision.

instructional systems design (ISD) An organized, systems approach to training.

integrative bargaining A type of bargaining that seeks win–win situations and solutions that are responsive to the needs of both the union and the employer.

internal equity The pay relationships among jobs in an organization and the extent to which workers are compensated fairly.

internal recruitment An approach to employee recruitment that emphasizes identifying and recruiting applicants who are already members of the organization.

intersectionality The aspects of social identity such as race, gender, gender identity, and class that overlap and create connected systems of privilege or discrimination.

intervention A series of activities and events designed to help an organization become more productive and effective.

intrinsic rewards Intangible aspects of compensation, such as public recognition; praise from a supervisor; and feelings of accomplishment, recognition, or belonging to an organization.

job A group of activities and duties that entail natural units of work that are similar and related.

job analysis The systematic process of determining the skills, duties, tasks, activities, competencies, and knowledge required to perform particular jobs.

job characteristics Job-related decision-making factors such as flexibility, compensation, hours, challenge and responsibility, advancement opportunities, job security, geographic location, and employee benefits.

job classification system A method of categorizing jobs based on predetermined job requirements wherein each job grade is associated with a salary range.

job description A detailed summary of a job's duties, tasks, responsibilities, reporting relationships, working conditions, and Fair Labor Standards Act (FLSA) exemption status.

job design The process of structuring jobs by determining the specific tasks to be performed, the methods used in performing these tasks, and how the job relates to other jobs.

job enlargement The horizontal expansion of job duties with the same level of autonomy and responsibility.

job enrichment The vertical expansion of job duties that includes additional autonomy, responsibility, achievement, and recognition to provide greater challenges to the employee.

job evaluation A formal process designed to determine the monetary value of a job based on job descriptions and specifications.

job-knowledge interview question A type of interview question asked to assess whether applicants have the knowledge needed to do the job.

job sharing An arrangement in which two part-time employees share a job that otherwise would be held by one full-time employee.

job specification A description of the personal qualifications, traits, and background an individual must possess to perform the duties and responsibilities contained in a job description satisfactorily and best reflect characteristics of the organization's culture.

Labor Management Reporting and Disclosure Act of 1959 A US labor law that regulates labor unions' internal affairs and their officials' relationships with employers.

labor relations process The process whereby management and the union jointly decide on and administer terms and conditions of employment.

learning collaboratives Cooperatives whereby people on multiple quality improvement (QI) teams come together to learn from the successes (or shortcomings) of others in similar organizations working on related QI projects.

lockout An act by an employer when it shuts down operations during or before a labor dispute.

locum tenens physician A temporarily employed physician; typically paid a fixed amount for services provided.

long-term care (LTC) insurance Insurance to help cover the cost of nursing homes, home care, and assisted living for older adults.

long-term disability (LTD) insurance A welfare benefit designed to provide employees with income if they become disabled and cannot work.

Magnet Recognition Program A program established by the American Nurses Credentialing Center to acknowledge and reward healthcare organizations that demonstrate and provide excellent nursing care.

management by objectives (MBO) A performance management method that involves setting performance goals for employees, coaching them to help them achieve their goals, and reviewing progress over a specified period.

mandatory bargaining issues Topics related to wages, hours, and other conditions of employment that must be negotiated as part of collective bargaining if raised by the union or management.

marginal job function A function that is incidental to the main function of the job—a matter of convenience, not a necessity.

market pricing A method of setting salaries based on market factors (supply and demand).

mediation A nonbinding type of dispute resolution in which a neutral third party called a *mediator* attempts to assist in negotiations between the two primary parties.

microlearning A training and development method that presents new information in small chunks (segments of ten minutes or less).

mission A statement created by an organization's board and senior managers specifying how the organization intends to manage itself to most effectively fulfill its purpose.

misuse A situation that occurs when care is provided incorrectly or when patients receive the wrong care altogether. Misuse typically either harms patients or prevents them from experiencing the full benefit of a treatment.

mobile learning Educational content delivery through smartphones, tablets, or laptops.

MOOCs Free online courses on a variety of topics that are available to anyone worldwide to enroll. MOOCs stands for *massive open online courses*.

multiskilled health practitioner (MSHP) A healthcare worker who is cross-trained to serve more than one function, often in multiple disciplines.

multisource appraisal A form of performance evaluation in which many individuals—such as supervisors, subordinates, other coworkers, customers, and patients—provide a richer description of an employee's performance than may be obtained from a single rater. Also referred to as *360-degree feedback* or *multirater assessment*.

National Labor Relations Act (NLRA) The legal framework for the labor relations process in the United States; it contains significant provisions intended to protect workers' rights to form and join unions and to engage in collective bargaining, and it defines unfair labor practices.

National Labor Relations Board (NLRB) An independent federal agency that protects the rights of private-sector employees to join together, with or without a union, to improve their wages and working conditions. It was established by the National Labor Relations Act (NLRA) to investigate alleged NLRA violations.

needs assessment A tool used to determine whether gaps exist between the desired and actual levels of performance, according to organizational requirements or performance standards.

negligent hiring A situation in which an employer could have discovered a new employee's problematic conduct through due diligence but failed to do so, making the employer liable for damages caused by the employee.

noncompetition and nonsolicitation clauses Statements of agreement in a contract that prevent a departed employee from posing a competitive risk or a confidentiality breach.

nonqualified retirement plan A type of retirement plan typically designed to meet the needs of key executives; not subject to as many government regulations as a qualified plan is.

occupation One's principal activity and means of support.

onboarding The process of integrating newly hired employees into the organization.

organizational development (OD) An organization's endeavor to increase its effectiveness through planned interventions related to the organization's processes and people.

organizational risk factors Results of organizational operational decision making that increase healthcare workers' susceptibility to stress and burnout.

orientation The completion of new-hire forms and other routine tasks for new employees.

overuse A situation that occurs when a drug or treatment is given without medical justification. Examples of overuse include treating people with antibiotics for simple infections or failing to follow effective options that cost less or cause fewer side effects.

paid time off (PTO) The number of paid days or hours off work for which an individual employee is eligible; it does not distinguish absences between vacation leave, sick leave, and personal leave.

patient safety Freedom from accidental, erroneous, or preventable injuries produced by medical care.

pay band A salary range for a particular job category.

pay-for-performance system A compensation system that rewards employees based on their job performance; managers evaluate their employees' work according to preestablished goals, standards, or company values.

performance appraisal Methods of assessing the level of employee performance.

performance management All the activities supervisors carry out to manage and improve employee performance; includes appraisal, supervision, rewards, and training.

performance standards Indicators of what a job is meant to accomplish, how performance is measured, and what the expected levels of job performance are.

personal leave A policy that allows employees to get paid time off without having to specify the reason.

person–job fit The traditional foundation for human resource selection, in which a successful applicant possesses the knowledge, skills, and abilities required for the job.

personnel replacement charts Lists of key personnel in an organization and their possible replacements in the organization, including information about their current performance and promotability.

person–organization fit An approach to employee selection that emphasizes the extent to which an applicant's attitudes, behaviors, values, and beliefs align with the culture, norms, and values of the organization.

Peter Principle The theory that employees in an organization will be promoted to their highest level of competence and then be promoted to and remain at a level at which they are incompetent.

picketing Outside patrolling by union members of any employer's premises for the purpose of achieving a specific objective.

point system A method in which jobs are assigned points based on compensable factors predetermined by the organization. Points are then translated into salary levels.

position Duties and responsibilities performed by only one employee.

predictive HR analytics Data mining and modeling techniques to identify potential causes for human resource outcomes, which then indicate future outcomes.

primary verification Information directly received from the licensing authority that verifies a new hire's license.

process analysis Breaking down an organizational process to identify bottlenecks, blockages, inefficiencies, and waste in an effort to understand how a process operates and how it may be improved.

productivity-focused pay for performance A compensation system that ties financial incentives to individual employee productivity.

profession A calling that requires specialized knowledge and training. Professionals have more authority and responsibility than people in an occupation and adhere to a code of ethics.

professional risk factors Inherent risks attributable to the nature of one's work.

protected class A group of individuals protected under a particular law.

psychological safety Belief that one will not be rejected or humiliated in a particular setting or role; also an atmosphere in which people feel free to express work-relevant thoughts and feelings.

punitive damages Payment to compensate a claimant in a court decision beyond actual damages suffered.

purpose An organization's basic reason for existence.

qualified retirement plan A type of retirement plan with strict eligibility and vesting requirements and strict taxable limits, in which employees receive more tax benefits than from nonqualified plans; typically the employee and employer are not taxed until the time a distribution is made.

quality The degree to which health services for individuals and populations increase the likelihood of desired health outcomes and are consistent with current professional knowledge.

quality-focused pay for performance An approach to compensation that rewards service quality.

quid pro quo sexual harassment When a benefit for an employee in the workplace is granted on condition of submission to sexual advances.

ranking A method of appraisal in which managers list employees in order from best to worst on some overall measure of employee performance.

rating errors In performance management, positive or negative distortions in performance appraisal ratings that reduce the accuracy of appraisals.

realistic job preview A process in which applicants are given a true picture of a job, including its strengths and weaknesses, through verbal information, discussions with job incumbents, employee shadowing, and other methods.

reasonable accommodation The concept that it is the employer's responsibility to make adjustments—within reasonable limits—for employees with physical or mental disabilities. Reasonableness is determined on a case by case basis.

recruitment The means by which organizations attract qualified individuals on a timely basis and in sufficient numbers and encourage them to apply for jobs.

reliability In performance appraisal, the consistency with which a manager rates an employee in successive ratings, assuming consistent performance, or the consistency with which two or more managers assess performance when they have comparable information.

retaliatory discharge When an employer takes action to attempt to prevent an employee from filing a claim of discrimination against the employer, or when an employer punishes an employee for participating in a legal activity.

retention Maintaining employee employment with an organization.

retention rate The percentage of specific individuals or cohorts that enter and exit the organization.

right-to-work laws Laws that prohibit union membership (and related union security clauses) as a condition of employment, in accordance with point 14(b) of the National Labor Relations Act.

risk factor Something that increases risk or susceptibility.

root cause analysis A structured approach to analyzing adverse events by identifying underlying factors that increase the probability of errors. This structure might include asking *why* consecutively to understand the deepest cause for a process or action.

scope creep The progressive expansion of the scope of practice for specific healthcare professional roles, encompassing responsibilities previously viewed as outside a specific role's scope of practice or pertaining to another healthcare professional role.

scope of practice The services a healthcare professional's role permits them to perform given their professional license.

secondary verification A copy of a document that indicates licensure has been granted and shows the license's expiration date.

selection The process of evaluating job applicants with the goal of identifying the best person for a position.

selection tools Information-gathering methods used in employee selection to obtain job-related information about applicants.

self-appraisal An evaluation done by an employee on the employee's own performance, usually in conjunction with the manager's performance appraisal.

self-insurance An insurance design wherein the employer budgets, underwrites, and administers a customized benefit rather than contracts for a standard plan.

severance agreement An agreement that ensures a terminated employee certain benefits from the former employer.

short-term disability insurance An optional benefit for which the employee must pay, in which an employee is covered from the time that an illness, a condition, or a disability starts to the time that the eligibility period for long-term disability has been satisfied.

sick leave A policy that allows employees to get paid during time off as a result of illness, injury, or medical appointments.

situational interview question A type of interview question in which applicants are asked how they would handle specific situations that may arise on the job.

skills-based or knowledge-based compensation system A compensation system in which employees are financially rewarded for mastering new skills or acquiring new knowledge.

skills inventory A manual or electronic system designed to keep track of employees' experiences, education, skills, knowledge, abilities, and other characteristics.

solo practice An approach to providing medical services in which a physician works as a single, office-based practitioner.

staffing strategy A set of activities used by an organization to determine its future human resources needs, recruit qualified applicants with an interest in the organization, and select the best of those applicants as new employees.

staff-model HMO A setup in which physicians and health professionals are salaried employees of a health maintenance organization (HMO), and the clinics or health centers in which they practice are owned by the HMO.

stop-loss insurance A kind of insurance that mitigates the risk to the employer in the event that there are large claims in a given plan year.

strategic human resources management (SHRM) The process of formulating and executing human resources (HR) policies and practices that produce employee competencies and behaviors required for the organization to achieve its strategic objectives.

strike A temporary stoppage of work by a group of employees for the purposes of expressing a grievance or forcing a demand.

structured interview An interview technique in which questions and related constructs (and sometimes, preferred answers) are developed in advance.

subordinate appraisal A performance evaluation of a manager by the manager's subordinates.

succession planning The process of identifying and developing employees for potential promotion or transfer into positions that are critical to operations.

SWOT analysis Analysis of the organization's strengths, weaknesses, opportunities, and threats.

Taft-Hartley Act Law that amended the National Labor Relations Act in 1947; it protects employers and gives states permission to enact right-to-work laws.

tax-deferred plan A savings plan that allows staff to contribute to their own retirement.

team-based appraisal Evaluation of the work of teams; used under the assumption that service or product quality is largely the result of team, not individual, efforts.

team-based compensation Rewards given to individual members of a team in recognition of the team's performance.

team-based incentives Variable compensation schemes based on the performance of a team. An individual's salary may be determined in part by the performance of the team.

team citizenship Employee behaviors and attitudes that are respectful of team norms and expectations.

team composition The size of the team, the backgrounds and competencies of team members, and other factors relevant to the particular tasks the team is facing. For example, a team may include people external to the organization, such as suppliers and patients.

technical conference method A job analysis method in which job attributes are obtained from supervisors who have extensive knowledge of the job (frequently called *subject matter experts*).

telecommuting Performing work away from the office enabled by technology to communicate and collaborate with coworkers and access desktop tools.

Title VII of the Civil Rights Act of 1964 That portion of the law prohibiting discrimination in employment on the basis of race, sex, religion, national origin, or color. This was the first nationwide antidiscrimination law.

total compensation All aspects of direct and indirect rewards given to employees, including money, benefits (such as health insurance and retirement plans), paid time off (such as vacation and sick time), and stock options.

training The acquisition of knowledge, skills, abilities, and competencies that are needed to perform a particular job.

training design The unifying thread of all training modes, in which the grand plan is established, timelines are set, and the overall project outline is created.

training development The step of the training design process in which the training materials, including the curriculum and learning outcomes, take shape; also includes a dry run and feedback.

training evaluation The step of the training design process in which the information collected after implementation is reviewed to determine whether objectives were met.

training implementation The step of the training design process in which rollout occurs and evaluation data are collected for analysis.

travel nurse A registered nurse who works in a short-term role at a hospital, clinic, or other healthcare facility that is experiencing a nursing shortage.

turnover Employee departures from an organization.

turnover rate A ratio providing a summary of the gross movement in and out of the organization during a specific time frame.

underuse A situation that occurs when providers fail to provide patients with medically necessary care or do not adhere to evidence-based guidelines. Examples include failure to provide beta-blockers to patients with coronary artery disease or failure to vaccinate elderly patients against pneumonia.

union An organization formed by employees to act as a single unit when dealing with management about workplace issues.

unstructured interview An interview technique in which questions are usually open-ended and guided by applicant answers and interviewer preferences.

US Equal Employment Opportunity Commission (EEOC) A federal agency responsible for ending employment discrimination. The EEOC files lawsuits on behalf of alleged victims of discrimination in the workplace.

vacation leave The number of days an individual employee is eligible to take for vacation with pay, based on the individual's years of service and employee category.

validity The extent to which appraisal criteria actually measure the performance dimension of interest.

value chain analysis An analysis that aims to identify new sources of advantage by suggesting how internal core competencies can be deployed to meet external environmental conditions and direct the best use of resources.

voluntary bargaining issues Topics, such as benefits for retired employees, that can be negotiated between the union and the employer as part of collective bargaining only if both parties so desire. Also called *permissive* or *nonmandatory* issues.

webinars Seminars posted on the internet, either conducted live or recorded and broadcast.

whistle-blower An employee who discloses or exposes to the government an illegal activity in the workplace.

worker-requirement interview question A type of interview question asked to determine whether applicants are able and willing to work under the specific conditions of the job.

workforce composition The demographics of the workforce, including factors such as gender, age, ethnicity, marital status, and disability status.

INDEX

ABOUT THE EDITORS

Bruce J. Fried, PhD, is professor emeritus in the Department of Health Policy and Management in the Gillings School of Global Public Health at the University of North Carolina at Chapel Hill, where he served as director of master's degree programs for more than 20 years. He has taught courses in human resources management, international and comparative health systems, and globalization and health. Bruce has written numerous journal articles, books and book chapters, commentaries, and book reviews and was coeditor of *World Health Systems: Challenges and Perspectives,* 2nd ed. (Health Administration Press, 2012) and *Human Resources in Healthcare: Managing for Success,* 5th ed. (Health Administration Press, 2021). His research interests include the impact of improvement teams and culture on quality in healthcare settings, the healthcare workforce, mental health services, and global health. Bruce has conducted workshops and management training courses in Europe, Asia, Latin America, Africa, the Middle East, and the Caribbean. He received his master's degree from the University of Chicago and his doctorate from the University of North Carolina at Chapel Hill.

Carla Jackie Sampson, PhD, MBA, FACHE, is clinical associate professor and director of the Health Policy and Management Program and online Master of Health Administration Program at New York University's Robert F. Wagner Graduate School of Public Service, where she teaches courses in strategy, executive leadership, human resources management, and healthcare system organization. Her research interests include healthcare workforce policy, the impact of structural racism on the social determinants of health, and anchor mission strategy development. She was coeditor of *Human Resources in Healthcare: Managing* *for Success,* 5th ed. (Health Administration Press, 2021). Carla received a master of business administration degree in healthcare management and a master of science degree in healthcare financial management from Temple University. She earned her doctorate in public affairs–health services management and research from the University of Central Florida, Orlando, and is board certified in healthcare management. Carla is a fellow of the American College of Healthcare Executives, for which she serves as editor of the quarterly publication *Frontiers of Health Services Management.*

ABOUT THE CONTRIBUTORS

Julene Campion, MS, is vice president of recruitment, organization development, and learning at Geisinger Health System. She previously worked for Lehigh Valley Health Network as director of talent acquisition and has more than 15 years of human resources leadership experience in integrated healthcare delivery systems. Julene is also an adjunct assistant professor of health administration at New York University's Robert Wagner Graduate School of Public Health Education. Julene received her master of science degree in organization development and leadership from Saint Joseph's University in Philadelphia, Pennsylvania.

John Cashion, JD, MPH, is an attorney whose primary focus is on law, health equity, and the social determinants of health. As a staff attorney at Pisgah Legal Services in Asheville, North Carolina, John worked on key programs addressing access to healthcare by marginalized populations. He also worked for the Public Health Division of the North Carolina Department of Health and Human Services, Emory Healthcare, and the University of North Carolina (UNC) at Chapel Hill. John received his law degree from the UNC School of Law and his master of public health degree from the UNC Gillings School of Global Public Health.

Dolores G. Clement, DrPH, FACHE, is Sentara Professor Emeritus and Distinguished Career Professor in the Department of Health Administration at Virginia Commonwealth University (VCU). She previously served as program director of the MHA and the MSHA programs and the program director of dual degree programs (MHA/MD and MHA/JD) at VCU and held a joint appointment in the Department of Preventive and Community Medicine at VCU's School of Medicine. She serves on the Governing Board of the Commission on Accreditation of Health Management Education (CAHME). She was American College of Healthcare Executives regent for Virginia–Central from 2013 to 2017. Dolores earned master's degrees in health systems management from Rush University and in international affairs from Ohio University and received her doctorate in health policy and administration from the University of California at Berkeley.

Brigid K. Grabert, PhD, JD, MPH, is a postdoctoral fellow in the Cancer Control Education Program at the University of North Carolina Lineberger Comprehensive Cancer Center. She is a health services researcher with research interests in primary and secondary human papilloma virus (HPV) cancer prevention, global health, health law and policy, and sexual and reproductive health. Brigid is particularly interested in implementing evidence-based interventions to increase HPV vaccine coverage. She holds a law degree from the UNC School of Law and is an adjunct assistant professor of health law in the Department of Health Policy and Management at the UNC Gillings School of Global Public Health for the Executive Master's Program.

Hillary K. Hecht, MSW, is a doctoral student at University of North Carolina at Chapel Hill. They are researching decolonial ethics of weight-affirming policies in healthcare organizations. Hillary completed a master of social work degree from the University of Michigan, where they explored gender expansive patients' access to care and complex family caregiving. Their research career is built after having worked in human resources within healthcare software and financial services industries and having studied dance and organizational science at George Washington University.

Donna Malvey, PhD, is an associate professor in the Department of Health Management and Informatics at the University of Central Florida. With Donna J. Slovensky, she coauthored *mHealth: Transforming Healthcare* (Springer, 2014). With Slovensky and Myron Fottler, she is a coeditor and contributor to *The Handbook of Healthcare Management* (Elgar, 2015). Donna earned her master's degree in health services administration from George Washington University and her doctorate in health services administration from the University of Alabama at Birmingham. She has completed a residency and health systems fellowship with the Veterans Administration.

Gabriella "Gabbi" J. Maris, MHA, is an administrative fellow at Houston Methodist. Gabbi has experience working in various healthcare settings including community hospitals, academic medical centers, outpatient clinics, and long-term care facilities. Gabbi earned a master of healthcare administration degree from the Gillings School of Global Public

Health at the University of North Carolina at Chapel Hill after receiving a bachelor's degree in public health from Texas A&M University.

Drake Maynard operates a human resources consulting service for state and local government agencies, providing technical advice and assistance, consultation in the area of employee relations, and training seminars on human resources issues of interest. He previously worked for the State of North Carolina for nearly 35 years, during that time serving in a number of positions, including director of employee relations and head of the local government services program team for the North Carolina Office of State Personnel.

Melissa G. McCraw, MHA, is a management associate at Atrium Health in Charlotte, North Carolina. She has several years of experience working with human resources and healthcare administration at academic medical centers, Veterans Affairs Health Systems, and community hospitals and outpatient practices. She also has extensive human resources experience in the manufacturing industry prior to entering the healthcare field. Melissa earned a master of healthcare administration degree from the University of North Carolina at Chapel Hill after receiving a bachelor's degree in Spanish and international public health from Clemson University.

Sean A. Newman, DBA, is an MBA and MHR lecturer at Rollins College in Winter Park, Florida. His research interests include human resource management, virtual team management, leader communication, organizational commitment and loyalty, and the impact of technology on the workplace. Sean has also worked for more than 25 years in human resource outsourcing at Aon. He has corporate experience leading business units through complex client relationships and business engagements. Sean has led numerous business transformation strategies, internally at Aon and for clients. He earned his doctor of business administration degree from the Crummer Graduate School of Business at Rollins College.

Paige N. Ocker, MHR, is a human resources professional at Think Food Group. Paige has previous experience in theme park operations as a training and development supervisor at SeaWorld Parks and Entertainment. She earned her master of human resources degree from Rollins College in Winter Park, Florida, and is currently exploring PhD programs.

Amanda Raffenaud, PhD, MSHSA, is an associate professor at AdventHealth University in Orlando, Florida. She has been teaching healthcare administration courses for more than 15 years. Her research interests include healthcare human resources, healthcare leadership, healthy work environments, and healthy communities. Amanda has published in numerous healthcare journals and contributed to multiple textbooks related to the health administration field. She holds a master of science in health services administration degree and a doctorate in public affairs, with a concentration in health management and research, from the University of Central Florida.

Patrick D. Shay, PhD, is an associate professor in the Department of Health Care Administration at Trinity University in San Antonio, Texas, where he teaches graduate courses on such topics as health services organization and policy, healthcare innovation, population health management, and healthcare organization theory and behavior. His research applies organization theory to healthcare organization phenomena, including the activities and configurations of local multihospital systems as well as the impact of regulation on post-acute care providers, among others. Prior to his doctoral studies, Patrick worked as a healthcare administrator for a post-acute care system in south Texas. He received his master of science degree in healthcare administration from Trinity University and his doctorate in health services organization and research from Virginia Commonwealth University.

Jeffrey Simms, MSPH, MDiv, is an assistant professor and director of professional development and alumni affairs for the Department of Health Policy and Management at the Gillings School of Global Public Health at the University of North Carolina at Chapel Hill. In 2022, he served as the interim associate dean for inclusive excellence at Gillings. Prior to transitioning to higher education, Jeffrey was in senior leadership with the North Carolina Department of Health and Human Services as assistant director of the North Carolina Medicaid Program and deputy director of the North Carolina Office of Rural Health. He received his master of science in public health degree from UNC Chapel Hill and also earned a master of divinity degree from Duke University. Throughout most of his healthcare career, Jeffrey has simultaneously served as pastor for two rural congregations in Wilson County, where he grew up.

Tina Yeung, PhD, is a clinical assistant professor at Florida International University. Her research focus areas include health policy, health disparities, health information technology, and other health-related topics. She previously worked for a health benefits administration company in Atlanta, Georgia. She holds a master's degree in health services administration and a doctorate in public affairs, with a concentration in health service management and research, from the University of Central Florida.